THE 8088 AND 8086 MICROPROCESSORS
Programming, Interfacing,
Software, Hardware,
and Applications

THE 8088 AND 8086 MICROPROCESSORS
Programming, Interfacing, Software, Hardware, and Applications

WALTER A. TRIEBEL

Intel Corporation

AVTAR SINGH

San Jose State University

PRENTICE HALL
Englewood Cliffs, New Jersey 07632

Library of Congress Cataloging-in-Publication Data

Avtar Singh
   The 8088 and 8086 microprocessors: programming, interfacing,
software, hardware, and applications/Avtar Singh, Walter A.
Triebel.
      p.   cm.
   Includes bibliographical references and index.
   ISBN 0-13-248337-8 (case)
      1. Intel 8088 (Microprocessor)   2. Intel 8086 (Microprocessor)
I. Triebel, Walter A. II.   Title.
QA76.8.I2924A96   1992
004.165—dc20   91-11145
                                                         CIP

Acquisitions Editor: Holly Hodder
Editorial/production supervision: Karen Winget
Cover design: Bruce Kenselaar
Prepress buyer: Mary McCartney
Manufacturing buyer: Ed O'Dougherty
Cover photograph reprinted by permission of
Intel Corporation, Copyright 1990

 © 1991 by Prentice-Hall, Inc.
A Simon & Schuster Company
Englewood Cliffs, New Jersey 07632

Printed in the United States of America
10 9 8 7 6 5 4 3 2

ISBN 0-13-248337-8

Prentice-Hall International (UK) Limited, *London*
Prentice-Hall of Australia Pty. Limited, *Sydney*
Prentice-Hall Canada Inc., *Toronto*
Prentice-Hall Hispanoamericana, S.A., *Mexico*
Prentice-Hall of India Private Limited, *New Delhi*
Prentice-Hall of Japan, Inc., *Tokyo*
Simon & Schuster Asia Pte. Ltd., *Singapore*
Editora Prentice-Hall do Brasil, Ltda., *Rio de Janeiro*

WALTER A. TRIEBEL
To my father Adolf A. Triebel

AVTAR SINGH
To my students

CONTENTS

PREFACE

The 8086 family of microprocessors is the most widely used architecture in modern personal computer systems. The family includes both 16-bit microprocessors, such as the 8088, 8086, and 80286, and 32-bit microprocessors, such as the 80386 and 80486. The 8088, which is the 8-bit bus version of the 8086, is the microprocessor employed in the original IBM personal computer (PC). The 8088 and 8086 microprocessors are also used in many other manufacturers' personal computers, as well as a wide variety of other electronic equipment. IBM's original personal computer advanced technology (PCAT) was designed with the 80286 microprocessor. Just like the PC, PCAT compatible personal computers are made by many other manufacturers and today they are built with 80286-, 80386-, and 80486-based microcomputers.

The 8088 and 8086 Microprocessors: Programming, Interfacing, Software, Hardware, and Applications is a thorough study of the 8088 and 8086 microprocessors, their microcomputer system architectures, and the circuitry used in the design of the microcomputer of the original IBM PC. It is written for use as a textbook in courses on microprocessors at vocational schools, colleges, and universities. The intended use is in a one-semester course in microprocessor technology that emphasizes both assembly language software and microcomputer circuit design.

Individuals involved in the design of microprocessor-based electronic equipment need a systems-level understanding of the 8088 and 8086 microcomputers, that is, a thorough understanding of both their software and hardware. The first half of this book explores the software architecture of the 8088 and 8086 microprocessors and teaches the reader how to write, execute, and debug assembly language programs. The things that one needs to learn to be successful at writing assembly language programs for the 8088/8086 are the following:

1. *Software architecture:* the internal registers, flags, memory organization and stack, and how they are used from a software point of view.
2. *Software development tools:* how to use the commands of the program debugger (DEBUG), available in PCDOS, to assemble, execute, and debug instructions and programs.
3. *Instruction set:* the function of each of the instructions in the instruction set, the allowed operand variations, and how to write statements using the instructions.
4. *Programming techniques:* basic techniques of programming, such as flow-charting, jumps, loops, strings, subroutines, parameter passing, and so on.
5. *Applications:* The step by step process of writing programs for practical applications. Examples are a block move routine, average calculating routine, and a data table sort routine.

All of this material is developed in detail in Chapters 2 through 5.

The study of software architecture, instruction set, and assembly language programming is closely coupled with use of the DEBUG program on the PC. That is, the line-by-line assembler in DEBUG is used to assemble instructions and programs into the memory of the PC, whereas other DEBUG commands are used to execute and debug the programs.

The second half of the book examines the hardware architecture of microcomputers built with the 8088 and 8086 microprocessors. To understand the hardware design of an 8088- or 8086-based microcomputer system, the reader must begin by first understanding the function and operation of each of its hardware interfaces: memory, input/output, and interrupt. After this, the role of each of these subsystems can be explored relative to overall microcomputer system operation. It is this material that is presented in Chapters 6 through 9.

We begin in Chapter 6 by examining the architecture of the 8088 and 8086 microprocessor from a hardware point of view. This includes information such as pin layout, minimum- and maximum-mode signal interfaces, signal functions, and clock requirements. The latter part of Chapter 6 covers the memory interface of the 8088/8086. This material includes extensive coverage of memory bus cycles, address maps, memory interface circuits, and program storage memory (ROM, PROM, and EPROM) and data storage memory (SRAM and DRAM). Practical bus interface circuit and memory subsystem design techniques are also examined.

This hardware introduction is followed by separate studies of the architectural characteristics, operation, and circuit designs for the input/output and interrupt interfaces of the 8088- and 8086-based microcomputer in Chapters 7 and 8, respectively. This material includes information such as the function of the signals at each of the interfaces, input/output and interrupt acknowledge bus cycle activity, and examples of typical interface circuit designs. Included in these chapters is detailed coverage of the very large-scale integrated peripheral ICs, such as the 8255A, 8253, 8237A, and 8259A.

The hardware design section closes in Chapter 9 with a study of the 8088-based microcomputer design used in the IBM PC. It presents the circuitry used in the design of the memory subsystem, input/output interfaces, and interrupt interface on the system processor board of the PC. This chapter demonstrates a practical implementation of the material presented in the prior chapters on microcomputer interfacing techniques.

Eleven laboratory exercises are included at the back of the book. These exercises can be performed on either an IBM PC or a PC compatible. The first three laboratories are to be done after completing Chapter 3. With these laboratory exercises, the reader explores the software architecture of the 8088-based microcomputer, assembles and disassembles instructions and programs, and loads, executes, and debugs a program. Laboratory exercises 4 and 5 study the operations performed by the instructions in the 8088's instruction set. Laboratory 4 should be performed after reading Chapter 4 and Laboratory 5 at the end of Chapter 5.

The next three laboratory exercises demonstrate the process of writing a complete program for an application. Laboratory 6 is an application in which a program is used to calculate the average of a series of numbers, 7 demonstrates how a table of random data can be sorted, and 8 shows how to generate the elements of a Fibonacci series.

The rest of the laboratory exercises examine hardware aspects of the IBM PC's 8088-based microcomputer. For example, laboratories 9, 10, and 11 explore the memory subsystem, I/O subsystem, and interrupt subsystem, respectively.

Supplementary materials available from Prentice Hall are a solutions manual, transparencies, and a DOS 3.1 compatible diskette that contains all the programs used in the book.

Walter A. Triebel
Avtar Singh

Introduction to Microprocessors and Microcomputers

1

1.1 INTRODUCTION

In the last few years, the important advances in computer system technology have been closely related to the development of high-performance 16-bit microprocessors and their microcomputer systems. During this period there has been a major change in direction of business away from minicomputers to smaller, lower-cost microcomputers. The IBM personal computer (the PC, as it has become known), which was introduced in mid-1981, was the first microcomputer introduced with a 16-bit microprocessor, the 8088, as its central processing unit. The PC quickly became the driving force in this evolutionary process, and today it stands as the industry standard architecture in the personal computer marketplace.

Since the introduction of the IBM PC, the 16-bit microprocessor market has matured significantly. Today, several complete 16-bit microprocessor families are available. They include support products such as large-scale integrated (LSI) peripheral devices, development systems, emulators, and high-level software languages. Over the same period of time, these higher-performance microprocessors have become more widely used in the design of new electronic equipment and computers. This book presents a detailed study of Intel Corporation's 8088 and 8086 microprocessors.

1

In this chapter we begin our study of microprocessors and microcomputers. The following topics are discussed:

1. The IBM personal computer, a general-purpose microcomputer
2. General architecture of a microcomputer system
3. Evolution of the microprocessor architecture

1.2 THE IBM PERSONAL COMPUTER: A GENERAL-PURPOSE MICROCOMPUTER

The IBM personal computer (the PC), which is shown in Fig. 1.1, was IBM's first entry into the microcomputer market. Since its introduction in mid-1981, market acceptance of the PC has grown by leaps and bounds so that today it is the leading personal computer architecture. An important key to its success is that an enormous amount of application software quickly became available for the machine. There are more than 20,000 off-the-shelf software packages available for use on the PC. They include business applications, software languages, educational programs, games, and even alternate operating systems.

The IBM PC is an example of a *general-purpose digital computer*. By *general purpose* we mean that it is intended to run programs for a wide variety of applications; by *digital computer* we mean that its intended use is for processing data or information. For instance, one user could use the PC with a standard application package for accounting or inventory control. In this type of application, the primary task of the microcomputer is to analyze and process a large amount of data, known as the *data base*. Another user could be running a word-

Figure 1.1 Original IBM personal computer. (Courtesy of International Business Machines Corporation)

processing software package. This is an example of an input/output-intensive task. The user enters text information, this information is reorganized by the microcomputer and then output to a diskette or printer. A third example is where a programmer uses a language, such as FORTRAN, to write programs for scientific applications. Here the primary function of the computer is to solve complex mathematical problems. The point we want to make is that the PC used for each of these applications is the same. The only difference is the software the computer is running.

The large success of the PC has caused IBM to spawn additional family members. IBM's *PCXT* is shown in Fig. 1.2, personal system 2 in Fig. 1.3 and the *PCAT* in Fig. 1.4. Each of these machines offers a wide variety of computing capabilities, range of performance, and software base for use in business and at home.

We have already mentioned that the IBM PC is a *microcomputer*. Let us now look at what a microcomputer is and how it differs from the other classes of computers.

Evolution of the computer marketplace over the last 25 years has taken us from very large *mainframe computers* to smaller *minicomputers* and now even smaller microcomputers. These three classes of computers do not replace each other. They all coexist in the marketplace. Today, computer users have the opportunity to select the computer that best meets their needs. For instance, a large university or institution still would select a mainframe computer for its data-processing center. On the other hand, a department at a university or in business

Figure 1.2 PCXT personal computer. (Courtesy of International Business Machines Corporation)

Figure 1.3 Personal System 2, Model 25. (Courtesy of International Business Machines Corporation)

might select a minicomputer for a multiuser-dedicated need such as application software development. Moreover, managers may select a microcomputer, such as the PC, for their personal needs such as word processing and data-base management.

Figure 1.4 PCAT personal computer. (Courtesy of International Business Machines Corporation)

Along the evolutionary path from mainframes to microcomputers, the basic concepts of computer architecture have not changed. Just like the mainframe and minicomputer, the microcomputer is a general-purpose electronic data-processing system intended for use in a wide variety of applications. The key difference is that microcomputers, such as the IBM PC, employ the newest *very large-scale integrated (VLSI) circuit technology* to implement a smaller, reduced-capability computer system, but with a much lower cost than a minicomputer. However, microcomputers, which are designed for the high-performance end of the microcomputer market, are beginning to capture part of the market that was traditionally supported with lower-performance minicomputers.

1.3 GENERAL ARCHITECTURE OF A MICROCOMPUTER SYSTEM

The *hardware* of a microcomputer system can be divided into four functional sections. The block diagram of Fig. 1.5 shows that they are the *input unit, microprocessing unit, memory unit,* and *output unit.* Each unit has a special function in terms of overall system operation. Let us now look at each of these sections in more detail.

The heart of a microcomputer is its microprocessing unit (MPU). The MPU of a microcomputer is implemented with a VLSI device known as a *microprocessor.* A microprocessor is a general-purpose processing unit built into a single integrated circuit. The microprocessor used in the IBM PC is Intel Corporation's 8088, which is shown in Fig. 1.6.

Earlier we indicated that the 8088 is a 16-bit microprocessor. To be more accurate, it is the 8-bit external bus version in Intel's 8086 family of 16-bit microprocessors. Even though the 8088 has an 8-bit external bus, its internal architecture is 16 bits in length and it can directly process 16-bit-wide data. For this reason, we consider the 8088 as a 16-bit microprocessor.

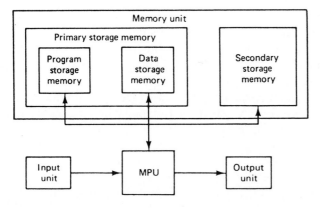

Figure 1.5 General architecture of a microcomputer system.

Figure 1.6 8088 microprocessor. (Courtesy of Intel Corp.)

The 8088 MPU is the part of the microcomputer that executes instructions of the program and processes data. It is responsible for performing all arithmetic operations and making the logical decisions initiated by the computer's program. In addition to arithmetic and logic functions, the MPU controls overall system operation.

The input and output units are the means by which the MPU communicates with the outside world. Input units, such as the *keyboard* on the PC, allow the user to input information or commands to the MPU. For instance, a programmer could key in the lines of a BASIC program from the keyboard. Many other input devices are available for the IBM PC. Two examples are a *mouse* for implementing a more user-friendly input interface and a *joy stick* for use when playing video games.

The most widely used devices on the PC are the *display* and *printer*. The output unit in a microcomputer is used to give feedback to the user and for producing documented results. For instance, key entries from the keyboard are echoed back to the display. This lets the user confirm that the correct entry was made. Moreover, the results produced by the MPU's processing can be displayed or printed. Alternate output devices are also available for the microcomputer; for instance, it can be equipped with a color video display instead of the standard monochrome video display.

The memory unit in a microcomputer is used to store information such as number or character data. By *store* we mean that memory has the ability to hold this information for processing or for outputting at a later time. Programs that define how the computer is to operate and process data also reside in memory.

In the microcomputer system, memory can be divided into two different sections, called *primary storage memory* and *secondary storage memory*. Primary storage memory is used for long-term storage of information that is not currently being used. For example, it can hold programs, files of data, and files of information. In the IBM PC, the *floppy disk drives* represent the long-term storage memory subsystem. If the system has 5¼-inch double-sided, double-density drives, each floppy diskette can store up to 360K bytes of data. The IBM PCXT employs another form of mass storage device. It has one of the floppy drives replaced with a *hard disk drive* capable of storing 10M, 20M, or 40M bytes.

Primary storage memory is normally smaller in size and used for temporary storage of active information, such as the operating system of the computer, the program that is currently being executed, and the data that are being processed. In Fig. 1.5 we see that primary storage memory is further subdivided into *program storage memory* and *data storage memory*. The program section of memory is used to store instructions of the operating system and programs. The data section normally contains data that are to be processed by the programs as they are executed. However, programs can also be loaded into RAM for execution.

Typically, primary storage memory is implemented with both *read-only memory* (ROM) and *random access read/write memory* (RAM) integrated circuits. The IBM PC has 48K bytes of ROM and can be configured with 256K bytes of RAM without adding memory expansion boards.

Data, whether they represent numbers, characters, or instructions, can be stored in either ROM or RAM. In the IBM PC a small part of the operating system and BASIC language are made resident to the computer by supplying them in ROM. By using ROM, this information is made *nonvolatile,* that is, the information is not lost if power is turned off.

On the other hand, data that are to be processed and information that frequently changes must be stored in a type of primary storage memory from which they can be read by the microprocessor, modified through processing, and written back for storage. For this reason they are stored in RAM instead of ROM. For instance, the *DOS 3.1 operating system* for the PC is provided on a diskette; to be used it must be loaded from diskette into the RAM of the microcomputer. RAM is a *volatile* memory. That is, when power is turned off, the data that it holds are lost. This is why the DOS operating system must be reloaded into the PC each time power is turned on.

1.4 EVOLUTION OF THE MICROPROCESSOR ARCHITECTURE

The principal way in which microprocessors and microcomputers are categorized is in terms of the number of binary bits in the data they process, that is, their word length. Four standard data widths have evolved for microprocessors and microcomputers over time, *4 bit, 8 bit, 16 bit,* and *32 bit.*

Figure 1.7 illustrates the evolution of Intel's microprocessors since their introduction in 1972. The first microprocessor, the *4004,* was designed to process data arranged as 4-bit words. This organization is also referred to as a *nibble* of data.

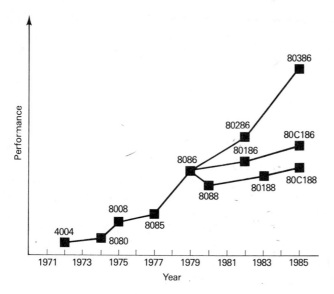

Figure 1.7 Evolution of the Intel microprocessor architecture.

The 4004 implemented a very low-performance microcomputer by today's standards. This low performance and limited system capability restricted its use to simpler, special-purpose applications, such as in calculators and electronic toys.

In 1974 second-generation microprocessors became available. These devices, such as the *8008, 8080,* and *8085* identified in Fig. 1.7, were 8-bit microprocessors; that is, they were all designed to process 8-bit (1-byte-wide) data instead of 4-bit data.

These newer 8-bit microprocessors were characterized by higher-performance operation, larger system capabilities, and greater ease of programming. They were able to provide the system requirements for many applications that could not be satisfied by the earlier 4-bit microprocessors. These extended capabilities led to widespread acceptance of multichip 8-bit microcomputers for special-purpose system designs. Examples of these dedicated applications are electronic instruments, cash registers, and printers.

The plans for development of third-generation 16-bit microprocessors were announced by many leading semiconductor manufacturers in the mid-1970s. Looking at Fig. 1.7 we see that Intel's first 16-bit microprocessor, the *8086,* became available in 1979; its 8-bit bus version, the *8088,* was available in 1980. This was the birth of Intel's 8086 family architecture. Other family members, such as the *80286, 80186,* and *80188,* were introduced in the years that followed.

These 16-bit microprocessors provide high performance and have the ability to satisfy a broad scope of special-purpose and general-purpose microcomputer applications. They all have the ability to handle 8-bit, 16-bit, and special-purpose data types, and their powerful instruction sets are more in line with those provided by minicomputers instead of an 8-bit microcomputer.

This evolution of microprocessors was made possible by advances in semiconductor process technology. During this period, semiconductor device geometries were decreased from about 5 microns in the early 1970s to submicron today. This has permitted integration of one order of magnitude more transistors into the same size chip and at the same time has led to higher operating speeds. In Fig. 1.8 we see that the 4004 contained about 10,000 transistors. Transistor density was increased to about 30,000 with the development of the 8086 in 1979, and with the introduction of the 80286, device transistor count was increased to approximately 140,000.

Microprocessors can be classified according to the type of application for which they have been designed. In Fig. 1.9 we have placed Intel microprocessors in two application-oriented categories: *embedded microcontrollers* and *reprogrammable microprocessors*. Initially devices such as the 8080 were most widely used as *special-purpose microcomputers*. These special-purpose microcomputers were used in embedded control applications, that is, an application in which the microcomputer performs a dedicated control function.

Embedded control applications are further devided into those that primarily involve *event control* and those that require *data control*. An example of an

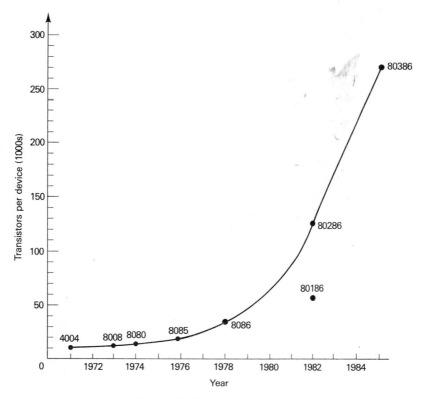

Figure 1.8   Device complexity.

embedded control application that is primarily event control is a microcomputer used for industrial process control. Here the program of the microprocessor is used to initiate a timed sequence of events. An application that focuses more on data control is a hard disk controller interface. In this case, a block of data that is to be processed, for example a data base, must be quickly transferred from external memory to internal memory.

The spectrum of embedded control applications requires a wide variety of system features and performance levels. Devices developed specifically for the needs of this marketplace have stressed low cost and high integration. In Fig. 1.9 we see that the earlier multichip 8080 solutions were initially replaced by the highly integrated 8-bit, single-chip microcomputer devices such as the 8048 and 8051. These devices were tailored to work best as event controllers. For instance, the 8051 offers one-order-of-magnitude-higher performance than the 8080, a more powerful instruction set, and special on-chip functions such as ROM, RAM, an interval/event timer, a universal asynchronous receiver/transmitter (UART), and programmable parallel I/O ports. Today these types of devices are called *microcontrollers*.

Later, devices such as the 80186 and 80188 were designed to better meet the needs of data-control applications. They are also highly integrated but have additional features, such as string instructions and direct memory access channels, which better handle the movement of data.

The category of reprogrammable microprocessors represents the class of applications in which a microprocessor is used to implement a *general-purpose microcomputer*. Unlike a special-purpose microcomputer, a general-purpose microcomputer is intended to run a wide variety of applications; that is, while it is in use it can be easily reprogrammed to run a different application. Two examples of reprogrammable microcomputers are the personal computer and the minicomputer. In Fig. 1.9 we see that the 8086, 8088, 80286, and 80386 are the Intel microprocessors in this category.

Architectural compatibility is a critical need of processors developed for use in reprogrammable applications. As shown in Fig. 1.10, the 80286 provides a super set of the 8086/8088 architecture. Actually both the 80286 and 80386 can operate in either of two modes—the *real-address mode* or *protected-address mode*. When in the real mode, they operate like a high-performance 8086/8088.

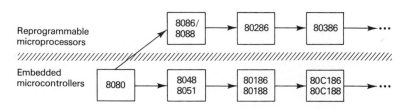

Figure 1.9   Embedded control and reprogrammable applications.

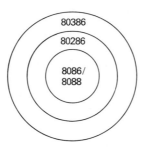

Figure 1.10 Code and system-level compatibility.

Either the 80286 or 80386 can be used to execute the base instruction set, which is object code compatible with the 8086/8088. For this reason, operating systems and programs written for the 8086 and 8088 can be run on the 80286 or 80386 without modification. However, a number of new instructions have been added in the instruction sets of the 80286 and 80386 to enhance performance and functionality. We say that object code is *upward compatible* within the 8086 architecture. This means that 8086/8088 code will run on the 80286 or 80386, but the reverse is not true if any of the new instructions are in use.

A microprocessor that is designed for implementing general-purpose micro-computers must offer more advanced system features than a microcontroller. For example, it needs to support and manage a large memory subsystem. The 80286 is capable of managing a 1G-byte (gigabyte) address space and the 80386 supports 64T-bytes (terabytes) of memory. Moreover, a reprogrammable microcomputer, such as a personal computer, normally runs an operating system. The architectures of the 80286 and 80386 have been enhanced with on-chip support for operating system functions such as memory management, protection, and multitasking. These new features become active only when the device is operated in the protected mode.

Reprogrammable microcomputers, such as those based on the 8086 family, require a wide variety of I/O resources. Figure 1.11 shows the kinds of interfaces that are frequently implemented in a personal computer or minicomputer system. A large family of VLSI peripheral ICs are needed to support a reprogrammable microprocessor such as the 8086, 80286, or 80386; for example, floppy disk controllers, hard disk controllers, local-area-network controllers, and communication controllers. For this reason, the 8086, 8088, 80286, and 80386 are designed to implement a multichip microcomputer system. In this way, a system can be easily configured with the appropriate set of I/O interfaces.

ASSIGNMENTS

Section 1.2

1. Which IBM personal computer employs the 8088 microprocessor?

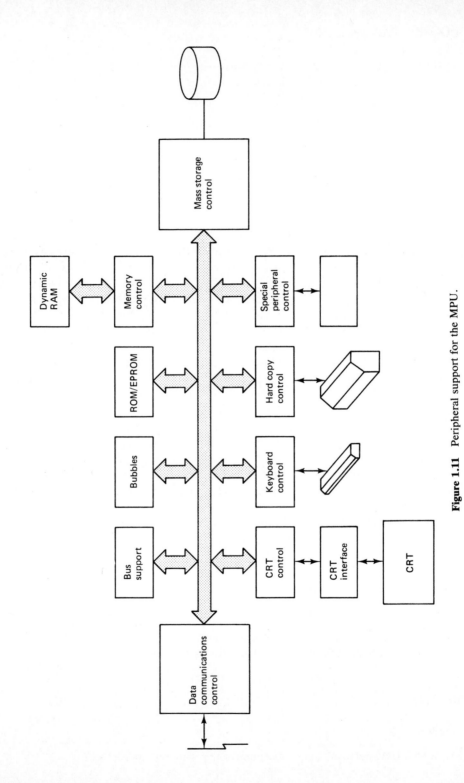

Figure 1.11 Peripheral support for the MPU.

2. What is a general-purpose microcomputer?

3. Name the three classes of computers.

4. What are the main similarities and differences between the minicomputer and the microcomputer?

5. What does VLSI stand for?

Section 1.3

6. What are the four building blocks of a microcomputer system?

7. What is the heart of the microcomputer system called?

8. What is an 8088?

9. What is the primary input unit of the PC? Give two other examples of input units available for the PC.

10. What are the primary output devices of the PC?

11. Into what two sections is the memory of a PC partitioned?

12. What is the storage capacity of the standard 5¼-inch floppy diskette for the PC? What is the storage capacity of the standard hard disk in the PC?

13. What do ROM and RAM stand for?

14. How much ROM is provided in the PC? What is the maximum amount of RAM that can be implemented on the system processor board?

15. Why must the operating system be reloaded from the DOS diskette each time power is turned on?

Section 1.4

16. What are the standard data word lengths for which microprocessors have been developed?

17. What was the first 4-bit microprocessor introduced by Intel Corporation? Eight-bit microprocessor? Sixteen-bit microprocessor?

18. Name five members of the 8086 family architecture.

19. Approximately how many transistors are used to implement the 8088 microprocessor? The 80286 microprocessor?

20. What is an embedded microcontroller?

21. Name the two types of embedded microcontrollers.

22. What is the difference between a multichip microcomputer and a single-chip microcomputer?

23. Name three 16-bit microprocessors intended for use in reprogrammable microcomputer applications.

24. Give the names of the 80386's two modes of operation.

25. What is meant by upward software compatibility relative to 8086 architecture microprocessors?

26. List three advanced architectural features provided by the 80386 microprocessor.

27. Give three types of VLSI peripheral support devices needed in a reprogrammable microcomputer system.

Software Architecture of the 8088 and 8086 Microprocessors

2.1 INTRODUCTION

In this chapter we begin our study of the 8088 and 8086 microprocessor and assembly language programming. To program either the 8088 or 8086 with assembly language, we must understand how the microprocessor and its memory subsystem operate from a software point of view. For this reason, we will examine the *software architecture* of the 8088 and 8086 microprocessors in this chapter. In the material that follows we will just refer to the 8088 microprocessor, but everything that is described for the 8088 also applies to the 8086. This is because the software architecture of the 8086 is identical to that of the 8088. The following topics are covered:

1. Software—the microcomputer program
2. Software model of the 8088/8086 microprocessor
3. Memory address space and data organization
4. Data types
5. Segment registers and memory segmentation
6. Dedicated and general use of memory
7. Instruction pointer

14

   8. Data registers
   9. Pointer and index registers
   10. Status, or flag, register
   11. Generating a memory address
   12. The stack
   13. Input/output address space
   14. Addressing modes of the 8088/8086 microprocessor

2.2 SOFTWARE—THE MICROCOMPUTER PROGRAM

In this section, we begin our study of the 8088's software architecture with the topics of software and the computer program. A computer cannot think about how to process data. It must be told exactly what to do, where to get data, what to do with the data, and where to put the results when it is done. This is the job of software in a microcomputer system.

The sequence of instructions that is used to tell a computer what to do is called a *program*. A program may be simple and include just a few instructions or very complex and contain more than 100,000 instructions. When the computer is operating, it fetches and executes one instruction of the program after the other. In this way, the instructions of the program guide it step by step through the task that it is to perform.

Software is a general name used to refer to a wide variety of programs that can be run by a microcomputer. Examples are *languages, operating systems, application programs,* and *diagnostics*.

The native language of the IBM PC is 8088 *machine language*. Programs must always be coded in this machine language before they can be executed by the 8088. The 8088 microprocessor understands and performs operations for more than 100 instructions. When expressed in machine code, an instruction is encoded using 0s and 1s. A single machine instruction can take anywhere from 1 to 6 bytes of code. Even though the 8088 only understands machine code, it is almost impossible to write programs directly in machine language. For this reason, programs are normally written in other languages, such as 8088 assembly language or a high-level language such as C.

In 8088 assembly language, each of the basic operations that can be performed by the 8088 microprocessor is described with alphanumeric symbols instead of with 0s and 1s. Each instruction is represented by one *assembly language statement* in a program. This statement must specify which operation is to be performed and what data operands are to be processed. For this reason, an instruction can be divided into two parts: its *opcode* and its *operands*. The opcode is the part of the instruction that identifies the operation that is to be performed. For example, typical operations are add, subtract, and move. Each opcode is assigned a unique one- through five-letter combination. This letter combination is referred to as the *mnemonic* for the instruction. For example, the mnemonics for the earlier operations are ADD, SUB, and MOV. Operands describe the data that are to be processed as the microprocessor carries out the operation specified by the opcode. They identify whether the source and destination of the data are registers within the MPU or storage locations in data memory.

An example of an instruction written in 8088 assembly language is

```
ADD AX,BX
```

This instruction says, "Add the contents of BX and AX together and put the sum in AX." AX is called the *destination operand* because it is the place where the result ends up, and BX is called the *source operand*.

Another example of an assembly language statement is

```
START: MOV AX,BX ;COPY BX INTO AX
```

This statement begins with the word START:. It is an address identifier for the instruction MOV AX,BX. This type of identifier is called a *label*. The instruction is followed by ;COPY BX INTO AX. This part of the statement is called a *comment*. Thus a general format for an assembly language statement is

```
LABEL: INSTRUCTION ;COMMENT
```

Programs written in assembly language are referred to as *source code*. An example of a short 8088 assembly language program is shown in Fig. 2.1(a). The assembly language statements are located on the left. Notice that labels are not used in most statements. On the other hand, a comment describing the statement is usually included on the right. This type of documentation makes it easier for a program to be read and debugged.

Assembly language programs cannot be directly executed on the 8088. They must still be converted to an equivalent machine language program for execution by the 8088. This conversion is automatically done by running the program through what is called an *assembler*. The machine language output produced by the assembler is called *object code*.

Figure 2.1(b) is the *listing* produced by assembling the assembly language source code in Fig. 2.1(a) with IBM's macroassembler for the PC. Reading from left to right, this listing contains line numbers, addresses of memory locations, the machine language instructions, the original assembly language statements, and comments. For example, line 53, which is

```
0013 8A24 NXTPT: MOV AH,[SI] ;MOVE A BYTE
```

shows that the assembly language instruction MOV AH,[SI] is encoded as 8A24 in machine language and that this 2-byte instruction is loaded into memory starting at

```
TITLE   BLOCK-MOVE PROGRAM

        PAGE    ,132

COMMENT *This program moves a block of specified number of bytes
        from one place to another place*


;Define constants used in this program

        N           =       16              ;Bytes to be moved
        BLK1ADDR=           100H            ;Source block offset address
        BLK2ADDR=           120H            ;Destination block offset addr
        DATASEGADDR=        1020H           ;Data segment start address


STACK_SEG   SEGMENT         STACK 'STACK'
            DB              64 DUP(?)
STACK_SEG   ENDS


CODE_SEG    SEGMENT         'CODE'
BLOCK       PROC            FAR
        ASSUME  CS:CODE_SEG,SS:STACK_SEG

;To return to DEBUG program put return address on the stack

        PUSH    DS
        MOV     AX, 0
        PUSH    AX

;Set up the data segment address

        MOV     AX, DATASEGADDR
        MOV     DS, AX

;Set up the source and destination offset addresses

        MOV     SI, BLK1ADDR
        MOV     DI, BLK2ADDR

;Set up the count of bytes to be moved

        MOV     CX, N

;Copy source block to destination block

NXTPT:  MOV     AH, [SI]                ;Move a byte
        MOV     [DI], AH
        INC     SI                      ;Update pointers
        INC     DI
        DEC     CX                      ;Update byte counter
        JNZ     NXTPT                   ;Repeat for next byte
        RET                             ;Return to DEBUG program
BLOCK       ENDP
CODE_SEG    ENDS
        END     BLOCK                   ;End of program
```

(a)

Figure 2.1 (a) Example of an 8088 assembly language program. (b) Assembled version of the program.

```
 1
 2
 3                                    TITLE   BLOCK-MOVE PROGRAM
 4
 5                                            PAGE    ,132
 6
 7                                    COMMENT *This program moves a block of specified number of bytes
 8                                            from one place to another place*
 9
10
11                                    ;Define constants used in this program
12
13       = 0010                               N        =      16          ;Bytes to be moved
14       = 0100                               BLK1ADDR=      100H         ;Source block offset address
15       = 0120                               BLK2ADDR=      120H         ;Destination block offset addr
16       = 1020                               DATASEGADDR=   1020H        ;Data segment start address
17
18
19       0000                         STACK_SEG     SEGMENT       STACK 'STACK'
20       0000      40 [                              DB            64 DUP(?)
21                      ??
22                       ]
23
24       0040                         STACK_SEG     ENDS
25
26
27       0000                         CODE_SEG      SEGMENT       'CODE'
28       0000                         BLOCK         PROC          FAR
29                                    ASSUME  CS:CODE_SEG,SS:STACK_SEG
30
31                                    ;To return to DEBUG program put return address on the stack
32
33       0000  1E                             PUSH    DS
34       0001  B8 0000                        MOV     AX, 0
35       0004  50                             PUSH    AX
36
37                                    ;Set up the data segment address
38
39       0005  B8 1020                        MOV     AX, DATASEGADDR
40       0008  8E D8                          MOV     DS, AX
41
42                                    ;Set up the source and destination offset adresses
43
44       000A  BE 0100                        MOV     SI, BLK1ADDR
45       000D  BF 0120                        MOV     DI, BLK2ADDR
46
47                                    ;Set up the count of bytes to be moved
48
49       0010  B9 0010                        MOV     CX, N
50
51                                    ;Copy source block to destination block
52
53       0013  8A 24                 NXTPT:   MOV     AH, [SI]              ;Move a byte
```

(b)

Figure 2.1   (Continued)

```
The IBM Personal Computer MACRO Assembler 02-22-88       PAGE    1-2
BLOCK-MOVE PROGRAM


54      0015  88 25                      MOV     [DI], AH
55      0017  46                         INC     SI              ;Update pointers
56      0018  47                         INC     DI
57      0019  49                         DEC     CX              ;Update byte counter
58      001A  75 F7                      JNZ     NXTPT           ;Repeat for next byte
59      001C  CB                         RET                     ;Return to DEBUG program
60      001D                   BLOCK     ENDP
61      001D           CODE_SEG          ENDS
62                               END      BLOCK                  ;End of program



    The IBM Personal Computer MACRO Assembler 02-22-88       PAGE    Symbols-1
BLOCK-MOVE PROGRAM


Segments and groups:

                N a m e              Size    align    combine class

CODE_SEG . . . . . . . . . . .       001D    PARA     NONE   'CODE'
STACK_SEG. . . . . . . . . . .       0040    PARA     STACK  'STACK'

Symbols:

                N a m e              Type    Value    Attr

BLK1ADDR . . . . . . . . . . .       Number  0100
BLK2ADDR . . . . . . . . . . .       Number  0120
BLOCK. . . . . . . . . . . . .       F PROC  0000     CODE_SEG      Length =001D
DATASEGADDR. . . . . . . . . .       Number  1020
N. . . . . . . . . . . . . . .       Number  0010
NXTPT. . . . . . . . . . . . .       L NEAR  0013     CODE_SEG


Warning Severe
Errors  Errors
0       0
```

(b)

Figure 2.1 (Continued)

address 0013_{16} and ending at address 0014_{16}. Note that for simplicity the machine language instructions are expressed in hexadecimal notation, not in binary. Use of assembly language makes it much easier to write a program. But notice that there is still a one-to-one relationship between assembly and machine language instructions.

High-level languages make writing programs even easier. In a language like BASIC, high-level commands such as FOR, NEXT, and GO are provided. These commands no longer correspond to a single machine language statement. In fact, they may require many assembly language statements to be implemented. Again, the program must be converted to machine code before it can be run on the 8088.

The program that converts high-level language statements to machine code instructions is called a *compiler*.

Some languages, for instance, BASIC, are not always compiled. Instead, *interpretive* versions of the language are available. When a program written in an interpretive form of BASIC is executed, each line of the program is interpreted just before it is executed and at that moment replaced with a corresponding machine language routine. It is this machine code routine that is executed by the 8088.

The question you may be asking yourself right now is that if it is so much easier to write programs with a high-level language, then why is it important to know how to program the 8088 in its assembly language? Let us now answer this question.

We just pointed out that if a program is written in a high-level language, it must be compiled into machine code before it can be run on the 8088. The general nature with which compilers must be designed usually results in inefficient machine code. That is, the quality of the machine code that is produced for the program depends on the quality of the compiler program in use. What is found is that a compiled machine code implementation of a program that was written in a high-level language results in many more machine code instructions than an assembled version of an equivalent assembly language program. This leads us to the two key benefits derived from writing programs in assembly language: first, the machine code program that is produced will take up less memory space than the compiled version of the program; second, it will execute much faster.

Now we know the benefits attained by writing programs in assembly language, but we still do not know when these benefits are important. To be important, they must outweigh the additional effort that must be put into writing the program in assembly language instead of a high-level language. One of the major uses of assembly language programming is in *real-time applications*. By *real time* we mean that the task required by the application must be completed before any other input to the program can occur that will alter its operation.

For example, the *device service routine* that controls the operation of the floppy disk drives of the PC is a good example of the kind of program that is usually written in assembly language. This is because it is a segment of program that must closely control hardware of the microcomputer in real time. In this case, a program that is written in a high-level language probably could not respond quickly enough to control the hardware, and even if it could, operations performed with the disk subsystem would be very slow. Some other examples of hardware-related operations typically performed by routines written in assembler are communication routines such as those that drive the display and printer and the I/O routines that scan the keyboard.

Assembly language is not only important for controlling hardware devices of the microcomputer system; its use is also important when performing pure software operations. For instance, applications frequently require the microcomputer to search through a large table of data in memory looking for a special string of characters, for instance, a person's name. This type of operation can be easily performed by writing a program in a high-level language; however, for large tables of data the search will take very long. By implementing the search routine through assembly language, the performance of the search operation is greatly improved. Other examples of software operations that may require implementation with high-performance routines derived from assembly language are *code translations,* such as from ASCII to EBCDIC, *table sort or search routines,* such as a bubble sort, and *mathematical routines,* such as those for floating-point arithmetic.

Not all parts of an application require real-time performance. For this reason, it is a common practice to mix routines developed through a high-level language and routines developed with assembly language in the same program. That is, assembler is used to code those parts of the application that must perform real-time operations; high-level language is used to write those parts that are not time critical. The machine codes obtained by assembling or compiling the two types of program segments are linked together to form the final application program.

2.3 INTERNAL ARCHITECTURE OF THE 8088/8086 MICROPROCESSOR

The internal architectures of the 8088 and 8086 microprocessors are similar. They both employ what is called *parallel processing;* that is, they are implemented with simultaneously operating multiple processing units. Figure 2.2(a) illustrates the internal architecture of the 8088 and 8086 microprocessors. Here we find that they contain two processing units: the *bus interface unit* (BIU) and the *execution unit* (EU). Each unit has dedicated functions and they both operate at the same time. In essence, this parallel processing effectively eliminates the time needed to fetch many of the instructions of the microcomputer's program. The results are efficient use of the system bus and higher performance for the 8088/8086 microcomputer system.

The bus interface unit is the 8088/8086's interface to the outside world; that is, it is responsible for performing all external bus operations. In general, the BIU performs bus operations, such as instruction fetching, reading and writing of data operands for memory, and inputting or outputting of data for input/output peripherals. These information transfers take place over the system bus. This bus includes an 8-bit bidirectional data bus (16 bits for the 8086) and a 20-bit address bus. The BIU is not just responsible for performing bus operations, it also performs other functions related to instruction and data acquisition. For instance, it is responsible for instruction queueing and address generation.

To implement these functions, the BIU contains the segment registers, the instruction pointer, address generation adder, bus control logic, and an instruction queue. Figure 2.2(b) shows the bus interface unit of the 8088/8086 in more detail.

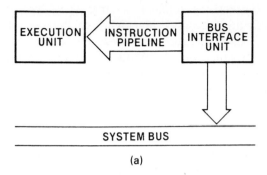

SYSTEM BUS

(a)

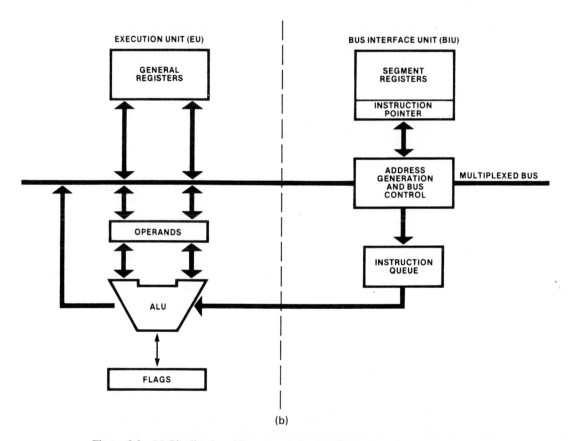

(b)

Figure 2.2 (a) Pipelined architecture of the 8088/8086 microprocessors (Reprinted with permission of Intel Corporation, © 1981); (b) execution and bus interface units (Reprinted with permission of Intel Corporation, © 1981).

The BIU uses a mechanism known as an *instruction queue* to implement a pipe-lined architecture. This queue permits prefetch of up to four bytes (six bytes for the 8086) of instruction code. Whenever the queue is not full, the BIU is free to look ahead in the program by prefetching the next sequential instructions. These prefetched instructions are held in the first-in, first-out (FIFO) queue. After a byte is loaded at the input end of the queue, it automatically shifts up through the FIFO to the empty location nearest the output. If the queue is full and the EU is not requesting access to data operands in memory, the BIU does not perform any bus cycles.

The execution unit is responsible for decoding and executing instructions. Notice in Fig. 2.2(b) that it consists of the *arithmetic logic unit* (ALU), status and control flags, general purpose registers, and temporary operand registers. The EU accesses instructions from the output end of the instruction queue and data from the general-purpose registers or memory. It reads one instruction byte after the other from the output of the queue, decodes them, generates operand addresses if necessary, passes them to the BIU and requests it to perform the read or write cycle to memory or I/O, and performs the operation specified by the instruction on operands. During execution of the instruction, the EU tests the status and control flags and updates these flags based on the results of executing the instruction. If the queue is empty, the EU waits for the next instruction byte to be fetched and shifted to the top of the queue.

2.4 SOFTWARE MODEL OF THE 8088/8086 MICROPROCESSOR

The purpose of developing a *software model* is to aid the programmer in understanding the operation of the microcomputer system from a software point of view. To be able to program a microprocessor, one does not need to know all of its hardware architecture features. For instance, we do not necessarily need to know the function of the signals at its various pins, their electrical connections, or their electrical switching characteristics. The function, interconnection, and operation of the internal circuits of the microprocessor also need not normally be considered.

What is important to the programmer is to know the various registers within the device and to understand their purpose, functions, operating capabilities, and limitations. Furthermore, it is essential to know how external memory is organized and how it is addressed to obtain instructions and data.

The software architecture of the 8088 microprocessor is illustrated with the software model shown in Fig. 2.3. Looking at this diagram, we see that it includes 13 16-bit internal registers: the *instruction pointer* (IP), *four data registers* (AX, BX, CX, and DX), *two pointer registers* (BP and SP), *two index registers* (SI and DI), and *four segment registers* (CS, DS, SS, and ES). In addition to these registers, there is another register called the *status register* (SR), with nine of its bits implemented for status and control flags. The model also includes a *1,048,576*

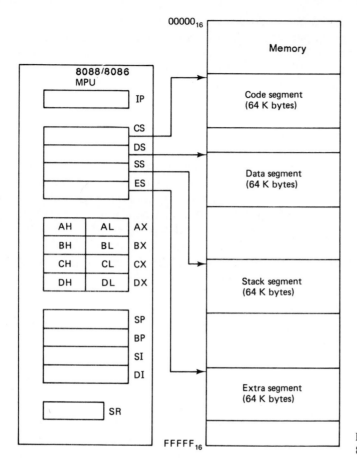

Figure 2.3 Software model of the 8088/8086 microprocessor.

(1M) *byte address space* for implementation of external memory. Our concern here is what can be done with this architecture and how to do it through software. For this purpose, we will now begin a detailed study of the elements of the model and their relationship to software.

2.5 MEMORY ADDRESS SPACE AND DATA ORGANIZATION

Now that we have introduced the idea of a software model, let us look at how information such as numbers, characters, and instructions are stored in memory. As shown in Fig. 2.4, the 8088 microcomputer supports 1M bytes of external memory. This memory space is organized as bytes of data stored at consecutive

Figure 2.4   Address space of the 8088. (Courtesy of Intel Corp.)

addresses over the address range 00000_{16} to $FFFFF_{16}$. From an addressing point of view, *even-* or *odd-addressed bytes of data* can be independently accessed. In this way, we see that the memory in an 8088-based microcomputer is actually organized as 8-bit bytes, not as 16-bit words. However, the 8088 can access any two consecutive bytes as a *word* of data. In this case, the *lower-addressed byte is the least significant byte* of the word and the *higher-addressed byte is its most significant byte.*

Figure 2.5(a) shows how a word of data is stored in memory. Notice that the storage location at the lower address, 00724_{16}, contains the value $00000010_2 = 02_{16}$. Moreover, the contents of the next-higher-addressed storage location 00725_{16} are $01010101_2 = 55_{16}$. These two bytes represent the word $0101010100000010_2 = 5502_{16}$.

To permit efficient use of memory, words of data can be stored at even- or odd-address boundaries. The least significant bit of the address determines the type of *word boundary*. If this bit is 0, the word is said to be held at an *even-address boundary*. That is, a word at an even-address boundary corresponds to two consecutive bytes, with the least significant byte located at an even address. For example, the word in Fig. 2.5(a) has its least significant byte at address 00724_{16}. Therefore, it is stored at an even-address boundary.

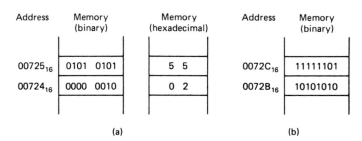

Figure 2.5   (a) Storing a word of data in memory. (b) An example.

EXAMPLE 2.1

What is the data word shown in Fig. 2.5(b)? Express the result in hexadecimal form. Is it stored at an even- or an odd-address boundary?

SOLUTION   The most significant byte of the word is stored at address $0072C_{16}$ and equals

$$11111101_2 = FD_{16}$$

Its least significant byte is stored at address $0072B_{16}$ and is

$$10101010_2 = AA_{16}$$

Together these two bytes give the word

$$1111110110101010_2 = FDAA_{16}$$

Expressing the address of the least significant byte in binary form gives

$$0072B_{16} = 0000000001110010101 1_2$$

Since the rightmost bit (LSB) is logic 1, the word is stored at an odd-address boundary in memory.

The *double word* is another data form that can be processed by the 8088 microcomputer. A double word corresponds to four consecutive bytes of data stored in memory. An example of double-word data is a *pointer*. A pointer is a two-word address element that is used to access data or code outside the current segment of memory. The word of this pointer that is stored at the higher address is called the *segment base address* and the word at the lower address is called the *offset value*.

An example showing the storage of a pointer in memory is given in Fig. 2.6(a). Here we find that the higher-addressed word, which represents the segment address, is stored starting at even-address boundary 00006_{16}. The most significant byte of this word is at address 00007_{16} and equals $00111011_2 = 3B_{16}$. Its least significant byte is at address 00006_{16} and equals $01001100_2 = 4C_{16}$. Combining these two values, we get the segment base address, which equals $0011101101001100_2 = 3B4C_{16}$.

The offset part of the pointer is the lower-addressed word. Its least significant byte is stored at address 00004_{16}. This location contains $01100101_2 = 65_{16}$. The most significant byte is at address 00005_{16}, which contains $00000000_2 = 00_{16}$. The resulting offset is $0000000001100101_2 = 0065_{16}$.

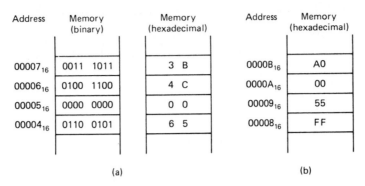

Figure 2.6 (a) Storing a 32-bit pointer in memory. (b) An example.

EXAMPLE 2.2

How should the pointer with segment-base address equal to $A000_{16}$ and offset address $55FF_{16}$ be stored at an even-address boundary starting at 00008_{16}?

SOLUTION   Storage of the two-word pointer requires four consecutive byte locations in memory starting at address 00008_{16}. The least significant byte of the offset is stored at address 00008_{16}. This value is shown as FF_{16} in Fig. 2.6(b). The most significant byte of the offset, which is 55_{16}, is stored at address 00009_{16}. These two bytes are followed by the least significant byte of the segment base address, 00_{16}, at address $0000A_{16}$, and its most significant byte, $A0_{16}$, at address $0000B_{16}$.

2.6 DATA TYPES

In the last section we identified the fundamental data formats of the 8088 as the byte (8 bits), word (16 bits), or double word (32 bits). As shown in Fig. 2.7, these basic formats represent data elements that span one, two, or four consecutive bytes of memory, respectively. Here we will continue by examining the types of data that can be coded into these formats for processing by the 8088 microprocessor.

The 8088 microprocessor can directly process data expressed in a number of different data types. Let us begin with the *integer data type*. The 8088 can process data as either *unsigned* or *signed* integer numbers; each type of integer can be

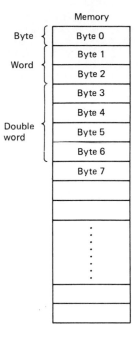

Figure 2.7   Byte, word, and double-word data organization.

either byte-wide or word-wide. Figure 2.8(a) represents an *unsigned byte integer*. This data type can be used to represent decimal numbers in the range 0 through 255. The *unsigned word integer* is shown in Fig. 2.8(b). It can be used to represent decimal numbers in the range 0 through 65,535.

The *signed byte integer* and *signed word integer* of Figs 2.9(a) and (b) are similar to the unsigned integer data types just introduced; however, here the most significant bit is a sign bit. A 0 in the MSB position identifies a positive number. For this reason, signed integers can represent decimal numbers in the ranges $+127$ to -128 and $+32767$ to -32768, respectively. For example $+3$ is expressed as $00000011_2(03_{16})$. On the other hand, the 8088 represents negative numbers in 2's-complement notation. Therefore, -3 is coded as $11111101_2(FD_{16})$.

The 8088 can also process data that is coded as *BCD numbers*. Figure 2.10(a) lists the BCD values for decimal numbers 0 through 9. BCD data can be stored in

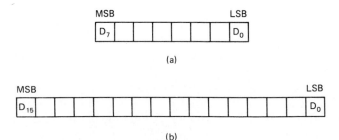

Figure 2.8   (a) Unsigned byte integer. (b) Unsigned word integer.

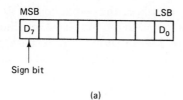

Sign bit

(a)

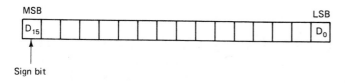

Sign bit

(b)

Figure 2.9 (a) Signed byte integer. (b) Signed word integer.

Decimal	BCD
0	0000
1	0001
2	0010
3	0011
4	0100
5	0101
6	0110
7	0111
8	1000
9	1001

(a)

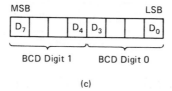

(c)

Figure 2.10 (a) BCD numbers. (b) Unpacked BCD byte. (c) Packed BCD digits.

either unpacked or packed form. For instance, the *unpacked BCD byte* in Fig. 2.10(b) shows that a single BCD digit is stored in the four least significant bits, and the upper four bits are set to 0. Figure 2.10(c) shows a byte with packed BCD digits. Here we find two BCD numbers stored in a byte. The upper four bits represent the most significant digit of a two-digit BCD number.

Information expressed in *ASCII (American Standard Code for Information Interchange)* can also be directly processed by the 8088 microprocessor. Figure 2.11(a) shows how numbers, letters, and control characters are coded in ASCII.

	b_7	0	0	0	0	1	1	1	1
	b_6	0	0	1	1	0	0	1	1
	b_5	0	1	0	1	0	1	0	1
b_4 b_3 b_2 b_1	H_1 / H_0	0	1	2	3	4	5	6	7
0 0 0 0	0	NUL	DLE	SP	0	@	P	'	p
0 0 0 1	1	SOH	DC1	!	1	A	Q	a	q
0 0 1 0	2	STX	DC2	"	2	B	R	b	r
0 0 1 1	3	ETX	DC3	#	3	C	S	c	s
0 1 0 0	4	EOT	DC4	$	4	D	T	d	t
0 1 0 1	5	ENQ	NAK	%	5	E	U	e	u
0 1 1 0	6	ACK	SYN	&	6	F	V	f	v
0 1 1 1	7	BEL	ETB	'	7	G	W	g	w
1 0 0 0	8	BS	CAN	(	8	H	X	h	x
1 0 0 1	9	HT	EM	)	9	I	Y	i	y
1 0 1 0	A	LF	SUB	*	:	J	Z	j	z
1 0 1 1	B	V	ESC	+	;	K	[	k	}
1 1 0 0	C	FF	FS	,	<	L	\	l	|
1 1 0 1	D	CR	GS	—	=	M	]	m	{
1 1 1 0	E	SO	RS	.	>	N	Λ	n	~
1 1 1 1	F	SI	US	/	?	O	-	o	DEL

(a)

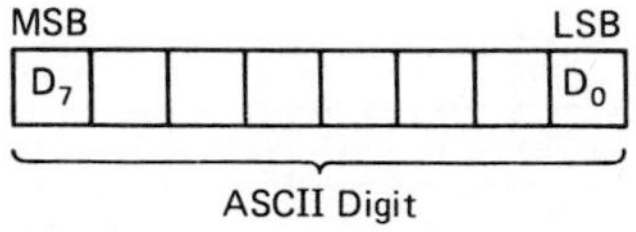

(b)

Figure 2.11 (a) ASCII table. (b) ASCII number.

For instance, the number 5 is coded as

$$H_1H_0 = 00110101_2 = 35H$$

where H denotes that the number is a hexadecimal number. As shown in Fig. 2.11(b), ASCII numbers are stored one number per byte.

2.7 SEGMENT REGISTERS AND MEMORY SEGMENTATION

Even though the 8088 has a 1M-byte memory address space, not all this memory can be active at one time. Actually, the 1M byte of memory can be partitioned into 64K (65,536) byte *segments*. Each segment represents an independently addressable unit of memory consisting of 64K consecutive byte-wide storage locations. Each segment is assigned a *base address* that identifies its starting point, that is, its lowest-addressed byte storage location.

Only four of these 64K-byte segments can be active at a time. They are called the *code segment, stack segment, data segment,* and *extra segment*. The locations of the segments of memory that are active, as shown in Fig. 2.12, are identified by the value of address held in the 8088's four internal segment registers: CS (*code segment*), SS (*stack segment*), DS (*data segment*), and ES (*extra segment*). Each contains a 16-bit base address that points to the lowest-addressed byte of the segment in memory. These four segments give a maximum of 256K

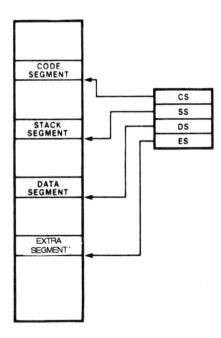

Figure 2.12 Active segments of memory. (Reprinted with permission of Intel Corporation, © 1979)

bytes of active memory. Of this, 64K bytes are allocated for code (*program storage*), 64K bytes for a *stack,* and 128K bytes for *data storage.*

The values held in these registers are usually referred to as the *current segment register values.* For example, the word in CS points to the first byte-wide storage location in the current code segment.

Figure 2.13 illustrates the *segmentation of memory.* In this diagram, we have identified 64K-byte segments with letters such as A, B, and C. The data segment (DS) register contains the value B. Therefore, the second 64K-byte segment of memory from the top, which is labeled B, acts as the current data storage segment. This is the segment in which data that are to be processed by the microcomputer are stored. Therefore, this part of the microcomputer's memory must contain read/write storage locations that can be accessed by instructions as storage locations for source and destination operands. Segment E is selected for the code segment. It is this segment of memory from which instructions of the program are currently being fetched for execution. The stack segment (SS) register contains H, thereby selecting the 64K-byte segment labeled as H for use as a stack. Finally, the extra segment register ES is loaded with J so that segment J of memory can function as a second 64K-byte data storage segment.

The segment registers are said to be *user accessible.* This means that the programmer can change the value they hold through software. Therefore, for a program to gain access to another part of memory, it just has to change the value of the appropriate register or registers. For instance, a new 128K-byte data space can be brought in by simply changing the values in DS and ES.

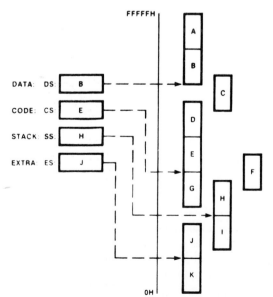

Figure 2.13 Contiguous, adjacent, disjointed, and overlapping segments. (Reprinted by permission of Intel Corp. Copyright/Intel Corp. 1979)

There is one restriction on the value that can be assigned to a segment as a base address: it must reside on a 16-byte address boundary. Valid examples are 00000_{16}, 00010_{16}, and 00020_{16}. Other than this restriction, segments can be *contiguous, adjacent, disjointed,* or even *overlapping.* For example, in Fig. 2.13, segments A and B are contiguous, whereas segments B and C are overlapping.

2.8 DEDICATED AND GENERAL USE OF MEMORY

Any part of the 8088 microcomputer's 1M-byte address space can be implemented; however, some address locations have *dedicated functions.* These locations should not be used as general memory where data or instructions of the program are stored. Let us now look at these reserved and general-use parts of memory.

Figure 2.14 shows the *reserved* and *general-use (open) parts* of the 8088's *address space.* Notice that storage locations from address 00000_{16} to 00013_{16} are dedicated and those from address 00014_{16} to $00007F_{16}$ are reserved. These 128 bytes of memory are used for storage of pointers to interrupt service routines. As indicated earlier, each pointer requires 4 bytes of memory. Two bytes hold the 16-bit segment address and the other two hold the 16-bit offset. Therefore, it can contain up to 32 pointers.

At the high end of the memory address space is another reserved pointer area. It is located from address $FFFFC_{16}$ through $FFFFF_{16}$. These four memory locations are reserved for use with future products and should not be used. Moreover, Intel Corporation, the manufacturer of the 8088, has identified the 12 storage locations from address $FFFF0_{16}$ through $FFFFB_{16}$ as dedicated for functions such as storage of the hardware reset jump instruction. For instance, physical address $FFFF0_{16}$ is where the 8088/8086 begins execution after a reset.

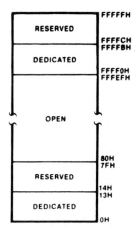

Figure 2.14 Dedicated and general use memory. (Reprinted by permission of Intel Corp. Copyright/Intel Corp. 1979)

2.9 INSTRUCTION POINTER

The next register from the 8088's software model of Fig. 2.3 that we will consider is the *instruction pointer* (IP). It is also 16 bits in length and identifies the location of the next instruction to be executed in the current code segment. It is similar to a *program counter;* however, IP contains an offset instead of the actual address of the next instruction. This is because the 8088 contains 16-bit registers, but requires a 20-bit address for addressing memory. Internal to the 8088, the offset in IP is combined with the contents of CS to generate the address of the instruction.

During normal operation, the 8088 fetches instructions one after the other from the code segment of memory and executes them. After an instruction is fetched from memory it is decoded within the 8088 and, if necessary, operands are read from either the data segment of memory or internal registers. Next the operation specified in the instruction is performed on the operands and the result is written back to either an internal register or a storage location in memory. The 8088 is now ready to execute the next instruction.

Every time an instruction is fetched from memory, the 8088 updates the value in IP such that it points to the first byte of the next sequential instruction. In this way, it is always ready to fetch the next instruction of the program. Actually, the 8088 has an internal *code queue* and *prefetches* up to 4 bytes of instruction code and holds them internal waiting for execution.

The active code segment can be changed by simply executing an instruction that loads a new value into the CS register. For this reason, we can use any 64K-byte segment of memory for storage of code.

2.10 DATA REGISTERS

As shown in Fig. 2.3, four *general-purpose data registers* are located within the 8088. During program execution, they are used for temporary storage of frequently used intermediate results. The advantage of storing these data in internal registers instead of memory is that they can be accessed much faster.

The data registers are shown in more detail in Fig. 2.15(a). Here we see that the four data registers are referred to as the *accumulator register* (A), the *base register* (B), the *count register* (C), and the *data register* (D). These names imply special functions that are performed by each register. Each of these registers can be accessed either as a whole for 16-bit data operations or as two 8-bit registers for byte-wide data operations. References to a register as a word are identified by an X after the register letter. For instance, the 16-bit accumulator is referenced as AX. In a similar way, the other three registers are referred to as BX, CX, and DX.

On the other hand, when referencing one of these registers on a byte-wide basis, its high byte and low byte are identified by following the register name with the letter H or L, respectively. For the A register, the most significant byte is

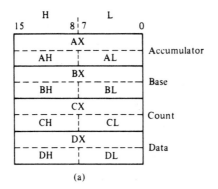

Register	Operations
AX	Word multiply, word divide, word I/O
AL	Byte multiply, byte divide, byte I/O, translate, decimal arithmetic
AH	Byte multiply, byte divide
BX	Translate
CX	String operations, loops
CL	Variable shift and rotate
DX	Word multiply, word divide, indirect I/O

(a)   (b)

Figure 2.15   (a) General-purpose data registers. (Reprinted by permission of Intel Corp. Copyright/Intel Corp. 1979) (b) Dedicated register functions. (Reprinted by permission of Intel Corp. Copyright/Intel Corp. 1979)

referred to as AH and the least significant byte as AL. The other byte-wide register pairs are BH and BL, CH and CL, and DH and DL.

Any of the general-purpose data registers can be used as the source or destination of an operand during an arithmetic operation such as ADD or a logic operation such as AND. However, for some operations, such as those performed by string instructions, specific registers are used. In the case of a string instruction, register C is used to store a count representing the number of bytes to be processed. This is the reason it is given the name *count register*. Another use of C is for the count of the number of bits by which the contents of an operand must be shifted or rotated during the execution of the multibit shift or rotate instructions.

Another example of dedicated use of data registers is that all I/O oeprations require the data that are to be input or output to be in the A register, while register D holds the address of the I/O port. Figure 2.15(b) summarizes the dedicated functions of the general-purpose data registers.

2.11 POINTER AND INDEX REGISTERS

There are four other general-purpose registers shown in Fig. 2.3: two *pointer registers* and two *index registers*. They are used to store offset addresses of memory locations relative to the segment registers. The values held in these registers can be read, loaded, or modified through software. This is done prior to executing the instruction that references the register for address offset. In this way, the instruction simply specifies which register contains the offset address.

Figure 2.16 shows that the two pointer registers are the *stack pointer* (SP) and *base pointer* (BP). The contents of SP and BP are used as offsets from the current value of SS during the execution of instructions that involve the stack segment of memory. In this way, they permit easy access to locations in the stack part of memory. The value in SP always represents the offset of the next stack

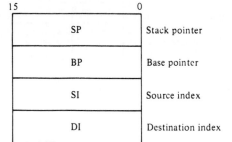

Figure 2.16 Pointer and index registers. (Reprinted by permission of Intel Corp. Copyright/Intel Corp. 1979)

location that can be accessed. That is, when combined with the value in SS, it results in a 20-bit address that points to the *top of the stack.*

BP also represents an offset relative to the SS register. Its intended use is for access of data within the stack segment of memory. BP is employed as the offset in an addressing mode called the based addressing mode.

One common use of BP is within a subroutine that must reference parameters that were passed to the subroutine by way of the stack. In this case, instructions are written that use based addressing to examine the values of parameters held in the stack.

The index registers are used to hold offset addresses for instructions that access data stored in the data segment of memory. For this reason, they are always combined with the value in the DS register. In instructions that use indexed type of addressing, the *source index* (SI) register is used to store an offset address for a source operand, and the *destination index* (DI) register is used for storage of an offset that identifies the location of a destination operand. For example, a string instruction that requires an offset to the location of a source or destination operand would use these registers.

The index registers can also be used as source or destination registers in arithmetic and logical operations. Unlike the general-purpose registers, these registers must always be used for 16-bit operations and cannot be accessed as two separate bytes.

2.12 STATUS REGISTER

The status register, which is also called the flag register, is a 16-bit register within the 8088. However, as shown in Fig. 2.17, just nine of its bits are implemented. Six of these bits represent status flags. They are the *carry flag* (CF), the *parity flag* (PF), the *auxiliary carry flag* (AF), the *zero flag* (ZF), the *sign flag* (SF), and the *overflow flag* (OF). The logic state of these *status flags* indicates conditions that are produced as the result of executing an arithmetic or logic instruction. That is, specific flag bits are reset (logic 0) or set (logic 1) at the completion of execution of the instruction.

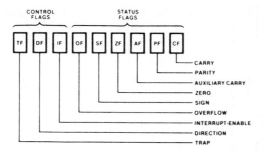

Figure 2.17 Status and control flags. (Reprinted by permission of Intel Corp. Copyright/Intel Corp. 1979)

Let us first summarize the operation of these flags:

1. The carry flag (CF): CF is set if there is a carry-out or a borrow-in for the most significant bit of the result during the execution of an arithmetic instruction. Otherwise, CF is reset.

2. The parity flag (PF): PF is set if the result produced by the instruction has even parity, that is, if it contains an even number of bits at the 1 logic level. If parity is odd, PF is reset.

3. The auxiliary carry flag (AF): AF is set if there is a carry-out from the low nibble into the high nibble or a borrow-in from the high nibble into the low nibble of the lower byte in a 16-bit word. Otherwise, AF is reset.

4. The zero flag (ZF): ZF is set if the result of an arithmetic or logic operation is zero. Otherwise, ZF is reset.

5. The sign flag (SF): The MSB of the result is copied into SF. Thus SF is set if the result is a negative number or reset if it is positive.

6. The overflow flag (OF): When OF is set, it indicates that the signed result is out of range. If the result is not out of range, OF remains reset.

For example, at the completion of execution of a byte-addition instruction, the carry flag (CF) could be set to indicate that the sum of the operands caused a carry-out condition. The auxiliary carry flag (AF) could also set due to the execution of the instruction. This depends on whether or not a carry-out occurred from the least significant nibble to the most significant nibble when the byte operands are added. The sign flag (SF) is also affected and it will reflect the logic level of the MSB of the result. The overflow flag (OF) is set if there is a carry-out of the sign bit but no carry into the sign bit.

The 8088 provides instructions within its instruction set that are able to use these flags to alter the sequence in which the program is executed. For instance, ZF equal to logic 1 could be tested as the condition that would initiate a jump to another part of the program.

The other three implemented flag bits are *control flags*. They are the *direction flag* (DF), the *interrupt enable flag* (IF), and the *trap flag* (TF). These three flags are provided to control functions of the 8088 as follows:

1. The trap flag (TF): If TF is set, the 8088 goes into the *single-step mode*. When in the single-step mode, it executes one instruction at a time. This type of operation is very useful for debugging programs.

2. The interrupt flag (IF): For the 8088 to recognize *maskable interrupt requests* at its INT input, the IF flag must be set. When IF is reset, requests at INT are ignored and the maskable interrupt interface is disabled.

3. The direction flag (DF): The logic level of DF determines the direction in which string operations will occur. When it is set, the string instruction automatically decrements the address. Therefore, the string data transfers proceed from high address to low address. On the other hand, resetting DF causes the string address to be incremented. In this way, transfers proceed from low address to high address.

The instruction set of the 8088 includes instructions for saving, loading, or manipulating specific bits of the status register. For instance, special instructions are provided to permit user software to set or reset CF, DF, and IF at any point in the program. For instance, just prior to the beginning of a string operation DF could be reset so that the string address automatically increments.

2.13 GENERATING A MEMORY ADDRESS

A *logical address* in the 8088 system is described by a segment and an offset. Both the segment and offset are 16-bit quantities. This is because all registers and memory locations are 16 bits long. However, the *physical addresses* that are used to access memory are 20 bits in length. The generation of the physical address involves combining a 16-bit offset value that is located in a base register, an index register, or a pointer register and a 16-bit base value that is located in one of the segment registers.

The source of the offset address depends on which type of memory reference is taking place. It can be the base pointer (BP) register, base (BX) register, source index (SI) register, destination index (DI) register, or instruction pointer (IP). On the other hand, the base value always resides in one of the segment registers: CS, DS, SS, or ES.

For instance, when an instruction acquisition takes place, the source of the base address is always the code segment (CS) register and the source of the offset is always the instruction pointer (IP). This physical address can be denoted as CS:IP. On the other hand, if the value of a variable is being written to memory during the execution of an instruction, typically, the base address will be in the data segment (DS) register and the offset will be in the destination index (DI) register. That is, the physical address is given as DS:DI. Segment override prefixes can be used to change the segment from which the variable is accessed.

Another example is the stack address that is needed when pushing parameters onto the stack. This address is formed from the contents of the stack segment (SS) register and stack pointer (SP).

Remember that the segment base address represents the starting location of the 64K-byte segment in memory, that is, the lowest-addressed byte in the segment. The offset identifies the distance in bytes that the storage location of interest resides from this starting address. Therefore, the lowest-addressed byte in a segment has an offset of 0000_{16} and the highest-addressed byte has an offset of $FFFF_{16}$.

Figure 2.18 shows how a segment address and offset value are combined to give a physical address. What happens is that the value in the segment register is shifted left by 4 bits with its LSBs being filled with 0s. Then the offset value is added to the 16 LSBs of the shifted segment address. The result of this addition is the 20-bit physical address.

The example in Fig. 2.19 represents a segment address of 1234_{16} and an offset address of 0022_{16}. First let us express the base address in binary form. This gives

$$1234_{16} = 0001001000110100_2$$

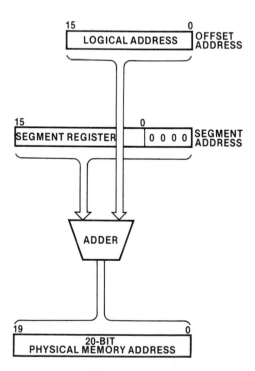

Figure 2.18 Generating a physical address. (Reprinted by permission of Intel Corp., Copyright/Intel 1981)

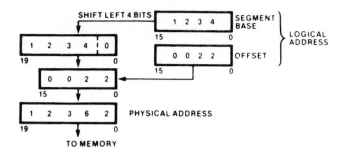

Figure 2.19 Physical address calculation example. (Reprinted by permission of Intel Corp. Copyright/Intel Corp. 1979)

Shifting left four times and filling with zeros results in

$$0001001000110100000_2 = 12340_{16}$$

The offset in binary form is

$$0022_{16} = 0000000000100010_2$$

Adding the shifted segment address and offset, we get

$$0001001000110100000_2 + 0000000000100010_2 = 0001001000110110010_2$$
$$= 12362_{16}$$

This address calculation is automatically done within the 8088 each time a memory access is initiated.

EXAMPLE 2.3

What would be the offset required to map to physical address location $002C3_{16}$ if the segment base address is $002A_{16}$?

SOLUTION   The offset value can be obtained by shifting the segment base address left 4 bits and then subtracting it from the physical address. Shifting left gives

$$002A0_{16}$$

Now subtracting, we get the value of the offset:

$$002C3_{16} - 002A0_{16} = 0023_{16}$$

Actually, many different logical addresses can be mapped to the same physical address location in memory. This is done by simply changing the values of the base address in the segment register and its corresponding offset. The diagram in Fig. 2.20 demonstrates this idea. Notice that base $002B_{16}$ with offset 0013_{16} maps

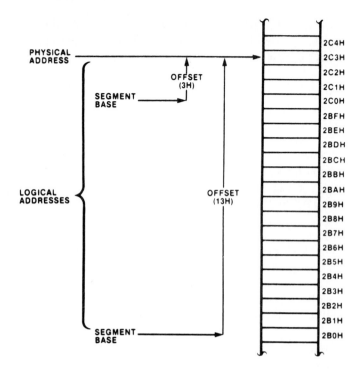

Figure 2.20 Relationship between logical and physical addresses. (Reprinted by permission of Intel Corp. Copyright/Intel Corp. 1979)

to physical address $002C3_{16}$ in memory. However, if the segment base address is changed to $002C_{16}$ with a new offset of 0003_{16}, the physical address is still $002C3_{16}$.

2.14 THE STACK

As indicated earlier, *stack* is implemented in the memory of the 8088 microcomputer. It is 64K bytes long and is organized from a software point of view as 32K words. Moreover, we found that the lowest-addressed byte in the current stack is pointed to by the base address in the SS register.

During a *subroutine call* the contents of certain internal registers of the 8088 are pushed to the stack part of memory. Here they are maintained temporarily. At the completion of the subroutine, these values are popped off the stack and put back into the same internal registers where they originally resided.

For instance, when a *call* instruction is executed, the 8088 automatically pushes the current values in CS and IP onto the stack. As part of the subroutine, the contents of other registers can also be saved on the stack by executing *push* instructions. An example is the instruction PUSH SI. When executed, it causes the contents of the source register to be pushed onto the stack.

At the end of the subroutine, *pop* instructions can be included to pop values from the stack back into their corresponding internal registers. For example, POP SI causes the value at the top of the stack to be popped back into the source index register.

Any number of stacks may exist in an 8088 microcomputer. A new stack can be brought in by simply changing the value in the SS register. For instance, executing the instruction MOV SS,DX loads a new value from DX into SS. Even though many stacks can exist, only one can be active at a time.

Another register, the stack pointer (SP), contains an offset from the value in SS. The address obtained from the contents of SS and SP is the physical address of the last storage location in the stack to which data were pushed. This is known as the *top of the stack*. The value in the stack pointer is initialized to $FFFF_{16}$ upon start-up of the microcomputer. Combining this value with the current value in SS gives the highest-addressed location in the stack, that is, the *bottom of the stack*.

The 8088 pushes data and addresses to the stack one word at a time. Each time the contents of a register are to be pushed onto the top of the stack, the value in the stack pointer is first automatically decremented by two and then the contents of the register are written into memory. In this way we see that the stack grows down in memory from the bottom of the stack, which corresponds to the physical address derived from SS and $FFFF_{16}$, toward the *end of the stack,* which corresponds to the physical address obtained from SS and offset 0002_{16}.

When a value is popped from the top of the stack, the reverse of this sequence occurs. The physical address defined by SS and SP points to the location of the last value pushed onto the stack. Its contents are first popped off the stack and put into the specific register within the 8088; then SP is automatically incremented by two. The top of the stack now corresponds to the previous value pushed onto the stack.

An example that shows how the contents of a register are pushed onto the stack is shown in Fig. 2.21(a). Here we find the state of the stack prior to execution of the PUSH instruction. Notice that the stack segment register contains 105_{16}. As indicated, the bottom of the stack resides at the physical address derived from SS with offset $FFFF_{16}$. This gives the bottom of stack address A_{BOS} as

$$A_{BOS} = 1050_{16} + FFFF_{16}$$

$$= 1104F_{16}$$

Furthermore, the stack pointer, which represents the offset from the beginning of the stack specified by the contents of SS to the top of the stack, equals 0008_{16}. Therefore, the current top of the stack is at physical address A_{TOS}, which equals

$$A_{TOS} = 1050_{16} + 0008_{16}$$

$$= 1058_{16}$$

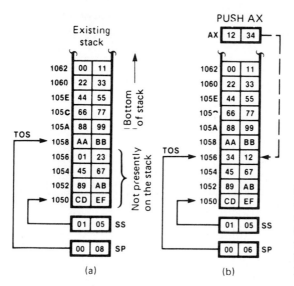

Figure 2.21 (a) Stack just prior to push operation. (Reprinted by permission of Intel Corp. Copyright/Intel Corp. 1979) (b) Stack after execution of the PUSH AX instruction. (Reprinted by permission of Intel Corp. Copyright/Intel Corp. 1979)

Addresses with higher values than that of the top of stack, 1058_{16}, contain valid stack data. Those with lower addresses do not yet contain valued stack data. Notice that the last value pushed to the stack in Fig. 2.21(a) was $BBAA_{16}$.

Figure 2.21(b) demonstrates what happens when the PUSH AX instruction is executed. Here we see that AX contains the value 1234_{16}. Notice that execution of the PUSH instruction causes the stack pointer to be decremented by two but does not affect the contents of the stack segment register. Therefore, the next location to be accessed in the stack corresponds to address 1056_{16}. It is to this location that the value in AX is pushed. Notice that the most significant byte of AX, which equals 12_{16}, now resides in the least significant byte of the word in stack, and the least significant byte of AX, which is 34_{16}, is held in the most significant byte.

Now let us look at an example in which stack data are popped back into the register from which they were pushed. Figure 2.22 illustrates this operation. In Fig. 2.22(a), the stack is shown to be in the state that resulted due to our prior PUSH AX example. This is, SP equals 0006_{16}, SS equals 105_{16}, the address of the top of the stack equals 1056_{16}, and the word at the top of the stack equals 1234_{16}.

Looking at Fig. 2.22(b), we see what happens when the instructions POP AX and POP BX are executed in that order. Here we see that execution of the first instruction causes the 8088 to read the value from the top of the stack and put it into the AX register as 1234_{16}. Next, SP is incremented to give 0008_{16} and another read cycle is initiated from the stack. This second read corresponds to the POP BX instruction, and it causes the value $BBAA_{16}$ to be loaded into the BX register. SP is incremented once more and now equals $000A_{16}$. Therefore, the new top of stack is at address $105A_{16}$.

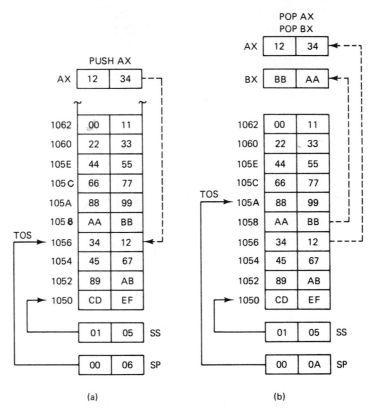

Figure 2.22 (a) Stack just prior to pop operation. (Reprinted by permission of Intel Corp. Copyright/Intel Corp. 1979) (b) Stack after execution of the POP AX and POP BX instructions. (Reprinted by permission of Intel Corp. Copyright/Intel Corp. 1979)

From Fig. 2.22(b), we see that the values read out of 1056_{16} and 1058_{16} still remain at these addresses. But now they reside at locations that are considered to be above the top of the stack. Therefore, they no longer represent valid stack data.

2.15 INPUT/OUTPUT ADDRESS SPACE

The 8088 has separate memory and input/output (I/O) address spaces. The *I/O address space* is the place where I/O interfaces, such as printer and terminal ports, are implemented. Figure 2.23 shows a map of the 8088's I/O address space. Notice that the address range is from 0000_{16} to $FFFF_{16}$. This represents just 64K byte addresses; therefore, unlike memory, I/O addresses are just 16 bits long. Each of the addresses corresponds to a byte-wide I/O port.

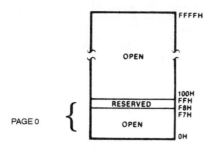

Figure 2.23 I/O address space. (Reprinted by permission of Intel Corp. Copyright/Intel Corp. 1979)

The part of the map from address 0000_{16} through $00FF_{16}$ is referred to as *page 0*. Certain of the 8088's I/O instructions can only perform operations to I/O devices located in this part of the I/O address space. Other I/O instructions can input or output data from devices located anywhere in the I/O address space. Notice that the eight locations from address $00F8_{16}$ through $00FF_{16}$ are specified as reserved by Intel Corporation and should not be used.

2.16 ADDRESSING MODES OF THE 8088/8086

When the 8088 executes an instruction, it performs the specified function on data. These data are called its *operands* and may be part of the instruction, reside in one of the internal registers of the microprocessor, stored at an address in memory, or held at an I/O port. To access these different types of operands, the 8088 is provided with various *addressing modes*. Addressing modes are categorized into three types: *register operand addressing, immediate operand addressing,* and *memory operand addressing.* Let us now consider in detail the addressing modes in each of these categories.

Register Operand Addressing Mode

With the *register addressing mode,* the operand to be accessed is specified as residing in an internal register of the 8088. Figure 2.24 shows that any of the internal registers can be used as a source or destination operand; however, only the data registers can be accessed as either a byte or word.

An example of an instruction that uses this addressing mode is

```
MOV AX,BX
```

This stands for move the contents of BX, the *source operand,* to AX, the *destination operand.* Both the source and destination operands have been specified as the contents of internal registers of the 8088.

Let us now look at the effect of executing the register addressing mode MOV instruction. In Fig. 2.25(a), we see the state of the 8088 just prior to fetching the

Register	Operand sizes	
	Byte (Reg 8)	Word (Reg 16)
Accumulator	AL, AH	AX
Base	BL, BH	BX
Count	CL, CH	CX
Data	DL, DH	DX
Stack pointer	—	SP
Base pointer	—	BP
Source index	—	SI
Destination index	—	DI
Code segment	—	CS
Data segment	—	DS
Stack segment	—	SS
Extra segment	—	ES

Figure 2.24 Direct addressing register and operand sizes.

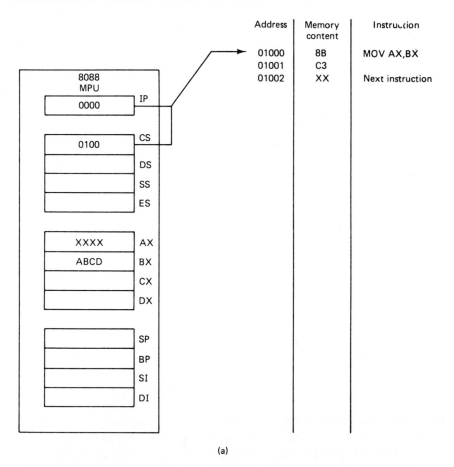

(a)

Figure 2.25 (a) Register addressing mode instruction before fetch and execution. (b) After execution.

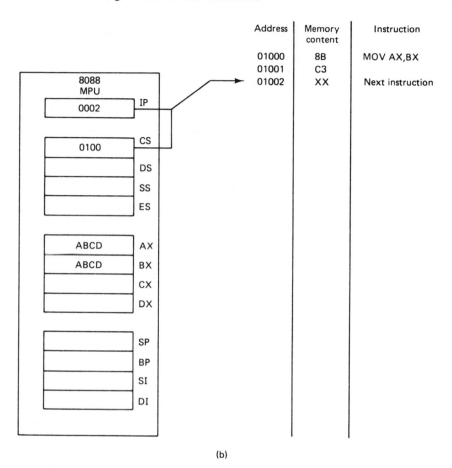

Address	Memory content	Instruction
01000	8B	MOV AX,BX
01001	C3	
01002	XX	Next instruction

(b)

Figure 2.25   (Continued)

instruction. Notice that IP and CS point to the MOV AX,BX instruction at address 01000_{16}. This instruction is fetched into the 8088's instruction queue where it is held waiting to be executed.

Prior to execution of this instruction, the contents of BX are $ABCD_{16}$ and the contents of AX represent a don't-care state. The instruction is read from the output side of the queue, decoded, and executed. As shown in Fig. 2.25(b), the result of executing the instruction is that $ABCD_{16}$ is copied into AX.

Immediate Operand Addressing Mode

If a source operand is part of the instruction instead of the contents of a register or memory location, it represents what is called an *immediate operand* and is accessed using the *immediate addressing mode*. Figure 2.26 shows that the operand,

Opcode	Immediate operand

Figure 2.26 Instruction encoded with an immediate operand.

which can be 8 bits (Imm8) or 16 bits (Imm16) in length, is encoded into the instruction following the opcode. Since the data are coded directly into the instruction, immediate operands represent constant data. This addressing mode can only be used to specify a source operand.

In the instruction

```
MOV AL,15H
```

the source operand 15H (= 15_{16}) is an example of a byte-wide immediate source

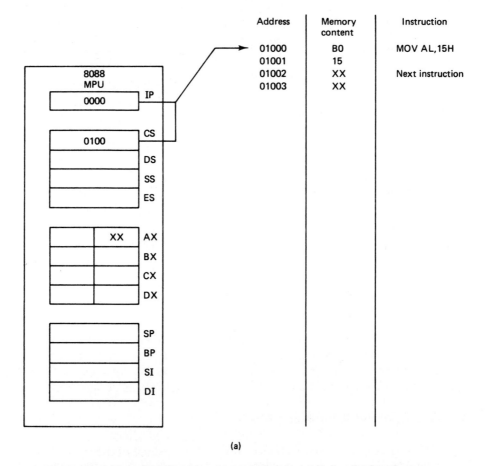

(a)

Figure 2.27 (a) Immediate addressing mode instruction before fetch and execution. (b) After execution.

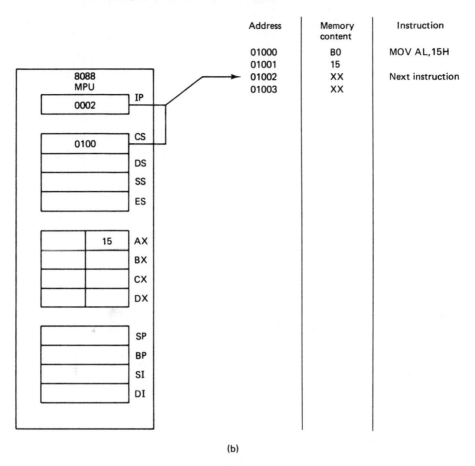

(b)

Figure 2.27   (Continued)

operand. The destination operand, which is the contents of AL, uses register addressing. Thus this instruction employs both the immediate and register addressing modes.

Figure 2.27(a) and (b) illustrates the fetch and execution of this instruction. Here we find that the immediate operand 15_{16} is stored in the code segment of memory in the byte location immediately following the opcode of the instruction. This value is fetched, along with the opcode for MOV, into the instruction queue within the 8088. When it performs the move operation, the source operand is fetched from the instruction queue and not from the memory, and no external memory operations are performed. Notice that the result produced by executing this instruction is that the immediate operand, which equals 15_{16}, is loaded into the lower-byte part of the accumulator (AL).

Memory Addressing Modes

To reference an operand in memory, the 8088 must calculate the physical address (PA) of the operand and then initiate a read or write operation to this storage location. Looking at Fig. 2.28 we see that the physical address is formed from a *segment base address* (SBA) and an *effective address* (EA). SBA identifies the starting location of the segment in memory and EA represents the offset of the operand from the beginning of this segment. Earlier we showed how SBA and EA are combined within the 8088 to form the physical address SBA:EA.

PA = SBA : EA

PA = Segment base : Base + Index + Displacement

$$PA = \begin{Bmatrix} CS \\ SS \\ DS \\ ES \end{Bmatrix} : \begin{Bmatrix} BX \\ BP \end{Bmatrix} + \begin{Bmatrix} SI \\ DI \end{Bmatrix} + \begin{Bmatrix} \text{8-bit displacement} \\ \text{16-bit displacement} \end{Bmatrix}$$

Figure 2.28   Physical and effective address computation for memory operands.

The value of the EA can be specified in a variety of ways. One way is to encode the effective address of the operand directly in the instruction. This represents the simplest type of memory addressing known as the direct addressing mode. Figure 2.28 shows that an effective address can be made up from as many as three elements. They are the *base, index,* and *displacement.* Using these elements, the effective address calculation is made by the general formula

$$EA = BASE + INDEX + DISPLACEMENT$$

Figure 2.28 also identifies the registers that can be used to hold the values of the segment base, base, and index. For example, it tells us that any of the four segment registers can be the source of the segment base for the physical address calculation and that the value of base for the effective address can be in either the base register (BX) or base pointer register (BP). Also identified in Fig. 2.28 are the sizes permitted for the displacement.

Not all of these elements are always used in the effective address calculation. In fact, a number of memory addressing modes are defined by using various combinations of these elements. They are called *register indirect addressing, based addressing, indexed addressing,* and *based-indexed addressing.* For instance, using based addressing mode, the effective address calculation includes just a base. These addressing modes provide the programmer with different ways of computing the effective address of an operand in memory. Next, we will examine each of the memory operand addressing modes in detail.

Direct addressing mode

Direct addressing is similar to immediate addressing in that information is directly encoded into the instruction. However, in this case, the instruction opcode is followed by an effective address, instead of the data. As shown in Fig. 2.29, this effective address is directly used as the 16-bit offset of the storage location of the operand from the location specified by the current value in the selected segment register. The default segment register is always DS. Therefore, the 20-bit physical address of the operand in memory is normally obtained as DS:EA. But, by using a segment override prefix (SEG) in the instruction, any of the four segment registers can be referenced.

PA = Segment base: Direct address

$$PA = \begin{Bmatrix} CS \\ DS \\ SS \\ ES \end{Bmatrix} : \begin{Bmatrix} Direct\ address \end{Bmatrix}$$

Figure 2.29 Computation of a direct memory address.

An example of an instruction that uses direct addressing for its source operand is

MOV CX,[BETA]   *address of data*

This stands for "move the contents of the memory location, which is labeled as BETA in the current data segment, into internal register CX." The assembler computes the offset of BETA from the beginning of the data segment and encodes it as part of the instruction's machine code.

In Fig. 2.30(a), we find that the value of the offset is stored in the two byte locations that follow the instruction. Notice that the value assigned to constant BETA is 1234_{16}. As the instruction is executed, the 8088 combines 1234_{16} with 0200_{16} to get the physical address of the source operand. This gives

$$PA = 02000_{16} + 1234_{16}$$
$$= 03234_{16}$$

Then it reads the word of data starting at this address, which is $BEED_{16}$, and loads it into the CX register. This result is illustrated in Fig. 2.30(b).

Register indirect addressing mode

Register indirect addressing is similar to the direct addressing we just described in that an effective address is combined with the contents of DS to obtain a physical address. However, it differs in the way the offset is specified. Figure 2.31 shows that this time EA resides in either a base register or an index register within the 8088. The base register can be either base register BX or base pointer register BP, and the index register can be source index register SI or destination index register DI. Another segment register can be referenced by using a segment override prefix.

An example of an instruction that uses register indirect addressing is

```
MOV AX,[SI]
```

This instruction moves the contents of the memory location offset by the value of EA in SI from the beginning of the current data segment to the AX register.

For instance, as shown in Fig. 2.32(a) and (b), if SI contains 1234_{16} and DS contains 0200_{16}, the result produced by executing the instruction is that the contents of memory location

$$PA = 02000_{16} + 1234_{16}$$

$$= 03234_{16}$$

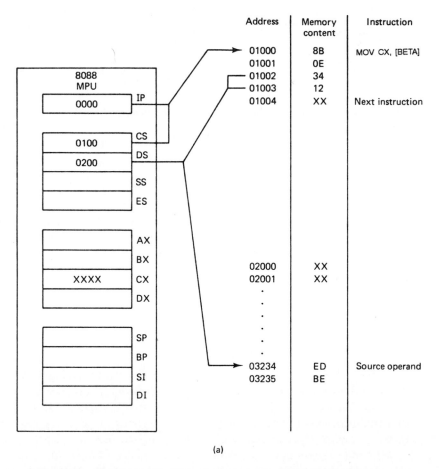

(a)

Figure 2.30 (a) Direct addressing mode instruction before fetch and execution. (b) After execution.

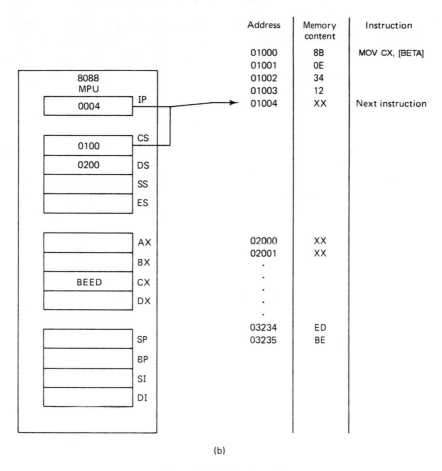

(b)

Figure 2.30   (Continued)

PA = Segment base: Indirect address

$$PA = \begin{Bmatrix} CS \\ DS \\ SS \\ ES \end{Bmatrix} : \begin{Bmatrix} BX \\ BP \\ SI \\ DI \end{Bmatrix}$$

Figure 2.31   Computation of an indirect memory address.

are moved to the AX register. Notice in Fig. 2.32(b) that this value is $BEED_{16}$. In this example, the value 1234_{16} that was found in the SI register must have been loaded with another instruction prior to executing the MOV instruction.

Notice that the result produced by executing this instruction and the example for the direct addressing mode are the same. However, they differ in the way in which the physical address was generated. The direct addressing method lends itself to applications where the value of EA is a constant. On the other hand, register indirect addressing can be used when the value of EA is calculated and stored, for example, in SI by a previous instruction. That is, EA is a variable. For example, the instructions executed just before our example instruction could have incremented the address in SI by two.

Based addressing mode

In the *based addressing* mode, the physical address of the operand is obtained by adding a direct or indirect displacement to the contents of either base register BX or base pointer register BP and the current value in DS or SS, respectively. This physical address calculation is shown in Fig. 2.33(a). Looking at Fig. 2.33(b), we

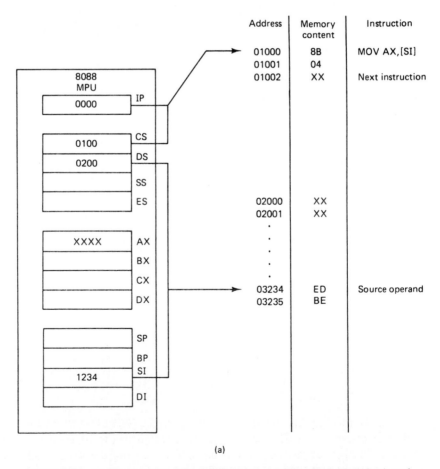

(a)

Figure 2.32   (a) Instruction using register indirect addressing before fetch and execution. (b) After execution.

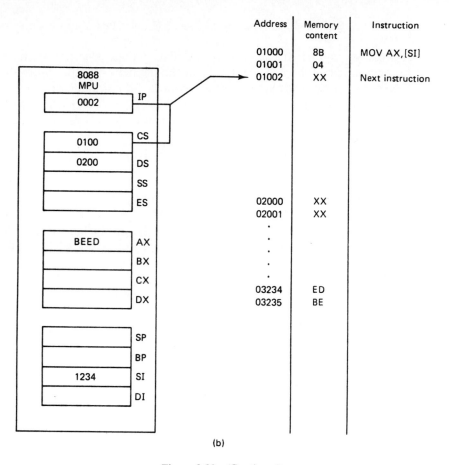

	Address	Memory content	Instruction
	01000	8B	MOV AX,[SI]
	01001	04	
	01002	XX	Next instruction
	02000	XX	
	02001	XX	
	03234	ED	
	03235	BE	

(b)

Figure 2.32 (Continued)

PA = Segment base: Base + Displacement

$$PA = \begin{Bmatrix} CS \\ DS \\ SS \\ ES \end{Bmatrix} : \begin{Bmatrix} BX \\ BP \end{Bmatrix} + \begin{Bmatrix} \text{8-bit displacement} \\ \text{16-bit displacement} \end{Bmatrix}$$

(a)

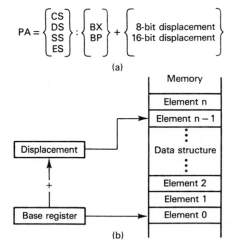

(b)

Figure 2.33 (a) Based addressing of a structure of data. (b) Computation of a based address.

55

see that the value in the base register defines a data structure, such as a record, in memory and the displacement selects the element of data within this structure. To access a different element in the record, the programmer simply changes the value of the displacement. On the other hand, to access the same element in another record, the programmer can change the value in the base register so that it points to the new record.

A MOV instruction that uses based addressing to specify the location of its destination operand is as follows:

```
MOV [BX]+BETA,AL
```

This instruction uses base register BX and direct displacement BETA to derive the EA of the destination operand. The based addressing mode is implemented by

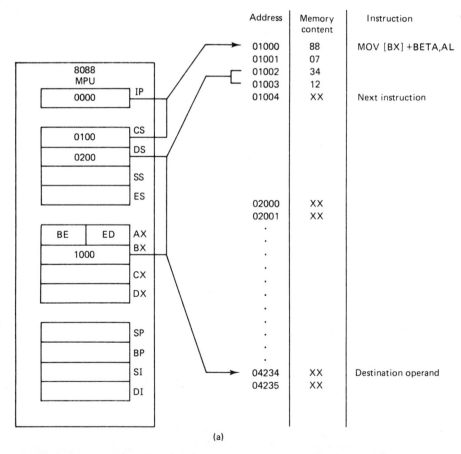

(a)

Figure 2.34 (a) Instruction using direct base pointer addressing before fetch and execution. (b) After execution.

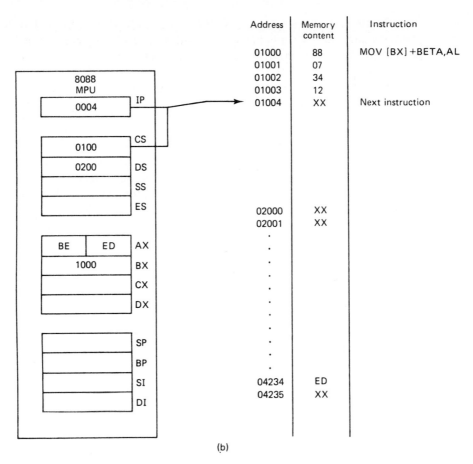

Address	Memory content	Instruction
01000	88	MOV [BX]+BETA,AL
01001	07	
01002	34	
01003	12	
01004	XX	Next instruction

(b)

Figure 2.34   (Continued)

specifying the base register in brackets followed by a + sign and the direct displacement. The source operand in this example is located in byte accumulator AL.

As shown in Fig. 2.34(a) and (b), the fetch and execution of this instruction causes the 8088 to calculate the physical address of the destination operand from the contents of DS, BX, and the direct displacement. The result is

$$PA = 02000_{16} + 1000_{16} + 1234_{16}$$

$$= 04234_{16}$$

Then it writes the contents of source operand AL into the storage location at 04234_{16}. The result is that ED_{16} is written into the destination memory location. Again, the default segment register can be changed with the segment override prefix.

If BP is used instead of BX, the calculation of the physical address is performed using the contents of the stack segment (SS) register instead of DS. This permits access to data in the stack segment of memory.

Indexed addressing mode

Indexed addressing mode works in a similar way to the based addressing mode we just described. However, as shown in Fig. 2.35(a), indexed addressing mode uses the value of the displacement as a pointer to the starting point of an array of data in memory and the contents of the specified index register as an index that selects the specific element in the array that is to be accessed. For instance, in Fig. 2.35(a), the index register holds the value *n*. In this way, it selects data element *n* in the array. Figure 2.35(b) shows how the physical address is obtained from the value in the DS register, an index in the SI or DI register, and a displacement.

Here is an example:

```
MOV AL,[SI]+ARRAY
```

The source operand has been specified using direct indexed addressing. Notice that the notation this time is such that ARRAY, which is a *direct displacement,* is added to the selected index register, SI. Just like for the base register in based addressing, the index register is enclosed in brackets.

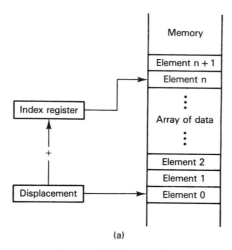

(a)

PA = Segment base: Index + Displacement

$$PA = \begin{Bmatrix} CS \\ DS \\ SS \\ ES \end{Bmatrix} : \begin{Bmatrix} SI \\ DI \end{Bmatrix} + \begin{Bmatrix} \text{8-bit displacement} \\ \text{16-bit displacement} \end{Bmatrix}$$

(b)

Figure 2.35   (a) Indexed addressing of an array of data elements. (b) Computation of an indexed address.

The effective address is calculated as

$$EA = (SI) + ARRAY$$

and the physical address is obtained by combining the contents of DS with EA.

The example in Fig. 2.36(a) and (b) shows the result of executing the MOV instruction. First the physical address of the source operand is calculated from DS, SI, and the direct displacement.

$$PA = 02000_{16} + 2000_{16} + 1234_{16}$$

$$= 05234_{16}$$

Then the byte of data stored at this location, which is BE_{16}, is read into the lower byte (AL) of the accumulator register.

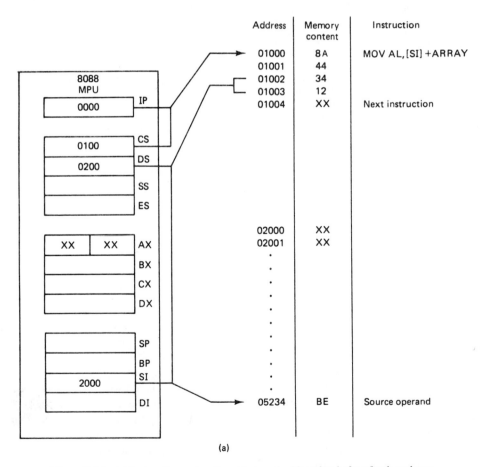

(a)

Figure 2.36   (a) Instruction using direct indexed addressing before fetch and execution. (b) After execution.

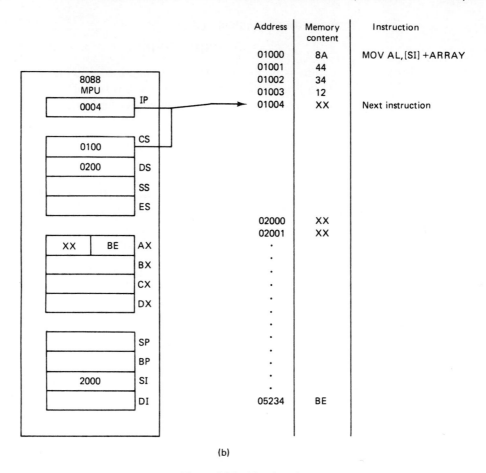

(b)

Figure 2.36   (Continued)

Based-indexed addressing mode

Combining the based addressing mode and the indexed addressing mode together results in a new, more powerful mode known as *based-indexed addressing*. This addressing mode can be used to access complex data structures such as two-dimensional arrays. Figure 2.37(a) shows how it can be used to access elements in an $m \times n$ array of data. Notice that the displacement, which is a fixed value, locates the array in memory. The base register specifies the m coordinate of the array and the index register identifies the n coordinate. Any element in the array can be accessed by simply changing the values in the base and index registers. The registers permitted in the based-indexed physical address computation are shown in Fig. 2.37(b).

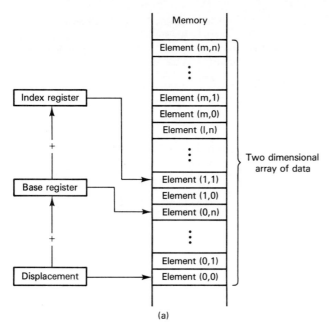

PA = Segment base: Base + Index + Displacement

$$PA = \begin{Bmatrix} CS \\ DS \\ SS \\ ES \end{Bmatrix} : \begin{Bmatrix} BX \\ BP \end{Bmatrix} + \begin{Bmatrix} SI \\ DI \end{Bmatrix} + \begin{Bmatrix} \text{8-bit displacement} \\ \text{16-bit displacement} \end{Bmatrix}$$

(b)

Figure 2.37 (a) Based-indexed addressing of a two-dimensional array of data. (b) Computation of a based-indexed address.

Let us consider an example of a MOV instruction using this type of addressing.

```
MOV AH,[BX][SI]+BETA
```

Notice that the source operand is accessed using based-indexed addressing mode. Therefore, the effective address of the source operand is obtained as

$$EA = (BX) + (SI) + BETA$$

and the physical address of the operand from the current DS and the calculated EA.

An example of executing this instruction is illustrated in Fig. 2.38(a) and (b). The address of the source operand is calculated as

$$PA = 02000_{16} + 1000_{16} + 2000_{16} + 1234_{16}$$

$$= 6234_{16}$$

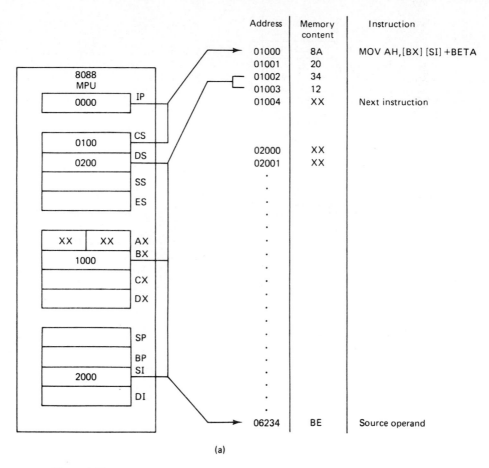

Figure 2.38   (a) Instruction using based-indexed addressing before fetch and execution. (b) After execution.

Execution of the instruction causes the value stored at this location to be read into AH.

ASSIGNMENTS

Section 2.2

1. What tells a computer what to do, where to get data, how to process the data, and where to put the results when done?

2. What is the name given to a sequence of instructions that is used to guide a computer through a task?

3. What is the native language of the 8088?

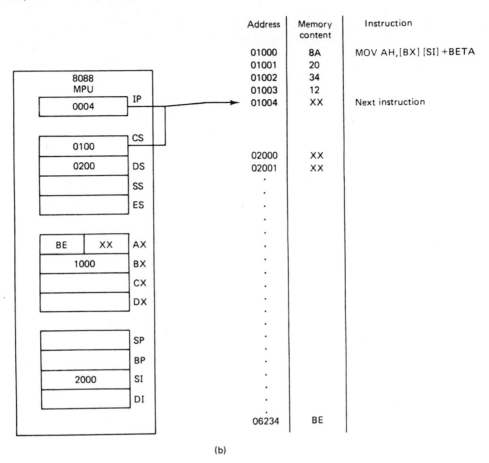

(b)

Figure 2.38   (Continued)

4. How does machine language differ from assembly language?
5. What does *opcode* stand for? Give two examples.
6. What is an *operand?* Give two types.
7. In the assembly language statement

$$\text{START: ADD AX,BX ;ADD BX TO AX}$$

what is the label?
8. What is the function of an assembler? A compiler?
9. What is *object code?* What is *source code?*
10. Give two benefits derived from writing programs in assembly language instead of a high-level language.
11. What is meant by the phrase *real-time application?*

12. List two hardware-related applications that require use of assembly language programming. Name two software-related applications.

Section 2.3

13. Name the two internal processing units of the 8088.

14. Which processing unit of the 8088 is the interface to the outside world?

15. How large is the instruction queue of the 8088? The 8086?

16. List the elements of the execution unit.

Section 2.4

17. What is the purpose of a software model for a microprocessor?

18. What must an assembly language programmer know about the registers within the 8088 microprocessor?

19. How many registers are located within the 8088?

20. How large is the 8088's memory address space?

Section 2.5

21. What is the highest address in the 8088's memory address space? Lowest address?

22. Is memory in the 8088 microcomputer organized as bytes, words, or double words?

23. The contents of memory location $B0000_{16}$ are FF_{16}, and those at $B0001_{16}$ are 00_{16}. What is the even-addressed data word stored at address $B0000_{16}$?

24. Show how the double word 12345678_{16} will be stored in memory starting at address $A001_{16}$.

Section 2.6

25. List five data types directly processed by the 8088.

26. Express each of the signed decimal integers that follow as either a byte or word hexadecimal number (use 2's-complement notation for negative numbers).

   (a) $+127$

   (b) -10

   (c) -128

   (d) $+500$

27. How would the integer in problem 26(d) be stored in memory starting at address $0A000_{16}$?

28. How would the decimal number -1000 be expressed for processing by the 8088?

29. Express the decimal numbers that follow as unpacked and packed BCD bytes.

   (a) 29

   (b) 88

30. How would the BCD number in problem 29(a) be stored in memory starting at address $0B000_{16}$? Assume that the least significant digit is stored at the lower address.

31. What is the statement that follows if it is coded in ASCII represented by the binary strings as

$$1001110$$

$$1000101$$

$$1011000$$

$$1010100$$

$$0100000$$

$$1001001$$

32. How would the decimal number 1234 be codes in ASCII and stored in memory starting at address $0C000_{16}$? Assume that the least significant digit is stored at the lower addressed memory location.

Section 2.7

33. How much memory can be active at a given time in the 8088 microcomputer?
34. Which of the 8088's internal registers are used for memory segmentation?
35. How much of the 8088's active memory is available as general-purpose data storage memory?
36. Which part of the 8088's memory address space is used to store instructions of a program?

Section 2.8

37. What is the dedicated use of the part of the 8088's address space from 00000_{16} through $0007F_{16}$?
38. What is stored at address $FFFF0_{16}$?

Section 2.9

39. What is the function of the instruction pointer register?
40. Give an overview of the fetch and the execution of an instruction by the 8088.
41. What happens to the value in IP each time the 8088 fetches instruction code?

Section 2.10

42. Make a list of the general-purpose data registers of the 8088.
43. How is the word value of a data register labeled?
44. How are the upper and lower bytes of a data register denoted?
45. What dedicated operations are assigned to the CX register?

Section 2.11

46. What kind of information is stored in the pointer and index registers?
47. Name the two pointer registers.
48. For which segment register are the contents of the pointer registers used as an offset?

49. For which segment register are the contents of the index registers used as an offset?

50. What is the difference between SI and DI?

Section 2.12

51. Categorize each flag bit of the 8088 as either a control flag or a flag that monitors the status due to execution of an instruction.

52. Describe the function of each of the status flags.

53. How are the status flags used by software?

54. Which flag determines whether the address for a string operation is incremented or decremented?

55. Can the state of the flags be modified through software?

Section 2.13

56. What is the word length of the 8088's physical address?

57. What two address elements are combined to form a physical address?

58. Calculate the value of each of the physical addresses that follows. Assume all numbers as hexadecimal numbers.

    (a) 1000:1234

    (b) 0100:ABCD

    (c) A200:12CF

    (d) B2C0:FA12

59. Find the unknown value for each of the following physical addresses. Assume all numbers as hexadecimal numbers.

    (a) A000:? = A0123

    (b) ?:14DA = 235DA

    (c) D765:? = DABC0

    (d) ?:CD21 = 32D21

60. If the current values in the code segment register and the instruction pointer are 0200_{16} and $01AC_{16}$, respectively, what is the physical address of the next instruction?

61. A data segment is to be located from address $A0000_{16}$ to $AFFFF_{16}$; what value must be loaded into DS?

62. If the data segment register contains the value found in problem 61, what value must be loaded into DI if it is to point to a destination operand stored at address $A1234_{16}$ in memory?

Section 2.14

63. What is the function of the stack?

64. If the current values in the stack segment register and stack pointer are $C000_{16}$ and $FF00_{16}$, respectively, what is the address of the top of the stack?

65. For the base and offset addresses in problem 64, how many words of data are currently held in the stack?

66. Show how the value $EE11_{16}$ from register AX would be pushed onto the top of the stack as it exists in problem 64.

Section 2.15

67. For the 8088 microprocessor, are the input/output and memory address spaces common or separate?

68. How large is the 8088's I/O address space?

69. What is the name given to the part of the I/O address space from 0000_{16} through $00FF_{16}$?

Section 2.16

70. Make a list of the addressing modes available on the 8088.

71. Identify the addressing modes used for the source and the destination operands in the instructions that follow.
   (a) MOV AL,BL
   (b) MOV AX,0FFH
   (c) MOV [DI],AX
   (d) MOV DI,[SI]
   (e) MOV [BX]+XYZ,CX
   (f) MOV [DI]+XYZ,AH
   (g) MOV [BX][DI]+XYZ,AL

72. Compute the physical address for the specified operand in each of the following instructions from problem 71. The register contents and variables are as follows: (CS) = $0A00_{16}$, (DS) = $0B00_{16}$, (SI) = 0100_{16}, (DI) = 0200_{16}, (BX) = 0300_{16}, and XYZ = 0400_{16}.
   (a) Destination operand of the instruction in (c)
   (b) Source operand of the instruction in (d)
   (c) Destination operand of the instruction in (e)
   (d) Destination operand of the instruction in (f)
   (e) Destination operand of the instruction in (g)

Machine Language Coding and the Software Development Tools of the IBM PC

3.1 INTRODUCTION

In Chapter 2 we examined the software architecture of the 8088 and 8086 micro-processors. This chapter describes how their assembly language instructions are encoded in machine language and how to use the DEBUG program on the IBM PC to load, assemble, execute, and debug programs. In this chapter we will once again describe the material with respect to the 8088 microprocessor. However, it also applies directly to the 8086. The topics discussed are as follows:

1. Converting assembly language instructions to machine language
2. Encoding a complete source program in machine code
3. The IBM PC and its DEBUG program
4. Examining and modifying the contents of memory
5. Loading, verifying, and saving machine code programs
6. Assembling instructions with the ASSEMBLE command
7. Executing instructions and programs with the TRACE and GO commands
8. Debugging a program

3.2 CONVERTING ASSEMBLY LANGUAGE INSTRUCTIONS TO MACHINE CODE

To convert an assembly language program to machine code, we must convert each assembly language instruction to its equivalent machine code instruction. In general, for an instruction, the machine code specifies things like what operation is to be performed, what operand or operands are to be used, whether the operation is performed on byte or word data, whether the operation involves operands that are located in registers or a register and a storage location in memory, and, if one of the operands is in memory, how its address is to be generated. All this information is encoded into the bits of the machine code instruction.

The machine code instructions of the 8088 vary in the number of bytes used to encode them. Some instructions can be encoded with just 1 byte, others in 2 bytes, and many require more. The maximum number of bytes an instruction might take is 6. Single-byte instructions generally specify a simpler operation with a register or a flag bit. For instance, *complement carry* (CMC) is an example of a single-byte instruction. It is specified by the machine code byte 11110101_2, which equals $F5_{16}$.

$$CMC = 11110101_2 = F5_{16}$$

The machine code for instructions can be obtained by following the formats that are used in encoding the instructions of the 8088 microprocessor. Most multi-byte instructions use the *general instruction format* shown in Fig. 3.1. Exceptions to this format will be considered separately later. For now, let us describe the functions of the various bits and fields (groups of bits) in each byte of this format.

Looking at Fig. 3.1, we see that byte 1 contains three kinds of information: the *operation code* (opcode), the *register direction bit* (D), and the *data size bit* (W). Let us summarize the function of each of these pieces of information.

1. Opcode field (6 bits) specifies the operation, such as add, subtract, or move, that is to be performed.

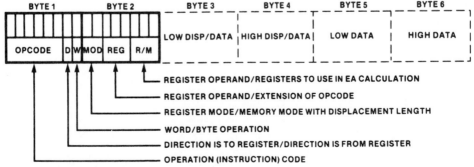

Figure 3.1   General instruction format. (Reprinted by permission of Intel Corp. Copyright/Intel Corp. 1979)

2. Register direction bit (D bit) specifies whether the register operand that is specified in byte 2 is the source or destination operand. A logic 1 at this bit position indicates that the register operand is a destination operand; a logic 0 indicates that it is a source operand.

3. Data size bit (W bit) specifies whether the operation will be performed on 8-bit or 16-bit data. Logic 0 selects 8 bits and 1 selects 16 bits.

For instance, if a 16-bit value is to be added to register AX, the 6 most significant bits specify the add register operation. This opcode is 000000_2. The next bit, D, will be at logic 1 to specify that a register, AX in this case, holds the destination operand. Finally, the least significant bit, W, will be logic 1 to specify a 16-bit data operation.

The second byte in Fig. 3.1 has three fields. They are the *mode* (MOD) *field*, the *register* (REG) *field*, and the *register/memory* (R/M) *field*. These fields are used to specify which register is used for the first operand and where the second operand is stored. The second operand can be in either a register or a memory location.

The 3-bit REG field is used to identify the register for the first operand. This is the operand that was defined as the source or destination by the D bit in byte 1. The encoding for each of the 8088's registers is shown in Fig. 3.2. Here we find that the 16-bit register AX and the 8-bit register AL are specified by the same binary code. Notice that the decision whether to use AX or AL is made based on the setting of the operation size (W) bit in byte 1.

For instance, in our earlier example, we said that the first operand, which is the destination operand, is register AX. For this case, the REG field is set to 000.

The 2-bit MOD field and 3-bit R/M field together specify the second operand. Encodings for these two fields are shown in Fig. 3.3(a) and (b), respectively. MOD indicates whether the operand is in a register or memory. Notice that in the case of a second operand that is in a register, the MOD field is always 11. The R/M field along with the W bit from byte 1 selects the register.

For example, if the second operand, the source operand, in our earlier addition example is to be in BX, the MOD and R/M fields will be made MOD = 11 and R/M = 011, respectively.

REG	W = 0	W = 1
000	AL	AX
001	CL	CX
010	DL	DX
011	BL	BX
100	AH	SP
101	CH	BP
110	DH	SI
111	BH	DI

Figure 3.2   Register (REG) field encoding. (Reprinted by permission of Intel Corp. Copyright/Intel Corp. 1979)

EXAMPLE 3.1

The instruction

MOV BL,AL

stands for "move the byte contents from source register AL to destination register BL." Using the general format in Fig. 3.1, show how to encode the instruction in machine code. Assume that the 6-bit opcode for the move operation is 100010.

SOLUTION   In byte 1 the first 6 bits specify the move operation and thus must be 100010.

$$OPCODE = 100010$$

The next bit, which is D, indicates whether the register that is specified by the REG part of byte 2 is a source or destination operand. Let us say that we will encode AL in the REG field of byte 2; therefore, D is set equal to 0 for source operand.

$$D = 0$$

The last bit (W) in byte 1 must specify a byte operation. For this reason, it is also set to 0.

$$W = 0$$

This leads to

$$BYTE\ 1 = 10001000_2 = 88_{16}$$

In byte 2, the source operand, which is specified by the REG field, is AL. The corresponding code from Fig. 3.2 is

$$REG = 000$$

Since the second operand is also a register, the MOD field is made 11. The R/M field specifies that the destination register is BL and the code from Fig. 3.3(b) is 011. This gives

$$MOD = 11$$

$$R/M = 011$$

Therefore, byte 2 is given by

$$BYTE\ 2 = 11000011_2 = C3_{16}$$

The entire hexadecimal code for the instruction is

MOV BL,AL = 88C3H

For a second operand that is located in memory, there are a number of different ways its location can be specified. That is, any of the addressing modes supported by the 8088 microprocessor can be used to generate its address. The addressing mode is also selected with the MOD and R/M fields.

Notice in Fig. 3.3(b) that the addressing mode for an operand in memory is indicated by one of the other three values (00, 01, and 10) in the MOD field and an appropriate R/M code. The different ways in which the operand's address can be generated are shown in the effective address calculation part of the table in Fig. 3.3(b). These different address calculation expressions correspond to the addressing modes we introduced in Chapter 2. For instance, if the base (BX) register contains the memory address, this fact is encoded into the instruction by making MOD = 00 and R/M = 111.

CODE	EXPLANATION
00	Memory Mode, no displacement follows*
01	Memory Mode, 8-bit displacement follows
10	Memory Mode, 16-bit displacement follows
11	Register Mode (no displacement)

*Except when R/M = 110, then 16-bit displacement follows

(a)

MOD = 11			EFFECTIVE ADDRESS CALCULATION			
R/M	W = 0	W = 1	R/M	MOD = 00	MOD = 01	MOD = 10
000	AL	AX	000	(BX) + (SI)	(BX) + (SI) + D8	(BX) + (SI) + D16
001	CL	CX	001	(BX) + (DI)	(BX) + (DI) + D8	(BX) + (DI) + D16
010	DL	DX	010	(BP) + (SI)	(BP) + (SI) + D8	(BP) + (SI) + D16
011	BL	BX	011	(BP) + (DI)	(BP) + (DI) + D8	(BP) + (DI) + D16
100	AH	SP	100	(SI)	(SI) + D8	(SI) + D16
101	CH	BP	101	(DI)	(DI) + D8	(DI) + D16
110	DH	SI	110	DIRECT ADDRESS	(BP) + D8	(BP) + D16
111	BH	DI	111	(BX)	(BX) + D8	(BX) + D16

(b)

Figure 3.3 (a) Mode (MOD) field encoding. (Reprinted by permission of Intel Corp. Copyright/Intel Corp. 1979) (b) Register/memory (R/M) field encoding. (Reprinted by permission of Intel Corp. Copyright/Intel Corp. 1979)

EXAMPLE 3.2

The instruction

ADD AX,[SI]

stands for "add the 16-bit contents of the memory location indirectly specified by SI to the contents of AX." Encode the instruction in machine code. The opcode for this add operation is 000000_2.

SOLUTION   To specify a 16-bit add operation with a register as the destination, the first byte of machine code will be

$$\text{BYTE } 1 = 00000011_2 = 03_{16}$$

The REG field bits in byte 2 are 000 to select AX as the destination register. The other operand is in memory and its address is specified by the contents of SI with no displacement. In Figs. 3.3(a) and (b), we find that for indirect addressing using SI with no displacement, MOD equals 00 and R/M equals 100.

$$\text{MOD} = 00$$

$$\text{R/M} = 100$$

This gives

$$\text{BYTE } 2 = 00000100_2 = 04_{16}$$

Thus the machine code for the instruction is

ADD AX,[SI] = 0304H

Some of the addressing modes of the 8088 need either data or an address displacement to be coded into the instruction. These types of information are encoded using additional bytes. For instance, looking at Fig. 3.1, we see that byte 3 is needed in the encoding of an instruction if it uses a byte-size address displacement, and both bytes 3 and 4 are needed if the instruction uses a word-size displacement.

The size of the displacement is encoded into the MOD field. For example, if the effective address is to be generated by the expression

$$(BX) + D8$$

where D8 stands for *8-bit displacement,* MOD is set to 01 to specify memory mode with an 8-bit displacement and R/M is set to 111 to select BX.

Bytes 3 and 4 are also used to encode byte-wide immediate operands, word-wide immediate operands, and direct addresses. For example, in an instruction where direct addressing is used to identify the location of an operand in memory, the MOD field must be 00 and the R/M field 110. The offset value of the operand's address is coded into the bytes that follow.

If both a 16-bit displacement and a 16-bit immediate operand are used in the same instruction, the displacement is encoded into bytes 3 and 4 and the immediate operand into bytes 5 and 6.

EXAMPLE 3.3

What is the machine code for the following instruction?

```
XOR CL,[1234H]
```

This instruction stands for exclusive-OR the byte of data at memory address 1234_{16} with the byte contents of CL. The opcode for exclusive-OR is 001100_2.

SOLUTION   Using the XOR opcode 001100_2, 1 for destination operand, and 0 for byte data, we get

$$\text{BYTE 1} = 00110010_2 = 32_{16}$$

The REG field has to specify CL, which makes it equal to 001. In this case a direct address has been specified for operand 2. This requires MOD = 00 and R/M = 110. Thus

$$\text{BYTE 2} = 00001110_2 = 0E_{16}$$

To specify the address 1234_{16}, we must use bytes 3 and 4. The least significant byte of the address is encoded first, followed by the most significant byte. This gives

$$\text{BYTE 3} = 34_{16}$$

and

$$\text{BYTE 4} = 12_{16}$$

The entire machine code form of the instruction is

```
XOR CL,[1234H] = 320E3412H
```

EXAMPLE 3.4

The instruction

$$\text{ADD [BX][DI]+DISP,AX}$$

means "add the word contents of AX to the contents of the memory location specified by based-indexed addressing mode." The opcode for the add operation is 000000_2 and assume that DISP equals 1234_{16}.

SOLUTION   The add opcode, which is 000000_2, a 0 for source operand, and a 1 for word data, gives

$$\text{BYTE 1} = 00000001_2 = 01_{16}$$

The REG field in byte 2 is 000 to specify AX as the source register. Since there is a displacement and it needs 16 bits for encoding, the MOD field obtained from Fig. 3.3(a) is 10. The R/M field, which is also obtained from Fig. 3.3(b), is set to 001 for an effective address generated from DI and BX. This gives the second byte as

$$\text{BYTE 2} = 10000001_2 = 81_{16}$$

The displacement 1234_{16} is encoded in the next 2 bytes, with the least significant byte first. Therefore, the machine code that results is

$$\text{ADD [BX][DI]+DISP,AX} = \text{01813412H}$$

As we indicated earlier, the general format in Fig. 3.1 cannot be used to encode all the instructions that can be executed by the 8088. Minor modifications must be made to this general format to encode a few instructions. In some instructions, one or more single-bit fields are needed. These 1-bit fields and their functions are shown in Fig. 3.4.

Field	Value	Function
S	0 1	No sign extension Sign extend 8-bit immediate data to 16 bits if W=1
V	0 1	Shift/rotate count is one Shift/rotate count is specified in CL register
Z	0 1	Repeat/loop while zero flag is clear Repeat/loop while zero flag is set

Figure 3.4 Additional 1-bit fields and their functions. (Reprinted by permission of Intel Corp. Copyright/Intel Corp. 1979)

For instance, the general format of the *repeat* (REP) instruction is

$$REP = 1111001Z$$

Here bit Z is made 1 or 0 depending on whether the repeat operation is to be done when the zero flag is set or when it is reset. Similarly, the other two bits, S and V, in Fig. 3.4 are used to encode sign extension for arithmetic instructions and to specify the source of the count for shift or rotate instructions, respectively.

The formats for all the instructions in the 8088's instruction set are shown in Fig. 3.5. This is the information that can be used to encode any 8088 instruction.

Instructions that involve a segment register need a 2-bit field to encode which register to be affected. This field is called the *SR field*. The four segment registers ES, CS, SS, and DS are encoded according to the table in Fig. 3.6.

DATA TRANSFER

MOV = Move:

	7 6 5 4 3 2 1 0	7 6 5 4 3 2 1 0	7 6 5 4 3 2 1 0	7 6 5 4 3 2 1 0	7 6 5 4 3 2 1 0	7 6 5 4 3 2 1 0
Register/memory to/from register	1 0 0 0 1 0 d w	mod reg r/m	(DISP-LO)	(DISP-HI)		
Immediate to register/memory	1 1 0 0 0 1 1 w	mod 0 0 0 r/m	(DISP-LO)	(DISP-HI)	data	data if w = 1
Immediate to register	1 0 1 1 w reg	data	data if w = 1			
Memory to accumulator	1 0 1 0 0 0 0 w	addr-lo	addr-hi			
Accumulator to memory	1 0 1 0 0 0 1 w	addr-lo	addr-hi			
Register/memory to segment register	1 0 0 0 1 1 1 0	mod 0 SR r/m	(DISP-LO)	(DISP-HI)		
Segment register to register/memory	1 0 0 0 1 1 0 0	mod 0 SR r/m	(DISP-LO)	(DISP-HI)		

PUSH = Push:

Register/memory	1 1 1 1 1 1 1 1	mod 1 1 0 r/m	(DISP-LO)	(DISP-HI)
Register	0 1 0 1 0 reg			
Segment register	0 0 0 SR 1 1 0			

POP = Pop:

Register/memory	1 0 0 0 1 1 1 1	mod 0 0 0 r/m	(DISP-LO)	(DISP-HI)
Register	0 1 0 1 1 reg			
Segment register	0 0 0 SR 1 1 1			

XCHG = Exchange:

Register/memory with register	1 0 0 0 0 1 1 w	mod reg r/m	(DISP-LO)	(DISP-HI)
Register with accumulator	1 0 0 1 0 reg			

Figure 3.5   8088 instruction encoding tables. (Reprinted by permission of Intel Corp. Copyright/Intel Corp. 1979)

IN = Input from:

Fixed port	`1 1 1 0 0 1 0 w`	DATA-8
Variable port	`1 1 1 0 1 1 0 w`	

OUT = Output to:

Fixed port	`1 1 1 0 0 1 1 w`	DATA-8		
Variable port	`1 1 1 0 1 1 1 w`			
XLAT = Translate byte to AL	`1 1 0 1 0 1 1 1`			
LEA = Load EA to register	`1 0 0 0 1 1 0 1`	mod reg r/m	(DISP-LO)	(DISP-HI)
LDS = Load pointer to DS	`1 1 0 0 0 1 0 1`	mod reg r/m	(DISP-LO)	(DISP-HI)
LES = Load pointer to ES	`1 1 0 0 0 1 0 0`	mod reg r/m	(DISP-LO)	(DISP-HI)
LAHF = Load AH with flags	`1 0 0 1 1 1 1 1`			
SAHF = Store AH into flags	`1 0 0 1 1 1 1 0`			
PUSHF = Push flags	`1 0 0 1 1 1 0 0`			
POPF = Pop flags	`1 0 0 1 1 1 0 1`			

ARITHMETIC

ADD = Add:

	7 6 5 4 3 2 1 0	7 6 5 4 3 2 1 0	7 6 5 4 3 2 1 0	7 6 5 4 3 2 1 0	7 6 5 4 3 2 1 0	7 6 5 4 3 2 1 0
Reg/memory with register to either	`0 0 0 0 0 0 d w`	mod reg r/m	(DISP-LO)	(DISP-HI)		
Immediate to register/memory	`1 0 0 0 0 0 s w`	mod 0 0 0 r/m	(DISP-LO)	(DISP-HI)	data	data if s: w=01
Immediate to accumulator	`0 0 0 0 0 1 0 w`	data	data if w=1			

ADC = Add with carry:

Reg/memory with register to either	`0 0 0 1 0 0 d w`	mod reg r/m	(DISP-LO)	(DISP-HI)		
Immediate to register/memory	`1 0 0 0 0 0 s w`	mod 0 1 0 r/m	(DISP-LO)	(DISP-HI)	data	data if s: w=01
Immediate to accumulator	`0 0 0 1 0 1 0 w`	data	data if w=1			

INC = Increment:

Register/memory	`1 1 1 1 1 1 1 w`	mod 0 0 0 r/m	(DISP-LO)	(DISP-HI)
Register	`0 1 0 0 0 reg`			
AAA = ASCII adjust for add	`0 0 1 1 0 1 1 1`			
DAA = Decimal adjust for add	`0 0 1 0 0 1 1 1`			

SUB = Subtract:

Reg/memory and register to either	`0 0 1 0 1 0 d w`	mod reg r/m	(DISP-LO)	(DISP-HI)		
Immediate from register/memory	`1 0 0 0 0 0 s w`	mod 1 0 1 r/m	(DISP-LO)	(DISP-HI)	data	data if s: w=01
Immediate from accumulator	`0 0 1 0 1 1 0 w`	data	data if w=1			

Figure 3.5 (Continued)

SBB = Subtract with borrow:

	7 6 5 4 3 2 1 0	7 6 5 4 3 2 1 0				
Reg/memory and register to either	0 0 0 1 1 0 d w	mod reg r/m	(DISP-LO)	(DISP-HI)		
Immediate from register/memory	1 0 0 0 0 0 s w	mod 0 1 1 r/m	(DISP-LO)	(DISP-HI)	data	data if s: w=01
Immediate from accumulator	0 0 0 1 1 1 0 w	data	data if w=1			

DEC Decrement:

Register/memory	1 1 1 1 1 1 1 w	mod 0 0 1 r/m	(DISP-LO)	(DISP-HI)
Register	0 1 0 0 1 reg			
NEG Change sign	1 1 1 1 0 1 1 w	mod 0 1 1 r/m	(DISP-LO)	(DISP-HI)

CMP = Compare:

Register/memory and register	0 0 1 1 1 0 d w	mod reg r/m	(DISP-LO)	(DISP-HI)		
Immediate with register/memory	1 0 0 0 0 0 s w	mod 1 1 1 r/m	(DISP-LO)	(DISP-HI)	data	data if s: w=1
Immediate with accumulator	0 0 1 1 1 1 0 w	data				
AAS ASCII adjust for subtract	0 0 1 1 1 1 1 1					
DAS Decimal adjust for subtract	0 0 1 0 1 1 1 1					
MUL Multiply (unsigned)	1 1 1 1 0 1 1 w	mod 1 0 0 r/m	(DISP-LO)	(DISP-HI)		

ARITHMETIC

	7 6 5 4 3 2 1 0	7 6 5 4 3 2 1 0	7 6 5 4 3 2 1 0	7 6 5 4 3 2 1 0	7 6 5 4 3 2 1 0	7 6 5 4 3 2 1 0
IMUL Integer multiply (signed)	1 1 1 1 0 1 1 w	mod 1 0 1 r/m	(DISP-LO)	(DISP-HI)		
AAM ASCII adjust for multiply	1 1 0 1 0 1 0 0	0 0 0 0 1 0 1 0	(DISP-LO)	(DISP-HI)		
DIV Divide (unsigned)	1 1 1 1 0 1 1 w	mod 1 1 0 r/m	(DISP-LO)	(DISP-HI)		
IDIV Integer divide (signed)	1 1 1 1 0 1 1 w	mod 1 1 1 r/m	(DISP-LO)	(DISP-HI)		
AAD ASCII adjust for divide	1 1 0 1 0 1 0 1	0 0 0 0 1 0 1 0	(DISP-LO)	(DISP-HI)		
CBW Convert byte to word	1 0 0 1 1 0 0 0					
CWD Convert word to double word	1 0 0 1 1 0 0 1					

LOGIC

NOT Invert	1 1 1 1 0 1 1 w	mod 0 1 0 r/m	(DISP-LO)	(DISP-HI)
SHL/SAL Shift logical/arithmetic left	1 1 0 1 0 0 v w	mod 1 0 0 r/m	(DISP-LO)	(DISP-HI)
SHR Shift logical right	1 1 0 1 0 0 v w	mod 1 0 1 r/m	(DISP-LO)	(DISP-HI)
SAR Shift arithmetic right	1 1 0 1 0 0 v w	mod 1 1 1 r/m	(DISP-LO)	(DISP-HI)
ROL Rotate left	1 1 0 1 0 0 v w	mod 0 0 0 r/m	(DISP-LO)	(DISP-HI)
ROR Rotate right	1 1 0 1 0 0 v w	mod 0 0 1 r/m	(DISP-LO)	(DISP-HI)
RCL Rotate through carry flag left	1 1 0 1 0 0 v w	mod 0 1 0 r/m	(DISP-LO)	(DISP-HI)
RCR Rotate through carry right	1 1 0 1 0 0 v w	mod 0 1 1 r/m	(DISP-LO)	(DISP-HI)

Figure 3.5 (Continued)

AND = And:

Reg/memory with register to either	0 0 1 0 0 0 d w	mod reg r/m	(DISP-LO)	(DISP-HI)		

Reg/memory with register to either	0 0 1 0 0 0 d w	mod reg r/m	(DISP-LO)	(DISP-HI)		
Immediate to register/memory	1 0 0 0 0 0 0 w	mod 1 0 0 r/m	(DISP-LO)	(DISP-HI)	data	data if w=1
Immediate to accumulator	0 0 1 0 0 1 0 w	data	data if w=1			

TEST = And function to flags no result:

Register/memory and register	0 0 0 1 0 0 d w	mod reg r/m	(DISP-LO)	(DISP-HI)		
Immediate data and register/memory	1 1 1 1 0 1 1 w	mod 0 0 0 r/m	(DISP-LO)	(DISP-HI)	data	data if w=1
Immediate data and accumulator	1 0 1 0 1 0 0 w	data				

OR = Or:

Reg/memory and register to either	0 0 0 0 1 0 d w	mod reg r/m	(DISP-LO)	(DISP-HI)		
Immediate to register/memory	1 0 0 0 0 0 0 w	mod 0 0 1 r/m	(DISP-LO)	(DISP-HI)	data	data if w=1
Immediate to accumulator	0 0 0 0 1 1 0 w	data	data if w=1			

XOR = Exclusive or:

Reg/memory and register to either	0 0 1 1 0 0 d w	mod reg r/m	(DISP-LO)	(DISP-HI)		
Immediate to register/memory	0 0 1 1 0 1 0 w	data	(DISP-LO)	(DISP-HI)	data	data if w=1
Immediate to accumulator	0 0 1 1 0 1 0 w	data	data if w=1			

STRING MANIPULATION

7 6 5 4 3 2 1 0   7 6 5 4 3 2 1 0   7 6 5 4 3 2 1 0   7 6 5 4 3 2 1 0   7 6 5 4 3 2 1 0   7 6 5 4 3 2 1 0

REP = Repeat	1 1 1 1 0 0 1 z
MOVS = Move byte/word	1 0 1 0 0 1 0 w
CMPS = Compare byte/word	1 0 1 0 0 1 1 w
SCAS = Scan byte/word	1 0 1 0 1 1 1 w
LODS = Load byte/wd to AL/AX	1 0 1 0 1 1 0 w
STDS = Stor byte/wd from AL/A	1 0 1 0 1 0 1 w

CONTROL TRANS. ...

CALL = Call:

Direct within segment	1 1 1 0 1 0 0 0	IP-INC-LO	IP-INC-HI
Indirect within segment	1 1 1 1 1 1 1 1	mod 0 1 0 r/m	(DISP-LO)	(DISP-HI)
Direct intersegment	1 0 0 1 1 0 1 0	IP-lo	IP-hi
		CS-lo	CS-hi
Indirect intersegment	1 1 1 1 1 1 1 1	mod 0 1 1 r/m	(DISP-LO)	(DISP-HI)

Figure 3.5 (Continued)

JMP = Unconditional Jump:

Direct within segment	1 1 1 0 1 0 0 1	IP-INC-LO	IP-INC-HI
Direct within segment-short	1 1 1 0 1 0 1 1	IP-INC8	
Indirect within segment	1 1 1 1 1 1 1 1	mod 1 0 0 r/m	(DISP-LO)	(DISP-HI)
Direct intersegment	1 1 1 0 1 0 1 0	IP-lo	IP-hi
		CS-lo	CS-hi
Indirect intersegment	1 1 1 1 1 1 1 1	mod 1 0 1 r/m	(DISP-LO)	(DISP-HI)

RET = Return from CALL:

Within segment	1 1 0 0 0 0 1 1		
Within seg adding immed to SP	1 1 0 0 0 0 1 0	data-lo	data-hi
Intersegment	1 1 0 0 1 0 1 1		
Intersegment adding immediate to SP	1 1 0 0 1 0 1 0	data-lo	data-hi
JE/JZ = Jump on equal/zero	0 1 1 1 0 1 0 0	IP-INC8	
JL/JNGE = Jump on less/not greater or equal	0 1 1 1 1 1 0 0	IP-INC8	
JLE/JNG = Jump on less or equal/not greater	0 1 1 1 1 1 1 0	IP-INC8	
JB/JNAE = Jump on below/not above or equal	0 1 1 1 0 0 1 0	IP-INC8	
JBE/JNA = Jump on below or equal/not above	0 1 1 1 0 1 1 0	IP-INC8	
JP/JPE = Jump on parity/parity even	0 1 1 1 1 0 1 0	IP-INC8	
JO = Jump on overflow	0 1 1 1 0 0 0 0	IP-INC8	
JS = Jump on sign	0 1 1 1 1 0 0 0	IP-INC8	
JNE/JNZ = Jump on not equal/not zer0	0 1 1 1 0 1 0 1	IP-INC8	

CONTROL TRANSFER (Cont'd.) 7 6 5 4 3 2 1 0   7 6 5 4 3 2 1 0   7 6 5 4 3 2 1 0   7 6 5 4 3 2 1 0   7 6 5 4 3 2 1 0   7 6 5 4 3 2 1 0

JNL/JGE = Jump on not less/greater or equal	0 1 1 1 1 1 0 1	IP-INC8
JNLE/JG = Jump on not less or equal/greater	0 1 1 1 1 1 1 1	IP-INC8
JNB/JAE = Jump on not below/above or equal	0 1 1 1 0 0 1 1	IP-INC8
JNBE/JA = Jump on not below or equal/above	0 1 1 1 0 1 1 1	IP-INC8
JNP/JPO = Jump on not par/par odd	0 1 1 1 1 0 1 1	IP-INC8
JNO = Jump on not overflow	0 1 1 1 0 0 0 1	IP-INC8
JNS = Jump on not sign	0 1 1 1 1 0 0 1	IP-INC8
LOOP = Loop CX times	1 1 1 0 0 0 1 0	IP-INC8
LOOPZ/LOOPE = Loop while zero/equal	1 1 1 0 0 0 0 1	IP-INC8
LOOPNZ/LOOPNE = Loop while not zero/equal	1 1 1 0 0 0 0 0	IP-INC8
JCXZ = Jump on CX zero	1 1 1 0 0 0 1 1	IP-INC8

Figure 3.5 (Continued)

80

INT = Interrupt:

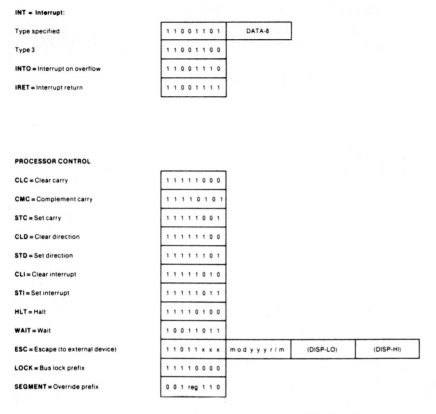

Type specified

| 1 1 0 0 1 1 0 1 | DATA-8 |

Type 3

| 1 1 0 0 1 1 0 0 |

INTO = Interrupt on overflow

| 1 1 0 0 1 1 1 0 |

IRET = Interrupt return

| 1 1 0 0 1 1 1 1 |

PROCESSOR CONTROL

CLC = Clear carry

| 1 1 1 1 1 0 0 0 |

CMC = Complement carry

| 1 1 1 1 0 1 0 1 |

STC = Set carry

| 1 1 1 1 1 0 0 1 |

CLD = Clear direction

| 1 1 1 1 1 1 0 0 |

STD = Set direction

| 1 1 1 1 1 1 0 1 |

CLI = Clear interrupt

| 1 1 1 1 1 0 1 0 |

STI = Set interrupt

| 1 1 1 1 1 0 1 1 |

HLT = Halt

| 1 1 1 1 0 1 0 0 |

WAIT = Wait

| 1 0 0 1 1 0 1 1 |

ESC = Escape (to external device)

| 1 1 0 1 1 x x x | m o d y y y r / m | (DISP-LO) | (DISP-HI) |

LOCK = Bus lock prefix

| 1 1 1 1 0 0 0 0 |

SEGMENT = Override prefix

| 0 0 1 reg 1 1 0 |

Figure 3.5   (Continued)

EXAMPLE 3.5

The instruction

```
MOV WORD PTR [BP][DI]+1234H,0ABCDH
```

stands for "move the immediate data word $ABCD_{16}$ into the memory location specified by based-indexed addressing mode." Express the instruction in machine code.

SOLUTION   Since this instruction does not involve one of the registers as an operand, it does not follow the general format we have been using. From Fig. 3.5 we find that the format of byte 1 in an immediate data-to-memory move is

$$1100011W$$

In our case, we are moving word-size data; therefore, W equals 1. This gives

$$\text{BYTE 1} = 11000111_2 = C7_{16}$$

Again from Fig. 3.5, we find that byte 2 has the form

$$\text{BYTE 2} = (\text{MOD})000(\text{R/M})$$

For a memory operand using a 16-bit displacement, Fig. 3.3(a) shows that MOD equals 10, and for based indexed addressing using BP and DI with a 16-bit displacement, Fig. 3.3(b) shows that R/M equals 011. This gives

$$\text{BYTE 2} = 10000011_2 = 83_{16}$$

Bytes 3 and 4 encode the displacement with its low byte first. Thus, for a displacement of 1234_{16}, we get

$$\text{BYTE 3} = 34_{16}$$

and

$$\text{BYTE 4} = 12_{16}$$

Last, bytes 5 and 6 encode the immediate data also with the least significant byte first. For data word $ABCD_{16}$, we get

$$\text{BYTE 5} = CD_{16}$$

and

$$\text{BYTE 6} = AB_{16}$$

The entire instruction in machine code is

```
MOV WORD PTR [BP][DI]+1234H,0ABCDH = C7833412CDABH
```

Register	SR
ES	00
CS	01
SS	10
DS	11

Figure 3.6   Segment register codes.

EXAMPLE 3.6

The instruction

$$\text{MOV [BP][DI]+1234H,DS}$$

stands for "move the contents of the data segment register to the memory location specified by based-indexed addressing mode." Express the instruction in machine code.

SOLUTION   From Fig. 3.5, we see that this instruction is encoded as

$$10001100(\text{MOD})0(\text{SR})(\text{R/M})(\text{DISP})$$

The MOD and R/M fields are the same as in Example 3.5. That is,

$$\text{MOD} = 10$$

and

$$\text{R/M} = 011$$

Moreover, the value of DISP is given as 1234_{16}. Finally, from Fig. 3.6 we find that to specify DS the SR field is

$$\text{SR} = 11$$

Therefore, the instruction is coded as

$$1000110010011011001101000001001 0_2 = 8\text{C}9\text{B}3412_{16}$$

3.3 ENCODING A COMPLETE PROGRAM IN MACHINE CODE

To encode a complete assembly language program in machine code, we must individually code each of its instructions. This can be done by using the instruction formats shown in Fig. 3.5 and the information in the tables of Figs. 3.2, 3.3, 3.4, and 3.6. We first identify the general machine code format for the instruction in Fig. 3.5. After determining the format, the bit fields can be evaluated using the tables of Figs. 3.2, 3.3, 3.4, and 3.6. Finally, the binary coded instruction can be expressed in hexadecimal form.

To execute a program on the PC, we must first store the machine code of the program in the code segment of memory. The bytes of machine code are stored in sequentially addressed locations in memory. The first byte of the program is stored at the lowest-value address; it is followed by the other bytes in the order in which they are encoded. That is, the address is incremented by one after storing each byte of machine code in memory.

EXAMPLE 3.7

Encode the "block move" program shown in Fig. 3.7(a) and show how it would be stored in memory starting at address 200_{16}.

	MOV AX,1020H	;LOAD AX REGISTER
	MOV DS,AX	;LOAD DATA SEGMENT ADDRESS
	MOV SI,100H	;LOAD SOURCE BLOCK POINTER
	MOV DI,120H	;LOAD DESTINATION BLOCK POINTER
	MOV CX,10H	;LOAD REPEAT COUNTER
NXTPT:	MOV AH,[SI]	;MOVE SOURCE BLOCK ELEMENT TO AH
	MOV [DI],AH	;MOVE ELEMENT FROM AH TO DESTINATION BLOCK
	INC SI	;INCREMENT SOURCE BLOCK POINTER
	INC DI	;INCREMENT DESTINATION BLOCK POINTER
	DEC CX	;DECREMENT REPEAT COUNTER
	JNZ NXTPT	;JUMP TO NXTPT IF CX NOT EQUAL TO ZERO
	NOP	;NO OPERATION

(a)

Instruction	Type of instruction	Machine code
MOV AX,1020H	Move immediate data to register	$1011100000010000000010000_2 = B82010_{16}$
MOV DS,AX	Move register to segment register	$1000111011011000_2 = 8ED8_{16}$
MOV SI,100H	Move immediate data to register	$1011111000000000000000001_2 = BE0001_{16}$
MOV DI,120H	Move immediate data to register	$1011111100100000000000001_2 = BF2001_{16}$
MOV CX,10H	Move immediate data to register	$1011100100010000000000000_2 = B91000_{16}$
MOV AH,[SI]	Move memory data to register	$1000101000100100_2 = 8A24_{16}$
MOV [DI],AH	Move register data to memory	$1000100000100101_2 = 8825_{16}$
INC SI	Increment register	$01000110_2 = 46_{16}$
INC DI	Increment register	$01000111_2 = 47_{16}$
DEC CX	Decrement register	$01001001_2 = 49_{16}$
JNZ NXTPT	Jump on not equal to zero	$0111010111110111_2 = 75F7_{16}$
NOP	No operation	$10010002_2 = 90_{16}$

(b)

Figure 3.7 (a) Block move program. (b) Machine coding of the block move program. (c) Storing the machine code in memory.

Memory address	Contents	Instruction
200H	B8H	MOV AX,1020H
201H	20H	
202H	10H	
203H	8EH	MOV DS,AX
204H	D8H	
205H	BEH	MOV SI,100H
206H	00H	
207H	01H	
208H	BFH	MOV DI,120H
209H	20H	
20AH	01H	
20BH	B9H	MOV CX,10H
20CH	10H	
20DH	00H	
20EH	8AH	MOV AH,[SI]
20FH	24H	
210H	88H	MOV [DI],AH
211H	25H	
212H	46H	INC SI
213H	47H	INC DI
214H	49H	DEC CX
215H	75H	JNZ $-9
216H	F7H	
217H	90H	NOP

(c)

Figure 3.7   (Continued)

SOLUTION   To encode this program into its equivalent machine code, we will use the instruction set table in Fig. 3.5. The first instruction

```
MOV AX,1020H
```

is a "move immediate data to register" instruction. In Fig. 3.5 we find it has the form

$$1011(W)(REG)(DATA)(DATA\ IF\ W = 1)$$

Since the move is to register AX, Fig. 3.2 shows that the W bit is 1 and REG is 000. The immediate data 1020_{16} follows this byte with the least significant byte coded first. This gives the machine code for the instruction as

$$1011100000010000000010000_2 = B82010_{16}$$

The second instruction

$$\texttt{MOV DS,AX}$$

represents a "move register to segment register" operation. This instruction has the general format

$$10001110(MOD)0(SR)(R/M)$$

From Fig. 3.3(a) and (b), we find that for this instruction MOD = 11 and R/M is 000 for AX. Furthermore, from Fig. 3.6, we find that SR = 11 for data segment register. This results in the code

$$1000111011011000_2 = 8ED8_{16}$$

for the second instruction.

The next three instructions have the same format as the first instruction. In the third instruction, REG is 110 for SI and the data is 0100_{16}. This gives

$$1011111000000000000000001_2 = BE0001_{16}$$

The fourth instruction has REG coded as 111 (DI) and the data as 0120_{16}. This results in

$$1011111100100000000000001_2 = BF2001_{16}$$

And in the fifth instruction REG is 001 for CX with 0010_{16} as the data. This gives

$$1011100100010000000000000_2 = B91000_{16}$$

Instruction six changes. It is a move of byte data from memory to a register. From Fig. 3.5, we find that its general format is

$$100010(D)(W)(MOD)(REG)(R/M)$$

Since AH is the destination and the instruction operates on bytes of data, the D and W bits are 1 and 0, respectively, and the REG field is 100. The contents of SI are used as a pointer to the source operand; therefore, MOD is 00 and R/M is 100. This gives

$$1000101000100100_2 = 8A24_{16}$$

The last MOV instruction has the same form. However, in this case, AH is the destination and DI is the address pointer. This makes D equal 0 and R/M equal 101. Therefore, we get

$$1000100000100101_2 = 8825_{16}$$

The next two instructions increment registers and have the general form

$$01000(REG)$$

For the first one, register SI is incremented. Therefore, REG equals 110. This results in

$$01000110_2 = 46_{16}$$

In the second, DI (REG = 111) is incremented and this gives

$$01000111_2 = 47_{16}$$

The two INC instructions are followed by a DEC instruction. Its general form is

$$01001(REG)$$

To decrement CX (REG = 001), we get

$$01001001_2 = 49_{16}$$

The next instruction is a jump to the location NXTPT. Its form is

$$01110101(IP{-}INC8)$$

We will not yet complete this instruction because it will be easier to determine the number of bytes to be jumped after the data have been coded for storage in memory. The final instruction is NOP and it is coded as

$$10010000_2 = 90_{16}$$

The entire machine code program is shown in Fig. 3.7(b). As shown in Fig. 3.7(c), our encoded program will be stored in memory starting from memory address 200_{16}. The choice of program beginning address establishes the address for the NXTPT label. Notice that the MOV AH,[SI] instruction, which has this label, starts at address $20E_{16}$. This is 9 bytes back from the value in IP after fetching the JNZ instruction. Therefore, the displacement (IP–INC8) in the JNZ instruction is -9, which is encoded as

$$0111010111110111_2 = 75F7_{16}$$

3.4 THE IBM PC AND ITS DEBUG PROGRAM

Now that we know how to convert an assembly language program to machine code and how this machine code is stored in memory, we are ready to enter the program into the PC; execute it; examine the results that it produces; and, if necessary, debug any errors in its operation. It is the *DEBUG program,* which is part of the PC's *DOS operating system,* that permits us to initiate these types of operations from the keyboard of the PC. In this section we will show how to load the DEBUG program from DOS, use it to examine or modify the contents of the 8088's internal registers, and how to return back to DOS from DEBUG.

   Using DEBUG, the programmer can issue commands to the 8088 microcomputer in the PC. DEBUG resides on the *DOS supplemental programs diskette.* Assuming that the DOS operating system has already been loaded and the supplemental programs diskette is in drive A, we load DEBUG by simply issuing the command

```
A > DEBUG (↵)
```

Actually, "DEBUG" can be typed in using either uppercase or lowercase characters. Therefore, DEBUG can also be brought up with the entry

A > debug (⏎)

For simplicity, we will use all uppercase characters in this book.

EXAMPLE 3.8

Initiate the DEBUG program from the keyboard of the PC. What prompt for command entry is displayed when in the debugger?

SOLUTION   When the DOS operating system has been loaded and the DOS supplemental programs diskette resides in drive A, DEBUG is brought up by entering

A > DEBUG (⏎)

Drive A is accessed to load the DEBUG program from the DOS diskette; DEBUG is then executed and its prompt, which is a "_", is displayed. DEBUG is now waiting to accept a command. Figure 3.8 shows what will be displayed on the screen.

A>DEBUG   **Figure 3.8**   Loading the DEBUG
_   program.

The keyboard is the input unit of the debugger and permits the user to enter commands that will load data, such as the machine code of a program; examine or modify the state of the 8088's internal registers; or execute a program. All we need to do is type in the command and then depress the enter (⏎) key. These debug commands are the tools a programmer needs to enter, execute, and debug programs.

When the command entry sequence is completed, the DEBUG program decodes the entry to determine which operation is to be performed, verifies that it is a valid command, and if valid, passes control to a routine that performs the operation. At the completion of the operation, results are displayed on the screen and the DEBUG prompt (_) is redisplayed. The PC remains in this state until a new entry is made from the keyboard.

Six kinds of information are typically entered as part of a command: *a command letter, an address, a register name, a file name, a drive name,* and *data.* The entire command set of DEBUG is shown in Fig. 3.9. This table gives the name for each command, its function, and its general *syntax.* By *syntax,* we mean the order in which key entries must be made to initiate the command.

Command	Syntax	Function
Register	R [REGISTER NAME]	Examine or modify the contents of an internal register
Quit	Q	End use of the DEBUG program
Dump	D [ADDRESS]	Dump the contents of memory to the display
Enter	E [ADDRESS] [LIST]	Examine or modify the contents of memory
Fill	F [STARTING ADDRESS] [ENDING ADDRESS] [LIST]	Fill a block in memory with the data in list
Move	M [STARTING ADDRESS] [ENDING ADDRESS] [DESTINATION ADDRESS]	Move a block of data from a source location in memory to a destination location
Compare	C [STARTING ADDRESS] [ENDING ADDRESS] [DESTINATION ADDRESS]	Compare two blocks of data in memory and display the locations that contain different data
Search	S [STARTING ADDRESS] [ENDING ADDRESS] [LIST]	Search through a block of data in memory and display all locations that match the data in list
Unassemble	U [STARTING ADDRESS] [ENDING ADDRESS]	Unassemble the machine code into its equivalent assembler instructions
Write	W [STARTING ADDRESS] [DRIVE] [STARTING SECTOR] [NUMBER OF SECTORS]	Save the contents of memory in a file on a diskette
Load	L [STARTING ADDRESS] [DRIVE] [STARTING SECTOR] [NUMBER OF SECTORS]	Load memory with the contents of a file on a diskette
Assemble	A [STARTING ADDRESS]	Assemble the instruction into machine code and store in memory
Trace	T = [ADDRESS] [NUMBER]	Trace the execution of the specified number of instructions
Go	G [STARTING ADDRESS] [BREAKPOINT ADDRESS]	Execute the instructions down through the breakpoint address

Figure 3.9 DEBUG program command set.

With the loading of DEBUG, the state of the 8088 microprocessor is initialized. This *initial state* is illustrated with the software model in Fig. 3.10. Notice that registers AX, BX, CX, DX, BP, SI, DI, and all the flags are reset to zero; IP is initialized to 0100_{16}; CS, DS, SS, and ES are all loaded with $0CDE_{16}$; and SP is loaded with $FFEE_{16}$. We can use the register command to verify this initial state.

Let us now look at the syntax for the *REGISTER* (R) *command.* This is the debugger command that allows us to examine or modify the contents of internal registers of the 8088. Notice that the syntax for this command is given in Fig. 3.9 as

```
R [REGISTER NAME]
```

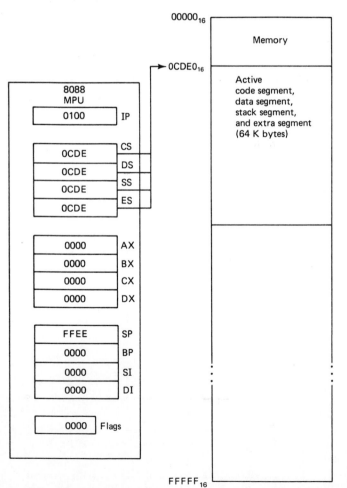

Figure 3.10   Software model of the 8088 microprocessor.

Symbol	Register
AX	Accumulator register
BX	Base register
CX	Count register
DX	Data register
SI	Source index register
DI	Destination index register
SP	Stack pointer register
BP	Base pointer register
CS	Code segment register
DS	Data segment register
SS	Stack segment register
ES	Extra segment register
F	Flag register

Figure 3.11 Register mnemonics for the R command.

Here the command letter is R. It is followed by the register name. Figure 3.11 shows what must be entered as the register name for each of the 8088's registers.

An example of the command entry needed to examine or modify the value in register AX is

$$\_R \ AX \ (\lrcorner)$$

Its execution causes the current value in AX to be displayed as

$$AX \ 0000$$
$$:\_$$

Here we see that AX contains 0000_{16}. The examine register command is not yet complete. Notice that a ":" followed by the cursor is displayed. We can now either depress ($\lrcorner$) to complete the command, leaving its value unchanged, or enter a new value for AX following the colon and then depress ($\lrcorner$). Let us load AX with a new value of $00FF_{16}$. This is done by the entry

$$:00FF \ (\lrcorner)$$
$$\_$$

EXAMPLE 3.9

Verify the initialized state of the 8088 by examining the contents of its registers with the register command.

SOLUTION   If we enter the register command without a specific register name, the debugger causes the state of all registers and flags to be displayed. That is, if we enter

$$\_R \quad (\hookleftarrow)$$

the information displayed is that shown in Fig. 3.12. Looking at Fig. 3.12, we see that all registers were initialized as expected. To verify that all flags other than IF were reset, we can compare the flag settings that are listed to the right of the value for IP with the values in the table of Fig. 3.13. Note that all but IP correspond to the reset state. The last line displays the machine code and assembly language statement of the instruction pointed to by the current values in CS and IP (CS:IP).

```
-R
AX=0000  BX=0000  CX=0000  DX=0000  SP=FFEE  BP=0000  SI=0000  DI=0000
DS=0CDE  ES=0CDE  SS=0CDE  CS=0CDE  IP=0100    NV UP EI PL NZ NA PO NC
0CDE:0100 DC37              FDIV    QWORD PTR [BX]                    DS:0000=CD
-
```

Figure 3.12 Displaying the initialized state of the 8088.

Flag	Meaning	Set	Reset
OF	Overflow	OV	NV
DF	Direction	DN	UP
IF	Interrupt	EI	DI
SF	Sign	NG	PL
ZF	Zero	ZR	NZ
AF	Auxiliary carry	AC	NA
PF	Parity	PE	PO
CF	Carry	CY	NC

Figure 3.13 Notations used for displaying the status flags.

EXAMPLE 3.10

Issue commands to the debugger on the PC that will cause the value in BX to be modified to $FF00_{16}$ and then verify that this new value exists in BX.

SOLUTION To modify the value in BX, all we need to do is issue the register command with BX and then respond to the :_ by entering the value $FF00_{16}$. This is done with the command sequence

                    _R BX (↵)
                    BX 0000
                    :FF00 (↵)

                    ─

We can verify that $FF00_{16}$ has been loaded into BX by issuing another register command as follows

                    _R BX (↵)
                    BX FF00
                    :_   (↵)

                    ─

The displayed information for this command sequence is shown in Fig. 3.14.

```
-R BX
BX 0000
:FF00
-R BX
BX FF00
:
```
Figure 3.14 Displayed information for Example 3.10.

The way in which the register command is used to modify flags is different from how it is used to modify the contents of a register. If we enter the command

                    _R F (↵)

the states of the flags are displayed as

            NV UP EI PL NZ NA PO NC-_

To modify one or more flags, just type in their new states (using the notations shown in Fig. 3.13) and depress the return key. For instance, to set the carry and zero flags, we enter

            NV UP EI PL NZ NA PO NC_ CY ZR (↵)

Note that the new flag states can be entered in any order.

EXAMPLE 3.11

Use the register command to set the parity flag to even parity. Verify that the flag has been changed.

SOLUTION   To set PF for even parity, we can issue the register command for the flag register and then enter PE as the new flag data. This is done with the command sequence

$$\_R \ F \ (\downarrow)$$
$$NV \ UP \ EI \ PL \ NZ \ NA \ PO \ NC\_ \ PE \ (\downarrow)$$

To verify that PF has been changed to its PE state, just initiate another register command for the flag register as follows:

$$\_R \ F \ (\downarrow)$$
$$NV \ UP \ EI \ PL \ NZ \ NA \ PE \ NC-\_ \ (\downarrow)$$

Notice that the state of the parity flag has changed from PO to PE. Figure 3.15 shows these commands and the displayed flag status that results.

```
-R F
NV UP EI PL NZ NA PO NC  -PE
-R F
NV UP EI PL NZ NA PE NC  -
```

Figure 3.15   Displayed information for Example 3.11.

The REGISTER command is very important for debugging programs. For instance, it can be used to check the contents of a register or flag prior to and again just after execution of an instruction. In this way, we can tell whether or not the instruction correctly performed the required operation.

If the command that was entered is identified as being invalid, an *error message* is displayed. Let us look at an example of an invalid command entry. To do this, we will repeat our earlier example in which AX was loaded with $00FF_{16}$, but in the entry of $00FF_{16}$ the uppercase letter O is keyed in instead of zeros. The result produced by issuing this command is shown in Fig. 3.16. Here we see that a warning "Error" is displayed and the symbol "^" is used to mark the starting location of the error in the command. To correct this error, the command is simply reentered.

```
-R AX
AX 0000
:00FF
  ^ Error
_
```

Figure 3.16 Invalid entry.

We will examine one more command before going on. We now know how to call up the DEBUG program from DOS, but we must also know how to return to DOS once in DEBUG. The debugger contains a special command to do this. It is called *QUIT* (Q). Therefore, to return to DOS we simply respond to the debug prompt with

```
_Q (↵)
```

3.5 EXAMINING AND MODIFYING THE CONTENTS OF MEMORY

In Section 3.4 we studied the command that permitted us to examine or modify the contents of the 8088's internal registers. Here we will continue our study of DEBUG's command set with those commands that can be used to examine and modify the contents of memory. The ability to do this is essential for debugging programs. For instance, the contents of a memory address can be examined just before and just after the execution of an instruction. In this way, we can verify that the instruction performs the operation correctly. Another use of this type of command is to load a program into the code segment of the 8088's memory. The complete command set of DEBUG was shown in Fig. 3.9. Six of these commands, DUMP, ENTER, FILL, MOVE, COMPARE, and SEARCH, are provided for use in examining or modifying the contents of storage locations in memory.

DUMP Command

The *DUMP* (D) *command* allows us to examine the contents of a memory location or a block of consecutive memory locations. Looking at Fig. 3.9, we see that the general syntax for DUMP is

```
D ADDRESS
```

The value of address entered is automatically referenced to the current value in the data segment (DS) register. For instance, issuing the command

```
D (↵)
```

causes the 128 consecutive bytes offset by 0100_{16} from the current value in DS to be displayed. Remember that when DEBUG is loaded DS is initialized as

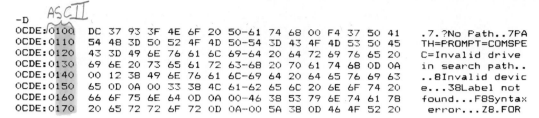

```
-D   ASCII
OCDE:0100   DC 37 93 3F 4E 6F 20 50-61 74 68 00 F4 37 50 41    .7.?No Path..7PA
OCDE:0110   54 48 3D 50 52 4F 4D 50-54 3D 43 4F 4D 53 50 45    TH=PROMPT=COMSPE
OCDE:0120   43 3D 49 6E 76 61 6C 69-64 20 64 72 69 76 65 20    C=Invalid drive
OCDE:0130   69 6E 20 73 65 61 72 63-68 20 70 61 74 68 0D 0A    in search path..
OCDE:0140   00 12 38 49 6E 76 61 6C-69 64 20 64 65 76 69 63    ..8Invalid devic
OCDE:0150   65 0D 0A 00 33 38 4C 61-62 65 6C 20 6E 6F 74 20    e...38Label not
OCDE:0160   66 6F 75 6E 64 0D 0A 00-46 38 53 79 6E 74 61 78    found...F8Syntax
OCDE:0170   20 65 72 72 6F 72 0D 0A-00 5A 38 0D 46 4F 52 20    error...Z8.FOR
```

Figure 3.17 Examining the contents of 128 consecutive bytes in memory.

$0CDE_{16}$. Therefore, issuing this command gives the memory dump shown in Fig. 3.17.

Notice that 16 bytes of data are displayed per line and only the address of the first byte is shown at the left. From Fig. 3.17 we see that this is denoted as 0CDE:0100. This stands for physical address $12C20_{16}$. The second byte of data displayed in the first line corresponds to the memory address 0CDE:0101 or $12C21_{16}$, and the last byte corresponds to the memory address 0CDE:010F or $12C2F_{16}$. Note that the values of the eighth and ninth bytes are separated by a hyphen.

For all memory dumps, an ASCII version of the memory data is also displayed. It is displayed to the right of the hexadecimal data. In Fig. 3.17, this results in a series of "." because all bytes that result in an unprintable ASCII character are displayed as the symbol ".".

The results shown in Fig. 3.17 could be obtained with several other forms of the DUMP command. One way is to enter the current value in DS, which is $0CDE_{16}$, and an offset of 0100_{16} in the address field. This results in the command

D 0CDE:100 (↵)

Another way is to enter DS instead of its value with the offset. This gives

D DS:100 (↵)

In fact, the same results can be obtained by just issuing the command

D 100 (↵)

EXAMPLE 3.12   *PA*

What is the physical address range of the bytes of data in the last line of data shown in Fig. 3.17?

SOLUTION In Fig. 3.17 we see that the first byte is at address 0CDE:0170. This is the physical address

$$PA = 0CDE_{16} + 0170_{16} = 0CF60_{16}$$

The last byte is at address 0CDE:017F and its physical address is

$$PA = 0CDE_{16} + 017F_{16} = 0CF6F_{16}$$

EXAMPLE 3.13

What happens if we repeat the entry D (↵) after obtaining the memory dump shown in Fig. 3.17?

step through memory

SOLUTION The contents of the next 128 consecutive bytes of memory are dumped to the display. The displayed information is shown in Fig. 3.18.

Frequently, we do not want to examine such a large block of memory. Instead, we may want to look at just a few bytes or a specific-sized block. The DUMP command can also do this. This time we enter two addresses. The first address defines the starting point of the block and the second address defines the end of the block. For instance, if we want to examine the two bytes of data that are at offsets equal to 200_{16} and 201_{16} in the current data segment, we enter the command

$$D \; DS:200 \; 201 \; (↵)$$

```
-D                ASCII
OCDE:0180  63 61 6E 6E 6F 74 20 62-65 20 6E 65 73 74 65 64   cannot be nested
OCDE:0190  0D 0A 00 6B 38 49 6E 73-75 66 66 69 63 69 65 6E   ...k8Insufficien
OCDE:01A0  74 20 6D 65 6D 6F 72 79-0D 0A 00 85 38 49 6E 74   t memory....8Int
OCDE:01B0  65 72 6D 65 64 69 61 74-65 20 66 69 6C 65 20 65   ermediate file e
OCDE:01C0  72 72 6F 72 20 64 75 72-69 6E 67 20 70 69 70 65   rror during pipe
OCDE:01D0  0D 0A 00 9D 38 43 61 6E-6E 6F 74 20 64 6F 20 62   ....8Cannot do b
OCDE:01E0  69 6E 61 72 79 20 72 65-61 64 73 20 66 72 6F 6D   inary reads from
OCDE:01F0  20 61 20 64 65 76 69 63-65 0D 0A 00 C5 38 42 52   a device....8BR
-
```

Figure 3.18 Displayed information for repeat of 128-byte memory dump command.

The result obtained by executing this command is given in Fig. 3.19.

```
-D DS:200 201
0CDE:0200   45 41
```
                                                                    EA

Figure 3.19 Displaying just two bytes of data.

EXAMPLE 3.14

Issue a dump command that will display the 32 bytes of memory that are located at offsets 0300_{16} through $031F_{16}$ in the current data segment.

SOLUTION   The command needed to display the contents of this part of memory is

$$D \ \ 300 \ \ 31F \ \ (\lrcorner)$$

and the information that is displayed is shown in Fig. 3.20.

```
-D 300 31F
0CDE:0300   0F 03 44 45 4C 01 68 0F-04 54 59 50 45 01 38 10   ..DEL.h..TYPE.8.
0CDE:0310   03 52 45 4D 02 04 01 04-43 4F 50 59 03 61 26 05   .REM....COPY.a&.
_
```

Figure 3.20 Displayed information for Example 3.14.

Up to now, all the data displayed with the DUMP command was contained in the data segment of memory. It is also possible to examine data that are stored in the code segment, stack segment, or extra segment. To do this, we simply use the appropriate segment register name in the command. For instance, the commands needed to dump the values in the first 16 bytes of the current code segment and extra segment are

$$D \ \ CS:0 \ \ F \ \ (\lrcorner)$$
$$D \ \ ES:0 \ \ F \ \ (\lrcorner)$$

EXAMPLE 3.15

Use the DUMP command to examine the 16 bytes of memory just below the top of the stack.

SOLUTION The top of the stack is defined by the contents of the SS and SP registers (SS:SP). Earlier we found that SP was initialized to $FFEE_{16}$ when debug was loaded. Therefore, the 16 bytes we are interested in reside at offset $FFEE_{16}$ through $FFFD_{16}$ from the current value in SS. This part of the stack is examined with the command

$$D \ SS:FFEE \ FFFD \ (\downarrow)$$

The result displayed by executing this command is shown in Fig. 3.21

```
-D SS:FFEE FFFD
0CDE:FFE0                                                        00 00                          ..
0CDE:FFF0   00 00 00 00 00 00 00 00-00 00 00 00 00 00                ..............
-
```

Figure 3.21 Displayed information for Example 3.15.

ENTER Command

The DUMP command allowed us to examine the contents of memory, but we also need to be able to modify the data stored in memory—for instance, to load a machine code program. It is for this purpose that the *ENTER* (E) *command* is provided in the DEBUG program.

In Fig. 3.9, we find that the syntax of the ENTER command is

$$E \ [ADDRESS] \ [LIST]$$

The address part of the E command is entered the same way we just described for the DUMP command. If no segment name is included with the offset, the DS register is assumed. The list that follows the address is the data that get loaded into memory.

As an example, let us write a command that will load five consecutive byte-wide memory locations that start at address DS:100 with the value FF_{16}. This is done with the command

$$E \ DS:100 \ FF \ FF \ FF \ FF \ FF \ (\downarrow)$$

To verify that the new values of data have been stored in memory, let us dump the contents of these locations to the display. To do this, we issue the command

$$D \ DS:100 \ 104 \ (\downarrow)$$

This series of commands and the displayed results are illustrated in Fig. 3.22.

```
-E DS:100 FF FF FF FF FF
-D DS:100 104
0CDE:0100   FF FF FF FF FF
-
```
                                                                    . . . . .

Figure 3.22 Modifying five consecutive bytes of memory and verifying the change of data.

Notice that the byte storage locations from address DS:100 through DS:104 now all contain the value FF_{16}.

The ENTER command can also be used in a way in which it either examines or modifies the contents of memory. If we issue the command with an address but no data, what happens is that the contents of the addressed storage location are displayed. For instance, the command

$$E \ DS:100 \ (\downarrow)$$

causes the value held at this address to be displayed as follows:

$$0CDE:0100 \ FF._$$

Notice that the value at address 0CDE:0100 is FF_{16}.

At this point we have several options; for one, the return key can be depressed. This terminates the ENTER command without changing the contents of the displayed memory location and causes the debug prompt to be displayed. Instead of depressing return, we can depress the space bar. Again, this would cause the contents of the displayed memory location not to be changed. Instead, it causes the contents of the next consecutive memory address to be displayed. Let us assume that this was done. Then the display would read

$$0CDE:0100 \ FF. \ FF._$$

Here we see that the data stored at address 0CDE:0101 are also FF_{16}. A third type of entry that could be made is to enter a new value of data and then depress the space bar or return key. For example, we could enter 11 and then depress space. This gives the display

$$0CDE:0100 \ FF. \ FF.11 \ FF._$$

The value pointed to by address 0CDE:101 has been changed to 11 and the contents of address 0CDE:0102, which are FF_{16}, are displayed. Now depress the return key to finalize the data entry sequence.

EXAMPLE 3.16

Start a data entry sequence by examining the contents of address DS:100 and then, without entering new data, depress the "−" key. What happens?

SOLUTION   The data entry sequence is initiated as

```
        E DS:100 (↵)
        0CDE:0100 FF._
```

Now entering "−" causes the address and data that follow to be displayed.

```
        0CDE:00FF 00._
```

Notice that the address of the previous storage location was displayed by entering minus (−). This result is illustrated in Fig. 3.23.

```
-E DS:100
0CDE:0100   FF.-
0CDE:00FF   00.
```

Figure 3.23   Using the "−" key to examine the contents of the previous memory location.

The ENTER command can also be used to enter ASCII data. This is done by simply enclosing the data entered in quotation marks. An example is the command

```
        E DS:200 "ASCII" (↵)
```

This command causes the ASCII data for letters A, S, C, I, and I to be stored in memory at addresses DS:200, DS:201, DS:202, DS:203, and DS:204, respectively. This character data entry can be verified with the command

```
        D DS:200 204 (↵)
```

Looking at the ASCII field of the data dump shown in Fig. 3.24, we see that the correct ASCII data were stored into memory. Actually, either single or double quote marks can be used. Therefore, the entry could also have been made as

```
        E DS:200 'ASCII' (↵)
```

FILL Command − *rewrite command*

Frequently, we want to fill a block of consecutive memory locations all with the same data. For example, we may need to initialize storage locations in an area of

```
-E DS:200 "ASCII"
-D DS:200 204
0CDE:0200   41 53 43 49 49                                    ASCII
-
```

Figure 3.24   Loading ASCII data into memory with the ENTER command.

memory with zeros. To do this by entering data address by address with the ENTER command would be very time-consuming. It is for this type of operation that the *FILL* (F) *command* is provided in the DEBUG program.

From Fig. 3.9, we find that the general form of the FILL command is

```
F [STARTING ADDRESS] [ENDING ADDRESS] [LIST]
```

Here *starting address* and *ending address* specify the block of storage locations in memory. They are followed by a *list* of data. An example is the command

```
F 100 11F 22 (↵)
```

Execution of this command causes the 32 byte locations in the range 0CDE:100 through 0CDE:11F to be loaded with 22_{16}. The fact that this change in memory contents has happened can be verified with the command

```
D 100 11F (↵)
```

Figure 3.25 shows the result of executing these two commands.

```
--F 100 11F 22
--D 100 11F
0CDE:0100  22 22 22 22 22 22 22 22-22 22 22 22 22 22 22 22   """"""""""""""""""
0CDE:0110  22 22 22 22 22 22 22 22-22 22 22 22 22 22 22 22   """"""""""""""""""
--
```

Figure 3.25   Initializing a block of memory with the FILL command.

EXAMPLE 3.17

Initialize all storage locations in the block of memory from DS:120 through DS:13F with the value 33_{16} and the block of storage locations from DS:140 through DS:15F with the value 44_{16}. Verify that the contents of these ranges of memory were correctly modified.

SOLUTION   The initialization operations can be done with the FILL commands that follow:

```
F 120 13F 33 (↵)
F 140 15F 44 (↵)
```

They are then verified with the DUMP command

```
D 120 15F (↵)
```

The information displayed by the command sequence is shown in Fig. 3.26.

```
-F 120 13F 33
-F 140 15F 44
-D 120 15F
OCDE:0120  33 33 33 33 33 33 33 33-33 33 33 33 33 33 33 33   3333333333333333
OCDE:0130  33 33 33 33 33 33 33 33-33 33 33 33 33 33 33 33   3333333333333333
OCDE:0140  44 44 44 44 44 44 44 44-44 44 44 44 44 44 44 44   DDDDDDDDDDDDDDDD
OCDE:0150  44 44 44 44 44 44 44 44-44 44 44 44 44 44 44 44   DDDDDDDDDDDDDDDD
-
```

Figure 3.26   Displayed information for Example 3.17.

MOVE Command — *relocate blocks of memory*

The *MOVE* (M) *command* allows us to copy a block of data from one part of
memory to another part. For instance, using this command, a 32-byte block of
data that resides in memory from address DS:100 to DS:11F can be copied to the
address range DS:200 through DS:21F with a single command.

The general form of the command is given in Fig. 3.9 as

```
M [STARTING ADDRESS] [ENDING ADDRESS] [DESTINATION ADDRESS]
```

Notice that it is initiated by depressing the M key. After this, we must enter three
addresses. The first two address are the starting address and ending address of
the source block of data, that is, the block of data that is to be copied. The third
address is the *destination starting address,* that is, the starting address of the
segment of memory to which the block of data is to be copied.

The command for our earlier example, which copied a 32-byte block of data
from DS:100 through DS:11F to DS:200, is written as

```
M 100 11F 200 (↵)
```

EXAMPLE 3.18

Fill each storage location in the block of memory from address DS:100 through
DS:11F with the value 11. Then copy this block of data to a destination block
starting at DS:160. Verify that the block move was correctly done.

SOLUTION   First, we will fill the source block with 11_{16} using the command

```
F 100 11F 11 (↵)
```

Next, it is copied to the destination with the command

```
M 100 11F 160 (↵)
```

Finally, we dump the complete range from DS:100 to DS:17F by issuing the command

D 100 17F (↵)

The result of this memory dump is given in Fig. 3.27. It verifies that the block move was successfully performed.

```
-F 100 11F 11
-M 100 11F 160
-D 100 17F
OCDE:0100  11 11 11 11 11 11 11 11-11 11 11 11 11 11 11 11    ................
OCDE:0110  11 11 11 11 11 11 11 11-11 11 11 11 11 11 11 11    ................
OCDE:0120  33 33 33 33 33 33 33 33-33 33 33 33 33 33 33 33    3333333333333333
OCDE:0130  33 33 33 33 33 33 33 33-33 33 33 33 33 33 33 33    3333333333333333
OCDE:0140  44 44 44 44 44 44 44 44-44 44 44 44 44 44 44 44    DDDDDDDDDDDDDDDD
OCDE:0150  44 44 44 44 44 44 44 44-44 44 44 44 44 44 44 44    DDDDDDDDDDDDDDDD
OCDE:0160  11 11 11 11 11 11 11 11-11 11 11 11 11 11 11 11    ................
OCDE:0170  11 11 11 11 11 11 11 11-11 11 11 11 11 11 11 11    ................
-
```

Figure 3.27 Displayed information for Example 3.18.

COMPARE Command — compare one block of data to another block of data

Another type of memory operation we sometimes need to perform is to compare the contents of two blocks of data to determine if they are or are not the same. This operation can be easily done with the *COMPARE* (C) *command* of the DEBUG program. Figure 3.9 shows that the general form of this command is

```
C [STARTING ADDRESS] [ENDING ADDRESS] [DESTINATION ADDRESS]
```

For example, to compare a block of data located from address DS:100 through DS:10F to an equal sized block of data starting at address DS:160, we issue the command

C 100 10F 160 (↵)

This command causes the contents of corresponding address locations in each block to be compared to each other. That is, the contents of address DS:100 are compared to those at address DS:160, those at address DS:101 are compared to those at address DS:161, and so on. Each time unequal elements are found, the address and contents of that byte in both blocks are displayed.

Since both of these blocks contain the same information, no data are displayed. However, if this source block is next compared to the destination block starting at address DS:120 by entering the command

C 100 10F 120 (↵)

```
-C 100 10F 120
OCDE:0100    11    33    OCDE:0120
OCDE:0101    11    33    OCDE:0121
OCDE:0102    11    33    OCDE:0122
OCDE:0103    11    33    OCDE:0123
OCDE:0104    11    33    OCDE:0124
OCDE:0105    11    33    OCDE:0125
OCDE:0106    11    33    OCDE:0126
OCDE:0107    11    33    OCDE:0127
OCDE:0108    11    33    OCDE:0128
OCDE:0109    11    33    OCDE:0129
OCDE:010A    11    33    OCDE:012A
OCDE:010B    11    33    OCDE:012B
OCDE:010C    11    33    OCDE:012C
OCDE:010D    11    33    OCDE:012D
OCDE:010E    11    33    OCDE:012E
OCDE:010F    11    33    OCDE:012F
-
```

Figure 3.28 Results produced when unequal data are found in a COMPARE command.

all elements in both blocks are unequal; therefore, the information shown in Fig. 3.28 is displayed.

SEARCH Command

The *SEARCH* (S) *command* can be used to scan through a block of data in memory to determine whether or not it contains certain data. The general form of this command is given in Fig. 3.9 as

S [STARTING ADDRESS] [ENDING ADDRESS] [LIST]

When the command is issued, the contents of each storage location in the block of memory between the starting address and the ending address are compared to the data in list. The address is displayed for each memory location where a match is found.

EXAMPLE 3.19

Perform a search of the block of data from address DS:100 through DS:17F to determine which memory locations contain 33_{16}.

SOLUTION The search command that must be issued is

S 100 17F 33 (↵)

Figure 3.29 shows that all addresses in the range 120_{16} through $13F_{16}$ contain this value of data.

```
-S 100 17F 33
OCDE:0120
OCDE:0121
OCDE:0122
OCDE:0123
OCDE:0124
OCDE:0125
OCDE:0126
OCDE:0127
OCDE:0128
OCDE:0129
OCDE:012A
OCDE:012B
OCDE:012C
OCDE:012D
OCDE:012E
OCDE:012F
OCDE:0130
OCDE:0131
OCDE:0132
OCDE:0133
OCDE:0134
OCDE:0135
OCDE:0136
OCDE:0137
OCDE:0138
OCDE:0139
OCDE:013A
OCDE:013B
OCDE:013C
OCDE:013D
OCDE:013E
OCDE:013F
--
```

Figure 3.29   Displayed information for Example 3.19.

3.6 LOADING, VERIFYING, AND SAVING MACHINE CODE PROGRAMS

Up to this point we have learned how to encode instructions and programs in machine code and how to use the register and memory commands of DEBUG to examine or modify the contents of the 8088's internal registers or data stored in memory. Let us now look at how we can load machine code instructions and programs into the memory of the PC.

In Section 3.5, we found that the ENTER command can be used to load either a single or a group of memory locations with data, such as the machine code for instructions. As an example, let us load the machine code $88C3_{16}$ that was found for the instruction MOV BL,AL in Example 3.1. This instruction is loaded into memory starting at address CS:100 with the ENTER command

```
E CS:100 88 C3 (↵)
```

Moreover, we can verify that it has been loaded correctly with the DUMP command

D CS:100 101 (↵)

This displays the data

0CDE:0100 88 C3

Let us now introduce another command that is important for loading and debugging machine code on the PC. It is the *UNASSEMBLE* (U) *command.* By *unassemble* we mean the process of converting machine code instructions to their equivalent assembly language source statements. The U command lets us specify a range in memory, and execution of the command causes the source statements for the memory data to be displayed on the screen.

Looking at Fig. 3.9, we find that the syntax of the UNASSEMBLE command is

U [STARTING ADDRESS] [ENDING ADDRESS]

We can use this command to verify that the machine code entered for an instruction is correct. To do this for our earlier example, the command that follows is issued

U CS:100 101 (↵)

This results in display of the starting memory location, followed by both the machine code and assembler forms of the instruction. This gives

0CDE:0100 88C3 MOV BL,AL

The entry sequence and displayed information for loading, verification, and unassembly of the instruction are shown in Fig. 3.30.

```
-E CS:100 88 C3
-D CS:100 101
0CDE:0100    88 C3
-U CS:100 101                                        ..
0CDE:0100 88C3          MOV       BL,AL
-
```

Figure 3.30 Loading, verifying, and unassembly of an instruction.

EXAMPLE 3.20

Use a series of commands to load, verify loading, and unassemble the machine code for the ADD instruction encoded in Example 3.2. Load the instruction at address CS:200.

SOLUTION   In Example 3.2, we found that the machine code for the instruction was 0304_{16}. It is loaded into the code segment of the microcomputer's memory with the command

$$E \ CS:200 \ 03 \ 04 \ (\hookleftarrow)$$

Next, we can verify that it was loaded correctly with the command

$$D \ CS:200 \ 201 \ (\hookleftarrow)$$

and finally unassemble the instruction with

$$U \ CS:200 \ 201 \ (\hookleftarrow)$$

The results produced by this sequence of commands are shown in Fig. 3.31. Here we see that the instruction entered is

$$ADD \ AX,[SI]$$

```
-E CS:200 03 04
-D CS:200 201
OCDE:0200   03 04                              ..
-U CS:200 201
OCDE:0200 0304          ADD     AX,[SI]
-
```

Figure 3.31   Displayed information for Example 3.20.

Before going further we will cover two more commands that are useful for loading programs. They are the *WRITE* (W) *command* and *LOAD* (L) *command*. These commands give the ability to save data stored in memory on a diskette and to reload memory from a diskette, respectively. We can load the machine code of a program with the E command the first time we use it and then save it on a diskette. In this way, we can simply reload the program from the diskette the next time we need to work with it.

Figure 3.9 shows that the general forms of W and L are

```
W [STARTING ADDRESS] [DRIVE] [STARTING SECTOR] [NUMBER OF SECTORS]
L [STARTING ADDRESS] [DRIVE] [STARTING SECTOR] [NUMBER OF SECTORS]
```

For instance, to save the ADD instruction we just loaded at address CS:200 in Example 3.20, we can issue the WRITE command

```
W CS:200 1 10 1 (↵)
```

Notice that we have selected for the specification disk drive 1 (drive B), 10 as an arbitrary starting sector on the diskette, and an arbitrary length of one sector. Before the command is issued, a formatted data diskette must be inserted into drive B. Then issuing the command causes one sector of data starting at address CS:200 to be read from memory and written into sector 10 on the diskette in drive B. Unlike the earlier commands we have studied, the W command automatically references the CS register instead of the DS register. For this reason, the command

```
W 200 1 10 1 (↵)
```

will perform the same operation.

Let us digress for a moment to examine the file specification of the W command in more detail. The diskettes for an IBM PC that has double-sided, double-density drives are organized into 10,001 sectors that are assigned sector numbers over the range 0_{16} through $27F_{16}$. Moreover, each sector is capable of storing 512 bytes of data. With the file specification in a W command, we can select any one of these sector numbers as the starting sector. The value of the number of sectors should be specified based on the number of bytes of data that are to be saved. The specification we made earlier for our example of a write command selected one sector (sector number 10_{16}) and for this reason could only save up to 512 bytes of data. The maximum value of sectors that can be specified with a write command is 80_{16}.

The LOAD command can be used to reload a file of data stored on a diskette anywhere in memory. As an example, let us load the instruction that we just saved on disk with a W command at a new address (CS:300). This is done with the L command

```
L 300 1 10 1 (↵)
```

The reloading of the instruction can be verified by issuing the UNASSEMBLE command

```
U CS:300 301 (↵)
```

This causes the display

```
0CDE:300 0301 ADD AX,[SI]
```

EXAMPLE 3.21

Show the sequence of keyboard entries needed to enter the machine code program of Fig. 3.7(c) into memory of the PC. The program is to be loaded into memory starting at address CS:100. Verify that the hexadecimal machine code was entered correctly and then unassemble the machine code to ensure that it represents the source program of Fig. 3.7(c). Save the program in sector 100 of a formatted data diskette.

SOLUTION   We will use the ENTER command to load the program

E CS:100 B8 20 10 8E D8 BE 0 01 BF 20 01 B9 10 0 8A 24 88 25 46 47 49 75 F7 90 (↵)

First, we verify that the machine code has loaded correctly with the command

D CS:100 117 (↵)

Comparing the displayed data in Fig. 3.32 to the machine code in Fig. 3.7(c), we see that it has been loaded correctly. Now the machine code can be unassembled by the command

U CS:100 117 (↵)

Comparing the displayed program of Fig. 3.32 to that in Fig. 3.7(c), it again verifies correct entry. Finally, the program is saved on the data diskette with the command

W CS:100 1 100 1   (↵)

```
-E CS:100 B8 20 10 8E D8 BE 0 01 BF 20 01 B9 10 0 8A 24 88 25 46 47 49 75 F7 90
-D CS:100 117
0CDE:0100   B8 20 10 8E D8 BE 00 01-BF 20 01 B9 10 00 8A 24     . ........ .....$
0CDE:0110   88 25 46 47 49 75 F7 90                             .%FGIu..
-U CS:100 117
0CDE:0100 B82010        MOV     AX,1020
0CDE:0103 8ED8          MOV     DS,AX
0CDE:0105 BE0001        MOV     SI,0100
0CDE:0108 BF2001        MOV     DI,0120
0CDE:010B B91000        MOV     CX,0010
0CDE:010E 8A24          MOV     AH,[SI]
0CDE:0110 8825          MOV     [DI],AH
0CDE:0112 46            INC     SI
0CDE:0113 47            INC     DI
0CDE:0114 49            DEC     CX
0CDE:0115 75F7          JNZ     010E
0CDE:0117 90            NOP
-W CS:100 1 100 1
```

Figure 3.32   Displayed information for Example 3.21.

3.7 ASSEMBLING INSTRUCTIONS WITH THE ASSEMBLE COMMAND

All the instructions we have worked with up to this point have been hand assembled into machine code. The DEBUG program has a command that lets us automatically assemble the instructions of a program, one after the other, and store them in memory. It is called the *ASSEMBLE* (A) *command.*

The general syntax of ASSEMBLE is given in Fig. 3.9 as

A [STARTING ADDRESS]

Here, "starting address" is the address at which the machine code of the first instruction of the program is to be stored. For example, to assemble the instruction ADD [BX + SI + 1234], AX and store its machine code in memory starting at address CS:100, the command entry is

A CS:100 (↵)

The response to this command input is the display of the starting address in the form

0CDE:0100_

The instruction to be assembled is typed in following this address, and when the (↵) key is depressed, the instruction is assembled into machine code; then it is stored in memory, and the starting address of the next instruction is displayed. As shown in Fig. 3.33, for our example, we get

```
0CDE:0100 ADD [BX+SI+1234],AX (↵)
0CDE:0104_
```

Now either the next instruction is entered or the (↵) key is depressed to terminate the ASSEMBLE command.

```
A>DEBUG
-A CS:100
0CDE:0100 ADD [BX+SI+1234],AX
0CDE:0104
-D CS:100 103
0CDE:0100  01 80 34 12                                    ..4.
-W CS:100 1 75 1
-Q

A>
```

Figure 3.33   Assembling the instruction ADD [BX+SI +1234],AX.

Assuming that the assemble operation we just performed was completed by entering (↵), we can view the machine code that was produced for the instruction by issuing a DUMP command. Notice that the address displayed as the starting point of the next instruction is 0CDE:0104. Therefore, the machine code for the ADD instruction took up 4 bytes of memory: CS:100, CS:101, CS:102, and CS:103. The command needed to display this machine code is

```
D CS:100 103 (↵)
```

In Fig. 3.33, we find that the machine code stored for the instruction is 01803412.

At this point, the instruction can be executed or saved on a diskette. For instance, to save the machine code at file specification 1 75 1 on a diskette, we can issue the command

```
W CS:100 1 75 1(↵)
```

Now that we have shown how to assemble an instruction, view its machine code, and save the machine code on a data diskette, let us look into how a complete program can be assembled with the A command. For this purpose, we will use the program shown in Fig. 3.34(a). This is the same program that was hand assembled to machine code in Example 3.7.

We will begin by assuming that the program is to be stored in memory starting at address CS:200. For this reason, the *line-by-line assembler* is invoked with the command

```
A CS:200 (↵)
```

This gives the response

```
0CDE:0200_
```

Now we type in instructions of the program as follows:

```
0CDE:0200 MOV AX,1020 (↵)
0CDE:0203 MOV DS,AX (↵)
0CDE:0205 MOV SI,0100 (↵)
       .        .        .
       .        .        .
       .        .        .
0CDE:0217 NOP (↵)
0CDE:0218 (↵)
```

The details of the instruction entry sequence are shown in Fig. 3.34(b).

Now that the complete program has been entered, let us verify that it has been assembled correctly. This can be done with an UNASSEMBLE command. Notice in Fig. 3.34(b) that the program resides in memory over the address range

```
MOV    AX,1020              A>DEBUG
                           -A CS:200
MOV    DS,AX               0CDE:0200 MOV AX,1020
MOV    SI,0100             0CDE:0203 MOV DS,AX
                           0CDE:0205 MOV SI,100
MOV    DI,0120             0CDE:0208 MOV DI,120
MOV    CX,010              0CDE:020B MOV CX,10
MOV    AH,[SI]             0CDE:020E MOV AH,[SI]
                           0CDE:0210 MOV [DI],AH
MOV    [DI],AH             0CDE:0212 INC SI
INC    SI                  0CDE:0213 INC DI
                           0CDE:0214 DEC CX
INC    DI                  0CDE:0215 JNZ 20E
DEC    CX                  0CDE:0217 NOP
                           0CDE:0218
JNZ    20E
                           -
NOP
        (a)                          (b)
```

```
-U CS:200 217
0CDE:0200 B82010        MOV    AX,1020
0CDE:0203 8ED8          MOV    DS,AX
0CDE:0205 BE0001        MOV    SI,0100
0CDE:0208 BF2001        MOV    DI,0120
0CDE:020B B91000        MOV    CX,0010
0CDE:020E 8A24          MOV    AH,[SI]
0CDE:0210 8825          MOV    [DI],AH
0CDE:0212 46            INC    SI
0CDE:0213 47            INC    DI
0CDE:0214 49            DEC    CX
0CDE:0215 75F7          JNZ    020E
0CDE:0217 90            NOP
              (c)
```

Figure 3.34   (a) Block move program. (b) Assembling the program. (c) Verifying the assembled program with the U command.

CS:200 through CS:217. To unassemble the machine code in this part of memory, we issue the command

$$\text{U CS:200 217 } (\downarrow)$$

The results produced with this command are shown in Fig. 3.34(c). Comparing the source statements to those in Fig. 3.34(a) confirms that the program has been assembled correctly.

3.8 EXECUTING INSTRUCTIONS AND PROGRAMS WITH THE TRACE AND GO COMMANDS

Once the program has been entered into the memory of the PC, it is ready to be executed. The DEBUG program allows us to execute the entire program with one *GO* (G) *command* or to execute the program in several segments of instructions by using *breakpoints* in the GO command. Moreover, by using the *TRACE* (T) *command,* the program can be stepped through by executing one or more instructions at a time.

Let us begin by examining the operation of the TRACE command in more detail. This command provides the programmer with the ability to execute one instruction at a time. This mode of operation is also known as *single-stepping the program;* it is very useful during early phases of program debugging. This is because the contents of registers or memory can be viewed both before and after the execution of each instruction to determine whether or not the correct operation was performed.

The general form of the command as shown in Fig. 3.9 is

```
T  =  [ADDRESS]  [NUMBER]
```

Notice that a *starting address* may be specified as part of the command. This is the address of the instruction at which execution is to begin. It is followed by a *number* that tells how many instructions are to be executed. If an instruction count is not specified in the command, just one instruction is executed. For instance, the command

```
T  =CS:100  (↵)
```

causes the instruction starting at address CS:100 to be executed. At completion of the instruction's execution, the complete state of the 8088's internal registers is automatically displayed. At this point, other debug commands can be issued, for instance, to display the contents of memory, or the next instruction can be executed.

The TRACE command can also be issued as

```
T  (↵)
```

In this case the instruction pointed to by the current values of CS and IP (CS:IP) is executed. This is the form of the TRACE command that is used to execute the next instruction.

If we want to single-step through several instructions, the TRACE command must include the number of instructions to be executed. This number is included after the address. For example, to trace through three instructions, the command is issued as

```
T  =CS:100  3  (↵)
```

Again, the internal state of the 8088 is displayed after each instruction is executed.

EXAMPLE 3.22

Load the instruction stored at file specification 1 10 1 at offset 100 of the current code segment. Unassemble the instruction. Then initialize AX = 1111_{16}, SI = 1234_{16}, and the contents of memory address 1234_{16} to 2222_{16}. Next, display the internal state of the 8088 and the contents of address 1234_{16} to verify their initialization. Finally, execute the instruction with the TRACE command. What operation is performed by the instruction?

SOLUTION   First, the instruction is loaded at CS:100 from the diskette with the command

L CS:100 1 10 1 (↵)

Now the machine code is unassembled to verify that the instruction has loaded correctly.

U 100 101 (↵)

Looking at the displayed information in Fig. 3.35, we see that it is an add instruction. Next we initialize the internal registers and memory with the command sequence

R AX (↵)
AX 0000
:1111 (↵)
R SI (↵)
SI 0000
:1234 (↵)
E DS:1234 22 22 (↵)

Now the initialization is verified with the commands

R (↵)
D DS:1234 1235 (↵)

In Fig. 3.35, we see that AX, SI, and the contents of address 1234_{16} were correctly initialized. Therefore, we are ready to execute the instruction. This is done with the command

T =CS:100 (↵)

From the displayed trace information in Fig. 3.35, we find that the value 2222_{16} at address 1234_{16} was added to the value 1111_{16} held in AX. Therefore, the new contents of AX are 3333_{16}.

```
-L CS:100 1 10 1
-U 100 101
0CDE:0100 0304          ADD      AX,[SI]
-R AX
AX 0000
:1111
-R SI
SI 0000
:1234
-E DS:1234 22 22
-R
AX=1111  BX=0000  CX=0000  DX=0000  SP=FFEE  BP=0000  SI=1234  DI=0000
DS=0CDE  ES=0CDE  SS=0CDE  CS=0CDE  IP=0100   NV UP EI PL NZ NA PO NC
0CDE:0100 0304          ADD      AX,[SI]                            DS:1234=2222
-D DS:1234 1235
0CDE:1230               22 22                                  " "
-T =CS:100

AX=3333  BX=0000  CX=0000  DX=0000  SP=FFEE  BP=0000  SI=1234  DI=0000
DS=0CDE  ES=0CDE  SS=0CDE  CS=0CDE  IP=0102   NV UP EI PL NZ NA PE NC
0CDE:0102 93            XCHG     BX,AX
-
```

Figure 3.35 Displayed information for Example 3.22.

The GO command is typically used to execute programs that are already debugged or to execute programs in the latter stages of debugging. For example, if the beginning part of a program is already operating correctly, a GO command can be issued to execute this group of instructions and then stop execution at a point in the program where additional debugging is to begin.

The table in Fig. 3.9 shows that the general form of the GO command is

```
G = [STARTING ADDRESS]  [BREAKPOINT ADDRESS]
```

The first address is the starting address of the program segment that is to be executed, that is, the address of the instruction at which execution is to begin. The second address, the *breakpoint address,* is the address of the end of the program segment, that is, the address of the instruction at which execution is to stop. The breakpoint address that is specified must correspond to the first byte of an instruction. A list of up to ten breakpoint addresses can be supplied with the command.

An example of the GO command is

```
G =CS:200 217 (↵)
```

This command loads the IP register with 0200_{16}, sets a breakpoint at address CS:217, and then begins program execution at address CS:200. Instruction execution proceeds until address CS:217 is accessed. When the breakpoint address is reached, program execution is terminated, the complete internal status of the 8088 is displayed, and control is returned to DEBUG.

Sometimes we just want to execute a program without using a breakpoint. This can also be done with the GO command. For instance, to execute a program that starts at offset 100_{16} in the current CS, we can issue the GO command without a breakpoint address as follows:

$$G \ = CS:100 \ (\dashv)$$

This command will cause the program to run to completion. In the case of a program where CS and IP are already initialized with the correct values, we can just enter

$$G \ (\dashv)$$

EXAMPLE 3.23

In Example 3.21, we saved the block move program at file specification 1 100 1 of a data diskette. Load this program into memory starting at address CS:200. Then initialize the microcomputer by loading the DS register with 1020_{16}; fill the block of memory from DS:100 through DS:10F with FF_{16}, and the block of memory from DS:120 through DS:12F with 00_{16}. Verify that the blocks of memory were initialized correctly. Load DS with $0CDE_{16}$, and display the state of the 8088's registers. Display the assembly language version of the program from CS:200 through CS:217. Use a GO command to execute the program through address CS:20E. What changes have occurred in the contents of the 8088's registers? Now execute down through address CS:215. What changes are found in the blocks of data? Next execute the program down to address CS:217. What new changes are found in the blocks of data?

SOLUTION   The command needed to load the program is

$$L \ CS:200 \ 1 \ 100 \ 1 \ (\dashv)$$

Next we initialize the DS register and memory.

```
R DS (↵)
DS 0CDE
:1020 (↵)
F DS:100 10F FF (↵)
F DS:120 12F 00 (↵)
```

Now the blocks of data in memory are displayed.

```
D DS:100 10F (↵)
D DS:120 12F (↵)
```

This displayed information is shown in Fig. 3.36. DS is loaded with $0CDE_{16}$ using the command

```
R DS (↵)
DS 1020
:0CDE (↵)
```

and the state of the 8088's registers is displayed with the command

```
R (↵)
```

Before beginning to execute the program, we will display the source code with the command

```
U CS:200 217 (↵)
```

The program that is displayed is shown in Fig. 3.36.

Now the first section of program is executed with the command

```
G =CS:200 20E (↵)
```

Looking at the displayed state of the 8088 in Fig. 3.36, we see that DS was loaded with 1020_{16}, AX was loaded with 1020_{16}, SI was loaded with 0100_{16}, and CX was loaded with 0010_{16}.

Next, another GO command is used to execute the program down through address CS:215.

```
G =CS:20E 215 (↵)
```

We can check the state of the blocks of memory with the commands

```
D DS:100 10F (↵)
D DS:120 12F (↵)
```

From the display information Fig. 3.36, we see that FF_{16} was copied from the first element of the source block to the first element of the destination block. Now we execute through CS:217 with the command

```
G =CS:215 217 (↵)
```

and examining the blocks of data with the commands

```
D DS:100 10F (↵)
D DS:120 12F (↵)
```

we find that the complete source block has been copied into the destination block.

```
-L CS:200 1 100 1
-R DS
DS 0CDE
:1020
-F DS:100 10F FF
-F DS:120 12F 00
-D DS:100 10F
1020:0100  FF FF FF FF FF FF FF FF-FF FF FF FF FF FF FF FF   ................
-D DS:120 12F
1020:0120  00 00 00 00 00 00 00 00-00 00 00 00 00 00 00 00   ................
-R DS
DS 1020
:0CDE
-R
AX=0000  BX=0000  CX=0000  DX=0000  SP=FFEE  BP=0000  SI=0000  DI=0000
DS=0CDE  ES=0CDE  SS=0CDE  CS=0CDE  IP=0100    NV UP EI PL NZ NA PO NC
0CDE:0100 DC37                FDIV    QWORD PTR [BX]             DS:0000=CD
-U CS:200 217
0CDE:0200 B82010        MOV    AX,1020
0CDE:0203 8ED8          MOV    DS,AX
0CDE:0205 BE0001        MOV    SI,0100
0CDE:0208 BF2001        MOV    DI,0120
0CDE:020B B91000        MOV    CX,0010
0CDE:020E 8A24          MOV    AH,[SI]
0CDE:0210 8825          MOV    [DI],AH
0CDE:0212 46            INC    SI
0CDE:0213 47            INC    DI
0CDE:0214 49            DEC    CX
0CDE:0215 75F7          JNZ    020E
0CDE:0217 90            NOP
-G =CS:200 20E

AX=1020  BX=0000  CX=0010  DX=0000  SP=FFEE  BP=0000  SI=0100  DI=0120
DS=1020  ES=0CDE  SS=0CDE  CS=0CDE  IP=020E    NV UP EI PL NZ NA PO NC
0CDE:020E 8A24          MOV    AH,[SI]                       DS:0100=FF
-G =CS:20E 215

AX=FF20  BX=0000  CX=000F  DX=0000  SP=FFEE  BP=0000  SI=0101  DI=0121
DS=1020  ES=0CDE  SS=0CDE  CS=0CDE  IP=0215    NV UP EI PL NZ AC PE NC
0CDE:0215 75F7          JNZ    020E
-D DS:100 10F
1020:0100  FF FF FF FF FF FF FF FF-FF FF FF FF FF FF FF FF   ................
-D DS:120 12F
1020:0120  FF 00 00 00 00 00 00 00-00 00 00 00 00 00 00 00   ................
-G =CS:215 217

AX=FF20  BX=0000  CX=0000  DX=0000  SP=FFEE  BP=0000  SI=0110  DI=0130
DS=1020  ES=0CDE  SS=0CDE  CS=0CDE  IP=0217    NV UP EI PL ZR NA PE NC
0CDE:0217 90            NOP
-D DS:100 10F
1020:0100  FF FF FF FF FF FF FF FF-FF FF FF FF FF FF FF FF   ................
-D DS:120 12F
1020:0120  FF FF FF FF FF FF FF FF-FF FF FF FF FF FF FF FF   ................
-
```

Figure 3.36 Displayed information for Example 3.23.

3.9 DEBUGGING A PROGRAM

In Sections 3.6, 3.7, and 3.8 we learned how to use DEBUG to load a machine code program into the memory of the PC, assemble a program, and execute the program. However, we did not determine if the program when run performed the operation for which it was written. It is common to have errors in programs, and even a single error can render the program useless. For instance, if the address to which a "jump" instruction passes control is wrong, the program may get hung up. Errors in a program are also referred to as *bugs;* the process of removing them is called *debugging.*

The two types of errors that can be made by a programmer are the *syntax error* and the *execution error*. A syntax error is an error caused by not following the rules for coding or entering an instruction. These types of errors are typically identified by the microcomputer and signaled to the user with an error message. For this reason, they are usually easy to find and correct. For example, if a DUMP command was keyed in as

```
D DS:100120 (↵)
```

an error condition exists. This is because the space between the starting and ending address is left out. This incorrect entry is signaled by the warning "Error" in the display and the spot where the error begins, the 1 in 120, is marked with the symbol "^".

An execution error is an error in the logic behind the development of the program. That is, the program is correctly coded and entered, but still it does not perform the operation for which it was planned. This type of error can be identified by entering the program into the microcomputer and observing its operation. Even when an execution error problem has been identified, it is usually not easy to find the exact cause of the problem.

Our ability to debug execution errors in a program is aided by the commands of the DEBUG program. For instance, the TRACE command allows us to step through the program by executing just one instruction at a time. We can use the display of the internal register state produced by TRACE and the memory dump command to determine the state of the 8088 and memory prior to execution of an instruction and again after its execution. This information will tell us whether the instruction has performed the operation planned for it. If an error is found, its cause can be identified and corrected.

To demonstrate the process of debugging a program, let us once again use the program that we stored at file specification 1 100 1 of the data diskette. We load it into the code segment at address CS:200 with the command

```
L CS:200 1 100 1 (↵)
```

Now the program resides in memory at addresses CS:200 through CS:217. The program is displayed with the command

$$U \quad CS:200 \quad 217 \quad (\dashv)$$

The program that is displayed is shown in Fig. 3.37. This program implements a block data transfer operation. The block of data to be moved starts at memory address DS:100 and is 16 bytes in length. It is to be moved to another block location starting at address DS:120. DS points to a segment starting at 10200_{16}.

```
A>DEBUG
-L CS:200 1 100 1
-U CS:200 217
0CDE:0200 B82010        MOV     AX,1020
0CDE:0203 8ED8          MOV     DS,AX
0CDE:0205 BE0001        MOV     SI,0100
0CDE:0208 BF2001        MOV     DI,0120
0CDE:020B B91000        MOV     CX,0010
0CDE:020E 8A24          MOV     AH,[SI]
0CDE:0210 8825          MOV     [DI],AH
0CDE:0212 46            INC     SI
0CDE:0213 47            INC     DI
0CDE:0214 49            DEC     CX
0CDE:0215 75F7          JNZ     020E
0CDE:0217 90            NOP
 -R DS
 DS 0CDE
 :1020
-F DS:100 10F FF
-F DS:120 12F 00
-R DS
DS 1020
:0CDE
-T =CS:200 4

AX=1020  BX=0000  CX=0000  DX=0000  SP=FFEE  BP=0000  SI=0110  DI=0130
DS=0CDE  ES=0CDE  SS=0CDE  CS=0CDE  IP=0203    NV UP EI PL ZR NA PE NC
0CDE:0203 8ED8          MOV     DS,AX

AX=1020  BX=0000  CX=0000  DX=0000  SP=FFEE  BP=0000  SI=0100  DI=0130
DS=1020  ES=0CDE  SS=0CDE  CS=0CDE  IP=0208    NV UP EI PL ZR NA PE NC
0CDE:0208 BF2001        MOV     DI,0120

AX=1020  BX=0000  CX=0000  DX=0000  SP=FFEE  BP=0000  SI=0100  DI=0120
DS=1020  ES=0CDE  SS=0CDE  CS=0CDE  IP=020B    NV UP EI PL ZR NA PE NC
0CDE:020B B91000        MOV     CX,0010

AX=1020  BX=0000  CX=0010  DX=0000  SP=FFEE  BP=0000  SI=0100  DI=0120
DS=1020  ES=0CDE  SS=0CDE  CS=0CDE  IP=020E    NV UP EI PL ZR NA PE NC
0CDE:020E 8A24          MOV     AH,[SI]                          DS:0100=FF
-D DS:120 12F
1020:0120  00 00 00 00 00 00 00 00-00 00 00 00 00 00 00 00    ................
-T 2

AX=FF20  BX=0000  CX=0010  DX=0000  SP=FFEE  BP=0000  SI=0100  DI=0120
DS=1020  ES=0CDE  SS=0CDE  CS=0CDE  IP=0210    NV UP EI PL ZR NA PE NC
0CDE:0210 8825          MOV     [DI],AH                          DS:0120=00
```

Figure 3.37 Program debugging demonstration.

```
AX=FF20  BX=0000  CX=0010  DX=0000  SP=FFEE  BP=0000  SI=0100  DI=0120
DS=1020  ES=0CDE  SS=0CDE  CS=0CDE  IP=0212    NV UP EI PL ZR NA PE NC
0CDE:0212 46                INC    SI
-D DS:120 12F
1020:0120  FF 00 00 00 00 00 00 00-00 00 00 00 00 00 00 00    ................
-T 3

AX=FF20  BX=0000  CX=0010  DX=0000  SP=FFEE  BP=0000  SI=0101  DI=0120
DS=1020  ES=0CDE  SS=0CDE  CS=0CDE  IP=0213    NV UP EI PL NZ NA PO NC
0CDE:0213 47                INC    DI

AX=FF20  BX=0000  CX=0010  DX=0000  SP=FFEE  BP=0000  SI=0101  DI=0121
DS=1020  ES=0CDE  SS=0CDE  CS=0CDE  IP=0214    NV UP EI PL NZ NA PE NC
0CDE:0214 49                DEC    CX

AX=FF20  BX=0000  CX=000F  DX=0000  SP=FFEE  BP=0000  SI=0101  DI=0121
DS=1020  ES=0CDE  SS=0CDE  CS=0CDE  IP=0215    NV UP EI PL NZ AC PE NC
0CDE:0215 75F7              JNZ    020E
-T

AX=FF20  BX=0000  CX=000F  DX=0000  SP=FFEE  BP=0000  SI=0101  DI=0121
DS=1020  ES=0CDE  SS=0CDE  CS=0CDE  IP=020E    NV UP EI PL NZ AC PE NC
0CDE:020E 8A24              MOV    AH,[SI]                        DS:0101=FF
-G =CS:20E 215

AX=FF20  BX=0000  CX=000E  DX=0000  SP=FFEE  BP=0000  SI=0102  DI=0122
DS=1020  ES=0CDE  SS=0CDE  CS=0CDE  IP=0215    NV UP EI PL NZ NA PO NC
0CDE:0215 75F7              JNZ    020E
-D DS:120 12F
1020:0120  FF FF 00 00 00 00 00 00-00 00 00 00 00 00 00 00    ................
-T

AX=FF20  BX=0000  CX=000E  DX=0000  SP=FFEE  BP=0000  SI=0102  DI=0122
DS=1020  ES=0CDE  SS=0CDE  CS=0CDE  IP=020E    NV UP EI PL NZ NA PO NC
0CDE:020E 8A24              MOV    AH,[SI]                        DS:0102=FF
-G =CS:20E 217

AX=FF20  BX=0000  CX=0000  DX=0000  SP=FFEE  BP=0000  SI=0110  DI=0130
DS=1020  ES=0CDE  SS=0CDE  CS=0CDE  IP=0217    NV UP EI PL ZR NA PE NC
0CDE:0217 90                NOP
-D DS:120 12F
1020:0120  FF FF FF FF FF FF FF FF-FF FF FF FF FF FF FF FF    ................
-
```

Figure 3.37 (Continued)

Before executing the program, let us issue commands to initialize the source block of memory locations from address 100_{16} through $10F_{16}$ with FF_{16}, and the bytes in the destination block starting at 120_{16} with 00_{16}. To do this, we issue the command sequence

```
R DS (↵)
DS 0CDE
:1020 (↵)
F DS:100 10F FF (↵)
F DS:120 12F 00 (↵)
```

Now we will reset DS to its original value

R DS (⏎)
DS 1020
:0CDE (⏎)

The first two instructions of the program in Fig. 3.37 are

MOV AX,1020

and

MOV DS,AX

These two instructions, when executed, load the data segment register with the value 1020_{16}. In this way, they define a data segment starting at address 10200_{16}. The next three instructions are used to load the SI, DI, and CX registers with 100_{16}, 120_{16}, and 10_{16}, respectively. Let us now show how to execute these instructions and then determine if they perform the correct function. They are executed by issuing the command

T =CS:200 4 (⏎)

To determine if the five instructions that were executed performed the correct operation, we just need to look at the trace display that they produce. This display trace is shown in Fig. 3.37. Here we see that the first instruction loads AX with 1020_{16} and the second moves this value into the DS register. Also notice in the last trace displayed that SI contains 0100_{16}, DI contains 0120_{16}, and CX contains 0010_{16}.

The next two instructions copy the contents of memory location 100_{16} into the storage location at address 120_{16}. Let us first check the contents of the destination block with the D command

D DS:120 12F (⏎)

Looking at the dump display in Fig. 3.37, we see that the original contents of these locations are 00_{16}. Now the two instructions are executed with the command

T 2 (⏎)

and the contents of address DS:120 are checked once again with the command

D DS:120 12F (⏎)

The display dump in Fig. 3.37 shows that the first element of the source block was copied to the location of the first element of the destination block. Therefore, both address 100_{16} and address 120_{16} now contain the value FF_{16}.

The next three instructions are used to increment pointers SI and DI and decrement block counter CX. To execute them, we issue the command

T 3 (↵)

Referring to the trace display in Fig. 3.37 to verify their operation, we find that the new values in SI and DI are 0101_{16} and 0121_{16}, respectively, and CX is now $000F_{16}$.

The jump instruction is next and it transfers control to the instruction 8 bytes back if CX did not become zero. It is executed with the command

T (↵)

Notice that the result of executing this instruction is that the value in IP is changed to $020E_{16}$. This corresponds to the location of the instruction

MOV AH,[SI]

In this way we see that control has been returned to the part of the program that performs the byte move operation.

The move operation performed by this part of the program was already checked; however, we must still determine if it runs to completion when the count in CX decrements to zero. Therefore, we will execute the complete loop with a GO command. This command is

G =CS:20E 215 (↵)

Correct operation is verified because the trace shows that CX has been decremented by one more and equals E. The fact that the second element has been moved can be verified by dumping the destination block with the command

D DS:120 12F (↵)

Now we are again at address CS:215. To execute the jump instruction at this location, we can again use the T command

T (↵)

This returns control to the instruction at CS:20E. The previous two commands can be repeated until the complete block is moved and CX equals 0_{16}. Or we can use the G command to execute to the address CS:217, which is the end of the program.

G CS:217

At completion, the overall operation of the program can be verified by examining the contents of the destination block with the command sequence

```
D DS:120 12F (↵)
```

FF_{16} should be displayed as the data held in each storage location.

ASSIGNMENTS

Section 3.2

1. Encode the following instruction using the information in Figs. 3.1 through 3.4.

```
ADD AX,DX
```

Assume that the opcode for the add operation is 000000_2.

2. Encode the following instructions using the information in the tables of Figs. 3.2 through 3.6.
   (a) MOV [DI],DX
   (b) MOV [BX+SI],BX
   (c) MOV DL,[BX+10H]

3. Encode the instructions that follow using the tables in Figs. 3.2 through 3.6.
   (a) PUSH DS
   (b) ROL BL,CL
   (c) ADD AX,[1234H]

Section 3.3

4. How many bytes are required to encode the instruction MOV SI,0100H?

5. How many bytes of memory are required to store the machine code for the program in Fig. 3.7(a)?

Section 3.4

6. On which DOS diskette does the DEBUG program reside?

7. Can DEBUG be brought up by typing the command using lowercase letters?

8. What would you expect to happen if the command R AXBX is entered at the keyboard?

9. Write the REGISTER command needed to change the value in CX to 10_{16}.

10. Write the command needed to change the state of the parity flag to PE.

11. Write a command that will dump the state of the 8088's internal registers.

Section 3.5

12. Write a DUMP command that will display the contents of the first 16 bytes of the current code segment.

13. Show an ENTER command that can be used to examine the contents of the same 16 bytes of memory that were displayed in problem 12.

14. Show the ENTER command needed to load five consecutive bytes of memory starting at address CS:100H of the current code segment with FF_{16}.

15. Show how an ENTER command can be used to initialize the first 32 bytes at the top of the stack to 00_{16}.

16. Write a sequence of commands that will fill the first six storage locations starting at address CS:100H with 11_{16}, the second six with 22_{16}, the third six with 33_{16}, the fourth six with 44_{16}, and the fifth six with 55_{16}, change the contents of storage locations CS:105H and CS:113H to FF_{16}, display the first 30 bytes of memory starting at CS:100H, and search the block of memory for those storage locations that contain FF_{16}.

Section 3.6

17. Show the sequence of commands needed to load the machine code found for the instruction in Example 3.3 starting at address CS:100H, unassemble it to verify that the correct instruction was loaded, and save it on a data diskette at file specification 1 50 1.

18. Write commands that will reload the instruction saved on the data diskette in problem 17 into memory at offset 400 in the current code segment and unassemble it to verify correct loading.

Section 3.7

19. Show how the instruction in problem 2(a) can be assembled into memory at address CS:100H.

20. Write a sequence of commands that will first assemble the instruction in problem 3(b) into memory starting at address CS:200H and then verify its entry by disassembling the instruction.

Section 3.8

21. Show a sequence of commands that will load the instruction saved on the data diskette in problem 17 at address CS:300H, unassemble it to verify correct loading, initialize the contents of register CX to $000F_{16}$ and the contents of the word memory location starting at DS:1234H to $00FF_{16}$, execute the instruction with the TRACE command, and verify its operation by examining the contents of CX and the word of data stored starting at DS:1234H in memory.

22. Write a sequence of commands to repeat Example 3.23; however, this time execute the complete program with one GO command.

Section 3.9

23. What is the difference between a syntax error and an execution error?

24. Write a sequence of commands to repeat the debug demonstration presented in Section 3.9, but this time use only GO commands to execute the program.

8088/8086 Microprocessor Programming 1

4.1 INTRODUCTION

Up to this point, we have studied the software architecture of the 8088 and 8086 microprocessors and the software development tools provided by the DEBUG program on the IBM PC. We found that the software architecture of the 8088 and 8086 microprocessors are identical and learned how to encode assembly language instructions in machine language and how to use the debugger to enter, execute, and debug programs.

In this chapter, we begin a detailed study of the instruction set of the 8088 and 8086 microprocessors. A large part of the instruction set is covered in this chapter. These instructions provide the ability to write straight-line programs. The rest of the instruction set and some more sophisticated programming concepts are covered in Chapter 5. The following topics are presented in this chapter:

1. The instruction set of the 8088/8086
2. Data transfer instructions
3. Arithmetic instructions
4. Logic instructions
5. Shift instructions
6. Rotate instructions

4.2 THE INSTRUCTION SET OF THE 8088/8086

The instruction set of a microprocessor defines the basic operations that a programmer can make the device perform. The 8088 and 8086 microprocessors have the same instruction set. This powerful instruction set contains 117 basic instructions. The wide range of operands and addressing modes permitted for use with these instructions further expands the instruction set into many more instructions executable at the machine code level. For instance, the basic MOV instruction expands into 28 different machine-level instructions.

For the purpose of discussion, the instruction set will be divided into a number of groups of functionally related instructions. In this chapter we consider the data transfer instructions, arithmetic instructions, the logic instructions, shift instructions, and rotate instructions. Advanced instructions such as those for program and processor control are described in Chapter 5.

4.3 DATA TRANSFER INSTRUCTIONS

The 8088 microprocessor has a group of *data transfer instructions* that are provided to move data either between its internal registers or between an internal register and a storage location in memory. This group includes the *move byte or word* (MOV) instruction, *exchange byte or word* (XCHG) instruction, *translate byte* (XLAT) instruction, *load effective address* (LEA) instruction, *load data segment* (LDS) instruction, and *load extra segment* (LES) instruction. These instructions are discussed in this section.

The MOV instruction

The MOV instruction shown in Fig. 4.1(a) is used to transfer a byte or a word of data from a source operand to a destination operand. These operands can be internal registers of the 8088 and storage locations in memory. Figure 4.1(b) shows the valid source and destination operand variations. This large choice of operands results in many different MOV instructions. Looking at this list of operands, we see that data can be moved between general-purpose registers, between a general-purpose register and a segment register, between a general-purpose register or segment register and memory, or between a memory location and the accumulator.

Notice that the MOV instruction cannot transfer data directly between a source and a destination that both reside in external memory. Instead, the data must first be moved from memory into an internal register, such as to the accumulator (AX), with one move instruction and then moved to the new location in memory with a second move instruction.

All transfers between general-purpose registers and memory can involve either a byte or word of data. The fact that the instruction corresponds to byte or

Mnemonic	Meaning	Format	Operation	Flags affected
MOV	Move	MOV D,S	(S) → (D)	None

(a)

Destination	Source
Memory	Accumulator
Accumulator	Memory
Register	Register
Register	Memory
Memory	Register
Register	Immediate
Memory	Immediate
Seg-reg	Reg16
Seg-reg	Mem16
Reg16	Seg-reg
Memory	Seg-reg

(b)

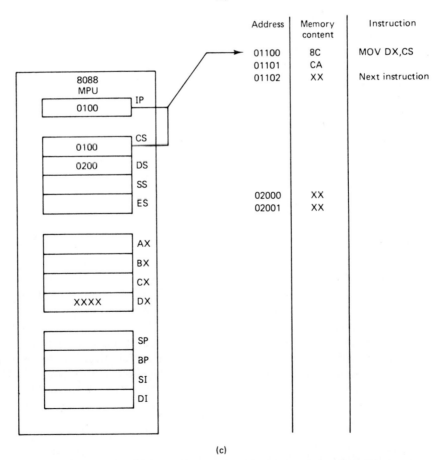

(c)

Figure 4.1 (a) MOV data transfer instruction. (b) Allowed operands. (c) MOV DX,CS instruction before execution. (d) After execution.

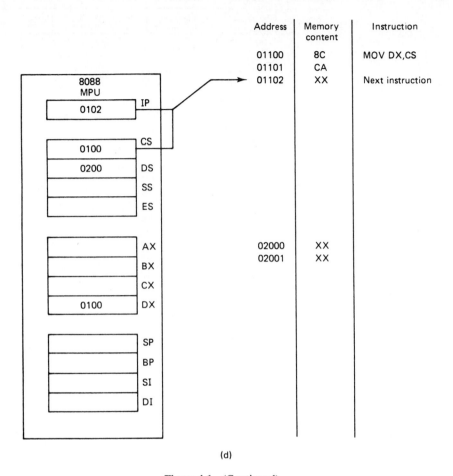

(d)

Figure 4.1 (Continued)

word data is designated by the way in which its operands are specified. For instance, AL or AH would be used to specify a byte operand, and AX, a word operand. On the other hand, data moved between one of the general-purpose registers and a segment register or between a segment register and a memory location must always be word-wide.

In Fig. 4.1(a), we also find additional important information. For instance, flag bits within the 8088 are not modified by execution of a MOV instruction.

An example of a segment register to general-purpose register MOV instruction shown in Fig. 4.1(c) is

```
MOV DX,CS
```

In this instruction, the code segment register is the source operand and the data register is the destination. It stands for "move the contents of CS into DX." That is.

$$(CS) \rightarrow (DX)$$

For example, if the contents of CS are 0100_{16}, execution of the instruction MOV DX,CS as shown in Fig. 4.1(d) makes

$$(DX) = (CS) = 0100_{16}$$

In all memory reference MOV instructions, the machine code for the instruction includes an offset address relative to the contents of the data segment register. An example of this type of instruction is

```
MOV [SUM],AX
```

In this instruction, the memory location identified by the variable SUM is specified using direct addressing. That is, the value of the offset is included in the two byte locations that follow its opcode in program memory.

Let us assume that the contents of DS equals 0200_{16} and that SUM corresponds to a displacement of 1212_{16}. Then this instruction means "move the contents of accumulator AX to the memory location offset by 1212_{16} from the starting location of the current data segment." The physical address of this location is obtained as

$$PA = 02000_{16} + 1212_{16} = 03212_{16}$$

Thus the effect of the instruction is

$$(AL) \rightarrow (Memory\ Location\ 03212_{16})$$

and

$$(AH) \rightarrow (Memory\ Location\ 03213_{16})$$

EXAMPLE 4.1

What is the effect of executing the instruction

```
MOV CX,[SOURCE_MEM]
```

where SOURCE_MEM is the memory location offset 20_{16} relative to the data segment starting at address $1A000_{16}$?

SOLUTION   Execution of this instruction results in the following:

$$((DS)0 + 20_{16}) \rightarrow (CL)$$

$$((DS)0 + 20_{16} + 1_{16}) \rightarrow (CH)$$

In other words, CL is loaded with the contents held at memory address

$$1A000_{16} + 20_{16} = 1A020_{16}$$

and CH is loaded with the contents of memory address

$$1A000_{16} + 20_{16} + 1_{16} = 1A021_{16}$$

EXAMPLE 4.2

Use the DEBUG program on the IBM PC to verify the operation of the instruction in Example 4.1. Initialize the word storage location pointed to by SOURCE_MEM to the value $AA55_{16}$ before executing the instruction.

SOLUTION   First, the DEBUG program is invoked by entering the command

A>DEBUG (↵)

As shown in Fig. 4.2, this results in the display of the debugger's prompt

$-$

To determine the memory locations the debugger assigns for use in entering instructions and data, we can examine the state of the internal registers with the command

−R (↵)

Looking at the displayed information for this command in Fig. 4.2, we find that the contents of CS and IP indicate that the starting address in the current code segment is 0CDE:0100 and the current data segment starts at address 0CDE:0000. Also note that the initial value in CX is 0000H.

To enter the instruction from Example 4.1 at location 0CDE:0100, we use the ASSEMBLE command

```
−A                        (↵)
0CDE:0100 MOV CX,[20]  (↵)
0CDE:0104                 (↵)
```

Note that we must enter the value of the offset address instead of the symbol SOURCE_MEM and that it must be enclosed in brackets to indicate that it is a direct address.

Let us now redefine the data segment so that it starts at $1A000_{16}$. This is done by loading the DS register with $1A00_{16}$ with the REGISTER command. As shown in Fig. 4.2, we do this with the entries

$$-R\ DS \qquad (\lrcorner)$$
$$DS\ 0CDE$$
$$:1A00 \qquad (\lrcorner)$$

Now we initialize the memory locations at addresses 1A00:20 and 1A00:21 to 55_{16} and AA_{16}, respectively, with the ENTER command

$$-E\ 20\ 55\ AA\ (\lrcorner)$$

Notice that the bytes of the word of data must be entered in the reverse order.

Finally, to execute the instruction, we issue the trace command

$$-T\ (\lrcorner)$$

The results of executing the instructions are shown in Fig. 4.2. Note that CX has been loaded with $AA55_{16}$.

```
A>DEBUG
-R
AX=0000  BX=0000  CX=0000  DX=0000  SP=FFEE  BP=0000  SI=0000  DI=0000
DS=0CDE  ES=0CDE  SS=0CDE  CS=0CDE  IP=0100    NV UP EI PL NZ NA PO NC
0CDE:0100 DC37              FDIV    QWORD PTR [BX]                      DS:0000=CD
-A
0CDE:0100 MOV CX,[20]
0CDE:0104
-R DS
DS 0CDE
:1A00
-E 20 55 AA
-T

AX=0000  BX=0000  CX=AA55  DX=0000  SP=FFEE  BP=0000  SI=0000  DI=0000
DS=1A00  ES=0CDE  SS=0CDE  CS=0CDE  IP=0104    NV UP EI PL NZ NA PO NC
0CDE:0104 4E                DEC     SI
-Q

A>
```

Figure 4.2 Display sequence for Example 4.2.

The XCHG Instruction

In our study of the move instruction, we found that it could be used to copy the contents of a register or memory location into a register or contents of a register into a storage location in memory. In all cases, the original contents of the source location are preserved and the original contents of the destination are destroyed. In some applications it is required to interchange the contents of two registers. For instance, we might want to exchange the data in the AX and BX registers.

This could be done using multiple move instructions and storage of the data in a temporary register such as DX. However, to perform the exchange function more efficiently, a special instruction has been provided in the instruction set of the 8088. This is the exchange (XCHG) instruction. The forms of the XCHG instruction and its allowed operands are shown in Fig. 4.3(a) and (b). Here we see that it can be used to swap data between two general-purpose registers or between a general-purpose register and a storage location in memory. In particular, it allows for the exchange of words of data between one of the general-purpose registers, including the pointers and index registers, and the accumulator (AX), exchange of a byte or word of data between one of the general-purpose registers and a location in memory, or between two of the general-purpose registers.

Let us consider an example of an exchange between two internal registers. Here is a typical instruction.

$$\text{XCHG AX,DX}$$

Its execution by the 8088 swaps the contents of AX with that of DX. That is,

$$(\text{AX original}) \rightarrow (\text{DX})$$

$$(\text{DX original}) \rightarrow (\text{AX})$$

or

$$(\text{AX}) \leftrightarrow (\text{DX})$$

EXAMPLE 4.3

For the data shown in Fig. 4.3(c), what is the result of executing the following instruction?

$$\text{XCHG [SUM],BX}$$

SOLUTION   Execution of this instruction performs the function

$$((\text{DS})0 + \text{SUM}) \leftrightarrow (\text{BX})$$

In Fig. 4.3(c), we see that $(\text{DS}) = 1200_{16}$ and the direct address $\text{SUM} = 1234_{16}$. Therefore, the physical address is

Mnemonic	Meaning	Format	Operation	Flags affected
XCHG	Exchange	XCHG D,S	(D) ↔ (S)	None

(a)

Destination	Source
Accumulator	Reg16
Memory	Register
Register	Register

(b)

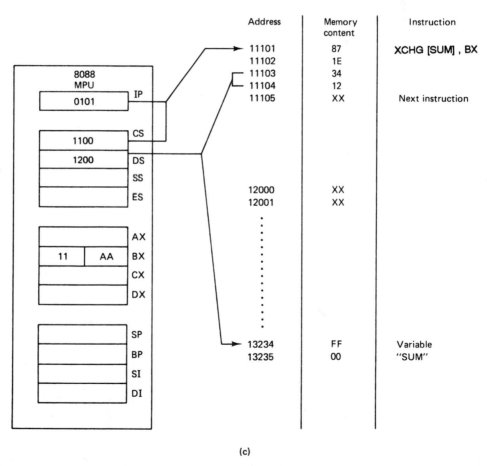

(c)

Figure 4.3 (a) Exchange data transfer instruction. (b) Allowed operands. (c) XCHG [SUM],BX instruction before fetch and execution. (d) After execution.

$$PA = 12000_{16} + 1234_{16} = 13234_{16}$$

Notice that this location contains FF_{16} and the address that follows contains 00_{16}. Moreover, note that BL contains AA_{16} and BH contains 11_{16}.

Execution of the instruction performs the following 16-bit swap.

$$(13234_{16}) \leftrightarrow (BL)$$

$$(13235_{16}) \leftrightarrow (BH)$$

As shown in Fig. 4.3(d), we get

$$(BX) = 00FF_{16}$$

$$(SUM) = 11AA_{16}$$

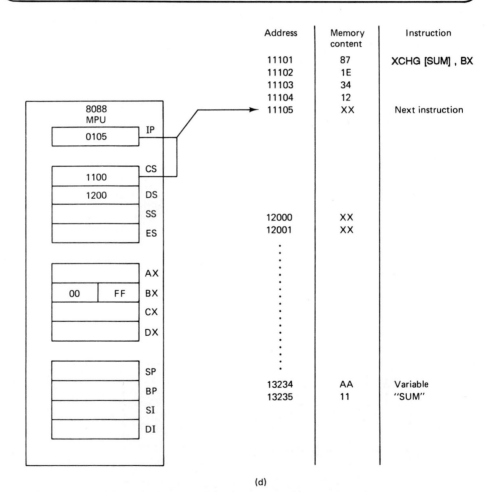

(d)

Figure 4.3   (Continued)

EXAMPLE 4.4

Use the IBM PC's DEBUG program to verify the operation of the instruction in Example 4.3.

SOLUTION   The DEBUG operations needed to enter the instruction, enter the data, execute the instruction, and verify the result of its operation are shown in Fig. 4.4. Here we see that, after invoking DEBUG and displaying the initial state of the 8088's registers, the instruction is loaded into memory with the command

```
-A 1100:101                    (↵)
1100:0101 XCHG [1234],BX       (↵)
1100:0105                      (↵)
-
```

Next, as shown in Fig. 4.4, R commands are used to initialize the contents of registers BX, DS, CS, and IP to $11AA_{16}$, 1200_{16}, 1100_{16} and 0101_{16}, respectively, and then the updated register states are verified with another R command. Now memory locations DS:1234H and DS:1235H are loaded with the values FF_{16} and 00_{16}, respectively, with the E command

```
-E 1234 FF 00      (↵)
-
```

Before executing the instruction, its loading is verified with an unassemble command. Looking at Fig. 4.4, we see that it has been correctly loaded. Therefore, the instruction is executed by issuing the TRACE command

```
-T          (↵)
```

The displayed trace information in Fig. 4.4 shows that BX now contains $00FF_{16}$. To verify that the memory location was loaded with data from BX, we must display the data held at address DS:1234H and DS:1235H. This is done with the DUMP command

```
-D 1234 1235 (↵)
0200:1234 AA 11
```

In this way, we see that the word contents of memory location DS:1234H have been exchanged with the contents of the BX register.

```
A>DEBUG
-R
AX=0000  BX=0000  CX=0000  DX=0000  SP=FFEE  BP=0000  SI=0000  DI=0000
DS=OCDE  ES=OCDE  SS=OCDE  CS=OCDE  IP=0100   NV UP EI PL NZ NA PO NC
OCDE:0100 8B0E2000       MOV    CX,[0020]                    DS:0020=FFFF
-A 1100:101
1100:0101 XCHG [1234],BX
1100:0105
-R BX
BX 0000
:11AA
-R DS
DS OCDE
:1200
-R CS
CS OCDE
:1100
-R IP
IP 0100
:101
-R
AX=0000  BX=11AA  CX=0000  DX=0000  SP=FFEE  BP=0000  SI=0000  DI=0000
DS=1200  ES=OCDE  SS=OCDE  CS=1100  IP=0101   NV UP EI PL NZ NA PO NC
1100:0101 871E3412       XCHG    BX,[1234]                   DS:1234=0000
-E 1234 FF 00
-U 101 104
1100:0101 871E3412       XCHG    BX,[1234]
-T

AX=0000  BX=00FF  CX=0000  DX=0000  SP=FFEE  BP=0000  SI=0000  DI=0000
DS=1200  ES=OCDE  SS=OCDE  CS=1100  IP=0105   NV UP EI PL NZ NA PO NC
1100:0105 0000           ADD     [BX+SI],AL                  DS:00FF=00
-D 1234 1235
1200:1230                AA 11                                .. 
-Q

A>
```

Figure 4.4 Display sequence for Example 4.4.

The XLAT Instruction

The translate (XLAT) instruction has been provided in the instruction set of the 8088 to simplify implementation of the lookup table operation. This instruction is described in Fig. 4.5. When using XLAT, the contents of register BX represent the offset of the starting address of the lookup table from the beginning of the current data segment. Also, the contents of AL represent the offset of the element to be accessed from the beginning of the lookup table. This 8-bit element address permits a table with up to 256 elements. The values in both of these registers must be initialized prior to execution of the XLAT instruction.

Execution of XLAT replaces the contents of AL by the contents of the accessed lookup table location. The physical address of this element in the table is derived as

$$PA = (DS)0 + (BX) + (AL)$$

Mnemonic	Meaning	Format	Operation	Flags affected
XLAT	Translate	XLAT	$((AL)+(BX)+(DS)0) \rightarrow (AL)$	None

Figure 4.5   Translate data transfer instruction.

An example of the use of this instruction would be for software code conversions, for instance, an ASCII-to-EBCDIC conversion. This requires an EBCDIC table in memory. The individual EBCDIC codes are located in the table at element displacements (AL) equal to their equivalent ASCII character values. That is, the EBCDIC code $C1_{16}$ for letter A would be positioned at displacement 41_{16}, which equals ASCII A, from the start of the table. The start of this ASCII-to-EBCDIC table in the current data segment is identified by the contents of BX.

As an illustration of XLAT, let us assume that $(DS) = 0300_{16}$, $(BX) = 0100_{16}$, and $(AL) = 0D_{16}$. $0D_{16}$ represents the ASCII character CR (carriage return). Execution of XLAT replaces the contents of AL by the contents of the memory location given by

$$PA = (DS)0 + (BX) + (AL)$$

$$= 03000_{16} + 0100_{16} + 0D_{16} = 0310D_{16}$$

Thus the execution can be described by

$$(0310D_{16}) \rightarrow (AL)$$

Assuming that this memory location contains 52_{16} (EBCDIC carriage return), this value is placed in AL.

$$(AL) = 52_{16}$$

The LEA, LDS, and LES Instructions

Another type of data transfer operation that is important is to load a segment or general-purpose register with an address directly from memory. Special instructions are provided in the instruction set of the 8088 to give a programmer this capability. These instructions are described in Fig. 4.6. They are load register with effective address (LEA), load register and data segment register (LDS), and load register and extra segment register (LES).

Looking at Fig. 4.6(a), we see that these instructions provide the ability to manipulate memory addresses by loading a specific register with a 16-bit offset address or a 16-bit offset address together with a 16-bit segment address into either DS or ES.

The LEA instruction is used to load a specified register with a 16-bit offset address. An example of this instruction is

```
LEA SI,[INPUT]
```

Mnemonic	Meaning	Format	Operation	Flags affected
LEA	Load effective address	LEA Reg16,EA	(EA) → (Reg16)	None
LDS	Load register and DS	LDS Reg16,Mem32	(Mem32) → (Reg16) (Mem32+2) → (DS)	None
LES	Load register and ES	LES Reg16,Mem32	(Mem32) → (Reg16) (Mem32+2) → (ES)	None

(a)

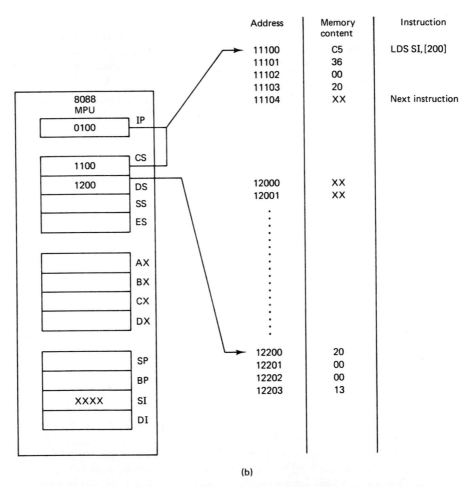

(b)

Figure 4.6 (a) LEA, LDS, and LES data transfer instructions. (b) LDS SI, [200] instruction before fetch and execution. (c) After execution.

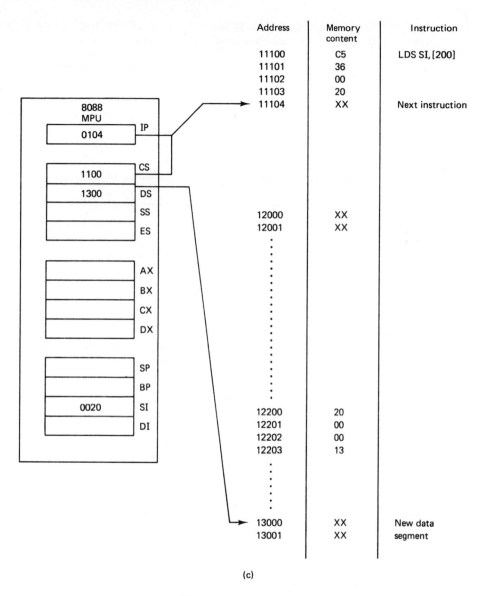

Address	Memory content	Instruction
11100	C5	LDS SI, [200]
11101	36	
11102	00	
11103	20	
11104	XX	Next instruction

8088 MPU

IP	0104
CS	1100
DS	1300
SS	
ES	
AX	
BX	
CX	
DX	
SP	
BP	
SI	0020
DI	

Address	Memory content	Instruction
12000	XX	
12001	XX	
12200	20	
12201	00	
12202	00	
12203	13	
13000	XX	New data
13001	XX	segment

(c)

Figure 4.6 (Continued)

When executed, it loads the SI register with an offset address value. The value of this offset is represented by the value of INPUT. INPUT is encoded following the instruction opcode in the code segment of memory.

The other two instructions, LDS and LES, are similar to LEA except that they load the specified register as well as the DS or ES segment register. That is, they are able to load a complete address pointer. In this way, a new data segment can be activated by executing a single instruction.

EXAMPLE 4.5

Assuming that the 8088 is set up as shown in Fig. 4.6(b), what is the result of executing the following instruction:

$$\text{LDS SI, [200]}$$

SOLUTION   Execution of the instruction loads the SI register from the word location in memory whose offset address with respect to the current data segment is 200_{16}. Figure 4.6(b) shows that the contents of DS are 1200_{16}. This gives a physical address of

$$PA = 12000_{16} + 0200_{16} = 12200_{16}$$

It is the contents of this location and the one that follows that are loaded into SI. Therefore, in Fig. 4.6(c) we find that SI contains 0020_{16}. The next two bytes, that is, the contents of addresses 12202_{16} and 12203_{16}, are loaded into the DS register. As shown, this defines a new data segment address of 13000_{16}.

EXAMPLE 4.6

Verify the execution of the instruction in Example 4.5 using the debugger of the IBM PC. The memory and register contents are to be those shown in Fig. 4.6(b).

SOLUTION   As shown in Fig. 4.7, DEBUG is first brought up and then REGISTER commands are used to initialize registers IP, CS, DS, and SI with values 0100_{16}, 1100_{16}, 1200_{16}, and 0000_{16}, respectively. Next the instruction is assembled at address CS:100 with the command

```
  -A CS:100              (↵)
  1100:0100 LDS SI,[200] (↵)
  1100:0104              (↵)
```

Before executing the instruction, we need to initialize two words of data starting at location DS:200 in memory. As shown in Fig. 4.7, this is done with an E command.

-E 200 20 00 00 13 (↵)

Then the instruction is executed with the TRACE command

-T (↵)

Looking at the displayed register status in Fig. 4.7, we see that SI has been loaded with the value 0020_{16} and DS with the value 1300_{16}.

```
A>DEBUG
-R IP
IP 0100
:
-R CS
CS 0CDE
:1100
-R DS
DS 0CDE
:1200
-R SI
SI 0000
:
-A CS:100
1100:0100 LDS SI,[200]
1100:0104
-E 200 20 00 00 13
-T

AX=0000  BX=0000  CX=0000  DX=0000  SP=FFEE  BP=0000  SI=0020  DI=0000
DS=1300  ES=0CDE  SS=0CDE  CS=1100  IP=0104    NV UP EI PL NZ NA PO NC
1100:0104 1200           ADC      AL,[BX+SI]                    DS:0020=00
-Q

A>
```

Figure 4.7 Display sequence for Example 4.6.

4.4 ARITHMETIC INSTRUCTIONS

The instruction set of the 8088 microprocessor contains a variety of *arithmetic instructions*. They include instructions for the *addition, subtraction, multiplication,* and *division* operations. These operations can be performed on numbers expressed in a variety of numeric data formats. They include *unsigned* or *signed binary bytes* or *words, unpacked* or *packed decimal bytes,* or *ASCII numbers.* By *packed decimal* we mean that two BCD digits are packed into a byte register or memory location. Unpacked decimal numbers are stored one BCD digit per byte. The decimal numbers are always unsigned. Moreover, ASCII numbers are expressed in ASCII code and stored one number per byte.

The status that results from the execution of an arithmetic instruction is recorded in the flags of the 8088. The flags that are affected by the arithmetic instructions are carry flag (CF), auxiliary flag (AF), sign flag (SF), zero flag (ZF), parity flag (PF), and overflow flag (OF). Each of these flags was discussed in Chapter 2.

For the purpose of discussion, we will divide the arithemetic instructions into the subgroups shown in Fig. 4.8.

Addition Instructions: ADD, ADC, INC, AAA, and DAA

The form of each of the instructions in the *addition group* is shown in Fig. 4.9(a); the allowed operand variations, for all but the INC instruction, are shown in Fig. 4.9(b). The allowed operands for the INC instruction are shown in Fig. 4.9(c). Let us begin by looking more closely at the *add* (ADD) instruction. Notice in Fig. 4.9(b) that it can be used to add an immediate operand to the contents of the accumulator, the contents of another register, or the contents of a storage location in memory. It also allows us to add the contents of two registers or the contents of a register and a memory location.

In general, the result of executing the instruction is expressed as

$$(S) + (D) \rightarrow (D)$$

Addition	
ADD	Add byte or word
ADC	Add byte or word with carry
INC	Increment byte or word by 1
AAA	ASCII adjust for addition
DAA	Decimal adjust for addition
Subtraction	
SUB	Subtract byte or word
SBB	Subtract byte or word with borrow
DEC	Decrement byte or word by 1
NEG	Negate byte or word
AAS	ASCII adjust for subtraction
DAS	Decimal adjust for subtraction
Multiplication	
MUL	Multiply byte or word unsigned
IMUL	Integer multiply byte or word
AAM	ASCII adjust for multiply
Division	
DIV	Divide byte or word unsigned
IDIV	Integer divide byte or word
AAD	ASCII adjust for division
CBW	Convert byte to word
CWD	Convert word to doubleword

Figure 4.8 Arithmetic instructions.

Mnemonic	Meaning	Format	Operation	Flags affected
ADD	Addition	ADD D,S	$(S) + (D) \rightarrow (D)$ carry $\rightarrow (CF)$	OF,SF,ZF,AF,PF,CF
ADC	Add with carry	ADC D,S	$(S)+(D)+(CF) \rightarrow (D)$ carry $\rightarrow (CF)$	OF,SF,ZF,AF,PF,CF
INC	Increment by 1	INC D	$(D)+1 \rightarrow (D)$	OF,SF,ZF,AF,PF,CF
DAA	Decimal adjust for addition	DAA		OF,SF,ZF,AF,PF,CF
AAA	ASCII adjust for addition	AAA		OF,SF,ZF,AF,PF,CF

(a)

Destination	Source
Register	Register
Register	Memory
Memory	Register
Register	Immediate
Memory	Immediate
Accumulator	Immediate

(b)

Destination
Reg16
Reg8
Memory

(c)

Figure 4.9 (a) Addition arithmetic instructions. (b) Allowed operands for ADD and ADC instructions. (c) Allowed operands for INC instruction.

That is, the contents of the source operand are added to those of the destination operand and the sum that results is put into the location of the destination operand.

EXAMPLE 4.7

Assume that the AX and BX registers contain 1100_{16} and $0ABC_{16}$, respectively. What are the results of executing the instruction ADD AX,BX?

SOLUTION   Execution of the ADD instruction causes the contents of source operand BX to be added to the contents of destination register AX. This gives

$$(BX) + (AX) = 0ABC_{16} + 1100_{16} = 1BBC_{16}$$

This sum ends up in destination register AX.

$$(AX) = 1BBC_{16}$$

Execution of this instruction is illustrated in Fig. 4.10(a) and (b).

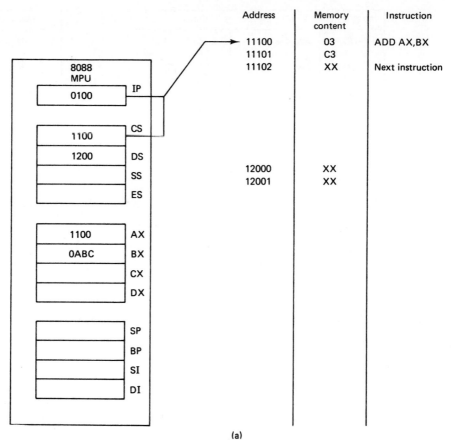

Address	Memory content	Instruction
11100	03	ADD AX,BX
11101	C3	
11102	XX	Next instruction
12000	XX	
12001	XX	

(a)

Figure 4.10 (a) ADD instruction before fetch and execution. (b) After execution.

EXAMPLE 4.8

Use the debugger on the IBM PC to verify the execution of the instruction in Example 4.7. Assume that the registers are to be initialized with the values shown in Fig. 4.10(a).

SOLUTION The debug sequence for this problem is shown in Fig. 4.11. After DEBUG is brought up, the instruction is assembled into memory with the command

```
–A 1100:0100        (↵)
1100:0100 ADD AX,BX (↵)
1100:0102           (↵)
–
```

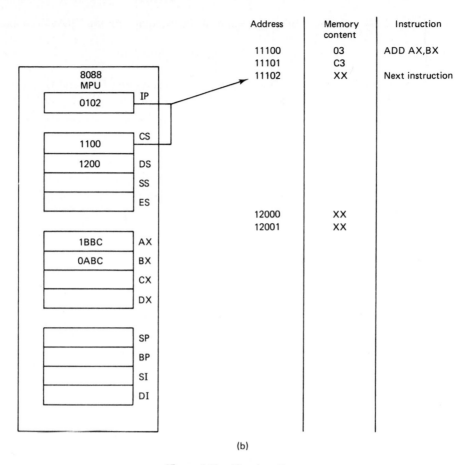

(b)

Figure 4.10   (Continued)

Next, as shown in Fig. 4.11, the AX and BX registers are loaded with the values 1100_{16} and $0ABC_{16}$, respectively, using R commands.

```
-R AX
AX 0000
:1100    (↵)
-R  BX
BX 0000
:0ABC    (↵)
```

Next, the loading of the instruction is verified with the unassemble command

```
-U 1100:0100 0100  (↵)
```

and is shown in Fig. 4.11 to be correct.

We are now ready to execute the instruction with the TRACE command

$$-T \ =1100:0100 \ (\lrcorner)$$

From the trace dump in Fig. 4.11, we see that the sum of AX and BX, which equals $1BBC_{16}$, is now held in destination register AX. Also note that no carry (NC) occurs.

```
A>DEBUG
-A 1100:100
1100:0100 ADD AX,BX
1100:0102
-R AX
AX 0000
:1100
-R BX
BX 0000
:0ABC
-U 1100:100 100
1100:0100 01D8           ADD      AX,BX
-T =1100:100

AX=1BBC  BX=0ABC  CX=0000  DX=0000  SP=FFEE  BP=0000  SI=0000  DI=0000
DS=0CDE  ES=0CDE  SS=0CDE  CS=1100  IP=0102    NV UP EI PL NZ NA PO NC
1100:0102 0002           ADD      [BP+SI],AL                    SS:0000=CD
-Q

A>
```

Figure 4.11 Display sequence for Example 4.8.

The instruction *add with carry* (ADC) works similarly to ADD. But in this case, the content of the carry flag is also added; that is.

$$(S) + (D) + (CF) \rightarrow (D)$$

The valid operand combinations are the same as those for the ADD instruction. ADC is primarily used for multiword add operation.

Another instruction that can be considered as part of the addition subgroup of arithmetic instructions is the *increment* (INC) instruction. As shown in Fig. 4.9(c), its operands can be the contents of a 16-bit internal register, an 8-bit internal register, or a storage location in memory. Execution of the INC instruction adds one to the specified operand. An example of an instruction that increments the high byte of AX is

```
INC AH
```

Looking at Fig. 4.9(a), we see how execution of these three instructions affects the earlier mentioned flags.

EXAMPLE 4.9

The original contents of AX, BL, memory location SUM, and carry flag (CF) are 1234_{16}, AB_{16}, $00CD_{16}$, and 0_{16}, respectively. Describe the results of executing the following sequence of instructions.

```
ADD AX,[SUM]
ADC BL,05H
INC [SUM]
```

SOLUTION   By executing the first instruction, we add the word in the accumulator and the word in the memory location identified as SUM. The result is placed in the accumulator. That is,

$$(AX) \leftarrow (AX) + (SUM) = 1234_{16} + 00CD_{16} = 1301_{16}$$

The carry flag remains reset.

The second instruction adds to the lower byte of the base register (BL), the immediate operand 5_{16}, and the carry flag, which is 0_{16}. This gives

$$(BL) \leftarrow (BL) + IOP + (CF) = AB_{16} + 5_{16} + 0_{16} = B0_{16}$$

Since no carry is generated, CF stays reset.

The last instruction increments the contents of memory location SUM by one. That is,

$$(SUM) \leftarrow (SUM) + 1_{16} = 00CD_{16} + 1_{16} = 00CE_{16}$$

These results are summarized in Fig. 4.12.

EXAMPLE 4.10

Verify the operation of the instruction sequence in Example 4.9 by executing it with DEBUG on the IBM PC. A source program that includes this sequence of instructions is shown in Fig. 4.13(a), and the source listing produced when the program is assembled is shown in Fig. 4.13(b). A run module that was produced by linking this program is stored in file EX410.EXE.

Instruction	(AX)	(BL)	(SUM)	(CF)
Initial state	1234	AB	00CD	0
ADD AX,SUM	1301	AB	00CD	0
ADC BL,05H	1301	B0	00CD	0
INC SUM	1301	B0	00CE	0

Figure 4.12 Results due to execution of arithmetic instructions in Example 4.9.

```
TITLE   EXAMPLE 4.10

        PAGE    ,132

STACK_SEG       SEGMENT         STACK 'STACK'
                DB              64 DUP(?)
STACK_SEG       ENDS


DATA_SEG        SEGMENT
SUM             DW              0CDH
DATA_SEG        ENDS

CODE_SEG        SEGMENT         'CODE'
EX410   PROC    FAR
        ASSUME  CS:CODE_SEG, SS:STACK_SEG, DS:DATA_SEG

;To return to DEBUG program put return address on the stack

        PUSH    DS
        MOV     AX, 0
        PUSH    AX


;Following code implements the Example 4.10

        MOV     AX, DATA_SEG    ;Establish data segment
        MOV     DS, AX

        ADD     AX, SUM
        ADC     BL, 5H
        INC     SUM

        RET                     ;Return to DEBUG program
EX410   ENDP

CODE_SEG        ENDS

        END     EX410
```

(a)

Figure 4.13 (a) Source program for Example 4.10. (b) Source listing produced by assembler. (c) Debug session for execution of program EX410,EXE.

```
                              TITLE    EXAMPLE 4.10

                                    PAGE     ,132

0000                          STACK_SEG      SEGMENT        STACK 'STACK'
0000     40 [                                DB             64 DUP(?)
            ??
              ]

0040                          STACK_SEG      ENDS


0000                          DATA_SEG       SEGMENT
0000   00CD                   SUM            DW             0CDH
0002                          DATA_SEG       ENDS

0000                          CODE_SEG       SEGMENT        'CODE'
0000                          EX410  PROC    FAR
                              ASSUME  CS:CODE_SEG, SS:STACK_SEG, DS:DATA_SEG

                              ;To return to DEBUG program put return address on the stack

0000   1E                            PUSH    DS
0001   B8 0000                       MOV     AX, 0
0004   50                            PUSH    AX

                              ;Following code implements the Example 4.10

0005   B8 ---- R                     MOV     AX, DATA_SEG    ;Establish data segment
0008   8E D8                         MOV     DS, AX

000A   03 06 0000 R                  ADD     AX, SUM
000E   80 D3 05                      ADC     BL, 5H
0011   FF 06 0000 R                  INC     SUM

0015   CB                            RET                     ;Return to DEBUG program
0016                          EX410  ENDP

0016                          CODE_SEG       ENDS

                              END     EX410
```

Segments and groups:

N a m e	Size	align	combine	class
CODE_SEG	0016	PARA	NONE	'CODE'
DATA_SEG	0002	PARA	NONE	
STACK_SEG.	0040	PARA	STACK	'STACK'

Symbols:

N a m e	Type	Value	Attr	
EX410.	F PROC	0000	CODE_SEG	Length =0016
SUM.	L WORD	0000	DATA_SEG	

```
Warning Severe
Errors  Errors
0       0
```

(b)

Figure 4.13 (Continued)

```
A>DEBUG B:EX410.EXE
-U 0 12
0D03:0000 1E             PUSH    DS
0D03:0001 B80000         MOV     AX,0000
0D03:0004 50             PUSH    AX
0D03:0005 B8050D         MOV     AX,0D05
0D03:0008 8ED8           MOV     DS,AX
0D03:000A 03060000       ADD     AX,[0000]
0D03:000E 80D305         ADC     BL,05
0D03:0011 FF060000       INC     WORD PTR [0000]
-G A

AX=0D05  BX=0000  CX=0022  DX=0000  SP=003C  BP=0000  SI=0000  DI=0000
DS=0D05  ES=0CF3  SS=0D06  CS=0D03  IP=000A    NV UP EI PL NZ NA PO NC
0D03:000A 03060000       ADD     AX,[0000]                          DS:0000=00CD
-R AX
AX 0D05
:1234
-R BX
BX 0000
:AB
-R F
NV UP EI PL NZ NA PO NC  -
-E 0 CD 00
-D 0 1
0D05:0000  CD 00                                           ..
-T

AX=1301  BX=00AB  CX=0022  DX=0000  SP=003C  BP=0000  SI=0000  DI=0000
DS=0D05  ES=0CF3  SS=0D06  CS=0D03  IP=000E    NV UP EI PL NZ AC PO NC
0D03:000E 80D305         ADC     BL,05
-T

AX=1301  BX=00B0  CX=0022  DX=0000  SP=003C  BP=0000  SI=0000  DI=0000
DS=0D05  ES=0CF3  SS=0D06  CS=0D03  IP=0011    NV UP EI NG NZ AC PO NC
0D03:0011 FF060000       INC     WORD PTR [0000]                    DS:0000=00CD
-T

AX=1301  BX=00B0  CX=0022  DX=0000  SP=003C  BP=0000  SI=0000  DI=0000
DS=0D05  ES=0CF3  SS=0D06  CS=0D03  IP=0015    NV UP EI PL NZ NA PO NC
0D03:0015 CB             RETF
-D 0 1
0D05:0000  CE 00                                           ..
-G

Program terminated normally
-Q

A>
```

(c)

Figure 4.13 (Continued)

SOLUTION The DEBUG program is brought up and at the same time the run module from file EX410.EXE is loaded with the command

$$>\text{DEBUG B:EX410.EXE} \qquad (\dashv)$$

Next, we will verify the loading of the program by unassembling it with the command

$$-\text{U 0 12} \qquad (\dashv)$$

Looking at the displayed instruction sequence in Fig. 4.13(c) and comparing it to the source listing in Fig. 4.13(b), we find that the program has loaded correctly.

Notice in Fig. 4.13(c) that the instructions for which we are interested in verifying operation start at address 0D03:000A. For this reason, a GO command will be used to execute down to this point in the program. This command is

$$-\text{G A} \qquad (\dashv)$$

Notice in the trace information displayed for this command that now CS contains $0D03_{16}$ and IP contains $000A_{16}$; therefore, the next instruction to be executed is at address 0D03:000A. This is the ADD instruction.

Now we need to initialize registers AX, BX, and the memory location pointed to by SUM (WORD PTR [0000]). We must also verify that the CF status flag is set to NC (no carry). In Fig. 4.13(c), we find that these operations are done with the following sequence of commands

```
-R AX                        (↵)
AX 0D05
:1234                        (↵)
-R BX                        (↵)
BX 0000
:AB                          (↵)
-R F                         (↵)
NV UP EI PL NZ NA PO NC  -  (↵)
-E 0 CD 00                   (↵)
-D 0 1                       (↵)
0D03:0000 CD 00
```

Now we are ready to execute the ADD instruction. This is done by issuing the TRACE command

$$-\text{T} \qquad (\dashv)$$

From the state information displayed for this command in Fig. 4.13(c), notice that the value CD_{16} has been added to the original value in AX, which was 1234_{16}, and the sum that results in AX is 1301_{16}.

Next the ADC instruction is executed with another T command.

$$-\text{T} \qquad (\downharpoonleft)$$

It causes the immediate operand value 05_{16} to be added to the original contents of BL, which is AB_{16}, and the sum that is produced in BL is $B0_{16}$.

The last instruction is executed with one more T command, and it causes the SUM (WORD PTR [0000]) to be incremented by one. This can be verified by issuing the DUMP command

$$-\text{D} \ 0 \ 1 \qquad (\downharpoonleft)$$

The addition instructions we just covered can also be used to directly add numbers expressed in ASCII code. This eliminates the need for doing a code conversion on ASCII data prior to processing it with addition operations. Whenever the 8088 does an addition on ASCII format data, an adjustment must be performed on the result to convert it to a decimal number. It is specifically for this purpose that the *ASCII adjust for addition* (AAA) instruction is provided in the instruction set of the 8088. The AAA instruction should be executed immediately after the instruction that adds ASCII data.

Assuming that AL contains the result produced by adding two ASCII coded numbers, execution of the AAA instruction causes the contents of AL to be replaced by its equivalent decimal value. If the sum is greater than nine, AL contains the LSD and AH is incremented by one. Otherwise, AL contains the sum and AH is unchanged. Both the AF and CF flags can be affected. Since AAA can only adjust data that are in AL, the destination register for ADD instructions that process ASCII numbers should be AL.

EXAMPLE 4.11

What is the result of executing the following instruction sequence?

```
ADD  AL,BL
AAA
```

Assume that AL contains 32_{16}, which is the ASCII code for number 2, BL contains 34_{16}, which is the ASCII code for number 4, and AH has been cleared.

SOLUTION   Executing the ADD instruction gives

$$(\text{AL}) \leftarrow (\text{AL}) + (\text{BL}) = 32_{16} + 34_{16} = 66_{16}$$

Next, the result is adjusted to give its equivalent decimal number. This is done by execution of the AAA instruction. The equivalent of adding 2 and 4 is decimal 6 with no carry. Therefore, the result after the AAA instruction is

$$(AL) = 06_{16}$$

$$(AH) = 00_{16}$$

and both AF and CF remain cleared.

The instruction set of the 8088 includes another instruction, called *decimal adjust for addition* (DAA). This instruction is used to perform an adjust operation similar to that performed by AAA but for the addition of packed BCD numbers instead of ASCII numbers. Information about this instruction is also provided in Fig. 4.9. Similar to AAA, DAA performs an adjustment on the value in AL. A typical instruction sequence is

```
ADD  AL,BL
DAA
```

Remember that the contents of AL and BL must be packed BCD numbers, that is, two BCD digits packed into a byte. The adjusted result in AL is again a packed BCD byte.

Subtraction Instructions: SUB, SBB, DEC, AAS, DAS, and NEG

The instruction set of the 8088 includes an extensive set of instructions provided for implementing subtraction. As shown in Fig. 4.14, the subtraction subgroup is similar to the addition subgroup. It includes instructions for subtracting a source and destination operand, decrementing an operand, and adjusting the result of subtractions of ASCII and BCD data. An additional instruction in this subgroup is negate.

The *subtract* (SUB) instruction is used to subtract the value of a source operand from a destination operand. The result of this operation in general is given as

$$(D) \leftarrow (D) - (S)$$

As shown in Fig. 4.14(b), it can employ the identical operand combinations as the ADD instruction.

The *subtract with borrow* (SBB) instruction is similar to SUB; however, it also subtracts the contents of the carry flag from the destination. That is,

$$(D) \leftarrow (D) - (S) - (CF)$$

Mnemonic	Meaning	Format	Operation	Flags affected
SUB	Subtract	SUB D,S	(D) − (S) → (D) Borrow → (CF)	OF, SF, ZF, AF, PF, CF
SBB	Subtract with borrow	SBB D,S	(D) − (S) − (CF) → (D)	OF, SF, ZF, AF, PF, CF
DEC	Decrement by 1	DEC D	(D) − 1 → (D)	OF, SF, ZF, AF, PF
NEG	Negate	NEG D	0 − (D) → (D) 1 → (CF)	OF, SF, ZF, AF, PF, CF
DAS	Decimal adjust for subtraction	DAS		OF, SF, ZF, AF, PF, CF
AAS	ASCII adjust for subtraction	AAS		OF, SF, ZF, AF, PF, CF

(a)

Destination	Source
Register	Register
Register	Memory
Memory	Register
Accumulator	Immediate
Register	Immediate
Memory	Immediate

(b)

Destination
Reg16
Reg8
Memory

(c)

Destination
Register
Memory

(d)

Figure 4.14 (a) Subtraction arithmetic instructions. (b) Allowed operands for SUB and SBB instructions. (c) Allowed operands for DEC instruction. (d) Allowed operands for NEG instruction.

EXAMPLE 4.12

Assuming that the contents of registers BX and CX are 1234_{16} and 0123_{16}, respectively, and the carry flag is 0, what will be the result of executing the following instruction?

$$\text{SBB BX,CX}$$

SOLUTION   Since the instruction implements the operation

$$(BX) - (CX) - (CF) \rightarrow (BX)$$

we get

$$(BX) = 1234_{16} - 0123_{16} - 0_{16}$$

$$= 1111_{16}$$

EXAMPLE 4.13

Verify the operation of the subtract instruction in Example 4.12 by repeating the example using the debugger on the IBM PC.

SOLUTION   As shown in Fig. 4.15, we first bring up the debugger and then dump the initial state of the 8088 with a REGISTER command. Next, we load registers BX, CX, and flag CF with the values 1234_{16}, 0123_{16}, and NC, respectively. Notice in Fig. 4.15 that this is done with three more R commands.

Now the instruction is assembled at address CS:100 with the command

```
-A                        ( ⏎)
0CDE:0100  SBB  BX,CX  ( ⏎)
0CDE:0102                 ( ⏎)
-
```

Before executing the instruction, we can verify the initialization of the registers and the entry of the instruction by issuing the commands

```
-R              ( ⏎)
```

and

```
-U 100 101  ( ⏎)
```

Looking at Fig. 4.15, we find that the registers have been correctly initialized and that the instruction SBB BX,CX has been correctly loaded.

Finally, the instruction is executed with a TRACE command. As shown in Fig. 4.15, the result of executing the instruction is that the contents of CX were subtracted from the contents of BX. The difference, which is 1111_{16}, resides in destination register BX.

Just as the INC instruction could be used to add one to an operand, the *decrement* (DEC) instruction can be used to subtract one from its operand. The allowed operands are shown in Fig. 4.14(c).

In Fig. 4.14(d), we see that the *negate* (NEG) instruction can operate on operands in a general-purpose register or a storage location in memory. Execution of this instruction causes the value of its operand to be replaced by its negative. The way this is actually done is through subtraction. That is, the contents of the specified operand are subtracted from zero (using 2's-complement arithmetic plus complementing carry), and the result is returned to the operand location.

```
A>DEBUG
-R
AX=0000  BX=0000  CX=0000  DX=0000  SP=FFEE  BP=0000  SI=0000  DI=0000
DS=0CDE  ES=0CDE  SS=0CDE  CS=0CDE  IP=0100    NV UP EI PL NZ NA PO NC
0CDE:0100 4D              DEC      BP
-R BX
BX 0000
:1234
-R CX
CX 0000
:0123
-R F
NV UP EI PL NZ NA PO NC   -
-A
0CDE:0100 SBB BX,CX
0CDE:0102
-R
AX=0000  BX=1234  CX=0123  DX=0000  SP=FFEE  BP=0000  SI=0000  DI=0000
DS=0CDE  ES=0CDE  SS=0CDE  CS=0CDE  IP=0100    NV UP EI PL NZ NA PO NC
0CDE:0100 19CB           SBB       BX,CX
-U 100 101
0CDE:0100 19CB           SBB       BX,CX
-T

AX=0000  BX=1111  CX=0123  DX=0000  SP=FFEE  BP=0000  SI=0000  DI=0000
DS=0CDE  ES=0CDE  SS=0CDE  CS=0CDE  IP=0102    NV UP EI PL NZ NA PE NC
0CDE:0102 0003           ADD       [BP+DI],AL                   SS:0000=CD
-Q

A>
```

Figure 4.15 Display sequence for Example 4.13.

EXAMPLE 4.14

Assuming that register BX contains $003A_{16}$, what is the result of executing the following instruction?

$$NEG \quad BX$$

SOLUTION   Executing the NEG instruction causes the 2's-complement subtraction that follows:

$$0000_{16} - (BX) = 0000_{16} + 2\text{'s complement of } 003A_{16}$$

$$= 0000_{16} + FFC6_{16}$$

$$= FFC6_{16}$$

This value is placed in BX.

$$(BX) = FFC6_{16}$$

EXAMPLE 4.15

Verify the operation of the NEG instruction in Example 4.14 by executing it with the debugger on the IBM PC.

SOLUTION   After loading the DEBUG program, we must initialize the contents of the BX register. This is done with the command

```
                    -R BX       (↵)
                    BX 0000
                    :3A         (↵)
                    -
```

Next the instruction is assembled with the command

```
                -A                      (↵)
                0CDE:0100 NEG BX (↵)
                0CDE:0102             (↵)
                -
```

At this point, we can verify the initialization of BX by issuing the command

```
                    -R BX       (↵)
                    BX 003A
                    :           (↵)
                    -
```

To check the assembly of the instruction, we can unassemble it with the command

```
                -U 100 101                  (↵)
                0CDE:0100 F7DB NEG BX
                -
```

Now the instruction is executed with the command

```
                    -T      (↵)
```

The information that is dumped by issuing this command is shown in Fig. 4.16. Here the new contents in register BX are verified as $FFC6_{16}$, which is the negative of $003A_{16}$. Also note that the carry flag is set.

```
A>DEBUG
-R BX
BX 0000
:3A
-A
OCDE:0100 NEG BX
OCDE:0102
-R BX
BX 003A
:
-U 100 101
OCDE:0100 F7DB            NEG       BX
-T

AX=0000  BX=FFC6  CX=0000  DX=0000  SP=FFEE  BP=0000  SI=0000  DI=0000
DS=OCDE  ES=OCDE  SS=OCDE  CS=OCDE  IP=0102  NV UP EI NG NZ AC PE CY
OCDE:0102 0003           ADD       [BP+DI],AL                    SS:0000=CD
-Q

A>
```

Figure 4.16   Display sequence for Example 4.15.

In our study of the addition instruction subgroup, we found that the 8088 is capable of directly adding ASCII and BCD numbers. The SUB and SBB instructions can also subtract numbers represented in these formats. Just as for addition, the results that are obtained must be adjusted to produce their corresponding decimal numbers. In the case of ASCII subtraction, we use the *ASCII adjust for subtraction* (AAS) instruction, and for packed BCD subtraction we use the *decimal adjust for subtract* (DAS) instruction.

An example of an instruction sequence for direct ASCII subtraction is

```
                    SUB AL,BL
                    AAS
```

ASCII numbers must be loaded into AL and BL before execution of the subtract instruction. Notice that the destination of the subtraction should be AL. After execution of AAS, AL contains the difference of the two numbers, and AH is unchanged if no borrow takes place or is decremented by one if a borrow occurs.

Multiplication and Division Instructions: MUL, DIV, IMUL, IDIV, AAM, AAD, CBW, and CWD

The 8088 has instructions to support multiplication and division of binary and BCD numbers. Two basic types of multiplication and division instructions, those for the processing of unsigned numbers and signed numbers, are available. To do these operations on unsigned numbers, the instructions are MUL and DIV. On the other hand, to multiply or divide signed numbers, the instructions are IMUL and IDIV.

Figure 4.17(a) describes these instructions. Notice in Fig. 4.17(b) that a single byte-wide or word-wide operand is specified in a multiplication instruc-

Mnemonic	Meaning	Format	Operation	Flags Affected
MUL	Multiply (unsigned)	MUL S	$(AL) \cdot (S8) \rightarrow (AX)$ $(AX) \cdot (S16) \rightarrow (DX),(AX)$	OF, SF, ZF, AF, PF, CF
DIV	Division (unsigned)	DIV S	(1) $Q((AX)/(S8)) \rightarrow (AL)$ $R((AX)/(S8)) \rightarrow (AH)$ (2) $Q((DX,AX)/(S16)) \rightarrow (AX)$ $R((DX,AX)/(S16)) \rightarrow (DX)$ If Q is FF_{16} in case (1) or $FFFF_{16}$ in case (2), then type 0 interrupt occurs	OF, SF, ZF, AF, PF, CF
IMUL	Integer multiply (signed)	IMUL S	$(AL) \cdot (S8) \rightarrow (AX)$ $(AX) \cdot (S16) \rightarrow (DX),(AX)$	OF, SF, ZF, AF, PF, CF
IDIV	Integer divide (signed)	IDIV S	(1) $Q((AX)/(S8)) \rightarrow (AL)$ $R((AX)/(S8)) \rightarrow (AH)$ (2) $Q((DX,AX)/(S16)) \rightarrow (AX)$ $R((DX,AX)/(S16)) \rightarrow (DX)$ If Q is $7F_{16}$ in case (1) or $7FFF_{16}$ in case (2), then type 0 interrupt occurs	OF, SF, ZF, AF, PF, CF
AAM	Adjust AL for multiplication	AAM	$Q((AL)/10) \rightarrow AH$ $R((AL)/10) \rightarrow AL$	OF, SF, ZF, AF, PF, CF
AAD	Adjust AX for division	AAD	$(AH) \cdot 10 + AL \rightarrow AL$ $00 \rightarrow AH$	OF, SF, ZF, AF, PF, CF
CBW	Convert byte to word	CBW	(MSB of AL) $\rightarrow$ (All bits of AH)	None
CWD	Convert word to double word	CWD	(MSB of AX) $\rightarrow$ (All bits of DX)	None

(a)

Source
Reg8
Reg16
Mem8
Mem16

(b)

Figure 4.17   (a) Multiplication and division instructions. (b) Allowed operands.

tion. It is the source operand. As shown in Fig. 4.17(a), the other operand, which is the destination, is assumed already to be in AL for 8-bit multiplications or in AX for 16-bit multiplications.

The result of executing a MUL or IMUL instruction on byte data can be represented as

$$(AX) \leftarrow (AL) \times (8\text{-bit operand})$$

That is, the resulting 16-bit product is produced in the AX register. On the other hand, for multiplications of data words, the 32-bit result is given by

$$(DX,AX) \leftarrow (AX) \times (16\text{-bit operand})$$

where AX contains the 16 LSBs and DX the 16 MSBs.

For the division operation, again just the source operand is specified. The other operand is either the contents of AX for 16-bit dividends or the contents of both DX and AX for 32-bit dividends. The result of a DIV or IDIV instruction for an 8-bit divisor is represented by

$$(AH),(AL) \leftarrow (AX)/(8\text{-bit operand})$$

where (AH) is the remainder and (AL) the quotient. For 16-bit divisions, we get

$$(DX),(AX) \leftarrow (DX,AX)/(16\text{-bit operand})$$

Here AX contains the quotient and DX contains the remainder.

EXAMPLE 4.16

If the contents of AL equals -1 and the contents of CL are -2, what will be the result produced in AX by executing the following instructions?

```
MUL CL
```

and

```
IMUL CL
```

SOLUTION   The first instruction multiplies the contents of AL and CL as unsigned numbers.

$$-1 = 11111111_2 = FF_{16}$$

$$-2 = 11111110_2 = FE_{16}$$

Thus, executing the MUL instruction, we get

$$(AX) = 11111111_2 \times 11111110_2 = 1111110100000010_2$$

$$= FD02_{16}$$

The second instruction multiplies the same two numbers as signed numbers and gives

$$(AX) = -1_{16} \times -2_{16}$$

$$= 2_{16}$$

EXAMPLE 4.17

Verify the operation of the MUL instruction in Example 4.16 by performing the same operation on the IBM PC with the debugger.

SOLUTION   First the DEBUG program is loaded and then registers AX and CX are initialized with the values FF_{16} and FE_{16}, respectively. These registers are loaded as follows:

```
           -R  AX     ( ↵ )
           AX  0000
            :FF       ( ↵ )
           -R  CX     ( ↵ )
           CX  0000
            :FE       ( ↵ )
            -
```

Next the instruction is loaded with the command

```
           -A                    ( ↵ )
           0CDE:0100  MUL  CL
           0CDE:0102            ( ↵ )
            -
```

Before executing the instruction, let us verify the loading of AX, CX, and the instruction. To do this, we use the commands

```
           -R  AX                    ( ↵ )
           AX  00FF
            :                        ( ↵ )
           -R  CX                    ( ↵ )
           CX  00FE
            :                        ( ↵ )
           -U  100  101              ( ↵ )
           0CDE:0100  F6E1  MUL  CL
            -
```

To execute the instruction, we issue the T command.

```
           -T       ( ↵ )
```

The displayed result in Fig. 4.18 shows that AX now contains $FD02_{16}$, which is the product that was expected.

```
A>DEBUG
-R AX
AX 0000
:FF
-R CX
CX 0000
:FE
-A
0CDE:0100 MUL CL
0CDE:0102
-R AX
AX 00FF
:
-R CX
CX 00FE
:
-U 100 101
0CDE:0100 F6E1              MUL      CL
-T

AX=FD02  BX=0000  CX=00FE  DX=0000  SP=FFEE  BP=0000  SI=0000  DI=0000
DS=0CDE  ES=0CDE  SS=0CDE  CS=0CDE  IP=0102   OV UP EI NG NZ NA PO CY
0CDE:0102 0003              ADD      [BP+DI],AL                       SS:0000=CD
-Q

A>
```

Figure 4.18 Display sequence for Example 4.17.

As shown in Fig. 4.17(a), adjust instructions for BCD multiplication and division are also provided. They are *adjust AX for multiply* (AAM) and *adjust AX for divide* (AAD). The multiplication performed just before execution of the AAM instruction is assumed to have been performed on two unpacked BCD numbers with the product produced in AL. The AAD instruction assumes that AH and AL contain unpacked BCD numbers.

The division instructions can also be used to divide an 8-bit dividend in AL by an 8-bit divisor. However, to do this, the sign of the dividend must first be extended to fill the AX register. That is, AH is filled with zeros if the number in AL is positive or with ones if it is negative. This conversion is automatically done by executing the *convert byte to word* (CBW) instruction.

In a similar way, the 32-bit by 16-bit division instructions can be used to divide a 16-bit dividend in AX by a 16-bit divisor. In this case, the sign bit of AX must be extended by 16 bits into the DX register. This can be done by another instruction, which is known as *convert word to double word* (CWD). These two sign extension instructions are also shown in Fig. 4.17(a).

Notice that the CBW and CWD instructions are provided to handle operations where the result or intermediate results of an operation cannot be held in the correct word length for use in other arithmetic operations. Using these instructions, we can extend a byte or word of data to its equivalent word or double word.

EXAMPLE 4.18

What is the result of executing the following sequence of instructions?

```
MOV AL,0A1H
CBW
CWD
```

SOLUTION   The first instruction loads AL with $A1_{16}$. This gives

$$(AL) = A1_{16} = 10100001_2$$

Executing the second instruction extends the most significant bit of AL, which is one, into all bits of AH. The result is

$$(AH) = 11111111_2 = FF_{16}$$

$$(AX) = 1111111110100001_2 = FFA1_{16}$$

This completes conversion of the byte in AL to a word in AX.

   The last instruction loads each bit of DX with the most significant bit of AX. This bit is also one. Therefore, we get

$$(DX) = 1111111111111111_2 = FFFF_{16}$$

Now the word in AX has been extended to the double word

$$(AX) - FFA1_{16}$$

$$(DX) = FFFF_{16}$$

EXAMPLE 4.19

Use an assembled version of the program in Example 4.18 to verify the results obtained when it is executed.

SOLUTION   The source program is shown in Fig. 4.19(a). Notice that this program differs from that described in Example 4.18 in that it includes the pseudo-op statements that are needed to assemble it and some additional instructions so that it can be executed through the debugger.

   This source file is assembled with the macroassembler and then linked with the LINK program to give a run module stored in the file EX419.EXE. The source listing (EX419.LST) produced by the assembly of this source file, which is called EX419.ASM, is shown in Fig. 4.19(b).

As shown in Fig. 4.19(c), the run module is loaded for execution as part of calling up the DEBUG program. This is done with the command

A>DEBUG B:EX419.EXE   (↵)

The program load can now be verified with the UNASSEMBLE command

−U 0 9   (↵)

Looking at the instructions displayed in Fig. 4.19(c), we see that the program is correct.

From the unassembled version of the program in Fig. 4.19(c), we find that the instructions we are interested in start at address 0D03:0005. Thus we will execute the instructions prior to the MOV AL,A1 instruction by issuing the command

−G 5   (↵)

The state information that is displayed in Fig. 4.19(c) shows that $(AX) = 0000_{16}$ and $(DX) = 0000_{16}$. Moreover, $(IP) = 0005_{16}$ and points to the first instruction that we are interested in. This instruction is executed with the command

−T   (↵)

In the trace dump information of Fig. 4.19(c), we see that AL has been loaded with $A1_{16}$ and DX contains 0000_{16}.

Now the second instruction is executed with the command

−T   (↵)

Again looking at the trace information, we see that AX now contains the value $FFA1_{16}$ and DX still contains 0000_{16}. This shows that the byte in AL has been extended to a word in AX.

To execute the third instruction, the command is

−T   (↵)

Then, looking at the trace information produced, we find that AX still contains $FFA1_{16}$ and the value in DX has changed to $FFFF_{16}$. This shows us that the word in AX has been extended to a double word in DX and AX.

To run the program to completion, enter the command

−G   (↵)

This executes the remaining instructions, which cause control to be returned to the DEBUG program.

```
                TITLE   EXAMPLE 4.19

                        PAGE        ,132

        STACK_SEG       SEGMENT         STACK 'STACK'
                        DB              64 DUP(?)
        STACK_SEG       ENDS


        CODE_SEG        SEGMENT         'CODE'
        EX419   PROC    FAR
                ASSUME  CS:CODE_SEG, SS:STACK_SEG

        ;To return to DEBUG program put return address on the stack

                        PUSH    DS
                        MOV     AX, 0
                        PUSH    AX

        ;Following code implements Example 4.19

                        MOV     AL, 0A1H
                        CBW
                        CWD

                        RET                     ;Return to DEBUG program
        EX419   ENDP

        CODE_SEG        ENDS

                        END     EX419
```

(a)

```
                        TITLE   EXAMPLE 4.19

                                PAGE        ,132

0000                            STACK_SEG       SEGMENT         STACK 'STACK'
0000    40 [                                    DB              64 DUP(?)
             ??
           ]

0040                            STACK_SEG       ENDS


0000                            CODE_SEG        SEGMENT         'CODE'
0000                            EX419   PROC    FAR
                                        ASSUME  CS:CODE_SEG, SS:STACK_SEG

                                ;To return to DEBUG program put return address on the stack

0000    1E                              PUSH    DS
0001    B8 0000                         MOV     AX, 0
0004    50                              PUSH    AX

                                ;Following code implements Example 4.19

0005    B0 A1                           MOV     AL, 0A1H
0007    98                              CBW
0008    99                              CWD
```

Figure 4.19 (a) Source program for Example 4.19. (b) Source listing produced by assembler. (c) Debug session for execution of program EX419,EXE.

```
0009  CB                          RET                          ;Return to DEBUG program
000A                   EX419      ENDP

000A                              CODE_SEG      ENDS
```

Segments and groups:

N a m e	Size	align	combine class
CODE_SEG	000A	PARA	NONE 'CODE'
STACK_SEG.	0040	PARA	STACK 'STACK'

Symbols:

N a m e	Type	Value	Attr
EX419.	F PROC	0000	CODE_SEG Length =000A

Warning Severe
Errors Errors
  0   0

(b)

```
A>DEBUG B:EX419.EXE
-U 0 9
0D03:0000 1E              PUSH     DS
0D03:0001 B80000          MOV      AX,0000
0D03:0004 50              PUSH     AX
0D03:0005 B0A1            MOV      AL,A1
0D03:0007 98              CBW
0D03:0008 99              CWD
0D03:0009 CB              RETF
-G 5

AX=0000  BX=0000  CX=000A  DX=0000  SP=003C  BP=0000  SI=0000  DI=0000
DS=0CF3  ES=0CF3  SS=0D04  CS=0D03  IP=0005   NV UP EI PL NZ NA PO NC
0D03:0005 B0A1            MOV      AL,A1
-T

AX=00A1  BX=0000  CX=000A  DX=0000  SP=003C  BP=0000  SI=0000  DI=0000
DS=0CF3  ES=0CF3  SS=0D04  CS=0D03  IP=0007   NV UP EI PL NZ NA PO NC
0D03:0007 98              CBW
-T

AX=FFA1  BX=0000  CX=000A  DX=0000  SP=003C  BP=0000  SI=0000  DI=0000
DS=0CF3  ES=0CF3  SS=0D04  CS=0D03  IP=0008   NV UP EI PL NZ NA PO NC
0D03:0008 99              CWD
-T

AX=FFA1  BX=0000  CX=000A  DX=FFFF  SP=003C  BP=0000  SI=0000  DI=0000
DS=0CF3  ES=0CF3  SS=0D04  CS=0D03  IP=0009   NV UP EI PL NZ NA PO NC
0D03:0009 CB              RETF
-G

Program terminated normally
-Q

A>
```

(c)

Figure 4.19 (Continued)

168

4.5 LOGIC INSTRUCTIONS

The 8088 has instructions for performing the logic operations *AND, OR, exclusive-OR,* and *NOT*. As shown in Fig. 4.20(a), the AND, OR, and XOR instructions perform their respective logic operations bit by bit on the specified source and destination operands, the result being represented by the final contents of the destination operand. Figure 4.20(b) shows the allowed operand combinations for the AND, OR, and XOR instructions.

For example, the instruction

$$AND \ AX,BX$$

causes the contents of BX to be ANDed with the contents of AX. The result is reflected by the new contents of AX. If AX contains 1234_{16} and BX contains $000F_{16}$, the result produced by the instruction is

$$1234_{16} \cdot 000F_{16} = 0001001000110100_2 \cdot 0000000000001111_2$$

$$= 0000000000000100_2$$

$$= 0004_{16}$$

Mnemonic	Meaning	Format	Operation	Flags Affected
AND	Logical AND	AND D,S	$(S) \cdot (D) \rightarrow (D)$	OF, SF, ZF, AF, PF, CF
OR	Logical Inclusive-OR	OR D,S	$(S) + (D) \rightarrow (D)$	OF, SF, ZF, AF, PF, CF
XOR	Logical Exclusive-OR	XOR D,S	$(S) \oplus (D) \rightarrow (D)$	OF, SF, ZF, AF, PF, CF
NOT	Logical NOT	NOT D	$(\overline{D}) \rightarrow (D)$	None

(a)

Destination	Source
Register	Register
Register	Memory
Memory	Register
Register	Immediate
Memory	Immediate
Accumulator	Immediate

(b)

Destination
Register
Memory

(c)

Figure 4.20   (a) Logic instructions. (b) Allowed operands for the AND, OR, and XOR instructions. (c) Allowed operands for the NOT instruction.

This result is stored in the destination operand.

$$(AX) = 0004_{16}$$

In this way we see that the AND instruction was used to mask off the 12 most significant bits of the destination operand.

The NOT logic instruction differs from those for AND, OR, and exclusive-OR in that it operates on a single operand. Looking at Fig. 4.20(c), which shows the allowed operands of the NOT instruction, we see that this operand can be the contents of an internal register or a location in memory.

EXAMPLE 4.20

Describe the result of executing the following sequence of instructions.

```
MOV  AL,01010101B
AND  AL,00011111B
OR   AL,11000000B
XOR  AL,00001111B
NOT  AL
```

SOLUTION   The first instruction moves the immediate operand 01010101_2 into the AL register. This loads the data that are to be manipulated with the logic instructions. The next instruction performs a bit-by-bit AND operation of the contents of AL with immediate operand 00011111_2. This gives

$$01010101_2 \cdot 00011111_2 = 00010101_2$$

$$(AL) = 00010101_2 = 15_{16}$$

This result is produced in destination register AL. Note that this operation has masked off the three most significant bits of AL. The next instruction performs a bit-by-bit logical OR of the present contents of AL with immediate operand $C0_{16}$. This gives

$$00010101_2 + 11000000_2 = 11010101_2$$

$$(AL) = 11010101_2 = D5_{16}$$

This operation is equivalent to setting the two most significant bits of AL.

The fourth instruction is an exclusive-OR operation of the contents of AL with immediate operand 00001111_2. We get

$$11010101_2 \oplus 00001111_2 = 11011010_2$$

$$(AL) = 11011010_2 = DA_{16}$$

Note that this operation complements the logic state of those bits in AL that are ones in the immediate operand.

The last instruction, NOT AL, inverts each bit of AL. Therefore, the final contents of AL become

$$(AL) = \overline{11011010_2} = 00100101_2 = 25_{16}$$

These results are summarized in Fig. 4.21.

Instruction	(AL)
MOV AL,01010101B	01010101
AND AL,00011111B	00010101
OR AL,11000000B	11010101
XOR AL,00001111B	11011010
NOT AL	00100101

Figure 4.21 Results of example program using logic instructions.

EXAMPLE 4.21

Use the IBM PC's debugger to verify the operation of the program in Example 4.20.

SOLUTION   After the debugger is brought up, the line-by-line assembler is used to enter the program as shown in Fig. 4.22. The first instruction is executed by issuing the T command

$$-T \qquad (\rlap{\_}\rfloor)$$

The trace dump given in Fig. 4.22 shows that the value 55_{16} has been loaded into the AL register.

The second instruction is executed by issuing another T command.

$$-T \qquad (\rlap{\_}\rfloor)$$

Execution of this instruction causes $1F_{16}$ to be ANDed with the value 55_{16} in AL. Looking at the trace information displayed in Fig. 4.22, we see that the three most significant bits of AL have been masked off to produce the result 15_{16}.

The third instruction is executed in the same way.

$$-T \qquad (\rlap{\_}\rfloor)$$

It causes the value $C0_{16}$ to be ORed with the value $1F_{16}$ in AL. This gives the result $D5_{16}$ in AL.

A fourth T command is used to execute the XOR instruction.

$$-T \qquad (\hookleftarrow)$$

and the trace dump that results shows that the new value in AL is DA_{16}.

The last instruction is a NOT instruction and its execution with the command

$$-T \qquad (\hookleftarrow)$$

causes the bits of DA_{16} to be inverted. This gives 25_{16} as the final result in AL.

```
A>DEBUG
-A
0CDE:0100 MOV AL,55
0CDE:0102 AND AL,1F
0CDE:0104 OR AL,C0
0CDE:0106 XOR AL,0F
0CDE:0108 NOT AL
0CDE:010A
-T

AX=0055  BX=0000  CX=0000  DX=0000  SP=FFEE  BP=0000  SI=0000  DI=0000
DS=0CDE  ES=0CDE  SS=0CDE  CS=0CDE  IP=0102    NV UP EI PL NZ NA PO NC
0CDE:0102 241F         AND      AL,1F
-T

AX=0015  BX=0000  CX=0000  DX=0000  SP=FFEE  BP=0000  SI=0000  DI=0000
DS=0CDE  ES=0CDE  SS=0CDE  CS=0CDE  IP=0104    NV UP EI PL NZ NA PO NC
0CDE:0104 0CC0         OR       AL,C0
-T

AX=00D5  BX=0000  CX=0000  DX=0000  SP=FFEE  BP=0000  SI=0000  DI=0000
DS=0CDE  ES=0CDE  SS=0CDE  CS=0CDE  IP=0106    NV UP EI NG NZ NA PO NC
0CDE:0106 340F         XOR      AL,0F
-T

AX=00DA  BX=0000  CX=0000  DX=0000  SP=FFEE  BP=0000  SI=0000  DI=0000
DS=0CDE  ES=0CDE  SS=0CDE  CS=0CDE  IP=0108    NV UP EI NG NZ NA PO NC
0CDE:0108 F6D0         NOT      AL
-T

AX=0025  BX=0000  CX=0000  DX=0000  SP=FFEE  BP=0000  SI=0000  DI=0000
DS=0CDE  ES=0CDE  SS=0CDE  CS=0CDE  IP=010A    NV UP EI NG NZ NA PO NC
0CDE:010A 68          DB       68
-Q

A>
```

Figure 4.22 Display sequence for Example 4.21.

4.6 SHIFT INSTRUCTIONS

The four *shift instructions* of the 8088 can perform two basic types of shift operations. They are the *logical shift* and the *arithmetic shift*. Moreover, each of these operations can be performed to the right or to the left. The shift instructions are *shift logical left* (SHL), *shift arithmetic left* (SAL), *shift logical right* (SHR), and *shift arithmetic right* (SAR).

The logical shift instructions, SHL and SHR, are described in Fig. 4.23(a). Notice in Fig. 4.23(b) that the destination operand, the data whose bits are to be shifted, can be either the contents of an internal register or a storage location in memory. Moreover, the source operand can be specified in two ways. If it is assigned the value of 1, a 1-bit shift will take place. For instance, as illustrated in Fig. 4.24(a), executing

```
SHL AX,1
```

causes the 16-bit contents of the AX register to be shifted one bit position to the left. Here we see that the vacated LSB location is filled with zero and the bit shifted out of the MSB is saved in CF.

Mnemonic	Meaning	Format	Operation	Flags Affected
SAL/SHL	Shift arithmetic left/shift logical left	SAL/SHL D,Count	Shift the (D) left by the number of bit positions equal to Count and fill the vacated bits positions on the right with zeros	OF, CF
SHR	Shift logical right	SHR D,Count	Shift the (D) right by the number of bit positions equal to Count and fill the vacated bit positions on the left with zeros	OF, CF
SAR	Shift arithmetic right	SAR D,Count	Shift the (D) right by the number of bit positions equal to Count and fill the vacated bit positions on the left with the original most significant bit	OF, SF, ZF, AF, PF, CF

(a)

Destination	Count
Register	1
Register	CL
Memory	1
Memory	CL

(b)

Figure 4.23   (a) Shift instructions. (b) Allowed operands.

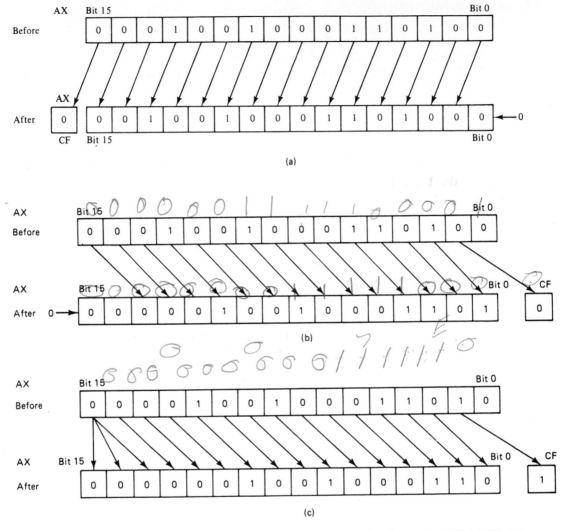

Figure 4.24   (a) Results of executing SHL AX,1. (b) Results of executing SHR AX,CL. (c) Results of executing SAR AX,CL.

On the other hand, if the source operand is specified as CL instead of one, the count in this register represents the number of bit positions the contents of the operand are to be shifted. This permits the count to be defined under software control and allows a range of shifts from 1 to 255 bits.

An example of an instruction specified in this way is

```
SHR AX,CL
```

Assuming that CL contains the value 02_{16}, the logical shift right that occurs is as shown in Fig. 4.24(b). Notice that the two MSBs have been filled with zeros and the last bit shifted out at the LSB, which is zero, is placed in the carry flag.

In an arithmetic shift to the left, SAL operation, the vacated bits at the right of the operand are filled with zeros, whereas in an arithmetic shift to the right, SAR operation, the vacated bits at the left are filled with the value of the original MSB of the operand. Thus, in an arithmetic shift to the right, the original sign of the number is extended. This operation is equivalent to division by powers of 2 as long as the bits shifted out of the LSB are zeros.

EXAMPLE 4.22

Assume that CL contains 02_{16} and AX contains $091A_{16}$. Determine the new contents of AX and the carry flag after the instruction

```
SAR AX,CL
```

is executed.

SOLUTION   Figure 4.24(c) shows the effect of executing the instruction. Here we see that since CL contains 02_{16} a shift right by two bit locations takes place, and the original sign bit, which is logic 0, is extended to the two vacated bit positions. Moreover, the last bit shifted out from the LSB location is placed in CF. This makes CF equal to 1. Therefore, the results produced by execution of the instruction are

$$(AX) = 0246_{16}$$

and

$$(CF) = 1_2$$

EXAMPLE 4.23

Verify the operation of the SAR instruction in Example 4.22 by executing with the DEBUG program on the IBM PC.

SOLUTION   After invoking the debugger, we enter the instruction by assembling it with the command

```
-A                       (↵)
0CDE:0100  SAR AX,CL  (↵)
0CDE:0102                (↵)
-
```

Next, registers AX and CL are loaded with data and the carry flag is reset. This is done with the command sequence

```
-R AX                        (↵)
AX 0000
:091A                        (↵)
-R CX                        (↵)
CX 0000
:2                           (↵)
-R F                         (↵)
NV UP EI PL NZ NA PO NC - (↵)
-
```

Notice that the carry flag was already clear, so no status entry was made.
  Now the instruction is executed with the T command

$$-T \qquad (↵)$$

Note in Fig. 4.25 that the value in AX has become 0246_{16} and a carry (CY) has occurred. These results are identical to those obtained in Example 4.22.

```
A>DEBUG
-A
0CDE:0100 SAR AX,CL
0CDE:0102
-R AX
AX 0000
:091A
-R CX
CX 0000
:2
-R F
NV UP EI PL NZ NA PO NC  -
-T

AX=0246  BX=0000  CX=0002  DX=0000  SP=FFEE  BP=0000  SI=0000  DI=0000
DS=0CDE  ES=0CDE  SS=0CDE  CS=0CDE  IP=0102   NV UP EI PL NZ NA PO CY
0CDE:0102 241F          AND      AL,1F
-Q

A>
```

Figure 4.25 Display sequence for Example 4.23.

4.7 ROTATE INSTRUCTIONS

Another group of instructions, known as the *rotate instructions,* are similar to the shift instructions we just introduced. This group, as shown in Fig. 4.26(a), includes the *rotate left* (ROL), *rotate right* (ROR), *rotate left through carry* (RCL), and *rotate right through carry* (RCR) instructions.

Mnemonic	Meaning	Format	Operation	Flags Affected
ROL	Rotate left	ROL D,Count	Rotate the (D) left by the number of bit positions equal to Count. Each bit shifted out from the leftmost bit goes back into the rightmost bit position.	OF, CF
ROR	Rotate right	ROR D,Count	Rotate the (D) right by the number of bit positions equal to Count. Each bit shifted out from the rightmost bit goes into the leftmost bit position.	OF, CF
RCL	Rotate left through carry	RCL D,Count	Same as ROL except carry is attached to (D) for rotation.	OF, CF
RCR	Rotate right through carry	RCR D,Count	Same as ROR except carry is attached to (D) for rotation.	OF, CF

(a)

Destination	Count
Register	1
Register	CL
Memory	1
Memory	CL

(b)

Figure 4.26   (a) Rotate instructions. (b) Allowed operands.

As shown in Fig. 4.26(b), the rotate instructions are similar to the shift instructions in several ways. They have the ability to rotate the contents of either an internal register or storage location in memory. Also, the rotation that takes place can be from 1 to 255 bit positions to the left or to the right. Moreover, in the case of a multibit rotate, the number of bit positions to be rotated is again specified by the contents of CL. Their difference from the shift instructions lies in the fact that the bits moved out at either the MSB or LSB end are not lost; instead, they are reloaded at the other end.

As an example, let us look at the operation of the ROL instruction. Execution of ROL causes the contents of the selected operand to be rotated left the specified number of bit positions. Each bit shifted out at the MSB end is reloaded at the LSB end. Moreover, the content of CF reflects the state of the last bit that was shifted out. For instance, the instruction

```
ROL AX,1
```

causes a 1-bit rotate to the left. Figure 4.27(a) shows the result produced by executing this instruction. Notice that the original value of bit 15 is zero. This value has been rotated into CF and bit 0 of AX. All other bits have been rotated one bit position to the left.

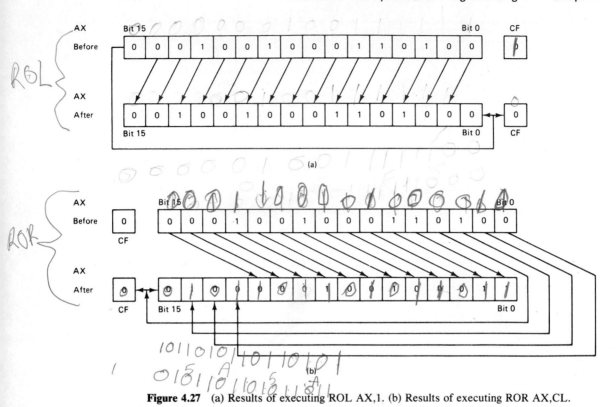

Figure 4.27 (a) Results of executing ROL AX,1. (b) Results of executing ROR AX,CL.

The ROR instruction operates the same way as ROL except that it causes data to be rotated to the right instead of to the left. For example, execution of

ROR AX,CL

causes the contents of AX to be rotated right by the number of bit positions specified in CL. The result for CL equal to four is illustrated in Fig. 4.27(b).

The other two rotate instructions, RCL and RCR, differ from ROL and ROR in that the bits are rotated through the carry flag. Figure 4.28 illustrates the rotation that takes place due to execution of the RCL instruction. Notice that the value returned to bit 0 is the prior contents of CF and not bit 15. The value shifted out of bit 15 goes into the carry flag. Thus the bits rotate through carry.

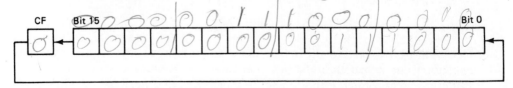

Figure 4.28 Rotation caused by execution of the RCL instruction.

EXAMPLE 4.24

What is the result in BX and CF after execution of the following instruction?

$$RCR \quad BX,CL$$

Assume that, prior to execution of the instruction, $(CL) = 04_{16}$, $(BX) = 1234_{16}$, and $(CF) = 0$.

SOLUTION   The original contents of BX are

$$(BX) = 0001001000110100_2 = 1234_{16}$$

Execution of the RCR instruction causes a 4-bit rotate right through carry to take place on the data in BX. Therefore, the original content of bit 3, which is zero, resides in carry; $CF = 0$ and 1000_2 has been reloaded from bit 15. The resulting contents of BX are

$$(BX) = 1000000100100011_2 = 8123_{16}$$

$$(CF) = 0_2$$

EXAMPLE 4.25

Use the IBM PC debugger to verify the operation of the RCR instruction in Example 4.24.

SOLUTION   After loading DEBUG, the instruction is assembled into memory with the command

```
        -A                      (↵)
        0CDE:0100 RCR BX,CL
        0CDE:0102               (↵)
```

Next, BX and CX are loaded with data and CF is cleared by issuing the commands

```
        -R BX                   (↵)
        BX 0000
        :1234                   (↵)
        -R CX                   (↵)
```

```
CX 0000
:4                                    (↵)
-R F                                  (↵)
NV UP EI PL NZ NA PO NC - (↵)
-
```

Notice that CF is already cleared (NC); therefore, no entry is made for the flag register command.

Now we can execute the instruction with the command

$$-T \qquad (↵)$$

Looking at the trace information displayed in Fig. 4.29, we see that the new contents of BX are 8123_{16} and CF equals NC. These are the same results as obtained in Example 4.24.

```
A>DEBUG
-A
OCDE:0100 RCR BX,CL
OCDE:0102
-R BX
BX 0000
:1234
-R CX
CX 0000
:4
-R F
NV UP EI PL NZ NA PO NC  -
-T

AX=0000  BX=8123  CX=0004  DX=0000  SP=FFEE  BP=0000  SI=0000  DI=0000
DS=OCDE  ES=OCDE  SS=OCDE  CS=OCDE  IP=0102   OV UP EI PL NZ NA PO NC
OCDE:0102 241F           AND      AL,1F
-Q

A>
```

Figure 4.29 Display sequence for Example 4.25.

ASSIGNMENTS

Section 4.2

1. List five groups of instructions.

Section 4.3

2. Explain what operation is performed by each of the instructions that follows.
  (a) MOV AX,0110H
  (b) MOV DI,AX

    (c) MOV BL,AL
    (d) MOV [0100H],AX
    (e) MOV [BX+DI],AX
    (f) MOV [DI]+4,AX
    (g) MOV [BX][DI]+4,AX

3. Assume that registers AX, BX, and DI are all initialized to 0000_{16} and that all data storage memory has been cleared. Determine the location and value of the destination operand as instructions (a) through (g) from problem 2 are executed as a sequence.

4. Write an instruction sequence that will initialize the ES register with the immediate value 1010_{16}.

5. Write an instruction that will save the contents of the ES register in memory at address DS:1000H.

6. Why will the instruction MOV CL,AX result in an error when it is assembled?

7. Describe the operation performed by each of the instructions that follows.
    (a) XCHG AX,BX
    (b) XCHG BX,DI
    (c) XCHG DATA,AX
    (d) XCHG [BX+DI],AX

8. If register BX contains the value 0100_{16}, register DI contains 0010_{16}, and register DS contains 1075_{16}, what physical memory location is swapped when the instruction in problem 7(d) is executed?

9. Assuming that (AL) = 0010_{16}, (BX) = 0100_{16}, and (DS) = 1000_{16}, what happens if the XLAT instruction is executed?

10. Write a single instruction that will load AX from address 0200_{16} and DS from address 0202_{16}.

11. Two code-conversion tables starting with offsets TABL1 and TABL2 in the current data segment are to be accessed. Write a routine that initializes the needed registers and then replaces the contents of memory locations MEM1 and MEM2 (offsets in the data segment) by the equivalent converted codes from the code-conversion tables.

Section 4.4

12. What operation is performed by each of the following instructions?
    (a) ADD   AX,00FFH
    (b) ADC   SI,AX
    (c) INC   BYTE PTR [0100H]
    (d) SUB   DL,BL
    (e) SBB   DL,[0200H]
    (f) DEC   BYTE PTR [DI+BX]
    (g) NEG   BYTE PTR [DI]+0010H
    (h) MUL   DX
    (i) IMUL BYTE PTR [BX+SI]
    (j) DIV   BYTE PTR [SI]+0030H
    (k) IDIV BYTE PTR [BX][SI]+0030H

13. Assume that the state of 8088's registers and memory is as follows just prior to the execution of each instruction in problem 12.

$$(AX) = 0010H$$
$$(BX) = 0020H$$
$$(CX) = 0030H$$
$$(DX) = 0040H$$
$$(SI) = 0100H$$
$$(DI) = 0200H$$
$$(CF) = 1H$$
$$(DS:100H) = 10H$$
$$(DS:101H) = 00H$$
$$(DS:120H) = FFH$$
$$(DS:121H) = FFH$$
$$(DS:130H) = 08H$$
$$(DS:131H) = 00H$$
$$(DS:150H) = 02H$$
$$(DS:151H) = 00H$$
$$(DS:200H) = 30H$$
$$(DS:201H) = 00H$$
$$(DS:210H) = 40H$$
$$(DS:211H) = 00H$$
$$(DS:220H) = 30H$$
$$(DS:221H) = 00H$$

What is the result produced in the destination operand by executing instructions (a) through (k)?

14. Write an instruction that will add the immediate value $111F_{16}$ and the carry flag to the contents of the data register.

15. Write an instruction that will subtract the word contents of the storage location pointed to by the base register and the carry flag from the accumulator.

16. Two word-wide unsigned integers are stored at the memory addresses $0A00_{16}$ and $0A02_{16}$, respectively. Write an instruction sequence that computes and stores their sum, difference, product, and quotient. Store these results at consecutive memory locations starting at address $0A10_{16}$ in memory. To obtain the difference, subtract the integer at $0A02_{16}$ from the integer at $0A00_{16}$. For the division, divide the integer at $0A00_{16}$ by the integer at $0A02_{16}$. Use register indirect relative addressing mode to store the various results.

17. Assuming that $(AX) = 0123_{16}$ and $(BL) = 10_{16}$, what will be the new contents of AX after executing the instruction DIV BL?

18. What instruction is used to adjust the result of an addition that processed packed BCD numbers?

19. Which instruction is provided in the instruction set of the 8088 to adjust the result of a subtraction that involved ASCII coded numbers?

20. If AL contains $A0_{16}$, what happens when the instruction CBW is executed?

21. If the value in AX is $7FFF_{16}$, what happens when the instruction CWD is executed?

22. Two byte-sized BCD integers are stored at the symbolic addresses NUM1 and NUM2, respectively. Write an instruction sequence to generate their difference and store it at NUM3. The difference is to be formed by subtracting the value at NUM1 from that at NUM2.

Section 4.5

23. Describe the operation performed by each of the following instructions.
  (a) AND BYTE PTR[0300H] , 0FH
  (b) AND DX,[SI]
  (c) OR   [BX+DI],AX
  (d) OR   BYTE PTR [BX][DI]+10H,0F0H
  (e) XOR AX,[SI + BX]
  (f) NOT BYTE PTR [0300H]
  (g) NOT WORD PTR [BX+DI]

24. Assume that the state of 8088's registers and memory is as follows just prior to execution of each instruction in problem 23.

$$(AX) = 5555H$$
$$(BX) = 0010H$$
$$(CX) = 0010H$$
$$(DX) = AAAAH$$
$$(SI) = 0100H$$
$$(DI) = 0200H$$
$$(DS:100H) = 0FH$$
$$(DS:101H) = F0H$$
$$(DS:110H) = 00H$$
$$(DS:111H) = FFH$$
$$(DS:200H) = 30H$$
$$(DS:201H) = 00H$$
$$(DS:210H) = AAH$$
$$(DS:211H) = AAH$$
$$(DS:220H) = 55H$$
$$(DS:221H) = 55H$$
$$(DS:300H) = AAH$$
$$(DS:301H) = 55H$$

What is the result produced in the destination operand by executing instructions (a) through (g)?

25. Write an instruction that when executed will mask off all but bit 7 of the contents of the data register.

26. Write an instruction that will mask off all but bit 7 of the word of data stored at address DS:0100H.

27. Specify the relation between the old and new contents of AX after executing the following instructions.

```
NOT AX
ADD AX,1
```

28. Write an instruction sequence that generates a byte-sized integer in the memory location identified by label RESULT. The value of the byte integer is to be calculated as from the logic equation:

$$(RESULT) = (AL) \cdot (NUM1) + (\overline{\overline{NUM2}}) \cdot (AL) + (BL)$$

Assume that all parameters are byte sized, NUM1 and NUM2 are the addresses of memory locations.

Section 4.6

29. Explain what operation is performed by each of the instructions that follows.
  (a) SHL DX, CL
  (b) SHL BYTE PTR [0400H],CL
  (c) SHR BYTE PTR [DI],1
  (d) SHR BYTE PTR [DI+BX],CL
  (e) SAR WORD PTR [BX+DI],1
  (f) SAR WORD PTR [BX] [DI]+10H,CL

30. Assume that the state of 8088's registers and memory is as follows just prior to execution of each instruction in problem 29.

$$
\begin{aligned}
(AX) &= 0000H \\
(BX) &= 0010H \\
(CX) &= 0105H \\
(DX) &= 1111H \\
(SI) &= 0100H \\
(DI) &= 0200H \\
(CF) &= 0 \\
(DS:100H) &= 0FH \\
(DS:200H) &= 22H \\
(DS:201H) &= 44H \\
(DS:210H) &= 55H \\
(DS:211H) &= AAH \\
(DS:220H) &= AAH \\
(DS:221H) &= 55H \\
(DS:400H) &= AAH \\
(DS:401H) &= 55H
\end{aligned}
$$

What is the result produced in the destination operand by executing instructions (a) through (f)?

31. Write an instruction that shifts the contents of the count register left by one bit position.

32. Write an instruction sequence that when executed shifts left by eight bit positions the contents of the word-wide memory location pointed to by the address in the destination index register.

33. Identify the condition under which the contents of AX would remain unchanged after executing any of the instructions that follow.

```
MOV CL,4
SHL AX,CL
SHR AX,CL
```

34. Implement the following operation using shift and arithmetic instructions.

$$7(AX) - 5(BX) - (BX)/8 \rightarrow (AX)$$

Assume that all parameters are word sized.

Section 4.7

35. Describe what happens as each of the instructions that follows is executed by the 8088.
  (a) ROL DX, CL
  (b) RCL BYTE PTR [0400H],CL
  (c) ROR BYTE PTR [DI],1
  (d) ROR BYTE PTR [DI+BX],CL
  (e) RCR WORD PTR [BX+DI],1
  (f) RCR WORD PTR [BX] [DI]+10H,CL

36. Assume that the state of 8088's registers and memory is as follows just prior to execution of each of the instructions in problem 35.

$$(AX) = 0000H$$
$$(BX) = 0010H$$
$$(CX) = 0105H$$
$$(DX) = 1111H$$
$$(SI) = 0100H$$
$$(DI) = 0200H$$
$$(CF) = 1$$
$$(DS:100H) = 0FH$$
$$(DS:200H) = 22H$$
$$(DS:201H) = 44H$$
$$(DS:210H) = 55H$$
$$(DS:211H) = AAH$$
$$(DS:220H) = AAH$$
$$(DS:221H) = 55H$$
$$(DS:400H) = AAH$$
$$(DS:401H) = 55H$$

What is the result produced in the destination operand by executing instructions (a) through (f)?

37. Write an instruction sequence that when executed rotates left through carry by one bit position the contents of the word-wide memory location pointed to by the address in the base register.

38. Write a program that saves the content of bit 5 in AL in BX as a word.

8088/8086 Microprocessor Programming 2

5.1 INTRODUCTION

In Chapter 4 we discussed many of the instructions that can be executed by the 8088 and 8086 microprocessors. Furthermore, we used these instructions in simple programs. In this chapter, we introduce the rest of the instruction set and at the same time cover some more complicated programming techniques. The following topics are discussed in this chapter:

1. Flag control instructions
2. Compare instruction
3. Jump instructions
4. Subroutines and subroutine handling instructions
5. The loop and loop handling instructions
6. Strings and string handling instructions

5.2 FLAG CONTROL INSTRUCTIONS

The 8088 microprocessor has a set of flags that either monitors the status of executing instructions or controls options available in its operation. These flags were described in detail in Chapter 2. The instruction set includes a group of instructions that when executed directly affects the state of the flags. These instructions, shown in Fig. 5.1, are *load AH from flags* (LAHF), *store AH into flags* (SAHF), *clear carry* (CLC), *set carry* (STC), *complement carry* (CMC), *clear interrupt* (CLI), and *set interrupt* (STI). A few more instructions exist that can directly affect the flags; however, we will not cover them until later in the chapter when we introduce the subroutine and string instructions.

Looking at Fig. 5.1, we see that the first two instructions, LAHF and SAHF, can be used either to read the flags or to change them, respectively. Notice that the data transfer that takes place is always between the AH register and the flag register. For instance, we may want to start an operation with certain flags set or reset. Assume that we want to preset all flags to logic 1. To do this, we can first load AH with FF_{16} and then execute the SAHF instruction.

Mnemonic	Meaning	Operation	Flags Affected
LAHF	Load AH from flags	(AH) ← (Flags)	None
SAHF	Store AH into flags	(Flags) ← (AH)	SF, ZF, AF, PF, CF
CLC	Clear carry flag	(CF) ← 0	CF
STC	Set carry flag	(CF) ← 1	CF
CMC	Complement carry flag	(CF) ← $(\overline{CF})$	CF
CLI	Clear interrupt flag	(IF) ← 0	IF
STI	Set interrupt flag	(IF) ← 1	IF

Figure 5.1   Flag control instructions.

EXAMPLE 5.1

Write an instruction sequence to save the current contents of the 8088's flags in memory location MEM1 and then reload the flags with the contents of memory location MEM2.

SOLUTION To save the current flags, we must first load them into the AH register and then move them to the location MEM1. The instructions that do this are

```
LAHF
MOV MEM1,AH
```

Similarly, to load the flags with the contents of MEM2, we must first copy the contents of MEM2 into AH and then store the contents of AH into the flags. The instructions for this are

```
MOV AH,MEM2
SAHF
```

The entire instruction sequence is shown in Fig. 5.2.

```
LAHF
MOV     MEM1,AH
MOV     AH,MEM2
SAHF
```

Figure 5.2 Instruction sequence for saving the contents of the flag register and reloading it from memory.

EXAMPLE 5.2

Use the DEBUG program on the IBM PC to enter the instruction sequence in Example 5.1 starting at memory address 00110_{16}. Assign memory addresses 00150_{16} and 00151_{16} to symbols MEM1 and MEM2, respectively. Then initialize the values of MEM1 and MEM2 to FF_{16} and 01_{16}, respectively. Verify the operation of the instructions by executing them one after the other with the TRACE command.

SOLUTION As shown in Fig. 5.3, the DEBUG program is called up with the DOS command

```
                A>DEBUG      (↵)
```

Now we are ready to assemble the program into memory. This is done by making the ASSEMBLE command entries

```
        -A 0:0110               (↵)
        0000:0110 LAHF          (↵)
        0000:0111 MOV [0150],AH (↵)
        0000:0115 MOV AH,[0151] (↵)
        0000:0119 SAHF          (↵)
```

Now the values of MEM1 and MEM2 are initialized with the ENTER command

```
-E 0:0150 FF 01          (↵)
```

Moreover, the registers CS, IP, and DS must be initialized with the values 0000_{16}, 0110_{16}, and 0000_{16}, respectively. This is done with the commands

```
-R CS     (↵)
CS 0CDE
:0        (↵)
-R IP     (↵)
IP 0100
:0110     (↵)
-R DS     (↵)
DS 0CDE
:0        (↵)
```

Before going further, let us verify the initialization of the internal registers. This is done by displaying their state with the R command

```
-R      (↵)
```

Looking at the information displayed in Fig. 5.3, we see that all three registers have been correctly initialized.

Now we are ready to step through the execution of the program. The first instruction is executed with the command

```
-T      (↵)
```

Notice from the displayed trace information in Fig. 5.3 that the contents of the status register, which are 02_{16}, have been copied into the AH register.

The second instruction is executed by issuing another T command

```
-T      (↵)
```

This instruction causes the status, which is now in AH, to be saved in memory at address 0000:0150. The fact that this operation has occurred is verified with the D command

```
-D 150 151    (↵)
```

In Fig. 5.3, we see that the data held at address 0000:0150 is displayed by this command as 02_{16}. This verifies that status was saved at MEM1.

The third instruction is now executed with the command

```
-T      (↵)
```

Its function is to copy the new status from MEM2 (0000:0151) into the AH register. From the data displayed in the earlier D command, we see that this value is 01_{16}. Looking at the displayed information for the third instruction, we find that 01_{16} has been copied into AH.

The last instruction is executed with another T command and, as shown by its trace information in Fig. 5.3, it has caused the carry flag to set. That is, CF is displayed with the value CY.

```
A>DEBUG
-A 0:0110
0000:0110 LAHF
0000:0111 MOV [0150],AH
0000:0115 MOV AH,[0151]
0000:0119 SAHF
0000:011A
-E 0:0150 FF 01
-R CS
CS 0CDE
:0
-R IP
IP 0100
:0110
-R DS
DS 0CDE
:0
-R
AX=0000  BX=0000  CX=0000  DX=0000  SP=FFEE  BP=0000  SI=0000  DI=0000
DS=0000  ES=0CDE  SS=0CDE  CS=0000  IP=0110   NV UP EI PL NZ NA PO NC
0000:0110 9F            LAHF
-T

AX=0200  BX=0000  CX=0000  DX=0000  SP=FFEE  BP=0000  SI=0000  DI=0000
DS=0000  ES=0CDE  SS=0CDE  CS=0000  IP=0111   NV UP EI PL NZ NA PO NC
0000:0111 88265001      MOV    [0150],AH                        DS:0150=FF
-T

AX=0200  BX=0000  CX=0000  DX=0000  SP=FFEE  BP=0000  SI=0000  DI=0000
DS=0000  ES=0CDE  SS=0CDE  CS=0000  IP=0115   NV UP EI PL NZ NA PO NC
0000:0115 8A265101      MOV    AH,[0151]                        DS:0151=01
-D 150 151
0000:0150  02 01                                                ..
-T

AX=0100  BX=0000  CX=0000  DX=0000  SP=FFEE  BP=0000  SI=0000  DI=0000
DS=0000  ES=0CDE  SS=0CDE  CS=0000  IP=0119   NV UP EI PL NZ NA PO NC
0000:0119 9E            SAHF
-T

AX=0100  BX=0000  CX=0000  DX=0000  SP=FFEE  BP=0000  SI=0000  DI=0000
DS=0000  ES=0CDE  SS=0CDE  CS=0000  IP=011A   NV UP EI PL NZ NA PO CY
0000:011A 0000          ADD    [BX+SI],AL                       DS:0000=E8
-Q

A>
```

Figure 5.3 Display sequence for Example 5.2.

The next three instructions, CLC, STC, and CMC, as shown in Fig. 5.1, are used to manipulate the carry flag. They permit CF to be cleared, set, or complemented to its inverse logic level, respectively. For example, if CF is 1 and the CMC instruction is executed, it becomes 0.

The last two instructions are used to manipulate the interrupt flag. Executing the clear interrupt (CLI) instruction sets IF to logic 0 and disables the interrupt interface. On the other hand, executing the STI instruction sets IF to 1, and the microprocessor starts accepting interrupts from that point on.

EXAMPLE 5.3

Of the three carry flag instructions CLC, STC, and CMC, only one is really an independent instruction. That is, the operation that it provides cannot be performed by a series of the other two instructions. Determine which one of the carry instructions is the independent instruction.

SOLUTION Let us begin with the CLC instruction. The clear carry operation can be performed by an STC instruction followed by a CMC instruction. Therefore, CLC is not an independent instruction. Moreover, the operation of the set carry (STC) instruction is equivalent to the operation performed by a CLC instruction, followed by a CMC instruction. Thus, STC is also not an independent instruction. On the other hand, the operation performed by the last instruction, complement carry (CMC), cannot be expressed in terms of the CLC and STC instructions. Therefore, it is the independent instruction.

EXAMPLE 5.4

Verify the operation of the following instructions that affect the carry flag,

```
CLC
STC
CMC
```

by executing them with the debugger on the IBM PC. Start with CF equal to one (CY).

SOLUTION After bringing up the debugger, we enter the instructions with the ASSEMBLE command as

```
                              −A                (↵)
                              0CDE:0100 CLC (↵)
                              0CDE:0101 STC (↵)
                              0CDE:0102 CMC (↵)
                              0CDE:0103         (↵)
                              −
```

These inputs are shown in Fig. 5.4.

Next, the carry flag is initialized to CY with the R command

```
              −R  F          (↵)
              NV UP EI PL NZ NA PO NC −CY        (↵)
```

and in Fig. 5.4 the updated status is displayed with another R command to verify that CF is set to the CY state.

Now the first instruction is executed with the TRACE command

```
                      −T       (↵)
```

Looking at the displayed state information in Fig. 5.4, we see that CF has been cleared and its new state is NC.

The other two instructions are also executed with T commands and, as shown in Fig. 5.4, the STC instruction sets CF (CY in the state dump) and CMC inverts CF (NC in the state dump).

```
A>DEBUG
−A
0CDE:0100 CLC
0CDE:0101 STC
0CDE:0102 CMC
0CDE:0103
−R F
NV UP EI PL NZ NA PO NC  −CY
−R F
NV UP EI PL NZ NA PO CY  −
−T

AX=0000  BX=0000  CX=0000  DX=0000  SP=FFEE  BP=0000  SI=0000  DI=0000
DS=0CDE  ES=0CDE  SS=0CDE  CS=0CDE  IP=0101  NV UP EI PL NZ NA PO NC
0CDE:0101 F9             STC
−T

AX=0000  BX=0000  CX=0000  DX=0000  SP=FFEE  BP=0000  SI=0000  DI=0000
DS=0CDE  ES=0CDE  SS=0CDE  CS=0CDE  IP=0102  NV UP EI PL NZ NA PO CY
0CDE:0102 F5             CMC
−T

AX=0000  BX=0000  CX=0000  DX=0000  SP=FFEE  BP=0000  SI=0000  DI=0000
DS=0CDE  ES=0CDE  SS=0CDE  CS=0CDE  IP=0103  NV UP EI PL NZ NA PO NC
0CDE:0103 1F             POP     DS
−Q

A>
```

Figure 5.4   Display sequence for Example 5.4.

5.3 COMPARE INSTRUCTION

An instruction is included in the instruction set of the 8088 that can be used to compare two 8-bit or 16-bit numbers. It is the *compare* (CMP) instruction of Fig. 5.5(a). Figure 5.5(b) shows that the operands can reside in a storage location in memory, a register within the MPU, or as part of the instruction. For instance, a byte-wide number in a register such as BL can be compared to a second byte-wide number that is supplied as immediate data.

The result of the comparison is reflected by changes in six of the status flags of the 8088. Notice in Fig. 5.5(a) that it affects the overflow flag, sign flag, zero flag, auxiliary carry flag, parity flag, and carry flag. The new logic state of these flags can be used by instructions in order to make a decision whether or not to alter the sequence in which the program executes.

The process of comparison performed by the CMP instruction is basically a subtraction operation. The source operand is subtracted from the destination operand. However, the result of this subtraction is not saved. Instead, based on the result, the appropriate flags are set or reset.

The subtraction is done using 2's-complement arithmetic. For example, let us assume that the destination operand equals $10011001_2 = -103_{10}$ and that the source operand equals $00011011_2 = +27_{10}$. Subtracting the source from the destination, we get

$$10011001_2 = -103_{10}$$

$$\underline{-00011011_2 = -(+27_{10})}$$

$$101111110_2 = +126_{10}$$

Mnemonic	Meaning	Format	Operation	Flags Affected
CMP	Compare	CMP D,S	(D) − (S) is used in setting or resetting the flags	CF, AF, OF, PF, SF, ZF

(a)

Destination	Source
Register	Register
Register	Memory
Memory	Register
Register	Immediate
Memory	Immediate
Accumulator	Immediate

(b)

Figure 5.5   (a) Compare instruction. (b) Operand combinations.

In the process of obtaining this result, we get the status that follows:

1. No carry is generated from bit 3 to bit 4; therefore, the auxiliary carry flag AF is at logic 0.
2. There is a carry-out from bit 7. Thus, carry flag CF is set.
3. Even though a carry-out of bit 7 is generated, there is no carry from bit 6 to bit 7. This is an overflow condition and the OF flag is set.
4. There are an even number of 1s; therefore, this makes parity flag PF equal to 1.
5. Bit 7 is zero and therefore sign flag SF is at logic 0.
6. The result that is produced is nonzero, which makes zero flag ZF logic 0.

Notice that the result produced by the subtraction of the two 8-bit numbers is not correct. This condition was indicated by setting the overflow flag.

EXAMPLE 5.5

Describe what happens to the status flags as the sequence of instructions that follows is executed.

```
MOV AX,1234H
MOV BX,0ABCDH
CMP AX,BX
```

Assume that flags ZF, SF, CF, AF, OF, and PF are all initially reset.

SOLUTION   The first instruction loads AX with 1234_{16}. No status flags are affected by the execution of a MOV instruction.

The second instruction puts $ABCD_{16}$ into the BX register. Again, status is not affected. Thus, after execution of these two move instructions, the contents of AX and BX are

$$(AX) = 1234_{16} = 0001001000110100_2$$

and

$$(BX) = ABCD_{16} = 1010101111001101_2$$

The third instruction is a 16-bit comparison with AX representing the destination and BX the source. Therefore, the contents of BX are subtracted from that of AX.

$$(AX) - (BX) = 0001001000110100_2 - 1010101111001101_2 = 0110011001100111_2$$

The flags are either set or reset based on the result of this subtraction. Notice that the result is nonzero and positive. This makes ZF and SF equal to zero. Moreover, the overflow condition has not occurred. Therefore, OF is also at logic 0. The carry and auxiliary carry conditions have occurred; therefore, CF and AF are 1. Finally, the result has odd parity; therefore, PF is 0. These results are summarized in Fig. 5.6.

Instruction	ZF	SF	CF	AF	OF	PF
Initial state	0	0	0	0	0	0
MOV AX,1234H	0	0	0	0	0	0
MOV BX,0ABCDH	0	0	0	0	0	0
CMP AX,BX	0	0	1	1	0	0

Figure 5.6 Effect on flags of executing instructions.

EXAMPLE 5.6

Verify the execution of the instruction sequence in Example 5.5 on the PC. Use DEBUG and a run module formed with the macroassembler (MASM) and linker (LINK) programs.

SOLUTION A source program written to implement a procedure that contains the instruction sequence executed in Example 5.5 is shown in Fig. 5.7(a). This program was assembled with MASM and linked with LINK to form a run module in file EX56.EXE. The source listing produced by the assembler is shown in Fig. 5.7(b).

To execute this program with DEBUG, we bring up the debugger and load the file from a data diskette in drive B with the DOS command

A>DEBUG B:EX56.EXE (↵)

To verify its loading, the UNASSEMBLE command that follows can be used

–U 0 D   (↵)

As shown in Fig. 5.7(c), the instructions of the source program are correctly displayed.

First, we will execute the instructions up to the CMP instruction. This is done with the GO command

–G B   (↵)

Note in Fig. 5.7(c) that AX has been loaded with 1234_{16} and BX with the value $ABCD_{16}$.

Next, the compare instruction is executed with the command

$$-T \qquad (\hookleftarrow)$$

By comparing the state information before and after execution of the CMP instruction, we find that auxiliary carry flag and carry flag are the only flags that have changed states and they have both been set. Their new states are identified as AC and CY, respectively. These results are identical to those found in Example 5.5.

```
TITLE    EXAMPLE 5.6

         PAGE     ,132

STACK_SEG    SEGMENT    STACK 'STACK'
             DB         64 DUP(?)
STACK_SEG    ENDS


CODE_SEG     SEGMENT    'CODE'
EX56    PROC    FAR
        ASSUME  CS:CODE_SEG, SS:STACK_SEG

;To return to DEBUG program put return address on the stack

        PUSH    DS
        MOV     AX, 0
        PUSH    AX

;Following code implements Example 5.6

        MOV     AX, 1234H
        MOV     BX, 0ABCDH
        CMP     AX, BX

        RET                     ;Return to DEBUG program
EX56    ENDP

CODE_SEG     ENDS

        END     EX56
```

(a)

Figure 5.7 (a) Source program for Example 5.6. (b) Source listing produced by assembler. (c) Execution of the program with DEBUG.

```
                              TITLE    EXAMPLE 5.6

                                 PAGE      ,132

0000                          STACK_SEG     SEGMENT      STACK 'STACK'
0000     40 [                               DB           64 DUP(?)
            ??
              ]

0040                          STACK_SEG     ENDS


0000                          CODE_SEG      SEGMENT      'CODE'
0000                          EX56   PROC   FAR
                              ASSUME CS:CODE_SEG, SS:STACK_SEG

                              ;To return to DEBUG program put return address on the stack

0000  1E                             PUSH   DS
0001  B8 0000                        MOV    AX, 0
0004  50                             PUSH   AX

                              ;Following code implements Example 5.6

0005  B8 1234                        MOV    AX, 1234H
0008  BB ABCD                        MOV    BX, 0ABCDH
000B  3B C3                          CMP    AX, BX

000D  CB                             RET                  ;Return to DEBUG program
000E                          EX56   ENDP

000E                          CODE_SEG      ENDS

                                 END    EX56
```

Segments and groups:

N a m e	Size	align	combine	class
CODE_SEG	000E	PARA	NONE	'CODE'
STACK_SEG.	0040	PARA	STACK	'STACK'

Symbols:

N a m e	Type	Value	Attr	
EX56	F PROC	0000	CODE_SEG	Length =000E

```
Warning Severe
Errors  Errors
0       0
```

(b)

Figure 5.7 (Continued)

```
A>DEBUG B:EX56.EXE
-U 0 D
0D03:0000 1E              PUSH     DS
0D03:0001 B80000          MOV      AX,0000
0D03:0004 50              PUSH     AX
0D03:0005 B83412          MOV      AX,1234
0D03:0008 BBCDAB          MOV      BX,ABCD
0D03:000B 3BC3            CMP      AX,BX
0D03:000D CB              RETF
-G B

AX=1234  BX=ABCD  CX=000E  DX=0000  SP=003C  BP=0000  SI=0000  DI=0000
DS=0CF3  ES=0CF3  SS=0D04  CS=0D03  IP=000B   NV UP EI PL NZ NA PO NC
0D03:000B 3BC3            CMP      AX,BX
-T

AX=1234  BX=ABCD  CX=000E  DX=0000  SP=003C  BP=0000  SI=0000  DI=0000
DS=0CF3  ES=0CF3  SS=0D04  CS=0D03  IP=000D   NV UP EI PL NZ AC PO CY
0D03:000D CB              RETF
-G

Program terminated normally
-Q

A>
```

(c)

Figure 5.7 (Continued)

5.4 JUMP INSTRUCTIONS

The purpose of a *jump* instruction is to alter the execution path of instructions in the program. In the 8088 microprocessor, the code segment register and instruction pointer keep track of the next instruction to be fetched for execution. Thus a jump instruction involves altering the contents of these registers. In this way, execution continues at an address other than that of the next sequential instruction. That is, a jump occurs to another part of the program. Typically, program execution is not intended to return to the next sequential instruction after the jump instruction. Therefore, no return linkage is saved when the jump takes place.

The Unconditional and Conditional Jump

The 8088 microprocessor allows two different types of jump instructions. They are the *unconditional jump* and the *conditional jump*. In an unconditional jump, no status requirements are imposed for the jump to occur. That is, as the instruction is executed, the jump always takes place to change the execution sequence.

This concept is illustrated in Fig. 5.8(a). Notice that, when the instruction JMP AA in part I is executed, program control is passed to a point in part III identified by the label AA. Execution resumes with the instruction corresponding to AA. In this way, the instructions in part II of the program have been bypassed; that is, they have been jumped over.

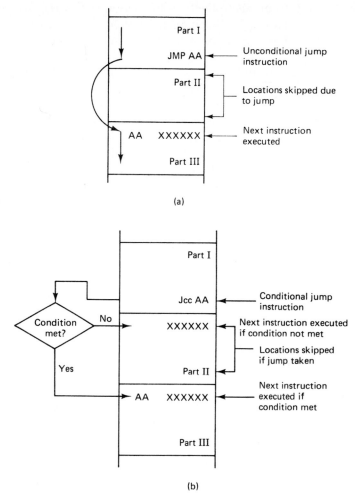

Figure 5.8 (a) Unconditional jump program sequence. (b) Conditional jump program sequence.

On the other hand, for a conditional jump instruction, status conditions that exist at the moment the jump instruction is executed decide whether or not the jump will occur. If this condition or conditions are met, the jump takes place; otherwise, execution continues with the next sequential instruction of the program. The conditions that can be referenced by a conditional jump instruction are status flags such as carry (CF), parity (PF), and overflow (OF).

Looking at Fig. 5.8(b), we see that execution of the conditional jump instruction in part I causes a test to be initiated. If the conditions of the test are not met, the NO path is taken and execution continues with the next sequential instruction. This corresponds to the first instruction in part II. However, if the result of the conditional test is YES, a jump is initiated to the segment of program identified as part III and the instructions in part II are bypassed.

Unconditional Jump Instruction

The unconditional jump instruction of the 8088 is shown in Fig. 5.9(a) together with its valid operand combinations in Fig. 5.9(b). There are two basic kinds of unconditional jumps. The first, called an *intrasegment jump,* is limited to addresses within the current code segment. This type of jump is achieved by just modifying the value in IP. The other kind of jump, the *intersegment jump,* permits jumps from one code segment to another. Implementation of this type of jump requires modification of the contents of both CS and IP.

Jump instructions specified with a *Short-label, Near-label, Memptr16,* or *Regptr16 operand* represent intrasegment jumps. The Short-label and Near-label operands specify the jump relative to the address of the jump instruction itself. For example, in a Short-label jump instruction an 8-bit number is coded as an immediate operand to specify the *signed displacement* of the next instruction to be executed from the location of the jump instruction. When the jump instruction is executed, IP is reloaded with a new value equal to the updated value in IP, which is (IP) + 2, plus the signed displacement. The new value of IP and current value in CS give the address of the next instruction to be fetched and executed. With an 8-bit displacement, the Short-label operand can only be used to initiate a jump in the range from −126 to +129 bytes from the location of the jump instruction.

On the other hand, Near-label operands specify a new value for IP with a 16-bit immediate operand. This size of offset corresponds to the complete range of

Mnemonic	Meaning	Format	Operation	Affected flags
JMP	Unconditional jump	JMP Operand	Jump is initiated to the address specified by the operand	None

(a)

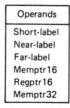

(b)

Figure 5.9   (a) Unconditional jump instruction. (b) Allowed operands.

the current code segment. The value of the offset is automatically added to IP upon execution of the instruction. In this way, program control is passed to the location identified by the new IP. An example is the instruction

```
JMP LABEL
```

This means jump to the point in the program corresponding to the tag LABEL. The programmer does not have to worry about counting the number of bytes from the jump instruction to the location to which control is to be passed. Moreover, the fact that it is coded as a Short- or Near-label displacement is also determined by the assembler.

The jump to address can also be specified indirectly by the contents of a memory location or the contents of a register. These two types correspond to the Memptr16 and Regptr16 operands, respectively. Just as for the Near-label operand, they both permit a jump to any address in the current code segment.

For example,

```
JMP BX
```

uses the contents of register BX for the displacement. That is, the value in BX is copied into IP. Then the physical address of the next instruction is obtained by using the current contents of CS and the new value in IP.

EXAMPLE 5.7

Verify the operation of the instruction JMP BX using the DEBUG program on the IBM PC. Let the contents of BX be 0010_{16}.

SOLUTION   As shown in Fig. 5.10, DEBUG is invoked and then the line-by-line assembler is used to load the instruction with the command

```
-A                    (↵)
0CDE:0100 JMP BX  (↵)
0CDE:0102         (↵)
```

Next, BX is initialized with the command

```
-R BX         (↵)
BX 0000
:10           (↵)
```

Let us check the value in IP before executing the JMP instruction. This is done with another R command as

-R   (↵)

Looking at the state information displayed in Fig. 5.10, we see that IP contains 0100_{16} and BX contains 0010_{16}.

Executing the instruction with the command

-T   (↵)

and then looking at Fig. 5.10, we see that the value in IP has become 10_{16}. Therefore, the address at which execution picks up is 0CDE:0010.

```
A>DEBUG
-A
OCDE:0100 JMP BX
OCDE:0102
-R BX
BX 0000
:10
-R
AX=0000  BX=0010  CX=0000  DX=0000  SP=FFEE  BP=0000  SI=0000  DI=0000
DS=OCDE  ES=OCDE  SS=OCDE  CS=OCDE  IP=0100   NV UP EI PL NZ NA PO NC
OCDE:0100 FFE3            JMP      BX
-T

AX=0000  BX=0010  CX=0000  DX=0000  SP=FFEE  BP=0000  SI=0000  DI=0000
DS=OCDE  ES=OCDE  SS=OCDE  CS=OCDE  IP=0010   NV UP EI PL NZ NA PO NC
OCDE:0010 43             INC      BX
-Q

A>
```

Figure 5.10   Display sequence for Example 5.7.

To specify an operand to be used as a pointer, the various addressing modes available with the 8088 can be used. For instance

JMP [BX]

uses the contents of BX as the address of the memory location that contains the offset address (Memptr16 operand). This offset is loaded into IP, where it is used together with the current contents of CS to compute the "jump to" address.

EXAMPLE 5.8

Use the DEBUG program to observe the operation of the instruction

JMP [BX]

Assume that the pointer held in BX is 1000_{16} and the value held at memory location DS:1000 is 200_{16}. What is the address of the next instruction to be executed?

SOLUTION   Figure 5.11 shows that first the debugger is brought up and then an ASSEMBLE command issued to load the instruction. This assemble command is

```
-A                        (↵)
0CDE:0100  JMP  [BX]       (↵)
0CDE:0102                  (↵)
```

Next BX is loaded with the pointer address using the R command

```
-R BX                     (↵)
BX 0000
:1000                     (↵)
```

and the memory location is initialized with the command

```
-E 1000 00 02             (↵)
```

As shown in Fig. 5.11, the loading of memory location DS:1000 and the BX register are next verified with D and R commands, respectively.

Now the instruction is executed with the command

```
-T           (↵)
```

Notice from the state information displayed in Fig. 5.11 that the new value in IP is 0200_{16}. This value was loaded from memory location 0CDE:1000. Therefore, program execution continues with the instruction at address 0CDE:0200.

```
A>DEBUG
-A
0CDE:0100  JMP  [BX]
0CDE:0102
-R BX
BX 0000
:1000
-E 1000 00 02
-D 1000 1001
0CDE:1000   00 02                                          ..
-R
AX=0000   BX=1000   CX=0000   DX=0000   SP=FFEE   BP=0000   SI=0000   DI=0000
DS=0CDE   ES=0CDE   SS=0CDE   CS=0CDE   IP=0100   NV UP EI PL NZ NA PO NC
0CDE:0100 FF27          JMP      [BX]                             DS:1000=0200
-T

AX=0000   BX=1000   CX=0000   DX=0000   SP=FFEE   BP=0000   SI=0000   DI=0000
DS=0CDE   ES=0CDE   SS=0CDE   CS=0CDE   IP=0200   NV UP EI PL NZ NA PO NC
0CDE:0200 0000          ADD      [BX+SI],AL                       DS:1000=00
-Q

A>
```

Figure 5.11 Display sequence for Example 5.8.

The intersegment unconditional jump instructions correspond to the *Far-label* and *Memptr32 operands* that are shown in Fig. 5.9(b). Far-label uses a 32-bit immediate operand to specify the jump to address. The first 16 bits of this 32-bit pointer are loaded into IP and are an offset address relative to the contents of the code-segment register. The next 16 bits are loaded into the CS register and define the new 64K-byte code segment.

An indirect way to specify the offset and code segment address for an intersegment jump is by using the Memptr32 operand. This time four consecutive memory bytes starting at the specified address contain the offset address and the new code segment address, respectively. Just like the Memptr16 operand, the Memptr32 operand may be specified using any one of the various addressing modes of the 8088.

An example is the instruction

```
JMP DWORD PTR [DI]
```

It uses the contents of DS and DI to calculate the address of the memory location that contains the first word of the pointer that identifies the location to which the jump will take place. The two-word pointer starting at this address is read into IP and CS to pass control to the new point in the program.

Conditional Jump Instruction

The second type of jump instruction is that which performs conditional jump operations. Figure 5.12(a) shows a general form of this instruction; Fig. 5.12(b) is a list of each of the conditional jump instructions in the 8088's instruction set. Notice that each of these instructions tests for the presence or absence of certain status conditions.

For instance, the *jump on carry* (JC) instruction makes a test to determine if carry flag (CF) is set. Depending on the result of the test, the jump to the location specified by its operand either takes place or does not. If CF equals zero, the test fails and execution continues with the instruction at the address following the JC instruction. On the other hand, if CF is set to one, the test condition is satisfied and the jump is performed.

Notice that for some of the instructions in Fig. 5.12(b) two different mnemonics can be used. This feature can be used to improve program readability. That is, for each occurrence of the instruction in the program, it can be identified with the mnemonic that best describes its function.

For instance, the instruction *jump on parity* (JP)/*jump on parity even* (JPE) can be used to test parity flag PF for logic 1. Since PF is set to one if the result from a computation has even parity, this instruction can initiate a jump based on the occurrence of even parity. The reverse instruction JNP/JPO is also provided. It can be used to initiate a jump based on the occurrence of a result with odd parity instead of even parity.

Mnemonic	Meaning	Format	Operation	Flags affected
Jcc	Conditional jump	Jcc Operand	If the specified condition cc is true the jump to the address specified by the operand is initiated; otherwise the next instruction is executed.	None

(a)

Mnemonic	Meaning	Condition
JA	above	CF = 0 and ZF = 0
JAE	above or equal	CF = 0
JB	below	CF = 1
JBE	below or equal	CF = 1 or ZF = 1
JC	carry	CF = 1
JCXZ	CX register is zero	(CF or ZF) = 0
JE	equal	ZF = 1
JG	greater	ZF = 0 and SF = OF
JGE	greater or equal	SF = OF
JL	less	(SF xor OF) = 1
JLE	less or equal	((SF xor OF) or ZF) = 1
JNA	not above	CF = 1 or ZF = 1
JNAE	not above nor equal	CF = 1
JNB	not below	CF = 0
JNBE	not below nor equal	CF = 0 and ZF = 0
JNC	not carry	CF = 0
JNE	not equal	ZF = 0
JNG	not greater	((SF xor OF) or ZF) = 1
JNGE	not greater nor equal	(SF xor OF) = 1
JNL	not less	SF = OF
JNLE	not less nor equal	ZF = 0 and SF = OF
JNO	not overflow	OF = 0
JNP	not parity	PF = 0
JNS	not sign	SF = 0
JNZ	not zero	ZF = 0
JO	overflow	OF = 1
JP	parity	PF = 1
JPE	parity even	PF = 1
JPO	parity odd	PF = 0
JS	sign	SF = 1
JZ	zero	ZF = 1

(b)

Figure 5.12 (a) Conditional jump instruction. (b) Types of conditional jump instructions.

In a similar manner, the instructions *jump if equal* (JE) and *jump if zero* (JZ) have the same function. Either notation can be used in a program to determine if the result of a computation was zero.

All other conditional jump instructions work in a similar way except that they test different conditions to decide whether or not the jump is to take place. Examples of these conditions are that the contents of CX are zero, an overflow has occurred, or the result is negative.

To distinguish between comparisons of signed and unsigned numbers by jump instructions, two different names, which seem to be the same, have been devised. They are *above* and *below* for comparison of unsigned numbers and *less* and *greater* for comparison of signed numbers. For instance, the number $ABCD_{16}$ is above the number 1234_{16} if considered as an unsigned number. On the other hand, if they are considered as signed numbers, $ABCD_{16}$ is negative and 1234_{16} is positive. Therefore, $ABCD_{16}$ is less than 1234_{16}.

As an example of the use of a conditional jump operation, let us write a program to move a block of N bytes of data starting at offset address BLK1ADDR to another block starting at offset address BLK2ADDR. We will assume that both blocks are in the same data segment, whose starting point is defined by the data segment address DATASEGADDR.

The steps to be implemented to solve this problem are outlined in the flow-chart in Fig. 5.13(a). It has four basic operations. The first operation is initialization. Initialization involves establishing the initial address of the data segment. This is done by loading the DS register with the value DATASEGADDR. Furthermore, source index register SI and destination index register DI are initialized with addresses BLK1ADDR and BLK2ADDR, respectively. In this way, they point to the beginning of the source block and the beginning of the destination block, respectively. To keep track of the count, register CX is initialized with N, the number of points to be moved. This leads us to the following assembly language statements.

```
MOV    AX,DATASEGADDR
MOV    DS,AX
MOV    SI,BLK1ADDR
MOV    DI,BLK2ADDR
MOV    CX,N
```

Notice that DS cannot be directly loaded by immediate data with a MOV instruction. Therefore, the segment address was first loaded into AX and then moved to DS. SI, DI, and CX can be loaded directly with immediate data.

The next operation that must be performed is the actual movement of data from the source block of memory to the destination block. The offset addresses are already loaded into SI and DI; therefore, move instructions that employ indirect addressing can be used to accomplish the data transfer operation. Remember that the 8088 does not allow direct memory-to-memory moves. For this

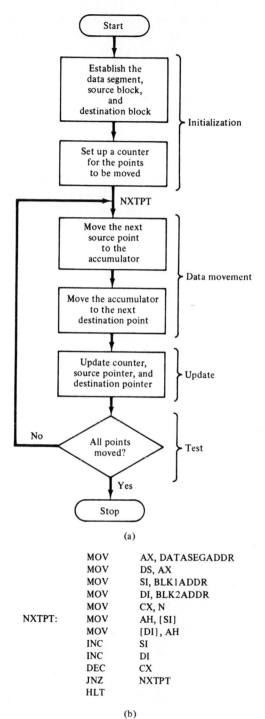

Figure 5.13 (a) Block transfer flow-chart. (b) Program.

(a)

```
                MOV     AX, DATASEGADDR
                MOV     DS, AX
                MOV     SI, BLK1ADDR
                MOV     DI, BLK2ADDR
                MOV     CX, N
NXTPT:          MOV     AH, [SI]
                MOV     [DI], AH
                INC     SI
                INC     DI
                DEC     CX
                JNZ     NXTPT
                HLT
```

(b)

reason, AX will be used as an intermediate storage location for data. The source byte is moved into AX with one instruction and then another instruction is needed to move it from AX to the destination location. Thus, the data move is accomplished by the following instructions.

```
NXTPT: MOV    AH,[SI]
       MOV    [DI],AH
```

Notice that for a byte move only the higher eight bits of AX are used. Therefore, the operand is specified as AH instead of AX.

The next operation is to update the pointers in SI and DI so that they are ready for the next byte move. Also, the counter must be decremented so that it corresponds to the number of bytes that remain to be moved. These updates can be done by the following sequence of instructions.

```
INC    SI
INC    DI
DEC    CX
```

The test operation involves determining whether or not all the data points have been moved. The contents of CX represent this condition. When its value is not 0, there still are points to be moved; whereas a value of 0 indicates that the block move is complete. This 0 condition is reflected by 1 in ZF. The instruction needed to perform this test is

```
JNZ NXTPT
```

Here NXTPT is a label that corresponds to the first instruction in the data move operation. The last instruction in the program can be a *halt* (HLT) instruction to indicate the end of the block move operation. The entire program is shown in Fig. 5.13(b).

EXAMPLE 5.9

The source program in Fig. 5.14(a) is used to implement the instruction sequence

```
        CMP AX,BX
        JC  DIFF2
DIFF 1: MOV DX,AX
        SUB DX,BX ;DX = AX - BX
        JMP DONE
DIFF 2: MOV DX,BX
        SUB DX,AX ;DX = BX - AX
  DONE: NOP
```

as a procedure. This sequence of instructions calculates the absolute difference between the contents of AX and BX and places it in DX. Use the run module produced by assembling and linking the source program in Fig. 5.14(a) to verify the operation of the program for the two cases that follow:

$$\text{(a) } (AX) = 6, \ (BX) = 2$$
$$\text{(b) } (AX) = 2, \ (BX) = 6$$

SOLUTION   The source program in Fig. 5.14(a) can be assembled with MASM and linked with LINK to produce a run module called EX59.EXE. The source listing produced as part of the assembly process is shown in Fig. 5.14(b).

As shown in Fig. 5.14(c), the run module can be loaded as part of calling up the debugger by issuing the DOS command

$$A> \ DEBUG \ B:EX59.EXE \quad (↵)$$

Next, the loading of the program is verified with the UNASSEMBLE command

$$-U \ 0 \ 15$$

Notice in Fig. 5.14(c) that the CMP instruction, which is the first instruction of the sequence that generates the absolute difference, is located at address 0D03:0005. Let us execute down to this statement with the GO command

$$-G \ 5 \quad (↵)$$

Now we will load AX and BX with the case (a) data. This is done with the R commands

$$
\begin{array}{ll}
-R \ AX & (↵) \\
AX \ 0000 & \\
:6 & (↵) \\
-R \ BX & (↵) \\
BX \ 0000 & \\
:2 & (↵)
\end{array}
$$

Next, we execute the compare instruction with the command

$$-T \quad (↵)$$

Note in the trace information display in Fig. 5.14(c) that the carry flag is reset (NC). Therefore, no jump will take place when the JB instruction is executed.

The rest of the program can be executed by inputting the command

$$-G \ 14 \quad (↵)$$

From Fig. 5.14(c), we find that DX contains 4. This result was produced by executing the SUB instruction at 0D03:000B. Before executing the program for the (b) set of data, the command

$$-G \qquad (\hookleftarrow)$$

must be issued. This command causes the program to terminate normally.

The R command shows that the value in IP must be reset and then we can execute down to the CMP instruction. This is done with the commands

```
-R  IP        (↵)
IP  0014
:0            (↵)
```

and

$$-G \; 5 \qquad (\hookleftarrow)$$

Notice in Fig. 5.14(c) that IP again contains 0005_{16} and points to the CMP instruction. Next, the data for case (b) are loaded with R commands. This gives

```
-R  AX        (↵)
AX  0000
:2            (↵)
-R  BX        (↵)
BX  0002
:6            (↵)
```

Now a T command is used to execute the CMP instruction. Notice that CY is set this time. Therefore, control is passed to the instruction at 0D03:0010.

A GO command is now used to execute down to the NOP instruction at 0D03:0014. This command is

$$-G \; 14 \qquad (\hookleftarrow)$$

Notice that DX again contains 4; however, this time it was calculated with the SUB instruction at 0D03:0012.

5.5 SUBROUTINES AND SUBROUTINE-HANDLING INSTRUCTIONS

A *subroutine* is a special segment of program that can be called for execution from any point in a program. Figure 5.15(a) illustrates the concept of a subroutine. Here we see a program structure where one part of the program is called the *main program.* In addition to this, we find a smaller segment attached to the main program, known as a subroutine. The subroutine is written to provide a function that must be performed at various points in the main program. Instead of including this piece of code in the main program each time the function is needed, it is put into the program just once as a subroutine.

Wherever the function must be performed, a single instruction is inserted into the main body of the program to "call" the subroutine. Remember that the physical address CS:IP identifies the next instruction to be executed. Thus, to branch to a subroutine that starts elsewhere in memory, the value in either IP or CS and IP must be modified. After executing the subroutine, we want to return control to the instruction that follows the one that called the subroutine. In this way, program execution resumes in the main program at the point where it left off due to the subroutine call. A return instruction must be included at the end of the subroutine to initiate the *return sequence* to the main program environment.

The instructions provided to transfer control from the main program to a subroutine and return control back to the main program are called *subroutine-*

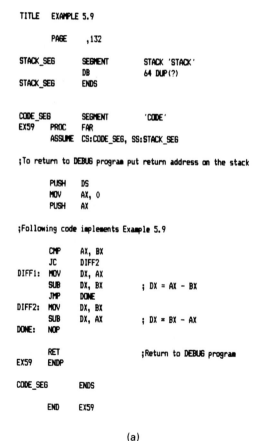

```
TITLE    EXAMPLE 5.9

        PAGE        ,132

STACK_SEG      SEGMENT        STACK 'STACK'
               DB             64 DUP(?)
STACK_SEG      ENDS


CODE_SEG       SEGMENT        'CODE'
EX59    PROC   FAR
        ASSUME CS:CODE_SEG, SS:STACK_SEG

;To return to DEBUG program put return address on the stack

        PUSH    DS
        MOV     AX, 0
        PUSH    AX

;Following code implements Example 5.9

        CMP     AX, BX
        JC      DIFF2
DIFF1:  MOV     DX, AX
        SUB     DX, BX         ; DX = AX - BX
        JMP     DONE
DIFF2:  MOV     DX, BX
        SUB     DX, AX         ; DX = BX - AX
DONE:   NOP

        RET                    ;Return to DEBUG program
EX59    ENDP

CODE_SEG       ENDS

        END     EX59
```

(a)

Figure 5.14   (a) Source program for Example 5.9. (b) Source listing produced by the assembler. (c) Executing the program with DEBUG.

```
AX=0002   BX=0006   CX=0016   DX=0004   SP=0038   BP=0000  SI=0000  DI=0000
DS=0CF3   ES=0CF3   SS=0D05   CS=0D03   IP=0007    NV UP EI NG NZ AC PE CY
0D03:0007 7207              JB         0010
-G 14

AX=0002   BX=0006   CX=0016   DX=0004   SP=0038   BP=0000  SI=0000  DI=0000
DS=0CF3   ES=0CF3   SS=0D05   CS=0D03   IP=0014    NV UP EI PL NZ NA PO NC
0D03:0014 90               NOP
-G

Program terminated normally
-Q

A>
```

(c)

Figure 5.14   (Continued)

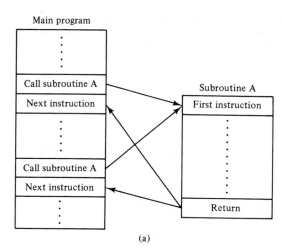

(a)

Mnemonic	Meaning	Format	Operation	Flags Affected
CALL	Subroutine call	CALL operand	Execution continues from the address of the subroutine specified by the operand. Information required to return back to the main program such as IP and CS are saved on the stack.	None

(b)

Operand
Near-proc
Far-proc
Memptr16
Regptr16
Memptr32

(c)

Figure 5.15   (a) Subroutine concept. (b) Subroutine call instruction. (c) Allowed operands.

214

handling instructions. Let us now examine the instructions provided for this purpose.

CALL and RET Instructions

There are two basic instructions in the instruction set of the 8088 for subroutine handling. They are the *call* (CALL) and *return* (RET) instructions. Together they provide the mechanism for calling a subroutine into operation and returning control back to the main program at its completion. We will first discuss these two instructions and later introduce other instructions that can be used in conjunction with subroutines.

Just like the JMP instruction, CALL allows implementation of two types of operations, the *intrasegment call* and the *intersegment call.* The CALL instruction is shown in Fig. 5.15(b), and its allowed operand variations are shown in Fig. 5.15(c).

It is the operand that initiates either an intersegment or an intrasegment call. The operands Near-proc, Memptr16, and Regptr16 all specify intrasegment calls to a subroutine. In all three cases, execution of the instruction causes the contents of IP to be saved on the stack. Then the stack pointer (SP) is decremented by two. The saved values of IP is the address of the instruction that follows the CALL instruction. After saving this return address, a new 16-bit value, which corresponds to the storage location of the first instruction in the subroutine, is loaded into IP.

The three types of intrasegment operands represent different ways of specifying this new value of IP. In a Near-proc operand, the offset of the first instruction of the subroutine in the current code segment is supplied directly by the instruction. An example is

```
                    CALL LABEL
```

Here LABEL identifies the 16-bit offset for a Near-proc operand that gets added to IP. This offset is coded as an immediate operand following the opcode for the call instruction. With a 16-bit offset, the subroutine can reside anywhere in the current code segment.

The Memptr16 and Regptr16 operands provide indirect subroutine addressing by specifying a memory location or an internal register, respectively, as the source of a new value for IP. The value specified is the actual offset that is to be loaded into IP. An example of a Regptr16 operand is

```
                    CALL BX
```

When this instruction is executed, the contents of BX are loaded into IP and execution continues with the subroutine starting at a physical address derived from CS and the new value of IP.

By using one of the various addressing modes of the 8088, an internal register can be used as pointer to an operand that resides in memory. This represents a Memptr16 type of operand. In this case, the value of the physical address of the offset is obtained from the current contents of the data segment register DS and the address or addresses held in the specified registers. For instance, the instruction

```
CALL [BX]
```

has its subroutine offset address at the memory location whose physical address is derived from the contents of DS and BX. The value stored at this memory location is loaded into IP. Again the current contents of CS and the new value in IP point to the first instruction of the subroutine. Again the current contents of CS and the new value in IP point to the first instruction of the subroutine.

Notice that in both intrasegment call examples the subroutine was located within the same code segment as the call instruction. The other type of CALL instruction, the intersegment call, permits the subroutine to reside in another code segment. It corresponds to the Far-proc and Memptr32 operands. These operands specify both a new offset address for IP and a new segment address for CS. In both cases, execution of the call instruction causes the contents of the CS and IP registers to be saved on the stack and then new values are loaded into IP and CS. The saved values of CS and IP permit return to the main program from a different code segment.

Far-proc represents a 32-bit immediate operand that is stored in the four bytes that follow the opcode of the call instruction in program memory. These two words are loaded directly from code segment memory into IP and CS with execution of the CALL instruction.

On the other hand, when the operand is Memptr32, the pointer for the subroutine is stored as four consecutive bytes in data memory. The location of the first byte of the pointer can be specified indirectly by one of the 8088's registers. An example is

```
CALL DWORD PTR [DI]
```

Here the physical address of the first byte of the 4-byte pointer in memory is derived from the contents of DS and DI.

Every subroutine must end by executing an instruction that returns control to the main program. This is the return (RET) instruction. It is described in Fig. 5.16(a) and (b). Notice that its execution causes the value of IP or both the values of IP and CS that were saved on the stack to be returned back to their corresponding registers. In general, an intrasegment return results from an intrasegment call and an intersegment return results from an intersegment call. In this way, pro-

Mnemonic	Meaning	Format	Operation	Flags Affected
RET	Return	RET or RET Operand	Return to the main program by restoring IP (and CS for fat-proc). If Operand is present, it is added to the contents of SP.	None

(a)

(b)

Figure 5.16   (a) Return instruction. (b) Allowed operands.

gram control is returned to the instruction that follows the call instruction in program memory.

There is an additional option with the return instruction. It is that a 2-byte code following the return instruction can be included. This code gets added to the stack pointer after restoring the return address either into IP (intrasegment return) or IP and CS (intersegment return). The purpose of this stack pointer displacement is to provide a simple mean by which the *parameters* that were saved on the stack before the call to the subroutine was initiated can be discarded. For instance, the instruction

```
RET 2
```

when executed adds 2 to SP. This discards one word parameter as part of the return sequence.

EXAMPLE 5.10

The source program in Fig. 5.17(a) can be used to demonstrate the use of the call and return instructions to implement a subroutine. This program was assembled and linked on the IBM PC to produce a run module in file EX510.EXE. Its source listing is provided for reference in Fig. 5.16(b). Trace the operation of the program by executing it with DEBUG for data (AX) = 2 and (BX) = 4.

SOLUTION We begin by calling up DEBUG and loading the program with the DOS command

$$A > DEBUG \ B:EX510.EXE \qquad (\hookleftarrow)$$

The loading of the program is now verified with the UNASSEMBLE command

$$-U \ 0 \ D \qquad (\hookleftarrow)$$

Looking at Fig. 5.17(c), we see that the program has correctly loaded. Moreover, we find that the CALL instruction is located at offset 0005_{16} of the current code segment. The command

$$-G \ 5 \qquad (\hookleftarrow)$$

executes the program down to the CALL instruction. The state information displayed in Fig. 5.17(c) shows that $(CS) = 0D03_{16}$, $(IP) = 0005_{16}$, and $(SP) = 003C_{16}$. Now let us load the AX and BX registers with R commands. This gives

```
-R  AX        (↵)
AX  0000
:2            (↵)
-R  BX        (↵)
BX  0000
:4            (↵)
```

Now the CALL instruction is executed with the T command

$$-T \qquad (\hookleftarrow)$$

and, looking at the displayed state information in Fig. 5.17(c), we find that CS still contains $0D03_{16}$, IP has been loaded with 0009_{16}, and SP has been decremented to $003A_{16}$. This information tells us that the next instruction to be executed is the move instruction at address 0D03:0009, and a word of data has been pushed to the stack.

Before executing another instruction, let us look at what got pushed onto the stack. This is done by issuing the memory dump command

$$-D \ SS:3A \ 3B \qquad (\hookleftarrow)$$

Note from Fig. 5.17(c) that the value 0008_{16} has been pushed onto the stack. This is the address offset of the RETF instruction that follows the CALL instruction and is the address of the instruction to which control is to be returned at completion of the subroutine.

Two more TRACE commands are used to execute the move and add instructions of the subroutine. From the state information displayed in Fig. 5.17(c), we see that their execution causes the value 2_{16} in AX to be copied into DX and then the value 4_{16} in BX to be added to the value in DX. This results in the value 6_{16} in DX.

Now the RET instruction is executed by issuing another T command. In Fig. 5.17(c), we see that execution of this instruction causes the value 0008_{16} to be popped off the stack and put back into the IP register. Therefore, the next instruction to be executed is that located at address 0D03:0008; this is the RETF instruction. Moreover, notice that, as the word is popped from the stack back into IP, the value in SP is incremented by two. After this, the program is run to completion by issuing a GO command.

```
TITLE    EXAMPLE 5.10

         PAGE      ,132

STACK_SEG    SEGMENT       STACK 'STACK'
             DB            64 DUP(?)
STACK_SEG    ENDS


CODE_SEG     SEGMENT       'CODE'
EX510   PROC    FAR
             ASSUME   CS:CODE_SEG, SS:STACK_SEG

;To return to DEBUG program put return address on the stack

         PUSH    DS
         MOV     AX, 0
         PUSH    AX

;Following code implements Example 5.10

         CALL    SUM
         RET

SUM     PROC    NEAR
         MOV     DX, AX
         ADD     DX, BX        ; DX = AX + BX
         RET
SUM     ENDP

EX510   ENDP
CODE_SEG         ENDS

         END     EX510

                (a)
```

Figure 5.17 (a) Source program for Example 5.10. (b) Source listing produced by assembler. (c) Executing the program with DEBUG.

```
                        TITLE   EXAMPLE 5.10

                                PAGE      ,132

0000                    STACK_SEG        SEGMENT         STACK 'STACK'
0000      40 [                           DB              64 DUP(?)
          ??
          ]

0040                    STACK_SEG        ENDS


0000                    CODE_SEG         SEGMENT         'CODE'
0000                    EX510   PROC     FAR
                                ASSUME   CS:CODE_SEG, SS:STACK_SEG

                        ;To return to DEBUG program put return address on the stack

0000  1E                         PUSH    DS
0001  B8 0000                    MOV     AX, 0
0004  50                         PUSH    AX

                        ;Following code implements Example 5.10

0005  E8 0009 R                  CALL    SUM
0008  CB                         RET

0009                    SUM      PROC    NEAR
0009  8B D0                      MOV     DX, AX
000B  03 D3                      ADD     DX, BX          ; DX = AX + BX
000D  C3                         RET
000E                    SUM      ENDP

000E                    EX510    ENDP
000E                    CODE_SEG          ENDS

                                 END     EX510


Segments and groups:

              N a m e               Size   align   combine class

CODE_SEG . . . . . . . . . . . .    000E   PARA    NONE    'CODE'
STACK_SEG. . . . . . . . . . . .    0040   PARA    STACK   'STACK'

Symbols:

              N a m e               Type   Value   Attr

EX510. . . . . . . . . . . . . .    F PROC 0000    CODE_SEG      Length =000E
SUM. . . . . . . . . . . . . .      N PROC 0009    CODE_SEG      Length =0005

Warning Severe
Errors  Errors
0       0
```

(b)

Figure 5.17 (Continued)

```
A>DEBUG B:EX510.EXE
-U 0 D
0D03:0000 1E                PUSH      DS
0D03:0001 B80000            MOV       AX,0000
0D03:0004 50                PUSH      AX
0D03:0005 E80100            CALL      0009
0D03:0008 CB                RETF
0D03:0009 8BD0              MOV       DX,AX
0D03:000B 03D3              ADD       DX,BX
0D03:000D C3                RET
-G 5

AX=0000  BX=0000  CX=000E  DX=0000  SP=003C  BP=0000  SI=0000  DI=0000
DS=0CF3  ES=0CF3  SS=0D04  CS=0D03  IP=0005   NV UP EI PL NZ NA PO NC
0D03:0005 E80100            CALL      0009
-R AX
AX 0000
:2
-R BX
BX 0000
:4
-T

AX=0002  BX=0004  CX=000E  DX=0000  SP=003A  BP=0000  SI=0000  DI=0000
DS=0CF3  ES=0CF3  SS=0D04  CS=0D03  IP=0009   NV UP EI PL NZ NA PO NC
0D03:0009 8BD0              MOV       DX,AX
-D SS:3A 3B
0D04:0030                                          08 00
-T

AX=0002  BX=0004  CX=000E  DX=0002  SP=003A  BP=0000  SI=0000  DI=0000
DS=0CF3  ES=0CF3  SS=0D04  CS=0D03  IP=000B   NV UP EI PL NZ NA PO NC
0D03:000B 03D3              ADD       DX,BX
-T

AX=0002  BX=0004  CX=000E  DX=0006  SP=003A  BP=0000  SI=0000  DI=0000
DS=0CF3  ES=0CF3  SS=0D04  CS=0D03  IP=000D   NV UP EI PL NZ NA PE NC
0D03:000D C3                RET
-T

AX=0002  BX=0004  CX=000E  DX=0006  SP=003C  BP=0000  SI=0000  DI=0000
DS=0CF3  ES=0CF3  SS=0D04  CS=0D03  IP=0008   NV UP EI PL NZ NA PE NC
0D03:0008 CB                RETF
-G

Program terminated normally
-Q

A>
```

(c)

Figure 5.17   (Continued)

PUSH and POP Instructions

After the context switch to a subroutine, we find that it is usually necessary to save the contents of certain registers or some other main program parameters. These values are saved by pushing them onto the stack. Typically, these data correspond to registers and memory locations that are used by the subroutine. In this way, their original contents are kept intact in the stack segment of memory during the execution of the subroutine. Before a return to the main program takes place, the saved registers and main program parameters are restored. This is done by popping the saved values from the stack back into their original locations. Thus a typical structure of a subroutine is that shown in Fig. 5.18.

The instruction that is used to save parameters on the stack is the *push* (PUSH) instruction and that used to retrieve them back is the *pop* (POP) instruction. Notice in Fig. 5.19(a) and (b) that the standard PUSH and POP instructions can be written with a general-purpose register, a segment register (excluding CS), or a storage location in memory as their operand.

Execution of a PUSH instruction causes the data corresponding to the operand to be pushed onto the top of the stack. For instance, if the instruction is

$$\text{PUSH AX}$$

the result is as follows:

$$((SP) - 1) \leftarrow (AH)$$
$$((SP) - 2) \leftarrow (AL)$$
$$(SP) \leftarrow (SP) - 2$$

This shows that the two bytes of AX are saved in the stack part of memory and the stack pointer is decremented by two so that it points to the new top of the stack.

On the other hand, if the instruction is

$$\text{POP AX}$$

its execution results in

$$(AL) \leftarrow ((SP))$$
$$(AH) \leftarrow ((SP) + 1)$$
$$(SP) \leftarrow (SP) + 2$$

In this manner, the saved contents of AX are restored back into the register.

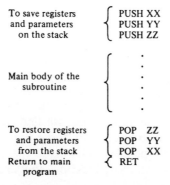

To save registers
and parameters
on the stack
$$\left\{ \begin{array}{l} \text{PUSH XX} \\ \text{PUSH YY} \\ \text{PUSH ZZ} \end{array} \right.$$

Main body of the
subroutine
$$\left\{ \begin{array}{l} \cdot \\ \cdot \\ \cdot \\ \cdot \\ \cdot \end{array} \right.$$

To restore registers
and parameters
from the stack
$$\left\{ \begin{array}{l} \text{POP ZZ} \\ \text{POP YY} \\ \text{POP XX} \end{array} \right.$$
Return to main   { RET
program

Figure 5.18 Structure of a subroutine.

Mnemonic	Meaning	Format	Operation	Flags Affected
PUSH	Push word onto stack	PUSH S	$((SP)) \leftarrow (S)$	None
POP	Pop word off stack	POP D	$(D) \leftarrow ((SP))$	None

(a)

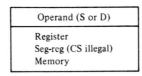

Operand (S or D)
Register Seg-reg (CS illegal) Memory

(b)

Figure 5.19   (a) PUSH and POP instructions. (b) Allowed operands.

EXAMPLE 5.11

Write a procedure named SUM that adds 31_{16} to the memory location TOTAL. The sum is to be formed using DX. Assume that this procedure is called from another procedure in the same code segment and that, at the time it is called, DX contains a value that must be saved at entry of the procedure and restored at its completion.

SOLUTION   The beginning of the procedure is defined with the pseudo-op statement

```
SUM PROC NEAR
```

At entry of the procedure, we must save the value currently held in DX. This is done by pushing its contents to the stack with the instruction

```
PUSH DX
```

Now we load DX with the value at TOTAL using the instruction

```
MOV DX,TOTAL
```

Add 31_{16} to it with the instruction

```
ADD DX,31H
```

and then place the result back in TOTAL.

MOV TOTAL,DX

This completes the addition operation; but before we return to the main part of the program, the original contents of DX that were saved on the stack are restored with the pop instruction

POP DX

Then a return instruction is used to pass control back to the main program.

RET

The procedure must be terminated with the end procedure pseudo-op statement that follows:

SUM ENDP

The complete instruction sequence is shown in Fig. 5.20.

```
SUM     PROC    NEAR
        PUSH    DX
        MOV     DX,TOTAL
        ADD     DX,31H
        MOV     TOTAL,DX
        POP     DX
        RET
SUM     ENDP
```

Figure 5.20 Program for Example 5.11.

EXAMPLE 5.12

A source program that can be used to demonstrate execution of the procedure written in Example 5.11 is shown in Fig. 5.21(a). The source listing produced when this program was assembled is given in Fig. 5.21(b), and the run module produced when it was linked is stored in file EX512.EXE. Use the DEBUG program to load this run module and verify its operation by executing it on the IBM PC.

SOLUTION The DEBUG program and run module can be loaded with the DEBUG DOS command. Looking at Fig. 5.21(c), we see that this command is

>DEBUG B:EX512.EXE   (↵)

After loading is completed, the instructions of the program are unassembled with the command

–U 0 1E   (↵)

The displayed information in Fig. 5.21(c) shows that the program did load correctly.

From the instruction sequence in Fig. 5.21(c), we find that the part of the program whose operation we are interested in observing starts with the CALL instruction at address 0D03:000D. Now we execute down to this point in the program with the GO command

–G D   (↵)

Looking at the trace information displayed, we see that DX has been initialized with the value $ABCD_{16}$.

Now the call instruction is executed with the command

–T   (↵)

Notice from the displayed information for this command in Fig. 5.21(c) that the value held in IP has been changed to 0011_{16}. Therefore, control has been passed to address 0D03:0011, which is the first instruction of procedure SUM. Moreover, note that stack pointer (SP) has been decremented to the value $003A_{16}$. The new top of the stack is at address SS:SP equal to 0D06:003A. The word held at the top of the stack can be examined with the command

–D SS:3A 3B   (↵)

Notice in Fig. 5.21(c) that its value is 0010_{16}. From the instruction sequence in Fig. 5.21(c), we see that this is the address of the RETF instruction. This is the instruction to which control is to be returned at the completion of the procedure.

Next, the PUSH DX instruction is executed with the command

–T   (↵)

and again, looking at the displayed state information, we find that SP has been decremented to the value 0038_{16}. Displaying the word at the top of the stack with the command

–D SS:38 39   (↵)

we find that it is the word $ABCD_{16}$. This confirms that the original contents of DX are saved on the stack.

Now we execute down to the POP DX instruction with the command

$$-G \quad 1D \qquad (\lrcorner)$$

Looking at the displayed state information in Fig. 5.21(c), we find that the sum $1234_{16} + 31_{16} = 1265_{16}$ has been formed in DX.

Next, the pop instruction is executed with the command

$$-T \qquad (\lrcorner)$$

and the displayed information shows that the value $ABCD_{16}$ has been popped off the stack and put back into DX. Moreover, the value in SP has been incremented to $003A_{16}$ so that once again the return address is at the top of the stack.

Finally, the RET instruction is executed with the command

$$-T \qquad (\lrcorner)$$

As shown in Fig. 5.21(c), this causes the value 0010_{16} to be popped from the top of the stack back into IP. Therefore, CS now equals 0010_{16} and IP equals 0010_{16}. In this way, we see that control has been returned to the instruction at address 0D03:0010 of the main program.

At times, we also want to save the contents of the flag register and if saved we will later have to restore them. These operations can be accomplished with *push flags* (PUSHF) and *pop flags* (POPF) instructions, respectively. These instructions are shown in Fig. 5.22. Notice that PUSHF saves the contents of the flag register on the top of the stack. On the other hand, POPF returns the flags from the top of the stack to the flag register.

5.6 THE LOOP AND THE LOOP-HANDLING INSTRUCTIONS

The 8088 microprocessor has three instructions specifically designed for implementing *loop operations*. These instructions can be used in place of certain conditional jump instructions and give the programmer a simpler way of writing loop sequences. The loop instructions are listed in Fig. 5.23.

The first instruction, *loop* (LOOP), works with respect to the contents of the CX register. CX must be preloaded with a count representing the number of times the loop is to be repeated. Whenever LOOP is executed, the contents of CX are first decremented by one and then checked to determine if they are equal to 0. If they are equal to 0, the loop is complete and the instruction following LOOP is executed; otherwise, control is returned to the instruction at the label specified in the loop instruction. In this way, we see that LOOP is a single instruction that functions the same as a decrement CX instruction followed by a JNZ instruction.

For example, the LOOP instruction sequence shown in Fig. 5.24(a) will cause the part of the program from the label NEXT through the instruction LOOP to be repeated a number of times equal to the value of count stored in CX. For

```
TITLE    EXAMPLE 5.12

         PAGE     ,132

STACK_SEG    SEGMENT    STACK 'STACK'
             DB         64 DUP(?)
STACK_SEG    ENDS


DATA_SEG     SEGMENT
TOTAL        DW         1234H
DATA_SEG     ENDS


CODE_SEG     SEGMENT    'CODE'
EX512  PROC  FAR
         ASSUME  CS:CODE_SEG, SS:STACK_SEG, DS:DATA_SEG

;To return to DEBUG program put return address on the stack

         PUSH   DS
         MOV    AX, 0
         PUSH   AX

;Setup the data segment

         MOV    AX, DATA_SEG
         MOV    DS, AX

;Following code implements Example 5.12

         MOV    DX, 0ABCDH    ;DX contents before call are ABCDH
         CALL   SUM           ;Call the procedure to add 31H to TOTAL
         RET                  ;Return to DEBUG program
EX512  ENDP

;Subroutine:   SUM
;Description:   Adds 31H to the current value held at TOTAL

SUM    PROC   NEAR
         PUSH   DX            ;Save the register to be used
         MOV    DX, TOTAL
         ADD    DX, 31H       ;DX = TOTAL + 31H
         MOV    TOTAL, DX
         POP    DX            ;Restore the register used
         RET
SUM    ENDP

CODE_SEG     ENDS

         END    EX512
                              (a)
```

Figure 5.21 (a) Source program for Example 5.12. (b) Source listing produced by the assembler. (c) DEBUG sequence for execution of run module EX512.EXE.

```
                        TITLE   EXAMPLE 5.12

                               PAGE    ,132

0000                    STACK_SEG    SEGMENT    STACK 'STACK'
0000    40 [                         DB         64 DUP(?)
            ??
          ]

0040                    STACK_SEG    ENDS


0000                    DATA_SEG     SEGMENT
0000  1234              TOTAL        DW         1234H
0002                    DATA_SEG     ENDS


0000                    CODE_SEG     SEGMENT    'CODE'
0000                    EX512  PROC  FAR
                               ASSUME  CS:CODE_SEG, SS:STACK_SEG, DS:DATA_SEG

                        ;To return to DEBUG program put return address on the stack

0000  1E                        PUSH   DS
0001  B8 0000                   MOV    AX, 0
0004  50                        PUSH   AX

                        ;Setup the data segment

0005  B8 ---- R                 MOV    AX, DATA_SEG
0008  8E D8                     MOV    DS, AX

                        ;Following code implements Example 5.12

000A  BA ABCD                   MOV    DX, 0ABCDH    ;DX contents before call are ABCDH
000D  E8 0011 R                 CALL   SUM           ;Call the procedure to add 31H to TOTAL
0010  CB                        RET                  ;Return to DEBUG program
0011                    EX512  ENDP

                        ;Subroutine:   SUM
                        ;Description:   Adds 31H to the current value held at TOTAL

0011                    SUM    PROC   NEAR
0011  52                       PUSH   DX            ;Save the register to be used
0012  8B 16 0000 R             MOV    DX, TOTAL
0016  83 C2 31                 ADD    DX, 31H        ;DX = TOTAL + 31H
0019  89 16 0000 R             MOV    TOTAL, DX
001D  5A                       POP    DX            ;Restore the register used
001E  C3                       RET
001F                    SUM    ENDP


001F                    CODE_SEG    ENDS

                               END    EX512

Segments and groups:

            N a m e            Size   align   combine class

CODE_SEG . . . . . . . . . . .  001F   PARA    NONE    'CODE'
DATA_SEG . . . . . . . . . . .  0002   PARA    NONE
STACK_SEG. . . . . . . . . . .  0040   PARA    STACK   'STACK'
```

(b)

Figure 5.21   (Continued)

N a m e	Type	Value	Attr	
EX512.	F PROC	0000	CODE_SEG	Length =0011
SUM.	N PROC	0011	CODE_SEG	Length =000E
TOTAL.	L WORD	0000	DATA_SEG	

Warning Severe
Errors Errors
0   0

(b)   (Continued)

```
A>DEBUG B:EX512.EXE
-U 0 1E
0D03:0000 1E            PUSH    DS
0D03:0001 B80000        MOV     AX,0000
0D03:0004 50            PUSH    AX
0D03:0005 B8050D        MOV     AX,0D05
0D03:0008 8ED8          MOV     DS,AX
0D03:000A BACDAB        MOV     DX,ABCD
0D03:000D E80100        CALL    0011
0D03:0010 CB            RETF
0D03:0011 52            PUSH    DX
0D03:0012 8B160000      MOV     DX,[0000]
0D03:0016 83C231        ADD     DX,+31
0D03:0019 89160000      MOV     [0000],DX
0D03:001D 5A            POP     DX
0D03:001E C3            RET
-G D

AX=0D05  BX=0000  CX=0022  DX=ABCD  SP=003C  BP=0000  SI=0000  DI=0000
DS=0D05  ES=0CF3  SS=0D06  CS=0D03  IP=000D   NV UP EI PL NZ NA PO NC
0D03:000D E80100        CALL    0011
-T

AX=0D05  BX=0000  CX=0022  DX=ABCD  SP=003A  BP=0000  SI=0000  DI=0000
DS=0D05  ES=0CF3  SS=0D06  CS=0D03  IP=0011   NV UP EI PL NZ NA PO NC
0D03:0011 52            PUSH    DX
-D SS:3A 3B
0D06:0030                                    10 00                        ..
-T

AX=0D05  BX=0000  CX=0022  DX=ABCD  SP=0038  BP=0000  SI=0000  DI=0000
DS=0D05  ES=0CF3  SS=0D06  CS=0D03  IP=0012   NV UP EI PL NZ NA PO NC
0D03:0012 8B160000      MOV     DX,[0000]                     DS:0000=1234
-D SS:38 39
0D06:0030                            CD AB                                ..
-G 1D

AX=0D05  BX=0000  CX=0022  DX=1265  SP=0038  BP=0000  SI=0000  DI=0000
DS=0D05  ES=0CF3  SS=0D06  CS=0D03  IP=001D   NV UP EI PL NZ NA PE NC
0D03:001D 5A            POP     DX
-T

AX=0D05  BX=0000  CX=0022  DX=ABCD  SP=003A  BP=0000  SI=0000  DI=0000
DS=0D05  ES=0CF3  SS=0D06  CS=0D03  IP=001E   NV UP EI PL NZ NA PE NC
0D03:001E C3            RET
-T

AX=0D05  BX=0000  CX=0022  DX=ABCD  SP=003C  BP=0000  SI=0000  DI=0000
DS=0D05  ES=0CF3  SS=0D06  CS=0D03  IP=0010   NV UP EI PL NZ NA PE NC
0D03:0010 CB            RETF
-G

Program terminated normally
```

(c)

Figure 5.21   (Continued)

Mnemonic	Meaning	Operation	Flags Affected
PUSHF	Push flags onto stack	$((SP)) \leftarrow (Flags)$	None
POPF	Pop flags from stack	$(Flags) \leftarrow ((SP))$	OF, DF, IF, TF, SF, ZF, AF, PF, CF

Figure 5.22 Push flags and pop flags instructions.

Mnemonic	Meaning	Format	Operation
LOOP	Loop	LOOP Short-label	$(CX) \leftarrow (CX) - 1$ Jump is initiated to location defined by short-label if $(CX) \neq 0$; otherwise, execute next sequential instruction
LOOPE/LOOPZ	Loop while equal/ loop while zero	LOOPE/LOOPZ Short-label	$(CX) \leftarrow (CX) - 1$ Jump to location defined by short-label if $(CX) \neq 0$ and $(ZF) = 1$; otherwise, execute next sequential instruction
LOOPNE/ LOOPNZ	Loop while not equal/ loop while not zero	LOOPNE/LOOPNZ Short-label	$(CX) \leftarrow (CX) - 1$ Jump to location defined by short-label if $(CX) \neq 0$ and $(ZF) = 0$; otherwise, execute next sequential instruction

Figure 5.23 LOOP instructions.

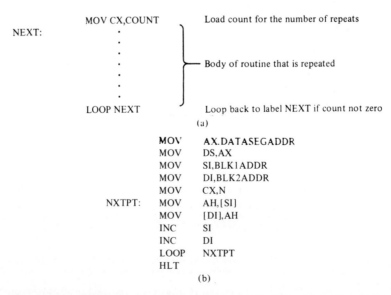

```
              MOV CX,COUNT        Load count for the number of repeats
NEXT:
                 .
                 .
                 .                — Body of routine that is repeated
                 .
                 .
                 .
              LOOP NEXT           Loop back to label NEXT if count not zero
```
(a)

```
         MOV     AX.DATASEGADDR
         MOV     DS,AX
         MOV     SI,BLK1ADDR
         MOV     DI,BLK2ADDR
         MOV     CX,N
NXTPT:   MOV     AH,[SI]
         MOV     [DI],AH
         INC     SI
         INC     DI
         LOOP    NXTPT
         HLT
```
(b)

Figure 5.24 (a) Typical loop routine structure. (b) Block move program employing the LOOP instruction.

example, if CX contains $000A_{16}$, the sequence of instructions included in the loop is executed 10 times.

Figure 5.24(b) shows a practical implementation of a loop. Here we find the block move program that was developed in Section 5.4 is rewritten using the LOOP instruction. Comparing this program with the one in Fig. 5.13(b), we see that the instruction LOOP NXTPT has replaced both the DEC and JNZ instructions.

EXAMPLE 5.13

The source program in Fig. 5.25(a) demonstrates the use of the LOOP instruction to implement a software loop operation. This program was assembled by the macroassembler on the IBM PC and linked to produce a run module called EX-513.EXE. The source listing is shown in Fig. 5.25(b). Observe the operation of the loop by executing the program through DEBUG.

SOLUTION   Looking at Fig. 5.25(c), we see that the run module is loaded with the DOS command

$$A>DEBUG\ B:EX513.EXE\qquad(\hookleftarrow)$$

Now the loading of the program is verified by unassembling it with the command

$$-U\ 0\ F\qquad(\hookleftarrow)$$

By comparing the instruction sequence displayed in Fig. 5.25(c) with the listing in Fig. 5.25(b), we find that the program has loaded correctly.

Also we find from the instruction sequence in Fig. 5.25(c) that the loop whose operation we want to observe is located from address 0D03:000B through 0D03:000D. Therefore, we will begin by executing the instructions down to address 0D03:000B with the GO command

$$-G\ B\qquad(\hookleftarrow)$$

Again, looking at Fig. 5.25(c), we see that these instructions initialize the count in CX to 0005_{16} and the contents of DX to 0000_{16}.

Now we execute the loop down to address 0D03:000D with another GO command

$$-G\ D\qquad(\hookleftarrow)$$

and, looking at the displayed information, we find that the pass count in DX has been incremented by one to indicate that the first pass through the loop is about to be completed.

Next the LOOP instruction is executed with the TRACE command

$$-T \qquad (\hookleftarrow)$$

From Fig. 5.25(c), we find that the loop count CX has decremented by one, meaning that the first pass through the loop is complete, and the value in IP has been changed to $000B_{16}$. Therefore, control has been returned to the NOP instruction that represents the beginning of the loop.

Now that we have observed the basic loop operation, let us execute the loop to completion with the command

$$-G \quad F \qquad (\hookleftarrow)$$

The displayed information for this command in Fig. 5.25(c) shows us that at completion of the program the loop count in CX has been decremented to 0000_{16} and the pass count in DX has been incremented to 0005_{16}.

```
TITLE   EXAMPLE 5.13

        PAGE    ,132

STACK_SEG    SEGMENT    STACK 'STACK'
             DB         64 DUP(?)
STACK_SEG    ENDS


CODE_SEG     SEGMENT    'CODE'
EX513   PROC  FAR
        ASSUME  CS:CODE_SEG, SS:STACK_SEG

;To return to DEBUG program put return address on the stack

        PUSH   DS
        MOV    AX, 0
        PUSH   AX

;Following code implements Example 5.13

        MOV    CX, 5H
        MOV    DX, 0H
AGAIN:  NOP
        INC    DX
        LOOP   AGAIN

        RET                     ;Return to DEBUG program
EX513   ENDP
CODE_SEG      ENDS

        END    EX513

             (a)
```

Figure 5.25 (a) Source program for Example 5.13. (b) Source listing produced by assembler. (c) Executing the program with DEBUG.

```
                          TITLE    EXAMPLE 5.13

                                   PAGE      ,132

0000                      STACK_SEG          SEGMENT       STACK 'STACK'
0000    40 [                                 DB            64 DUP(?)
               ??
                  ]

0040                      STACK_SEG          ENDS


0000                      CODE_SEG           SEGMENT       CODE
0000                      EX513    PROC      FAR
                                   ASSUME  CS:CODE_SEG, SS:STACK_SEG

                          ;To return to DEBUG program put return address on the stack

0000  1E                           PUSH      DS
0001  B8 0000                      MOV       AX, 0
0004  50                           PUSH      AX

                          ;Following code implements Example 5.13

0005  B9 0005                      MOV       CX, 5H
0008  BA 0000                      MOV       DX, OH
000B  90               AGAIN:      NOP
000C  42                           INC       DX
000D  E2 FC                        LOOP      AGAIN

000F  CB                           RET                     ;Return to DEBUG program
0010                      EX513    ENDP
0010                      CODE_SEG           ENDS

                                   END       EX513
```

Segments and groups:

N a m e	Size	align	combine	class
CODE_SEG	0010	PARA	NONE	'CODE'
STACK_SEG.	0040	PARA	STACK	'STACK'

Symbols:

N a m e	Type	Value	Attr	
AGAIN.	L NEAR	000B	CODE_SEG	
EX513.	F PROC	0000	CODE_SEG	Length =0010

Warning	Severe
Errors	Errors
0	0

(b)

Figure 5.25   (Continued)

```
A>DEBUG B:EX513.EXE
-U 0 F
0D03:0000 1E            PUSH     DS
0D03:0001 B80000        MOV      AX,0000
0D03:0004 50            PUSH     AX
0D03:0005 B90500        MOV      CX,0005
0D03:0008 BA0000        MOV      DX,0000
0D03:000B 90            NOP
0D03:000C 42            INC      DX
0D03:000D E2FC          LOOP     000B
0D03:000F CB            RETF
-G B

AX=0000  BX=0000  CX=0005  DX=0000  SP=003C  BP=0000  SI=0000  DI=0000
DS=0CF3  ES=0CF3  SS=0D04  CS=0D03  IP=000B   NV UP EI PL NZ NA PO NC
0D03:000B 90            NOP
-G D

AX=0000  BX=0000  CX=0005  DX=0001  SP=003C  BP=0000  SI=0000  DI=0000
DS=0CF3  ES=0CF3  SS=0D04  CS=0D03  IP=000D   NV UP EI PL NZ NA PO NC
0D03:000D E2FC          LOOP     000B
-T

AX=0000  BX=0000  CX=0004  DX=0001  SP=003C  BP=0000  SI=0000  DI=0000
DS=0CF3  ES=0CF3  SS=0D04  CS=0D03  IP=000B   NV UP EI PL NZ NA PO NC
0D03:000B 90            NOP
-G F

AX=0000  BX=0000  CX=0000  DX=0005  SP=003C  BP=0000  SI=0000  DI=0000
DS=0CF3  ES=0CF3  SS=0D04  CS=0D03  IP=000F   NV UP EI PL NZ NA PE NC
0D03:000F CB            RETF
-G

Program terminated normally
-Q

A>
```

(c)

Figure 5.25   (Continued)

The other two instructions in Fig. 5.23 operate in a similar way except that they check for two conditions. For instance, the instruction *loop while equal* (LOOPE)/*loop while zero* (LOOPZ) checks the contents of both CX and the ZF flag. Each time the loop instruction is executed, CX decrements by one without affecting the flags, its contents are checked for 0, and the state of ZF that results from execution of the previous instruction is tested for 1. If CX is not equal to 0 and ZF equals 1, a jump is initiated to the location specified with the Short-label operand and the loop continues. If either CX or ZF is 0, the loop is complete and the instruction following the loop instruction is executed.

Instruction *loop while not equal* (LOOPNE)/*loop while not zero* (LOOPNZ) works in a similar way to the LOOPE/LOOPZ instruction. The difference is that it checks ZF and CX looking for ZF equal to 0 together with CX not equal to 0. If these conditions are met, the jump back to the location specified with the Short-label operand is performed and the loop continues.

EXAMPLE 5.14

Given the following sequence of instructions, explain what happens as they are executed.

```
                    MOV  DL,05
                    MOV  AX,0A00H
                    MOV  DS,AX
                    MOV  SI,0
                    MOV  CX,0FH
        AGAIN:      INC  SI
                    CMP  [SI],DL
                    LOOPNE AGAIN
```

SOLUTION   The first five instructions are for initializing internal registers. Data register DL is loaded with 05_{16}; data segment register DS is loaded via AX with the value $0A00_{16}$; source index register SI is loaded with 0000_{16}; and count register CX is loaded with $0F_{16}$ (15_{10}). After initialization, a data segment is set up at address $0A000_{16}$ and SI points to the memory location at address 0000_{16} in this data segment. Moreover, DL contains the data 5_{10} and the CX register contains the loop count 15_{10}.

The part of the program that starts at the label AGAIN and ends with the LOOPNE instruction is a software loop. The first instruction in the loop increments SI by one. Therefore, the first time through the loop SI points to the memory address $A001_{16}$. The next instruction compares the contents of this memory location with the contents of DL, which are 5_{10}. If the data held at $A001_{16}$ are 5_{10}, the zero flag is set; otherwise, it is left at logic 0. The LOOPNE instruction then decrements CX (making it E_{16}) and then checks for CX = 0 or ZF = 1. If neither of these two conditions is satisfied, program control is returned to the instruction with the label AGAIN. This causes the comparison to be repeated for the examination of the contents of the next byte in memory. On the other hand, if either condition is satisfied, the loop is complete. In this way, we see that the loop is repeated until either a number 5_{16} is found or all locations in the address range $A001_{16}$ through $A00F_{16}$ have been tested and all are found not to contain 5_{16}.

EXAMPLE 5.15

Figure 5.26(a) shows the source version of a program that is written to implement the memory-compare routine in Example 5.14. This program was assembled by the macroassembler on the IBM PC and linked to produce run module EX-515.EXE. The source listing that resulted from the assembly process is shown in Fig. 5.26(b). Verify the operation of the program by executing it with the GO DEBUG command.

SOLUTION   As shown in Fig. 5.26(a), the run module is loaded with the DEBUG DOS command

A>DEBUG B:EX515.EXE   (↵)

The program loaded is verified with the command

—U 0 17   (↵)

Comparing the sequence of instructions displayed in Fig. 5.26(c) with those in the source listing of Fig. 5.26(b), we find that the program has loaded correctly.

Notice that the loop that performs the memory-compare operation starts at address 0D03:0012. Let us begin by executing down to this point with the GO command

—G 12   (↵)

From the state information displayed in Fig. 5.26(c), we see that DL has been loaded with 0005_{16}, AX with $0A00_{16}$, DS with $0A00_{16}$, SI with 0000_{16}, and CX with $000F_{16}$.

Next, the table of data is loaded with the E command

—E A00:0 4,6,3,9,5,6,D,F,9   (↵)

The nine values in this list are loaded into consecutive bytes of memory over the range 0A00:0000 through 0A00:0008. The compare routine actually also checks the storage locations from 0A00:0009 through 0A00:000F. Let us dump the data held in this part of memory to verify that it has been initialized correctly. In Fig. 5.26(c), we see that this is done with the command

—D A00:0 F   (↵)

and, looking at the displayed data, we find that it has loaded correctly.

Now the loop is executed with the command

—G 17   (↵)

In the display dump for this command in Fig. 5.26(c), we find that SI has incremented to the value 0004_{16}; therefore, the loop was only run four times. The fourth time through the loop SI equals four and the memory location pointed to by [SI], which is the address 0A00:0005, contains the value 5. This value is equal to the value in DL; therefore, the instruction CMP [SI],DL results in a difference of zero and the zero flag is set. Notice in Fig. 5.26(c) that this flag is identified as ZR in the display dump. For this reason, execution of the LOOPNZ instruction causes the loop to be terminated, and control is passed to the RETF instruction.

5.7 STRINGS AND STRING-HANDLING INSTRUCTIONS

The 8088 microprocessor is equipped with special instructions to handle *string operations*. By *string* we mean a series of data words (or bytes) that reside in consecutive memory locations. The string instructions of the 8088 permit a programmer to implement operations such as to move data from one block of memory to a block elsewhere in memory. A second type of operation that is easily performed is to scan a string of data elements stored in memory looking for a specific value. Other examples are to compare the elements of two strings together in order to determine whether they are the same or different, and to initialize a set of consecutive memory locations. Complex operations such as these typically require several nonstring instructions to be implemented.

There are five basic string instructions in the instruction set of the 8088. These instructions, as listed in Fig. 5.27, are *move byte* or *word string* (MOVSB/ MOVSW), *compare string* (CMPSB/CMPSW), *scan string* (SCASB/SCASW), *load string* (LODSB/LODSW), and *store string* (STOSB/STOSW). They are

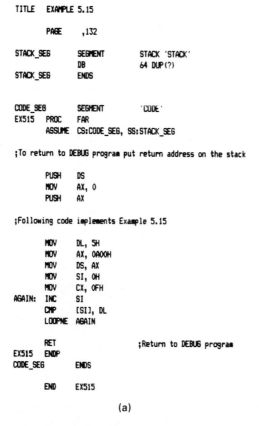

```
TITLE   EXAMPLE 5.15

        PAGE    ,132

STACK_SEG   SEGMENT     STACK 'STACK'
            DB          64 DUP(?)
STACK_SEG   ENDS


CODE_SEG    SEGMENT     'CODE'
EX515   PROC    FAR
        ASSUME  CS:CODE_SEG, SS:STACK_SEG

;To return to DEBUG program put return address on the stack

        PUSH    DS
        MOV     AX, 0
        PUSH    AX

;Following code implements Example 5.15

        MOV     DL, 5H
        MOV     AX, 0A00H
        MOV     DS, AX
        MOV     SI, OH
        MOV     CX, OFH
AGAIN:  INC     SI
        CMP     [SI], DL
        LOOPNE  AGAIN

        RET                 ;Return to DEBUG program
EX515   ENDP
CODE_SEG    ENDS

        END     EX515
```

(a)

Figure 5.26 (a) Source program for Example 5.15. (b) Source listing produced by assembler. (c) Executing the program with DEBUG.

```
                    TITLE   EXAMPLE 5.15

                         PAGE      ,132

0000                     STACK_SEG     SEGMENT     STACK 'STACK'
0000      40 [                         DB          64 DUP(?)
              ??
                  ]

0040                     STACK_SEG     ENDS


0000                     CODE_SEG      SEGMENT         'CODE'
0000                     EX515   PROC  FAR
                             ASSUME  CS:CODE_SEG, SS:STACK_SEG

                         ;To return to DEBUG program put return address on the stack

0000  1E                           PUSH    DS
0001  B8 0000                      MOV     AX, 0
0004  50                           PUSH    AX

                         ;Following code implements Example 5.15

0005  B2 05                        MOV     DL, 5H
0007  B8 0A00                      MOV     AX, 0A00H
000A  8E D8                        MOV     DS, AX
000C  BE 0000                      MOV     SI, OH
000F  B9 000F                      MOV     CX, 0FH
0012  46               AGAIN:      INC     SI
0013  38 14                        CMP     [SI], DL
0015  E0 FB                        LOOPNE  AGAIN

0017  CB                           RET                    ;Return to DEBUG program
0018                     EX515   ENDP
0018                     CODE_SEG      ENDS

                             END     EX515
```

Segments and groups:

N a m e	Size	align	combine	class
CODE_SEG	0018	PARA	NONE	'CODE'
STACK_SEG.	0040	PARA	STACK	'STACK'

Symbols:

N a m e	Type	Value	Attr	
AGAIN.	L NEAR	0012	CODE_SEG	
EX515.	F PROC	0000	CODE_SEG	Length =0018

```
Warning Severe
Errors  Errors
0       0
```

(b)

Figure 5.26   (Continued)

```
A>DEBUG B:EX515.EXE
-U 0 17
0D03:0000 1E          PUSH    DS
0D03:0001 B80000      MOV     AX,0000
0D03:0004 50          PUSH    AX
0D03:0005 B205        MOV     DL,05
0D03:0007 B8000A      MOV     AX,0A00
0D03:000A 8ED8        MOV     DS,AX
0D03:000C BE0000      MOV     SI,0000
0D03:000F B90F00      MOV     CX,000F
0D03:0012 46          INC     SI
0D03:0013 3814        CMP     [SI],DL
0D03:0015 E0FB        LOOPNZ  0012
0D03:0017 CB          RETF
-G 12

AX=0A00  BX=0000  CX=000F  DX=0005  SP=003C  BP=0000  SI=0000  DI=0000
DS=0A00  ES=0CF3  SS=0D05  CS=0D03  IP=0012   NV UP EI PL NZ NA PO NC
0D03:0012 46          INC     SI
-E A00:0 4,6,3,9,5,6,D,F,9
-D A00:0 F
0A00:0000   04 06 03 09 05 06 0D 0F-09 BA AB 32 E9 4C F7 80   ...........2.L..
-G 17

AX=0A00  BX=0000  CX=000B  DX=0005  SP=003C  BP=0000  SI=0004  DI=0000
DS=0A00  ES=0CF3  SS=0D05  CS=0D03  IP=0017   NV UP EI PL ZR NA PE NC
0D03:0017 CB          RETF
-G

Program terminated normally
-Q

A>
```

(c)

Figure 5.26 (Continued)

Mnemonic	Meaning	Format	Operation	Flags Affected
MOVS	Move string	MOVS Operand	$((ES)0 + (DI)) \leftarrow ((DS)0 + (SI))$ $(SI) \leftarrow (SI) \pm 1$ or 2 $(DI) \leftarrow (DI) \pm 1$ or 2	None
MOVSB	Move string byte	MOVSB	$((ES)0 + (DI)) \leftarrow ((DS)0 + (SI))$ $(SI) \leftarrow (SI) \pm 1$ $(DI) \leftarrow (DI) \pm 1$	None
MOVSW	Move string word	MOVSW	$((ES)0 + (DI)) \leftarrow ((DS)0 + (SI))$ $((ES)0 + (DI) + 1) \leftarrow ((DS)0 + (SI) + 1)$ $(SI) \leftarrow (SI) \pm 2$ $(DI) \leftarrow (DI) \pm 2$	None
CMPS	Compare string	CMPS Operand	Set flags as per $((DS)0 + (SI)) - ((ES)0 + (DI))$ $(SI) \leftarrow (SI) \pm 1$ or 2 $(DI) \leftarrow (DI) \pm 1$ or 2	CF, PF, AF, ZF, SF, OF
SCAS	Scan string	SCAS Operand	Set flags as per $(AL$ or $AX) - ((ES)0 + (DI))$ $(DI) \leftarrow (DI) \pm 1$ or 2	CF, PF, AF, ZF, SF, OF
LODS	Load string	LODS Operand	$(AL$ or $AX) \leftarrow ((DS)0 + (SI))$ $(SI) \leftarrow (SI) \pm 1$ or 2	None
STOS	Store string	STOS Operand	$((ES)0 + (DI)) \leftarrow (AL$ or $AX) \pm 1$ or 2 $(DI) \leftarrow (DI) \pm 1$ or 2	None

Figure 5.27 Basic string instructions.

called the *basic string instructions* because each defines an operation for one element of a string. Thus these operations must be repeated to handle a string of more than one element. Let us first look at the basic operations performed by these instructions.

Move String—MOVSB, MOVSW

The instructions MOVSB and MOVSW perform the same basic operation. An element of the string specified by the source index (SI) register with respect to the current data segment (DS) register is moved to the location specified by the destination index (DI) register with respect to the current extra segment (ES) register. The move can be performed on a byte or a word of data. After the move is complete, the contents of both SI and DI are automatically incremented or decremented by one for a byte move and by two for a word move. Remember the fact that the address pointers in SI and DI increment or decrement depending on how the direction flag DF is set.

For example to move a byte the instruction

```
MOVSB
```

can be used.

An example of a program that uses MOVSB is shown in Fig. 5.28. This program is a modified version of the block move program of Fig. 5.24(b). Notice that the two MOV instructions that performed the data transfer and INC instructions that update the pointer have been replaced with one move string byte instruction. We have also made DS equal to ES.

Compare String and Scan String—CMPSB/CMPSW and SCASB/SCASW

The compare strings instruction can be used to compare two elements in the same or different strings. It subtracts the destination operand from the source operand and adjusts flags CF, PF, AF, ZF, SF, and OF accordingly. The result of subtraction is not saved; therefore, the operation does not affect the operands in any way.

```
            MOV     AX,DATASEGADDR
            MOV     DS,AX
            MOV     ES,AX
            MOV     SI,BLK1ADDR
            MOV     DI,BLK2ADDR
            MOV     CX,N
            CLD
   NXTPT:   MOVSB
            LOOP    NXTPT
            HLT
```

Figure 5.28 Block move program using the move string instruction.

An example of a compare strings instruction for bytes of data is

```
CMPSB
```

Again, the source element is pointed to by the address in SI with respect to the current value in DS and the destination element is specified by the contents of DI relative to the contents of ES. When executed, the operands are compared, the flags are adjusted, and both SI and DI are updated so that they point to the next elements in their respective strings.

The scan string instruction is similar to compare strings; however, it compares the byte or word element of the destination string at the physical address derived from DI and ES to the contents of AL or AX, respectively. The flags are adjusted based on this result and DI incremented or decremented.

A program using the SCASB instruction that implements a string scan operation similar to that described in Example 5.14 is shown in Fig. 5.29. Notice that we have made DS equal to ES.

Load and Store String—LODSB/LODSW and STOSB/STOSW

The last two instructions in Fig. 5.27, load string and store string, are specifically provided to move string elements between the accumulator and memory. LODSB loads a byte from a string in memory into AL. The address in SI is used relative to DS to determine the address of the memory location of the string element; SI is incremented by one after loading. Similarly the instruction

```
LODSW
```

indicates that the word string element at the physical address derived from DS and SI is to be loaded into AX. Then the index in SI is automatically incremented by two.

On the other hand, STOSB stores a byte from AL into a string location in memory. This time the contents of ES and DI are used to form the address of the storage location in memory. For example, the program in Fig. 5.30 will load the block of memory locations from $0A000_{16}$ through $0A00F_{16}$ with number 5.

```
            MOV      AX,0
            MOV      DS,AX
            MOV      ES,AX
            MOV      AL,05
            MOV      DI,0A000H
            MOV      CX,0FH
            CLD
AGAIN:      SCASB
            LOOPNE   AGAIN
NEXT:
```

Figure 5.29 Block scan operation using the SCAS instruction.

```
           MOV      AX,0
           MOV      DS,AX
           MOV      ES,AX
           MOV      AL,05
           MOV      DI,A000H
           MOV      CX,0FH
           CLD
AGAIN:     STOSB
           LOOPNE   AGAIN
NEXT:
```

Figure 5.30 Initializing a block of memory with a store string operation.

Repeat String—REP

In most applications, the basic string operations must be repeated in order to process arrays of data. This is done by inserting a repeat prefix before the instruction that is to be repeated. The *repeat prefixes* of the 8088 are shown in Fig. 5.31.

The first prefix, REP, causes the basic string operation to be repeated until the contents of register CX become equal to zero. Each time the instruction is executed, it causes CX to be tested for 0. If CX is found not to be 0, it is decremented by one and the basic string operation is repeated. On the other hand, if it is 0, the repeat string operation is done and the next instruction in the program is executed. The repeat count must be loaded into CX prior to executing the repeat string instruction. Figure 5.32 is the memory load routine of Fig. 5.30 modified by using the REP prefix.

The prefixes REPE and REPZ stand for the same function. They are meant for use with the CMPS and SCAS instructions. With REPE/REPZ, the basic compare or scan operation can be repeated as long as both the contents of CX are not equal to 0 and the zero flag is 1. The first condition, CX not equal to 0, indicates that the end of the string has not yet been reached and the second condition, ZF = 1, indicates that the elements that were compared are equal.

The last prefix, REPNE/REPNZ, works similarly to REPE/REPZ except that now the operation is repeated as long as CX is not equal to 0 and ZF is 0. That is, the comparison or scanning is to be performed as long as the string elements are unequal and the end of the string is not yet found.

Prefix	Used with:	Meaning
REP	MOVS STOS	Repeat while not end of string CX ≠ 0
REPE/REPZ	CMPS SCAS	Repeat while not end of string and strings are equal CX ≠ 0 and ZF = 1
REPNE/REPNZ	CMPS SCAS	Repeat while not end of string and strings are not equal CX ≠ 0 and ZF = 0

Figure 5.31 Prefixes for use with the basic string operations.

```
            MOV        AX,0
            MOV        DS,AX
            MOV        ES,AX
            MOV        AL,05
            MOV        DI,A000H
            MOV        CX,0FH
            CLD
            REPSTOSB
NEXT:
```

Figure 5.32 Initializing a block of memory repeating STOSB instruction.

Autoindexing for String Instructions

Earlier we pointed out that during the execution of a string instruction the address indices in SI and DI are either automatically incremented or decremented. Moreover, we indicated that the decision to increment or decrement is made based on the setting of the direction flag DF. The 8088 provides two instructions, clear direction flag (CLD) and set direction flag (STD), to permit selection between *autoincrement* and *autodecrement mode* of operation. These instructions are shown in Fig. 5.33. When CLD is executed, DF is set to 0. This selects autoincrement mode and each time a string operation is performed SI and/or DI are incremented by one if byte data are processed and by two if word data are processed.

Mnemonic	Meaning	Format	Operation	Flags Affected
CLD	Clear DF	CLD	(DF) ← 0	DF
STD	Set DF	STD	(DF) ← 1	DF

Figure 5.33 Instructions for autoincrementing and autodecrementing in string instructions.

EXAMPLE 5.16

Describe what happens as the following sequence of instructions is executed.

```
        CLD
        MOV  AX,DATA_SEGMENT
        MOV  DS,AX
        MOV  AX,EXTRA_SEGMENT
        MOV  ES,AX
        MOV  CX,20H
        MOV  SI,OFFSET MASTER
        MOV  DI,OFFSET COPY
        REPMOVSB
```

SOLUTION The first instruction clears the direction flag and selects autoincrement mode of operation for string addressing. The next two instructions initialize DS with the value DATA_SEGMENT. It is followed by two instructions that load ES with the value EXTRA_SEGMENT. Then the number of repeats, 20_{16}, is loaded into CX. The next two instructions load SI and DI with beginning offset addresses MASTER and COPY for the source and destination strings. Now we are ready to perform the string operation. Execution of REP MOVSB moves a block of 32 consecutive bytes from the block of memory locations starting at offset address MASTER with respect to the current data segment (DS) to a block of locations starting at offset address COPY with respect to the current extra segment (ES).

EXAMPLE 5.17

The source program in Fig. 5.34(a) implements the block move operation of Example 5.16. This program was assembled by the macroassembler on the IBM PC and linked to produce a run module called EX517.EXE. The source listing that was produced during the assembly process is shown in Fig. 5.34(b). Execute the program using DEBUG and verify its operation.

SOLUTION The program is loaded with the DEBUG command

$$A > DEBUG \ B:EX517.EXE \qquad (\lrcorner)$$

and verified by the UNASSEMBLE command

$$-U \ 0 \ 18 \qquad (\lrcorner)$$

Comparing the displayed instruction sequence in Fig. 5.34(c) with the source listing in Fig. 5.34(b), we find that the program has loaded correctly.

First, we execute down to the REPZ instruction with the G command

$$-G \ 16 \qquad (\lrcorner)$$

and, looking at the state information displayed in Fig. 5.34(c), we see that CX has been loaded with 0020_{16}, SI with 0000_{16}, and DI with 0020_{16}.

Now the storage locations in the 32-byte source block that starts at address DS:0000 are loaded with the value FF_{16} using the FILL command

$$-F \ DS:0 \ 1F \ FF \ (\lrcorner)$$

and the 32 bytes of the destination block, which start at DS:0020, are loaded with the value 00_{16} with the FILL command

```
TITLE   EXAMPLE 5.17

        PAGE    ,132

STACK_SEG       SEGMENT         STACK 'STACK'
                DB              64 DUP(?)
STACK_SEG       ENDS


DATA_SEG        SEGMENT         'DATA'
MASTER          DB              32 DUP(?)
COPY            DB              32 DUP(?)
DATA_SEG        ENDS


CODE_SEG        SEGMENT         'CODE'
EX517   PROC    FAR
        ASSUME  CS:CODE_SEG, SS:STACK_SEG, DS:DATA_SEG, ES:DATA_SEG

;To return to DEBUG program put return address on the stack

        PUSH    DS
        MOV     AX, 0
        PUSH    AX

;Following code implements Example 5.17

        MOV     AX, DATA_SEG    ;Set up data segment
        MOV     DS, AX
        MOV     ES, AX          ;Set up extra segment

        CLD
        MOV     CX, 20H
        MOV     SI, OFFSET MASTER
        MOV     DI, OFFSET COPY
REP     MOVS    COPY, MASTER

        RET                     ;Return to DEBUG program
EX517   ENDP
CODE_SEG        ENDS

        END     EX517
```

(a)

Figure 5.34 (a) Source program for
Example 5.17. (b) Source listing produced by the assembler. (c) Executing
the program with DEBUG.

```
                          TITLE    EXAMPLE 5.17

                                   PAGE      ,132

0000                               STACK_SEG      SEGMENT      STACK 'STACK'
0000    40 [                                      DB           64 DUP(?)
        ??
            ]

0040                               STACK_SEG      ENDS


0000                               DATA_SEG       SEGMENT      'DATA'
0000    20 [                       MASTER         DB           32 DUP(?)
        ??
            ]

0020    20 [                       COPY           DB           32 DUP(?)
        ??
            ]

0040                               DATA_SEG       ENDS


0000                               CODE_SEG       SEGMENT      'CODE'
0000                               EX517   PROC   FAR
                                           ASSUME CS:CODE_SEG, SS:STACK_SEG, DS:DATA_SEG, ES:DATA_SEG

                                   ;To return to DEBUG program put return address on the stack

0000  1E                                   PUSH   DS
0001  B8 0000                              MOV    AX, 0
0004  50                                   PUSH   AX

                                   ;Following code implements Example 5.17

0005  B8  ---- R                           MOV    AX, DATA_SEG      ;Set up data segment
0008  8E D8                                MOV    DS, AX
000A  8E C0                                MOV    ES, AX            ;Set up extra segment

000C  FC                                   CLD
000D  B9 0020                              MOV    CX, 20H
0010  BE 0000 R                            MOV    SI, OFFSET MASTER
0013  BF 0020 R                            MOV    DI, OFFSET COPY
0016  F3/ A4                       REP     MOVS   COPY, MASTER

0018  CB                                   RET                      ;Return to DEBUG program
0019                               EX517   ENDP
0019                               CODE_SEG       ENDS

                                           END    EX517

Segments and groups:

            N a m e                Size     align   combine class

CODE_SEG . . . . . . . . . . . .   0019     PARA    NONE    'CODE'
DATA_SEG . . . . . . . . . . . .   0040     PARA    NONE    'DATA'
STACK_SEG. . . . . . . . . . . .   0040     PARA    STACK   'STACK'
```

(b)

Figure 5.34 (Continued)

Symbols:

Name	Type	Value	Attr	
COPY	L BYTE	0020	DATA_SEG	Length =0020
EX517.	F PROC	0000	CODE_SEG	Length =0019
MASTER	L BYTE	0000	DATA_SEG	Length =0020

Warning Severe
Errors Errors
0   0

(b)   (Continued)

```
A>DEBUG B:EX517.EXE
-U 0 18
0D03:0000 1E            PUSH    DS
0D03:0001 B80000        MOV     AX,0000
0D03:0004 50            PUSH    AX
0D03:0005 B8050D        MOV     AX,0D05
0D03:0008 8ED8          MOV     DS,AX
0D03:000A 8EC0          MOV     ES,AX
0D03:000C FC            CLD
0D03:000D B92000        MOV     CX,0020
0D03:0010 BE0000        MOV     SI,0000
0D03:0013 BF2000        MOV     DI,0020
0D03:0016 F3            REPZ
0D03:0017 A4            MOVSB
0D03:0018 CB            RETF
-G 16

AX=0D05  BX=0000  CX=0020  DX=0000  SP=003C  BP=0000  SI=0000  DI=0020
DS=0D05  ES=0D05  SS=0D09  CS=0D03  IP=0016   NV UP EI PL NZ NA PO NC
0D03:0016 F3            REPZ
0D03:0017 A4            MOVSB
-F DS:0 1F FF
-F DS:20 3F 00
-D DS:0 3F
0D05:0000  FF FF FF FF FF FF FF FF-FF FF FF FF FF FF FF FF   ................
0D05:0010  FF FF FF FF FF FF FF FF-FF FF FF FF FF FF FF FF   ................
0D05:0020  00 00 00 00 00 00 00 00-00 00 00 00 00 00 00 00   ................
0D05:0030  00 00 00 00 00 00 00 00-00 00 00 00 00 00 00 00   ................
-G 18

AX=0D05  BX=0000  CX=0000  DX=0000  SP=003C  BP=0000  SI=0020  DI=0040
DS=0D05  ES=0D05  SS=0D09  CS=0D03  IP=0018   NV UP EI PL NZ NA PO NC
0D03:0018 CB            RETF
-D DS:0 3F
0D05:0000  FF FF FF FF FF FF FF FF-FF FF FF FF FF FF FF FF   ................
0D05:0010  FF FF FF FF FF FF FF FF-FF FF FF FF FF FF FF FF   ................
0D05:0020  FF FF FF FF FF FF FF FF-FF FF FF FF FF FF FF FF   ................
0D05:0030  FF FF FF FF FF FF FF FF-FF FF FF FF FF FF FF FF   ................
-G

Program terminated normally
-Q

A>
```

(c)

Figure 5.34   (Continued)

-F DS:20 3F 00 (↵)

Now a memory dump command is used to verify the initialization of memory

-D DS:0 3F   (↵)

Looking at the displayed information in Fig. 5.34(c), we see that memory has been initialized correctly.

Now we execute the string move operation with the command

-G 18   (↵)

Again looking at the display in Fig. 5.34(c), we see that the repeat count in CX has been decremented to zero and that the source and destination pointers have been incremented to $(SI) = 0020_{16}$ and $(DI) = 0040_{16}$. In this way, we see that the string move instruction was executed 32 times and that the source and destination addresses were correctly incremented to complete the block transfer. The block transfer operation is verified by repeating the DUMP command

-D DS:0 3F   (↵)

Notice that both the source and destination blocks now contain FF_{16} in all byte storage locations.

ASSIGNMENTS

Section 5.2

1. Explain what happens when the instruction sequence

```
LAHF
MOV    [BX+DI],AH
```

is executed.

2. What operation is performed by the instruction sequence that follows?

```
MOV    AH, [BX+SI]
SAHF
```

3. What instruction should be executed to ensure that the carry flag is in the set state? The reset state?

4. Which instruction when executed disables the interrupt interface?

5. Write an instruction sequence to configure the 8088 as follows: interrupts not accepted; save the original contents of flags SF, ZF, AF, PF, and CF at the address $A000_{16}$; and then clear CF.

Section 5.3

6. Describe the difference in operation and the effect on status flags due to the execution of the subtract words and compare words instructions.

7. Describe the operation performed by each of the instructions that follow.
(a) CMP   [0100H],AL
(b) CMP   AX,[SI]
(c) CMP   WORD PTR [DI],1234H

8. What is the state of the 8088's flags after executing the instructions in problem 7 (a) through (c)? Assume the following initial state exists before executing the instructions.

$$(AX) = 8001H$$
$$(SI) = 0200H$$
$$(DI) = 0300H$$
$$(DS:100H) = F0H$$
$$(DS:200H) = F0H$$
$$(DS:201H) = 01H$$
$$(DS:300H) = 34H$$
$$(DS:301H) = 12H$$

9. What happens to the ZF and CF satus flags as the following sequence of instructions is executed? Assume that they are both initially cleared.

```
MOV BX,1111H
MOV AX,0BBBBH
CMP BX,AX
```

Section 5.4

10. What is the key difference between the unconditional jump instruction and conditional jump instruction?

11. Which registers have their contents changed during an intrasegment jump? Intersegment jump?

12. How large is a Short-label displacement? Near-label displacement? Memptr16 operand?

13. Is a Far-label used to initiate an intrasegment jump or an intersegment jump?

14. Identify the type of jump, the type of operand, and operation performed by each of the instructions that follow.
(a) JMP   10H
(b) JMP   1000H
(c) JMP   WORD PTR [SI]

15. If the state of the 8088 is as follows after executing each instruction in problem 14, to what address is program control passed?

$$(CS) = 0175H$$

$$(IP) = 0300H$$

$$(SI) = 0100H$$

$$(DS:100H) = 00H$$

$$(DS:101H) = 10H$$

16. Which flags are tested by the various conditional jump instructions?

17. What flag condition is tested for by the instruction JNS?

18. What flag conditions are tested for by the instruction JA?

19. Identify the type of jump, the type of operand, and operation performed by each of the instructions that follows.

   (a) `JNC 10H`

   (b) `JNP PARITY_ERROR`

   (c) `JO DWORD PTR [BX]`

20. What value must be loaded into BX such that execution of the instruction JMP BX transfers control to the memory location offset from the beginning of the current code segment by 256_{10}?

21. The program that follows implements what is known as a *delay loop*.

```
           MOV   CX,1000H
    DLY:   DEC   CX
           JNZ   DLY
    NXT:   ---   ---
```

   (a) How many times does the JNZ DLY instruction get executed?

   (b) Change the program so that JNZ DLY is executed just 17 times.

   (c) Change the program so that JNZ DLY is executed 2^{32} times.

22. Given a number N in the range $0 < N \le 5$, write a program that computes its factorial and saves the result in memory location FACT.

23. Write a program that compares the elements of two arrays, A(I) and B(I). Each array contains 100 16-bit signed numbers. The comparison is to be done by comparing the corresponding elements of the two arrays until either two elements are found to be unequal or all elements of the arrays have been compared and found to be equal. Assume that the arrays start at addresses $A000_{16}$ and $B000_{16}$, respectively. If the two arrays are found to be unequal, save the address of the first unequal element of A(I) in memory location FOUND; otherwise, write all 0s into this location.

24. Given an array A(I) of 100 16-bit signed numbers that are stored in memory starting at address $A000_{16}$, write a program to generate two arrays from the given array such that one P(J) consists of all the positive numbers and the other N(K) contains all the negative numbers. Store the array of positive numbers in memory starting at address $B000_{16}$ and the array of negative numbers starting at address $C000_{16}$.

25. Given a 16-bit binary number in DX, write a program that converts it to its equivalent BCD number in DX. If the result is bigger than 16 bits, place all 1s in DX.

26. Given an array A(I) with 100 16-bit signed integer numbers, write a program to generate a new array B(I) as follows:

$$B(I) = A(I), \quad \text{for I} = 1, 2, 99, \text{ and } 100$$

and

$$B(I) = \text{median value of } A(I - 2), A(I - 1), A(I), A(I + 1),$$

$$\text{and } A(I + 2), \quad \text{for all other Is}$$

Section 5.5

27. Describe the difference between a jump and call instruction.

28. Why are intersegment and intrasegment call instructions provided in the 8088?

29. What is saved on the stack when a call instruction with a Memptr16 operand is executed? A Memptr32 operand?

30. Identify the type of call, the type of operand, and operation performed by each of the instructions that follows.
   (a) CALL 1000H
   (b) CALL WORD PTR [100H]
   (c) CALL DWORD PTR [BX+SI]

31. The state of the 8088 is as follows. To what address is program control passed after executing each instruction in problem 30?

$$(CS) = 1075H$$

$$(IP) = 0300H$$

$$(BX) = 0100H$$

$$(SI) = 0100H$$

$$(DS:100H) = 00H$$

$$(DS:101H) = 10H$$

$$(DS:200H) = 00H$$

$$(DS:201H) = 01H$$

$$(DS:202H) = 00H$$

$$(DS:203H) = 10H$$

32. What function is performed by the RET instruction?

33. Describe the operation performed by each of the instructions that follows.
   (a) PUSH DS
   (b) PUSH [SI]
   (c) POP DI
   (d) POP [BX+DI]
   (e) POPF

34. At what addresses will the bytes of the immediate operand in problem 33 (a) be stored after the instruction is executed?

35. Write a subroutine that converts a given 16-bit BCD number to its equivalent binary number. The BCD number is to be passed to a subroutine through register DX and the routine returns the equivalent binary number in DX.

36. When is it required to include PUSHF and POPF instructions in a subroutine?

37. Given an array A(I) of 100 16-bit signed integer numbers, write a subroutine to generate a new array B(I) so that

$$B(I) = A(I), \qquad \text{for I} = 1 \text{ and } 100$$

and

$$B(I) = \frac{1}{4} [A(I-1) - 5A(I) + 9A(I+1)], \qquad \text{for all other Is}$$

The values of A(I − 1), A(I), and A(I + 1) are to be passed to the subroutine in registers AX, BX, and CX and the subroutine returns the result B(I) in register AX.

38. Write a segment of main program and show its subroutine structure to perform the following operations. The program is to check continuously the three most significant bits in register DX and, depending on their setting, execute one of three subroutines: SUBA, SUBB, or SUBC. The subroutines are selected as follows:

(a) If bit 15 of DX is set, initiate SUBA.
(b) If bit 14 of DX is set and bit 15 is not set, initiate SUBB.
(c) If bit 13 of DX is set and bits 14 and 15 are not set, initiate SUBC.

If the subroutine is executed, the corresponding bits of DX are to be cleared and then control returned to the main program. After returning from the subroutine, the main program is repeated.

Section 5.6

39. Which flags are tested by the various conditional loop instructions?

40. What two conditions can terminate the operation performed by the instruction LOOPNE?

41. How large a jump can be employed in a loop instruction?

42. What is the maximum number of repeats that can be implemented with a loop instruction?

43. Using loop instructions, implement the program in problem 22.

44. Using loop instructions, implement the program in problem 23.

Section 5.7

45. What determines whether the SI and DI registers increment or decrement during a string operation?

46. Which segment register is used to form the destination address for a string instruction?

47. Write equivalent string instruction sequences for each of the following:

```
(a) MOV  AL,[SI]    (c) MOV  AL,[DI]
    MOV  [DI],AL        CMP  AL,[SI]
    INC  SI             DEC  SI
    INC  DI             DEC  DI
(b) MOV  AX,[SI]
    INC  SI
    INC  SI
```

48. Use string instructions to implement the program in problem 23.

49. Write a program to convert a table of 100 ASCII characters that are stored starting at offset address ASCII_CHAR into their equivalent table of EBCDIC characters and store them at offset address EBCDIC_CHAR. The translation is to be done using an ASCII-to-EBCDIC conversion table starting at offset address ASCII_TO_EBCDIC. Assume that all three tables are located in different segments of memory.

The 8088 and 8086 Microprocessors and Their Memory Interfaces

6.1 INTRODUCTION

Up to this point, we have studied the 8088 and 8086 microprocessors from a software point of view. We covered their software architecture, instruction set, and how to write programs in assembly language, and found that the 8088 and 8086 were identical from the software point of view. This is not true of the hardware architectures of the 8088 and 8086 microcomputer systems. Now we will begin to examine the 8088 and 8086 microcomputer from the hardware point of view. The focus will be on the 8088-based microcomputer, but the differences of the 8086 microprocessor and microcomputer will also be described. This chapter is devoted to signal interfaces, memory interfaces, memory devices, and external memory subsystems. The following topics are presented in this chapter:

1. The 8088 and 8086 microprocessors
2. Minimum-mode and maximum-mode systems
3. Minimum-system-mode interface
4. Maximum-system-mode interface
5. Electrical characteristics
6. System clock

  7. Bus cycle

  8. Hardware organization of the memory address space

  9. Memory bus status codes

 10. Memory control signals

 11. Read and write bus cycles

 12. Memory interface circuits

 13. Programmable logic arrays

 14. Program storage memory—ROM, PROM, and EPROM

 15. Data storage memory—SRAM and DRAM

 16. Program storage memory and data storage memory circuits

6.2 THE 8088 AND 8086 MICROPROCESSORS

The 8086, which was first announced as a product in 1978, was the first 16-bit microprocessor introduced by Intel Corporation. It was followed by a second member of the 8086 family, the 8088 microprocessor, in 1979. The 8088 is fully software compatible with its predecessor, the 8086. The difference between these two devices is in their hardware architecture. Just like the 8086, the 8088 is internally a 16-bit MPU. However, externally the 8086 has a 16-bit data bus and the 8088 has an 8-bit data bus. This is the key hardware difference. Both devices have the ability to address up to 1M byte of memory via their 20-bit address buses. Moreover, they can address up to 64K of byte-wide input/output ports.

The 8088 and 8086 are both manufactured using *high-performance metal-oxide semiconductor (HMOS) technology,* and the circuitry on their chips is equivalent to approximately 29,000 transistors. They are enclosed in 40-pin packages as shown in Fig. 6.1(a) and (b), respectively. Many of their pins have multiple functions. For example, in the pin layout diagram of the 8088 we see that address bus lines A_0 through A_7 and data bus lines D_0 through D_7 are multiplexed. For this reason, these leads are labeled AD_0 through AD_7.

6.3 MINIMUM-MODE AND MAXIMUM-MODE SYSTEMS

The 8088 and 8086 microprocessors can be configured to work in either of two modes. These modes are known as the *minimum system mode* and the *maximum system mode*. The minimum system mode is selected by applying logic 1 to the $MN/\overline{MX}$ input lead. Minimum 8088/8086 systems are typically smaller and contain a single microprocessor. Changing $MN/\overline{MX}$ to logic 0 selects the maximum mode of operation. This configures the 8088/8086 system for use in larger systems and with multiple processors. This mode-selection feature lets the 8088 or 8086 better meet the needs of a wide variety of system requirements.

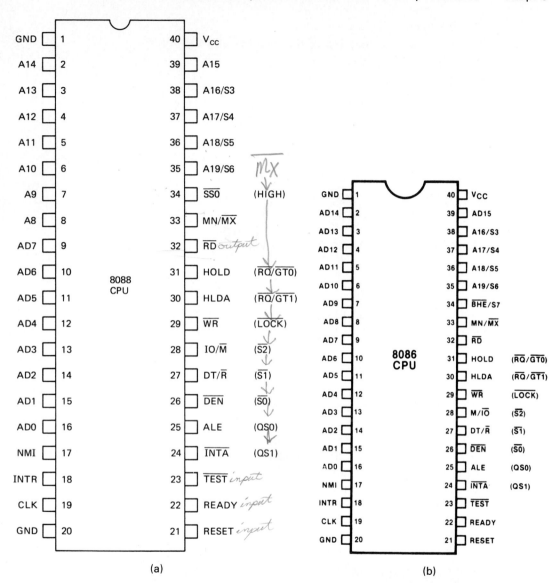

Figure 6.1 (a) Pin layout of the 8088 microprocessor. (Reprinted with permission of Intel Corporation, © 1981) (b) Pin layout of the 8086 microprocessor. (Reprinted with permission of Intel Corporation, © 1979)

Depending on the mode of operation selected, the assignments for a number of the pins on the microprocessor package are changed. As shown in Fig. 6.1(a), the pin functions of the 8088 specified in parentheses are those that pertain to a maximum-mode system.

The signals of the 8088 microprocessor that are common to both modes of operation, those unique to minimum mode and those unique to maximum mode, are listed in Fig. 6.2(a), (b), and (c), respectively. Here we find the name, function, and type for each signal. For example, the signal $\overline{RD}$ is in the common group. It functions as a read control output and is used to signal memory or I/O devices when the 8088's system bus is set up for input of data. Moreover, notice that the signals hold request (HOLD) and hold acknowledge (HLDA) are produced only in the minimum-mode system. If the 8088 is set up for maximum mode, they are replaced by the request/grant bus access control lines $\overline{RQ/GT}_0$ and $\overline{RQ/GT}_1$.

Minimum mode signals (MN/$\overline{MX}$ = V$_{cc}$)		
Name	Function	Type
HOLD	Hold request	Input
HLDA	Hold acknowledge	Output
$\overline{WR}$	Write control	Output, 3-state
IO/$\overline{M}$	IO/memory control	Output, 3-state
DT/$\overline{R}$	Data transmit/receive	Output, 3-state
$\overline{DEN}$	Data enable	Output, 3-state
$\overline{SSO}$	Status line	Output, 3-state
ALE	Address latch enable	Output
$\overline{INTA}$	Interrupt acknowledge	Output

(b)

Common signals		
Name	Function	Type
AD7–AD0	Address/data bus	Bidirectional, 3-state
A15–A8	Address bus	Output, 3-state
A19/S6–A16/S3	Address/status	Output, 3-state
MN/$\overline{MX}$	Minimum/maximum Mode control	Input
$\overline{RD}$	Read control	Output, 3-state
$\overline{TEST}$	Wait on test control	Input
READY	Wait state control	Input
RESET	System reset	Input
NMI	Nonmaskable Interrupt request	Input
INTR	Interrupt request	Input
CLK	System clock	Input
V$_{cc}$	+5 V	Input
GND	Ground	

(a)

Maximum mode signals (MN/$\overline{MX}$ = GND)		
Name	Function	Type
$\overline{RQ/GT}1, 0$	Request/grant bus access control	Bidirectional
$\overline{LOCK}$	Bus priority lock control	Output, 3-state
$\overline{S2}$–$\overline{S0}$	Bus cycle status	Output, 3-state
QS1, QS0	Instruction queue status	Output

(c)

Figure 6.2   (a) Signals common to both minimum and maximum modes. (b) Unique minimum-mode signals. (c) Unique maximum-mode signals.

EXAMPLE 6.1

Which pins provide different signal function in the minimum-mode 8088 and 8086?

SOLUTION Comparing the pin layouts of the 8088 and 8086 in Fig. 6.1, we find the following:

(a) Pins 2 through 8 on the 8088 are address lines A_{14} through A_8, but on the 8086 they are address/data bus lines AD_{14} through AD_8.

(b) Pin 28 on the 8088 is $IO/\overline{M}$ and on the 8086 it is the $M/\overline{IO}$.

(c) Pin 34 of the 8088 is the $\overline{SSO}$ output and on the 8086 this pin supplies the $\overline{BHE}/S_7$ output.

6.4 MINIMUM-SYSTEM-MODE INTERFACE

When the minimum system mode of operation is selected, the 8088 or 8086 itself provides all the control signals needed to implement the memory and I/O interfaces. Figure 6.3(a) and (b) shows block diagrams of a minimum-mode configuration of the 8088 and 8086 MPU, respectively. The minimum-mode signals can be divided into the following basic groups: address/data bus, status, control, interrupt, and DMA. For simplicity in the diagram, multiplexed signal lines are shown to be independent.

Address/Data Bus

Let us first look at the address/data bus. In an 8088-based microcomputer system these lines serve two functions. As an *address bus,* they are used to carry address information to the memory and I/O ports. The address bus is 20 bits long and consists of signal lines A_0 through A_{19}. Of these, A_{19} represents the MSB and A_0 the LSB. A 20-bit address gives the 8088 a 1M-byte memory address space. However, only address lines A_0 through A_{15} are used when accessing I/O. This gives the 8088 an independent I/O address space that is 64K bytes in length.

The eight *data bus* lines D_0 through D_7 are actually multiplexed with address lines A_0 through A_7, respectively. By *multiplexed* we mean that the bus works as an address bus during one period of time and as a data bus during another period. D_7 is the MSB and D_0 the LSB. When acting as a data bus, they carry read/write data for memory, input/output data for I/O devices, and interrupt-type codes from an interrupt controller.

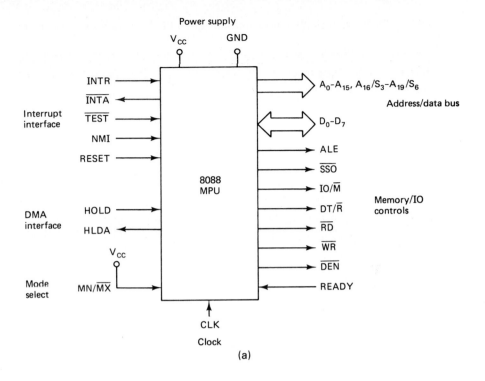

(a)

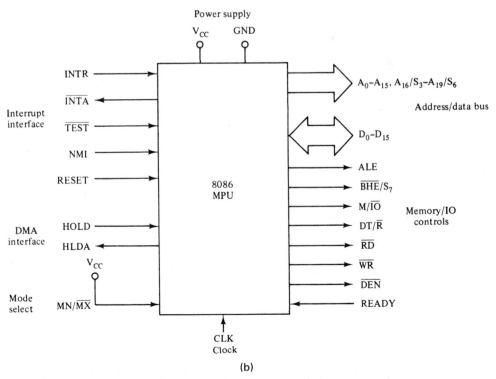

(b)

Figure 6.3 (a) Block diagram of the minimum-mode 8088 MPU. (b) Block diagram of a minimum-mode 8086 MPU.

Looking at Fig. 6.3(b), we see that the 8086 has 16 data bus lines instead of 8 like the 8088. Data bus lines D_0 through D_{15} are multiplexed with address bus lines A_0 through A_{15}.

Status Signals

The four most significant address lines, A_{19} through A_{16} of both the 8088 and 8086 are also multiplexed, but in this case with status signals S_6 through S_3. These status bits are output on the bus at the same time that data are transferred over the other bus lines. Bits S_4 and S_3 together form a 2-bit binary code that identifies which of the internal segment registers was used to generate the physical address that was output on the address bus during the current bus cycle. These four codes and the register they represent are shown in Fig. 6.4. Notice that the code $S_4S_3 = 00$ identifies a register known as the *extra segment register* as the source of the segment address.

Status line S_5 reflects the status of another internal characteristic of the MPU. It is the logic level of the internal interrupt enable flag. The last status bit S_6 is always at the 0 logic level.

Control Signals

The *control signals* are provided to support the memory and I/O interfaces of the 8088 and 8086. They control functions such as when the bus is to carry a valid address, in which direction data are to be transferred over the bus, when valid write data are on the bus, and when to put read data on the system bus. For example, *address latch enable* (ALE) is a pulse to logic 1 that signals external circuitry when a valid address word is on the bus. This address must be latched in external circuitry on the 1-to-0 edge of the pulse at ALE.

Using the IO/$\overline{\text{M}}$ (IO/memory) line, DT/$\overline{\text{R}}$ (*data transmit/receive*) line, and status line $\overline{\text{SSO}}$, the 8088 signals which type of bus cycle is in progress and in which direction data are to be transferred over the bus. The logic level of IO/$\overline{\text{M}}$ tells external circuitry whether a memory or I/O transfer is taking place over the bus. Logic 0 at this output signals a memory operation, and logic 1 an I/O operation. The direction of data transfer over the bus is signaled by the logic level output at DT/$\overline{\text{R}}$. When this line is logic 1 during the data transfer part of a bus cycle, the bus is in the transmit mode. Therefore, data are either written into

S_3	S_4	Address Status
0	0	Alternate (relative to the ES segment)
1	0	Stack (relative to the SS segment)
0	1	Code/None (relative to the CS segment or a default of zero)
1	1	Data (relative to the DS segment)

Figure 6.4   Address bus status code. (Reprinted with permission of Intel Corporation, © 1979)

memory or output to an I/O device. On the other hand, logic 0 at DT/$\overline{\text{R}}$ signals that the bus is in the receive mode. This corresponds to reading data from memory or input of data from an input port.

Comparing Fig. 6.3(a) and 6.3(b), we find two differences between the minimum-mode 8088 and 8086 microprocessors. First, the 8086's memory/IO control (M/$\overline{\text{IO}}$) signal is the complement of the equivalent signal of the 8088. Second, the 8088's $\overline{\text{SSO}}$ status signal is replaced by *bank high enable* ($\overline{\text{BHE}}$) on the 8086. Logic 0 on this line is used as a memory enable signal for the most significant byte half of the data bus, D_8 through D_{15}. This line also serves a second function, which is as the S_7 status line.

The signals *read* ($\overline{\text{RD}}$) and *write* ($\overline{\text{WR}}$), respectively, indicate that a read bus cycle or a write bus cycle is in progress. The MPU switches $\overline{\text{WR}}$ to logic 0 to signal external devices that valid write or output data are on the bus. On the other hand, $\overline{\text{RD}}$ indicates that the MPU is performing a read of data off the bus. During read operations, one other control signal is also supplied. This is $\overline{\text{DEN}}$ (*data enable*), and it signals external devices when they should put data on the bus.

There is one other control signal that is involved with the memory and I/O interface. This is the READY signal. It can be used to insert wait states into the bus cycle so that it is extended by a number of clock periods. This signal is provided by way of an external clock generator device and can be supplied by the memory or I/O subsystem to signal the MPU when they are ready to permit the data transfer to be completed.

Interrupt Signals

The key interrupt interface signals are *interrupt request* (INTR) and *interrupt acknowledge* ($\overline{\text{INTA}}$). INTR is an input to the 8088 and 8086 that can be used by an external device to signal that it needs to be serviced. This input is sampled during the final clock period of each *instruction acquisition cycle*. Logic 1 at INTR represents an active interrupt request. When an interrupt request has been recognized by the MPU it indicates this fact to external circuits with pulses to logic 0 at the $\overline{\text{INTA}}$ output.

The $\overline{\text{TEST}}$ input is also related to the external interrupt interface. For example, execution of a WAIT instruction causes the 8088 or 8086 to check the logic level at the $\overline{\text{TEST}}$ input. If logic 1 is found, the MPU suspends operation and goes into what is known as the *idle state*. The MPU no longer executes instructions; instead, it repeatedly checks the logic level of the $\overline{\text{TEST}}$ input waiting for its transition back to logic 0. As $\overline{\text{TEST}}$ switches to 0, execution resumes with the next instruction in the program. This feature can be used to synchronize the operation of the MPU to an event in external hardware.

There are two more inputs in the interrupt interface: the *nonmaskable interrupt* (NMI) and the *reset interrupt* (RESET). On the 0-to-1 transition of NMI, control is passed to a nonmaskable interrupt service routine at completion of execution of the current instruction. The RESET input is used to provide a hardware reset for the MPU. Switching RESET to logic 0 initializes the internal registers of the MPU and initiates a reset service routine.

DMA Interface Signals

The *direct memory access* (DMA) interface of the 8088/8086 minimum-mode microcomputer system consists of the HOLD and HLDA signals. When an external device wants to take control of the system bus, it signals this fact to the MPU by switching HOLD to the 1 logic level. For example, when the HOLD input of the 8088 becomes active, it enters the hold state at the completion of the current bus cycle. When in the hold state, signal lines AD_0 through AD_7, A_8 through A_{15}, A_{16}/S_3 through A_{19}/S_6, $\overline{SSO}$, $IO/\overline{M}$, $DT/\overline{R}$, $\overline{RD}$, $\overline{WR}$, $\overline{DEN}$, and INTR are all in the high-Z state. The 8088 signals external devices that it is in this state by switching its HLDA output to the 1 logic level.

6.5 MAXIMUM-SYSTEM-MODE INTERFACE

When the 8088 or 8086 microprocessor is set for the maximum-mode configuration, it produces signals for implementing a *multiprocessor/coprocessor system environment*. By *multiprocessor environment* we mean that more than one microprocessor exists in the system and that each processor is executing its own program. Usually in this type of system environment, some system resources are common to all processors. They are called *global resources*. There are also other resources that are assigned to specific processors. These dedicated resources are known as *local* or *private resources*.

Coprocessor also means that there is a second processor in the system. However, in this case, the two processors do not access the bus at the same time. One passes control of the system bus to the other and then may suspend its operation. In the maximum-mode system, facilities are provided for implementing allocation of global resources and passing bus control to other microcomputers or coprocessors.

8288 Bus Controller: Bus Commands and Control Signals

Looking at the maximum-mode block diagram in Fig. 6.5(a), we see that the 8088 does not directly provide all the signals that are required to control the memory, I/O, and interrupt interfaces. Specifically, the $\overline{WR}$, $IO/\overline{M}$, $DT/\overline{R}$, $\overline{DEN}$, ALE, and $\overline{INTA}$ signals are no longer produced by the 8088. Instead, it outputs three status signals $\overline{S}_0$, $\overline{S}_1$, and $\overline{S}_2$ prior to the initiation of each bus cycle. This 3-bit *bus status code* identifies which type of bus cycle is to follow. $\overline{S}_2\overline{S}_1\overline{S}_0$ are input to the external *bus controller* device, the 8288, which decodes them to identify the type of MPU bus cycle. The block diagram and pin layout of the 8288 are shown in Fig. 6.6(a) and (b), respectively. In response, the bus controller generates the appropriately timed command and control signals.

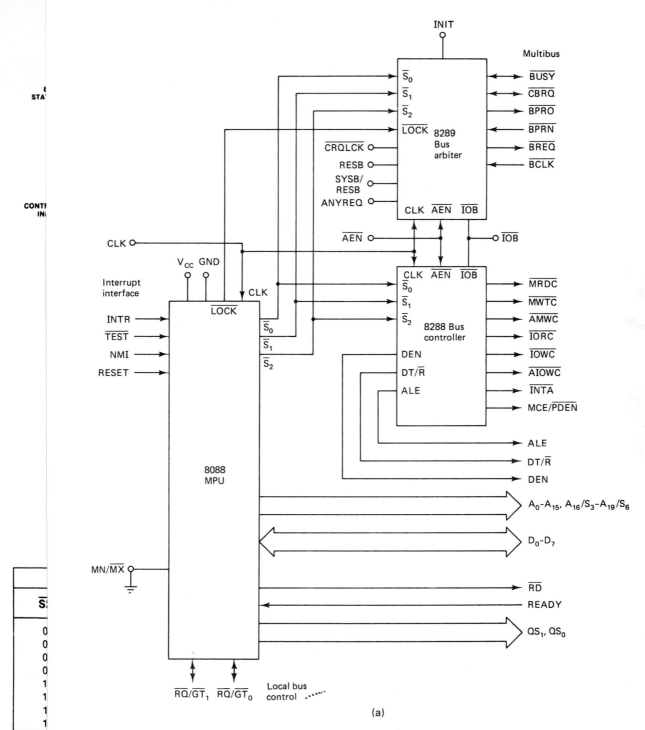

Figure 6.5 (a) 8088 maximum-mode block diagram. (b) 8086 maximum-mode block diagram.

The control outputs produced by the 8288 are DEN, DT/R̄, and ALE. These three signals provide the same functions as those described for the minimum system mode. This set of bus commands and control signals is compatible with the *Multibus*, an industry standard for interfacing microprocessor systems.

Figure 6.5(b) shows that the 8288 bus controller connects to the 8086 in the same way as it does to the 8088 and it also produces the same output signals.

8289 Bus Arbiter: Bus Arbitration and Lock Signals

Looking at Fig. 6.5(a), we see that an 8289 *bus arbiter* has also been added in the maximum-mode system. It is this device that permits multiple processors to reside on the system bus. It does this by implementing the *Multibus arbitration protocol* in an 8088-based system. Figure 6.8(a) and (b) show a block diagram and pin layout of the 8289, respectively.

Addition of the 8288 bus controller and 8289 bus arbiter frees a number of the 8088's pins for use to produce control signals that are needed to support multiple processors. *Bus priority lock* (LOCK) is one of these signals. It is input to the bus arbiter together with status signals $\bar{S}_0$ through $\bar{S}_2$. The control signals implemented by the 8289 are bus arbitration signals: *bus busy* (BUSY), *common bus request* (CBRQ), *bus priority out* (BPRO), *bus priority in* (BPRN), *bus request* (BREQ), and *bus clock* (BCLK). They correspond to the *bus exchange* signals of the Multibus and are used to lock other processors off the system bus during the execution of an instruction by the 8088. In this way the processor can be assured of uninterrupted access to *common system resources* such as *global memory*.

In Fig. 6.5(b), we see that the 8289 bus arbiter connects to the 8086 microprocessor just like it attaches to the 8088. Moreover, it produces the identical bus exchange signals at the Multibus interface.

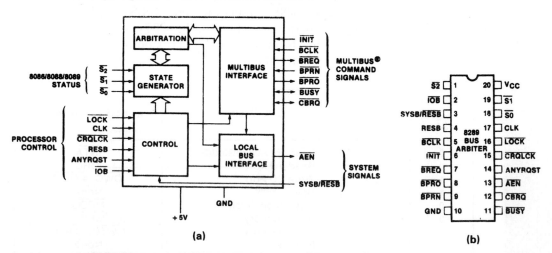

(a)   **(b)**

Figure 6.8   (a) Block diagram of the 8289. (Reprinted with permission of Intel Corporation, © 1979) (b) Pin layout. (Reprinted with permission of Intel Corporation, © 1979)

QS1	QS0	Queue Status
0 (low)	0	No Operation. During the last clock cycle, nothing was taken from the queue.
0	1	First Byte. The byte taken from the queue was the first byte of the instruction.
1 (high)	0	Queue Empty. The queue has been reinitialized as a result of the execution of a transfer instruction.
1	1	Subsequent Byte. The byte taken from the queue was a subsequent byte of the instruction.

Figure 6.9 Queue status codes. (Reprinted with permission of Intel Corporation, © 1979)

Queue Status Signals

Two new signals that are produced by the 8088 and 8086 in the maximum-mode microcomputer system are queue status outputs QS_0 and QS_1. Together they form a 2-bit *queue status code*, QS_1QS_0. This code tells the external circuitry what type of information was removed from the queue during the previous clock cycle. Figure 6.9 shows the four different queue statuses. Notice that $QS_1QS_0 = 01$ indicates that the first byte of an instruction was taken off the queue. As shown, the next byte of the instruction that is fetched is identified by the code 11. Whenever the queue is reset due to a transfer of control, the reinitialization code 10 is output.

Local Bus Control Signals: Request/Grant Signals

In a maximum-mode configuration, the minimum-mode HOLD and HLDA interface of the 8088/8086 is also changed. These two signals are replaced by *request/grant lines* $\overline{RQ/GT_0}$ and $\overline{RQ/GT_1}$, respectively. They provide a prioritized bus access mechanism for accessing the *local bus*.

6.6 ELECTRICAL CHARACTERISTICS

In the preceding sections, the pin layout and minimum- and maximum-mode interface signals of the 8088 and 8086 microprocessors were introduced. Here we will first look at their power supply ratings and then their input and output electrical characteristics.

Symbol	Meaning	Minimum	Maximum	Test condition
V_{IL}	Input low voltage	−0.5 V	+0.8 V	
V_{IH}	Input high voltage	+2.0 V	V_{cc} + 0.5 V	
V_{OL}	Output low voltage		+0.45 V	I_{OL} = 2.0mA
V_{OH}	Output high voltage	+2.4 V		I_{OH} = −400 uA

Figure 6.10   I/O voltage levels.

A power supply voltage must be applied to a microprocessor in order for its circuitry to operate. Looking at Fig. 6.1(a) we find that power is applied between pin 40 (V_{cc}) and pins 1 and 20, which are grounds (GND). Pins 1 and 20 should be connected electrically. The nominal value of V_{cc} is specified as +5 V dc with a tolerance of ±10%. This means that the 8088 or 8086 will operate correctly as long as the difference in voltage between V_{cc} and GND is greater than 4.5 V dc and less than 5.5 V dc. At room temperature (25°C), both the 8088 and 8086 will draw a maximum of 340 mA from the supply.

Let us now look at the dc I/O characteristics of the microprocessor, that is, its input and output logic levels. These ratings tell the minimum and maximum voltages for the 0 and 1 logic states for which the circuit will operate correctly. Different values are specified for the inputs and outputs.

The I/O voltage specifications for the 8088 are shown in Fig. 6.10. Notice that the minimum logic 1 (high-level) voltage at an output (V_{OH}) is 2.4 V. This voltage is specified for a test condition that identifies the amount of current being sourced by the output (I_{OH}) as −400 μA. All 8088s must be tested during manufacturing to ensure that under this test condition the voltages at all outputs will remain above the value of V_{OHmin}.

Input voltage levels are specified in a similar way. Except here the ratings identify the range of voltage that will be correctly identified as a logic 0 or logic 1 at all inputs. For instance, voltages in the range V_{ILmin} = −0.5 V to V_{ILmax} = +0.8 V represent a valid logic 0 (lower level) at an input of the 8088.

The I/O voltage levels of the 8086 microprocessor are identical to those given for the 8088 in Fig. 6.10. However, there is one difference in the test conditions. For the 8086, V_{OL} is measured at 2.5 mA instead of 2.0 mA.

6.7 SYSTEM CLOCK

The time base for synchronization of the internal and external operations of the microprocessor in a microcomputer system is provided by the CLK input signal. At present, the 8088 is available in two different speeds. The standard part operates at 5 MHz and the 8088-2 operates at 8 MHz. On the other hand, the 8086 microprocessor is manufactured in three speeds. They are the 5-MHz 8086, the 8-MHz 8086-2, and the 10-MHz 8086-1. CLK is externally generated by the 8284 clock generator and driver IC. Figure 6.11 is a block diagram of this device.

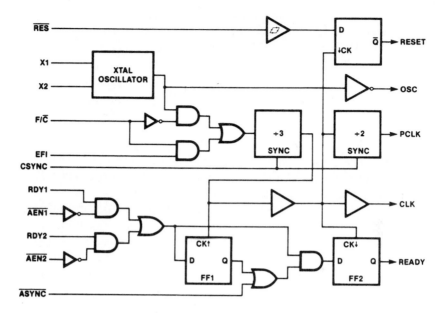

Figure 6.11   Block diagram of the 8284 clock generator. (Reprinted with permission of Intel Corporation, © 1979)

The normal way in which this clock chip is used with the 8088 is to connect either a 15- or 24-MHz crystal between its X_1 and X_2 inputs. This circuit connection is shown in Fig. 6.12. Notice that a series capacitor C_L is also required. Its typical value when used with the 15-MHz crystal is 12 pF. The *fundamental crystal frequency* is divided by 3 within the 8284 to give either a 5- or 8-MHz clock signal. This signal is buffered and output at CLK. CLK can be directly connected to CLK of the 8088. The 8284 connects to the 8086 in exactly the same way.

The waveform of CLK is shown in Fig. 6.13. Here we see that the signal is at Metal Oxide Semiconductor (*MOS*)-*compatible voltage levels* and not Transistor Transistor Logic (TTL) levels. Its minimum and maximum low logic levels are $V_{Lmin} = -0.5$ V and $V_{Lmax} = 0.6$ V, respectively. Moreover, the minimum and

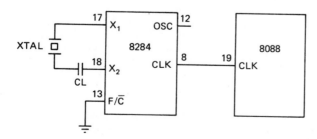

Figure 6.12   Connecting the 8284 to the 8088. (Reprinted with permission of Intel Corporation, © 1979)

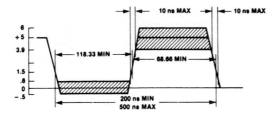

Figure 6.13 CLK voltage and timing characteristics. (Reprinted with permission of Intel Corporation, © 1979)

maximum high logic levels are $V_{Hmin} = 3.9$ V and $V_{Hmax} = V_{CC} + 1$ V, respectively. The *period* of the clock signal of the 8088 can range from a minimum of 200 ns to a maximum of 500 ns, and the maximum *rise* and *fall times* of its edges equal 10 ns.

In Fig. 6.11 we see that there are two more clock outputs on the 8284. They are the *peripheral clock* (PCLK) and *oscillator clock* (OSC). These signals are provided to drive peripheral ICs. The clock signal output at PCLK is always half the frequency of CLK. For instance, if an 8088 is operated at 5 MHz, PCLK is 2.5 MHz. Also, it is at TTL-compatible levels rather than MOS levels. On the other hand, the OSC output is at the fundamental clock frequency, which is three times that of CLK. These relationships are illustrated in Fig. 6.14.

The 8284 can also be driven from an external clock source. The external clock signal is applied to the external frequency input (EFI). Input $F/\overline{C}$ is provided for clock source selection. When it is strapped to the 0 logic level, the crystal between X_1 and X_2 is used. On the other hand, applying logic 1 to $F/\overline{C}$ selects EFI as the source of the clock. The clock sync (CSYNC) input can be used for external synchronization in systems that employ multiple clocks.

6.8 BUS CYCLE

The *bus cycle* of the 8088/8086 is used to access memory, I/O devices, or the interrupt controller. As shown in Fig. 6.15(a), it corresponds to a sequence of events that starts with an address being output on the system bus followed by a read or write data transfer. During these operations, a series of control signals are also produced by the MPU to control the direction and timing of the bus.

The bus cycle of the 8088 and 8086 microprocessors consists of at least four

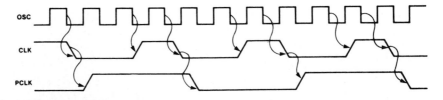

Figure 6.14 Relationship between CLK and PCLK. (Reprinted with permission of Intel Corporation, © 1979)

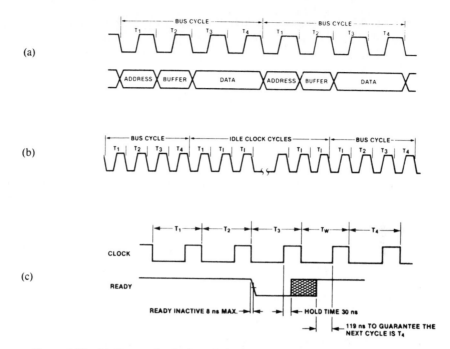

Figure 6.15 (a) Bus cycle clock periods. (Reprinted with permission of Intel Corporation, © 1979) (b) Bus cycle with idle states. (Reprinted with permission of Intel Corporation, © 1979) (c) Bus cycle with wait states. (Reprinted with permission of Intel Corporation, © 1979)

clock periods. These four time states are called T_1, T_2, T_3, and T_4. During T_1, the MPU puts an address on the bus. For a write memory cycle, data are put on the bus during period T_2 and maintained through T_3 and T_4. When a read cycle is to be performed, the bus is first put in the high-Z state during T_2 and then the data to be read must be put on the bus during T_3 and T_4. These four clock states give a *bus cycle duration* of 125 ns × 4 = 500 ns in an 8-MHz 8088 system.

If no bus cycles are required, the microprocessor performs what are known as *idle states*. During these states, no bus activity takes place. Each idle state is one clock period long, and any number of them can be inserted between bus cycles. Figure 6.15(b) shows two bus cycles separated by idle states. Idle states are also performed if the instruction queue inside the microprocessor is full and it does not need to read or write operands from memory.

Wait states can also be inserted into a bus cycle. This is done in response to a request by an event in external hardware instead of an internal event such as a full queue. In fact, the READY input of the MPU is provided specifically for this purpose. Figure 6.15(c) shows that logic 0 at this input indicates that the current bus cycle should not be completed. As long as READY is held at the 0 level, wait states are inserted between periods T_3 and T_4 of the current bus cycle, and the data that were on the bus during T_3 are maintained. The bus cycle is not completed until the external hardware returns READY back to the 1 logic level. This extends the duration of the bus cycle, thereby permitting the use of slower memory devices in the system.

6.9 HARDWARE ORGANIZATION OF THE MEMORY ADDRESS SPACE

From a hardware point of view, the memory address spaces of the 8088- and 8086-based microcomputers are organized differently. Figure 6.16(a) shows that the 8088's memory subsystem is implemented as a single $1M \times 8$ memory bank. Looking at the block diagram in Fig. 6.16(a), we see that these byte-wide storage locations are assigned to consecutive addresses over the range from 00000_{16} through $FFFFF_{16}$. During memory operations, a 20-bit address is applied to the memory bank over signal lines A_0 through A_{19}. It is this address that selects the storage location that is to be accessed. Bytes of data are transferred between the 8088 and memory over data bus lines D_0 through D_7.

On the other hand, the 8086's memory address space as shown in Fig. 6.16(b) is implemented as two independent 512K-byte banks. They are called the *low (even) bank* and the *high (odd) bank*. Data bytes associated with an even address (00000_{16}, 00002_{16}, etc.) reside in the low bank and those with odd addresses (00001_{16}, 00003_{16}, etc.) reside in the high bank.

Looking at the circuit diagram in Fig. 6.16(b), we see that address bits A_1 through A_{19} select the storage location that is to be accessed. Therefore, they are applied to both banks in parallel. A_0 and bank high enable ($\overline{BHE}$) are used as bank

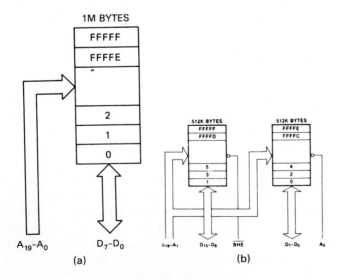

Figure 6.16   (a) $1M \times 8$ memory bank of the 8088. (b) High and low memory banks of the 8086. (Reprinted with permission of Intel Corporation, © 1979)

select signals. Logic 0 at A_0 identifies an even-addressed byte of data and causes the low bank of memory to be enabled. On the other hand, $\overline{\text{BHE}}$ equal to 0 enables the high bank of access of an odd-addressed byte of data. Each of the memory banks provides half of the 8086's 16-bit data bus. Notice that the lower bank transfers bytes of data over data lines D_0 through D_7, while data transfers for a high bank use D_8 through D_{15}.

We just saw that the memory subsystem of the 8088-based microcomputer system is actually organized as 8-bit bytes, not as 16-bit words. However, the contents of any two consecutive byte storage locations can be accessed as a word. The lower-addressed byte is the least significant byte of the word, and the higher-addressed byte is its most significant byte. Let us now look at how a byte and a word of data are read from memory.

Figure 6.17(a) shows how a byte memory operation is performed to the storage location at address X. As shown in the diagram, the address is supplied to

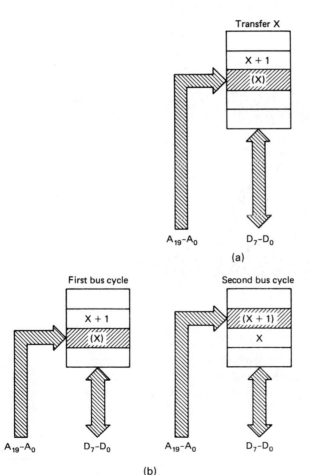

(a)

Figure 6.17   (a) Byte transfer by the 8088. (b) Word transfer by the 8088.

(b)

the memory bank over lines A_0 through A_{19}, and the bytes of data are written into or read from storage location X over lines D_0 through D_7. D_7 carries the MSB of the byte of data and D_0 carries the LSB. This shows that bytes of data are accessed by the 8088 in one bus cycle. With an 8088 running at 5 MHz, this memory cycle takes 800 ns.

When a word of data is to be transferred between the 8088 and memory, we must perform 2-byte accesses of memory. Figure 6.17(b) illustrates how the word storage location starting at address X is accessed. Two bus cycles are required to access this word of data. During the first bus cycle, the least significant byte of the word, which is located at address X, is accessed. Again the address is applied to the memory bank over A_0 through A_{19}, and the byte of data is transferred to or from storage location X over D_0 through D_7.

Next, the 8088 automatically increments the address so that it now points to byte address X + 1. This address points to the next consecutive byte storage location in memory, which corresponds to the most significant byte of the word of data at X. Now a second memory bus cycle is initiated. During this second cycle, data are written into or read from the storage location at address X + 1. Since word accesses of memory take two bus cycles instead of one, it takes 1.6 μs to access a word of data when the 8088 is operating at a 5-MHz clock rate.

The 8086 microprocessor performs byte and word data transfers differently from the 8088. Let us next examine the data transfers that can take place in an 8086-based microcomputer.

Figure 6.18(a) shows that when a byte memory operation is performed to address X, which is an even address, a storage location in the low bank is accessed. Therefore, A_0 is set to logic 0 to enable the low bank of memory and $\overline{BHE}$ to logic 1 to disable the high bank. As shown in the circuit diagram, data are transferred to or from the lower bank over data bus lines D_0 through D_7. D_7 carries the MSB of the byte and D_0 the LSB.

On the other hand, to access a byte of data at an odd address such as X + 1 in Fig. 6.18(b), A_0 is set to logic 1 and $\overline{BHE}$ to logic 0. This enables the high bank of memory and disables the low bank. Data are transferred between the 8086 and the high bank over bus lines D_8 through D_{15}. Here D_{15} represents the MSB and D_8 the LSB.

Whenever an even-addressed word of data is accessed, both the high and low banks are accessed at the same time. Figure 6.18(c) illustrates how a word at even address X is accessed. Notice that both A_0 and $\overline{BHE}$ equal 0; therefore, both banks are enabled. In this case, two bytes of data are transferred from or to one each low and high banks at the same time. This 16-bit word is transferred over the complete data bus D_0 through D_{15}. The bytes of an even-addressed word are said to be aligned and can be transferred with a memory operation that takes just one bus cycle.

A word at an odd-addressed boundary is different. It is said to be unaligned. That is, the least significant byte is at the lower address location in the high memory bank. This is demonstrated in Fig. 6.18(d). Here we see that

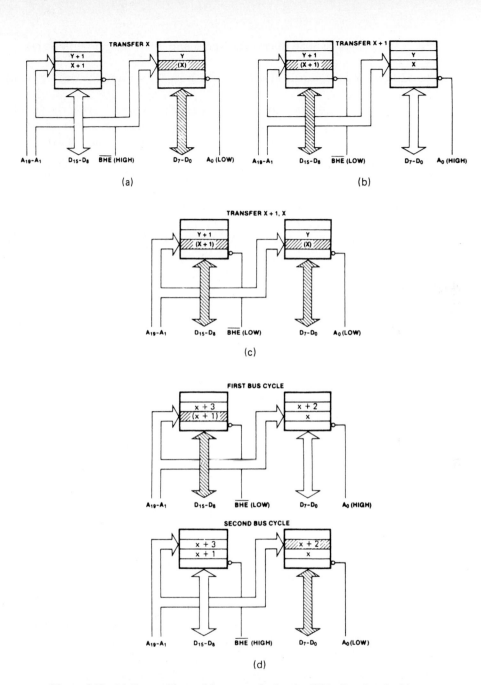

Figure 6.18 (a) Even-addressed byte transfer by the 8086. (Reprinted with permission of Intel Corporation, © 1979) (b) Odd-addressed byte transfer by the 8086. (Reprinted with permission of Intel Corporation, © 1979) (c) Even-addressed word transfer by the 8086. (Reprinted with permission of Intel Corporation, © 1979) (d) Odd-addressed word transfer by the 8086. (Reprinted with permission of Intel Corporation, © 1979)

the odd byte of the word is located at address $X + 1$ and the even byte at address $X + 2$.

Two bus cycles are required to access this word. During the first bus cycle, the odd byte of the word, which is located at address $X + 1$ in the high bank, is accessed. This is accompanied by select signals $A_0 = 1$ and $\overline{BHE} = 0$ and a data transfer over D_8 through D_{15}.

Next the 8086 automatically increments the address so that $A_0 = 0$. This represents the next address in memory which is even. Then a second memory bus cycle is initiated. During this second cycle, the even byte located at $X + 2$ in the low bank is accessed. The data transfer takes place over bus lines D_0 through D_7. This transfer is accompanied by $A_0 = 0$ and $\overline{BHE} = 1$.

6.10 MEMORY BUS STATUS CODES

Whenever a memory bus cycle is in progress, an address bus status code S_3S_4 is output on the 8088/8086's multiplexed address lines A_{16} and A_{17}. This two-bit code is output at the same time the data are carried over the other bus lines.

Bits S_3 and S_4 together form a 2-bit binary code that identifies which one of the four segment registers was used to generate the physical address that was output during the address period in the current bus cycle. The four *address bus status codes* are listed in Fig. 6.19. Here we find that code $S_3S_4 = 00$ identifies the extra segment register, 10 identifies the stack segment register, 01 identifies the code segment register, and 11 identifies the data segment register.

These status codes are output in both the minimum- and the maximum-system modes. The codes can be examined by external circuitry. For example, they can be decoded with external circuitry to enable separate 1M-byte address spaces for ES, SS, CS, and DS. In this way, the memory address reach of the microprocessor can be expanded to 4M bytes.

6.11 MEMORY CONTROL SIGNALS

Earlier in the chapter we saw that similar control signals are produced in the maximum- and minimum-mode systems. Moreover, we found that in the minimum system mode, the 8088 and 8086 microprocessors produce all the control

S_4	S_3	Segment register
0	0	Extra
0	1	Stack
1	0	Code/none
1	1	Data

Figure 6.19 Address bus status codes.

signals. But in the maximum system mode, they are produced by the 8288 bus controller. Here we will look more closely at each of these signals and their function with respect to memory interface operation.

Minimum-System Memory Control Signals

In the 8088 microcomputer system of Fig. 6.20, which is configured for the minimum system mode of operation, we find that the control signals provided to support the interface to the memory subsystem are ALE, IO/$\overline{\text{M}}$, DT/$\overline{\text{R}}$, $\overline{\text{RD}}$, $\overline{\text{WR}}$, and $\overline{\text{DEN}}$. These control signals are required to tell the memory subsystem when the bus is carrying a valid address, in which direction data are to be transferred over the bus, when valid write data are on the bus, and when to put read data on the bus. For example, *address latch enable* (ALE) signals external circuitry that a valid address is on the bus. It is a pulse to the 1 logic level and is used to latch the address in external circuitry.

The IO/$\overline{\text{M}}$ (input-output/memory) and *data transmit/receive* (DT/$\overline{\text{R}}$) lines signal external circuitry whether a memory or I/O bus cycle is in progress and whether the 8088 will transmit or receive data over the bus. During all memory bus cycles. IO/$\overline{\text{M}}$ is held at the 0 logic level. Moreover, when the 8088 switches DT/$\overline{\text{R}}$ to logic 1 during the data transfer part of the bus cycle, the bus is in the transmit mode and data are written into memory. On the other hand, it sets DT/$\overline{\text{R}}$ to logic 0 to signal that the bus is in the receive mode. This corresponds to reading of memory.

The signals *read* ($\overline{\text{RD}}$) and *write* ($\overline{\text{WR}}$), respectively, identify that a read or write bus cycle is in progress. The 8088 switches $\overline{\text{WR}}$ to logic 0 to signal memory that a write cycle is taking place over the bus. On the other hand, $\overline{\text{RD}}$ is switched

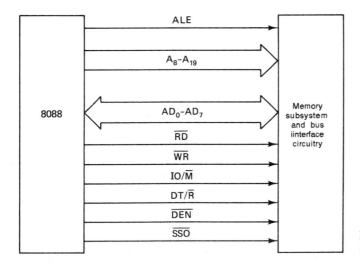

Figure 6.20   Minimum mode 8088 system memory interface.

to logic 0 whenever a read cycle is in progress. During all memory operations, the 8088 produces one other control signal. It is *data enable* ($\overline{DEN}$). Logic 0 at this output is used to enable the data bus.

Status line $\overline{SSO}$ is also part of the minimum-mode memory interface. The logic level that is output on this line during read bus cycles identifies whether a code or data access is in progress. $\overline{SSO}$ is set to logic 0 whenever instruction code is read from memory.

The control signals for the 8086's minimum-mode memory interface differ in three ways. First, the 8088's IO/$\overline{M}$ signal is replaced by *memory/input-output* (M/$\overline{IO}$). Whenever a memory bus cycle is in progress, the M/$\overline{IO}$ output is switched to logic 1. Second, the signal $\overline{SSO}$ is removed from the interface. Third, a new signal, *bank high enable* ($\overline{BHE}$) has been added to the interface. $\overline{BHE}$ is used as a select input for the high bank of memory in the 8086's memory subsystem. That is, logic 0 is output on this line during the address part of all the bus cycle in which data in the high-bank part of memory is to be accessed.

Maximum-System Memory Control Signals

When the 8088 is configured to work in the maximum mode, it does not directly provide all the control signals to support the memory interface. Instead, an external *bus controller,* the 8288, provides memory commands and control signals that are compatible with the *Multibus.* Figure 6.21 shows an 8088 connected in this way.

Specifically, the $\overline{WR}$, IO/$\overline{M}$, DT/$\overline{R}$, $\overline{DEN}$, ALE, $\overline{SSO}$, and $\overline{INTA}$ signal lines on the 8088 are changed. They are replaced with *multiprocessor lock* signal ($\overline{LOCK}$), a *bus status code* ($\overline{S}_2$ through $\overline{S}_0$), and a *queue status code* (QS$_1$QS$_0$).

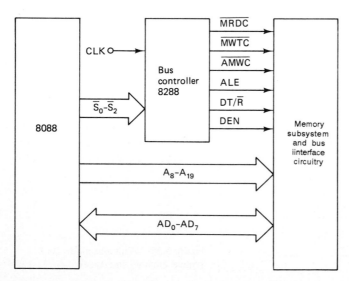

Figure 6.21 Maximum mode 8088 system memory interface.

Status Inputs			CPU Cycle	8288 Command
$\overline{S}_2$	$\overline{S}_1$	$\overline{S}_0$		
0	0	0	Interrupt acknowledge	$\overline{INTA}$
0	0	1	Read I/O port	$\overline{IORC}$
0	1	0	Write I/O port	$\overline{IOWC}$, $\overline{AIOWC}$
0	1	1	Halt	None
1	0	0	Instruction fetch	$\overline{MRDC}$
1	0	1	Read memory	$\overline{MRDC}$
1	1	0	Write memory	$\overline{MWTC}$, $\overline{AMWC}$
1	1	1	Passive	None

Figure 6.22 Memory bus cycle status codes. (Reprinted with permission of Intel Corporation, © 1979)

The 8088 still does produce the signal $\overline{RD}$. Moreover, this signal provides the same function as it did in minimum system mode.

The 3-bit bus status code $\overline{S}_2\overline{S}_1\overline{S}_0$ is output prior to the initiation of each bus cycle. It identifies which type of bus cycle is to follow. This code is input to the 8288 bus controller. Here it is decoded to identify which type of bus cycle command signals must be generated.

Figure 6.22 shows the relationship between the bus status codes and the types of 8088 bus cycle produced. Also shown in this chart are the names of the corresponding command signals that are generated at the outputs of the 8288. For instance, the input code $\overline{S}_2\overline{S}_1\overline{S}_0$ equal to 100 indicates that an instruction fetch bus cycle is to take place. This memory read makes the $\overline{MRDC}$ command output switch to logic 0.

Another bus command that is provided for the memory subsystem is $\overline{S}_2\overline{S}_1\overline{S}_0$ equal to 110. This represents a memory write cycle and it causes both the *memory write command* ($\overline{MWTC}$) and *advanced memory write command* ($\overline{AMWC}$) outputs to switch to the 0 logic level.

The control outputs produced by the 8288 are DEN, DT/$\overline{R}$, and ALE. These signals provide the same functions as those produced by the corresponding pins on the 8088 in the minimum system mode.

The other two status signals, QS_0 and QS_1, form an instruction queue code. This code tells external circuitry what type of information was removed from the queue during the previous clock cycle. Figure 6.23 shows the four different queue

QS_1	QS_0	Queue status
0	0	No operation
0	1	First byte of an instruction
1	0	Queue empty
1	1	Subsequent byte of an instruction

Figure 6.23 Queue status code.

statuses. Notice that $QS_1QS_0 = 01$ indicates that the first byte of an instruction was taken from the queue. The next byte of the instruction that is fetched is identified by queue status code 11. Whenever the queue is reset, for instance, due to a transfer of control, the reinitialization code 10 is output. Moreover, if no queue operation occurred, status code 00 is output.

The last signal is *bus priority lock* ($\overline{\text{LOCK}}$). This signal is to be used as an input to the 8289 bus arbiter together with bus status code $\overline{S}_0$ through $\overline{S}_2$ and CLK. They are used to lock other processors off the system bus during execution of an instruction. In this way the processor can be assured of uninterrupted access to common system resources such as *global memory*.

The *bus arbitration* signals produced by the 8289 are *bus clock* ($\overline{\text{BCLK}}$), *bus request* ($\overline{\text{BREQ}}$), *bus priority in* ($\overline{\text{BPRN}}$), *bus priority out* ($\overline{\text{BPRO}}$), and *I/O busy* ($\overline{\text{BUSY}}$). These are the bus exchange signals of the Multibus. It is this bus arbiter that permits multiple processors to reside on the system bus by implementing the Multibus arbitration protocol in the 8088 microcomputer system.

All of the memory control signals we just described for the 8088-based microcomputer system serve the same function in the maximum-mode 8086 microcomputer. However, there is one additional control signal in the 8086's memory interface. This is $\overline{\text{BHE}}$. $\overline{\text{BHE}}$ performs the same function as it did in the minimum-mode system. That is, it is used as an enable input to the high bank of memory.

6.12 READ AND WRITE BUS CYCLES

In the preceding section we introduced the status and control signals associated with the memory interface. Here we continue by studying the sequence in which they occur during the read and write bus cycles of memory.

Read Cycle

The memory interface signals of a minimum-mode 8088 system are shown in Fig. 6.24. Here their occurrence is illustrated relative to the four *time states* T_1, T_2, T_3, and T_4 of the 8088's bus cycle. Let us trace through the events that occur as data or instructions are read from memory.

The *read bus cycle* begins with state T_1. During this period, the 8088 outputs the 20-bit address of the memory location to be accessed on its multiplexed address/data bus AD_0 through AD_7 and A_8 through A_{19}. Notice that at the same time a pulse is also produced at ALE. The trailing edge of this pulse should be used to latch the address in external circuitry.

Also we see that at the start of T_1, signals IO/$\overline{\text{M}}$ and DT/$\overline{\text{R}}$ are set to the 1 and 0 logic levels, respectively. This indicates to circuitry in the memory subsystem that a memory cycle is in progress and that the 8088 is going to receive data from the bus. Status $\overline{\text{SSO}}$ is also output at this time. Notice that all three of these

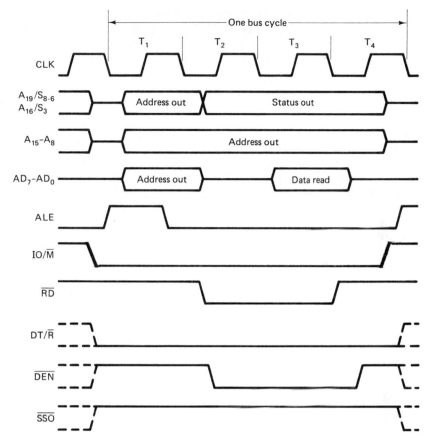

Figure 6.24 Minimum mode memory read bus cycle of the 8088. (Reprinted with permission of Intel Corporation, © 1979)

signals are maintained at these logic levels throughout all four periods of the bus cycle.

Beginning with state T_2, status bits S_3 through S_6 are output on the upper four address bus lines A_{16} through A_{19}. Remember that bits S_3 and S_4 identify to external circuitry which segment register was used to generate the address just output. This status information is maintained through periods T_3 and T_4. The part of the address output on address bus lines A_8 through A_{15} is maintained through states T_2, T_3, and T_4. On the other hand, address/data bus lines AD_0 through AD_7 are put in the high-Z state during T_2.

Late in period T_2, $\overline{RD}$ is switched to logic 0. This indicates to the memory subsystem that a read cycle is in progress. Then $\overline{DEN}$ is switched to logic 0 to tell external circuitry to put the data that are to be read from memory onto the bus.

As shown in the waveforms, input data are read by the 8088 during T_3, after which, as shown in T_4, the 8088 returns $\overline{RD}$ and $\overline{DEN}$ to the 1 logic level. The read cycle is now complete.

A timing diagram for the 8086's memory read cycle is given in Fig. 6.25(a). Comparing these waveforms to those of the 8088 in Fig. 6.24, we find just four differences. They are that $\overline{BHE}$ is output along with the address during T_1; the data read by the 8086 during T_3 can be carried over all 16 data bus lines; $M/\overline{IO}$, which replaces $IO/\overline{M}$, is switched to logic 1 at the beginning of T_1 and is held at this level for the duration of the bus cycle; and the $\overline{SSO}$ status signal is not produced.

Figure 6.25(b) shows a read cycle of 8-bit data in a maximum-mode 8086-based microcomputer system. These waveforms are similar to those given for the minimum mode read cycle in Fig. 6.25(a). Comparing these two timing diagrams, we see that the address and data transfers that take place are identical. In fact, the only difference found in the maximum mode waveforms is that a bus cycle status code, $\overline{S_2}\overline{S_1}\overline{S_0}$, is output just prior to the beginning of the bus cycle. This status information is decoded by the 8288 to produce control signals ALE, $\overline{MRDC}$, $DT/\overline{R}$, and DEN.

Write Cycle

The *write bus cycle* timing of the 8088 shown in Fig. 6.26 is similar to that given for a read cycle in Fig. 6.24. Looking at the write cycle waveforms, we find that during T_1 the address is output and latched with the ALE pulse. This is identical to the read cycle. Moreover, $IO/\overline{M}$ is set to logic 1 to indicate that a memory cycle

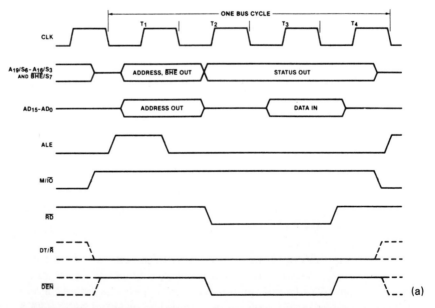

Figure 6.25 (a) Minimum mode memory read bus cycle of the 8086. (Reprinted with permission of Intel Corporation, © 1979) (b) Maximum mode memory read bus cycle of the 8086. (Reprinted with permission of Intel Corporation, © 1979)

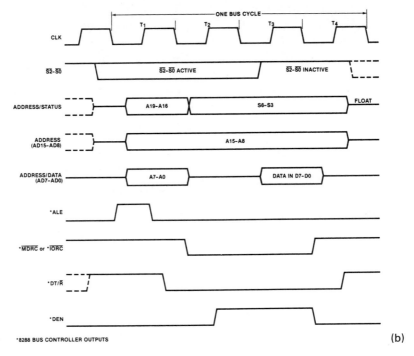

Figure 6.25   (Continued)

is in progress and status information is output at $\overline{\text{SSO}}$. However, this time DT/$\overline{\text{R}}$ is switched to logic 1. This signals external circuits that the 8088 is going to transfer data over the bus.

As T_2 starts, the 8088 switches $\overline{\text{WR}}$ to logic 0. This tells the memory subsystem that a write operation is to follow over the bus. The 8088 puts the data on the bus late in T_2 and maintains the data valid through T_4. The write of data into memory should be initiated as $\overline{\text{WR}}$ returns from 0 to 1 early in T_4. This completes the write cycle.

Just as we described for the read bus cycle, the write cycle of the 8086 differs from that of the 8088 in four ways. Again, $\overline{\text{SSO}}$ is not produced; $\overline{\text{BHE}}$ is output along with the address; data are carried over all 16 data bus lines; and finally, M/$\overline{\text{IO}}$ is the complement of the 8088's IO/$\overline{\text{M}}$ signal. The waveforms in Fig. 6.26(b) illustrate a write cycle of word data in a maximum mode 8086 system.

Wait States in the Memory Bus Cycle

Wait states can be inserted to lengthen the memory bus cycles of the 8088 or 8086. This is done with the *ready input* signal. Upon request from an event in hardware, for instance, slow memory, the READY input is switched to logic 0. This signals the MPU that the current bus cycle should not be completed. In-

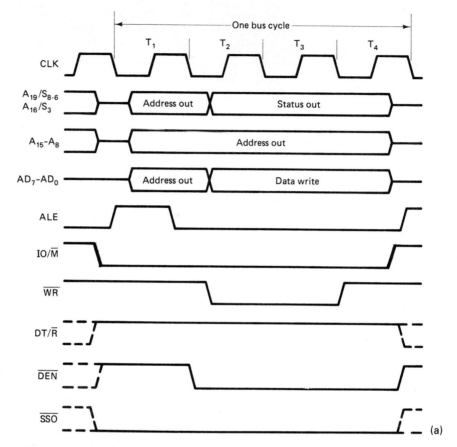

Figure 6.26 (a) Minimum mode memory write bus cycle of the 8088. (Reprinted with permission of Intel Corporation, © 1979) (b) Maximum mode memory write bus cycle of the 8086. (Reprinted with permission of Intel Corporation, © 1979)

stead, it is extended by inserting wait states with duration T_w equal to 125 ns (for 8-MHz clock operation) between periods T_3 and T_4. The data that were on the bus during T_3 are maintained throughout the wait-state period. In this way, the bus cycle is not completed until READY is returned back to logic 1.

In the microcomputer system, the READY input of the MPU is supplied by the READY output of the 8284 clock generator circuit.

EXAMPLE 6.2

What is the duration of the bus cycle in the 8088-based microcomputer if the clock is 8 MHz and two wait states are inserted through wait state logic?

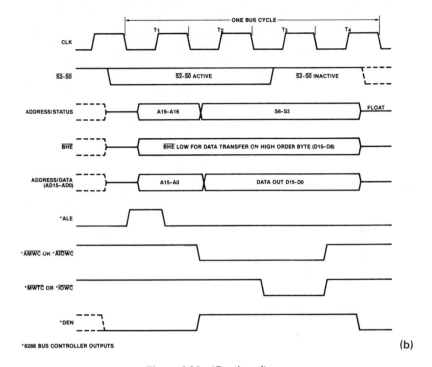

Figure 6.26   (Continued)

SOLUTION   The duration of the bus cycle in an 8-MHz system is given in general by the expression

$$t_{cyc} = 500 \text{ ns} + N (125 \text{ ns})$$

In this expression N stands for the number of wait states. For a bus cycle with two wait states, we get

$$t_{cyc} = 500 \text{ ns} + 2(125 \text{ ns}) = 500 \text{ ns} + 250 \text{ ns}$$

$$= 750 \text{ ns}$$

6.13 MEMORY INTERFACE CIRCUITS

In this section, we will describe the memory interface circuits of an 8086-based microcomputer system. The 8086 system was selected instead of an 8088 micro-computer because it is more complex. A memory interface diagram for a maxi-mum-mode 8086-based microcomputer system is shown in Fig. 6.27. Here we

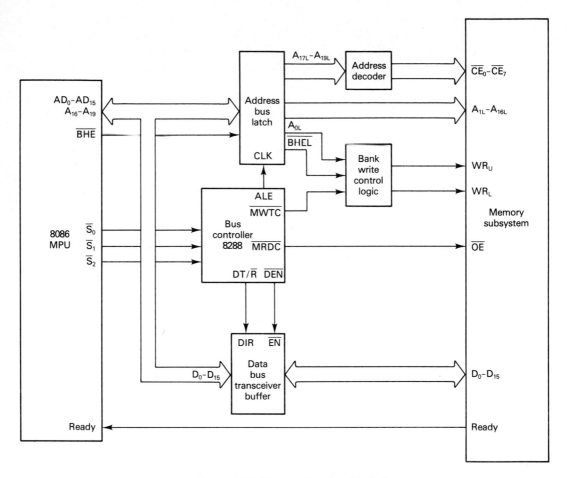

Figure 6.27 Memory interface block diagram.

find that the interface includes the 8288 bus controller, address bus latches and an address decoder, data bus transceiver/buffers, and bank write control logic. The 8088 microcomputer is simpler in that it does not require bank write control logic. Remember that the 8088's memory address space is organized as a single bank.

Looking at Fig. 6.27, we see that bus status code signals $\overline{S}_0$, $\overline{S}_1$, and $\overline{S}_2$, which are outputs of the 8086, are supplied directly to the 8288 bus controller. Here they are decoded to produce the command and control signals needed to control data transfers over the bus. In Fig. 6.22, the status codes that relate to the memory interface are highlighted. For example, the code $\overline{S}_2\overline{S}_1\overline{S}_0 = 101$ indicates that a data memory read bus cycle is in progress. This code makes the $\overline{\text{MRDC}}$

command output of the bus control logic switch to logic 0. Notice in Fig. 6.27 that $\overline{MRDC}$ is applied directly to the $\overline{OE}$ input of the memory subsystem.

Next let us look at how the address bus is latched, decoded, and buffered. Looking at Fig. 6.27, we see that address lines A_0 through A_{19} are latched along with and control signal $\overline{BHE}$ in the address bus latch. The value on latched address lines A_{17L} through A_{19L} is decoded to produce chip enable outputs $\overline{CE}_0$ through $\overline{CE}_7$. Notice that the 8288 bus controller produces the address latch enable (ALE) control signal from $\overline{S}_2\overline{S}_1\overline{S}_0$. ALE is applied to the CLK input of the latches and strobes the bits of the address and bank high enable signal into the address bus latches. These signals are buffered by the address latch devices. Latched address lines A_{0L} through A_{16} and $\overline{CE}_0$ and $\overline{CE}_7$ are applied directly to the memory subsystem.

During read bus cycles, the $\overline{MRDC}$ output of the bus control logic enables the byte of data at the outputs of the memory subsystem onto data bus lines D_0 through D_{15}. On the other hand, during write operations to memory, the bank write control logic determines into which of the two memory banks the data are written. This depends on whether a byte or word data transfer is taking place over the bus.

Notice in Fig. 6.27 that the latched bank high enable signal $\overline{BHEL}$ and address line A_{0L} are gated with the memory write command signal $\overline{MWTC}$ to produce a separate write enable signal for each bank. These signals are denoted as $\overline{WR}_U$ through $\overline{WR}_L$. For example, if a word of data is to be written to memory over data bus lines D_0 through D_{15}, both $\overline{WR}_U$ and $\overline{WR}_L$ are switched to their active 0 logic level.

The bus transceivers control the direction of data transfer between the MPU and memory subsystem. In Fig. 6.27, we see that the operation of the transceivers is controlled by the DT/$\overline{R}$ and DEN outputs of the bus controller. DEN is applied to the EN input of the transceivers and enables them for operation. This happens during all read and write bus cycles. DT/$\overline{R}$ selects the direction of data transfer through the devices. Notice that it is supplied to the DIR input of the data bus transceivers. When a read cycle is in progress, DT/$\overline{R}$ is set to 0 and data are passed from the memory subsystem to the MPU. On the other hand, when a write cycle is taking place, DT/$\overline{R}$ is switched to logic 1 and data are carried from the MPU to the memory subsystem.

Address Latches and Buffers

The 74F373 is an example of an octal latch device that can be used to implement the address latch section of the 8086's memory interface circuit. A block diagram of this device is shown in Fig. 6.28(a) and its internal circuitry is shown in Fig. 6.28(b). Notice that it accepts eight inputs DI_0 through DI_7. As long as the clock (CLK) input is at logic 1, the outputs of the D-type flip-flops follow the logic level of the data applied to their corresponding inputs. When CLK is switched to logic

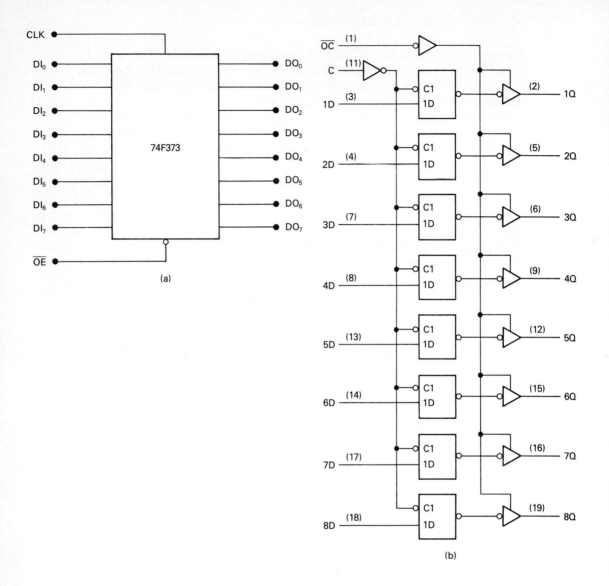

Figure 6.28 (a) Block diagram of an octal D-type latch. (b) Circuit diagram of the 74F373. (Courtesy of Texas Instruments Incorporated) (c) Operation of the 74F373. (Courtesy of Texas Instruments Incorporated)

	Inputs		Output
$\overline{OC}$	Enable C	D	Q
L	H	H	H
L	H	L	L
L	L	X	Q_0
H	X	X	Z

(c)

0, the current contents of the D-type flip-flops are latched. The latched information in the flip-flops are not output at data outputs DO_0 through DO_7 unless the output enable $(\overline{OE})$ input is at logic 0. If $\overline{OE}$ is at logic 1, the outputs are in the high-impedance state. Figure 6.28(c) summarizes this operation.

In the 8086 microcomputer system, the 20 address lines (AD_0–AD_{15}, A_{16}–A_{19}) and the bank high enable signal $\overline{BHE}$ are normally latched in the address bus latch. The circuit configuration shown in Fig. 6.29 can be used to latch these signals. Notice that the latched outputs A_{0L} through A_{19L} and $\overline{BHEL}$ are permanently enabled by fixing $\overline{OE}$ at the 0 logic level. Moreover, the address information is latched at the outputs as the ALE signal from the bus controller returns to logic 0—that is, when the CLK input of all devices is switched to logic 0.

In general, it is important to minimize the propagation delay of the address signals as they go through the bus interface circuit. The switching property of the 74F373 latches that determines this delay for the circuit of Fig. 6.29 is called *enable-to-output propagation delay* and has a maximum value of 13 ns. By selecting fast latches, that is, latches with a short propagation delay time, a maximum

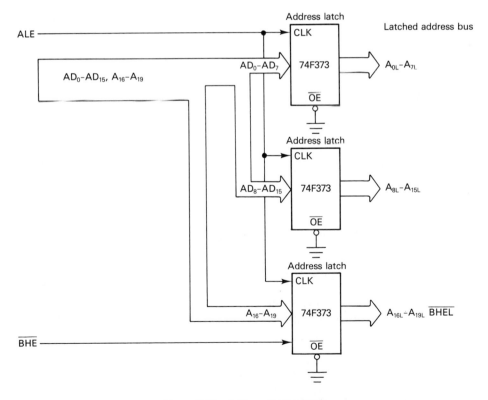

Figure 6.29 Address latch circuit.

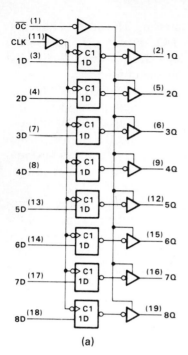

FUNCTION TABLE (EACH FLIP-FLOP)

INPUTS			OUTPUT
$\overline{OC}$	CLK	D	Q
L	↑	H	H
L	↑	L	L
L	L	X	Q_0
H	X	X	Z

(a)

(b)

Figure 6.30 (a) Circuit diagram of the 74F374. (Courtesy Texas Instruments Incorporated) (b) Operation of the 74F374. (Courtesy of Texas Instruments Incorporated)

amount of the 8086's bus cycle time is preserved for the access time of the memory devices. In this way slower, lower cost memory ICs can be used. These latches also provide buffering for the 8086's address lines. The outputs of the latch can sink a maximum of 24 mA.

The 74F374 is another IC that is frequently used as an address latch in microcomputer systems. The circuit within this device is shown in Fig. 6.30(a). This circuit is similar to the 74F373 we just introduced in that it is an octal latch device. However, the flip-flops used to implement the latches are edge triggered instead of transparent. Notice in Fig. 6.30(b) that when $\overline{OC}$ is logic 0 the data outputs become equal to the value of the data inputs synchronous with a low to high transition at the CLK input.

In some applications, additional buffering is required on the latched address lines. For example, the diagram in Fig. 6.31(a) shows that some of the address lines may be buffered to provide an independent I/O address bus. In this case, a simple octal buffer/line driver device such as the 74F244 can be used as the I/O bus buffer. Figure 6.31(b) shows the buffer circuitry provided by the 74F244. The outputs of this device can sink a maximum of 64 mA.

Data Bus Transceivers

The data bus transceiver block of the bus interface circuit can be implemented with 74F245 octal bus transceivers ICs. Figure 6.32(a) shows a block diagram of this device. Notice that its bidirectional input/output lines are called A_0 through

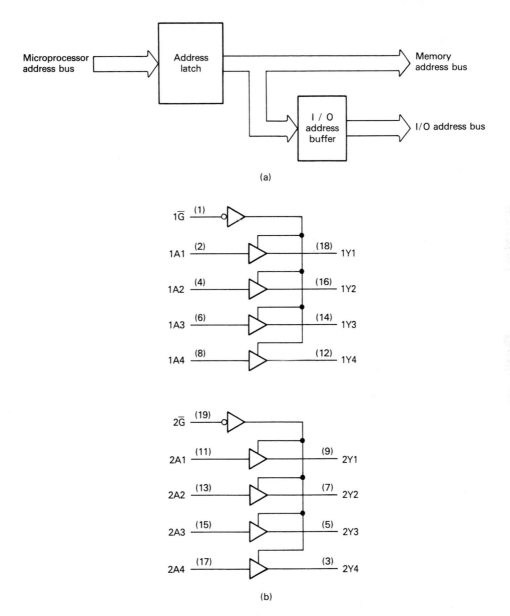

Figure 6.31 (a) Buffering the I/O address. (b) 74F244 circuit diagram. (Courtesy of Texas Instruments Incorporated)

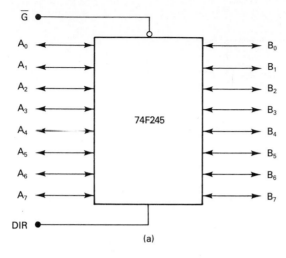

(a)

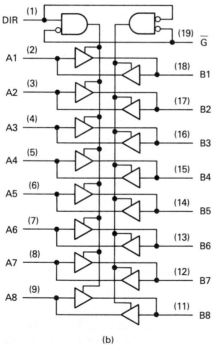

(b)

Figure 6.32 (a) Block diagram of the 74F245 octal bidirectional bus transceiver. (b) Circuit diagram of the 74F245. (Courtesy of Texas Instruments Incorporated)

A_7 and B_0 through B_7. Looking at the circuit diagram in Fig. 6.32(b), we see that the $\overline{G}$ input is used to enable the buffer for operation. On the other hand, the logic level at the direction (DIR) input selects the direction in which data are transferred through the device. For instance, logic 0 at this input sets the transceiver to pass data from the B lines to the A lines. Switching DIR to logic 1 reverses the direction of data transfer.

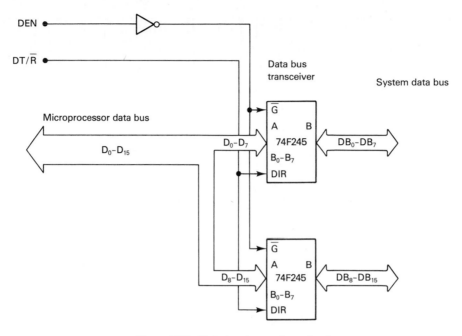

Figure 6.33 Data bus transceiver circuit.

Figure 6.33 shows a circuit that implements the data bus transceiver block of the bus interface circuit using the 74F245. For the 16-bit data bus of the 8086 microcomputer two devices are required. Here the DIR input is driven by the signal data transmit/receive (DT/$\overline{R}$), and $\overline{G}$ is supplied by data bus enable (DEN). These signals are outputs of the 8288 bus controller. Another key function of the data bus transceiver circuit is to buffer the data bus lines. This capability is defined by how much current the devices can sink at their outputs. The I_{OL} rating of the 74F245 is 64 mA.

The 74F646 device is an octal bus transceiver with registers. This device is more versatile than the 74F245 we just described. It can be configured to operate either as a simple bus transceiver or as a registered bus transceiver. Figure 6.34(a) shows the operations that can occur when used as a simple transceiver. Notice that logic 0 at the SAB or SBA input selects the direction of data transfer through the device. The diagram in Fig. 6.34(b) shows that when configured for the registered mode of operation data do not directly transfer between the A and B buses. Instead, data are passed from the bus to an internal register with one control signal sequence and from the internal register to the other bus with another control signal. Notice that lines CAB and CBA control the storage of the data from the A or B bus into the register and SAB and SBA control the transfer of stored data from the registers to the A or B bus. The table in Fig. 6.34(c) summarizes all of the operations performed by the 74F646.

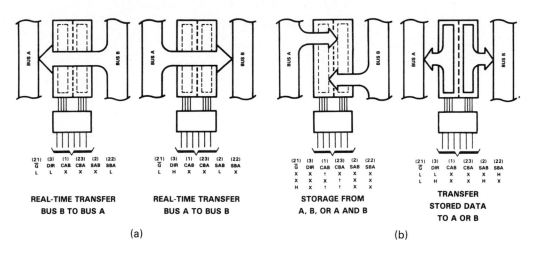

(21)	(3)	(1)	(23)	(2)	(22)
$\overline{G}$	DIR	CAB	CBA	SAB	SBA
L	L	X	X	X	L

REAL-TIME TRANSFER
BUS B TO BUS A

(21)	(3)	(1)	(23)	(2)	(22)
$\overline{G}$	DIR	CAB	CBA	SAB	SBA
L	H	X	X	L	X

REAL-TIME TRANSFER
BUS A TO BUS B

(a)

(21)	(3)	(1)	(23)	(2)	(22)
$\overline{G}$	DIR	CAB	CBA	SAB	SBA
X	X	↑	X	X	X
X	X	X	↑	X	X
H	X	↑	↑	X	X

STORAGE FROM
A, B, OR A AND B

(21)	(3)	(1)	(23)	(2)	(22)
$\overline{G}$	DIR	CAB	CBA	SAB	SBA
L	L	X	X	X	H
L	H	X	X	H	X

TRANSFER
STORED DATA
TO A OR B

(b)

INPUTS						DATA I/O*		OPERATION OR FUNCTION	
$\overline{G}$	DIR	CAB	CBA	SAB	SBA	A1 THRU A8	B1 THRU B8	'ALS646, 'ALS647 'AS646	'ALS648, 'ALS649 'AS648
X	X	↑	X	X	X	Input	Not specified	Store A, B unspecified	Store A, B unspecified
X	X	X	↑	X	X	Not specified	Input	Store B, A unspecified	Store B, A unspecified
H	X	↑·	↑	X	X	Input	Input	Store A and B Data	Store A and B Data
H	X	H or L	H or L	X	X	Input	Input	Isolation, hold storage	Isolation, hold storage
L	L	X	X	X	L	Output	Input	Real-Time B Data to A Bus	Real-Time $\overline{B}$ Data to A Bus
L	L	X	X	X	H	Output	Input	Stored B Data to A Bus	Stored $\overline{B}$ Data to A Bus
L	H	X	X	L	X	Input	Output	Real-Time A Data to B Bus	Real-Time $\overline{A}$ Data to B Bus
L	H	X	X	H	X	Input	Output	Stored A Data to B Bus	Stored $\overline{A}$ Data to B Bus

(c)

Figure 6.34 (a) Transceiver mode data transfers of the 74F646. (Courtesy of Texas Instruments Incorporated) (b) Register mode data transfers. (Courtesy of Texas Instruments Incorporated) (c) Control signals and data transfer operations. (Courtesy of Texas Instruments Incorporated)

Address Decoders

As shown in Fig. 6.35, the address decoder in the 8086 microcomputer system is located at the output side of the address latch. A typical device that is used to perform this decode function is the 74F139 dual 2-line to 4-line decoder. Figure 6.36(a) and (b) show a block diagram and circuit diagram for this device, respectively. When the enable ($\overline{G}$) input is at its active 0 logic level, the output corresponding to the code at the BA inputs switches to the 0 logic level. For instance, when BA = 01, output Y_1 is logic 0. The operation of the 74F139 is summarized in the table of Fig. 6.37.

The circuit in Fig. 6.38 employs the address decoder configuration of Fig. 6.35. Notice that address lines A_{19L} and A_{18L} are applied to the B and A inputs of the 74F139 decoder. Here they are decoded to produce chip enable outputs $\overline{CE}_0$

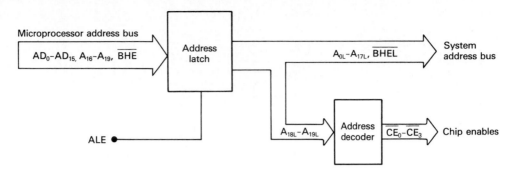

Figure 6.35 Address bus configuration with address decoding.

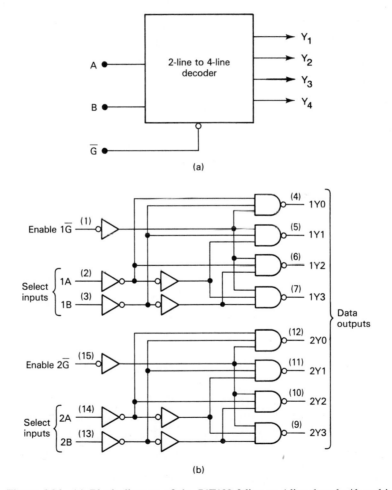

(a)

(b)

Figure 6.36 (a) Block diagram of the 74F139 2-line to 4-line decoder/demultiplexer. (b) Circuit diagram of the 74F139. (Courtesy of Texas Instruments Incorporated)

INPUTS			OUTPUTS			
ENABLE	SELECT					
$\overline{G}$	B	A	Y0	Y1	Y2	Y3
H	X	X	H	H	H	H
L	L	L	L	H	H	H
L	L	H	H	L	H	H
L	H	L	H	H	L	H
L	H	H	H	H	H	L

Figure 6.37 Operation of the 74F139 decoder. (Courtesy of Texas Instruments Incorporated)

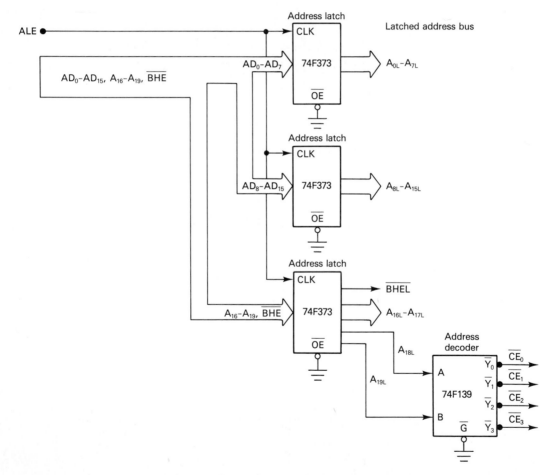

Figure 6.38 Address bus latch and decoder circuit.

through $\overline{CE}_3$. In some applications, independent decoders are used for memory and I/O. In this case, one of the decoders in the 74F139 can be used to produce four memory chip enables and the other decoder to provide four I/O device chip selects.

The 74F138 is similar to the 74F139, except that it is a single 3-line to 8-line decoder. The circuit used in this device is shown in Fig. 6.39(a). Notice that it can be used to produce eight $\overline{CE}$ outputs. The operation of the 74F138 is described by the table in Fig. 6.39(b). Here we find that when enabled only the output that corresponds to the code at the CBA inputs switches to the active 0 logic level.

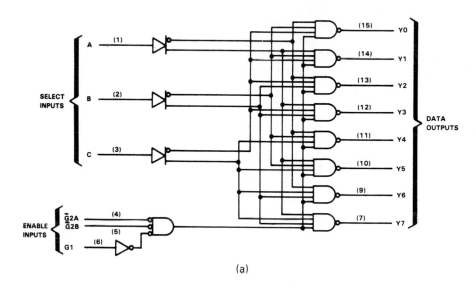

(a)

ENABLE INPUTS			SELECT INPUTS			OUTPUTS							
G1	$\overline{G2A}$	$\overline{G2B}$	C	B	A	Y0	Y1	Y2	Y3	Y4	Y5	Y6	Y7
X	H	X	X	X	X	H	H	H	H	H	H	H	H
X	X	H	X	X	X	H	H	H	H	H	H	H	H
L	X	X	X	X	X	H	H	H	H	H	H	H	H
H	L	L	L	L	L	L	H	H	H	H	H	H	H
H	L	L	L	L	H	H	L	H	H	H	H	H	H
H	L	L	L	H	L	H	H	L	H	H	H	H	H
H	L	L	L	H	H	H	H	H	L	H	H	H	H
H	L	L	H	L	L	H	H	H	H	L	H	H	H
H	L	L	H	L	H	H	H	H	H	H	L	H	H
H	L	L	H	H	L	H	H	H	H	H	H	L	H
H	L	L	H	H	H	H	H	H	H	H	H	H	L

(b)

Figure 6.39   (a) 74F138 circuit diagram. (Courtesy of Texas Instruments Incorporated) (b) Operation of the 74F138 decoder. (Courtesy of Texas Instruments Incorporated)

6.14 PROGRAMMABLE LOGIC ARRAYS

In the last section we found that basic logic devices such as latches, transceivers, and decoders are required in the bus interface section of the 8086 microcomputer system. We showed that these functions were performed with standard logic devices such as the 74F373 octal transparent latch, 74F245 octal bus transceiver, and 74F139 2-line to 4-line decoder, respectively. Today *programmable logic array* (PLA) devices are becoming very important in the design of microcomputer systems. For example, address and control signal decoding in the memory interface in Fig. 6.27 can be implemented with PLAs, instead of with separate logic ICs. Unlike the earlier mentioned devices, PLAs do not implement a specific logic function. Instead, they are general-purpose logic devices that have the ability to perform a wide variety of specialized logic functions. PLA contains a general purpose AND-OR-NOT array of logic gate circuits. The user has the ability to interconnect the inputs to the AND gates of this array. The definition of these inputs determines the logic function that is implemented. The process used to connect or disconnect inputs of the AND gate array is known as *programming*.

Block Diagram of a PLA

The block diagram in Fig. 6.40 represents a typical PLA. Looking at this diagram, we see that it has 16 input leads, marked I_0 through I_{15}. Moreover, there are eight output leads. These leads are labeled F_0 through F_7. This PLA is equipped with three-state outputs. For this reason, it has a chip enable control lead. In the block diagram, this control input is marked $\overline{CE}$. The logic level of $\overline{CE}$ determines if the outputs are enabled or disabled.

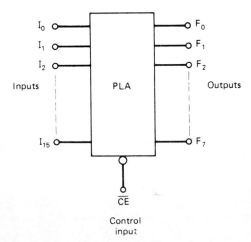

Figure 6.40 Block diagram of a PLA. (Walter A. Triebel and Alfred E. Chu, *Handbook of Semiconductor and Bubble Memories,* © 1982. Adapted with the permission of Prentice-Hall, Inc., Englewood Cliffs, N.J.)

When a PLA is used to implement random logic functions, the inputs represent Boolean variables, and the outputs are used to provide eight separate random logic functions. The internal AND-OR-NOT array is programmed to define a sum-of-product equation for each of these outputs in terms of the inputs and their complements. In this way, we see that the logic levels applied at inputs I_0 through I_{15} and the programming of the AND array determine what logic levels are produced at outputs F_0 through F_7. Therefore, the capacity of a PLA is measured by three properties—the number of inputs, the number of outputs, and the number of product terms (P-terms).

Architecture of a PLA

We just pointed out that the circuitry of a PLA is a general purpose AND-OR-NOT array. Figure 6.41(a) shows this architecture. Here we see that the input buffers supply input signals A and B and their complements $\overline{A}$ and $\overline{B}$. Programmable connections in the AND array permit any combination of these inputs to be combined to form a P-term. The product term outputs of the AND array are supplied to fixed inputs of the OR array. The output of the OR gate produces a sum-of-products function. Finally, the inverter complements this function.

The circuit of Fig. 6.41(b) shows how the function $F = (A\overline{B} + \overline{A}B)$ is implemented with the AND-OR-NOT array. Notice that an X marked into the AND array means that the fuse is left intact, and no marking means that it has been blown to form an open circuit. For this reason, the upper AND gate is connected to A and $\overline{B}$ and produces the product term $A\overline{B}$. The second AND gate from the top connects to $\overline{A}$ and B to produce $\overline{A}B$. The bottom AND gate is

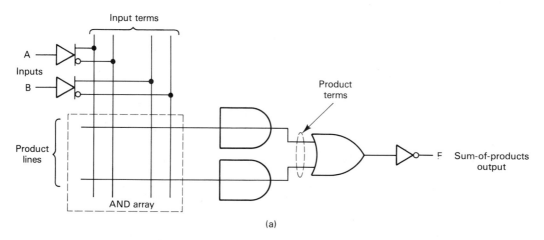

(a)

Figure 6.41 (a) Basic PLA architecture. (b) Implementing the logic function $F = A\overline{B} + A\overline{B}$.

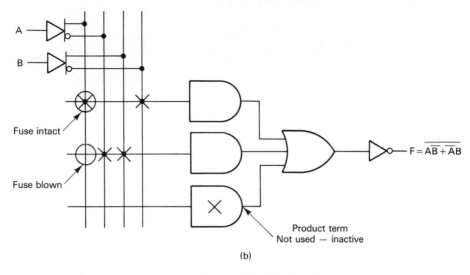

(b)

Figure 6.41 (Continued)

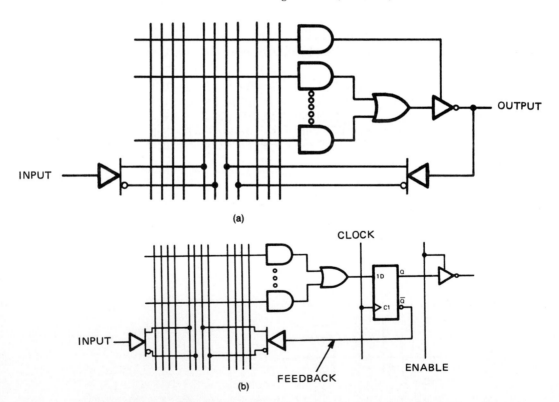

(a)

(b)

Figure 6.42 (a) Typical PLA architecture. (Courtesy of Texas Instruments Incorporated) (b) PLA with output latch. (Courtesy of Texas Instruments Incorporated)

marked with an X to indicate that it is not in use. Gates like this that are not to be active should have all of their input fuse links left intact.

In Fig. 6.42(a), we have shown the circuit structure that is most widely used in PLAs. It differs from the circuit shown in Fig. 6.41(a) in two ways. First, the inverter has a programmable three-state control and can be used to isolate the logic function from the output. Second, the buffered output is fed back to form another set of inputs to the AND array. This new output configuration permits the output pin to be programmed to work as a *standard output, standard input,* or *logic-controlled input/output.* For instance, if the upper AND gate, which is the control gate for the output buffer, is set up to permanently enable the inverter and the fuse links for its inputs that are fed back from the outputs are all blown open, the output functions as a standard output.

PLAs are also available in which the outputs are latched with registers. A circuit for this type of device is shown in Fig. 6.42(b). Here we see that the output of the OR gate is applied to the D input of a clocked D-type flip-flop. In this way, the logic level produced by the AND-OR array is not presented at the output until a pulse is first applied at the CLOCK input. Furthermore, the feedback input is produced from the complemented output of the flip-flop, not the output of the inverter. This configuration is known as a *PLA with registered outputs* and is designed to simplify implementation of *state machines* designs.

Standard PAL™ Devices

Now that we have introduced the block diagram of the PLA, types of PLAs, and internal architecture of the PLA, let us continue by examining a few of the widely used PAL devices. A PAL or a programmable array logic is a PLA in which OR array is fixed, only AND array is programmable.

The 16L8 is one of the more widely used PAL ICs. Its internal circuitry and pin numbering are shown in Fig. 6.43(a). This device is housed in a 20-pin package as shown in Fig. 6.43(b). Looking at this diagram, we see that it employs the PLA architecture that was illustrated in Fig. 6.42(a). Notice that it has ten dedicated input pins. All of these pins are labeled I. There are also two dedicated outputs, which are labeled with the letter O, and six programmable I/O lines, which are labeled I/O. Using the programmable I/O lines, the number of input lines can be expanded to as many as 16 inputs or the number of outputs can be increased to as many as 8 lines.

All of the 16L8's inputs are buffered and produce both the original form of the signal and its complement. The outputs of the buffers are applied to the inputs of the AND array. This array is capable of producing 64 product terms. Notice that the AND gates are arranged into eight groups of eight. The outputs of seven gates in each of these groups are used as inputs to an OR gate, and the eighth is used to produce an enable signal for the corresponding three-state output buffer. In this way, we see that the 16L8 is capable of producing up to seven product

PAL is a trademark of Monolithic Memory Devices.

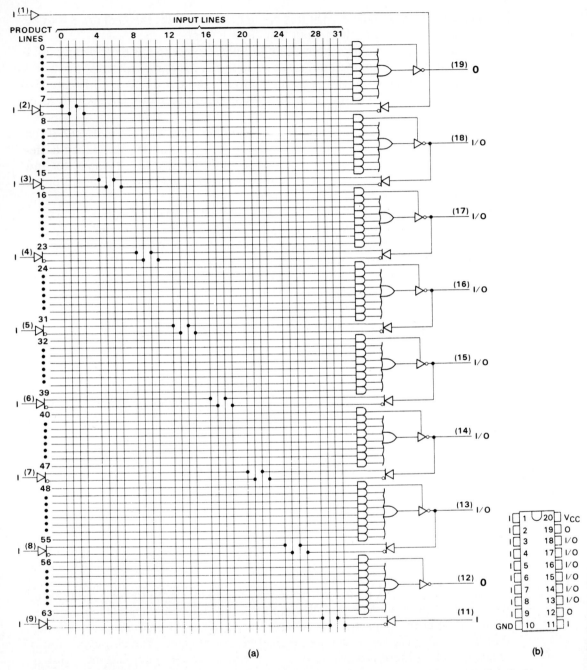

Figure 6.43 (a) 16L8 circuit diagram. (Courtesy of Texas Instruments Incorporated) (b) 16L8 pin layout. (Courtesy of Texas Instruments Incorporated)

terms for each output and the product terms can be formed using any combination of the 16 inputs.

The 16L8 is manufactured with bipolar technology. It operates from a $+5$ V $\pm 10\%$ dc power supply and draws a maximum of 180 mA. Moreover, all of its inputs and outputs are at TTL compatible voltage levels. This device exhibits high-speed input-output propagation delays. In fact, the maximum I-to-O propagation delay is rated as 7 ns.

Another widely used PAL is the 20L8 device. Looking at the circuitry of this device in Fig. 6.44(a), we see that it is similar to that of the 16L8 just described. However, the 20L8 has a maximum of 20 inputs, 8 outputs, and 64 P-terms. The device's 24-pin package is shown in Fig. 6.44(b).

The 16R8 is also a popular 20-pin PLA. The circuit diagram and pin layout for this device are shown in Fig. 6.45(a) and (b), respectively. From Fig. 6.45(a), we find that its eight fixed I inputs and AND-OR array are essentially the same as that of the 16L8. There is one change. The outputs of eight AND gates, instead of seven, are supplied to the inputs of each OR gate.

A number of changes have been made at the output side of the 16R8. Notice that the outputs of the OR gates are first latched in D-type flip-flops with the CLK signal. They are then buffered and supplied to the eight Q outputs. Another change is that the enable signals for the output inverters are no longer programmable. Now all three-state outputs are enabled by the logic level of the $\overline{OE}$ control input.

The last change is in the part of the circuit that produces the feedback inputs. In the 16R8, these eight input signals are derived from the complementary outputs work of the corresponding latches instead of the outputs of the buffers. For this reason, the output leads can no longer be programmed to work as direct inputs.

The 20R8 is the register output version of the 20L8 PAL. Its circuit diagram and pin layout are given in Fig. 6.46(a) and (b), respectively.

Expanding PLA Capacity

Some applications have requirements that exceed the capacity of a single PLA IC. For instance, a 16L8 device has the ability to supply a maximum of 16 inputs, 8 outputs, and 64 product terms. Capacity can be expanded by connecting several devices together. Let us now look at the way in which PLAs are interconnected to expand the number of inputs, outputs, and product terms.

If a single PLA does not have enough outputs, two or more devices can be connected together into the configuration of Fig. 6.47(a). Here we see that the inputs I_0 through I_{15} on the two devices are individually connected in parallel. This connection does not change the number of inputs.

On the other hand, the eight outputs of the two PLAs are separately used to form the upper and lower bytes of a 16-bit output word. The bits of this word are

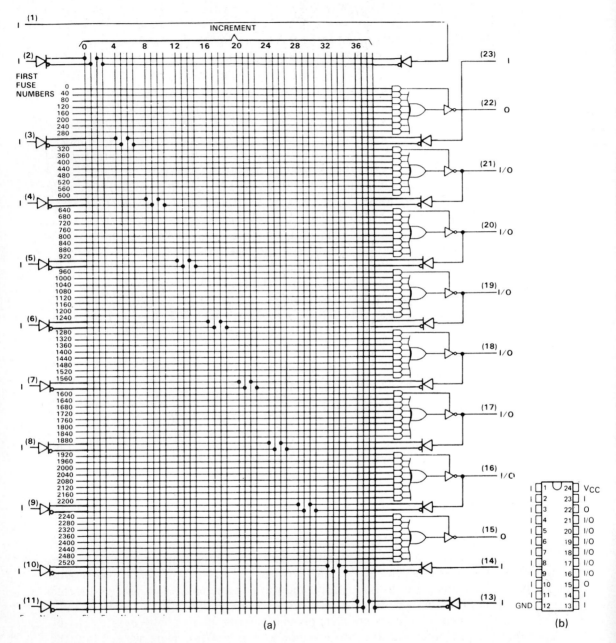

Figure 6.44 (a) 20L8 circuit diagram. (Courtesy of Texas Instruments Incorporated) (b) 20L8 pin layout. (Courtesy of Texas Instruments Incorporated)

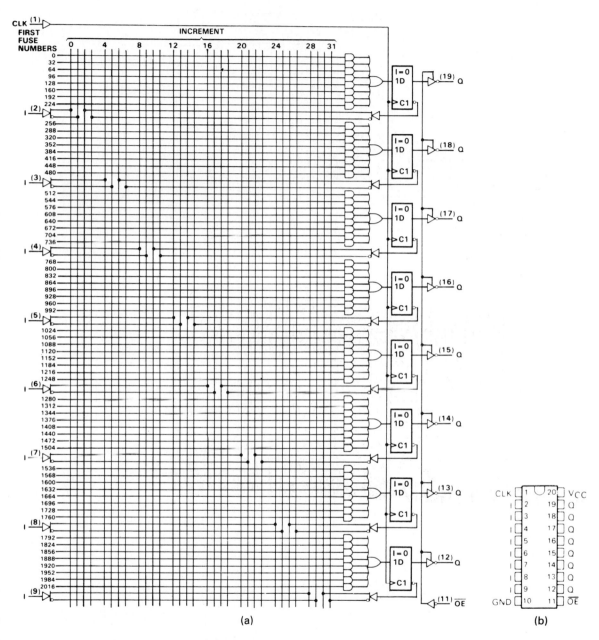

Figure 6.45 (a) 16R8 circuit diagram. (Courtesy of Texas Instruments Incorporated) (b) 16R8 pin layout. (Courtesy of Texas Instruments Incorporated)

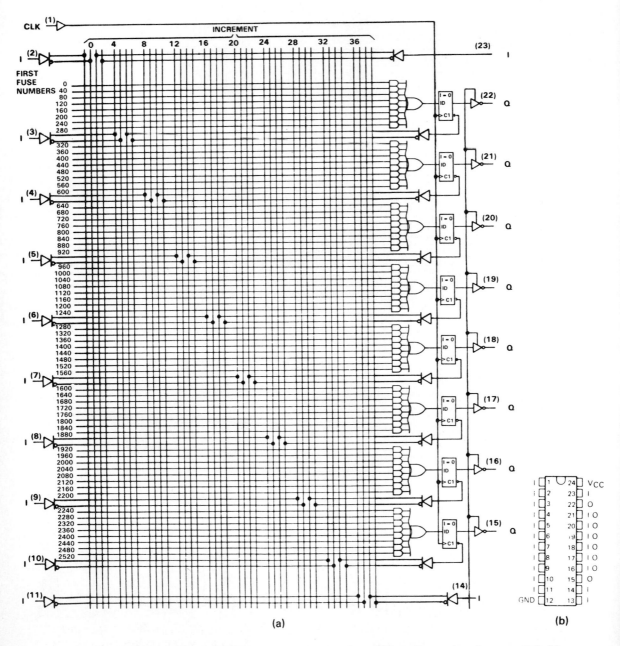

Figure 6.46 (a) 20R8 circuit diagram. (Courtesy of Texas Instruments Incorporated) (b) 20R8 pin layout. (Courtesy of Texas Instruments Incorporated)

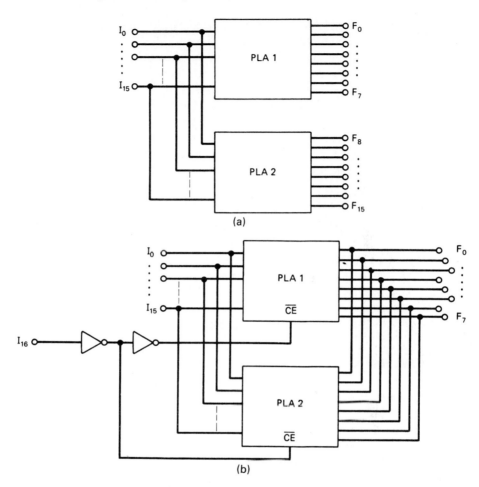

Figure 6.47   (a) Expanding output word length. (b) Expanding input word length. (Walter A. Triebel and Alfred E. Chu, *Handbook of Semiconductor and Bubble Memories,* © 1982. Adapted with the permission of Prentice-Hall, Inc., Englewood Cliffs, N.J.)

denoted as O_0 through O_{15}. So with this connection, we have doubled the number of outputs.

When data are applied to the inputs, PLA 1 outputs the eight least significant bits of data. At the same instant PLA 2 outputs the eight most significant bits. These outputs can be used to represent individual logic functions.

Another limitation on the application of PLAs is the number of inputs. The maximum number of inputs on a single 16L8 is 16. However, additional ICs can be connected to expand the capacity of inputs. Figure 6.47(b) shows how one additional input is added. This permits a 17-bit input denoted as I_0 through I_{16}. The new bit I_{16} is supplied through inverters to the $\overline{\text{CE}}$ inputs on the two PLAs.

At the output side of the PLAs, outputs O_0 through O_7 of the two devices are individually connected in parallel. To use this connection, PLA devices with open-collector or three-state outputs must be used.

When I_{16} is logic 0, $\overline{CE}$ on PLA 1 is logic 0. This enables the device for operation, and the output functions coded for input I_0 through I_{15} are output at O_0 through O_7. At the same instant, $\overline{CE}$ on PLA 2 is logic 1 and it remains disabled. Making the logic level of I_{16} equal to 1 disables PLA 1 and enables PLA 2. Now the input at I_0 through I_{15} causes the output function defined by PLA 2 to be output at O_0 through O_7. Actually, this connection doubles the number of product terms as well as increases the number of inputs.

6.15 PROGRAM STORAGE MEMORY—ROM, PROM, AND EPROM

Read-only memory (ROM) is one type of semiconductor memory device. It is most widely used in microcomputer systems for storage of the program that determines overall system operation. The information stored within a ROM integrated circuit is permanent—or *nonvolatile*. This means that when the power supply of the device is turned off, the stored information is not lost.

ROM, PROM, and EPROM

For some ROM devices, information (the microcomputer program) must be built in during manufacturing and for others the data must be electrically entered. The process of entering data into a ROM is called *programming*. As the name ROM implies, once entered into the device this information can be read only. Three types of ROM devices exist. They are known as the *mask-programmable read-only memory* (ROM), the *one-time programmable read-only memory* (PROM), and the *erasable programmable read-only memory* (EPROM).

Let us continue by looking more closely into the first type of device, the mask programmable read-only memory. This device has its data pattern programmed as part of the manufacturing process. This is known as *mask programming*. Once the device is programmed, its contents can never be changed. Because of this and the cost for making the programming masks, ROMs are used mainly in high-volume applications where the data will not change frequently.

The other two types of read-only memories, the PROM and EPROM, differ from the ROM in that the data contents are electrically entered by the user. Programming is usually done with equipment called a *programmer*. Both the PROM and EPROM are programmed in the same way. Once a PROM is programmed, its contents cannot be changed. This is the reason they are sometimes called one-time programmable PROMs. On the other hand, the contents of an EPROM can be erased by exposing it to ultraviolet light. In this way, the device can be used over and over again simply by erasing and reprogramming. PROMs

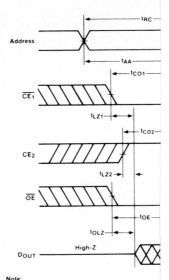

Note:
[1] $\overline{WE}$ is a high for a read cycle.
[2] The address inputs are valid prior to or coincide
and the CE_2 transition high.

write, has a minimum value o
remain valid for an interval of
time, however, just like addre
short recovery period takes p
cycle is complete. This inter
minimum value equals 5 ns.

The read cycle of a stat
ROM. Waveforms of a read c

Standard Dynamic RAM ICs

Dynamic RAMs are available i
most widely used DRAMs are
6.61 is a list of a number of pop
organized as 64K × 1 bit, the 2
which is organized as 64K × 4

DRAM	D
2164B	6
21256	2!
21464	2!
421000	
424256	

and EPROMs are most often used during the design of a product and for early production, when the code of the microcomputer may need to be changed frequently.

Block Diagram of a ROM

A block diagram of a typical ROM is shown in Fig. 6.48. Here we see that the device has three sets of signal lines: the address inputs, data outputs, and control inputs. This block diagram is valid for a ROM, PROM, or EPROM. Let us now look at the function of each of these sets of signal lines.

The address bus is used to input the signals that select between the data storage locations within the ROM device. In Fig. 6.48, we find that this bus consists of 11 address lines, A_0 through A_{10}. The bits in the address are arranged so that A_{10} is the MSB and A_0 is the LSB. With an 11-bit address, the memory device has $2^{11} = 2048$ unique data storage locations. The individual storage locations correspond to addresses over the range $00000000000_2 = 000_{16}$ through $11111111111_2 = 7FF_{16}$.

Each bit of data is stored inside a ROM, PROM, or EPROM as either a binary 0 or binary 1. Actually, 8 bits of data are stored at every address. Therefore the total storage capacity of the device we are describing is $2048 \times 8 = 16,384$ bits; that is, the device we are describing is really a 16K-bit ROM. By applying the address of a storage location to the address inputs of the ROM, the byte of data held at the addressed location is read out onto the data lines. In the block diagram of Fig. 6.48, we see that the data bus consists of eight lines labeled D_0 through D_7.

The control bus represents the control signals that are required to enable or disable the ROM, PROM, or EPROM device. In the block diagram of Fig. 6.48, two control leads, output enable ($\overline{OE}$) and chip enable ($\overline{CE}$), are identified. For example, logic 0 at $\overline{OE}$ enables the three state outputs, D_0 through D_7, of the

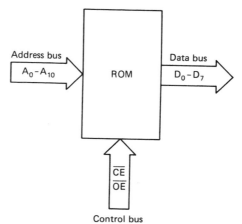

Figure 6.48 Block diagram of a ROM.

The waveforms for a t
now trace the events that ta
critical timing is referenced
Notice that the minimum di
the 100 ns *write cycle time* o
complete interval of time.

Next $\overline{CE}_1$ and CE_2 bec
write cycle. The durations
(t_{CW1}) time and CE_2 *to end*
are assuming here that they
but before the leading edge
80 ns. On the other hand, $\overline{W}$
This is the *address setup ti*
address inputs must be stabl
however, this parameter is
identified as t_{WP} and its min

Data applied to the D_1
with the trailing edge of $\overline{W}$.
equal to t_{DW} before this edg

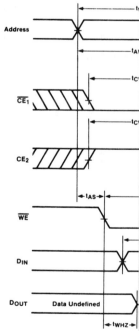

Note:
[1] A write occurs during the overlap of a low
[2] $\overline{CE}_1$ or $\overline{WE}$ (or CE_2) must be high (low) d
[3] If $\overline{OE}$ is high the I/O pins remain in a high

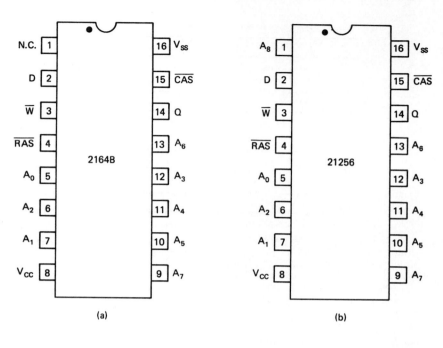

(a)   (b)

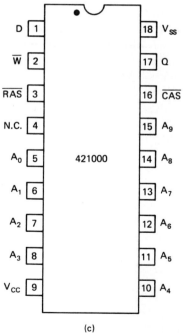

(c)

Figure 6.62 (a) 2164B pin layout. (b) 21256 pin layout. (c) 421000 pin layout.

and the 424256, which is organized as 256K × 4 bits. Pin layouts for the 2164B, 21256, and 421000 are shown in Fig. 6.62(a), (b), and (c), respectively.

Some other benefits of using DRAMs over SRAMs are that they cost less, consume less power, and their 16- and 18-pin packages take up less space. For these reasons, DRAMs are normally used in applications that require a large amount of memory. For example, most systems that support at least 1M byte of data memory are designed using DRAMs.

The 2164B is one of the older NMOS DRAM devices. A block diagram of the device is shown in Fig. 6.63. Looking at the block diagram we find that it has eight address inputs, A_0 through A_7, a data input and data output marked D and Q, respectively, and three control inputs, *row address strobe* ($\overline{RAS}$), *column address strobe* ($\overline{CAS}$), and *read/write* ($\overline{W}$).

The storage array within the 2164B is capable of storing 65,536 (64K) individual bits of data. To address this many storage locations, we need a 16-bit address; however, this device's package has just 16 pins. For this reason, the 16-bit address is divided into two separate parts: an 8-bit *row address* and an 8-bit *column address*. These two parts are time-multiplexed into the device over a single set of address lines, A_0 through A_7. First the row address is applied to A_0 through A_7. Then $\overline{RAS}$ is pulsed to logic 0 to latch it into the device. Next, the column address is applied and $\overline{CAS}$ strobed to logic 0. This 16-bit address selects which one of the 64K storage locations is to be accessed.

Data are either written into or read from the addressed storage location in the DRAMs. Write data are applied to the D input and read data are output at Q. The logic levels of control signals $\overline{W}$, $\overline{RAS}$, and $\overline{CAS}$ tell the DRAM whether a read or write data transfer is taking place and control the three-state outputs. For example, during a write operation, the logic level at D is latched into the addressed storage location at the falling edge of either $\overline{CAS}$ or $\overline{W}$. If $\overline{W}$ is switched to logic 0 before $\overline{CAS}$, an early write cycle is performed. During this type of write cycle, the outputs are maintained in the high-Z state throughout the complete bus cycle. The fact that the output is put in the high-Z state during the write operation allows the D input and Q output of the DRAM to be tied together. The Q output is also in the high-Z state whenever $\overline{CAS}$ is logic 1. This is the connection and mode

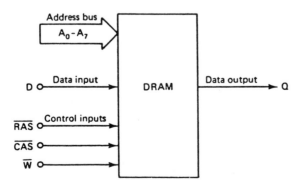

Figure 6.63 Block diagram of the 2164B DRAM.

of operation normally used when attaching DRAMs to the bidirectional data bus of a microprocessor. Figure 6.64 shows how 16 2164B devices are connected to make a 64K × 16-bit DRAM array.

The 2164B also has the ability to perform what are called *page mode* accesses. If RAS is left at logic 0 after the row address is latched inside the device,

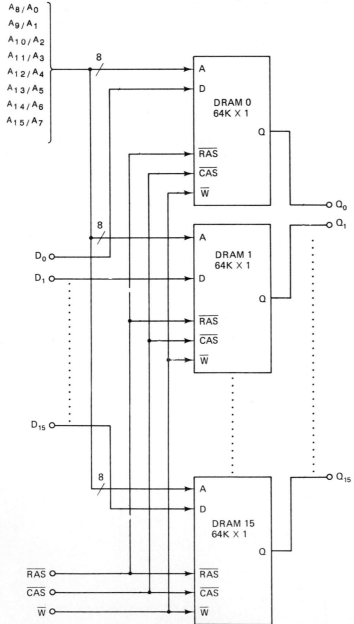

Figure 6.64   64K × 16-bit DRAM array.

the address is maintained within the device. Then data cells along the selected row can be accessed by simply supplying successive column addresses. This permits faster access of memory by eliminating the time needed to set up and strobe additional row addresses.

Earlier we pointed out that the key difference between the DRAM and SRAM is that the storage cells in the DRAM need to be periodically refreshed; otherwise, they lose their data. To maintain the integrity of the data in a DRAM, each of the rows of the storage array must typically be refreshed every 2 ms. All of the storage cells in an array are refreshed by simply cycling through the row addresses. As long as $\overline{CAS}$ is held at logic 1 during the refresh cycle, no data are output.

External circuitry is required to perform the address multiplexing, $\overline{RAS}/\overline{CAS}$ generation, and refresh operations for a DRAM subsystem. *DRAM refresh controller* ICs are available to permit easy implementation of these functions. An example of such a device is the 8208 DRAM refresh controller.

6.17 PROGRAM STORAGE MEMORY AND DATA STORAGE MEMORY CIRCUITS

In Section 6.13 we showed how the multiplexed bus is demultiplexed to give a system bus consisting of an independent 20-bit address bus and 8-bit or 16-bit data bus. Here we will look at some simple 8088 and 8086 microcomputer systems.

Program Storage Memory

The program storage memory part of a microcomputer is used to store fixed information such as instructions of the program or tables of data. Typically, it is read only, and for this reason is implemented with ROM, PROM, or EPROM devices. EPROM devices, such as the 2716, 2764, and 27256, are organized with a byte-wide output; therefore, a single device is required to supply the 8-bit data bus of the 8088.

Figure 6.65(a) shows how a 2716 is connected to the demultiplexed system bus of a minimum-mode 8088-based microcomputer. This device supplies 2K-bytes of program storage memory. To select one of the 2K of storage locations within the 2716, 11 bits of address are applied to address inputs A_0 through A_{10} of the EPROM. Assuming that bits A_0 through A_{10} of the 8088's address bus supply these inputs, the address range corresponding to program memory is from

$$A_{10}A_9 \ldots A_0 = 00000000000_2 = 00000_{16}$$

to

$$A_{10}A_9 \ldots A_0 = 11111111111_2 = 007FF_{16}$$

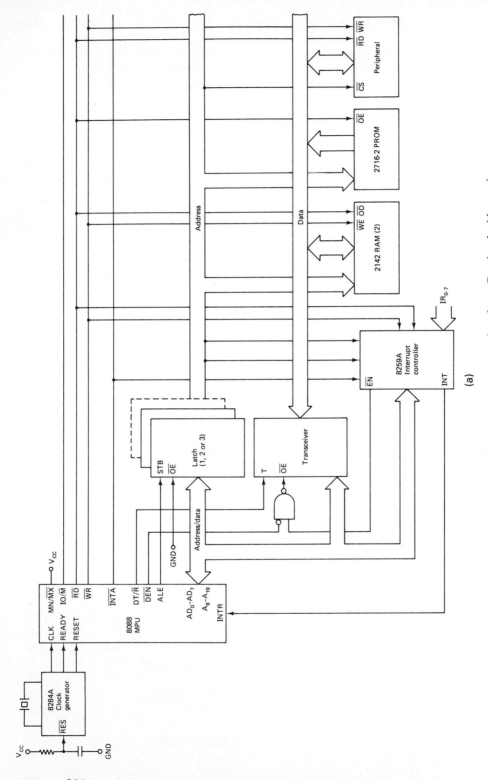

Figure 6.65 (a) Minimum-mode 8088 system memory interface. (Reprinted with permission of Intel Corp., Copyright/Intel Corp. 1981) (b) Minimum-mode 8086 system memory interface. (Reprinted with permission of Intel Corp., Copyright/Intel Corp. 1979) (c) Maximum-mode 8088 system memory interface. (Reprinted with permission of Intel Corp., Copyright/Intel Corp. 1981)

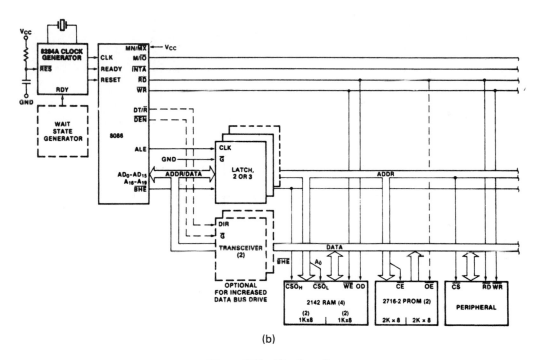

(b)

Figure 6.65 (Continued)

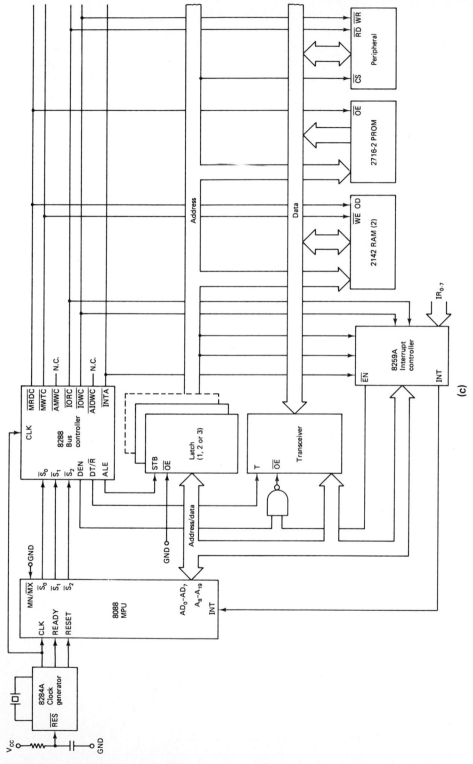

Figure 6.65 (Continued)

Data outputs D_0 through D_7 of the EPROM are applied to data bus lines D_0 through D_7, respectively, of the 8088's system data bus. Data held at the addressed storage location are enabled onto the data bus by the control signal $\overline{RD}$ (read), which is applied to the $\overline{OE}$ (output enable) input of the EPROM.

In most applications, the capacity of program storage memory is expanded by attaching several EPROM devices to the system bus. In this case, additional high-order bits of the 8088's address are decoded to produce chip select signals. For instance, two address bits, A_{11} and A_{12}, can be decoded to provide four chip select signals. Each of these chip selects is applied to the $\overline{CE}$ (chip enable) input of one EPROM. When an address is on the bus, just one of the outputs of the decoder becomes active and enables the corresponding EPROM for operation. By using four 2716s, the program storage memory is increased to 8K bytes.

Now that we have explained how EPROMs are attached to the 8088's system bus, let us trace through the operation of the circuit for a bus cycle in which a byte of code is fetched from program storage memory. During an instruction acquisition bus cycle, the instruction fetch sequence of the 8088 causes the instruction to be read from memory byte by byte. The values in CS and IP are combined within the 8088 to give the address of a storage location in the address range of the program storage memory. This address is output on A_0 through A_{19} and latched into the address latches synchronously with the signal ALE. Bits A_0 through A_{10} of the system address bus are applied to the address inputs of the 2716. This part of the address selects the byte of code to be output. When the 8088 switches $\overline{RD}$ to logic 0, the outputs of the 2716 are enabled and the byte of data at the addressed storage location is output onto system data bus lines D_0 through D_7. Early in the read bus cycle, the 8088 switches $DT/\overline{R}$ to logic 0 to signal the bus transceiver that data are to be input to the microprocessor, and later in the bus cycle $\overline{DEN}$ is switched to logic 0 to enable the transceiver for operation. Now the byte of data is passed from the system data bus onto the multiplexed address/data bus from which it is read by the MPU.

The circuit in Fig. 6.65(b) shows a similar circuit for a minimum-mode 8086 microcomputer system. Notice that because of the 16-bit data bus two octal transceivers and two EPROMs are required.

Figure 6.65(c) shows the program storage memory implementation for a maximum-mode 8088 microcomputer system. Let us look at how this circuit differs from the minimum mode circuit of Fig. 6.65(a). The key difference in this circuit is that the 8288 bus controller is used to produce the control signals for the memory interface. Remember that in maximum mode the code output on status lines $\overline{S}_0$ through $\overline{S}_2$ identifies the type of bus cycle that is in progress. During all read operations of program memory, the 8088 outputs the instruction fetch memory bus status code, $\overline{S}_2\overline{S}_1\overline{S}_0 = 101$, to the 8288. In response to this input, the bus controller produces the memory read command ($\overline{MRDC}$) output. This output is used as the $\overline{OE}$ input of the 2716 EPROM and enables it for operation.

In the maximum mode circuit, the 8288, rather than the 8088, produces the control signals for the address latches and data bus transceiver. Notice that three address latches are again used, but this time the ALE output of the 8288 is used to strobe the memory address into these latches. ALE is applied to the STB input of all three latch devices in parallel. Moreover, the direction of data transfer through the data bus transceiver is set by the DT/$\overline{\text{R}}$ output of the bus controller and the DEN output is used to generate the $\overline{\text{OE}}$ input of the transceiver. Since DEN, not $\overline{\text{DEN}}$, is produced by the 8288, an inverter is no longer required at its input of the NAND gate that drives $\overline{\text{OE}}$ of the transceiver.

Data Storage Memory

Information that frequently changes is stored in the data storage part of the microcomputer's memory subsystem. Examples of information typically stored in data storage memory are application programs and data bases. This part of the memory subsystem is normally implemented with random access read/write memory (RAM). If the amount of memory required in the microcomputer is small, for instance, less than 32K bytes, the memory subsystem will usually be designed with static RAMs. On the other hand, systems that require a larger amount of data storage memory normally use dynamic RAMs (DRAMs). This is because most DRAMs are organized as 64K by 1 bit, 256K by 1 bit, or 1M by 1 bit. Moreover, DRAMs require refresh support circuits. This additional circuitry is not warranted if storage requirements are small.

A 1K-byte random access read/write memory is also implemented in the minimum-mode 8088-based microcomputer circuit of Fig. 6.65(a). This part of the memory subsystem is implemented with two 2142 static RAM ICs. Each 2142 contains 1K, 4-bit storage locations; therefore, they both supply storage for just 4 bits of the byte. The storage location to be accessed is selected by a 10-bit address, which is applied to both RAMs in parallel over address lines A_0 through A_9. Data are read from or written into the selected storage location over data bus lines D_0 through D_7. Of course, through software, the 8088 can read data from memory either as bytes, words, or double words. The logic level of $\overline{\text{WR}}$ (write), which is applied to the write enable ($\overline{\text{WE}}$) input of both RAMs in parallel, signals whether a read or write bus cycle is in progress. Moreover, $\overline{\text{RD}}$ is applied to the OD (output disable) input of both RAMs in parallel. When a write cycle is in progress, $\overline{\text{RD}}$ is at logic 1 and disables the outputs of the RAMs. Now the data lines act as inputs.

Just as for program storage memory, data storage memory can be expanded by simply attaching additional banks of static RAMs to the system bus. Once again, high-order address bits can be decoded to produce chip select signals. Each chip select output is applied to the chip enable input of both RAMs in a bank and, when active, it enables that bank of RAMs for operation.

Let us assume that the value of a byte-wide data operand is to be updated in memory. In this case, the 8088 must perform a write bus cycle to the address of the operand's storage location. First, the address of the operand is formed and output on the multiplexed address/data bus. When the address is stable, a pulse at

ALE is used to latch it into the address latches. Bits A_0 through A_9 of the system address bus are applied to the address inputs of the 2142s. This part of the address selects the storage location into which the byte of data is to be written. Next the 8088 switches DT/$\overline{R}$ to logic 1 to signal the octal transceivers that data are to be output to memory. Later in the bus cycle, $\overline{DEN}$ is switched to logic 0 to enable the data bus transceiver for operation. Now the byte of data is output on the multiplexed address/data bus and passed through the transceiver to the system data bus and data inputs of the RAMs. Finally, the byte of data is written into the addressed storage location synchronously with the occurrence of the $\overline{WR}$ control signal.

The data storage memory circuitry of a minimum-mode 8086 system is also shown in Fig. 6.65(b). Here we see that two banks of RAM ICs are required.

The data storage memory circuit of a maximum-mode 8088 microcomputer is also shown in Fig. 6.65(c). Just like in our description of the program storage memory part of this circuit, the difference between the maximum mode and minimum mode data storage memory circuits lies in the fact that the 8288 bus controller produces the control signals for the memory and bus interface logic devices. When the 8088 is accessing data storage memory, it outputs either the read memory (101) or write memory (110) bus status code. These codes are decoded by the 8288 to produce appropriate memory control signals. For instance, an input of 110 (write memory) causes the memory write command ($\overline{MWTC}$) and advance memory write command ($\overline{AMWC}$) outputs to become active during all write bus cycles. In Fig. 6.65(c), we find that $\overline{MWTC}$ is used to drive the $\overline{WE}$ input of the 2142 SRAMs. When $\overline{MWTC}$ is at its active 0 logic level, the input buffers of the SRAMs are enabled for operation. On the other hand, during read bus cycles, $\overline{MRDC}$ is used to enable the outputs of the SRAMs.

ASSIGNMENTS

Section 6.2

1. Name the technology used to fabricate the 8088 and 8086 microprocessors.
2. What is the transistor count of the 8088?
3. Which pin is used as the NMI input on the 8088?
4. Which pin provides the $\overline{BHE}$ and S_7 output signals on the 8086?
5. How much memory can the 8088 and 8086 directly address?
6. How large is the I/O address space of the 8088 and 8086?

Section 6.3

7. How is minimum or maximum mode of operation selected?
8. Describe the difference between the minimum-mode 8088 system and maximum-mode 8088 system.

9. What output function is performed by pin 29 of the 8088 when in the minimum mode? Maximum mode?

10. Is the signal $M/\overline{IO}$ an input or output of the 8086?

11. Name one signal that is supplied by the 8088 but not by the 8086.

12. Are the signals QS_0 and QS_1 produced in the minimum mode or maximum mode?

Section 6.4

13. What are the word lengths of the 8088's address bus and data bus? The 8086's address bus and data bus?

14. Does the 8088 have a multiplexed address/data bus or independent address and data buses?

15. What mnemonic is used to identify the least significant bit of the 8088's address bus? The most significant bit of the 8088's data bus?

16. What does status code $S_4S_3 = 01$ mean in terms of the memory segment being accessed?

17. Which output is used to signal external circuitry that a byte of data is available on the upper half of the 8086's data bus?

18. What does the logic level on $M/\overline{IO}$ signal to external circuitry in an 8086 microcomputer?

19. Which output is used to signal external circuitry in an 8088-based microcomputer that valid data is on the bus during a write cycle?

20. What signal does a minimum-mode 8088 respond with when it acknowledges an active interrupt request?

21. Which signals implement the DMA interface in an 8088 or 8086 microcomputer system?

22. List the signals of the 8088 that go to the high-Z state in response to a DMA request.

Section 6.5

23. Identify the signal lines of the 8088 that are different for the minimum-mode and maximum-mode interfaces.

24. What status outputs of the 8088 are input to the 8288?

25. What maximum-mode control signals are generated by the 8288?

26. What function is served by the 8289 in a maximum-mode 8088 microcomputer system?

27. What status code is output by the 8088 to the 8288 if a memory read bus cycle is taking place?

28. What command output becomes active if the status inputs of the 8288 are 100_2?

29. If the 8088 executes a jump instruction, what queue status code would be output?

30. Which pins provide signals for local bus control in a maximum-mode 8088 system?

Section 6.6

31. What is the range of power supply voltage over which the 8088 is guaranteed to work correctly?

32. What is the maximum value of voltage that could be output as a valid logic 0 at bit D_0 of the 8088's data bus? Assume that the output is sinking 2 mA.

33. What is the minimum value of voltage that would represent a valid logic 1 at the INTR input of the 8088?

34. At what current value is V_{OLmax} measured on the 8086?

Section 6.7

35. What speed 8088s are available today?

36. What frequency crystal must be connected between the X_1 and X_2 inputs of the clock generator if an 8088-2 is to run at full speed?

37. What clock outputs are produced by the 8284? What would be their frequencies if a 30 MHz crystal is used?

38. What are the logic levels of the clock waveforms applied to the 8088?

Section 6.8

39. How many clock states are in an 8088 bus cycle that has no wait states? How are these states denoted?

40. What is the duration of the bus cycle for a 5 MHz 8088 that is running at full speed and with no wait states?

41. What is an idle state?

42. What is a wait state?

43. If an 8086 running at 10 MHz performs bus cycles with two wait states, what is the duration of the bus cycle?

Section 6.9

44. How is the memory bank of an 8088 microcomputer organized from a hardware point of view? The memory of an 8086 microcomputer?

45. Overview how a byte of data is read from memory address $B0003_{16}$ of an 8088-based microcomputer. List the memory control signals along with their active logic levels that occur during the memory read bus cycle.

46. Overview how a word of data is written to memory starting at address $A0000_{16}$ of an 8088-based microcomputer. List the memory control signals together with their active logic levels that occur during the memory write cycle.

47. In which bank of memory in an 8086-based microcomputer are odd-addressed bytes of data stored? What bank select signal is used to enable this bank of memory?

48. Over which of the 8086's data bus lines are even-addressed bytes of data transferred and which bank select signal is active?

49. List the memory control signals together with their active logic levels that occur when a word of data is written to memory address $A0000_{16}$ in an 8086 microcomputer system.

50. List the memory control signals together with their active logic levels that occur when a byte of data is written to memory address $B0003_{16}$ in an 8086 microcomputer. Over which data lines is the byte of data transferred?

Section 6.10

51. In a maximum-mode 8088 microcomputer, what code is output on S_3S_4 when an instruction-fetch bus cycle is in progress?

52. What is the value of S_3S_4 if the operand of a pop instruction is being read from memory? The microcomputer employs the 8088 in the maximum mode.

Section 6.11

53. Which of the 8088's memory control signals is complemented on the 8086?

54. What memory control output of the 8088 is not provided on the 8086? What signal replaces it on the 8086?

55. In a maximum-mode 8088-based microcomputer, what memory bus status code is output when a word of instruction code is fetched from memory? Which memory control output(s) is produced by the 8288?

56. In maximum mode, what memory bus status code is output when a destination operand is written to memory? Which memory control output(s) is (are) produced by the 8288?

57. When the instruction PUSH AX is executed, what address bus status code and memory bus cycle code are output by the 8088 in a maximum-mode microcomputer system? Which command signals are output by the 8288?

Section 6.12

58. How many clock states are in a read bus cycle that has no wait states? What would be the duration of this bus cycle if the 8086 is operating at 10 MHz?

59. What happens in the T_1 part of the 8088's bus cycle?

60. Describe the bus activity that takes place as the 8088 writes a byte of data into memory address $B0010_{16}$.

61. What input of the 8088 is used to initiate a wait state?

62. If an 8088 running at 5 MHz performs a write bus cycle with one wait state, what is the duration of the bus cycle?

Section 6.13

63. Overview the function of each of the blocks in the memory interface diagram of Fig. 6.27.

64. When the instruction PUSH AX is executed, what bus status code is output by the 8086, what are the logic levels of A_0 and $\overline{BHE}$, and what read/write control signals are produced by the bus controller?

65. What type of logic function is implemented by the 74F373 and 74F374 ICs?

66. What is the key difference between the 74F373 and 74F374?

67. Make a drawing to show how the address latch with I/O address buffer circuit in Fig. 6.31(a) can be constructed with 74F374 and 74F244 ICs. Assume that the latches and buffer circuits will be permanently enabled.

68. What logic function is implemented by the 74F245 IC?

69. In the circuit of Fig. 6.33, what logic levels must be applied to the $\overline{\text{DEN}}$ and DT/$\overline{\text{R}}$ inputs to cause data on the system data bus to be transferred to the microprocessor data bus?

70. Make a drawing like that in Fig. 6.33 to show the data bus transceiver circuit needed in an 8088-based microcomputer system.

71. What are the logic levels of the $\overline{\text{G}}$, DIR, CAB, CBA, SAB, and SBA inputs of the 74F646 when stored data in the A register are transferred to the B bus?

72. Name an IC that implements a 2-line to 4-line decoder logic function.

73. If the inputs to a 74F138 decoder are $G_1 = 1$, $\overline{\text{G}}_{2A} = 0$, $\overline{\text{G}}_{2B} = 0$, and CBA = 101, which output is active?

74. Make a drawing like that in Fig. 6.38 for an 8088-based microcomputer for which a 74F138 decoder is used to decode address line A_{17} through A_{19} into memory chip selects.

Section 6.14

75. What does PLA stand for?

76. List three properties that measure the capacity of a PLA.

77. What is the programming mechanism used in PAL called?

78. Give the key difference between a PAL and a PLA.

79. What does PAL stand for?

80. Redraw the circuit in Fig. 6.41(b) to show how it can implement the logic function $F = (\overline{AB} + AB)$.

81. How many dedicated inputs, dedicated outputs, programmable input/outputs, and product terms are supported on the 16L8 PAL?

82. What is the maximum number of inputs on a 20L8 PAL? The maximum number of outputs?

83. How do the outputs of the 16R8 differ from those of the 16L8?

Section 6.15

84. What is meant by the term *nonvolatile memory*?

85. What does PROM stand for? EPROM?

86. What must an EPROM be exposed to in order to erase its stored data?

87. If the block diagram of Fig. 6.48 has address lines A_0 through A_{16} and data lines D_0 through D_7, what are its bit density and byte capacity?

88. Summarize the read cycle of an EPROM. Assume that both $\overline{\text{CE}}$ and $\overline{\text{OE}}$ are active before the address is applied.

89. Which standard EPROM stores 64K 8-bit words?

90. What is the difference between a 2764A and a 2764A-1?

91. What are the values of V_{CC} and V_{pp} for the Intelligent Programming algorithm™?

92. What is the duration of the programming pulses used for the Intelligent Programming algorithm™?

Section 6.16

93. What do SRAM and DRAM stand for?

94. Are RAM ICs examples of nonvolatile or volatile memory devices?

95. What must be done to maintain the data in a DRAM valid?

96. Find the total storage capacity of the circuit in Fig. 6.55 if the devices are 43256As.

97. List the minimum values of each of the write cycle parameters that follow for the 4364-10 SRAM: t_{WC}, t_{CW1}, t_{CW2}, t_{WP}, t_{DW}, and t_{WR}.

98. Give two benefits of DRAMs over SRAMs.

99. Name the two parts of a DRAM address.

100. Show how the circuit in Fig. 6.64 can be expanded to 128K × 16 bits.

101. Give a disadvantage of the use of DRAMs in an application that does not require a large amount of memory.

Section 6.17

102. Make a diagram showing how four 2764 EPROMs are connected to form a 16K-byte program storage memory subsystem. Also show a 16K-word program memory subsystem.

103. If we assume that the high-order address bits in the circuits formed in problem 102 are all logic 0, what is the address range of the program memory subsystems?

104. How many 2142 static RAMs would be needed in the memory array of the circuit in Fig. 6.65(a) if the capacity of data storage memory is to be expanded to 64K bytes?

105. How many 2716 EPROMs would be needed in the program memory array in the circuit of Fig. 6.65(a) to expand its capacity to 96K bits? If 2732s were used instead of 2716s, how many devices are needed to implement the 96K-bit program memory?

Input/Output Interface of the 8088 and 8086 Microprocessors

7.1 INTRODUCTION

In Chapter 6, we studied the memory interface of the 8088 and 8086 microprocessors. Here we will study another important interface of 8088- and 8086-based microcomputer systems, the input/output (I/O) interface. Types of I/O, I/O interface, I/O data transfers, I/O instructions, I/O bus cycles, and LSI peripheral ICs, such as the 8255A programmable peripheral interface, 8253 programmable interval timer, and the 8237A direct memory access controllers, are described. Again, the focus will be on the description of the 8088's I/O interface and the differences between it and that of the 8086. Following are the topics that are covered:

1. Types of Input/Output
2. The isolated I/O interface
3. I/O data transfers
4. I/O instructions
5. I/O bus cycles
6. Eight-byte-wide output ports using isolated I/O
7. Eight-byte-wide input ports using isolated I/O
8. Input/Output handshaking

  9. 8255A programmable peripheral interface
 10. 8255A implementation of parallel I/O ports
 11. Memory-mapped I/O ports
 12. 8253 programmable interval timer
 13. 8237A direct memory access controller

7.2 TYPES OF INPUT/OUTPUT

The 8088 and 8086 microcomputers can employ two different types of input/output. They are known as *isolated I/O* and *memory-mapped I/O*. These I/O methods differ in how I/O ports are mapped into the 8088/8086's address spaces. Practical microcomputer systems usually employ both kinds of I/O. That is, some peripheral ICs are treated as isolated I/O devices and others as memory mapped I/O devices. Let us now look at each of these types of I/O.

When using isolated I/O in a microcomputer system, the I/O devices are treated separate from memory. This is achieved because the software and hardware architectures support separate memory and I/O address spaces. Figure 7.1(a) illustrates these memory and I/O address spaces. In our study of 8088/8086 software architecture in Chapter 2, we examined these address spaces from a software point of view. We found that information in memory or at I/O ports are organized as bytes of data; that the memory address space contains 1M consecutive byte addresses in the range 00000_{16} through $FFFFF_{16}$; and that the I/O address space contains 64K consecutive byte addresses in the range 0000_{16} through $FFFF_{16}$. Moreover, the contents of two consecutive memory or I/O addresses could be accessed as word-wide data. For instance, in Fig. 7.1(b), I/O address 0000_{16} or 0001_{16} can be treated as independent byte-wide I/O ports, port 0 and port 1, or they may be considered together as word-wide port 0.

This isolated method of I/O offers some advantages. First, the complete 1 MB memory address space is available for use with memory. Second, special instructions have been provided in the instruction set of the 8088/8086 to perform isolated I/O input and output operations. These instructions have been tailored to maximize I/O performance. A disadvantage of this type of I/O is that all input and output data transfers must take place between the AL or AX register and the I/O port.

I/O devices can be placed in the memory address space of the microcomputer, as well as in the independent I/O address space. In this case, the MPU looks at the I/O port as though it is a memory location. For this reason, the method is known as *memory-mapped I/O*.

In a microcomputer system with memory-mapped I/O, some of the memory address space is dedicated to I/O ports. For example, in Fig. 7.2 the 4096 memory addresses in the range from $E0000_{16}$ through $E0FFF_{16}$ are assigned to I/O devices. Here the contents of address $E0000_{16}$ represent byte-wide port 0 and the contents of addresses $E0000_0$ and $E0001_{16}$ correspond to word-wide port 0.

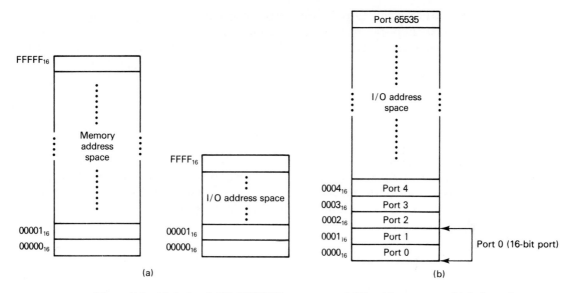

Figure 7.1 (a) Isolated I/O 8088/8086 memory and I/O address space. (b) Independent bytewide I/O ports.

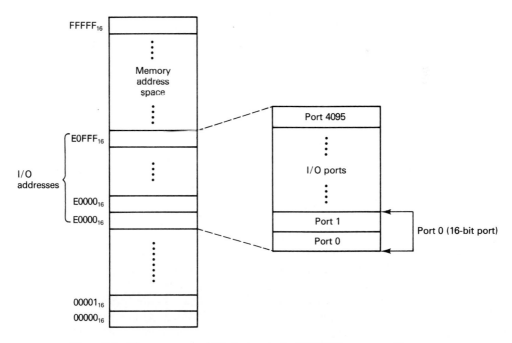

Figure 7.2 Memory-mapped I/O devices in the 8088/8086 memory address space.

When I/O is configured in this way, instructions that affect data in memory are used instead of the special input/output instructions. This is an advantage in that many more instructions and addressing modes are available to perform I/O operations. For instance, the contents of a memory-mapped I/O port can be directly ANDed with a value in an internal register. In addition, I/O transfers can now take place between an I/O port and an internal register other than just AL or AX. However, this also leads to a disadvantage. That is, the memory instructions tend to execute slower than those specifically designed for isolated I/O. Therefore, a memory-mapped I/O routine may take longer to execute than an equivalent program using the input/output instructions.

Another disadvantage of using this method is that part of the memory address space is lost. For instance, in Fig. 7.2 addresses in the range from $E0000_{16}$ through $E0FFF_{16}$ cannot be used to implement memory.

7.3 THE ISOLATED INPUT/OUTPUT INTERFACE

The isolated *input/output interface* of the 8088 and 8086 microcomputers permits them to communicate with the outside world. The way in which the MPU deals with input/output circuitry is similar to the way in which it interfaces with memory circuitry. That is, input/output data transfers also take place over the multiplexed address/data bus. This parallel bus permits easy interface to LSI peripherals such as parallel I/O expanders. Through this I/O interface, the MPU can input or output data in bit, byte, or word formats.

Minimum-Mode Interface

Let us begin by looking at the isolated I/O interface for a minimum-mode 8088 system. Figure 7.3 shows this minimum-mode interface. Here we find the 8088, interface circuitry, and I/O ports for devices 0 through N. The circuits in the interface section must perform functions such as select the I/O port, latch output data, sample input data, synchronize data transfers, and translate between TTL voltage levels and those required to operate the I/O devices.

The data path between the 8088 and I/O interface circuits is the multiplexed address/data bus. Unlike the memory interface, this time just the 16 least significant lines of the bus, AD_0 through AD_7 and A_8 through A_{15}, are in use. This interface also involves the control signals that we discussed as part of the memory interface. They are ALE, $\overline{SSO}$, $\overline{RD}$, $\overline{WR}$, IO/$\overline{M}$, DT/$\overline{R}$, and $\overline{DEN}$.

The isolated I/O interface of a minimum-mode 8086-based microcomputer system is shown in Fig. 7.3(b). Looking at this diagram, we find that the interface differs from that of the 8088 microcomputer in several ways. First, the complete data bus AD_0 through AD_{15} is used for input and output data transfers; second, the M/$\overline{IO}$ control signal is the complement of the equivalent signal IO/$\overline{M}$ in the 8088's interface; and third, status signal $\overline{SSO}$ is replaced by $\overline{BHE}$.

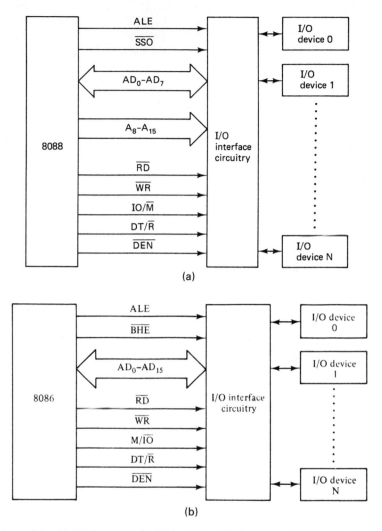

Figure 7.3 (a) Minimum-mode 8088 system I/O interface. (b) Minimum-mode 8086 system I/O interface.

Maximum-Mode Interface

When the 8088 is strapped to operate in the maximum mode, the interface to the I/O circuitry changes. Figure 7.4(a) illustrates this configuration.

As in the maximum-mode memory interface, the 8288 bus controller produces the control signals for the I/O subsystem. The 8288 decodes bus command status codes output by the 8088 at $\overline{S}_2\overline{S}_1\overline{S}_0$. These codes tell which type of bus cycle is in progress. If the code corresponds to an I/O read bus cycle, the 8288

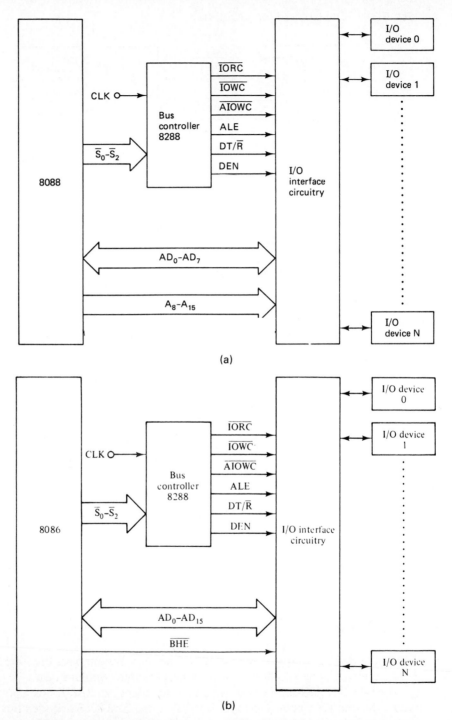

Figure 7.4 (a) Maximum-mode 8088 system I/O interface. (b) Maximum-mode 8086 system I/O interface.

Status inputs			CPU cycle	8288 command
$\overline{S}_2$	$\overline{S}_1$	$\overline{S}_0$		
0	0	0	Interrupt acknowledge	$\overline{INTA}$
0	0	1	Read I/O port	$\overline{IORC}$
0	1	0	Write I/O port	$\overline{IOWC}$, $\overline{AIOWC}$
0	1	1	Halt	None
1	0	0	Instruction fetch	$\overline{MRDC}$
1	0	1	Read memory	$\overline{MRDC}$
1	1	0	Write memory	$\overline{MWTC}$, $\overline{AMWC}$
1	1	1	Passive	None

Figure 7.5   I/O bus cycle status codes. (Reprinted with permission of Intel Corp., Copyright/Intel Corp. 1979)

generates the I/O *read command output* ($\overline{IORC}$) and for an I/O write cycle it generates I/O *write command outputs* ($\overline{IOWC}$) and ($\overline{AIOWC}$). The 8288 also produces control signals ALE, DT/$\overline{R}$, and DEN. Moreover, the address and data transfer path between 8088 and maximum-mode I/O interface remains address/data bus lines AD_0 through AD_7 and A_8 through A_{15}.

Figure 7.4(b) shows the maximum-mode isolated I/O interface of an 8086 microcomputer system. There are only two differences between this interface diagram and that for the 8088 microcomputer. As in the minimum mode, the full 16-bit data bus is the path for data transfers. Moreover, the signal $\overline{BHE}$, which is not supplied by the 8088, is included in the interface.

The table in Fig. 7.5 shows the bus command status codes together with the command signals that they produce. Those for I/O bus cycles have been highlighted. The MPU indicates that data are to be input (read I/O port) by code $\overline{S}_2\overline{S}_1\overline{S}_0 = 001$. This input causes the bus controller to produce control output I/O read command ($\overline{IORC}$). There is one other code that represents an output bus cycle. This is the write I/O port code $\overline{S}_2\overline{S}_1\overline{S}_0 = 010$. It produces two output command signals I/O write cycle ($\overline{IOWC}$) and advanced I/O write cycle ($\overline{AIOWC}$). These command signals are used to enable data from the I/O circuitry onto the system bus and control the direction in which data are transferred.

7.4 INPUT/OUTPUT DATA TRANSFERS

Input/output ports in the 8088 and 8086 microcomputers can be either byte-wide or word-wide. The port that is accessed for input or output of data is selected by an *I/O address*. This address is specified as part of the instruction that performs the I/O operation.

I/O addresses are 16 bits in length and are output by the 8088 to the isolated I/O interface over bus lines AD_0 through AD_7 and A_8 through A_{15}. As for memory addresses, AD_0 represents the LSB and A_{15} the MSB. The most significant bits, A_{16} through A_{19}, of the memory address are held at the 0 logic level during the address period (T_1) of all I/O bus cycles. Since 16 address lines are used to address I/O ports, the 8088's I/O address space consists of 64K byte-wide I/O ports.

The 8088 signals to external circuitry that the address on the bus is for an I/O port instead of a memory location by switching the $IO/\overline{M}$ control line to the 1 logic level. This signal is held at the 1 level during the complete input or output bus cycle. For this reason, it can be used to enable the address latch or address decoder in external I/O circuitry.

Data transfers between the 8088 and I/O devices are performed over the data bus. Data transfers to byte-wide I/O ports always require one bus cycle. Byte data transfers to a port are performed over bus lines D_0 through D_7. Word transfers also take place over the data bus, D_0 through D_7. However, this type of operation is performed as two consecutive byte-wide data transfers and takes two bus cycles.

For the 8086 microcomputer, I/O addresses are output on address/data bus lines AD_0 through AD_{15}. The logic levels of signals A_0 and $\overline{BHE}$ determine whether data are input/output for an odd-addressed byte-wide port, even-addressed byte-wide port, or a word-wide port. For example, if $A_0 \overline{BHE} = 10$, an odd-addressed byte-wide I/O port is accessed. Byte data transfers to a port at an even address are performed over bus lines D_0 through D_7 and those to an odd-addressed port are performed over D_8 through D_{15}. Data transfers to byte-wide I/O ports always take place in one bus cycle.

Word data transfers between the 8086 and I/O devices are accompanied by the code $A_0 \overline{BHE} = 00$ and are performed over the complete data bus, D_0 through D_{15}. A word transfer can require either one or two bus cycles. To ensure that just one bus cycle is required for the word data transfer, word-wide I/O ports should be aligned at even-address boundaries.

7.5 INPUT/OUTPUT INSTRUCTIONS

Input/output operations are performed by the 8088 and 8086 microprocessors that employ isolated I/O using the *in* (IN) and *out* (OUT) instructions. There are two types of IN and OUT instructions: the *direct I/O instructions* and *variable I/O instructions*. These instructions are listed in the table of Fig. 7.6. Their mnemonics and names are provided together with a brief description of their operations.

Either of these two types of instructions can be used to transfer a byte or word of data. In the case of byte transfers, data are input/output over data bus lines D_0 through D_7. Word data are input or output as two consecutive byte transfers over the data bus.

Mnemonic	Meaning	Format	Operation	
IN	Input direct	IN Acc,Port	$(Acc) \leftarrow (Port)$	$Acc = AL$ or AX
	Input indirect (variable)	IN Acc,DX	$(Acc) \leftarrow ((DX))$	
OUT	Output direct	OUT Port,Acc	$(Port) \leftarrow (Acc)$	
	Output indirect (variable)	OUT DX,Acc	$((DX)) \leftarrow (Acc)$	

Figure 7.6 Input/output instructions.

All data transfers take place between I/O devices and the MPU's AL or AX register. For this reason, this method of performing I/O is known as *accumulator I/O*. Byte transfers involve the AL register and word transfers the AX register. In fact, specifying AL as the source or destination register in an I/O instruction indicates that it corresponds to a byte transfer instead of a word transfer.

In a direct I/O instruction, the address of the I/O port is specified as part of the instruction. Eight bits are provided for this direct address. For this reason, its value is limited to the address range from $0_{10} = 0000_{16}$ to $255_{10} = 00FF_{16}$. This range corresponds to page 0 in the I/O address space. An example is the instruction

```
IN AL,0FEH
```

Execution of this instruction causes the contents of the byte-wide I/O port at address FE_{16} of the I/O address space to be input to the AL register.

EXAMPLE 7.1

Write a sequence of instructions that will output FF_{16} to a byte-wide output port at address AB_{16} of the I/O address space.

SOLUTION   First, the AL register is loaded with FF_{16} as an immediate operand in the instruction

```
MOV AL,0FFH
```

Now the data in AL can be output to the byte-wide output port with the instruction

```
OUT 0ABH,AL
```

The difference between the direct and variable I/O instructions lies in the way in which the address of the I/O port is specified. We just saw that for direct I/O instructions an 8-bit address is specified as part of the instruction. On the other hand, the variable I/O instructions use a 16-bit address that resides in the DX register within the MPU. The value in DX is not an offset. It is the actual address that is to be output on AD_0 through AD_7 and A_8 through A_{15} during the I/O bus cycle. Since this address is a full 16 bits in length, variable I/O instructions can access ports located anywhere in the 64K-byte I/O address space.

When using either type of I/O instruction, the data must be loaded into or removed from the AL or AX register before another input or output operation can be performed. Moreover, in the case of the variable I/O instructions, the DX register must be loaded with an address. This requires execution of additional instructions.

For instance, the instruction sequence.

```
MOV    DX,0A000H
IN     AL,DX
```

inputs the contents of the byte-wide input port at $A000_{16}$ of the I/O address space.

EXAMPLE 7.2

Write a series of instructions that will output FF_{16} to an output port located at address $B000_{16}$ of the I/O address space.

SOLUTION   The DX register must first be loaded with the address of the output port. This is done with the instruction

```
MOV    DX,0B000H
```

Next, the data that are to be output must be loaded into AL:

```
MOV    AL,0FFH
```

Finally, the data are output with the instruction

```
OUT    DX,AL
```

EXAMPLE 7.3

Data are to be read in from two byte-wide input ports at addresses AA_{16} and $A9_{16}$, respectively, and then output as a word to a word-wide output port at address $B000_{16}$. Write a sequence of instructions to perform this input/output operation.

SOLUTION   We can first read in the byte from the port at address AA_{16} into AL and move it to AH. This is done with the instructions

```
        IN      AL,0AAH
        MOV     AH,AL
```

Now the other byte can be read into AL by the instruction

```
        IN      AL,0A9H
```

To write out the word of data in AX, we can load DX with the address $B000_{16}$ and use a variable output instruction. This leads to the following

```
        MOV     DX,0B000H
        OUT,    DX,AX
```

7.6 INPUT/OUTPUT BUS CYCLES

In Section 7.3, we found that the isolated I/O interface signals for the minimum-mode 8088 and 8086 microcomputer systems are essentially the same as those involved in the memory interface. In fact, the function, logic levels, and timing of all signals other than IO/$\overline{M}$ (M/$\overline{IO}$) are identical to those already described for the memory interface in Chapter 6.

Waveforms for the 8088's *I/O input (I/O read) bus cycle* and *I/O output (I/O write) bus cycle* are shown in Figs. 7.7 and 7.8, respectively. Looking at the input and output bus cycle waveforms, we see that the timing of IO/$\overline{M}$ does not change. The 8088 switches it to logic 1 to indicate that an I/O bus cycle is in progress. It is maintained at the 1 logic level for the duration of the I/O bus cycle. As in memory cycles, the address (ADDRESS OUT) is output together with ALE during clock period T_1. For the input bus cycle, $\overline{DEN}$ is switched to logic 0 to signal the I/O interface circuitry when to put the data onto the bus and the 8088 reads data off the bus during period T_3.

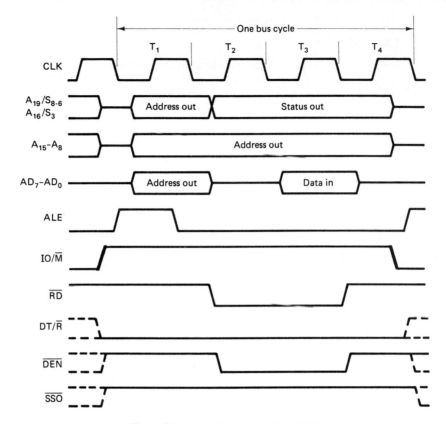

Figure 7.7 Input bus cycle of the 8088.

On the other hand, for the output bus cycle in Fig. 7.6, the 8088 puts write data (DATA OUT) on the bus late in T_2 and maintains it during the rest of the bus cycle. This time $\overline{WR}$ switches to logic 0 to signal the I/O section that valid data are on the bus.

The waveforms of the 8086's input and output bus cycles are shown in Figs. 7.9 and 7.10, respectively. Let us just look at the differences between the input cycle of the 8086 and that of the 8088. Comparing the waveforms in Fig. 7.9 to those in Fig. 7.7, we see that the 8086 outputs the signal $\overline{BHE}$ along with the address in T-state T_1. Remember that in the 8086 microcomputer this signal is used along with A_0 to select the byte-wide or word-wide port. Next, the 8086's data transfer path to the I/O interface is the 16-bit address/data bus, not 8 bits like in the 8088 system. Therefore, data transfers, which take place during T_3, can take place over the lower 8 data bus lines, upper 8 data bus lines, or all 16 data bus lines. Third, the 8086 outputs logic 0 on the M/$\overline{IO}$ line, while the 8088 outputs logic 1 on the IO/$\overline{M}$ line. That is, the M/$\overline{IO}$ control signal of the 8086 is the complement of that of the 8088. Finally, the 8086 does not produce an $\overline{SSO}$ output signal like the 8088.

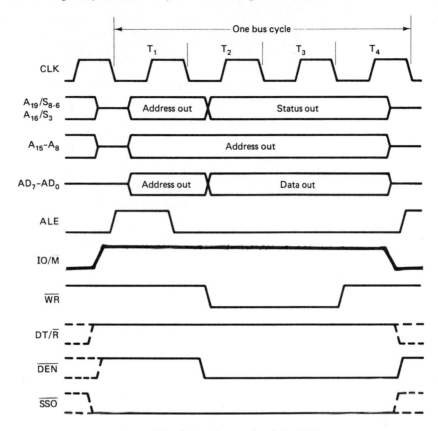

Figure 7.8   Output bus cycle of the 8088.

7.7 EIGHT-BYTE-WIDE OUTPUT PORTS USING ISOLATED I/O

Up to this point, we have introduced the isolated I/O interface of the 8088 and 8086 microprocessors, the I/O instructions, and I/O bus cycles. Now we will show circuits that can be used to implement parallel output ports in a microcomputer system employing isolated I/O. Figure 7.11(a) is such a circuit for an 8088-based microcomputer. It provides 8-byte-wide output ports that are implemented with 74F373 octal latches. In this circuit, the ports are labeled port 0 through port 7. These eight ports give a total of 64 parallel output lines, which are labeled O_0 through O_{63}.

Looking at the circuit, we see that the 8088's address/data bus is demultiplexed just as was done for the memory interface. Notice that two 74F373 octal latches are used to form a 16-bit address latch. These devices latch the address A_0 through A_{15} synchronously with the ALE pulse. The latched address outputs are labeled A_{0L} through A_{15L}. Remember that address lines A_{16} through A_{19} are not

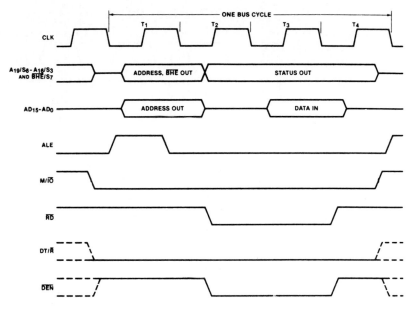

Figure 7.9 Input bus cycle of the 8086.

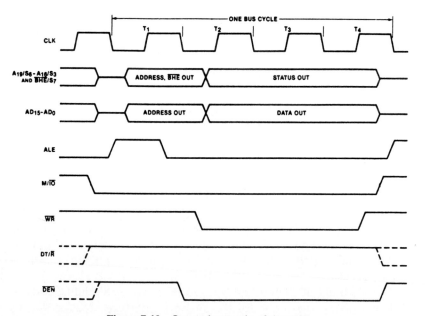

Figure 7.10 Output bus cycle of the 8086.

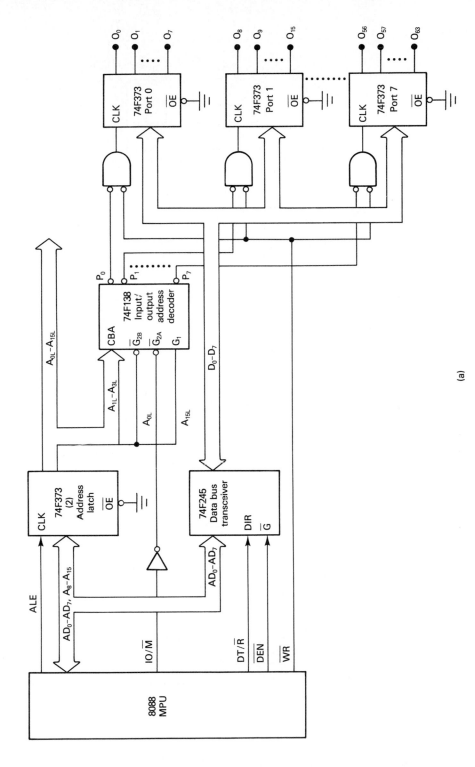

Figure 7.11 (a) Sixty-four-line output circuit for an 8088-based Microcomputer. (b) I/O address decoding for ports 0 through 7. (c) Sixty-four-line output circuit.

(a)

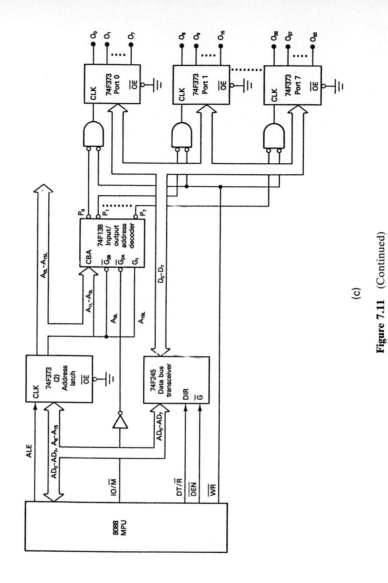

I/O port	I/O address
Port 0	1XXXXXXXXXXX0000₂
Port 1	1XXXXXXXXXXX0010₂
Port 2	1XXXXXXXXXXX0100₂
Port 3	1XXXXXXXXXXX0110₂
Port 4	1XXXXXXXXXXX1000₂
Port 5	1XXXXXXXXXXX1010₂
Port 6	1XXXXXXXXXXX1100₂
Port 7	1XXXXXXXXXXX1110₂

(b)

(c)

Figure 7.11 (Continued)

involved in the I/O interface. For this reason, they are not shown in the circuit diagram.

Address/data bus lines AD_0 through AD_7 are also applied to one side of the 74F245 bus transceiver. At the other side of the transceiver, data bus lines D_0 through D_7 are shown connecting to the output latches. It is over these lines that the 8088 writes data into the output ports.

Address lines A_{0L} and A_{15L} provide two of the three enable inputs of the 74F138 input/output address decoder. These signals are applied to enable inputs $\overline{G}_{2B}$ and G_1, respectively. The decoder requires one more enable signal at its $\overline{G}_{2A}$ input. It is supplied by the complement of IO/$\overline{M}$. These enable inputs must be $\overline{G}_{2B}\overline{G}_{1B}G_1$ = to 001 to enable the decoder for operation. The condition $\overline{G}_{2B} = 0$ corresponds to an even address and $\overline{G} = 0$ represents the fact that an I/O bus cycle is in progress. The third condition, $G_1 = 1$, is an additional requirement that A_{15L} be at logic 1 during all data transfers for this section of parallel output ports.

Notice that the 3-bit code $A_{3L}A_{2L}A_{1L}$ is applied to select inputs CBA of the 74F138 1-of-8 decoder. When the decoder is enabled, the P output corresponding to this select code switches to logic 0. Notice that logic 0 at this output enables the $\overline{WR}$ signal to the clock (CLK) input of the corresponding output latch. In this way, just one of the eight ports is selected for operation.

When valid output data are on D_0 through D_7, the 8088 switches $\overline{WR}$ to logic 0. This change in logic level causes the selected 74F373 device to latch in the data from the bus. The outputs of the latches are permanently enabled by the 0 logic level at the bus. The outputs of the latches are permanently enabled by the 0 logic level at their $\overline{OE}$ inputs. Therefore, the data appear at the appropriate port outputs.

The 74F245 in the circuit allows data to pass from the 8088 to the output ports. This is accomplished by enabling the 74F245's DTR and $\overline{G}$ inputs with the DT/$\overline{R}$ and $\overline{DEN}$ signals, which are at logic 1 and 0, respectively.

Notice in Fig. 7.11(a) that not all address bits are used in the I/O address decoding. Here only latched address bits A_{0L}, A_{1L}, A_{2L}, A_{3L}, and A_{15L} are decoded. Figure 7.11(b) shows the addresses that select each of the I/O ports. Unused bits are shown as don't care states. In this way, we see that many addresses decode to select each of the I/O ports. For instance, if all of the don't-care address bits are made 0, the address of PORT 0 is

$$1000000000000000_{16} = 8000_{16}$$

However, if these bits are all made equal to 1 instead of 0, the address is

$$1111111111110000_{16} = FFF0_{16}$$

and still decodes to enable PORT 0. In fact, every I/O address in the range from 8000_{16} through $FFF0_{16}$ that has its lower four bits equal to 0000_2 decodes to enable PORT 0.

EXAMPLE 7.4

To which output port in Fig. 7.11(a) are data written when the address put on the bus during an output bus cycle is 8002_{16}?

SOLUTION   Expressing the address in binary form, we get

$$A_{15} \ldots A_0 = A_{15L} \ldots A_{0L} = 1000000000000010_{16}$$

The important address bits are

$$A_{15L} = 1$$
$$A_{0L} = 0$$

and

$$A_{3L}A_{2L}A_{1L} = 001$$

Moreover, whenever an output bus cycle is in progress, $IO/\overline{M}$ is logic 1. Therefore, the enable inputs of the 74F138 decoder are

$$\overline{G}_{2B} = A_{0L} = 0$$
$$\overline{G}_{2A} = \overline{IO/\overline{M}} = 0$$
$$G_1 = A_{15L} = 1$$

These inputs enable the decoder for operation. At the same time, its select inputs are supplied with the code 001. This input causes output P_1 to switch to logic 0.

$$P_1 = 0$$

The gate at the CLK input of port 1 has as its inputs P_1 and $\overline{WR}$. When valid data are on the bus, $\overline{WR}$ switches to logic 0. Since P_1 is also 0, the CLK input of the 74F373 for port 1 switches to logic 1. This causes the data on D_0 through D_7 to be latched at output lines O_8 through O_{15} of port 1.

EXAMPLE 7.5

Write a series of instructions that will output the byte contents of the memory location called DATA to output port 0 in the circuit of Fig. 7.11(b).

SOLUTION   To write a byte to output port 0, the address that must be output on the 8088's address bus must be

$$A_{15}A_{14} \ldots A_0 = 1XXXXXXXXXXX0000_2$$

Assuming that the don't-care bits are all made logic 0, we get

$$A_{15}A_{14} \ldots A_0 = 1000000000000000_2$$

$$= 8000_{16}$$

Then the instruction sequence needed to output the contents of memory location DATA is

```
MOV    DX,8000H
MOV    AL,DATA
OUT    DX,AL
```

Figure 7.11(b) shows a similar output circuit for an 8086-based microcomputer system. Here again 64 output lines are implemented as eight byte-wide parallel ports, port 0 through port 7. Comparing this circuit to that for an 8088-based microcomputer in Fig.7.11(a), we find just one difference. This is that the control signal M/$\overline{\text{IO}}$ is applied directly to the $\overline{G}_{2A}$ input of the 74F138 input/output address decoder. Since M/$\overline{\text{IO}}$ is the complement of the 8088's IO/$\overline{\text{M}}$ signal, it does not have to be inverted.

7.8 EIGHT-BYTE-WIDE INPUT PORTS USING ISOLATED I/O

In Section 7.7, we showed circuits that implemented eight byte-wide output ports for the 8088 and 8086 microcomputer systems. These circuits used the 74F373 octal latch to provide the output ports. Here we will examine a similar circuit that implements input ports for the microcomputer system.

The circuit in Fig. 7.12 provides eight byte-wide input ports for an 8088-based microcomputer system employing isolated I/O. Just like in Fig. 7.11(a), the ports are labeled port 0 through port 7; however, this time the 64 parallel port lines are inputs, I_0 through I_{63}. Notice that eight 74F244 octal buffers are used to implement the ports. These buffers are equipped with three-state outputs.

When an input bus cycle is in progress, the I/O address is first latched into the 74F373 address latches. This address is accompanied by logic 1 on the IO/$\overline{\text{M}}$ control line. Notice that IO/$\overline{\text{M}}$ is inverted and applied to the $\overline{G}_{2A}$ input of the I/O address decoder. If during the bus cycle address bit $A_{0L} = 0$ and $A_{15L} = 1$, the address decoder is enabled for operation. Then the code $A_{3L}A_{2L}A_{1L}$ is decoded to produce an active logic level at one of the decoder's outputs. For instance, an

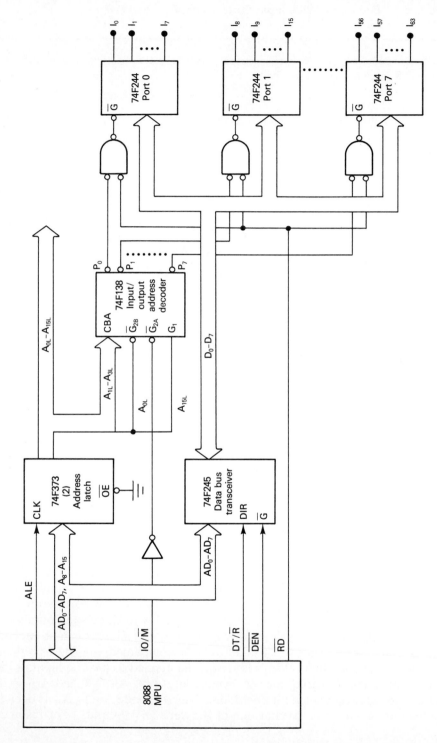

Figure 7.12 Sixty-four-line input circuit for an 8088 microcomputer.

input of $A_{3L}A_{2L}A_{1L} = 001$ switches the P_1 output to logic 0. P_1 is gated with $\overline{RD}$ to produce the $\overline{G}$ enable input for the port 1 buffer. If both $IO/\overline{M}$ and P_1 are logic 0, the $\overline{G}$ output of the control gate for port 1 is switched to logic 0 and the outputs of the 74F244 are enabled. In this case, the logic levels at inputs I_8 through I_{15} are passed onto data bus lines D_0 through D_7, respectively. This byte of data is carried through the enabled data bus transceiver to the data bus of the 8088. As part of the input operation, the 8088 reads this byte of data into the AL register.

EXAMPLE 7.6

What is the I/O address of port 7 in the circuit of Fig. 7.12? Assume that all unused address bits are at logic 0.

SOLUTION   For the I/O address decoder to be enabled, address bits A_{15} and A_0 must be

$$A_{15} = 1$$

and

$$A_0 = 0$$

Moreover, to select port 7, the address applied to CBA inputs of the decoder must be

$$A_{3L}A_{2L}A_{1L} = 111$$

Filling the unused bits with 0s gives the address

$$A_{15L} \ldots A_{1L}A_{0L} = 1000000000001110_2$$

$$= 800E_{16}$$

EXAMPLE 7.7

For the circuit of Fig. 7.12, write an instruction sequence that will input the byte contents of input port 7 to the memory location DATA_7.

SOLUTION   In Example 7.6 we found that the address of port 7 is $800E_{16}$. This address is loaded into the DX register with the instruction

```
MOV DX,800EH
```

Now the contents of this port are input to the AL register by executing the instruction

```
IN AL,DX
```

Finally, the byte of data is copied to memory location DATA-7 with the instruction.

```
MOV DATA_7,AL
```

In practical applications, it is sometimes necessary within an I/O service routine to repeatedly read the logic level of an input line and test it for a specific logic level. For instance, input I_3 at port 0 in Fig. 7.12 could be checked to determine if it is at the 1 logic level. Normally, the I/O routine does not continue until the input under test switches to the appropriate logic level. This mode of operation is known as *polling* an input. The polling technique can be used to synchronize the execution of an I/O routine to an event in external hardware.

Let us now look at how a polling software routine is written. The first step in the polling operation is to read the contents of the input port. For instance, the instructions needed to read the contents of port 0 in the circuit of Fig. 7.10 are

```
POLL_I3: MOV DX,8000H
         IN  AL,DX
```

A label has been added to identify the beginning of the polling routine. After executing these instructions, the byte contents of port 0 are held in the AL register. Let us assume that input I_3 at this port is the line that is being polled. Therefore, all other bits in AL are masked off with the instruction

```
AND AL,08H
```

After this instruction is executed, the contents of AL will be either 00H or 08H. Moreover the zero flag is 1 if AL contains 00H, else it is 0. The state of the zero flag can be tested with a jump on zero instruction.

```
JZ POLL_I3
```

If zero flag is 1, a jump is initiated to POLL_I3 and the sequence repeats. On the other hand, if it is 0, the jump is not made; instead, the instruction following the jump instruction is executed. That is, the polling loop repeats until input I_3 is tested and found to be logic 1.

7.9 INPUT/OUTPUT HANDSHAKING

In some applications, the microcomputer must synchronize the input or output of information to a peripheral device. Two examples of interfaces that normally require a synchronized data transfer are a serial communications interface and a parallel printer interface. Synchronization is achieved by implementing what is known as *handshaking* as part of the input/output interface.

A block diagram of a parallel printer interface is shown in Fig. 7.13(a). Here we find 8 data output lines D_0 through D_7, and the two handshake control signals strobe ($\overline{\text{STB}}$) and busy (BUSY). The MPU outputs data representing the character to be printed through the parallel printer interface. Character data are latched at the outputs of the parallel interface and are carried to the data inputs of the printer over data lines D_0 through D_7. The $\overline{\text{STB}}$ output of the parallel printer interface is used to signal the printer that new character data is available. Whenever the printer is already busy printing a character, it signals this fact to the MPU with the BUSY input of the parallel printer interface. These handshake signals are illustrated in Fig. 7.13(b).

Let us now look at the sequence of events that take place at the parallel printer interface when data are output to the printer. Figure 7.13(c) is a flowchart of a subroutine that performs a parallel printer interface character transfer operation. First the BUSY input of the parallel printer interface is tested. Notice that this is done with a polling operation. That is, the MPU tests the logic level of BUSY repeatedly until it is found to be at the *not busy* logic level. *Busy* means that the printer is currently printing a character. On the other hand, *not busy* signals that the printer is ready to receive another character for printing. After finding a not busy condition, a count of the number of characters in the printer buffer (microprocessor memory) is read; a byte of character data is read from the printer buffer; the character is output to the parallel interface; and then a pulse is produced at $\overline{\text{STB}}$. This pulse tells the printer to read the character off the data bus lines. The printer is again printing a character and signals this fact at BUSY. The handshake sequence is now complete. Now the count that represents the number of characters in the buffer is decremented and checked to see if the buffer is empty. If empty, the print operation is complete. Otherwise, the character transfer sequence is repeated.

The circuit in Fig. 7.13(d) implements a parallel printer interface like that in Fig. 7.13(a).

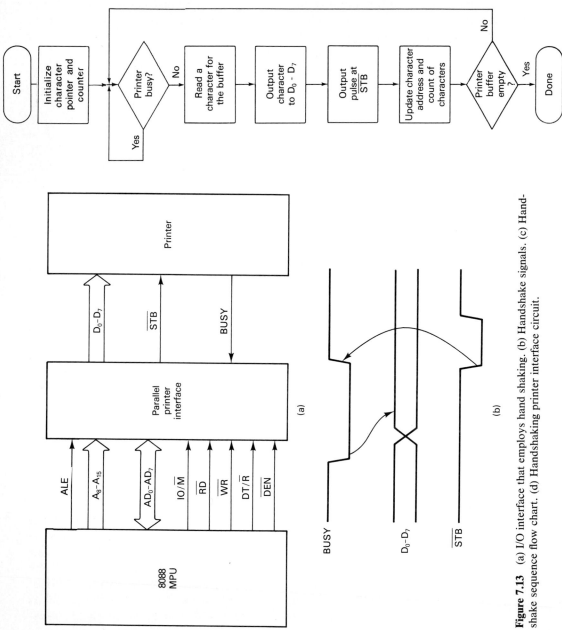

Figure 7.13 (a) I/O interface that employs hand shaking. (b) Handshake signals. (c) Handshake sequence flow chart. (d) Handshaking printer interface circuit.

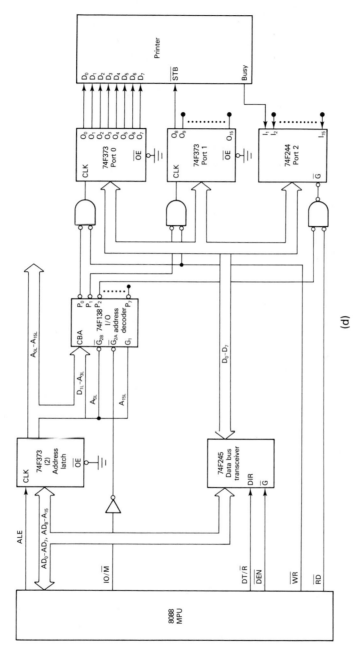

Figure 7.13 (Continued)

EXAMPLE 7.8

What are the addresses of the data lines, strobe output, and busy input in the circuit of Fig. 7.13(d)? Assume that all unused address bits are 0.

SOLUTION   The I/O addresses that enable ports 0, 1, and 2 are found as

$$\text{Port } 0 = 1000000000000000_2 = 8000_{16}$$
$$\text{Port } 1 = 1000000000000010_2 = 8002_{16}$$
$$\text{Port } 2 = 1000000000000100_2 = 8004_{16}$$

EXAMPLE 7.9

Write a program that will implement the sequence in Fig. 7.13(c) for the circuit in Fig. 7.13(d). Character data are held in memory starting at address PRNT_BUFF and the number of characters held in the buffer is identified by the count at address CHAR_COUNT. Use the port addresses from Example 7.8

SOLUTION   First the character counter and the character pointer are set up with the instructions

```
MOV CL,[CHAR_COUNT]
MOV SI,PRNT_BUFF
```

Next the BUSY input is checked with the instructions

```
POLL_BUSY: MOV DX,8004H
           IN  AL,DX
           AND AL,01H
           JNZ POLL_BUSY
```

Next the character is copied into AL, and then it is output to port 0.

```
            MOV AL,[SI]
            MOV DX,8000H
            OUT DX,AL
```

Now a strobe pulse is generated at port 1 with the instructions

```
            MOV AL,00H
            MOV DX,8002H
            OUT DX,AL
            MOV BX,0FH
STROBE:     DEC BX
            JNZ STROBE
            MOV AL,01H
            OUT DX,AL
```

At this point, the value of PRNT_BUFF must be incremented and the value of CHAR_COUNT must be decremented. This is done with

```
            INC SI
            DEC CL
```

Finally, a check is made to see if the printer buffer is empty. To do this, we execute the instructions

```
            JNZ POLL_BUSY
DONE:       -
```

7.10 8255A PROGRAMMABLE PERIPHERAL INTERFACE (PPI)

The *8255A* is an LSI peripheral designed to permit easy implementation of *parallel I/O* in the 8088 and 8086 microcomputer systems. It provides a flexible parallel interface, which includes features such as single-bit, 4-bit, and byte-wide input and output ports; level-sensitive inputs; latched outputs; strobed inputs or outputs; and strobed bidirectional input/outputs. These features are selected under software control.

A block diagram of the 8255A is shown in Fig. 7.14(a) and its pin layout in Fig. 7.14(b). The left side of the block represents the *microprocessors interface*. It includes an *8-bit bidirectional data bus* D_0 through D_7. Over these lines, commands, status information, and data are transferred between the MPU and 8255A. These data are transferred whenever the MPU performs an input or output bus cycle to an address of a register within the device. Timing of the data transfers to the 8255A is controlled by the *read/write* ($\overline{RD}$ and $\overline{WR}$) *control* signals.

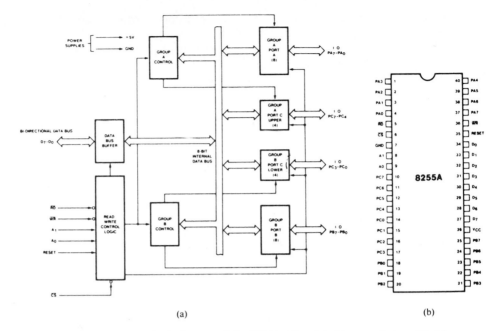

(a)   (b)

Figure 7.14   (a) Block diagram of the 8255A. (Reprinted by permission of Intel Corp. Copyright/Intel Corp. 1980) (b) Pin layout. (Reprinted by permission of Intel Corp. Copyright/Intel Corp. 1980)

The source or destination register within the 8255A is selected by a 2-bit *register select code*. The MPU must apply this code to the *register select inputs* A_0 and A_1 of the 8255A. The *port A, port B,* and *port C registers* correspond to codes $A_1A_0 = 00$, $A_1A_0 = 01$, and $A_1A_0 = 10$, respectively.

Two other signals are shown on the microprocessor interface side of the block diagram. They are the *reset* (RESET) and *chip select* ($\overline{CS}$) inputs. $\overline{CS}$ must be logic 0 during all read or write operations to the 8255A. It enables the microprocessor interface circuitry for an input or output operation.

On the other hand, RESET is used to initialize the device. Switching it to logic 0 at power-up causes the internal registers of the 8255A to be cleared. *Initialization* configures all I/O ports for input mode of operation.

The other side of the block corresponds to three *byte-wide I/O ports*. They are called port A, port B, and port C and represent *I/O lines* PA_0 through PA_7, PB_0 through PB_7, and PC_0 through PC_7, respectively. These ports can be configured for input or output operation. This gives a total of 24 I/O lines.

We already mentioned that the operating characteristics of the 8255A can be configured under software control. It contains an 8-bit internal control register for this purpose. This register is represented by the *group A* and *group B control blocks* in Fig. 7.14(a). Logic 0 or 1 can be written to the bit positions in this register to configure the individual ports for input or output operation and to enable one of its three modes of operation. The control register is write only and its contents are modified under software control by initiating a write bus cycle to the 8255A with register select code $A_1A_0 = 11$.

The bits of the control register and their control functions are shown in Fig. 7.15. Here we see that bits D_0 through D_2 correspond to the group B control block in the diagram of Fig. 7.14(a). Bit D_0 configures the lower four lines of port C for input or output operation. Notice that logic 1 at D_0 selects input operation, and logic 0 selects output operation. The next bit, D_1, configures port B as an 8-bit-wide input or output port. Again, logic 1 selects input operation and logic 0 selects output operation.

The D_2 bit is the mode select bit for port B and the lower 4 bits of port C. It permits selection of one of two different modes of operation called *mode 0* and *mode 1*. Logic 0 in bit D_2 selects mode 0, while logic 1 selects mode 1. These modes will be discussed in detail shortly.

The next four bits in the control register, D_3 through D_6, correspond to the group A control block in Fig. 7.14(a). Bits D_3 and D_4 of the control register are used to configure the operation of the upper half of port C and all of port A,

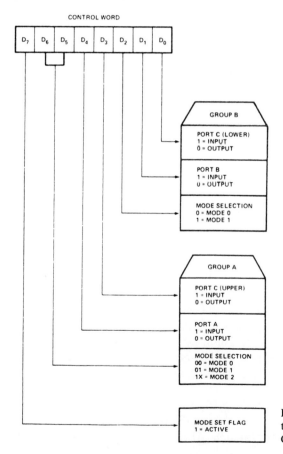

CONTROL WORD

| D_7 | D_6 | D_5 | D_4 | D_3 | D_2 | D_1 | D_0 |

GROUP B

PORT C (LOWER)
1 = INPUT
0 = OUTPUT

PORT B
1 = INPUT
0 = OUTPUT

MODE SELECTION
0 = MODE 0
1 = MODE 1

GROUP A

PORT C (UPPER)
1 = INPUT
0 = OUTPUT

PORT A
1 = INPUT
0 = OUTPUT

MODE SELECTION
00 = MODE 0
01 = MODE 1
1X = MODE 2

MODE SET FLAG
1 = ACTIVE

Figure 7.15 Control word bit functions. (Reprinted by permission of Intel Corp. Copyright/Intel Corp. 1980)

Pin	MODE 0	
	IN	OUT
PA$_0$	IN	OUT
PA$_1$	IN	OUT
PA$_2$	IN	OUT
PA$_3$	IN	OUT
PA$_4$	IN	OUT
PA$_5$	IN	OUT
PA$_6$	IN	OUT
PA$_7$	IN	OUT
PB$_0$	IN	OUT
PB$_1$	IN	OUT
PB$_2$	IN	OUT
PB$_3$	IN	OUT
PB$_4$	IN	OUT
PB$_5$	IN	OUT
PB$_6$	IN	OUT
PB$_7$	IN	OUT
PC$_0$	IN	OUT
PC$_1$	IN	OUT
PC$_2$	IN	OUT
PC$_3$	IN	OUT
PC$_4$	IN	OUT
PC$_5$	IN	OUT
PC$_6$	IN	OUT
PC$_7$	IN	OUT

Figure 7.16 Mode 0 port pin functions.

respectively. These bits work in the same way as D_0 and D_1 configure the lower half of port C and port B. However, there are now two mode select bits D_5 and D_6 instead of just one. They are used to select between three modes of operation known as *mode 0, mode 1,* and *mode 2*.

The last control register bit, D_7, is the *mode set flag*. It must be at logic 1 (active) whenever the mode of operation is to be changed.

Mode 0 selects what is called *simple I/O operation*. By simple I/O, we mean that the lines of the port can be configured as level-sensitive inputs or latched outputs. To set all ports for this mode of operation, load bit D_7 of the control register with logic 1, bits $D_6D_5 = 00$, and $D_2 = 0$. Logic 1 at D_7 represents an active mode set flag. Now port A and port B can be configured as 8-bit input or output ports, and port C can be configured for operation as two independent 4-bit input or output ports. This is done by setting or resetting bits D_4, D_3, D_1, and D_0. Figure 7.16 summarizes the port pins and the functions they can perform in mode 0.

For example, if $80_{16} = 10000000_2$ is written to the control register, the 1 in D_7 activates the mode set flag. Mode 0 operation is selected for all three ports because bits D_6, D_5, and D_2 are logic 0. At the same time, the 0s in D_4, D_3, D_1, and D_0

set up all port lines to work as outputs. This configuration is illustrated in Fig. 7.17(a).

By writing different binary combinations into bit locations D_4, D_3, D_1, and D_0, any one of 16 different mode 0 I/O configurations can be obtained. The control words and I/O setups for the rest of these combinations are shown in Fig. 7.17(b) through (p).

EXAMPLE 7.10

What is the mode and I/O configuration for ports A, B, and C of an 8255A after its control register is loaded with 82_{16}?

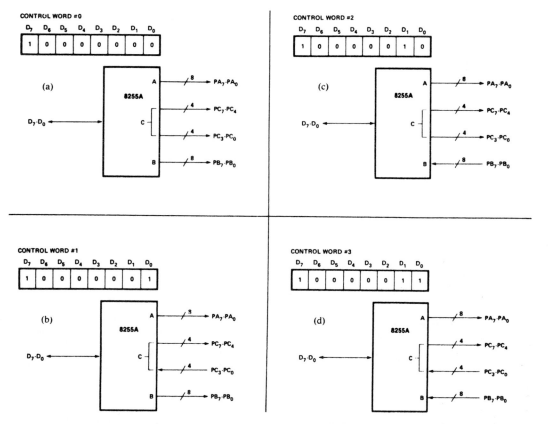

Figure 7.17 Mode 0 control words and corresponding input/output configuration. (Reprinted by permission of Intel Corp. Copyright/Intel Corp. 1980)

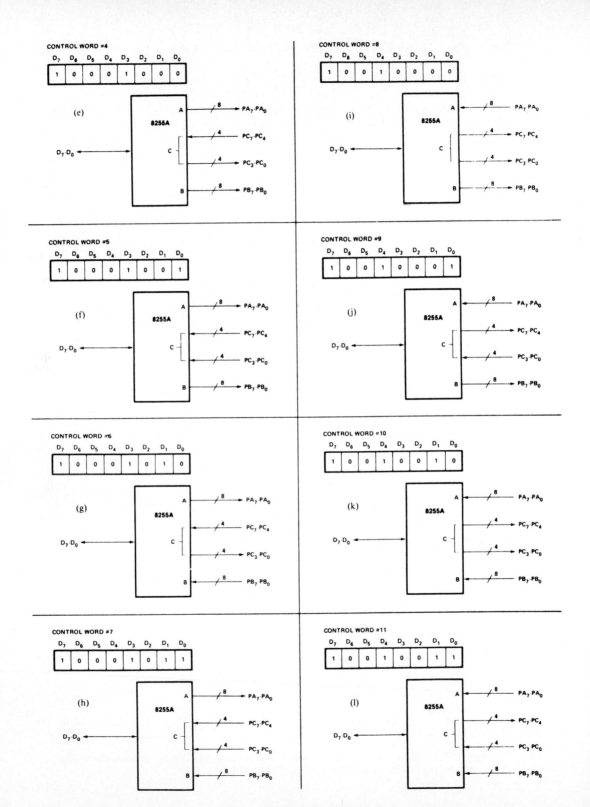

Figure 7.17 (Continued)

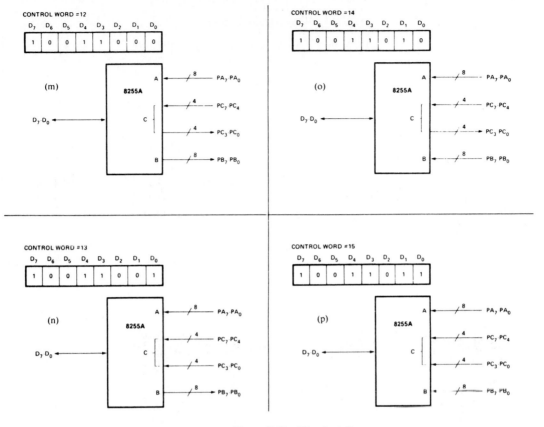

CONTROL WORD = 12

D_7	D_6	D_5	D_4	D_3	D_2	D_1	D_0
1	0	0	1	1	0	0	0

(m)

CONTROL WORD = 14

D_7	D_6	D_5	D_4	D_3	D_2	D_1	D_0
1	0	0	1	1	0	1	0

(o)

CONTROL WORD = 13

D_7	D_6	D_5	D_4	D_3	D_2	D_1	D_0
1	0	0	1	1	0	0	1

(n)

CONTROL WORD = 15

D_7	D_6	D_5	D_4	D_3	D_2	D_1	D_0
1	0	0	1	1	0	1	1

(p)

Figure 7.17   (Continued)

SOLUTION   Expressing the control register contents in binary form, we get

$$D_7 D_6 D_5 D_4 D_3 D_2 D_1 D_0 = 10000010_2$$

Since D_7 is 1, the modes of operation of the ports are selected by the control word. The three least significant bits of the word configure port B and the lower four bits of port C. They give

$D_0 = 0$ Lower four bits of port C are outputs

$D_1 = 1$ Port B are inputs

$D_2 = 0$ Mode 0 operation for both port B
            and the lower four bits of port C

The next four bits configure the upper part of port C and port A.

$D_3 = 0$ Upper four bits of port C are outputs

$D_4 = 0$ Port A are outputs

$D_6D_5 = 00$ Mode 0 operation for both port
A and the upper part of port C

This mode 0 I/O configuration is shown in Fig. 7.17(c).

Mode 1 operation represents what is known as *strobed I/O*. The ports of the 8255A are put into this mode of operation by setting $D_7 = 1$ to activate the mode set flag and setting $D_6D_5 = 01$ and $D_2 = 1$.

In this way, the A and B ports are configured as two independent *byte-wide I/O ports,* each of which has a *4-bit control/data port* associated with it. The control/data ports are formed from the lower and upper nibbles of port C, respectively. Figure 7.18 lists the mode 1 functions of each pin at ports A, B, and C.

When configured in this way, data applied to an input port must be strobed in with a signal produced in external hardware. Moreover, an output port is provided with handshake signals that indicate when new data are available at its outputs and when an external device has read these values.

	MODE 1	
Pin	IN	OUT
PA_0	IN	OUT
PA_1	IN	OUT
PA_2	IN	OUT
PA_3	IN	OUT
PA_4	IN	OUT
PA_5	IN	OUT
PA_6	IN	OUT
PA_7	IN	OUT
PB_0	IN	OUT
PB_1	IN	OUT
PB_2	IN	OUT
PB_3	IN	OUT
PB_4	IN	OUT
PB_5	IN	OUT
PB_6	IN	OUT
PB_7	IN	OUT
PC_0	$INTR_B$	$INTR_B$
PC_1	$\overline{IBF_B}$	$\overline{OBF_B}$
PC_2	$\overline{STB_B}$	$\overline{ACK_B}$
PC_3	$\underline{INTR_A}$	$INTR_A$
PC_4	$\overline{STB_A}$	I/O
PC_5	IBF_A	$\underline{I/O}$
PC_6	I/O	$\overline{ACK_A}$
PC_7	I/O	$\overline{OBF_A}$

Figure 7.18 Mode 1 port pin functions.

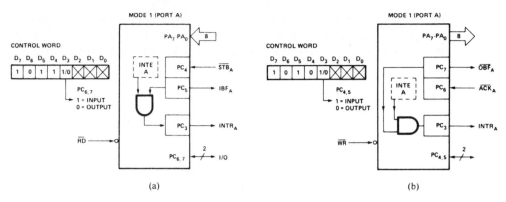

Figure 7.19 (a) Mode 1, port A input configuration. (Reprinted by permission of Intel Corp. Copyright/Intel Corp. 1980) (b) Mode 1, port A output configuration. (Reprinted by permission of Intel Corp. Copyright/Intel Corp. 1980)

As an example, let us assume for the moment that the control register of an 8255A is loaded with $D_7D_6D_5D_4D_3D_2D_1D_0 = 10111XXX$. This configures port A as a mode 1 input port. Figure 7.19(a) shows the function of the signal lines for this example. Notice that PA_7 through PA_0 form an 8-bit input port. On the other hand, the function of the upper port C leads are reconfigured to provide the port A control/data lines. The PC_4 line becomes $\overline{STB}_A$ (*strobe input*), which is used to strobe data at PA_7 through PA_0 into the input latch. Moreover, PC_5 becomes IBF_A (*input buffer full*). Logic 1 at this output indicates to external circuitry that a word has already been strobed into the latch.

The third control signal is at PC_3 and is labeled $INTR_A$ (*interrupt request*). It switches to logic 1 as long as $\overline{STB}_A = 1$, $IBF_A = 1$, and an internal signal $INTE_A$ (*interrupt enable*) = 1. $INTE_A$ is set to logic 0 or 1 under software control by using the bit set/reset feature of the 8255A. Looking at Fig. 7.19(a), we see that logic 1 in $INTE_A$ enables the logic level of IBF_A to the $INTR_A$ output. This signal can be applied to an interrupt input of the MPU to signal it that new data are available at the input port. The corresponding interrupt service routine can read the data and clear the interrupt request.

As another example, let us assume that the contents of the control register are changed to $D_7D_6D_5D_4D_3D_2D_1D_0 = 10100XXX$. This I/O configuration is shown in Fig. 7.19(b). Notice that port A is now configured for output operation instead of input operation. PA_7 through PA_0 are now an 8-bit output port. The control line at PC_7 is $\overline{OBF}_A$ (*output buffer full*). When data have been written into the output port, $\overline{OBF}_A$ switches to the 0 logic level. In this way, it signals external circuitry that new data are available at the port outputs.

Signal line PC_6 becomes $\overline{ACK}_A$ (*acknowledge*), which is an input. An external device can signal the 8255A that it has accepted the data provided at the output port by switching this input to logic 0. The last signal at the control port is output $INTR_A$, which is produced at the PC_3 lead. This output is switched to logic 1 when the $\overline{ACK}_A$ input is active. It is used to signal the MPU with an interrupt that indicates that an external device has accepted the data from the outputs. $INTR_A$ switches to the 1 level when $\overline{OBF}_A = \overline{ACK}_A = 0$, and $INTE_A = 1$. Again the interrupt enable ($INTE_A$) bit must be set to 1 under software control.

EXAMPLE 7.11

Figure 7.20(a) and (b) show how port B can be configured for mode 1 operation. Describe what happens in Fig. 7.20(a) when the $\overline{STB}_B$ input is pulsed to logic 0. Assume that $INTE_B$ is already set to 1.

SOLUTION   As $\overline{STB}_B$ is pulsed, the byte of data at PB_7 through PB_0 is latched into the port B register. This causes the IBF_B output to switch to 1. Since $INTE_B$ is 1, $INTR_B$ also switches to logic 1.

The last mode of operation, mode 2, represents what is known as *strobed bidirectional I/O*. The key difference is that now the port works as either inputs or outputs and control signals are provided for both functions. Only port A can be configured to work in this way. The I/O port and control signal pins are shown in Fig. 7.21.

To set up this mode, the control register is set to $D_7D_6D_5D_4D_3D_2D_1D_0 = 11XXXXXX$. The I/O configuration that results is shown in Fig. 7.22. Here we find that PA_7 through PA_0 operate as an *8-bit bidirectional port* instead of a unidirectional port. Its control signals are $\overline{OBF}_A$ at PC_7, $\overline{ACK}_A$ at PC_6, $\overline{STB}_A$ at PC_4, IBF_A at PC_5, and $INTR_A$ at PC_3. Their functions are similar to those already discussed for mode 1. One difference is that $INTR_A$ is produced by either gating $\overline{OBF}_A$ with $INTE_1$ or IBF_A with $INTE_2$.

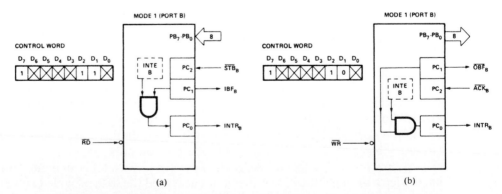

Figure 7.20   (a) Mode 1, port B input configuration. (Reprinted by permission of Intel Corp. Copyright/Intel Corp. 1980) (b) Mode 1, port B output configuration. (Reprinted by permission of Intel Corp. Copyright/Intel Corp. 1980)

Pin	MODE 2 GROUP A ONLY
PA$_0$	↔
PA$_1$	↔
PA$_2$	↔
PA$_3$	↔
PA$_4$	↔
PA$_5$	↔
PA$_6$	↔
PA$_7$	↔
PB$_0$	—
PB$_1$	—
PB$_2$	—
PB$_3$	—
PB$_4$	—
PB$_5$	—
PB$_6$	—
PB$_7$	—
PC$_0$	I/O
PC$_1$	I/O
PC$_2$	I/O
PC$_3$	INTR$_A$
PC$_4$	$\overline{\text{STB}}_A$
PC$_5$	IBF$_A$
PC$_6$	$\overline{\text{ACK}}_A$
PC$_7$	$\overline{\text{OBF}}_A$

MODE 0
OR MODE 1
ONLY

Figure 7.21 Mode 2 port pin functions.

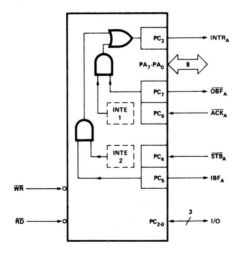

Figure 7.22 Mode 2 I/O configuration.
(Reprinted by permission of Intel Corp.
Copyright/Intel Corp. 1980)

373

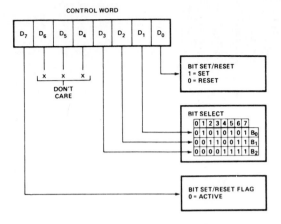

Figure 7.23 Bit set/reset format. (Reprinted by permission of Intel Corp. Copyright/Intel Corp. 1980)

In our discussion of mode 1, we mentioned that the *bit set/reset* feature could be used to set the INTE bit to logic 0 or 1. This feature also allows the individual bits of port C to be set or reset. To do this, we write logic 0 to bit D_7 of the control register. This resets the bit set/reset flag. The logic level that is to be latched at a port C line is included as bit D_0 of the control word. This value is latched at the I/O line of port C, which corresponds to the 3-bit code at $D_3D_2D_1$.

The relationship between the set/reset control word and input/output lines is illustrated in Fig. 7.23. For instance, writing $D_7D_6D_5D_4D_3D_2D_1D_0 = 00001111_2$ into the control register of the 8255A selects bit 7 and sets it to 1. Therefore, output PC_7 at port C is switched to the 1 logic level.

EXAMPLE 7.12

The interrupt control flag $INTE_A$ is controlled by bit set/reset of PC_6. What command code must be written to the control register of the 8255A to set its value to logic 1?

SOLUTION   To use the set/reset feature, D_7 must be logic 0. Moreover, $INTE_A$ is to be set to logic 1; therefore, D_0 must be logic 1. Finally, to select PC_6, the code at bits $D_3D_2D_1$ must be 110. The rest of the bits are don't-care states. This gives the control word

$$D_7D_6D_5D_4D_3D_2D_1D_0 = 0XXX1101_2$$

Replacing the don't-care states with the 0 logic level, we get

$$D_7D_6D_5D_4D_3D_2D_1D_0 = 00001101_2 = 0D_{16}$$

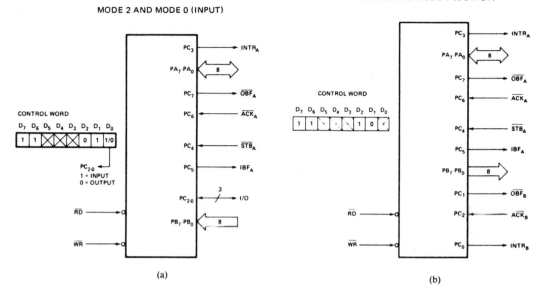

Figure 7.24   (a) Combined mode 2 and mode 0 (input) control word and I/O configuration. (Reprinted by permission of Intel Corp. Copyright/Intel Corp. 1980) (b) Combined mode 2 and mode 1 (output) control word and I/O configuration. (Reprinted by permission of Intel Corp. Copyright/Intel Corp. 1980)

We have just described and given examples of each of the modes of operation that can be assigned to the ports of the 8255A. In practice, the A and B ports are frequently configured with different modes. For example, Fig. 7.24(a) shows the control word and port configuration of an 8255A set up for bidirectional mode 2 operation of port A and input mode 0 operation of port B.

EXAMPLE 7.13

What control word must be written into the control register of the 8255A so that port A is configured for bidirectional operation and port B is set up with mode 1 outputs?

SOLUTION   To configure the mode of operation of the ports of the 8255A, D_7 must be 1.

$$D_7 = 1$$

Port A is set up for bidirectional operation by making D_6 logic 1. In this case, D_5 through D_3 are don't care states.

$$D_6 = 1$$

$$D_5D_4D_3 = XXX$$

Mode 1 is selected for port B by logic 1 in bit D_2 and output operation by logic 0 in D_1. Since mode 1 operation has been selected, D_0 is a don't-care state.

$$D_2 = 1$$

$$D_1 = 0$$

$$D_0 = X$$

This gives the control word

$$D_7D_6D_5D_4D_3D_2D_1D_0 = 11XXX10X_2$$

Assuming logic 0 for the don't-care states, we get

$$D_7D_6D_5D_4D_3D_2D_1D_0 = 11000100_2 = C4_{16}$$

This configuration is shown in Figure 7.24(b).

EXAMPLE 7.14

Write the sequence of instructions needed to load the control register of an 8255A with the control word formed in Example 7.13. Assume that the 8255A resides at address $0F_{16}$ of the I/O address space.

SOLUTION   First we must load AL with $C4_{16}$. This is the value of the control word that is to be output to the control register at address $0F_{16}$. The move instruction used to load Al is

```
MOV   AL,0C4H
```

These data are output to the control register with the OUT instruction

```
OUT   0FH,AL
```

7.11 8255A IMPLEMENTATION OF PARALLEL INPUT/OUTPUT PORTS

In Section 7.7, we showed how parallel output ports can be implemented for the 8088 and 8086 microcomputer systems using 74F373 octal latches. Even through logic ICs can be used to implement parallel input and output ports, the 8255A PPI, which was introduced in Section 7.9, produces a more versatile I/O interface. This is because its ports can be configured either as inputs or outputs under software control. Here we will show how the 8255A is used to design isolated parallel I/O interfaces for 8088- and 8086-based microcomputers.

The circuit in Fig. 7.25 shows how PPI devices can be connected to the bus of the 8088 to implement parallel input/output ports. This circuit configuration is for a minimum-mode 8088 microcomputer. Here we find a group of eight 8255A devices connected to the data bus. A 74F138 address decoder is used to select one of the devices at a time for input or output data transfers. The ports are located at even-address boundaries. Each of these PPI devices provides up to three byte-wide ports. In the circuit, they are labeled port A, port B, and port C. These ports can be individually configured as inputs or outputs through software. Therefore, this circuit is capable of implementing up to 192 I/O lines.

Let us look more closely at the connection of the 8255As. Starting with the inputs of the 74F138 address decoder, we see that its enable inputs are $\overline{G}_{2B} = A_0$

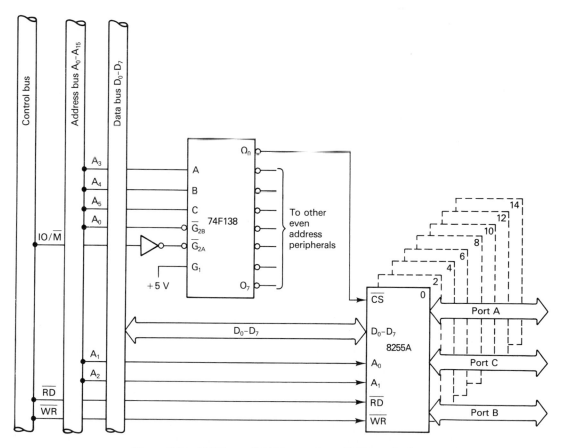

Figure 7.25   8255A parallel I/O ports in an 8088-based microcomputer.

and $\overline{G}_{2A} = \overline{\text{IO}/\text{M}}$. A_0 is logic 0 whenever the 8088 outputs an even address on the bus. Moreover, IO/M is switched to logic 1 whenever an I/O bus cycle is in progress. This logic level is inverted and applies logic 0 to the $\overline{G}_{2A}$ input. For this reason, the decoder is enabled for all I/O bus cycles to an even address.

When the 74F138 decoder is enabled, the code at its A_0 through A_2 inputs causes one of the eight 8255A PPIs to get enabled for operation. Bits A_5 through A_3 of the I/O address are applied to these inputs of the decoder. It responds by switching the output corresponding to this 3-bit code to the 0 logic level. Decoder outputs O_0 through O_7 are applied to the chip select ($\overline{CS}$) inputs of the PPIs. For instance, $A_5A_4A_3 = 000$ switches output O_0 to logic 0. This enables the first 8255A, which is numbered 0 in Fig. 7.25.

At the same time that the PPI chip is selected, the 2-bit code A_2A_1 at inputs A_1A_0 of the 8255A selects the port for which data are input or output. For example, $A_2A_1 = 00$ indicates that port A is to be accessed. Input/output data transfers take place over data bus lines D_0 through D_7. The timing of these read/write transfers is controlled by signals $\overline{RD}$ and $\overline{WR}$.

EXAMPLE 7.15

What must be the address inputs of the circuit in Fig. 7.25 if port C of PPI 14 is to be accessed?

SOLUTION   To enable PPI 14, the 74F138 must be enabled for operation and its O_7 output switched to logic 0. This requires enable input $A_0 = 0$ and chip select code $A_5A_4A_3 = 111$.

$$A_0 = 0 \qquad \text{Enables 74F138}$$

$$A_5A_4A_3 = 111 \qquad \text{Selects PPI 14}$$

Port C of PPI 14 is selected with $A_1A_0 = 10$.

$$A_2A_1 = 10 \qquad \text{Accesses port C}$$

The rest of the address bits are don't-care states.

EXAMPLE 7.16

Assume that in Fig. 7.25, PPI 14 is configured so that port A is an output port, both ports B and C are input ports, and all three ports are set up for mode 0 operation. Write a program that will input the data at ports B and C, find the difference $C - B$, and output this difference to port A.

SOLUTION From the circuit diagram in Fig. 7.25, we find that the addresses of the three I/O ports of PPI 14 are

$$\text{Port A} = 00111000_2 = 38_{16}$$

$$\text{Port B} = 00111010_2 = 3A_{16}$$

$$\text{Port C} = 00111100_2 = 3C_{16}$$

The data at ports B and C can be input with the instruction sequence

```
IN   AL,3AH ;READ PORT B
MOV  BL,AL  ;SAVE DATA FROM PORT B
IN   AL,3CH ;READ PORT C
```

Now the data from port B are subtracted from the data at port C with the instruction

```
SUB AL,BL    ;SUBTRACT B FROM C
```

Finally, the difference is output to port A with the instruction

```
OUT 38H,AL    ;WRITE TO PORT A
```

A similar circuit that implements parallel input/output ports for a minimum-mode 8086-based microcomputer system is given in Fig. 7.26. Let us now look at the differences between this circuit and the 8088 microcomputer circuit that is shown in Fig. 7.25. In Fig. 7.26, we find that the I/O circuit has two groups of eight 8255A devices, one connected to the lower eight data bus lines, and the other to the upper eight data bus lines. Each of these groups is capable of implementing up to 192 I/O lines to give a total I/O capability of 384 I/O lines.

Each of the groups of 8255As has its own 74F138 I/O address decoder. As in the 8088 microcomputer circuit, the address decoder is used to select one of the devices in a group at a time. The ports in the upper group are connected at odd-address boundaries and those in the lower group are at even-address boundaries. Let us first look more closely at the connection of the upper group of the 8255As. Starting with the inputs of the 74F138 decoder, we see that its $\overline{G}_{2B}$ input is driven by control signal $\overline{BHE}$, the $\overline{G}_{2A}$ input is supplied by control signal $M/\overline{IO}$, and the G_1 input is permanently enabled by fixing it at the 1 logic level. $\overline{BHE}$ is logic 0 whenever the 8086 outputs an odd address on the bus. Moreover, $M/\overline{IO}$ is switched to logic 0 whenever an I/O bus cycle is in progress. In this way, we see that the upper decoder is enabled for I/O bus cycles that access a byte of data at an odd I/O address. Actually, it is also enabled during all word-wide I/O data accesses.

The code on address lines A_3 through A_5 selects one of the eight 8255As for operation. When the upper 74F138 is enabled, the address code applied at the

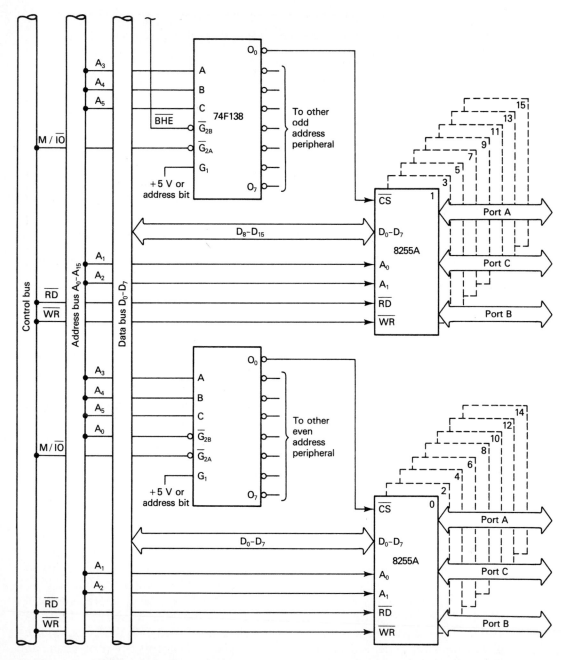

Figure 7.26 8255A parallel I/O ports at even- and odd-address boundaries in an 8086 based microcomputer.

CBA inputs causes the corresponding output to switch to logic 0. This output is used as a chip select ($\overline{CS}$) input to one of the 8255As and enables it for input/output operation. The port that is accessed in the enabled PPI is selected by the code on line A_1 and A_2 of the I/O address. Finally, the I/O data transfer takes place over data bus lines D_8 through D_{15}.

The connection of the lower group of PPIs in Fig. 7.26 is similar to that shown in Fig. 7.25. The only difference is that no inverter is required in the connection of the $M/\overline{IO}$ signal to the $\overline{G}_{2A}$ input of the 74F138 decoder. This bank is enabled for all byte-wide data accesses to an even address and for all word-wide data accesses.

7.12 MEMORY-MAPPED INPUT/OUTPUT

The *memory-mapped I/O interface* of a minimum-mode 8088 system is essentially the same as that employed in the accumulator I/O circuit of Fig. 7.27. Figure 7.27 shows the equivalent memory-mapped circuit. Ports are still selected by an address on the address bus and data are transferred between the 8088 and I/O device over the data bus. One difference is that now the full 20-bit address is available for addressing I/O. Therefore, memory-mapped I/O devices can reside anywhere in the 1M address space of the 8088.

Another difference is that during I/O operations memory read and write bus cycles are initiated instead of I/O bus cycles. This is because we are using memory instructions, not input/output instructions, to perform the data transfers. Furthermore, $IO/\overline{M}$ stays at the 0 logic level throughout the bus cycle. This indicates that a memory operation is in progress instead of an I/O operation.

Since memory-mapped I/O devices reside in the memory address space and are accessed with read and write cycles, additional I/O address latch, address buffer, data bus transceiver, and address decoder circuitry is not needed. The circuitry provided for the memory interface can be used. However, in some situations it may be practical to provide a separate I/O address decoder.

The key difference between the circuits in Figs. 7.25 and 7.27 is that $IO/\overline{M}$ is no longer inverted. Instead, it is applied directly to the $\overline{G}_{2A}$ input of the decoder. Another difference is that address line A_{10} supplies the G_1 input of the decoder. The I/O circuits are accessed whenever $IO/\overline{M}$ is equal to logic 0, A_{10} is equal to logic 1, and A_0 equals 0.

EXAMPLE 7.17

Which I/O port in Fig. 7.27 is selected for operation when the memory address output on the bus is 00402_{16}?

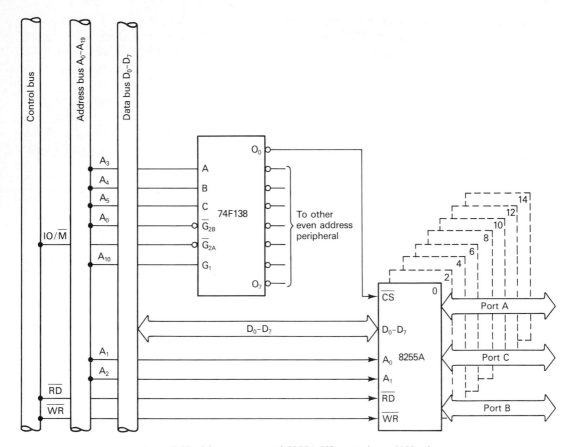

Figure 7.27   Memory-mapped 8255A I/O ports in an 8088 microcomputer.

SOLUTION   We begin by converting the address to binary form. This gives

$$A_{19} \ldots A_1 A_0 = 00000000010000000010_2$$

In this address, bits $A_{10} = 1$ and $A_0 = 0$. Therefore, the 74F138 address decoder is enabled.

$$\mathrm{IO/\overline{M}} = 0 \quad \text{Enables the 74F138 decoder}$$

$$A_{10} = 1$$

$$A_0 = 0$$

A memory-mapped I/O operation takes place at the port selected by $A_5 A_4 A_3 = 000$. This input code switches decoder output O_0 to logic 0 and chip selects PPI 0 for operation.

$$A_5A_4A_3 = 000 \quad \text{Selects PPI 0}$$

$$O_0 = 0$$

The address bits applied to the port select inputs of the PPI are $A_2A_1 = 01$. These inputs cause port B to be accessed.

$$A_2A_1 = 01 \quad \text{port B accessed}$$

Thus the address 00402_{16} selects port B on PPI 0.

EXAMPLE 7.18

Write the sequence of instructions needed to initialize the control register of PPI 0 in the circuit of Fig. 7.27 so that port A is an output port, ports B and C are input ports, and all three ports are configured for mode 0 operation.

SOLUTION   Referring to Fig. 7.15, we find that the control byte required to provide this configuration is

$10001011_2 = 8B_{16}$

— Lower half of port C as input

— Port B as input

— Mode 0

— Upper half of port C as input

— Port A as output

— Mode 0

— Mode set flag active

From the circuit diagram, the memory address of the control register for PPI 0 is found to be

$$\text{CONTROL REGISTER} = 0000000010000000110_2 = 00406_{16}$$

Since PPI 0 is memory mapped, move instructions can be used to initialize the control register.

```
MOV AX,0        ;CREATE DATA SEGMENT AT 00000₁₆
MOV DS,AX
MOV AL,08BH     ;LOAD AL WITH CONTROL BYTE
MOV [406H],AL   ;WRITE CONTROL BYTE TO PPI 0
```

EXAMPLE 7.19

Assume that PPI 0 in Fig. 7.27 is configured as described in Example 7.18. Write a program that will input the contents of ports B and C, AND them together, and output the results to port A.

SOLUTION   From the circuit diagram, we find that the addresses of the three I/O ports on PPI 0 are

$$\text{Port A} = 00400_{16}$$

$$\text{Port B} = 00402_{16}$$

$$\text{Port C} = 00404_{16}$$

Now we set up a data segment at 00000_{16} and input the data from ports B and C.

```
MOV AX,0          ;CREATE DATA SEGMENT AT 00000₁₆
MOV DS,AX
MOV BL,[402H]     ;READ PORT B
MOV AL,[404H]     ;READ PORT C
```

Next the contents of AL and BL must be ANDed and the result output to port A.

```
AND AL,BL         ;AND DATA AT PORTS B AND C
MOV [400H],AL     ;WRITE TO PORT A
```

Figure 7.28 shows a memory-mapped parallel I/O interface circuit for an 8086-based microcomputer system. Just like the accumulator-mapped circuit in Fig. 7.26, this circuit is capable of implementing up to 384 parallel I/O lines.

7.13 8253 PROGRAMMABLE INTERVAL TIMER

The 8253 is an LSI peripheral designed to permit easy implementation of timer and counter functions in a microcomputer system. It contains three independent 16-bit counters that can be programmed to operate in a variety of ways to implement timing functions. For instance, they can be set up to work as a one-shot pulse generator, square-wave generator, or rate generator.

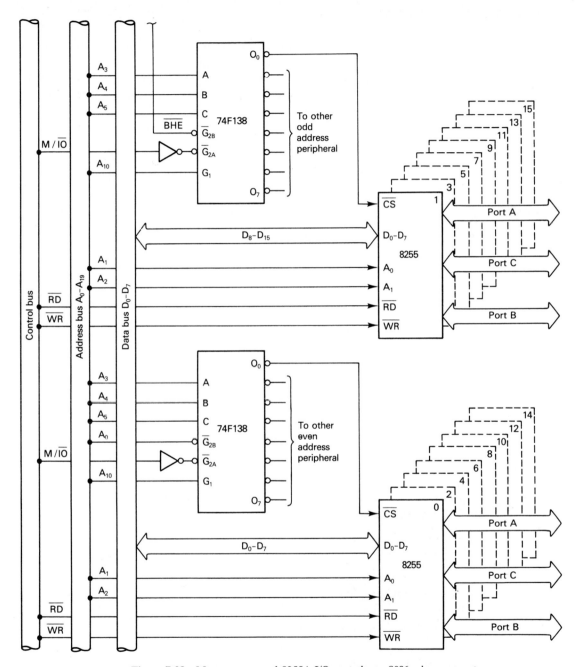

Figure 7.28 Memory-mapped 8255A I/O ports in an 8086 microcomputer.

Block Diagram of the 8253

Let us begin our study of the 8253 by looking at the signal interfaces shown in its block diagram of Fig. 7.29(a). The actual pin location for each of these signals is given in Fig. 7.29(b). In a microcomputer system, the 8253 is treated as a peripheral device. Moreover, it can be memory mapped into the memory address space or I/O mapped into the I/O address space. The microprocessor interface of the 8253 allows the MPU to read from or write to its internal registers. In this way, it

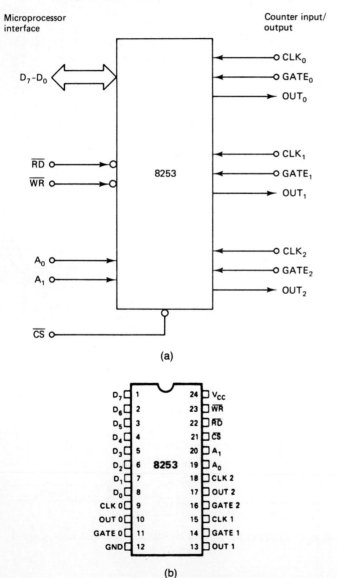

(a)

(b)

Figure 7.29 (a) Block diagram of the 8253 interval timer. (b) Pin layout. (Reprinted by permission of Intel Corp. Copyright/Intel Corp. 1987)

can configure the mode of operation for the timers, load initial values into the counters, or read the current value from a counter.

Now we will look at the signals of the microprocessor interface. The microprocessor interface includes an 8-bit bidirectional data bus, D_0 through D_7. It is over these lines that data are transferred between the MPU and 8253. Register address inputs A_0 and A_1 are used to select the register to be accessed, and control signals read ($\overline{RD}$) and write ($\overline{WR}$) indicate whether it is to be read from or written into, respectively. A chip select ($\overline{CS}$) input is also provided to enable the 8253's microprocessor interface. This input allows the designer to locate the device at a specific memory or I/O address.

At the other side of the block in Fig. 7.29(a), we find three signals for each counter. For instance, counter 0 has two inputs that are labeled CLK_0 and $GATE_0$. Pulses applied to the clock input are used to decrement counter 0. The gate input is used to enable or disable the counter. $GATE_0$ must be switched to logic 1 to enable counter 0 for operation. For example, in the square-wave mode of operation, the counter is to run continuously; therefore, $GATE_0$ is fixed at the 1 logic level and a continuous clock signal is applied to CLK_0. The 8253 is rated for a maximum clock frequency of 3 MHz. Counter 0 also has an output line that is labeled OUT_0. The counter produces either a clock or a pulse at OUT_0, depending on the mode of operation selected. For instance, when configured for the square-wave mode of operation, this output is a clock.

Architecture of the 8253

The internal architecture of the 8253 is shown in Fig. 7.30. Here we find the *data bus buffer, read/write logic, control word register,* and three *counters.* The data bus buffer and read/write control logic represent the microprocessor interface we just described.

The *control word register* section actually contains three 8-bit registers that are used to configure the operation of counters 0, 1, and 2. The format of a *control word* is shown in Fig. 7.31. Here we find that the two most significant bits are a code that assigns the control word to a counter. For instance, making these bits 01 selects counter 1. Bits D_1 through D_3 are a 3-bit mode select code, $M_2M_1M_0$, that selects one of six modes of counter operation. The least significant bit D_0 is labeled BCD and selects either binary or BCD mode of counting. For instance, if this bit is set to logic 0, the counter acts as a 16-bit binary counter. Finally, the 2-bit code RL_1RL_0 is used to set the sequence in which bytes are read from or loaded into the 16-bit count registers.

EXAMPLE 7.20

An 8253 receives the control word 10010000_2 over the bus. What configuration is set up for the counter?

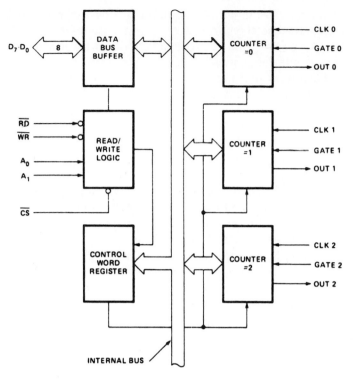

Figure 7.30   Internal architecture of the 8253. (Reprinted by permission of Intel Corp. Copyright/Intel Corp. 1987)

SOLUTION   Since the SC bits are 10, the rest of the bits are for setting up the configuration of counter 2. Following the format in Fig. 7.31, we find that 01 in the RL bits sets counter 2 for the read/load sequence identified as the least significant byte only. This means that the next write operation performed to counter 2 will load the data into the least significant byte of its count register. Next the mode code is 000 and this selects mode 0 operation for this counter. The last bit, BCD, is also set to 0 and selects binary counting.

The three counters shown in Fig. 7.30 are each 16 bits in length and operate as *down counters*. That is, when enabled by an active gate input, the clock decrements the count. Each counter contains a 16-bit *count register* that must be loaded as part of the initialization cycle. The value held in the count register can be read at any time through software.

To read from or write to the counters of the 8253 or load its control word register, the microprocessor needs to execute instructions. Figure 7.32 shows the bus control information needed to access each register. For example, to write to

Control Word Format

D$_7$	D$_6$	D$_5$	D$_4$	D$_3$	D$_2$	D$_1$	D$_0$
SC1	SC0	RL1	RL0	M2	M1	M0	BCD

Definition Of Control

SC—SELECT COUNTER:

SC1	SC0	
0	0	Select Counter 0
0	1	Select Counter 1
1	0	Select Counter 2
1	1	Illegal

RL—READ/LOAD:

RL1	RL0	
0	0	Counter Latching operation (see READ/WRITE Procedure Section).
1	0	Read/Load most significant byte only.
0	1	Read/Load least significant byte only.
1	1	Read/Load least significant byte first, then most significant byte.

M—MODE:

M2	M1	M0	
0	0	0	Mode 0
0	0	1	Mode 1
X	1	0	Mode 2
X	1	1	Mode 3
1	0	0	Mode 4
1	0	1	Mode 5

BCD:

0	Binary Counter 16-Bits
1	Binary Coded Decimal (BCD) Counter (4 Decades)

Figure 7.31 Control word format. (Reprinted by permission of Intel Corp. Copyright/Intel Corp. 1987)

$\overline{CS}$	$\overline{RD}$	$\overline{WR}$	A_1	A_0	
0	1	0	0	0	Load Counter No. 0
0	1	0	0	1	Load Counter No. 1
0	1	0	1	0	Load Counter No. 2
0	1	0	1	1	Write Mode Word
0	0	1	0	0	Read Counter No. 0
0	0	1	0	1	Read Counter No. 1
0	0	1	1	0	Read Counter No. 2
0	0	1	1	1	No-Operation 3-State
1	X	X	X	X	Disable 3-State
0	1	1	X	X	No-Operation 3-State

Figure 7.32 Accessing the registers of the 8253. (Reprinted by permission of Intel Corp. Copyright/Intel Corp. 1987)

the control register, the register address lines must be $A_1A_0 = 11$ and the control lines must be $\overline{WR} = 0$, $\overline{RD} = 1$, and $\overline{CS} = 0$.

EXAMPLE 7.21

Write an instruction sequence to set up the three counters of an 8253 located at I/O address 40H as follows:

Counter 0: Binary counter operating in mode 0 with an initial value of 1234H.

Counter 1: BCD counter operating in mode 2 with an initial value of 100H.

Counter 2: Binary counter operating in mode 4 with initial value of 1FFFH.

SOLUTION   Since the base address of the 8253 is 40H, the mode register is at address 43H. The three counters 0, 1, and 2 are at addresses 40H, 41H, and 42H, respectively. Let us first determine the mode words for the three counters. Following the bit definitions in Fig. 7.31, we get

$$\text{Mode word for counter } 0 = 00110000_2 = 30_{16}$$

$$\text{Mode word for counter } 1 = 01010101_2 = 55_{16}$$

$$\text{Mode word for counter } 2 = 10111000_2 = B8_{16}$$

The following instruction sequence can be used to set up the 8253 with the modes and counts:

```
MOV AL,30H      ;SET UP COUNTER 0 MODE
OUT 43H,AL
MOV AL,55H      ;SET UP COUNTER 1 MODE
```

```
OUT 43H,AL
MOV AL,0B8H        ;SET UP COUNTER 2 MODE
OUT 43H,AL
MOV AL,34H         ;LOAD COUNTER 0
OUT 40H,AL
MOV AL,12H
OUT 40H,AL
MOV AL,01H         ;LOAD COUNTER 1
OUT 41,AL
MOV AL,00H
OUT 41,AL
MOV AL,0FFH        ;LOAD COUNTER 2
OUT 42,AL
MOV AL,1FH
OUT 42,AL
```

Earlier we pointed out that the contents of a count register can be read at any time. Let us now look at how this is done in software. One approach is to simply read the contents of the corresponding register with an input instruction. In Fig. 7.32 we see that to read the contents of count register 0 the control inputs must be $\overline{CS} = 0$, $\overline{RD} = 0$, and $\overline{WR} = 1$, and the register address code must be $A_1A_0 = 00$. To ensure that a valid count is read out of count register 0, the counter must be inhibited before the read operation takes place. The easiest way to do this is to switch the $GATE_0$ input to logic 0 before performing the input operation. The count is read as two separate bytes, low byte first followed by the high byte.

The contents of the count registers can also be read without first inhibiting the counter. That is, the count can be read on the fly. To do this in software, a command must first be issued to the mode register to capture the current value of the counter into a temporary storage register. In Fig. 7.31, we find that setting bits D_5 and D_4 of the mode byte to 00 specifies the latch mode of operation. Once this mode byte has been written to the 8253, the contents of the temporary storage register for the counter can be read just as before.

EXAMPLE 7.22

Write an instruction sequence to read the contents of counter 2 on the fly. The count is to be loaded into the AX register. Assume that the 8253 is located at I/O address 40H.

SOLUTION   First, we will latch the contents of counter 2 and then this value is read from the temporary storage register. This is done with the following sequence of instructions:

```
MOV AL,10000000B        ;LATCH COUNTER 2
OUT 43H,AL
IN AL,42H                ;READ THE LOW BYTE
MOV BL,AL
IN AL,42H                ;READ THE HIGH BYTE
MOV AH,AL
MOV AL,BL
```

MODE 0: INTERRUPT ON TERMINAL COUNT

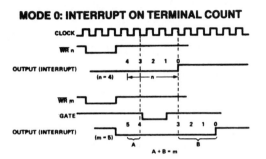

MODE 1: PROGRAMMABLE ONE-SHOT

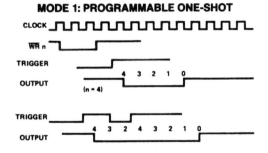

MODE 2: RATE GENERATOR

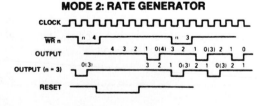

MODE 3: SQUARE WAVE GENERATOR

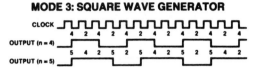

MODE 4: SOFTWARE TRIGGERED STROBE

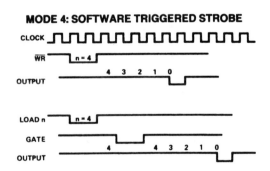

MODE 5: HARDWARE TRIGGERED STROBE

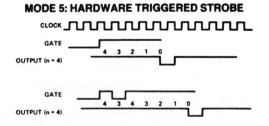

Figure 7.33 Operating modes of the 8253. (Reprinted by permission of Intel Corp. Copyright/Intel Corp. 1987)

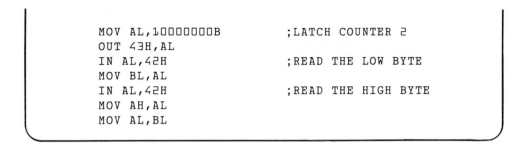

Signal Status Modes	Low Or Going Low	Rising	High
0	Disables counting	—	Enables counting
1	—	1) Initiates counting 2) Resets output after next clock	—
2	1) Disables counting 2) Sets output immediately high	1) Reloads counter 2) Initiates counting	Enables counting
3	1) Disables counting 2) Sets output immediately high	1) Reloads counter 2) Initiates counting	Enables counting
4	Disables counting	—	Enables counting
5	—	Initiates counting	—

Figure 7.34 Effect of the GATE input for each mode. (Reprinted by permission of Intel Corp. Copyright/Intel Corp. 1987)

Operating Modes of 8253 Counters

As indicated earlier, each of the 8253's counters can be configured to operate in one of six modes. Figure 7.33 shows waveforms that summarize operation for each mode. Notice that mode 0 operation is known as interrupt on terminal count and mode 1 is called programmable one-shot. The GATE input of a counter takes on different functions, depending on which mode of operation is selected. The effect of the gate input is summarized in Fig. 7.34. For instance, in mode 0, GATE disables counting when set to logic 0 and enables counting when set to 1. Let us now discuss each of these modes of operation in more detail.

The *interrupt on terminal count* mode of operation is used to generate an interrupt to the microprocessor after a certain interval of time has elapsed. As shown in the waveforms for mode 0 operation in Fig. 7.33, a count of 4 is written into the count register synchronously with the pulse at $\overline{WR}$. After the write operation is complete, the count is decremeted by one for each clock pulse. When the count reaches 0, the terminal count, a 0-to-1 transition occurs at OUTPUT. This signal is used as the interrupt input to the microprocessor.

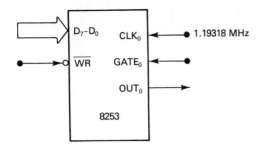

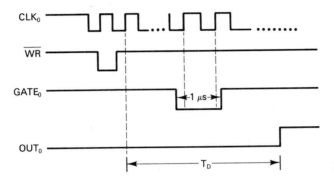

Figure 7.35   Mode 0 configuration.

Earlier we found in Fig. 7.34 that GATE must be at logic 1 to enable the counter for interrupt on terminal count mode of operation. Figure 7.33 also shows waveforms for the case in which GATE is switched to logic 0. Here we see that the counter does not decrement below the value 4 until GATE returns to 1.

EXAMPLE 7.23

The counter of Fig. 7.35 is programmed to operate in mode 0. Assuming that the decimal value 100 is written into the counter, compute the time delay (TD) that occurs until the positive transition takes place at the counter 0 output. Assume the relationship between the GATE and the CLK signal as shown in the figure.

SOLUTION   Once loaded, counter 0 needs to decrement down for 100 pulses at the clock input. During this period, the counter is disabled by logic 0 at the GATE input for 2 clock periods. Therefore, the time delay is calculated as

$$TD = (2 + 100)(T_{CLK0})$$

$$= (2 + 100)(1/1.19318) \ \mu s$$

$$= 85.5 \ \mu s$$

Mode 1 operation implements what is known as a *programmable one-shot*. As shown in Fig. 7.33, when set for this mode of operation, the counter produces a single pulse at its output. The waveforms show that an initial count, which in this example is the number 4, is written into the counter synchronous with a pulse at $\overline{WR}$. When GATE, called TRIGGER in the waveshapes, switches from logic 0 to 1, OUTPUT switches to logic 0 on the next pulse at CLOCK and the count begins to decrement with each successive clock pulse. The pulse is completed as OUTPUT returns to logic 1 when the terminal count, which is zero, is reached. In this way, we see that the duration of the pulse is determined by the value loaded into the counter.

The pulse generator produced with an 8253 counter is what is called a *retriggerable one-shot*. By *retriggerable* we mean that, if after an output pulse has been started another rising edge is experienced at TRIGGER, the count is reloaded and the pulse width is extended by the full pulse duration. The lower one-shot waveform in Fig. 7.33 shows this type of operation. Notice that after the count is decremented to 2, a second rising edge occurs at TRIGGER. This edge reloads the value 4 into the counter to extend the pulse width to 7 clock cycles.

EXAMPLE 7.24

Counter 1 of an 8253 is programmed to operate in mode 1 and is loaded with the decimal value 10. The gate and clock inputs are as shown in Fig. 7.36. How long is the output pulse?

SOLUTION   The GATE input in Fig. 7.36 shows that the counter is operated as a nonretriggerable one-shot. Therefore, the pulse width is given by

$$T = \text{(counter contents)} \times \text{(clock period)}$$

$$= 10 \times 1/1.19318 \text{ MHz}$$

$$= 8.38 \ \mu s$$

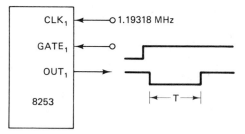

Figure 7.36   Mode 1 configuration.

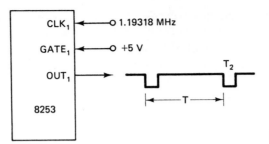

Figure 7.37 Mode 2 configuration.

When set for mode 2, *rate generator* operation, the counter within the 8253 is set to operate as a divide-by-N counter. Here N stands for the value of the count loaded into the counter. Figure 7.37 shows counter 1 of an 8253 set up in this way. Notice that the gate input is fixed at the 1 logic level. As shown in the table of Fig. 7.34, this enables counting operation. Looking at the waveforms for mode 2 operation in Fig. 7.33, we see that OUTPUT is at logic 1 until the count decrements to zero. Then the output switches to the active 0 logic level for just one clock pulse width. In this way, we see that there is one clock pulse at the output for every N clock pulses at the input. This is why it is called a divide-by-N counter.

EXAMPLE 7.25

Counter 1 of the 8253, as shown in Fig. 7.37, is programmed to operate in mode 2 and is loaded with the decimal number 18. Describe the signal produced at OUT_1.

SOLUTION   In mode 2 the output goes low for one period of the input clock after the counter contents decrement to zero. Therefore,

$$T_2 = 1/1.19318 \text{ MHz} = 838 \text{ ns}$$

and

$$T = 18 \times T_2 = 15.094 \ \mu s$$

Mode 3 sets the counter of the 8253 to operate as a *square-wave rate genera-tor*. In this mode, the output of the counter is a square wave with 50% duty cycle whenever the counter is loaded with an even number. That is, the output is at the 1 logic level for exactly the same amount of time that it is at the 0 logic level. As shown in Fig. 7.33, all transitions of the output take place with respect to the negative edge of the input clock. The period of the symmetrical square wave at the output equals the number loaded into the counter multiplied by the period of the input clock.

If an odd number (N) is loaded into the counter instead of an even number, the time for which the output is high is given by $(N + 1)/2$, and the time for which the output is low is given by $(N - 2)/2$.

EXAMPLE 7.26

The counter in Fig. 7.38 is programmed to operate in mode 3 and is loaded with the decimal value 15. Determine the characteristics of the square wave at OUT_1.

SOLUTION

$$T_{CLK1} = 1/1.19318 \text{ MHz} = 838 \text{ ns}$$

$$T_1 = T_{CLK1}(N + 1)/2 = 838 \text{ ns} \times [(15 + 1)/2]$$

$$= 6.704 \ \mu s$$

$$T_2 = T_{CLK1}(N - 1)/2 = 838 \text{ ns} \times [(15 - 1)/2]$$

$$= 5.866 \ \mu s$$

$$T = T_1 + T_2 = 6.704 \ \mu s + 5.866 \ \mu s$$

$$= 12.57 \ \mu s$$

Selecting mode 4 operation for a counter configures the counter to work as a *software triggered strobed counter.* When in this mode, the counter automatically begins to decrement immediately upon loading with its initial value through software. Again, it decrements at a rate set by the clock input signal. At the moment the terminal count is reached, the counter generates a single strobe pulse with duration equal to one clock pulse at its output. This pulse can be used to perform a timed operation. Figure 7.33 shows waveforms illustrating this mode of

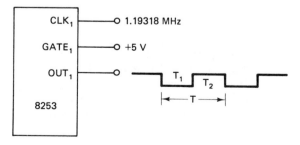

Figure 7.38   Mode 3 configuration.

operation initiated by writing the value 4 into a counter. Moreover, in the table of Fig. 7.34, we find that the gate input needs to be at logic 1 for the counter to operate.

This mode of operation can be used to implement a long-duration interval timer or a free-running timer. In either application, the strobe at the output can be used as an interrupt input to a microprocessor. In response to this pulse, an interrupt service routine can be used to reload the timer and restart the timing cycle. Frequently, the service routine also counts the strobes as they come in by decrementing the contents of a register. Software can test the value in this register to determine if the timer has timed out a certain number of times, for instance, to determine if the contents of the register have decremented to zero. When it reaches zero, a specific operation, such as a jump or call, can be initiated. In this way, we see that software has been used to extend the interval of time at which a function occurs beyond the maximum duration of the 16-bit counter within the 8253.

EXAMPLE 7.27

Counter 1 of Fig. 7.39 is programmed to operate in mode 4. What value must be loaded into the counter to produce a strobe signal 10 μs after the counter is loaded?

SOLUTION   The strobe pulse occurs after counting down the counter to zero. The number of input clock periods required for a period of 10 μs is given by

$$N = T/T_{\text{CLK}}$$

$$= 10 \ \mu\text{s}/(1/1.19318 \text{ MHz})$$

$$= 12_{10} = C_{10} = 00001100_2$$

Thus the counter should be loaded with the number $0C_{16}$ to produce a strobe pulse 10 μs after loading.

The last mode of 8253 counter operation, mode 5, is called the *hardware triggered strobe*. This mode is similar to mode 4 except that now counting is initiated by a signal at the gate input. That is, it is hardware triggered instead of software triggered. As shown in the waveforms of Fig. 7.33 and the table of Fig. 7.34, a rising edge at GATE starts the countdown process. Just as for software triggered strobed operation, the strobe pulse is output after the count decrements to zero.

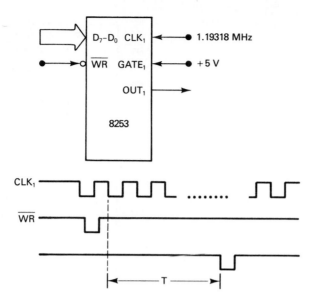

Figure 7.39   Mode 4 configuration.

7.14 8237A PROGRAMMABLE DIRECT MEMORY ACCESS CONTROLLER

The 8327A is the LSI controller IC that is most widely used to implement the *direct memory access* (DMA) function in 8088- and 8086-based microcomputer systems. DMA capability permits devices, such as peripherals, to perform high-speed data transfers between either two sections of memory or between memory and an I/O device. In a microcomputer system, the memory or I/O bus cycles initiated as part of a DMA transfer are not performed by the MPU; instead, they are performed by a device known as a *DMA controller,* such as the 8237A. DMA mode of operation is most frequently used when blocks or packets of data are to be transferred. For instance, disk controllers, local area network controllers, and communication controllers are devices that normally process data as blocks or packets. A single 8237A supports up to four peripheral devices for DMA operation.

Microprocessor Interface of the 8237A

A block diagram that shows the interface signals of the 8237A DMA controller is given in Fig. 7.40(a). The pin layout in Fig. 7.40(b) identifies the pins at which these signals are available. Let us now look briefly at the operation of the microprocessor interface of the 8237A.

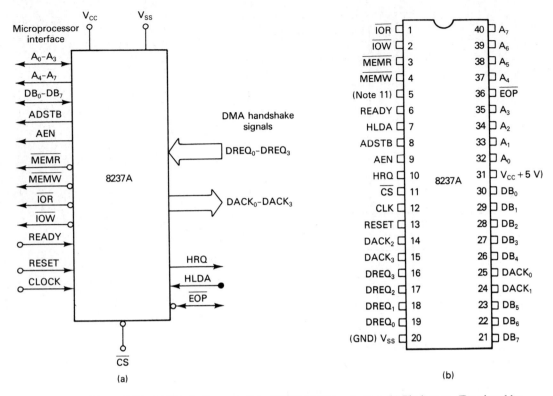

Figure 7.40 (a) Block diagram of the 8237A DMA controller. (b) Pin layout. (Reprinted by permission of Intel Corp. Copyright/Intel Corp. 1987)

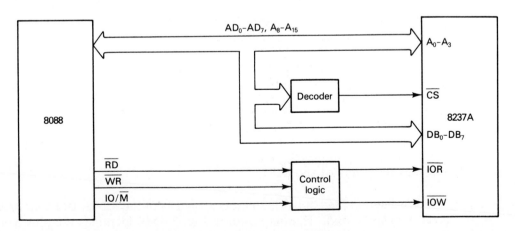

Figure 7.41 Microprocessor interface.

In a microcomputer system, the 8237A acts as a peripheral device and its operation must be initialized through software. This is done by reading from or writing to the bits of its internal registers. These data transfers take place through its microprocessor interface. Figure 7.41 shows how the 8088 connects to the 8237A's microprocessor interface.

Whenever the 8237A is not in use by a peripheral device for DMA operation, it is in a state known as the *idle state*. When in this state, the microprocessor can issue commands to the DMA controller and read from or write to its internal registers. Data bus lines DB_0 through DB_7 are the path over which these data transfers take place. Which register is accessed is determined by a 4-bit register address that is applied to address inputs A_0 through A_3. As shown in Fig. 7.41 these inputs are directly supplied by address bits A_0 through A_3 of the microprocessor.

During the data transfer bus cycle, other bits of the address are decoded in external circuitry to produce a chip select ($\overline{CS}$) input for the 8237A. When in the idle state, the 8237A continuously samples this input, waiting for it to become active. Logic 0 at this input enables the microprocessor interface. The microprocessor tells the 8237A whether an input or output bus cycle is in progress with the signal $\overline{IOR}$ or $\overline{IOW}$, respectively. In this way, we see that the 8237A is intended to be mapped into the I/O address space of the 8088 microcomputer.

DMA Interface of the 8237A

Now that we have described how a microprocessor talks to the registers of the 8237A, let us continue by looking at how peripheral devices initiate DMA service. The 8237A contains four independent DMA channels, channels 0 through 3. Typically, each of these channels is dedicated to a specific device, such as a peripheral. In Fig. 7.42, we see that the device has four DMA request inputs, denoted as $DREQ_0$ through $DREQ_3$. These DREQ inputs correspond to channels 0 through 3, respectively. In the idle state, the 8237A continuously tests these inputs to see if one is active. When a peripheral device wants to perform DMA operations, it makes a request for service at its DREQ input by switching it to its active state.

In response to the DMA request, the DMA controller switches the hold request (HRQ) output to logic 1. Normally, this output is supplied to the HOLD input of the 8088 and signals the microprocessor that the DMA controller needs to take control of the system bus. When the 8088 is ready to give up control of the bus, it puts its bus signals into the high-impedance state and signals this fact to the 8237A by switching the HLDA (hold acknowledge) output to logic 1. HLDA of the 8088 is applied to the HLDA input of the 8237A and signals that the system bus is now available for use by the DMA controller.

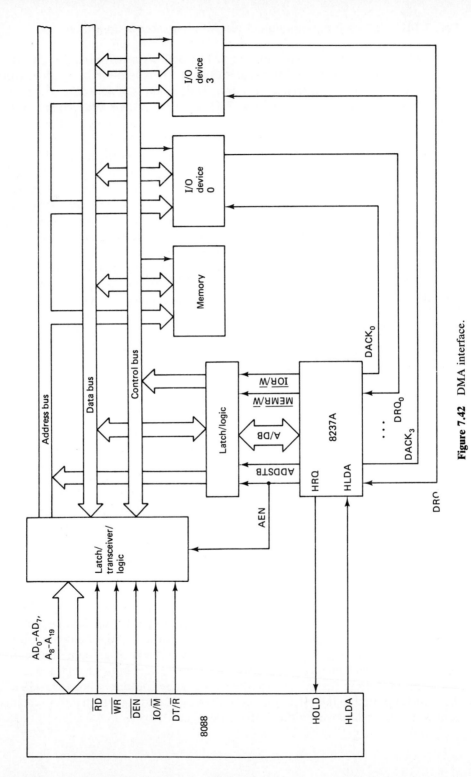

Figure 7.42 DMA interface.

The 8237A tells the requesting peripheral device that it is ready by outputting a DMA acknowledge (DACK) signal. Notice in Fig. 7.42 that each of the four DMA request inputs, $DREQ_0$ through $DREQ_3$, has a corresponding DMA acknowledge output, $DACK_0$ through $DACK_3$. Once this DMA request/acknowledge handshake sequence is complete, the peripheral device gets direct access to the system bus and memory under control of the 8237A.

During DMA bus cycles, the system bus is driven by the DMA controller, not the MPU. The 8237A generates the address and all control signals needed to perform the memory or I/O data transfers. At the beginning of all DMA bus cycles, a 16-bit address is output on lines A_0 through A_7 and DB_0 through DB_7. The upper 8 bits of the address, which are available on the data bus lines, appear at the same time that address strobe (ADSTB) becomes active. Thus ADSTB is intended to be used to strobe the most significant byte of the address into an external address latch. This 16-bit address gives the 8237A the ability to directly address up to 64K bytes of storage locations. The address enable (AEN) output signal is active during the complete DMA bus cycle and can be used to both enable the address latch and disable other devices connected to the bus.

Let us assume for now that an I/O peripheral device is to transfer data to memory. That is, the I/O device wants to write data to memory. In this case, the 8237A uses the $\overline{IOR}$ output to signal the I/O device to put the data onto data bus lines DB_0 through DB_7. At the same time, it asserts $\overline{MEMW}$ to signal that the data available on the bus are to be written into memory. In this case, the data are transferred directly from the I/O device to memory and do not go through the 8237A.

In a similar way, DMA transfers of data can take place from memory to an I/O device. Now the I/O device reads data from memory. For this data transfer, the 8237A activates the $\overline{MEMR}$ and $\overline{IOW}$ control signals.

The 8237A performs both the memory-to-I/O and I/O-to-memory DMA bus cycles in just four clock periods. The duration of these clock periods is determined by the frequency of the clock signal applied to the CLOCK input. For instance, at 5 MHz the clock period is 200 ns and the bus cycle takes 800 ns.

The 8237A is also capable of performing memory-to-memory DMA transfers. In such a data transfer, both the $\overline{MEMR}$ and $\overline{MEMW}$ signals are utilized. Unlike the I/O-to-memory operation, this memory-to-memory data transfer takes eight clock cycles. This is because it is actually performed as a separate four-clock read bus cycle from the source memory location to a temporary register within the 8237A and then another four-clock write bus cycle from the temporary register to the destination memory location. At 5 MHz, a memory-to-memory DMA cycle takes 1.6 μs.

The READY input is used to accommodate for the slow memory of I/O devices. READY must go active, logic 1, before the 8237A will complete a memory or I/O bus cycle. As long as READY is at logic 0, wait states are inserted to extend the duration of the current bus cycle.

Internal Architecture of the 8237A

Figure 7.43 is a block diagram of the internal architecture of the 8237A DMA controller. Here we find the following functional blocks: the timing and control, the priority encoder and rotating priority logic, the command control, and 12 different types of registers. Let us now look briefly at the functions performed by each of these sections of circuitry and registers.

The timing and control part of the 8237A generates the timing and control signals needed by the external bus interface. For instance, it accepts as inputs the READY and $\overline{CS}$ signals and produces as outputs signals such as ADSTB and AEN. These signals are synchronized to the clock signal that is input to the controller. The highest-speed version of the 8237A available today operates at a maximum clock rate of 5 MHz.

If multiple requests for DMA service are received by the 8237A, they are accepted on a priority basis. One of two priority schemes can be selected for the 8237A under software control. They are called *fixed priority* and *rotating priority*. The fixed priority mode assigns priority to the channels in descending numeric order. That is, channel 0 has the highest priority and channel 3 the lowest priority. Rotating priority starts with the priority levels initially the same way as in fixed priority. However, after a DMA request for a specific level gets serviced, priority is rotated so that the previously active channel is reassigned to the lowest priority level. For instance, assuming that channel 1, which was initially at priority level 1, was just serviced, then $DREQ_2$ is now at the highest priority level and $DREQ_1$ rotates to the lowest level. The priority logic circuitry shown in Fig. 7.43

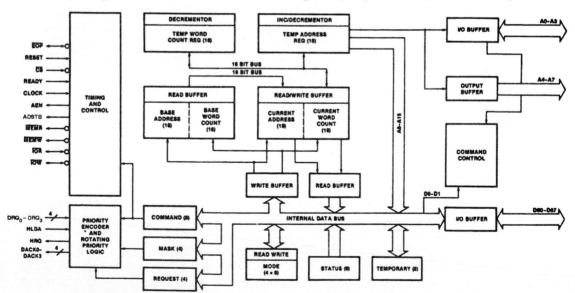

Figure 7.43 Internal architecture of the 8237A. (Reprinted by permission of Intel Corp. Copyright/Intel Corp. 1987)

resolves priority for simultaneous DMA requests from peripheral devices based on the enabled priority scheme.

The command control circuit decodes the register commands applied to the 8237A through the microprocessor interface. In this way it determines which register is to be accessed and what type of operation is to be performed. Moreover, it is used to decode the programmed operating modes of the device during DMA operation.

Looking at the block diagram in Fig. 7.43, we find that the 8237A has 12 different types of internal registers. Some examples are the current address register, current count register, command register, mask register, and status register. The names for all the internal registers are listed in Fig. 7.44, along with their sizes and how many are provided in the 8237A. Note that there are actually four current address registers and they are all 16 bits long. That is, there is one current address register for each of the four DMA channels. We will now describe the function served by each of these registers in terms of overall operation of the 8237A DMA controller. Addressing information for the internal registers is summarized in Fig. 7.45.

Each DMA channel has two address registers. They are called the *base address register* and the *current address register*. The base address register holds the starting address for the DMA operation, and the current address register contains the address of the next storage location to be accessed. Writing a value to the base address register automatically loads the same value into the current address register. In this way, we see that initially the current address register points to the starting I/O or memory address.

These registers must be loaded with appropriate values prior to initiating a DMA cycle. To load a new 16-bit address into the base register, we must write two separate bytes, one after the other, to the address of the register. The 8237A has an internal flip-flop called the *first/last flip-flop*. This flip-flop identifies which byte of the address is being written into the register. As shown in the table of Fig. 7.45, if the beginning state of the internal flip-flop (FF) is logic 0, then software must write the low byte of the address word to the register. On the other hand, if it is logic 1, the high byte must be written to the register. For example, to write the address 1234_{16} into the base address register and the current address register

Name	Size	Number
Base Address Registers	16 bits	4
Base Word Count Registers	16 bits	4
Current Address Registers	16 bits	4
Current Word Count Registers	16 bits	4
Temporary Address Register	16 bits	1
Temporary Word Count Register	16 bits	1
Status Register	8 bits	1
Command Register	8 bits	1
Temporary Register	8 bits	1
Mode Registers	6 bits	4
Mask Register	4 bits	1
Request Register	4 bits	1

Figure 7.44   Internal registers of the 8237A. (Reprinted by permission of Intel Corp. Copyright/Intel Corp. 1987)

Channel(s)	Register	Operation	I/O address	Internal FF	Data bus
0	Base and current address	Write	0_{16}	0 1	Low High
	Current address	Read	0_{16}	0 1	Low High
	Base and current count	Write	1_{16}	0 1	Low High
	Current count	Read	1_{16}	0 1	Low High
1	Base and current address	Write	2_{16}	0 1	Low High
	Current address	Read	2_{16}	0 1	Low High
	Base and current count	Write	3_{16}	0 1	Low High
	Current count	Read	3_{16}	0 1	Low High
2	Base and current address	Write	4_{16}	0 1	Low High
	Current address	Read	4_{16}	0 1	Low High
	Base and current count	Write	5_{16}	0 1	Low High
	Current count	Read	5_{16}	0 1	Low High
3	Base and current address	Write	6_{16}	0 1	Low High
	Current address	Read	6_{16}	0 1	Low High
	Base and current count	Write	7_{16}	0 1	Low High
	Current count	Read	7_{16}	0 1	Low High
All	Command register	Write	8_{16}	X	Low
All	Status register	Read	8_{16}	X	Low
All	Request register	Write	9_{16}	X	Low
All	Mask register	Write	A_{16}	X	Low
All	Mode register	Write	B_{16}	X	Low
All	Temporary register	Read	B_{16}	X	Low
All	Clear internal FF	Write	C_{16}	X	Low
All	Master clear	Write	D_{16}	X	Low
All	Clear mask register	Write	E_{16}	X	Low
All	Mask register	Write	F_{16}	X	Low

Figure 7.45 Accessing the registers of the 8237A.

for channel 0 of a DMA controller located at I/O address 'DMA' (where DMA $\leq$ F0H), the following instructions may be executed:

```
MOV AL,34H     ;WRITE LOW BYTE
OUT DMA+0,AL
MOV AL,12H     ;WRITE HIGH BYTE
OUT DMA+0,AL
```

This routine assumes that the internal flip-flop was initially set to 0. Looking at Fig. 7.45, we find that a command can be issued to the 8237A to clear the internal flip-flop. This is done by initiating an output bus cycle to address DMA + C_{16}.

If we read the contents of register address C_{16}, the value obtained is the contents of the current address register. Once loaded, the value in the base address register cannot be read out of the device.

The 8237A also has two word count registers for each of its DMA channels. They are called the *base count register* and the *current count register*. In Fig. 7.44, we find that these registers are also 16 bits in length, and Fig. 7.45 identifies their address as 1_{16}. The number of bytes of data that are to be transferred during a DMA operation is specified by the value in the base word count register. Actually, the number of bytes transferred is always one more than the value programmed into this register. This is because the end of a DMA cycle is detected by the rollover of the current word count from 0000_{16} to $FFFF_{16}$. At any time during the DMA cycle, the value in the current word count register tells how many bytes remain to be transferred.

The count registers are programmed in the same way as was just described for the address registers. For instance, to program a count of $0FFF_{16}$ into the base and current count registers for channel 1 of a DMA controller located at address 'DMA,' (where DMA $\leq$ F0H), the instructions that follow can be executed:

```
MOV AL,0FFH    ;WRITE LOW BYTE
OUT DMA+2,AL
MOV AL,0FH     ;WRITE HIGH BYTE
OUT DMA+2,AL
```

Again we have assumed that the internal flip-flop was initially cleared.

In Fig. 7.44, we find that the 8237A has a single 8-bit command register. The bits in this register are used to control operating modes that apply to all channels of the DMA controller. Figure 7.46 identifies the function of each of its control bits. Notice that the settings of the bits are used to select or deselect operating features such as memory-to-memory, DMA transfer, and the priority scheme. For instance, when bit 0 is set to logic 1, the memory-to-memory mode of DMA transfer is enabled, and when it is logic 0, DMA transfers take place between I/O and memory. Moreover, setting bit 4 to logic 0 selects the fixed priority scheme for all four channels or logic 1 in this location selects rotating priority. Looking at

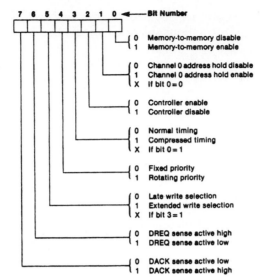

Figure 7.46 Command register format. (Reprinted by permission of Intel Corp. Copyright/Intel Corp. 1987)

Fig. 7.45, we see that the command register is loaded by outputting the command code to register address 8_{16}.

EXAMPLE 7.28

If the command register of an 8237A is loaded with 00_{16}, how does the controller operate?

SOLUTION Representing the command word as a binary number, we get

$$00_{16} = 00000000_2$$

Referring to Fig. 7.46, we find that the DMA operation can be described as follows:

Bit $0 = 0 =$ Memory-to-memory transfers are disabled

Bit $1 = 0 =$ Channel 0 address increments/decrements normally

Bit $2 = 0 =$ 8237A is enabled

Bit $3 = 0 =$ 8237A operates with normal timing

Bit $4 = 0 =$ Channels have fixed priority, channel 0 having the highest priority and channel 3 the lowest priority

Bit $5 = 0 =$ Write operation occurs late in the DMA bus cycle

Bit $6 = 0 =$ DREQ is an active high (logic 1) signal

Bit $7 = 0 =$ DACK is an active low (logic 0) signal

The *mode registers* are also used to configure operational features of the 8237A. In Fig. 7.44, we find that there is a separate mode register for each of the four DMA channels and that they are each 6 bits in length. Their bits are used to select various operational features for the individual DMA channels. A typical mode register command is shown in Fig. 7.47. As shown in the diagram, the two least significant bits are a 2-bit code that identifies the channel to which the mode command byte applies. For instance, in a mode register command written for channel 1, these bits must be made 01. Bits 2 and 3 specify whether the channel is to perform data write or data read or verify bus cycles. For example, if these bits are set to 01, the channel will only perform write data transfers (DMA data transfers from an I/O device to memory).

The next 2 bits of the mode register affect how the values in the current address and current count registers are updated at the end of a DMA cycle and DMA data transfer, respectively. Bit 4 enables or disables the autoinitialization function. When autoinitialization is enabled, the current address and current count registers are automatically reloaded from the base address and base count registers, respectively, at the end of a DMA cycle. In this way, the channel is prepared for the next cycle to begin. The setting of bit 5 determines whether the value in the current address register is automatically incremented or decremented at completion of each DMA data transfer.

The two most significant bits of the mode register select one of four possible modes of DMA operation for the channel. The four modes are called *demand mode, single mode, block mode,* and *cascade mode.* These modes allow for either one byte of data to be transferred at a time or a block of bytes. For example, when in the demand transfer mode, once the DMA cycle is initiated, bytes are continuously transferred as long as the DREQ signal remains active and the terminal count (TC) is not reached. By reaching the terminal count, we mean that the value in the current word count register, which automatically decrements after each data transfer, rolls over from 0000_{16} to $FFFF_{16}$.

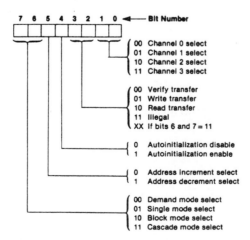

Figure 7.47 Mode register format. (Reprinted by permission of Intel Corp. Copyright/Intel Corp. 1987)

Block transfer mode is similar to demand transfer mode in that, once the DMA cycle is initiated, data are continuously transferred until the terminal count is reached. However, they differ in that, when in the demand mode, the return of DREQ to its inactive state halts the data transfer sequence. But, when in block transfer mode, DREQ can be released at any time after the DMA cycle begins, and the block transfer will still run to completion.

In the single transfer mode, the channel is set up such that it performs just one data transfer at a time. At the completion of the transfer, the current word count is decremented and the current address either incremented or decremented (based on an option setting). Moreover, an autoinitialize, if enabled, will not occur unless the terminal count has been reached at the completion of the current data transfer. If the DREQ input becomes inactive before the completion of the current data transfer, another data transfer will not take place until DREQ once more becomes active. On the other hand, if DREQ remains active during the complete data transfer cycle, the HRQ output of the 8237A is switched to its inactive 0 logic level to allow the microprocessor to gain control of the system bus for one bus cycle before another single transfer takes place. This mode of operation is typically used when it is necessary to not lock the microprocessor off the bus for the complete duration of the DMA cycle.

EXAMPLE 7.29

Specify the mode byte for DMA channel 2 if it is to transfer data from an input peripheral device to a memory buffer starting at address $A000_{16}$ and ending at $AFFF_{16}$. Ensure that the microprocessor is not completely locked off the bus during the DMA cycle. Moreover, at the end of each DMA cycle, the channel is to be reinitialized so that the same buffer is to be filled when the next DMA operation is initiated.

SOLUTION   For DMA channel 2, bit 1 and bit 0 must be loaded with 10_2.

$$B_1B_0 = 10$$

Transfer of data from an I/O device to memory represents a write bus cycle. Therefore, bit 3 and bit 2 must be set to 01.

$$B_3B_2 = 01$$

Selecting autoinitialization will set up the channel to automatically reset so that it points to the beginning of the memory buffer at completion of the current DMA cycle. This feature is enabled by making bit 4 equal to 1.

$$B_4 = 1$$

The address that points to the memory buffer must increment after each data transfer. Therefore, bit 5 must be set to 0.

$$B_5 = 0$$

Finally, to ensure that the 8088 is not locked off the bus during the complete DMA cycle, we will select the single transfer mode of operation. This is done by making bits B_7 and B_6 equal to 01.

$$B_7B_6 = 01$$

Thus the mode register byte is $01010110_2 = 56_{16}$.

Up to now, we have discussed how DMA cycles can be initiated by a hardware request at a DREQ input. However, the 8237A is also able to respond to software-initiated requests for DMA service. The *request register* has been provided for this purpose. Figure 7.44 shows that the request register has just 4 bits, one for each of the DMA channels. When the request bit for a channel is set, DMA operation is started, and when reset, the DMA cycle is stopped. Any channel used for software-initiated DMA must be programmed for block transfer mode of operation.

The bits in the request register can be set or reset by issuing software commands to the 8237A. The format of a request register command is shown in Fig. 7.48. For instance, if a command is issued to the address of the request register with bits 0 and 1 equal to 01 and with bit 3 at logic 1, a block mode DMA cycle is initiated for channel 1. In Fig. 7.45, we find that the request register is located at register address 9_{16}.

A 4-bit *mask register* is also provided within the 8237A. One bit is provided in this register for each of the DMA channels. When a mask bit is set, the DREQ input for the corresponding channel is disabled. That is, hardware requests to the channel are ignored and the channel is masked out. On the other hand, if the mask bit is cleared, the DREQ input is enabled and its channel can be activated by an external device.

The format of a software command that can be used to set or reset a single bit in the mask register is shown in Fig. 7.49(a). For example, to enable the DREQ input for channel 2, the command is issued with bits 0 and 1 set to 10 to select channel 2 and with bit 3 equal to 0 to clear the mask bit. For this example,

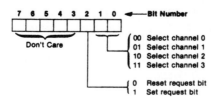

Figure 7.48   Request register format. (Reprinted by permission of Intel Corp. Copyright/Intel Corp. 1987)

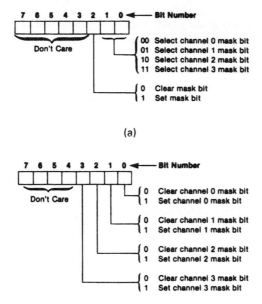

(a)

(b)

Figure 7.49 (a) Single channel mask register command format. (Reprinted by permission of Intel Corp. Copyright/Intel Corp. 1987) (b) Four channel mask register command format. (Reprinted by permission of Intel Corp. Copyright/Intel Corp. 1987)

the software command byte could be 03_{16}. The table in Fig. 7.45 shows that this command byte must be issued to the 8237A with register address A_{16}.

A second mask register command is shown in Fig. 7.49(b). This command can be used to load all 4 bits of the register at once. In Fig. 7.49, we find that this command is issued to register address F_{16} instead of A_{16}. For instance, to mask out channel 2 while enabling channels 0, 1, and 3, the command code 04_{16} is output to F_{16}. Either of these two methods can be used to mask or enable the DREQ input for a channel.

At system initialization, it is a common practice to clear the mask register. Looking at Fig. 7.49, we see that a special command is provided to perform this operation. Notice that the mask register can be cleared by executing an output cycle to register address E_{16}.

The 8237A has a *status register* that contains information about the operating state of its four DMA channels. Figure 7.50 shows the bits of the status register and defines their functions. Here we find that the four least significant bits identify whether or not channels 0 through 3 have reached their terminal count. When the DMA cycle for a channel reaches the terminal count, this fact is recorded by setting the corresponding TC bit to the 1 logic level. The four most significant bits of the register tell if a request is pending for the corresponding channel. For instance, if a DMA request has been issued for channel 0 either through hardware or software, bit 4 is set to 1. The 8088 can read the contents of the status register through software. This is done by initiating an input bus cycle for register address 8_{16}.

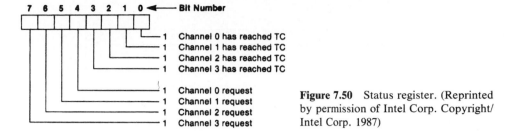

Figure 7.50   Status register. (Reprinted by permission of Intel Corp. Copyright/ Intel Corp. 1987)

Earlier we pointed out that during memory-to-memory DMA transfers, the data read from the source address are held in a register known as the *temporary register,* and then a write cycle is initiated to write the data to the destination address. At the completion of the DMA cycle, this register contains the last byte that was transferred. The value in this register can be read by the microprocessor.

EXAMPLE 7.30

Write an instruction sequence to issue a master clear to the 8237A and then enable all its DMA channels. Assume that the device is located at I/O address 'DMA < F0H.'

SOLUTION   In Fig. 7.45, we find that a special software command is provided to perform a master reset of the 8237A's registers. Since the contents of the data bus are a don't-care state when executing the master clear command, it is performed by simply writing to register address D_{16}. For instance, the instruction

```
OUT DMA+0DH,AL
```

can be used. To enable the DMA request inputs, all four bits of the mask register must be cleared. The clear mask register command is issued by performing a write to register address E_{16}. Again, the data put on the bus during the write cycle are a don't-care state. Therefore, the command can be performed with the instruction

```
OUT DMA+0EH,AL
```

DMA Interface for the 8088-Based Microcomputer Using the 8237A

Figure 7.51 shows how the 8237A is connected to the 8088 microprocessor to form a simplified DMA interface. Here we see that both the 8088 MPU and the 8237A DMA controller drive the three system buses, address bus, data bus, and control

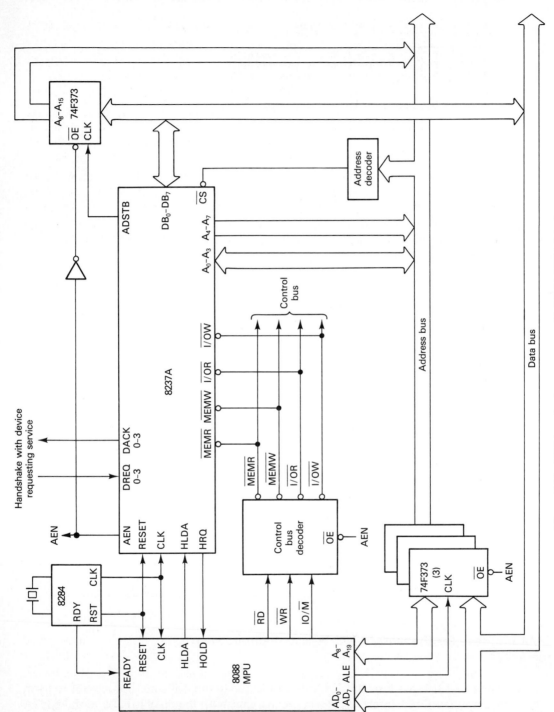

Figure 7.51 8088-based microcomputer with 8237A DMA interface.

bus. Let us now look at how each of these devices attaches to the system bus. The 8088's multiplexed address/data bus is demultiplexed using three 74F373 latches to form independent system address and data buses. The address bus is 20 bits in length and these lines are identified as A_0 through A_{19}. On the other hand, the data bus is byte-wide, with lines D_0 through D_7. Notice that the ALE output of the 8088 is used as the CLK input to the latches.

Looking at the 8237A, we find that the lower byte of its address, which is identified by A_0 through A_3 and A_4 through A_7, is supplied directly to the system address bus. On the other hand, the most significant byte of its address, A_8 through A_{15}, is demultiplexed from data bus lines DB_0 through DB_7 by another 74F373 latch. This latch is enabled by the AEN output of the DMA controller, and the address is loaded into the latch with the signal ADSTB. DB_0 through DB_7 are also directly attached to the system data bus.

Finally, let us look at how the system control bus signals are derived. The $IO/\overline{M}$, $\overline{RD}$, and $\overline{WR}$ control outputs of the microprocessor are gated together to produce the signals $\overline{MEMR}$, $\overline{MEMW}$, $\overline{IOR}$, and $\overline{IOW}$. These signals are combined to form the system control bus. Notice that these same four signals are generated as outputs of the 8237A and are also supplied to the control bus.

Now that we have shown how the independent address, data, and control signals of the 8088 and 8237A are combined to form the system address, data, and control buses, let us continue by looking at how the DMA request/acknowledge interface is implemented. I/O devices request DMA service by activating one of the 8237A's DMA request inputs, $DREQ_0$ through $DREQ_3$. When the 8237A receives a valid DMA request on one of these lines, it sends a hold request to the HOLD input of the 8088. It does this by setting the HRQ output to logic 1. After the 8088 gives up control of the system buses, it acknowledges this fact to the 8237A by switching its HLDA output to the 1 logic level. This signal is received by the DMA controller at its HLDA input and tells it that the system buses are available. The 8237A is now ready to take over control of the system buses, and it signals this fact to the device that is requesting service by activating its DMA acknowledge (DACK) line.

ASSIGNMENTS

Section 7.2

1. Name the two types of input/output.
2. What type of I/O is in use when peripheral devices are mapped to the 8088's I/O address space?
3. Which type of I/O has the disadvantage that part of the address space must be given up to implement I/O ports?
4. Which type of I/O has the disadvantage that all I/O data transfers must take place through the AL or AX register?

Section 7.3

5. What are the functions of the 8088's address and data bus lines relative to I/O operation?

6. In a minimum-mode 8088 microcomputer, which signal indicates to external circuitry that the current bus cycle is for the I/O interface and not the memory interface?

7. List the differences between the 8088's minimum-mode I/O interface in Fig. 7.3(a) and that of the 8086 in Fig. 7.3(b).

8. What is the logic relationship between the signals $IO/\overline{M}$ and $M/\overline{IO}$?

9. In a maximum-mode system, which device produces the input (read), output (write), and bus control signals for the I/O interface?

10. Briefly describe the function of each block in the I/O interface circuit in Fig. 7.4(a).

11. In a maximum-mode 8086 microcomputer, which signals tell external circuitry that an input/output bus cycle is in progress? What code identifies an input bus cycle?

12. In the maximum-mode I/O interface of Fig. 7.4(a), what are the logic levels of $\overline{IORC}$, $\overline{IOWC}$, and $\overline{AIOWC}$ during an output bus cycle?

Section 7.4

13. How many bits are in the 8088's I/O address?

14. What is the range of byte addresses in the 8088's I/O address space?

15. What is the size of the 8086's I/O address space in terms of word-wide I/O ports?

16. In an 8086-based microcomputer system, what are the logic levels of A_0 and $\overline{BHE}$ when a byte of data is being written to I/O address $A000_{16}$? If a word of data is being written to address $A000_{16}$?

17. In an 8088 microcomputer system, how many bus cycles are required to output a word of data to I/O address $A000_{16}$? In an 8086 microcomputer system?

Section 7.5

18. Describe the operation performed by the instruction IN AX,1AH.

19. Write an instruction sequence to perform the same operation as that of the instruction in problem 18, but this time use register DX to address the I/O port.

20. Describe the operation performed by the instruction OUT 2AH,AL.

21. Write an instruction sequence that will output the byte of data $0F_{16}$ to an output port at address 1000_{16}.

22. Write a sequence of instructions that will input the byte of data from input ports at addresses $A000_{16}$ and $B000_{16}$, add these values together, and save the sum in memory location IO_SUM.

23. Write a sequence of instructions that will input the contents of the input port at address $B0_{16}$, mask off all but the least significant bit (bit 0), shift the value of bit 0 into the carry flag, and jump to the beginning of a service routine identified by the label ACTIVE_INPUT if carry flag is 1.

Section 7.6

24. In the 8088's input bus cycle, during which T state do the IO/$\overline{\text{M}}$, ALE, $\overline{\text{RD}}$, and $\overline{\text{DEN}}$ control signals become active?

25. During which T state in the 8088's input bus cycle is the address output on the bus? Are data read from the bus by the MPU?

26. If an 8088 is running at 5 MHz, what is the duration of the output bus operation performed by executing the instruction OUT 0C0H,AX?

27. If an 8086 running at 10 MHz inserts two wait states into all I/O bus cycles, what is the duration of a bus cycle in which a byte of data is being output?

28. If the 8086 in problem 27 was outputting a word of data to a word-wide port at I/O address $1A1_{16}$, what would be the duration of the bus cycle?

Section 7.7

29. What is the address of port 7 in the circuit of Fig. 7.11(a)?

30. What are the inputs of the I/O address decoder in Fig. 7.11(a) when the I/O address on the bus is $800A_{16}$? Which output is active? Which output port does this enable?

31. What operation does the instruction sequence

```
MOV  AL,0FFH
MOV  DX,8004H
OUT  DX,AL
```

perform to the circuit in Fig. 7.11(a)?

32. Write a sequence of instructions to output the word contents of the memory location called DATA to output ports 0 and 1 in the circuit of Fig. 7.11(b).

Section 7.8

33. Which input port in the circuit of Fig. 7.12 is selected for operation if the I/O address output on the bus is 8008_{16}?

34. What operation is performed to the circuit in Fig. 7.12 when the instruction sequence

```
MOV  DX,8000H
IN   AL,DX
AND  AL,0FH
MOV  LOW_NIBBLE,AL
```

is executed?

35. Write a sequence of instructions to read in the contents of ports 1 and 2 in the circuit of Fig. 7.12 and save them at consecutive memory addresses $A0000_{16}$ and $A0001_{16}$ in memory.

36. Write an instruction sequence that will poll input 0_{63} in the circuit of Fig. 7.12 checking for it to switch to logic 0.

Section 7.9

37. Name a method that can be used to synchronize the input or output of information to a peripheral device.

38. List the control signals in the parallel printer interface circuit of Fig. 7.13(a). Identify whether they are an input or output of the printer and briefly describe their function.

39. Overview what happens when a write bus cycle of byte-wide data is performed to I/O address 8000_{16}.

40. Show what push and pop instructions are needed in the program written in Example 7.9 to preserve the contents of registers used by it so that it can be used as a subroutine.

Section 7.10

41. What kind of input/output interface does a PPI implement?

42. How many I/O lines are available on the 8255A?

43. If the value $A4_{16}$ is written to the control register of an 8255A, what is the mode and I/O configuration of port A? Port B?

44. What is the function of the port B lines of the 8255A when port A is configured for mode 2 operation?

45. Describe the mode 0, mode 1, and mode 2 I/O operations of the 8255A PPI.

46. What should be the control word if ports A, B, and C are to be configured for mode 0 operation? Moreover, ports A and B are to be used as inputs and C as an output.

47. Assume that the control register of an 8255A resides at memory address 00100_{16}. Write an instruction sequence to load it with the control word formed in problem 46.

48. If the value 03_{16} is written to the control register of an 8255A set for mode 2 operation, what bit at port C is affected by the bit set/reset operation? Is it set to 1 or cleared to 0?

49. Assume that the control register of an 8255A is at I/O address 0100_{16}. Write an instruction sequence that will load it with the bit set/reset value given in problem 48.

Section 7.11

50. If I/O address $003D_{16}$ is applied to the circuit in Fig. 7.25 during a write cycle and the data output on the bus is 98_{16}, which 8255A is being accessed? Are data being written into port A, port B, port C, or the control register of this device?

51. If the instruction

```
IN AL,08H
```

is executed to the I/O interface circuit in Fig. 7.25, what operation is performed?

52. What are the addresses of the A, B, and C ports of PPI 2 in the circuit of Fig. 7.26?

53. Assume that PPI 2 in Fig. 7.26 is configured as defined in problem 46. Write a program that will input the data at ports A and B, add these values together, and output the sum to port C.

Section 7.12

54. Distinguish between memory-mapped I/O and accumulator-mapped I/O.

55. What address inputs must be applied to the circuit in Fig. 7.27 in order to access port B of device 4? Assuming that all unused bits are 0, what would be the memory address?

56. Write an instruction that will load the control register of the port identified in problem 55 with the value 98_{16}.

57. Repeat problem 53 for the circuit in Fig. 7.28.

Section 7.13

58. What are the inputs and outputs of counter 2 of an 8253?

59. Write a control word for counter 1 that selects the following options: load least significant byte only, mode 5 of operation, and binary counting.

60. What are the logic levels of inputs $\overline{CS}$, $\overline{RD}$, $\overline{WR}$, A_1, and A_0 when the byte in problem 59 is written to an 8253?

61. Write an instruction sequence that will load the control word in problem 59 into an 8253 that is located starting at address 01000_{16} of the memory address space.

62. Write an instruction sequence that will write the value 12_{16} into the least significant byte of the count register for counter 2 of an 8253 located starting at memory address 01000_{16}.

63. Repeat Example 7.22 for the 8253 located at memory address 01000_{16}, but this time just read the least significant byte of the counter.

64. What is the maximum time delay that can be generated with the timer in Fig. 7.35? What will be the maximum time delay if the clock frequency is increased to 2 MHz?

65. What is the resolution of pulses generated with the 8253 in Fig. 7.35? What will be the resolution if the clock frequency is increased to 2 MHz?

66. Find the pulse width of the one-shot in Fig. 7.33 if the counter is loaded with the value 1000_{16}.

67. What count must be loaded into the square-wave generator of Fig. 7.38 to produce a 25-KHz output?

68. If the counter in Fig. 7.39 is loaded with the value 120_{16}, how long of a delay occurs before the strobe pulse is output?

Section 7.14

69. Are signal lines $\overline{MEMR}$ and $\overline{MEMW}$ of the 8237A used in the microprocessor interface?

70. Summarize the 8237A's DMA request/acknowledge handshake sequence.

71. What is the total number of user accessible registers in the 8237A?

72. Write an instruction sequence that will read the value of the address from the current address register into the AX register.

73. Assuming that an 8237A is located at I/O address DMA, what is the address of the command register?

74. Write an instruction sequence that will write the command word 00_{16} into the command register of an 8237A that is located at address DMA in the I/O address space.

75. Write an instruction sequence that will load the mode register for channel 2 with the mode byte obtained in Example 7.29. Assume that the 8237A is located at I/O address DMA.

76. What must be output to the mask register in order to disable all the DREQ inputs?

77. Write an instruction that will read the contents of the status register into the AL register. Assume that the 8237A is located at address DMA where DMA $> FF_{16}$.

Interrupt Interface of the 8088 and 8086 Microprocessors

8.1 INTRODUCTION

In Chapter 7 we covered the input/output interface of the 8088 and 8086 microcomputer systems. Here we continue with a special input interface, the *interrupt interface*. The following topics are presented in this chapter:

1. Types of interrupts
2. Interrupt address pointer table
3. Interrupt instructions
4. Enabling/disabling of interrupts
5. External hardware interrupt interface
6. External hardware interrupt sequence
7. 8259A programmable interrupt controller
8. 8259A interrupt interface circuits
9. Software interrupts
10. Nonmaskable interrupt
11. Reset
12. Internal interrupt functions

8.2 TYPES OF INTERRUPTS

Interrupts provide a mechanism for changing program environment. Transfer of program control is initiated by either the occurrence of an event internal to the microprocessor or an event in its external hardware. For instance, when an interrupt signal occurs indicating that an external device, such as a printer, requires service, the MPU must suspend what it is doing in the main part of the program and pass control to a special routine that performs the function required by the device.

The section of program to which control is passed is called the *interrupt service routine*. When the MPU terminates execution in the main program, it remembers the location where it left off and then picks up execution with the first instruction in the service routine. After this routine has run to completion, program control is returned to the point where the MPU originally left the main body of the program.

The 8088 and 8086 microcomputers are capable of implementing any combination of up to 256 interrupts. They are divided into four groups: *external hardware interrupts, software interrupts, internal interrupts,* and the *nonmaskable interrupt.* The function of the external hardware, software, and nonmaskable interrupts can be defined by the user. On the other hand, the internal interrupts have dedicated system functions.

Hardware, software, and internal interrupts are serviced on a *priority* basis. Priority is achieved in two ways. First, the interrupt processing sequence implemented in the 8088/8086 tests for the occurrence of the various groups based on the hierarchy that follows: internal interrupt, nonmaskable interrupt, software interrupt, and external hardware interrupt. Thus we see that internal interrupts are the *highest-priority group* and the external hardware interrupts are the *lowest-priority group*. Second, the various interrupts are given different priority levels within a group by assigning to each a *type number*. *Type 0* identifies the highest-priority interrupt and *type 255* identifies the lowest-priority interrupt. Actually, a few of the type numbers are not available for use with software or hardware interrupts. This is because they are reserved for special interrupt functions of the 8088/8086, such as internal interrupts. For instance, within the internal interrupt group an interrupt known as divide error is assigned to type number 0. Therefore, it has the highest priority of the internal interrupts. Another internal interrupt is called overflow and is assigned the type number 4. Overflow is the lowest-priority internal interrupt.

The importance of priority lies in the fact that, if an interrupt service routine has been initiated to perform a function at a specific priority level, only devices with higher priority can interrupt the active service routine. Lower-priority devices will have to wait until the routine is completed before their request for service can be acknowledged. For this reason, the user normally assigns tasks that must not be interrupted frequently to higher-priority levels and those that can be interrupted to lower-priority levels. An example of a high-priority service routine that should not be interrupted is that for a power failure.

We just pointed out that once an interrupt service routine is initiated, it can be interrupted only by a function that corresponds to a higher-priority level. For example, if a type 50 external hardware interrupt is in progress, it can be interrupted by any software interrupt, the nonmaskable interrupt, all internal interrupts, or any external interrupt with type number less than 50. That is, external hardware interrupts with priority levels equal to 50 or greater are *masked out*.

8.3 INTERRUPT ADDRESS POINTER TABLE

An *address pointer table* is used to link the interrupt type numbers to the locations of their service routines in the program storage memory. Figure 8.1 shows a map of the pointer table in the memory of the 8088 or 8086 microcomputer system. Looking at this table, we see that it contains 256 *address pointers (vectors)*. One pointer corresponds to each of the interrupt types 0 through 255. These address

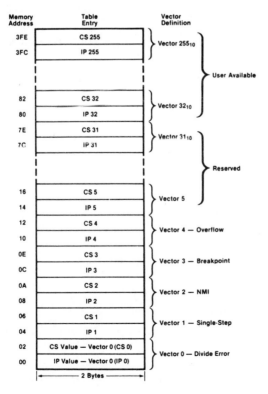

Figure 8.1 Interrupt vector table of the 8088/8086. (Reprinted by permission of Intel Corp. Copyright/Intel Corp. 1979)

pointers identify the starting locations of their service routines in program memory.

Notice that the pointer table is located at the low-address end of the memory address space. It starts at address 00000_{16} and ends at $003FE_{16}$. This represents the first 1K bytes of memory.

Each of the 256 pointers requires two words (4 bytes) of memory. These words are stored at even-address boundaries. The higher-addressed word of the two-word vector is called the *base address*. It identifies the program memory segment in which the service routine resides. For this reason, it is loaded into the code segment (CS) register within the MPU. The lower-addressed word of the vector is the *offset* of the first instruction of the service routine from the beginning of the code segment defined by the base address loaded into CS. This offset is loaded into the instruction pointer (IP) register. For example, the vector for type number 255, IP_{255} and CS_{255}, is stored at addresses $003FC_{16}$ and $003FE_{16}$.

Looking more closely at the table in Fig. 8.1, we find that the first five pointers have *dedicated functions*. Pointers 0, 1, 3, and 4 are required for the 8088's and 8086's internal interrupts: *divide error, single step, breakpoint,* and *overflow*. Pointer 2 is used to identify the starting location of the nonmaskable interrupt's service routine. The next 27 pointers, 5 through 31, represent a *reserved portion* of the pointer table and should not be used. The rest of the table, the 224 pointers in the address range 00080_{16} through $003FF_{16}$, is available to the user for storage of interrupt vectors. These pointers correspond to type numbers 32 through 255 and can be employed by hardware or software interrupts. In the case of external hardware interrupts, the type number (priority level) is associated with an interrupt input level.

EXAMPLE 8.1

At what address should vector 50, CS_{50}, and IP_{50}, be stored in memory?

SOLUTION   Each vector requires four consecutive bytes of memory for storage. Therefore, its address can be found by multiplying the type number by 4. Since CS_{50} and IP_{50} represent the words of the type 50 interrupt pointer, we get

$$\text{Address} = 4 \times 50 = 200$$

Converting to binary form gives

$$\text{Address} = 11001000_2$$

and expressing it as a hexadecimal number results in

$$\text{Address} = C8_{16}$$

Therefore, IP_{50} is stored starting at $000C8_{16}$ and CS_{50} starting at $000CA_{16}$.

8.4 INTERRUPT INSTRUCTIONS

A number of instructions are provided in the instruction set of the 8088 and 8086 microprocessors for use with interrupt processing. These instructions are listed with a brief description of their functions in Fig. 8.2.

For instance, the first two instructions, which are STI and CLI, permit manipulation of the interrupt flag through software. STI stands for *set interrupt enable flag*. Execution of this instruction enables the external interrupt input (INTR) for operation. That is, it sets interrupt flag (IF). On the other hand, execution of CLI (*clear interrupt enable flag*) disables the external interrupt input. It does this by resetting IF.

The next instruction listed in Fig. 8.2 is the *software interrupt* instruction INT n. It is used to initiate a software vector call of a subroutine. Executing the instruction causes transfer of program control to the subroutine pointed to by the vector for type number n specified in the instruction.

For example, execution of the instruction INT 50 initiates execution of a subroutine whose starting point is identified by vector 50 in the pointer table. That is, the MPU reads IP_{50} and CS_{50} from addresses $000C8_{16}$ and $000CA_{16}$, respectively, in memory, loads these values into IP and CS, calculates a physical address, and starts to fetch instructions from this new location in program memory.

An *interrupt return* (IRET) instruction must be included at the end of each interrupt service routine. It is required to pass control back to the point in the

Mnemonic	Meaning	Format	Operation	Flags Affected
CLI	Clear interrupt flag	CLI	$0 \rightarrow (IF)$	IF
STI	Set interrupt flag	STI	$1 \rightarrow (IF)$	IF
INT n	Type n software interrupt	INT n	$(Flags) \rightarrow ((SP) - 2)$ $0 \rightarrow TF,IF$ $(CS) \rightarrow ((SP) - 4)$ $(2 + 4 \cdot n) \rightarrow (CS)$ $(IP) \rightarrow ((SP) - 6)$ $(4 \cdot n) \rightarrow (IP)$	TF, IF
IRET	Interrupt return	IRET	$((SP)) \rightarrow (IP)$ $((SP) + 2) \rightarrow (CS)$ $((SP) + 4) \rightarrow (Flags)$ $(SP) + 6 \rightarrow (SP)$	All
INTO	Interrupt on overflow	INTO	INT 4 steps	TF, IF
HLT	Halt	HLT	Wait for an external interrupt or reset to occur	None
WAIT	Wait	WAIT	Wait for $\overline{TEST}$ input to go active	None

Figure 8.2 Interrupt instructions.

program where execution was terminated due to the occurrence of the interrupt. When executed, IRET causes the three words IP, CS, and flags to be popped from the stack back into the internal registers of the MPU. This restores the original program environment.

INTO is the *interrupt on overflow* instruction. This instruction must be included after arithmetic instructions that can generate an overflow condition, such as divide. It tests the overflow flag, and if the flag is found to be set, a type 4 internal interrupt is initiated. This causes program control to be passed to an overflow service routine that is located at the starting address identified by the vector IP_4 at 00010_{16} and CS_4 at 00012_{16} of the pointer table.

The last two instructions associated with the interrupt interface are *halt* (HLT) and *wait* (WAIT). They produce similar responses by the 8088/8086 and permit their operation to be synchronized to an event in external hardware. For instance, when HLT is executed, the MPU suspends operation and enters the idle state. It no longer executes instructions; instead, it remains idle waiting for the occurrence of an external hardware interrupt or reset interrupt. With the occurrence of either of these two events, the MPU resumes execution with the corresponding service routine.

If the WAIT instruction is used instead of the HLT instruction, the MPU checks the logic level of the $\overline{TEST}$ input prior to going into the idle state. Only if $\overline{TEST}$ is at logic 1 will the MPU go into the idle state. While in the idle state, the MPU continues to check the logic level at $\overline{TEST}$, looking for its transition to the 0 logic level. As $\overline{TEST}$ switches to 0, execution resumes with the next sequential instruction in the program.

8.5 ENABLING/DISABLING OF INTERRUPTS

An interrupt enable flag bit is provided within the 8088 and 8086 MPUs. Earlier we found that it is identified as IF. It affects only the external hardware interrupt interface, not the software or internal interrupts. The ability to initiate an external hardware interrupt at the INTR input is enabled by setting IF or masked out by resetting it. Through software, this can be done by executing the STI instruction or the CLI instruction, respectively.

During the initiation sequence of an interrupt service routine, the MPU automatically clears IF. This masks out the occurrence of any additional external hardware interrupt. If necessary, the interrupt flag bit can be set with an STI instruction at the beginning of the service routine to reenable the INTR input. Otherwise, it should be set at the end of the service routine to reenable the external hardware interrupt interface.

8.6 EXTERNAL HARDWARE INTERRUPT INTERFACE

Up to this point, we have introduced the interrupts of the 8088, its pointer table, interrupt instructions, and masking of interrupts. Let us now look at the *external hardware interrupt interface* of the 8088 and 8086 microcomputer systems.

Minimum System Interrupt Interface

We will begin with an 8088 microcomputer configured for the minimum system mode. The interrupt interface for this system is illustrated in Fig. 8.3(a). Here we see that it includes the multiplexed address/data bus and dedicated interrupt signal

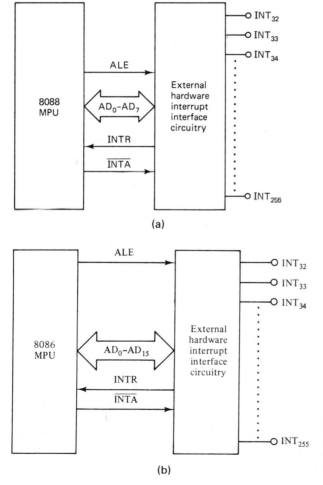

(a)

(b)

Figure 8.3 (a) Minimum-mode 8088 system external hardware interrupt interface. (b) Minimum-mode 8086 system external hardware interrupt interface.

lines INTR and $\overline{\text{INTA}}$. Moreover, external circuitry is required to interface the interrupt inputs, INT_{32} through INT_{255}, to the 8088's interrupt interface. This interface circuitry must identify which of the pending active interrupts has the highest priority and then pass its type number to the 8088.

In this circuit we see that the key interrupt interface signals are *interrupt request* (INTR) and *interrupt acknowledge* ($\overline{\text{INTA}}$). The logic level input at the INTR line signals the 8088 that an external device is requesting service. The 8088 samples this input during the last clock period of each instruction execution cycle. Logic 1 represents an active interrupt request. INTR is *level triggered;* therefore, its active 1 level must be maintained until tested by the 8088. If it is not maintained, the request for service may not be recognized. Moreover, the 1 at INTR must be removed before the service routine runs to completion; otherwise, the same interrupt may be acknowledged a second time.

When an interrupt request has been recognized by the 8088, it signals this fact to external circuitry. It does this with pulses to logic 0 at its $\overline{\text{INTA}}$ output. Actually, there are two pulses produced at $\overline{\text{INTA}}$ during the *interrupt acknowledge bus cycle*. The first pulse signals external circuitry that the interrupt request has been acknowledged and to prepare to send its type number to the 8088. The second pulse tells the external circuitry to put the type number on the data bus.

Notice that the lower eight lines of the address/data bus, AD_0 through AD_7, are also part of the interrupt interface. During the second cycle in the interrupt acknowledge bus cycle, external circuitry must put an 8-bit type number on bus lines AD_0 through AD_7. The 8088 reads this number off the bus to identify which external device is requesting service. It uses the type number to generate the address of the interrupt's vector in the pointer table and to read the new values of CS and IP into the corresponding internal registers. CS and IP are transferred over the data bus. The old values of CS, IP, and the internal flags are automatically pushed to the stack part of memory.

Figure 8.3(b) shows the interrupt interface of a minimum-mode 8086 microcomputer system. Comparing this diagram to that in Fig. 8.3(a), we find that the only difference is that the data path between the MPU and interrupt interface is now 16 bits in length.

Maximum-Mode Interrupt Interface

The maximum-mode interrupt interface of the 8088 microcomputer is shown in Fig. 8.4(a). The primary difference between this interrupt interface and that shown for the minimum mode in Fig. 8.3(a) is that the 8288 bus controller has been added. In the maximum mode system, the bus controller produces the $\overline{\text{INTA}}$ and ALE signals. Whenever the 8088 outputs an interrupt acknowledge bus status code, the 8288 generates pulses at its $\overline{\text{INTA}}$ output to signal external circuitry that the 8088 has acknowledged an interrupt request. This interrupt acknowledge bus status code, $\overline{S}_2\overline{S}_1\overline{S}_0 = 000$, is highlighted in Fig. 8.5.

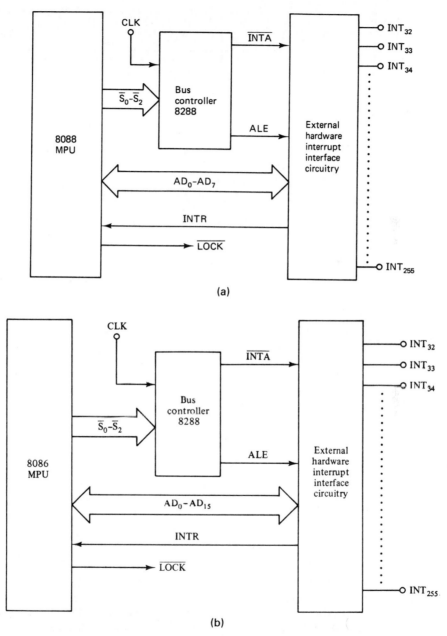

Figure 8.4 (a) Maximum-mode 8088 system external hardware interrupt interface. (b) Maximum-mode 8086 system external hardware interrupt interface.

Status inputs			CPU cycle	8288 command
$\overline{S}_2$	$\overline{S}_1$	$\overline{S}_0$		
0	0	0	Interrupt acknowledge	$\overline{\text{INTA}}$
0	0	1	Read I/O port	$\overline{\text{IORC}}$
0	1	0	Write I/O port	$\overline{\text{IOWC}}$, $\overline{\text{AIOWC}}$
0	1	1	Halt	None
1	0	0	Instruction fetch	$\overline{\text{MRDC}}$
1	0	1	Read memory	$\overline{\text{MRDC}}$
1	1	0	Write memory	$\overline{\text{MWTC}}$, $\overline{\text{AMWC}}$
1	1	1	Passive	None

Figure 8.5 Interrupt bus status code. (Reprinted by permission of Intel Corp. Copyright/Intel Corp. 1979)

A second change in Fig. 8.4(a) is that the 8088 provides a new signal for the interrupt interface. This output, which is labeled $\overline{\text{LOCK}}$, is called the *bus priority lock* signal. $\overline{\text{LOCK}}$ is applied as an input to the *bus arbiter circuit*. In response to this signal, the arbitration logic ensures that no other device can take over control of the system bus until the interrupt acknowledge bus cycle is completed.

Figure 8.4(b) illustrates the interrupt interface of a maximum-mode 8086 microcomputer system. Again, the only difference between this circuit and that of the 8088 microcomputer is that the complete 16-bit data bus is used to transfer data between the MPU and interrupt interface circuits.

8.7 EXTERNAL HARDWARE INTERRUPT SEQUENCE

In the preceding section we showed the interrupt interfaces for the external hardware interrupts in minimum-mode and maximum-mode 8088 and 8086 microcomputer systems. Now we will continue by describing in detail the events that take place during the interrupt request, interrupt acknowledge bus cycle, and device service routine. The events that take place in the external hardware interrupt service sequence are identical for an 8088-based or 8086-based microcomputer system. Here we will describe this sequence relative to the 8088 microcomputer.

The interrupt sequence begins when an external device requests service by activating one of the interrupt inputs, INT_{32} through INT_{255}, of the 8088's external interrupt interface circuit in Fig. 8.3. For example, the INT_{50} input could be switched to the 1 logic level. This signals that the device associated with priority level 50 wants to be serviced.

The external circuitry evaluates the priority of this input. If there is no interrupt already in progress or if this interrupt is of higher priority than that which is presently active, the external circuitry must issue a request for service to the MPU.

Let us assume that INT_{50} is the only active interrupt input. In this case, the external circuitry switches INTR to logic 1. This tells the 8088 that an interrupt is pending for service. To ensure that it is recognized, the external circuitry must maintain INTR active until an interrupt acknowledge pulse is issued by the 8088.

Figure 8.6 is a flow diagram that outlines the events that take place when the 8088 processes an interrupt. The 8088 tests for an active interrupt during the last clock state of the current instruction. Note that it tests first for the occurrence of an internal interrupt, then the occurrence of the nonmaskable interrupt, and finally checks the logic level of INTR to determine if an external hardware interrupt has occurred.

If INTR is logic 1, a request for service is recognized. Before the 8088 initiates the interrupt acknowledge sequence, it checks the setting of IF (interrupt flag). If it is logic 0, external interrupts are masked out and the request is ignored. In this case, the next sequential instruction is executed. On the other hand, if IF is at logic 1, external hardware interrupts are enabled and the service routine is to be initiated.

Let us assume that IF is set to permit interrupts to occur when INTR is tested as 1. The 8088 responds by initiating the interrupt acknowledge bus cycles. This bus cycle is illustrated in Fig. 8.7. During T_1 of the first bus cycle, we see that a pulse is output on ALE, but at the same time the address/data bus is put in the high-Z state. It stays in this state for the rest of the bus cycle. During periods T_2 and T_3, $\overline{INTA}$ is switched to logic 0. This signals external circuitry that the request for service has been granted. In response to this pulse, the logic 1 at INTR can be removed.

The signal identified as $\overline{LOCK}$ is produced only in maximum-mode systems. Notice that $\overline{LOCK}$ is switched to logic 0 during T_2 of the first INTA bus cycle and is maintained at this level until T_2 of the second INTA bus cycle. During this time, the 8088 is prevented from accepting a HOLD request. Moreover, the $\overline{LOCK}$ output is used in external logic to lock other devices off the system bus, thereby ensuring that the interrupt acknowledge sequence continues through to completion without interruption.

During the second interrupt acknowledge bus cycle, a similar signal sequence occurs. However, this interrupt acknowledge pulse tells the external circuitry to put the type number of the active interrupt on the data bus. External circuitry gates one of the interrupt codes $32 = 20_{16}$ through $255 = FF_{16}$ onto data bus lines AD_0 through AD_7. This code must be valid during periods T_3 and T_4 of the second interrupt acknowledge bus cycle.

The 8088 sets up its bus control signals for an input data transfer to read the type number off the data bus. $DT/\overline{R}$ and $\overline{DEN}$ are set to logic 0 to enable the external data bus circuitry and set it for input of data. Also, $IO/\overline{M}$ and $\overline{SSO}$ are set to 1, indicating that data are to be input from the interrupt interface. During this input operation, the byte interrupt code is read off the data bus. For the case of INT_{50}, this code would be $00110010_2 = 32_{16}$. This completes the interrupt acknowledge part of the interrupt sequence.

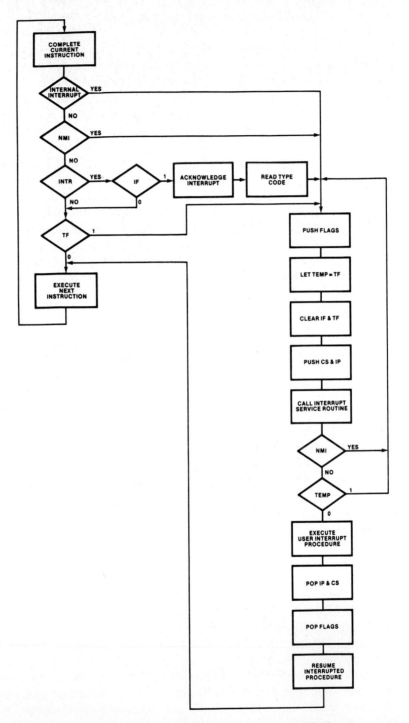

Figure 8.6 Interrupt processing sequence of the 8088 and 8086 microprocessors. (Reprinted by permission of Intel Corp. Copyright/Intel Corp. 1979)

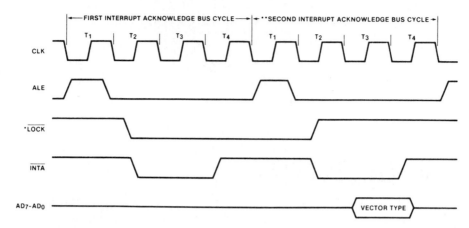

Figure 8.7   Interrupt acknowledge bus cycle. (Reprinted by permission of Intel Corp. Copyright/Intel Corp. 1979)

Looking at Fig. 8.6, we see that the 8088 first saves the contents of the flag register by pushing it to the stack. This requires two write cycles and two bytes of stack. Then it clears IF. This disables further external interrupts from requesting service. Actually, the TF flag is also cleared. This disables the single-step mode of operation if it happens to be active. Next, the 8088 automatically pushes the contents of the CS and IP onto the stack. This requires four write cycles to take place over the system bus. The current value of the stack pointer is decremented by two as each of these values is put onto the top of the stack.

Now the 8088 knows the type number associated with the external device that is requesting service. It must next call the service routine by fetching the vector that defines its starting point from memory. The type number is internally multiplied by 4, and this result is used as the address of the first word of the interrupt vector in the pointer table. Two word read operations (four bus cycles) are performed to read the two-word vector from memory. The first word, which is the lower-addressed word, is loaded into IP. The second, higher-addressed word, is loaded into CS. For instance, the vector for INT_{50} would be read from addresses $000C8_{16}$ and $000CA_{16}$.

The service routine is now initiated. That is, execution resumes with the first instruction of the service routine. It is located at the address generated from the new value in CS and IP. Figure 8.8 shows the structure of a typical interrupt service routine. The service routine must include PUSH instructions to save the contents of those internal registers that it will use. In this way, their original contents are saved in the stack during execution of the routine.

At the end of the service routine, the original program environment must be restored. This is done by first popping the contents of the appropriate registers from the stack by executing POP instructions. An IRET instruction must be executed as the last instruction of the service routine. This instruction reenables the interrupt interface and causes the old contents of the flags, CS, and IP to be

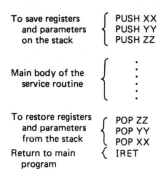

To save registers
and parameters
on the stack { PUSH XX
PUSH YY
PUSH ZZ

Main body of the
service routine { ⋮

To restore registers
and parameters
from the stack { POP ZZ
POP YY
POP XX

Return to main
program { IRET

Figure 8.8 Structure of an interrupt service routine.

popped from the stack back into the internal registers of the 8088. The original program environment has now been completely restored, and execution resumes at the point in the program where it was interrupted.

Earlier we pointed out that the events that take place during the external hardware interrupt service sequence of the 8086 microcomputer are identical to those of the 8088 microcomputer. However, because the 8086 has a 16-bit data bus, slight changes are found in the external bus cycles that are produced as part of the program context switch sequence. For example, as the interrupt's program environment is initiated, three word write cycles, instead of six byte write cycles, are required to save the old values of the flags, instruction pointer, and code segment registers on the stack. Moreover, when the new values of CS and IP are fetched from the address pointer table in memory, just two bus cycles take place. Because five bus cycles take place, not ten, the new program environment is entered faster by the 8086 microcomputer.

The same is true when the original program environment is restored at the completion of the service routine. Remember that this is done by popping the old flags, old CS, and old IP from the stack back into the MPU with an IRET instruction. This operation is performed with three word read cycles by the 8086 and six byte read cycles by the 8088.

8.8 8259A PROGRAMMABLE INTERRUPT CONTROLLER

The 8259A is an LSI peripheral IC that is designed to simplify the implementation of the interrupt interface in the 8088- and 8086-based microcomputer systems. This device is known as a *programmable interrupt controller* or *PIC*. It is manufactured using the NMOS technology.

The operation of the PIC is programmable under software control and it can be configured for a wide variety of applications. Some of its programmable features are the ability to accept level-sensitive or edge-triggered inputs, the ability to be easily cascaded to expand from 8 to 64 interrupt inputs, and its ability to be configured to implement a wide variety of priority schemes.

Block Diagram of the 8259A

Let us begin our study of the PIC with its block diagram in Fig. 8.9(a). We just mentioned that the 8259A is treated as a peripheral in the microcomputer. There-fore, its operation must be initialized by the microprocessor. The *host processor interface* is provided for this purpose. This interface consists of eight *data bus* lines D_0 through D_7 and control signals *read* ($\overline{RD}$), *write* ($\overline{WR}$), and *chip select* ($\overline{CS}$). The data bus is the path over which data are transferred between the MPU and 8259A. These data can be command words, status information, or interrupt type numbers. Control input $\overline{CS}$ must be at logic 0 to enable the host processor interface. Moreover, $\overline{WR}$ and $\overline{RD}$ signal the 8259A whether data are to be written into or read from its internal registers. They also control the timing of these data transfers.

Two other signals are identified as part of the host processor interface. They are INT and $\overline{INTA}$. Together, these two signals provide the handshake mecha-nism by which the 8259A can signal the MPU of a request for service and receive an acknowledgment that the request has been accepted. INT is the interrupt request output of the 8259A. It is applied directly to the INTR input of the 8088 or 8086. Logic 1 is produced at this output whenever the 8259A receives a valid interrupt request.

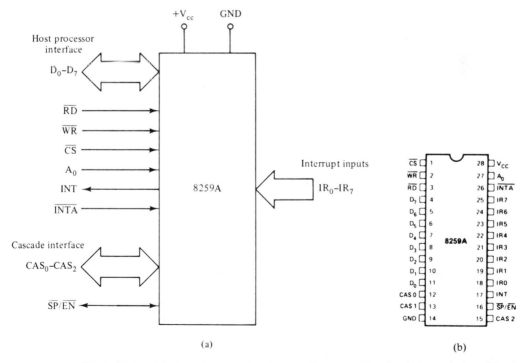

Figure 8.9 (a) Block diagram of the 8259A. (b) Pin layout. (Reprinted by permission of Intel Corp. Copyright/Intel Corp. 1979)

On the other hand, $\overline{\text{INTA}}$ is an input of the 8259A. It is connected to the $\overline{\text{INTA}}$ output of the 8088 or 8086. The MPU pulses this input of the 8259A to logic 0 twice during the interrupt acknowledge bus cycle, thereby signaling the 8259A that the interrupt request has been acknowledged and that it should output the type number of the highest-priority active interrupt on data bus lines D_0 through D_7 so that it can be read by the MPU. The last signal line involved in the host processor interface is the A_0 input. This input is normally supplied by an address line of the microprocessor such as A_0. The logic level at this input is involved in the selection of the internal register that is accessed during read and write operations.

At the other side of the block in Fig. 8.9(a), we find the eight *interrupt inputs* of the PIC. They are labeled IR_0 through IR_7. It is through these inputs that external devices issue a request for service. One of the software options of the 8259A permits these inputs to be configured for *level-sensitive* or *edge-triggered operation*. When configured for level-sensitive operation, logic 1 is the active level of the IR inputs. In this case, the request for service must be removed before the service routine runs to completion. Otherwise, the interrupt will be requested a second time and the service routine initiated again. Moreover, if the input returns to logic 0 before it is acknowledged by the MPU, the request for service will be missed.

Some external devices produce a short-duration pulse instead of a fixed logic level for use as an interrupt request signal. If the MPU is busy servicing a higher-priority interrupt when the pulse is produced, the request for service could be completely missed. To overcome this problem, the edge-triggered mode of operation is used.

Inputs of the 8259A that are set up for edge-triggered operation become active on the transition from the inactive 0 logic level to the active 1 logic level. This represents what is known as a *positive edge-triggered input*. The fact that this transition has occurred at an IR line is latched internal to the 8259A. If the IR input remains at the 1 logic level even after the service routine is completed, the interrupt is not reinitiated. Instead, it is locked out. To be recognized a second time, the input must first return to the 0 logic level and then be switched back to 1. The advantage of edge-triggered operation is that if the request at the IR input is removed before the MPU acknowledges service of the interrupt, its request is maintained latched internal to the 8259A until it can be serviced.

The last group of signals on the PIC implement what is known as the *cascade interface*. As shown in Fig. 8.9(a), it includes bidirectional *cascading bus lines* CAS_0 through CAS_2 and a multifunction control line labeled $\overline{\text{SP}/\text{EN}}$. The primary use of these signals is in cascaded systems where a number of 8259A ICs are interconnected in a master/slave configuration to expand the number of IR inputs from 8 to as high as 64.

In a cascaded system, the CAS lines of all 8259As are connected to provide a private bus between the master and slave devices. In response to the first $\overline{\text{INTA}}$ pulse during the interrupt acknowledge bus cycle, the master PIC outputs a 3-bit code on the CAS lines. This code identifies the highest-priority slave that is to be serviced. It is this device that is to be acknowledged for service. All slaves read this code off the *private cascading bus* and compare it to their internal ID code. A match condition at one slave tells the PIC that it has the highest-priority input. In response, it must put the type number of its highest-priority active input on the data bus during the second interrupt acknowledge bus cycle.

When the PIC is configured through software for the cascaded mode, the $\overline{SP}/\overline{EN}$ line is used as an input. This corresponds to its $\overline{SP}$ (*slave program*) function. The logic level applied at $\overline{SP}$ tells the device whether it is to operate as a master or slave. Logic 1 at this input designates master mode and logic 0 designates slave mode.

If the PIC is configured for single mode instead of cascade mode, $\overline{SP}/\overline{EN}$ takes on another function. In this case, it becomes an enable output that can be used to control the direction of data transfer through the bus transcciver that buffers the data bus.

A pin layout of the 8259A is given in Fig. 8.9(b).

Internal Architecture of the 8259A

Now that we have introduced the input/output signals of the 8259A, let us look at its internal architecture. Figure 8.10 is a block diagram of the PIC's internal circuitry. Here we find eight functional parts: the *data bus buffer, read/write*

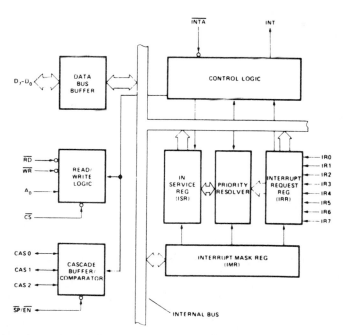

Figure 8.10   Internal architecture of the 8259A. (Reprinted by permission of Intel Corp. Copyright/Intel Corp. 1979)

logic, control logic, in-service register, interrupt request register, priority re-solver, interrupt mask register, and *cascade buffer/comparator.*

We will begin with the function of the data bus buffer and read/write logic sections. It is these parts of the 8259A that let the MPU have access to the internal registers. Moreover, they provide the path over which interrupt type numbers are passed to the microprocessor. The data bus buffer is an 8-bit bidirectional three-state buffer that interfaces the internal circuitry of the 8259A to the data bus of the MPU. The direction, timing, and source or destination for data transfers through the buffer are under control of the outputs of the read/write logic block. These outputs are generated in response to control inputs $\overline{RD}$, $\overline{WR}$, A_0, and $\overline{CS}$.

The interrupt request register, in-service register, priority resolver, and interrupt mask register are the key internal blocks of the 8259A. The interrupt mask register (IMR) can be used to enable or mask out individually the interrupt request inputs. It contains eight bits identified by M_0 through M_7. These bits correspond to interrupt inputs IR_0 through IR_7, respectively. Logic 0 in a mask register bit position enables the corresponding interrupt input and logic 1 masks it out. The register can be read from or written into under software control.

On the other hand, the interrupt request register (IRR) stores the current status of the interrupt request inputs. It also contains one bit position for each of the IR inputs. The values in these bit positions reflect whether the interrupt inputs are active or inactive.

Which of the active interrupt inputs is identified as having the highest priority is determined by the priority resolver. This section can be configured to work using a number of different priority schemes through software. Following this scheme, it identifies the highest priority of the active interrupt inputs and signals the control logic that an interrupt is active. In response, the control logic causes the INT signal to be issued to the 8088 or 8086 microprocessor.

The in-service register differs in that it stores the interrupt level that is presently being serviced. During the first $\overline{INTA}$ pulse in an interrupt acknowledge bus cycle, the level of the highest active interrupt is strobed into ISR. Loading of ISR occurs in response to output signals of the control logic section. This register cannot be written into by the microprocessor; however, its contents may be read as status.

The cascade buffer/comparator section provides the interface between master and slave 8259As. As we mentioned earlier, this interface permits easy expansion of the interrupt interface using a master/slave configuration. Each slave has an *ID code* that is stored in this section.

Programming the 8259A

The way in which the 8259A operates is determined by how the device is programmed. Two types of command words are provided for this purpose. They are the *initialization command words* (ICW) and the *operational command words*

(OCW). ICW commands are used to load the internal control registers of the 8259A. There are four such command words and they are identified as ICW_1, ICW_2, ICW_3, and ICW_4. On the other hand, the three OCW commands permit the 8088 or 8086 microprocessor to initiate variations in the basic operating modes defined by the ICW commands. These three commands are called OCW_1, OCW_2, and OCW_3.

Depending on whether the 8259A is I/O mapped or memory mapped, the MPU issues commands to the 8259A by initiating output or write cycles. This can be done by executing either the OUT instruction or MOV instruction, respectively. The address put on the system bus during the output bus cycle must be decoded with external circuitry to chip select the peripheral. When an address assigned to the 8259A is on the bus, the output of the decoder must produce logic 0 at the $\overline{CS}$ input. This signal enables the read/write logic within the PIC, and data applied at D_0 through D_7 are written into the command register within the control logic section synchronously with a write strobe at $\overline{WR}$.

The interrupt request input (INTR) of the 8088 or 8086 must be disabled whenever commands are being issued to the 8259A. This can be done by clearing the interrupt enable flag by executing the CLI (clear interrupt enable flag) instruction. After completion of the command sequence, the interrupt input must be reenabled. To do this, the microprocessor must execute the STI (set interrupt enable flag) instruction.

The flow diagram in Fig. 8.11 shows the sequence of events that must take place to initialize the 8259A with ICW commands. The cycle begins with the

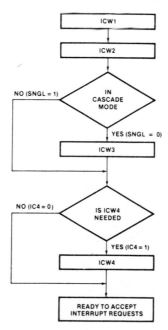

Figure 8.11 Initialization sequence of the 8259A. (Reprinted by permission of Intel Corp. Copyright/Intel Corp. 1979)

MPU outputting initialization command word ICW_1 to the address of the 8259A.

The moment that ICW_1 is written into the control logic section of the 8259A certain internal setup conditions automatically occur. First, the internal sequence logic is set up so that the 8259A will accept the remaining ICWs as designated by ICW_1. It turns out that if the least significant bit of ICW_1 is logic 1, command word ICW_4 is required in the initialization sequence. Moreover, if the next least significant bit of ICW_1 is logic 0, the command word ICW_3 is also required.

In addition to this, writing ICW_1 to the 8259A clears ISR and IMR. Also three operation command word bits, *special mask mode* (SMM) in OCW_3, *interrupt request register* (IRR) in OCW_3, and *end of interrupt* (EOI) in OCW_2, are cleared to logic 0. Furthermore, the *fully masked mode* of interrupt operation is entered with an initial priority assignment so that IR_0 is the highest-priority input and IR_7 the lowest-priority input. Finally, the edge-sensitive latches associated with the IR inputs are all cleared.

If the LSB of ICW_1 was initialized to logic 0, one additional event occurs. This is that all bits of the control register associated with ICW_4 are cleared.

In Fig. 8.11 we see that once the MPU starts initialization of the 8259A by writing ICW_1 into the control register, it must continue the sequence by writing ICW_2 and then optionally ICW_3 and ICW_4 in that order. Notice that it is not possible to modify just one of the initialization command registers. Instead, all words that are required to define the device's operating mode must be output once again.

We found that all four words need not always be used to initialize the 8259A. However, for its use in an 8088 or 8086 microcomputer system, words ICW_1, ICW_2, and ICW_4 are always required. ICW_3 is optional and is needed only if the 8259A is to function in the cascade mode.

Initialization Command Words

Now that we have introduced the initialization sequence of the 8259A, let us look more closely at the functions controlled by each of the initialization command words. We will begin with ICW_1. Its format and bit functions are identified in Fig. 8.12(a). Notice that address bit A_0 is included as a ninth bit and it must be logic 0. This corresponds to an even-address boundary.

Here we find that the logic level of the LSB D_0 of the initialization word indicates to the 8259A whether or not ICW_4 will be included in the programming sequence. As we mentioned earlier, logic 1 at D_0 (IC_4) specifies that it is needed. The next bit, D_2 (SNGL), selects between *single device* or *multidevice cascaded mode* of operation. When D_1 is set to logic 0, the internal circuitry of the 8259A is configured for cascaded mode. Selecting this state also sets up the initialization sequence such that ICW_3 must be issued as part of the initialization cycle. Bit D_2 has functions specified for it in Fig. 8.12(a). However, it can be ignored when the 8259A is being connected to the 8088/8086 and is a don't-care state. D_3, which is

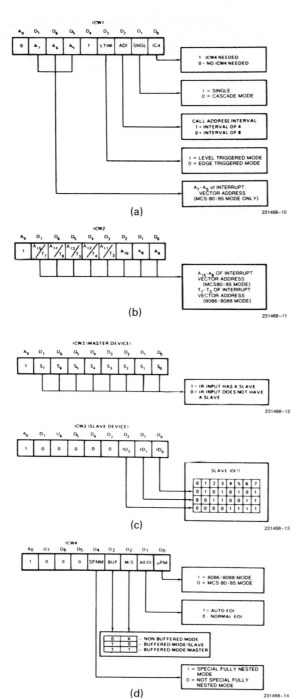

Figure 8.12   (a) ICW$_1$ format. (Reprinted by permission of Intel Corp. Copyright/Intel Corp. 1979) (b) ICW$_2$ format. (Reprinted by permission of Intel Corp. Copyright/Intel Corp. 1979) (c) ICW$_3$ format. (Reprinted by permission of Intel Corp. Copyright/Intel Corp. 1979) (d) ICW$_4$ format. (Reprinted by permission of Intel Corp. Copyright/Intel Corp. 1979)

NOTE:
Slave ID is equal to the corresponding master IR input.

labeled LTIM, defines whether the eight IR inputs operate in the level-sensitive or edge-triggered mode. Logic 1 in D_3 selects level-triggered operation and logic 0 selects edge-triggered operation. Finally, bit D_4 is fixed at the 1 logic level and the three MSBs D_5 through D_7 are not required in 8088- or 8086-based systems.

EXAMPLE 8.2

What value should be written into ICW_1 in order to configure the 8259A so that ICW_4 is needed in the initialization sequence, the system is going to use multiple 8259As, and its inputs are to be level sensitive? Assume that all unused bits are to be logic 0. Give the result in both binary and hexadecimal form.

SOLUTION Since ICW_4 is to be initialized, D_0 must be logic 1.

$$D_0 = 1$$

For cascaded mode of operation, D_1 must be 0.

$$D_1 = 0$$

And for level-sensitive inputs, D_3 must be 1.

$$D_3 = 1$$

Bits D_2 and D_5 through D_7 are don't-care states and are all made logic 0.

$$D_2 = D_5 = D_6 = D_7 = 0$$

Moreover, D_4 must be fixed at the 1 logic level.

$$D_4 = 1$$

This gives the complete command word

$$D_7D_6D_5D_4D_3D_2D_1D_0 = 00011001_2 = 19_{16}$$

The second initialization word, ICW_2, has a single function in the 8088 or 8086 microcomputer. As shown in Fig. 8.12(b), its five most significant bits D_7 through D_3 define a fixed binary code T_7 through T_3 that is used as the most significant bits of its type number. Whenever the 8259A puts the 3-bit interrupt type number corresponding to its active input onto the bus, it is automatically combined with the value T_7 through T_3 to form an 8-bit type number. The three least significant bits of ICW_2 are not used. Notice that logic 1 must be output on A_0 when this command word is put on the bus.

EXAMPLE 8.3

What should be programmed into register ICW_2 if the type numbers output on the bus by the device are to range from $F0_{16}$ through $F7_{16}$?

SOLUTION   To set the 8259A up so that type numbers are in the range of $F0_{16}$ through $F7_{16}$, its device code bits must be

$$D_7D_6D_5D_4D_3 = 11110_2$$

The lower three bits are don't-care states and all can be 0s. This gives the command word

$$D_7D_6D_5D_4D_3D_2D_1D_0 = 11110000_2 = F0_{16}$$

The information of initialization word ICW_3 is required by only those 8259As that are configured for the cascaded mode of operation. Figure 8.12(c) shows its bits. Notice that ICW_3 is used for different functions depending on whether the device is a master or slave. In the case of a master, bits D_0 through D_7 of the word are labeled S_0 through S_7. These bits correspond to IR inputs IR_0 through IR_7, respectively. They identify whether or not the corresponding IR input is supplied by either the INT output of a slave or directly by an external device. Logic 1 loaded in an S position indicates that the corresponding IR input is supplied by a slave.

On the other hand, ICW_3 for a slave is used to load the device with a 3-bit identification code $ID_2ID_1ID_0$. This number must correspond to the IR input of the master to which the slave's INT output is wired. The ID code is required within the slave so that it can be compared to the cascading code output by the master on CAS_0 through CAS_2.

EXAMPLE 8.4

Assume that a master PIC is to be configured so that its IR_0 through IR_3 inputs are to accept inputs directly from external devices, but IR_4 through IR_7 are to be supplied by the INT outputs of slaves. What code should be used for the initialization command word ICW_3?

SOLUTION   For IR_0 through IR_3 to be configured to allow direct inputs from external devices, bits D_0 through D_3 of ICW_3 must be logic 0.

$$D_3D_2D_1D_0 = 0000_2$$

The other IR inputs of the master are to be supplied by INT outputs of slaves. Therefore, their control bits must be all 1.

$$D_7D_6D_5D_4 = 1111_2$$

This gives the complete command word

$$D_7D_6D_5D_4D_3D_2D_1D_0 = 11110000_2 = F0_{16}$$

The fourth control word, ICW_4, which is shown in Fig. 8.12(d), is used to configure the device for use with the 8088 and selects various features that are available in its operation. The LSB D_0, which is called microprocessor mode (μPM), must be set to logic 1 whenever the device is connected to the 8088. The next bit, D_1, is labeled AEOI for *automatic end of interrupt*. If this mode is enabled by writing logic 1 into the bit location, the EOI (*end of interrupt*) command does not have to be issued as part of the service routine.

Of the next two bits in ICW_4, BUF is used to specify whether or not the 8259A is to be used in a system where the data bus is buffered with a bidirectional bus transceiver. When buffered mode is selected, the $\overline{SP}/\overline{EN}$ line is configured as $\overline{EN}$. As indicated earlier, $\overline{EN}$ is a control output that can be used to control the direction of data transfer through the bus transceiver. It switches to logic 0 whenever data are transferred from the 8259A to the 8088.

If buffered mode is not selected, the $\overline{SP}/\overline{EN}$ line is configured to work as the master/slave mode select input. In this case, logic 1 at the $\overline{SP}$ input selects master mode operation and logic 0 selects slave mode.

Assume that the buffered mode was selected; then the $\overline{SP}$ input is no longer available to select between the master and slave modes of operation. Instead, the MS bit of ICW_4 defines whether the 8259A is a master or slave device.

Bit D_4 is used to enable or disable another operational option of the 8259A. This option is known as the *special fully nested mode*. This function is only used in conjunction with the cascaded mode. Moreover, it is enabled only for the master 8259A, not for the slaves. This is done by setting the SFNM bit to logic 1.

The 8259A is put into the fully nested mode of operation as command word ICW_1 is loaded. When an interrupt is initiated in a cascaded system that is configured in this way, the occurrence of another interrupt at the slave corresponding to the original interrupt is masked out even if it is of higher priority. This is because the bit in ISR of the master 8259A that corresponds to the slave is already set; therefore, the master 8259A ignores all interrupts of equal or lower priority.

This problem is overcome by enabling special fully nested mode of operation at the master. In this mode, the master will respond to those interrupts that are at lower or higher priority than the active level.

The last three bits of ICW_4, D_5 through D_7, must be logic 0.

Operational Command Words

Once the appropriate ICW commands have been issued to the 8259A, it is ready to operate in the fully nested mode. Three operational command words are also provided for controlling the operation of the 8259A. These commands permit further modifications to be made to the operation of the interrupt interface after it has been initialized. Unlike the initialization sequence, which requires that the ICWs be output in a special sequence after power-up, the OCWs can be issued under program control whenever needed and in any order.

The first operational command word, OCW_1, is used to access the contents of the interrupt mask register (IMR). A read operation can be performed to the register to determine its present status. Moreover, write operations can be performed to set or reset its bits. This permits selective masking of the interrupt inputs. Notice in Fig. 8.13(a) that bits D_0 through D_7 of command word OCW_1 are identified as mask bits M_0 through M_7, respectively. In hardware, these bits correspond to interrupt inputs IR_0 through IR_7, respectively. Setting a bit to logic 1 masks out the associated interrupt input. On the other hand, clearing it to logic 0 enables the interrupt input.

For instance, writing $F0_{16} = 11110000_2$ into the register causes inputs IR_0 through IR_3 to be enabled and IR_4 through IR_7 to be disabled. Input A_0 must be logic 1 whenever the OCW_1 command is issued.

EXAMPLE 8.5

What should be the OCW_1 code if interrupt inputs IR_0 through IR_3 are to be disabled and IR_4 through IR_7 enabled?

SOLUTION   For IR_0 through IR_3 to be disabled, their corresponding bits in the mask register must be made logic 1.

$$D_3D_2D_1D_0 = 1111_2$$

On the other hand, for IR_4 through IR_7 to be enabled, D_4 through D_7 must be logic 0.

$$D_7D_6D_5D_4 = 0000_2$$

Therefore, the complete word for OCW_1 is

$$D_7D_6D_5D_4D_3D_2D_1D_0 = 00001111_2 = 0F_{16}$$

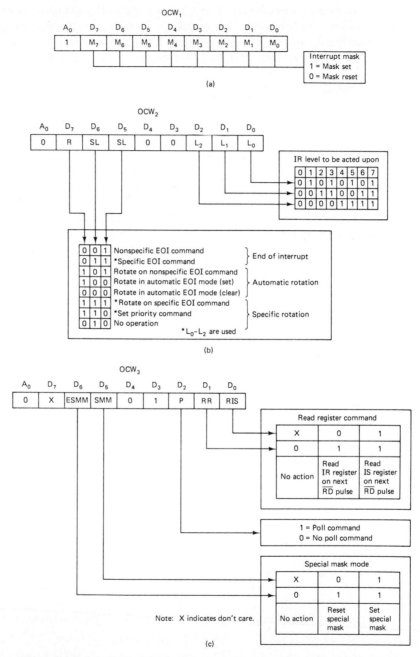

Figure 8.13 (a) OCW₁ format. (Reprinted by permission of Intel Corp. Copyright/Intel Corp. 1979) (b) OCW₂ format. (Reprinted by permission of Intel Corp. Copyright/Intel Corp. 1979) (c) OCW₃ format. (Reprinted by permission of Intel Corp. Copyright/Intel Corp. 1979)

The second operational command word, OCW_2, selects the appropriate priority scheme and assigns an IR level for those schemes that require a specific interrupt level. The format of OCW_2 is given in Fig. 8.13(b). Here we see that the three LSBs define the interrupt level. For example, using $L_2L_1L_0 = 000_2$ in these locations specifies interrupt level 0, which corresponds to input IR_0.

The other three active bits of the word D_7, D_6, and D_5 are called *rotation* (R), *specific level* (SL), and *end of interrupt* (EOI), respectively. They are used to select a priority scheme according to the table in Fig. 8.13(b). For instance, if these bits are all logic 1, the priority scheme known as *rotate on specific EOI command* is enabled. Since this scheme requires a specific interrupt, its value must be included in $L_2L_1L_0$. A_0 must be logic 0 whenever this command is issued to the 8259A.

EXAMPLE 8.6

What OCW_2 must be issued to the 8259A if the priority scheme rotate on nonspecific EOI command is to be selected?

SOLUTION   To enable the rotate on nonspecific EOI command priority scheme, bits D_7 through D_5 must be set to 101. Since a specific level does not have to be specified, the rest of the bits in the command word can be 0. This gives OCW_2 as

$$D_7D_6D_5D_4D_3D_2D_1D_0 = 10100000_2 = A0_{16}$$

The last control word, OCW_3, which is shown in Fig. 8.13(c), permits reading of the contents of the ISR or IRR registers through software, issue of the poll command, and enable/disable of the special mask mode. Bit D_1, which is called *read register* (RR), is set to 1 to initiate reading of either the in-service register (ISR) or interrupt request register (IRR). At the same time, bit D_0, which is labeled RIS, selects between ISR and IRR. Logic 0 in RIS selects IRR and logic 1 selects IRS. In response to this command, the 8259A makes the contents of the selected register available so that they can be read by the MPU.

If the next bit, D_2, in OCW_3 is logic 1, a *poll command* is issued to the 8259A. The result of issuing a poll command is that the next RD pulse to the 8259A is interpreted as an interrupt acknowledge. In turn, the 8259A causes the ISR register to be loaded with the value of the highest-priority active interrupt. After this, a *poll word* is automatically put on the data bus. The MPU must read it off the bus.

Figure 8.14 illustrates the format of the poll word. Looking at this word, we see that the MSB is labeled I for interrupt. The logic level of this bit indicates to the MPU whether or not an interrupt input was active. Logic 1 indicates that an

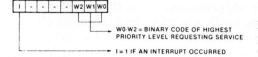

Figure 8.14 Poll word format. (Reprinted by permission of Intel Corp. Copyright/Intel Corp. 1979)

interrupt is active. The three LSBs $W_2 W_1 W_0$ identify the priority level of the highest-priority active interrupt input. This poll word can be decoded through software, and when an interrupt is found to be active, a branch is initiated to the starting point of its service routine. The poll command represents a software method of identifying whether or not an interrupt has occurred; therefore, the INTR input of the 8088 or 8086 should be disabled.

D_5 and D_6 are the remaining bits of OCW_3 for which functions are defined. They are used to enable or disable the special mask mode. ESMM (*enable special mask mode*) must be logic 1 to permit changing of the status of the special mask mode with the SMM (*special mask mode*) bit. Logic 1 at SMM enables the special mask mode of operation. If the 8259A is initially configured for the fully nested mode of operation, only interrupts of higher priority are allowed to interrupt an active service routine. However, by enabling the special mask mode, interrupts of higher or lower priority are enabled, but those of equal priority remain masked out.

EXAMPLE 8.7

Write a program that will initialize an 8259A with the initialization command words ICW_1, ICW_2, and ICW_3 derived in Examples 8.2, 8.3, and 8.4, respectively. Moreover, ICW_4 is to be equal to $1F_{16}$. Assume that the 8259A resides at address $A000_{16}$ in the memory address space.

SOLUTION Since the 8259A resides in the memory address space, we can use a series of move instructions to write the initialization command words into its registers. However, before doing this, we must first disable interrupts. This is done with the instruction

```
CLI                  ;DISABLE INTERRUPTS
```

Next we will set up a data segment starting at address 00000_{16}.

```
MOV AX,0             ;CREATE A DATA SEGMENT AT 00000₁₆
MOV DS,AX
```

Now we are ready to write the command words to the 8259A.

```
        MOV AL,19H          ;LOAD ICW 1
        MOV 0A000H,AL       ;WRITE ICW 1 TO 8259A
        MOV AL,0F0H         ;LOAD ICW 2
        MOV 0A001H,AL       ;WRITE ICW 2 TO 8259A
        MOV AL,0F0H         ;LOAD ICW 3
        MOV 0A001H,AL       ;WRITE ICW 3 TO 8259A
        MOV AL,1FH          ;LOAD ICW 4
        MOV 0A001H,AL       ;WRITE ICW 4 TO 8259A
```

Initialization is now complete and the interrupts can be enabled.

```
        STI                 ;ENABLE INTERRUPTS
```

8.9 INTERRUPT INTERFACE CIRCUITS USING THE 8259A

Now that we have introduced the 8259A programmable interrupt controller, let us look at how it is used to implement the interrupt interface in 8088- and 8086-based microcomputer systems.

Figure 8.15(a) shows an interrupt interface circuit for a minimum-mode microcomputer system. Notice that data bus lines, D_0 through D_7, of the 8259A are connected directly to the 8088's multiplexed address/data bus. It is over these lines that the 8088 initializes the internal registers of the 8259A, reads the contents of these registers, and reads the type number of the active interrupt during the interrupt acknowledge bus cycle. In this circuit, the registers of the 8259A are assigned to unique memory addresses. During read or write bus cycles to one of these addresses, bits of the demultiplexed address are applied to the $\overline{CS}$ and A_0 inputs of the 8259A to enable the microprocessor interface and select the register, respectively. The 8088's read and write control signals are supplied to the $\overline{RD}$ and $\overline{WR}$ inputs of the 8259A, respectively. These signals tell whether a read or write bus operation is to take place.

Let us trace the sequence of events that takes place as a device requests service through the interrupt interface circuit. The interrupt request inputs are identified as IR_0 through IR_7 in the circuit of Fig. 8.15(a). Whenever an interrupt input becomes active and either no other interrupts are active or the priority level of the new interrupt is higher than that of the already active interrupt, the 8259A switches its INT output to logic 1. This output is returned to the INT input of the 8088, where it signals that an external device needs to be serviced. As long as the interrupt flag within the 8088 is set to 1, the interrupt interface is enabled, the interrupt request is accepted, and the interrupt acknowledge bus cycle is initiated. As a second pulse is output at $\overline{INTA}$, the 8259A is signaled to put the type number of its highest-priority active interrupt onto the data bus. The 8088 reads

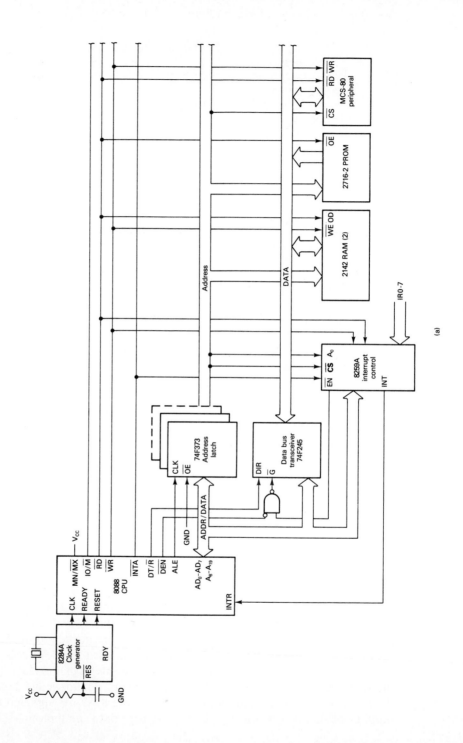

(a)

450

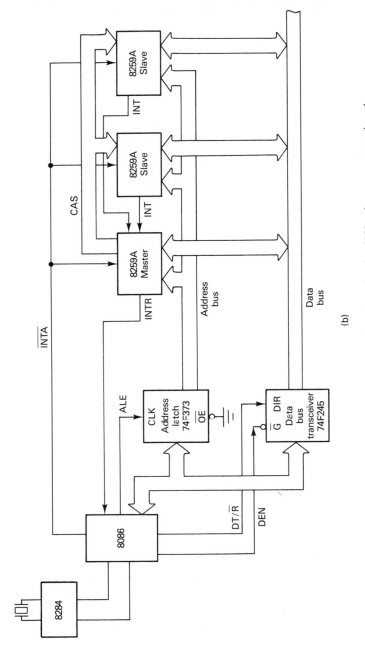

Figure 8.15 Minimum-mode interrupt interface for the 8088 microcomputer using the 8259A. (Reprinted by permission of Intel Corp. Copyright/Intel Corp. 1979) (b) Minimum-mode interrupt interface for the 8086 microcomputer system using cascaded 8259As. (Reprinted by permission of Intel Corp. Copyright/Intel Corp. 1979) (c) Master/slave connection. (Reprinted by permission of Intel Corp. Copyright/Intel Corp. 1979)

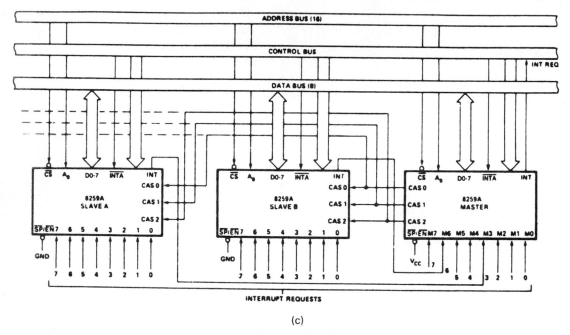

(c)

Figure 8.15 (Continued)

this number off the bus and then initiates a vectored transfer of control to the starting point of the corresponding service routine in program memory.

The circuit in Fig. 8.15(b) shows three 8259A devices connected in a *master/ slave configuration* to construct an interrupt interface for a minimum-mode 8086 microcomputer system. A request for interrupt service is initiated at an IR input of a slave. This causes the INT output of the corresponding slave to switch to logic 1. Looking at the circuit, we see that the INT outputs of the slave PICs are applied to separate interrupt inputs on the master PIC. Then the INT output of the master is supplied directly to the interrupt request input of the 8086. Unlike the 8088 minimum-mode circuit in Fig. 8.15(a), this circuit has the three 8259As connected to the demultiplexed address and data bus lines. Each device must reside at unique addresses in the I/O or memory address space. In this way, during read or write bus cycles to the interrupt interface, the address output on the bus can be decoded to produce a chip enable signal to select the appropriate device.

The last group of signals in the interrupt interface is the CAS bus. Notice that these lines on all three PICs are connected in parallel. It is over these lines that the master signals the slaves whether or not the interrupt request has been acknowledged. The master/slave connection is shown in more detail in Fig. 8.15(c). Here we find that the rightmost device is identified as the master and the devices to the left as slave A and slave B. At the interrupt request side of the devices, we find that slaves A and B are cascaded to the master 8259A by attaching their INT outputs to the M_3 (IR_3) and M_6 (IR_6) inputs, respectively. This means that the identification code for slave A is 3 and that of slave B is 6. Moreover, the CAS lines on all three PICs are tied in parallel. Over these CAS lines, the master signals the slaves whether or not their interrupt request has been acknowledged.

Whenever an interrupt input is active at the master or at a slave and the priority is higher than that of an already active interrupt, the master controller switches INTR to logic 1, this signals the 8086 that an external device needs to be serviced. If the interrupt flag within the 8086 is set to 1, the interrupt interface is enabled and the interrupt request will be accepted. Therefore, the interrupt acknowledge bus cycle sequence is initiated. As the first pulse is output at interrupt acknowledge ($\overline{INTA}$), the master PIC is signaled to output the 3-bit cascade code of the device whose interrupt request is being acknowledged on the CAS bus. The slaves read this code and compare it to their internal code. In this way, the slave corresponding to the code is signaled to output the type number of its highest-priority active interrupt onto the data bus during the second interrupt acknowledge bus cycle. The 8086 reads this number off the bus and passes program control to the beginning of the corresponding service routine.

Figure 8.16(a) and (b) illustrate similar interrupt interface implemented in a maximum-mode 8088 and 8086 microcomputer system, respectively.

EXAMPLE 8.8

Analyze the circuit in Fig. 8.17(a) and write an appropriate main program and a service routine that counts as a decimal number the positive edges of the 60 Hz clock signal applied to IR_0 input of the 8259A.

SOLUTION   The microprocessor addresses to which the 8259A in the circuit of Fig. 8.17(a) responds depend on how the $\overline{CS}$ signal for the 8259A is generated as well as the logic level of A_1 which is connected to its A_0. Notice that the A_0 of the microprocessor is not used in the circuit and therefore it is a don't care address bit. Thus if A_0 is taken as 0 the 8259A responds to

$$A_{15}\ A_{14}\ A_{13}\ A_{12}\ A_{11}\ A_{10}\ A_9\ A_8\ A_7\ A_6\ A_5\ A_4\ A_3\ A_2\ A_1\ A_0$$
$$= 111111110000000 \text{ for } A_1 = 0 \text{ and}$$
$$= 111111110000010 \text{ for } A_1 = 1.$$

These two addresses are FF00H and FF02H respectively. The address FF00H is for the ICW_1 and FF02H is for the ICW_2, ICW_3, ICW_4, and OCW_1 command words. Let us now determine the ICWs and OCWs for the 8259A.

From the circuit diagram we can see that the 8259 interfaces with the 8086 microprocessor, there is only one 8259A in the system, and the interrupt input is an edge. This information leads to the following ICW_1:

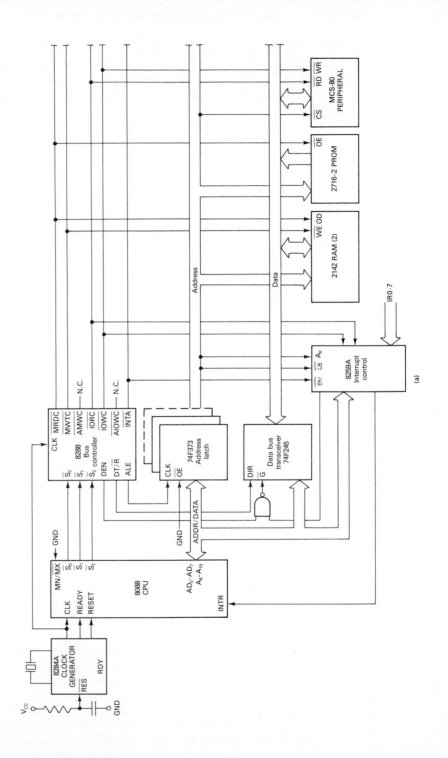

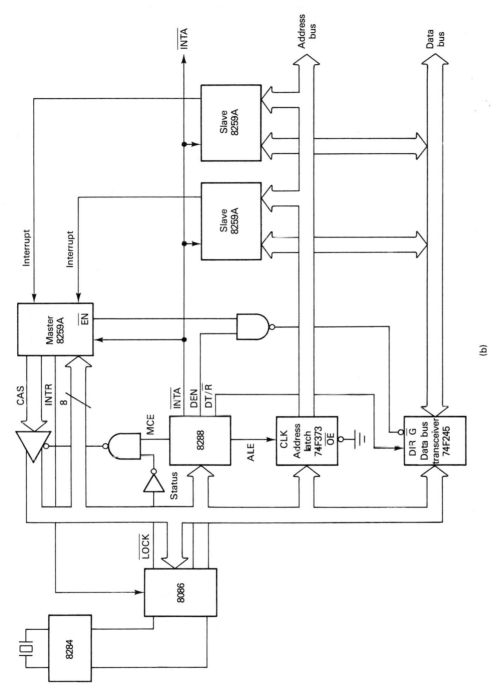

Figure 8.16 (a) Maximum-mode interrupt interface for the 8088 microcomputer using the 8259A. (Reprinted by permission of Intel Corp. Copyright/Intel Corp. 1979) (b) Maximum-mode interface for the 8083 microcomputer using cascaded 8259As. (Reprinted by permission of Intel Corp. Copyright/Intel Corp. 1979)

(b)

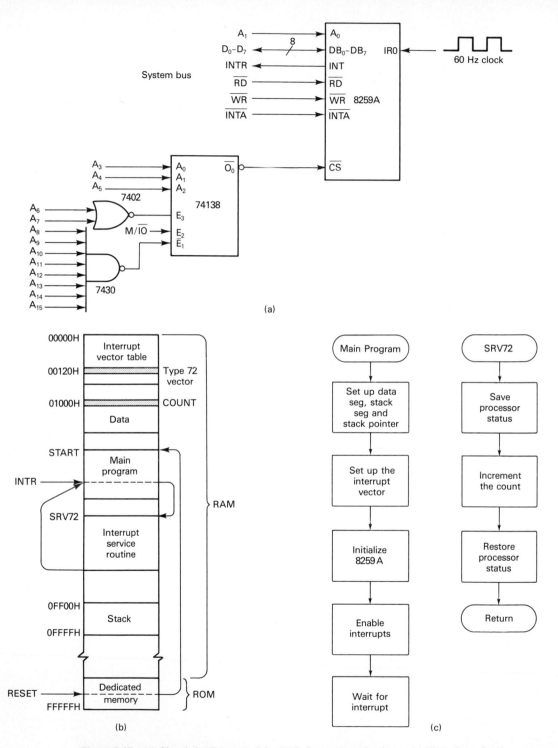

Figure 8.17 (a) Circuit for Example 8.8. (b) Software organizations. (c) Flowcharts for the main program and service routine.

$$ICW_1 = 00010011 = 13H$$

Let us assume that we will use interrupt type 72 to service an interrupt generated by an edge presented to the IR_0. This leads to the following ICW_2:

$$ICW_2 = 01001000 = 48H$$

For a single 8259A ICW_3 is not needed. To determine ICW_4 let us assume that we will use auto EOI and non buffered mode of operation. This leads to the following ICW_4:

$$ICW_4 = 00000011 = 03H$$

For OCWs we will use only OCW_1 to mask all other interrupts but IR_0. This gives OCW_1 as

$$OCW_1 = 11111110 = FEH$$

Figure 8.17(b) shows the memory organization for the software. Let us understand the information presented in this memory organization. In the interrupt vector table we need to set up the type 72 vector. The type 72 vector is located at $4 \times 72 = 288 = 120H$. At address 120H we need to place the offset of the service routine and at address 122H the code segment value of the service routine.

In the data area we need a location to keep a decimal count of the edges of the input clock. Let us assume that it is location 01000H. The stack starts at 0FF00H and ends at 0FFFFH. The start address of the main program is denoted as START and that of the service routine as SRV72.

The flowcharts in Fig. 8.17(c) are for the main program and the service routine. The main program initializes the microprocessor and the 8259A. First of all we establish various segments for data and stack. This can be done using the following instructions:

```
;MAIN PROGRAM
START:  MOV     AX,0            ;EXTRA SEGMENT AT 00000H
        MOV     ES,AX
        MOV     AX,100H         ;DATA SEGMENT AT 01000H
        MOV     DS,AX
        MOV     AX,0FF0H        ;STACK SEGMENT AT 0FF00H
        MOV     SS,AX
        MOV     SP,1000H        ;STACK END AT 10000H
```

Next we can set up the IP and CS for the type 72 vector in the interrupt vector table. This can be accomplished using the following instructions:

```
MOV   AX,OFFSET SRV72  ;GET OFFSET FOR THE SERVICE ROUTINE
MOV   [ES:120H],AX     ;SETUP THE IP
MOV   [ES:122H],CS     ;SETUP THE CS
```

Having set up the interrupt type vector let us proceed now to initialize the 8259A. Using the analyzed information the following instructions can be executed to initialize the 8259A:

```
MOV     DX,OFFOOH        ;ICW1 ADDRESS
MOV     AL,13H           ;EDGE TRIG INPUT, SINGLE 8259
OUT     DX,AL
MOV     DX,OFFO2H        ;ICW2,ICW4,OCW1 ADDRESS
MOV     AL,48H           ;ICW2, TYPE 72
OUT     DX,AL
MOV     AL,O3H           ;ICW4, AEOI, NON-BUFF MODE
OUT     DX,AL
MOV     AL,OFEH          ;OCW1, MASK ALL BUT IRO
OUT     DX,AL
STI                      ;ENABLE THE INTERRUPTS
```

Now the processor is ready to accept interrupts. We can write an endless loop to wait for the interrupt to occur. In a real situation we may be doing some other operation in which the interrupt will be received and serviced. For simplicity let us use the following instruction to wait for the interrupt;

```
HERE:   JMP     HERE     ;WAIT FOR INTERRUPT
```

Figure 8.17(c) shows the flow chart for the interrupt service routine as well. The operations shown in the flowchart can be implemented using the following instructions:

```
SRV72:  PUSH    AX            ;SAVE REGISTER TO BE USED
        MOV     AL,[COUNT]    ;GET THE COUNT
        INC     AL            ;INCREMENT THE COUNT
        DAA                   ;DECIMAL ADJUST THE COUNT
        MOV     [COUNT],AL    ;SAVE THE NEW COUNT
        POP     AX            ;RESTORE THE REGISTER USED
        IRET                  ;RETURN FROM INTERRUPT
```

8.10 SOFTWARE INTERRUPTS

The 8088 and 8086 microcomputer systems are capable of implementing up to 256 software interrupts. They differ from the external hardware interrupts in that their service routines are initiated in response to the execution of a software interrupt instruction, not an event in external hardware.

The INT n instruction is used to initiate a software interrupt. Earlier in this chapter we indicated that n represents the type number associated with the service routine. The software interrupt service routines are vectored to, using pointers from the same memory locations as the corresponding external hardware interrupts. These locations are shown in the pointer table of Fig. 8.1. Our earlier example was INT 50. It has a type number of 50 and causes a vector in program control to the service routine whose starting address is defined by the values of IP and CS stored at addresses $00C8_{16}$ through $00CA_{16}$, respectively.

The mechanism by which a software interrupt is initiated is similar to that described for the external hardware interrupts. However, no external interrupt -acknowledge bus cycles are initiated. Instead, control is passed to the start of the service routine immediately upon completion of execution of the interrupt instruction. As usual, the old flags, old CS, and old IP are automatically saved on the stack, and then IF and trap flag (TF) are cleared.

If necessary, the contents of other internal registers can be saved on the stack by including the appropriate PUSH instructions at the beginning of the service routine. Toward the end of the service routine, POP instructions must be included to restore these registers. Finally, IRET instruction is included to restore the original program environment.

Software interrupts are of higher priority than the external interrupts and are not masked out by IF. The software interrupts are actually *vectored subroutine calls*. A common use of these software routines is as *emulation routines* for more complex functions. For instance, INT_{50} could define a *floating-point addition instruction* and INT_{51} a *floating-point subtraction instruction*. These emulation routines are written using assembly language instructions, are assembled into machine code, and then are stored in the main memory of the 8088 microcomputer system. Other examples of their use are for *supervisor calls* from an operating system and for *testing* of external hardware interrupt service routines.

8.11 NONMASKABLE INTERRUPT

The nonmaskable interrupt (NMI) is another interrupt that is initiated from external hardware. However, it differs from the other external hardware interrupts in several ways. First, it cannot be masked out with the IF flag. Second, requests for service by this interrupt are signaled to the 8088 or 8086 microprocessor by applying logic 1 at the NMI input, not the INTR input. Third, the NMI input is positive edge triggered. Therefore, a request for service is latched internal to the MPU.

If the contents of the NMI latch are sampled as being active for two consecutive clock cycles, it is recognized and the nonmaskable interrupt sequence initiated. Initiation of NMI causes the current flags, current CS, and current IP to be pushed onto the stack. Moreover, the interrupt enable flag is cleared to disable all external hardware interrupts and the trap flag is cleared to disable the single-step mode of operation.

As shown in Fig. 8.1, NMI has a dedicated type number. It automatically vectors from the type 2 vector location in the pointer table. This vector is stored in memory at word addresses 0008_{16} and $000A_{16}$.

Typically, the NMI is assigned to hardware events that must be responded to immediately. Two examples are the detection of a power failure and detection of a memory read error.

8.12 RESET

The RESET input provides hardware means for initializing the 8088 or 8086 microcomputer. This is typically done at power-up to provide an orderly start-up of the system.

Figure 8.18(a) shows that the reset interface of the 8088 includes part of the 8284 clock generator device. The 8284 contains circuitry that makes it easy to implement the hardware reset function. Notice that the $\overline{\text{RES}}$ input (pin 11) of the clock generator is attached to an *RC* circuit. The signal at $\overline{\text{RES}}$ is applied to the input of a Schmitt trigger circuit. If the voltage across the capacitor is below the

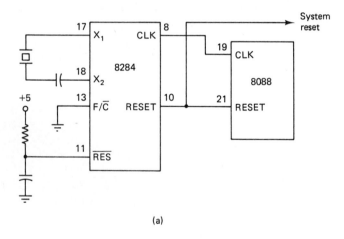

(a)

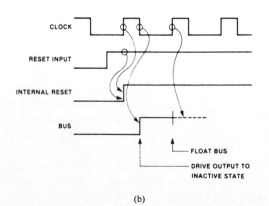

(b)

Figure 8.18 (a) Reset interface of the 8088. (Reprinted by permission of Intel Corp. Copyright/Intel Corp. 1979) (b) Reset timing sequence. (Reprinted by permission of Intel Corp. Copyright/Intel Corp. 1979)

1-logic-level threshold of the Schmitt trigger, the RESET output (pin 10) stays at logic 1. This output is supplied to the RESET input at pin 21 of the 8088. It can also be applied in parallel to reset inputs on LSI peripheral devices so that they are also initialized at power-on.

At power-on, $\overline{RES}$ of the 8284 is shorted to ground through the capacitor. This represents logic 0 at the input of the Schmitt trigger and RESET switches to logic 1. At the RESET input of the 8088, this signal is synchronized to the 0-to-1 edge of CLK. This is shown in the waveforms of Fig. 8.18(b). RESET must be held at logic 1 for a minimum of four clock cycles; otherwise, it will not be recognized.

The 8088 terminates operation on the 0-to-1 edge of the internal reset signal. Its bus is put in the high-Z state and the control signals are switched to their inactive states. These signal states are summarized in Fig. 8.19(a). Here we see that in a minimum-mode system, signals AD_0 through AD_7, A_8 through A_{15}, and $A_{16}/\overline{S_3}$ through $A_{19}/\overline{S_6}$, are immediately put in the high-Z state. On the other hand, signal lines $\overline{SSO}$, $IO/\overline{M}$, $DT/\overline{R}$, $\overline{DEN}$, $\overline{WR}$, $\overline{RD}$, and $\overline{INTA}$ are first forced to logic 1 for one clock interval and then they are put in the high-Z state synchronously with the positive edge of the next clock pulse. Moreover, signal lines ALE and HLDA are forced to their inactive 0 logic level. The 8088 remains in this state until the RESET input is returned to logic 0.

The hardware of the reset interface in an 8086 microcomputer system is identical to that just shown for the 8088 microprocessor. In fact, the reset and clock inputs, which are found at pins 21 and 19 of the 8088, respectively, in Fig. 8.18(a), are at these same pins on the 8086. Moreover, the waveforms given in Fig. 8.18(b) also describe the timing sequence that occurs when the reset input of the 8086 is activated. Remember that the 8086 produces some different signals than the 8088. For example, it has a $\overline{BHE}$ output instead of an $\overline{SSO}$ output. The state of the 8086's bus and control signals during reset is shown in Fig. 8.19(b).

In the maximum-mode system, the 8088 and 8086 respond in a similar way to an active reset request. However, this time the $\overline{S_2}\overline{S_1}\overline{S_0}$ outputs, which are inputs to the 8288 bus controller, are also forced to logic 1 and then put into the high-Z state. These inputs of the 8288 have internal pull-up resistors. Therefore, with the signal lines in the high-Z state, the input to the bus controller is $\overline{S_2}\overline{S_1}\overline{S_0} = 111$. In response, its control outputs are set to ALE = 0, DEN = 0, $DT/\overline{R}$ = 1, MCE/ $\overline{PDEN}$ = 0/1, and all its command outputs are switched to the 1 logic level. Moreover, outputs QS_0 and QS_1 of the MPU are both held at logic 0 and the $\overline{RQ/GT_0}$ and $\overline{RQ/GT_1}$, lines are held at logic 1.

When RESET returns to logic 0, the MPU initiates its internal initialization routine. The flags are all cleared; the instruction pointer is set to 0000_{16}; the CS register is set to $FFFF_{16}$; the DS register is set to 0000_{16}; the SS register is set to 0000_{16}; the ES register is set to 0000_{16}; and the instruction queue is emptied. The table in Fig. 8.20 summarizes this state.

Since the flags were all cleared as part of initialization, the external hardware interrupts are disabled. Moreover, the code segment register contains $FFFF_{16}$

Signals	Condition
AD_{7-0}	Three-state
A_{15-8}	Three-state
A_{19-16}/S_{6-3}	Three-state
$\overline{SSO}$	Driven to 1, then three-state
$\overline{S}_2/(IO/\overline{M})$	Driven to 1, then three-state
$\overline{S}_1/(DT/\overline{R})$	Driven to 1, then three-state
$\overline{S}_0/\overline{DEN}$	Driven to 1, then three-state
$\overline{LOCK}/\overline{WR}$	Driven to 1, then three-state
$\overline{RD}$	Driven to 1, then three-state
$\overline{INTA}$	Driven to 1, then three-state
ALE	0
HLDA	0
$\overline{RQ}/\overline{GT}_0$	1
$\overline{RQ}/\overline{GT}_1$	1
QS_0	0
QS_1	0

(a)

Signals	Condition
AD_{15-0}	Three-state
A_{19-16}/S_{6-3}	Three-state
BHE/S_7	Three-state
$\overline{S}_2/(M/\overline{IO})$	Driven to "1" then three-state
$\overline{S}_1/(DT/\overline{R})$	Driven to "1" then three-state
$\overline{S}_0/\overline{DEN}$	Driven to "1" then three-state
$\overline{LOCK}/\overline{WR}$	Driven to "1" then three-state
$\overline{RD}$	Driven to "1" then three-state
$\overline{INTA}$	Driven to "1" then three-state
ALE	0
HLDA	0
$\overline{RQ}/\overline{GT}_0$	1
$\overline{RQ}/\overline{GT}_1$	1
QS_0	0
QS_1	0

(b)

Figure 8.19 (a) Bus and control signal status of the 8088 during system reset. (b) Bus and control signal status of the 8086 during system reset. (Reprinted by permission of Intel Corp. Copyright/Intel Corp. 1979)

and the instruction pointer contains 0000_{16}. Therefore, execution begins after reset at $FFFF0_{16}$. This location can contain an instruction that will cause a jump to the start-up program that is used to initialize the rest of the system's resources, such as I/O ports, the interrupt flag, and data memory. After system-level initiali-

CPU COMPONENT	CONTENT
Flags	Clear
Instruction Pointer	0000H
CS Register	FFFFH
DS Register	0000H
SS Register	0000H
ES Register	0000H
Queue	Empty

Figure 8.20   Internal state of the 8088/ 8086 after reset. (Reprinted by permission of Intel Corp. Copyright/Intel Corp. 1979)

zation is complete, another jump can be performed to the starting point of the microcomputer's application program.

8.13 INTERNAL INTERRUPT FUNCTIONS

Earlier we indicated that 4 of the 256 interrupts of the 8088 and 8086 are dedicated to the internal functions: divide error, overflow error, single step, and break-point. They are assigned unique type numbers, as shown in Fig. 8.21. Notice that they are the highest-priority type numbers. Moreover, in Fig. 8.6 we find that they are not masked out with the interrupt enable flag.

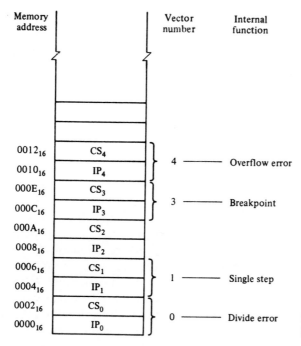

Figure 8.21   Internal interrupt vector locations.

The occurrence of any one of these internal conditions is automatically detected by the MPU and causes an interrupt of program execution and a vectored transfer of control to a corresponding service routine. During the control transfer sequence, no external bus cycles are produced. Let us now look at each of these internal functions in more detail.

Divide Error

The *divide error* function represents an error condition that can occur in the execution of the division instructions. If the quotient that results from a DIV (divide) instruction or an IDIV (integer divide) instruction is larger than the specified destination, a divide error has occurred. This condition causes automatic initiation of a type 0 interrupt and passes control to a service routine whose starting point is defined by the values of IP_0 and CS_0 at addresses 0000_{16} and 0002_{16}, respectively, in the pointer table.

Overflow Error

The *overflow error* is an error condition similar to that of divide error. However, it can result from the execution of any arithmetic instruction. Whenever an overflow occurs, the overflow flag gets set. In this case, the transfer of program control to a service routine is not automatic at occurrence of the overflow condition. Instead, the INTO (interrupt on overflow) instruction must be executed to test the overflow flag and determine if the overflow service routine should be initiated. If the overflow flag is found to be set, a type 4 interrupt service routine is initiated. Its vector consists of IP_4 and CS_4, which are stored at 0010_{16} and 0012_{16}, respectively, in memory. The routine pointed to by this vector can be written to service the overflow condition. For instance, it could cause a message to be displayed to identify that an overflow has occurred.

Single Step

The *single-step* function relates to an operating option of the 8088 or 8086. If the trap flag (TF) bit is set, the single-step mode of operation is enabled. This flag bit can be set or rest under software control.

When TF is set, the MPU initiates a type 1 interrupt to the service routine defined by IP_1 and CS_1 at 0004_{16} and 0006_{16}, respectively, at the completion of execution of every instruction. This permits implementation of the single-step mode of operation so that the program can be executed one instruction at a time. For instance, the service routine could include a WAIT instruction. In this way, a transition to logic 0 at the $\overline{TEST}$ input of the 8088 or 8086 could be used as the mechanism for stepping through a program one instruction at a time. This single-step operation can be used as a valuable software debugging tool.

Breakpoint Interrupt

The *breakpoint* function can also be used to implement a software diagnostic tool. A breakpoint interrupt is initiated by execution of the breakpoint instruction (*one-byte instruction*). This instruction can be inserted at strategic points in a program that is being debugged to cause execution to be stopped. This option can be used in a way similar to that of the single-step option. The service routine could again be put in the wait state, and resumption of execution down to the next breakpoint can be initiated by applying logic 0 to the $\overline{\text{TEST}}$ input.

ASSIGNMENTS

Section 8.2

1. What are the five groups of interrupts supported on the 8088 and 8086 MPUs?
2. What name is given to the special software routine to which control is passed when an interrupt occurs?
3. List in order the interrupt groups; start with the lowest priority and end with the highest priority.
4. What is the range of type numbers assigned to the interrupts in the 8088 and 8086 microcomputer systems?
5. Is the interrupt assigned to type 21 at a higher or lower priority than the interrupt assigned to type 35?

Section 8.3

6. Where are the interrupt pointers held?
7. How many bytes of memory does an interrupt vector take up?
8. What two elements make up an interrupt vector?
9. Which interrupt function's service routine is specified by $CS_4:IP_4$?
10. The breakpoint routine in an 8086 microcomputer system starts at address $AA000_{16}$ in the code segment located at address $A0000_{16}$. Specify how the breakpoint vector will be stored in the interrupt vector table.
11. At what addresses is the interrupt vector for type 40 stored in memory?

Section 8.4

12. What does STI stand for?
13. Which type of instruction does INTO normally follow? Which flag does it test?
14. What happens when the instruction HLT is executed?

Section 8.5

15. Explain how the CLI and STI instructions can be used to mask out external hardware interrupts during the execution of an uninterruptible subroutine.

16. How can the interrupt interface be reenabled during the execution of an interrupt service routine?

Section 8.6

17. Explain the function of the INTR and $\overline{\text{INTA}}$ signals in the circuit diagram of Fig. 8.4(a).

18. Which device produces $\overline{\text{INTA}}$ in a minimum-mode 8088 microcomputer system? In a maximum-mode 8088 microcomputer system?

19. Over which data bus lines does external circuitry send the type number of the active interrupt to the 8086?

20. What bus status code is assigned to interrupt acknowledge?

Section 8.7

21. Give an overview of the events in the order they take place during the interrupt request, interrupt acknowledge, and interrupt vector-fetch cycles of an 8088 microcomputer system.

22. If an 8086-based microcomputer is running at 10 MHz with two wait states, how long does it take to perform the interrupt acknowledge bus cycle sequence?

23. How long does it take the 8086 in problem 22 to push the values of the flags CS and IP to the stack? How much stack space do these values use?

24. How long does it take the 8086 in problem 22 to fetch its vector from memory?

Section 8.8

25. Specify the value of ICW_1 needed to configure an 8259A as follows: ICW_4 not needed, single-device interface, and edge-triggered inputs.

26. Specify the value of ICW_2 if the type numbers produced by the 8259A are to be in the range 70_{16} through 77_{16}.

27. Specify the value of ICW_4 so that the 8259A is configured for use in an 8086 system, with normal EOI, buffered-mode master, and special fully nested mode disabled.

28. Write a program that will initialize an 8259A with the initialization command words derived in problems 25, 26, and 27. Assume that the 8259A resides at address $0A000_{16}$ in the memory address space.

29. Write an instruction that when executed will read the contents of OCW_1 and place it in the AL register. Assume that the 8259A has been configured by the software of problem 28.

30. What priority scheme is enabled if OCW_2 equals 67_{16}?

31. Write an instruction sequence that when executed will toggle the state of the read register bit in OCW_3. Assume that the 8259A is located at memory address $0A000_{16}$.

Section 8.9

32. How many interrupt inputs can be directly accepted by the circuit in Fig. 8.15(a)?

33. How many interrupt inputs can be directly accepted by the circuit in Fig. 8.15(b)?

34. Summarize the interrupt request/acknowledge handshake sequence for an interrupt initiated at an input to slave B in the circuit of Fig. 8.16(b).

Section 8.10

35. Give another name for a software interrupt.

36. If the instruction INT 80 is to pass control to a subroutine at address $A0100_{16}$ in the code segment starting at address $A0000_{16}$, what vector should be loaded into the interrupt vector table?

37. At what address would the vector for the instruction INT 80 be stored in memory?

Section 8.11

38. What type number and interrupt vector table addresses are assigned to NMI?

39. What are the key differences between NMI and the other external-hardware-initiated interrupts?

40. Give a common use of the NMI input.

Section 8.12

41. What device is normally used to generate the signal for the RESET input of the 8088?

42. List the states of the address/data bus lines and control signals $\overline{BHE}$, ALE, $\overline{DEN}$, DT/$\overline{R}$, $\overline{RD}$, and $\overline{WR}$, in a minimum-mode 8086 system when reset is at its active level.

43. To what address does a reset operation pass control?

44. Write a reset subroutine that initializes the block of memory locations from address $0A000_{16}$ to $0A100_{16}$ to zero. The initialization routine is at address 01000_{16}.

Section 8.13

45. List the internal interrupts serviced by the 8088.

46. Which vector numbers are reserved for internal interrupts?

47. What mode of operation is enabled with the trap flag? Which pointer holds the entry point for this service routine?

48. If the starting point of the service routine for problem 47 is defined by CS:IP = A000H: 0200H, at what addresses in memory are the values of CS and IP held? At what physical address does the service routine start?

IBM PC Microcomputer Hardware

9.1 INTRODUCTION

Having learned about the 8088 and 8086 microprocessors, their memory, input/output, and interrupt interfaces, we now turn our attention to a microcomputer system designed using this hardware. The microcomputer we will study in this chapter is the one found in the IBM PC, the popular personal computer manufactured by IBM Corporation. The material covered in this chapter is organized as follows:

1. Architecture of the IBM PC system processor board
2. System processor circuitry
3. Wait state logic and NMI circuitry
4. I/O and memory chip select circuitry
5. Memory circuitry
6. Direct memory access circuitry
7. Timer circuitry
8. I/O circuitry
9. I/O channel interface
10. High-integration PCXT compatible peripheral ICs

9.2 ARCHITECTURE OF THE IBM PC SYSTEM PROCESSOR BOARD

The IBM PC is a practical application of the 8088 microprocessor and its peripheral chip set as a general-purpose microcomputer. A block diagram of the system processor board (main circuit board) of the PC is shown in Fig. 9.1(a). This diagram identifies the major functional elements of the PC: MPU, PIC, DMA, PIT, PPI, ROM, and RAM. We will describe the circuitry used in each of these blocks in detail in the following sections of this chapter; however, for now let us begin here with an overview of the architecture of the PC's microcomputer system.

The heart of the PC's system processor board is the 8088 microprocessor unit (MPU). It is here that instructions of the program are fetched and executed. To interface to the peripherals and other circuitry such as memory, the 8088 microprocessor generates address, data, status, and control signals. Together these signals form what is called the *local bus* in Fig. 9.1(a). Notice that the local address and data bus lines are both buffered and demultiplexed to provide a separate 20-bit *system address bus* and 8-bit *system data bus*.

At the same time, the status and control lines of the local bus are decoded by the bus controller to generate the *system control bus*. This control bus consists of memory and I/O read and write control signals. The bus controller also produces the signals that control the direction of data transfer through the data bus buffers, that is, the signals needed to make the data bus lines work as inputs to the microprocessor during memory and I/O read operations and as outputs during write operations.

The operation of the microprocessor and other devices in a microcomputer system must be synchronized. The circuitry in the clock generator block of the PC in Fig. 9.1(a) generates clock signals for this purpose. The clock generator section also produces a power-on reset signal that is needed for initialization of the microprocessor and peripherals at power-up. Moreover, the clock generator section works in conjunction with the wait state logic to synchronize the MPU to slow peripheral devices. In Fig. 9.1(a), we see that the wait state logic circuitry monitors the system control bus signals and generates a wait signal for input to the clock generator. In turn, the clock generator synchronizes the wait input to the system clock to produce a ready signal at its output. This ready signal is input to the 8088 MPU and provides the ability to automatically extend bus cycles that are performed to slow devices by inserting wait states.

The memory subsystem of the PC system processor board we are studying in this chapter has 256K bytes of dynamic R/W memory (RAM) and 48K bytes of read-only memory (ROM). A memory map for the PC's memory is shown in Fig. 9.1(b). From the map, we find that the RAM address range is from 00000_{16} through $3FFFF_{16}$. This part of the memory subsystem can be implemented using 64K $\times$ 1-bit or 256K $\times$ 1-bit dynamic RAMs and is used to store operating system routines, application programs, and data that are to be processed. These programs and data are typically loaded into RAM from a mass storage device such as a diskette or hard disk.

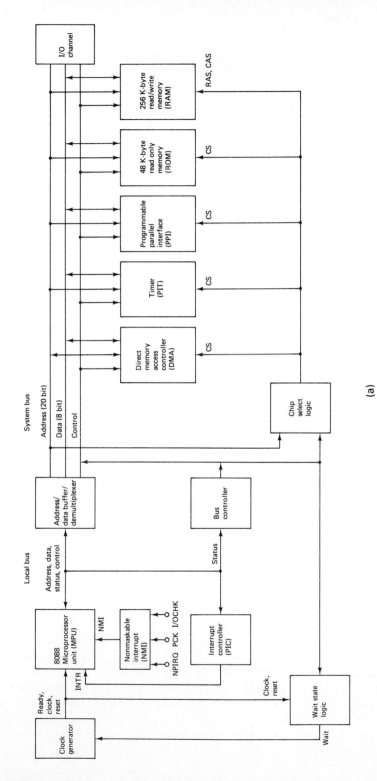

Figure 9.1 (a) IBM PC microcomputer block diagram. (b) Memory map. (c) PC system processor board peripheral addresses. (d) 8255A I/O map. (e) Interrupts. (Parts b, c, d, and e courtesy of International Business Machines Corporation)

(a)

Start Address		Function
Decimal	Hex	
0	00000	
16K	04000	
32K	08000	
48K	0C000	
64K	10000	
80K	14000	
96K	18000	
112K	1C000	64 to 256K Read/Write Memory
128K	20000	on System Board
144K	24000	
160K	28000	
176K	2C000	
192K	30000	
208K	34000	
224K	38000	
240K	3C000	
256K	40000	
272K	44000	
288K	48000	
304K	4C000	
320K	50000	
336K	54000	
352K	58000	
368K	5C000	
384K	60000	
400K	64000	
416K	68000	Up to 384K Read/Write
432K	6C000	Memory in I/O Channel
448K	70000	Up to 384K in I/O Channel
464K	74000	
480K	78000	
496K	7C000	
512K	80000	
528K	84000	
544K	88000	
560K	8C000	
576K	90000	
592K	94000	
608K	98000	
624K	9C000	

(b)

Figure 9.1 (Continued)

Start Address		Function
Decimal	**Hex**	
640K	A0000	
656K	A4000	
672K	A8000	128K Reserved
688K	AC000	
704K	B0000	Monochrome
720K	B4000	
736K	B8000	Color/Graphics
752K	BC000	
768K	C0000	
784K	C4000	
800K	C8000	Fixed Disk Control
816K	CC000	
832K	D0000	
848K	D4000	192K Read Only Memory
864K	D8000	Expansion and Control
880K	DC000	
896K	E0000	
912K	E4000	
928K	E8000	
944K	EC000	
960K	F0000	Reserved
976K	F4000	
992K	F8000	48K Base System ROM
1008K	FC000	

(b)

Figure 9.1 (Continued)

Hex Range	Usage
000-00F	DMA Chip 8237A-5
020-021	Interrupt 8259A
040-043	Timer 8253-5
060-063	PPI 8255A-5
080-083	DMA Page Registers
0Ax*	NMI Mask Register
0Cx	Reserved
0Ex	Reserved
100-1FF	Not Usable
200-20F	Game Control
210-217	Expansion Unit
220-24F	Reserved
278-27F	Reserved
2F0-2F7	Reserved
2F8-2FF	Asynchronous Communications (Secondary)
300-31F	Prototype Card
320-32F	Fixed Disk
378-37F	Printer
380-38C**	SDLC Communications
380-389**	Binary Synchronous Communications (Secondary)
3A0-3A9	Binary Synchronous Communications (Primary)
3B0-3BF	IBM Monochrome Display/Printer
3C0-3CF	Reserved
3D0-3DF	Color/Graphics
3E0-3F7	Reserved
3F0-3F7	Diskette
3F8-3FF	Asynchronous Communications (Primary)

* At power-on time, the Non Mask Interrupt into the 8088 is masked off. This mask bit can be set and reset through system software as follows:

Set mask: Write hex 80 to I/O Address hex A0 (enable NMI)

Clear mask: Write hex 00 to I/O Address hex A0 (disable NMI)

** SDLC Communications and Secondary Binary Synchronous Communications cannot be used together because their hex addresses overlap.

(c)

Figure 9.1 (Continued)

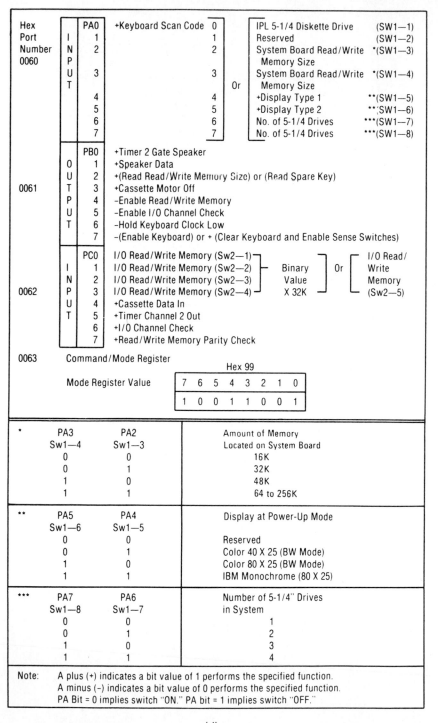

Hex Port Number 0060	INPUT	PA0	+Keyboard Scan Code	0		IPL 5-1/4 Diskette Drive	(SW1—1)
		1		1		Reserved	(SW1—2)
		2		2		System Board Read/Write	*(SW1—3)
						Memory Size	
		3		3	Or	System Board Read/Write	*(SW1—4)
						Memory Size	
		4		4		+Display Type 1	**(SW1—5)
		5		5		+Display Type 2	**(SW1—6)
		6		6		No. of 5-1/4 Drives	***(SW1—7)
		7		7		No. of 5-1/4 Drives	***(SW1—8)

0061	OUTPUT	PB0	+Timer 2 Gate Speaker
		1	+Speaker Data
		2	+(Read Read/Write Memory Size) or (Read Spare Key)
		3	+Cassette Motor Off
		4	−Enable Read/Write Memory
		5	−Enable I/O Channel Check
		6	−Hold Keyboard Clock Low
		7	−(Enable Keyboard) or + (Clear Keyboard and Enable Sense Switches)

0062	INPUT	PC0	I/O Read/Write Memory (Sw2—1)	Binary Value X 32K	Or	I/O Read/ Write Memory (Sw2—5)
		1	I/O Read/Write Memory (Sw2—2)			
		2	I/O Read/Write Memory (Sw2—3)			
		3	I/O Read/Write Memory (Sw2—4)			
		4	+Cassette Data In			
		5	+Timer Channel 2 Out			
		6	+I/O Channel Check			
		7	+Read/Write Memory Parity Check			

0063   Command/Mode Register

Mode Register Value

Hex 99

7	6	5	4	3	2	1	0
1	0	0	1	1	0	0	1

*	PA3 Sw1—4	PA2 Sw1—3	Amount of Memory Located on System Board
	0	0	16K
	0	1	32K
	1	0	48K
	1	1	64 to 256K

**	PA5 Sw1—6	PA4 Sw1—5	Display at Power-Up Mode
	0	0	Reserved
	0	1	Color 40 X 25 (BW Mode)
	1	0	Color 80 X 25 (BW Mode)
	1	1	IBM Monochrome (80 X 25)

***	PA7 Sw1—8	PA6 Sw1—7	Number of 5-1/4" Drives in System
	0	0	1
	0	1	2
	1	0	3
	1	1	4

Note: A plus (+) indicates a bit value of 1 performs the specified function.
A minus (−) indicates a bit value of 0 performs the specified function.
PA Bit = 0 implies switch "ON." PA bit = 1 implies switch "OFF."

(d)

Figure 9.1 (Continued)

Number	Usage
NMI	Parity
0	Timer
1	Keyboard
2	Reserved
3	Asynchronous Communications (Secondary)
	SDLC Communications
	BSC (Secondary)
4	Asynchronous Communications (Primary)
	SDLC Communications
	BSC (Primary)
5	Fixed Disk
6	Diskette
7	Printer

(e)

Figure 9.1   (Continued)

Furthermore, the memory map shows that ROM is located in the address range from $F4000_{16}$ to $FFFFF_{16}$. This part of the memory subsystem contains the basic system ROM of the PC. Included in these ROMs are fixed programs such as the *BASIC interpreter, power-on system procedures,* and *I/O device drivers,* or *BIOS* as it is better known.

The chip select logic section that is shown in the block diagram of Fig. 9.1(a) is used to select and enable the appropriate peripheral or memory devices whenever a bus cycle takes place over the system bus. To select a device in the I/O address space, such as the DMA controller, timer, or PPI, it decodes the address on the system bus along with the I/O read/write control signals to generate a chip select (CS) signal for the corresponding I/O device. This chip select signal is applied to the I/O device to enable it for operation. The ROM chip selects are produced in a similar way. But this time CS is produced by decoding the address in conjunction with the memory read control signal.

The LSI peripherals included on the PC system processor board are the 8237A direct memory access (DMA) controller, 8253 programmable interval timer (PIT), 8255A programmable peripheral interface (PPI), and 8259A programmable interrupt controller (PIC). Note that each of these devices is identified with a separate block in Fig. 9.1(a). These peripherals are all located in the 8088's I/O address space, and their registers are accessed through software using the address ranges given in Fig. 9.1(c). For instance, the four registers within the PIT are located at addresses 0040_{16}, 0041_{16}, 0042_{16}, and 0043_{16}.

To support high-speed memory and I/O data transfers, the 8237A direct memory access controller is provided on the PC system board. This DMA chip contains four DMA channels, *DMA channel 0 through DMA channel 3*. One channel, DMA 0, is used to refresh the dynamic R/W memory (RAM), and the other three channels are available for use with peripheral devices. For instance, DMA 2 is used to support floppy disk drive data transfers through the I/O channel.

The 8253-based timer circuitry is used to generate time-related functions and signals in the PC. There are three 16-bit counters in the 8253, and they are driven by a 1.19-MHz clock signal. Timer 0 is used to generate an interrupt to the microprocessor approximately every 55 ms. This timing function is used by the system to keep track of time of the day. On the other hand, timer 1 is used to produce a DMA request every 15.12 μs to initiate refresh of the dynamic RAM. The last timer has multiple functions. It is used to generate programmable tones when driving the speaker and a record tone for use when sending data to the cassette for storage on tape.

The parallel I/O section of the PC's microcomputer, which is identified as PPI in Fig. 9.1(a), is implemented with the 8255A programmable peripheral interface controller. This device is configured through software to provide two 8-bit input ports and one 8-bit output port. The functions of the individual I/O lines of the PPI are given in Fig. 9.1(d). Here we see that these I/O lines are used to input data from the keyboard (keyboard scan code), output tones to the speaker (speaker data), and read in the state of memory and system configuration switches (SW1-1 through SW1-8). Through the PPI's ports, the microcomputer also controls the cassette motor and enables or disables I/O channel check. Note in Fig. 9.1(d) that switch inputs SW1-3 and SW1-4 are used to tell the MPU how much RAM is implemented on the system processor board. In the lower part of this table, we find that for a system with 64K bytes or 256K bytes they are both set to the 1 position.

The circuitry in the nonmaskable interrupt (NMI) logic block allows nonmaskable interrupt requests derived from three sources to be applied to the microprocessor. As shown in Fig. 9.1(a), these interrupt sources are the *numeric coprocessor interrupt request* (NPIRQ), *R/W memory parity check* (PCK), and *I/O channel check* (I/O CHK). If any of these inputs are active, the NMI logic outputs a request for service to the 8088 over the NMI signal line.

In addition to the nonmaskable interrupt interface, the PC architecture provides for requests for service to the MPU by interrupts at another interrupt input called *interrupt request* (INTR). Note in Fig. 9.1(a) that this signal is supplied to the 8088 by the output of the interrupt controller (PIC) block. The 8259A LSI interrupt controller that is used in the PC provides for eight additional prioritized interrupt inputs. The inputs of the interrupt controller are supplied by peripherals such as the timer, keyboard, diskette drive, printer, and communication devices. Interrupt priority assignments for these devices are given in Fig. 9.1(e). For example, the timer (actually just timer 2 of the 8253) is at priority level 0.

I/O channel, which is a collection of address, data, control, and power lines, is provided to support expansion of the PC system. The chassis of the PC has five 62-pin I/O channel card slots. In this way, the system configuration can be expanded by adding special function adapter cards, such as boards to control a monochrome or color display, floppy disk drives, a hard disk drive, expanded memory, or to attach a printer. In Fig. 9.1(b), we see that I/O channel expanded RAM resides in the part of the memory address space from 40000_{16} through $9FFFF_{16}$.

9.3 SYSTEM PROCESSOR CIRCUITRY

The system processor circuitry section of the IBM PC is shown in Fig. 9.2. It consists of the 8088 microprocessor, the 8284A clock generator, the 8288 bus controller, and the 8259A programmable interrupt controller. Here we will examine the operation of each of these sections of circuitry.

Clock Generator Circuitry

In Section 9.2, we pointed out that the clock generator circuitry serves three functions in terms of overall microcomputer system operation. They are *clock signal generation, reset signal generation,* and *ready signal generation.* Let us now explore the operation of the circuit for each of these functions in more depth.

The first function performed by the clock generator circuitry is the generation of the various clock signals that are needed to drive the 8088 microprocessor (U_3) and other circuits within the PC. As shown in Fig. 9.2, the 8284A clock generator/driver (U_{11}) has a 14.31818-MHz crystal (Y_1) connected between its X_1 and X_2 pins. This crystal causes the oscillator circuitry within the 8284A to run and generate three clock output signals. They are oscillator clock (OSC), which is 14.31818 MHz, TTL peripheral clock (PCLK), which is 2.385 MHz, and 8088 microprocessor clock (CLK88), which is 4.77 MHz. Note in Fig. 9.2 that the CLK88 output at pin 8 of the 8284A is connected to the CLK input of the 8088 at pin 19. In this way, we see that the 8088 in the IBM PC is run at 4.77 MHz.

The second purpose served by the clock generator circuitry is to generate a power-on reset signal for the system. When power is first turned on, the power supply section of the PC tells the clock generator that power is not yet stable by setting its power good (PWR GOOD) output to logic 0. Looking at Fig. 9.2, we find that this signal is applied to the $\overline{RES}$ input at pin 11 of the 8284A. Logic 0 at $\overline{RES}$ represents an active input to the power-on reset circuit within the 8284A; therefore, the RESET output at pin 10 switches to its active level, logic 1, to signal that a reset operation is to take place. Notice that the RESET output of the 8284A is applied directly to the RESET input at pin 21 of the 8088. When this input is at the 1 logic level, reset of the MPU is initiated.

As the voltage of the power supply builds up and becomes stable, the power supply switches PWR GOOD to logic 1. In response to this change in input, the RESET output of the 8284A returns to its inactive 0 logic level and the power-on reset is complete.

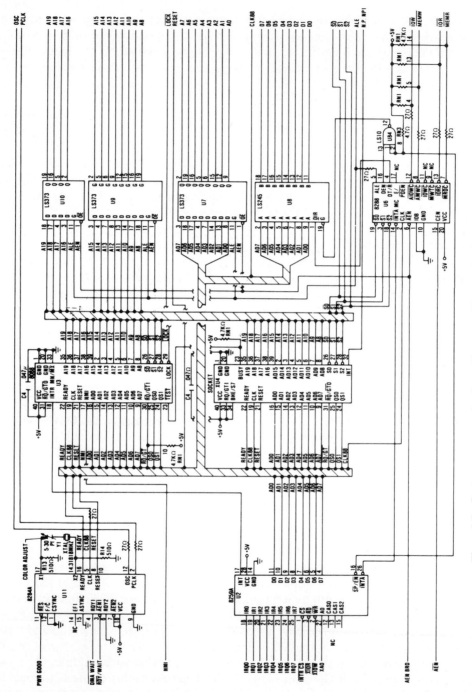

Figure 9.2 System processor circuitry. (Courtesy of International Business Machines Corporation)

478

The last function served by the clock generator circuitry is to provide for synchronization of the 8088's bus operations with its memory and I/O peripherals. This synchronization is required to support the use of slow memory or peripheral devices on the system bus and is achieved by inserting wait states into the bus cycle to extend its duration. Let us now look at how and for what devices wait states are initiated in the microcomputer of the IBM PC.

The READY input at pin 22 of the 8088 is the signal that determines whether or not wait states are inserted into a bus cycle. If this input is at the 1 logic level, bus cycles are run to completion without inserting wait states. However, if its logic level is switched to 0, wait states will be inserted into the current bus cycle until READY returns back to 1. In Fig. 9.2, we see that the READY input of the 8088 is directly supplied by the READY output (pin 5) of the 8284A. The logic level of this output is determined by inputs $\overline{\text{DMA WAIT}}$ and $\overline{\text{RDY}}$/WAIT. Whenever input $\overline{\text{DMA WAIT}}$ is logic 0, the READY output is switched to logic 0. This means that wait states are automatically inserted whenever DMA transfer bus cycles are performed. On the other hand, logic 1 at the $\overline{\text{RDY}}$/WAIT input also causes READY to switch to logic 0. This signals that a slow memory or I/O device is being accessed and wait states are needed to extend the bus cycle. In the IBM PC, both I/O and DMA data transfers have one wait state inserted into each bus cycle.

Microprocessor, System Data Bus, and Bus Controller

The 8088 microprocessor (U_3) used in the PC is rated to operate at a maximum clock rate of 5 MHz. However, we just found that the CLK88 signal that is applied to its CLK input actually runs it at 4.77 MHz. At power up, the RESET input of the 8088 is activated by the 8284A to initiate a power-on reset of the MPU. This reset operation causes the status, DS, SS, ES, and IP registers within the 8088 to be cleared, the instruction queue to be emptied, and the code segment register to be initialized to $FFFF_{16}$. When RESET returns to its inactive level, the 8088 begins to fetch instructions from program memory starting at address $FFFF0_{16}$. The instruction at this location passes control to the PC's power-up program, which causes the rest of the system resources to be initialized, diagnostic tests to be run on the hardware, and the operating system loaded from diskette or hard disk. At this point, the microcomputer is up and running. Let us now look at how it accesses memory and I/O devices.

Earlier we pointed out that the microcomputer of the IBM PC is architected to have both a multiplexed local bus and a demultiplexed system bus. In general, memory and I/O peripherals are attached to the 8088 microprocessor at the system bus. However, there are some exceptions; both the 8259A interrupt controller and 8087 numerics coprocessor are attached directly to the local bus.

In Fig. 9.2, we find that the local bus includes the 8088's multiplexed address data bus lines AD_0 through AD_7, address lines A_8 through A_{19}, and maximum-mode status lines $\overline{S}_0$ through $\overline{S}_2$. Note that the local bus lines are distributed to the

8259A programmable interrupt controller (U_2) and the socket for the 8087 numerics coprocessor (XU_4).

Let us now turn our attention to how the local bus lines are demultiplexed and decoded to form the system bus. Looking at Fig. 9.2, we see that the upper address lines are latched using 74LS373 devices U_9 and U_{10} to give system address bus lines A_8 through A_{19}. Another 74LS373 latch (U_7) is used to demultiplex low address signals A_0 through A_7 from the data signals to complete the system address bus. Finally, the separate system data bus lines, D_0 through D_7, are implemented with the 74LS245 bus transceiver U_8. These latches and transceivers also buffer the address and data bus lines to increase the drive capability at the system bus.

The 8288 bus controller U_5 monitors the codes output on the 8088's status lines $\overline{S}_0$ through $\overline{S}_2$. Based on these codes, it produces appropriate system bus control signals. For example, in Fig. 9.2 we see that the address latch enable (ALE) signal is output at pin 5 of the 8288 and supplied to the system bus. To ensure that address information is latched at the appropriate time when demultiplexing the local bus, ALE is also applied to the enable input (G) of all three 74LS373 latches. The 8288 also produces the DEN and DT/$\overline{R}$ signals that are used to control operation of the 74LS245 system data bus transceiver. Logic 1 at DEN (pin 16) signals when a data transfer is to take place over the data bus; therefore, it is inverted and applied to the enable input ($\overline{G}$) of the transceiver. On the other hand, the logic level of DT/$\overline{R}$ (pin 4) identifies whether data are to be input or output over the system bus. For this reason, it is applied to the direction (DIR) input of the 74LS245.

The 8288 also produces I/O and memory read and write control signals. The outputs $\overline{IOR}$ and $\overline{IOW}$ are used to identify I/O read and write operations, respectively. Moreover, $\overline{MEMR}$ or $\overline{MEMW}$ is output to tell that a memory read or write operation is in progress, respectively. These signals are made available on the system bus.

Address enable inputs AEN BRD and $\overline{AEN}$ are active during all DMA cycles. These signals are applied to enable inputs $\overline{AEN}$ and CEN, respectively, of the 8288 and disable it when DMA transfers are to take place over the system bus. When disabled, the 8288 stops producing the I/O and memory read/write control signals. Signal AEN BRD is also used to disable the address latches and data transceiver so that the system address lines float when the 8237A DMA controller is to use the bus.

Interrupt Controller

As shown in Fig. 9.2, an external hardware interrupt interface is implemented for the IBM PC with the 8259A programmable interrupt controller device U_2. It monitors the state of interrupt request lines IRQ_0 through IRQ_7 to determine if any external device is requesting service. In Fig. 9.1(c), the functions of the priority 0 through priority 7 interrupts are listed. For example, in this list we find that the

IRQ_0 input is used to service the 8253 timer and IRQ_1 is dedicated to servicing the keyboard.

If an interrupt request input becomes active, the PIC switches its interrupt request (INT) output to the 1 logic level. Note in Fig. 9.2 that the INT output at pin 17 of the 8259A is supplied to the INTR input at pin 18 of the 8088. At completion of execution of the current instruction, the 8088 samples the logic level of its INT input. Assuming that it is active, the 8088 responds to the request for service by outputting the interrupt acknowledge status code to the 8288 bus controller. In turn, the 8288 outputs logic 0 on interrupt acknowledge ($\overline{INTA}$), pin 14 of U_5. This signal is sent to the $\overline{INTA}$ input at pin 26 of the interrupt controller. Upon receiving this signal, the 8259A generates an active 0 level at $\overline{SP/EN}$, which, in conjunction with the data enable (DEN) output of the 8288, is used to float the system data bus lines. Now the interrupt controller outputs the type number of the active interrupt over the local data bus to the 8088. After this, the MPU fetches the vector of the service routine for this interrupt from memory, loads it into CS and IP, and then executes the service routine.

The operating configuration of the 8259A needs to be initialized at power-on of the system. This initialization is achieved by writing to the 8259A's internal registers over the local bus. Earlier we pointed out that the peripherals in the PC are located in the I/O address space. For this reason, I/O instructions are used to access the registers of the PIC. This is why its read ($\overline{RD}$) and write ($\overline{WR}$) inputs are supplied by the I/O read ($\overline{XIOR}$) and I/O write ($\overline{XIOW}$) control signals, respectively. Moreover, when inputting data from or outputting data to the 8259A, the address of the register, which is either 20_{16} or 21_{16}, is output on the address bus. This address is decoded in the chip select logic circuit to produce chip select signal $\overline{INTR\ CS}$. This signal is applied to the $\overline{CS}$ input of the 8259A and enables its microprocessor interface. In the sections of this chapter that follow, we will trace the operation of each of these segments of circuitry in detail.

9.4 WAIT STATE LOGIC AND NMI CIRCUITRY

The control logic circuitry shown in Fig. 9.3 provides several functions in terms of overall PC system operation. It consists of the wait state control circuit that is needed to extend memory and I/O bus cycles, the wait state and hold acknowledge logic that is used to grant the 8237A DMA controller access to the system bus, and the circuitry that generates the nonmaskable interrupt request.

Wait State Logic Circuitry

The wait state logic circuitry is used to insert one wait state into all I/O channel, I/O, and DMA bus cycles. Two wait state control signals, $\overline{RDY/WAIT}$ and $\overline{DMA\ WAIT}$, are produced by the circuit. $\overline{RDY/WAIT}$ is applied to the $\overline{AEN_1}$ input of the 8284A clock generator (see Fig. 9.2). Logic 1 at this input makes the

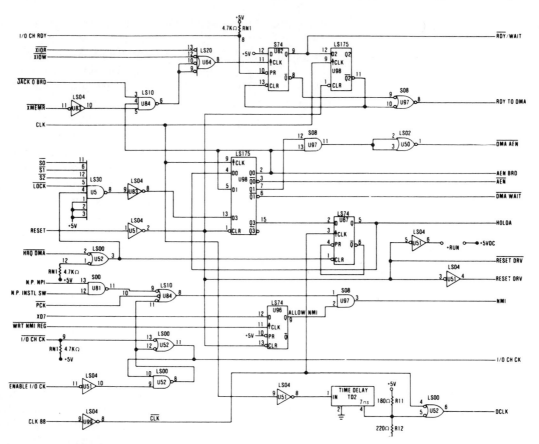

Figure 9.3 Wait state logic and NMI circuitry. (Courtesy of International Business Machines Corporation)

READY output of the 8284A switch to logic 0. This output is applied to the READY input of the 8088 and initiates a wait state for the current bus cycle. On the other hand, signal $\overline{\text{DMA WAIT}}$ switches to logic 0 whenever a DMA bus cycle is initiated. It is applied to the RDY_1 input of the 8284A and, when at logic 0, it causes the READY output to switch to logic 0. In this way, it extends the current bus cycle with wait states and allows the DMA controller to take over control of the system bus. Let us now examine just how the signal $\overline{\text{RDY}}$/WAIT is produced.

I/O CH RDY (I/O channel ready) is one signal that can insert wait states into the processor's bus cycle. I/O CH RDY is used by cards located in the slots of the I/O channel interface. In Fig. 9.3, we find that this signal is applied to the preset (PR) input of the 74S74 flip-flop U_{82}. As long as I/O CH RDY is logic 0 the flip-flop is set and its Q output, which is the signal $\overline{\text{RDY}}$/WAIT, is held at logic 1, and wait states are inserted into the current bus cycle. With this signal, I/O channel devices can insert up to ten wait states into a bus cycle.

Let us now look at how $\overline{\text{RDY}}$/WAIT is produced for an I/O read, I/O write, or memory refresh cycle. Note in Fig. 9.3 that the CLR input at pin 1 of D-type flip-flop U_{98} is tied to the RESET input through inverter U_{51}. This signal clears the flip-flop at power-up and initializes its $\overline{Q}_2$ output to logic 1. As long as the I/O CH RDY input is logic 1, flip-flop U_{82} will set whenever a 0-to-1 transition occurs at its CLK input (pin 11). This causes its Q output to switch to logic 1 and its $\overline{Q}$ output to switch to logic 1. $\overline{\text{RDY}}$/WAIT is now logic 1 and signals the 8088 that a wait state is to be inserted into the current bus cycle.

We will now look at what inputs cause an active transition at CLK. CLK is produced by the signals $\overline{\text{XIOR}}$ (I/O read), $\overline{\text{XIOW}}$ (I/O write), DACK 0 BRD (DMA acknowledge channel 0), $\overline{\text{XMEMR}}$ (memory read), and AEN BRD (DMA cycle in progress) with a logic circuit formed from gates U_{83}, U_{84}, and U_{64}. If any input of NAND gate U_{64} switches to logic 0, a 0-to-1 transition is produced at CLK and flip-flop U_{82} sets. In this way, we see that if either an I/O read ($\overline{\text{XIOR}}$ = 0) or I/O write ($\overline{\text{XIOW}}$ = 0) cycle is initiated, a wait state is generated. Moreover, a wait state is initiated if a memory read ($\overline{\text{XMEMR}}$ = 0) occurs when a memory refresh is not in progress ($\overline{\text{DACK 0 BRD}}$ = 1) and a DMA cycle is in progress (AEN BRD = 1).

Now that we see how the wait state is entered, let us look at how it is terminated so that just one wait state is inserted into the bus cycle. Since the logic 1 at $\overline{\text{RDY}}$/WAIT is also the data input (pin 12) of the 74LS175 flip-flop U_{98}, the next pulse at the CLK input (pin 9) causes its outputs to set. Therefore, output $\overline{Q}_2$ switches to the 0 logic level. This logic 0 is returned to the CLR input at pin 13 of flip-flop U_{82} and causes it to reset. $\overline{\text{RDY}}$/WAIT returns to logic 0, signaling ready, and the bus cycle proceeds to completion after just one wait state.

Hold/Hold Acknowledge Circuitry

The 8088 in the PC is configured to operate in the maximum mode. When configured this way, there is no hold/hold acknowledge interface available for use by the 8237A DMA controller. The $\overline{\text{DMA WAIT}}$ signal we mentioned earlier is coupled with a HOLDA signal produced in the control circuitry of Fig. 9.3 to implement a *simulated HOLD/HOLDA interface* in the PC. Let us look at how DMA requests produce the $\overline{\text{DMA WAIT}}$ and HOLDA signals.

Peripheral devices issue a request for DMA service through the 8237A DMA controller. The 8237A signals the 8088 that it wants control of the system bus to perform DMA transfers by outputting the signal $\overline{\text{HRQ DMA}}$ (hold request DMA). In Fig. 9.3, we find that this signal is an input to NAND gate U_{52}. Whenever $\overline{\text{HRQ DMA}}$ is at its inactive 1 logic level, the output at pin 3 of U_{52} is logic 0. This signal is applied to the CLR input of the 74LS74 flip-flop U_{67} and holds it cleared. Therefore, HOLDA is at its inactive 0 logic level. The output at pin 3 of U_{52} is also applied to one input of NAND gate U_5. Here it is synchronized to status code $\overline{S}_2\overline{S}_1\overline{S}_0$. If the status output is 111_2 and $\overline{\text{LOCK}}$ = 1, the output of U_5 switches to 0 and signals that the 8088's bus is in the passive state and DMA is permitted to take over control of the bus. On the next pulse at the CLK input, flip-flop 3 in latch U_{98} sets, and its Q_3 output switches to the 1 level. Q_3 is applied to the data input of the 74LS74 flip-flop U_{67}, and on the next pulse at CLK88, its Q output, which is HOLDA, becomes active. This output remains latched at the 1 logic level until the DMA request is removed. HOLDA is sent to the HLDA input of the 8237A (see Fig. 9.8) and signals that the 8088 has given up control of the system bus.

At the same time, the logic 1 at HOLDA is returned to the Q_0 input (pin 4) of 74LS175 latch U_{98}. On the next pulse at CLK, signals AEN BRD and $\overline{\text{AEN}}$ become active and signal that a DMA cycle is in progress. These signals are used to disable and tristate the 8288 bus controller and system bus address latches (see Fig. 9.2), thereby isolating the 8088 microprocessor from the system bus. $\overline{\text{AEN}}$ also disables the decoder that generates peripheral chip selects for the I/O address space [see Fig. 9.4(a)]. AEN BRD is returned to the Q_1 input at pin 5 of latch U_{98}, and on the next pulse at CLK the $\overline{\text{DMA WAIT}}$ signal becomes active. The logic 0 at $\overline{\text{DMA WAIT}}$ is sent to the 8284A, where it activates the READY input to ensure that a new bus cycle cannot be activated. Finally, AEN BRD and the complement of $\overline{\text{DMA WAIT}}$ are gated together by the 74S08 AND gate U_{97} to produce the signal $\overline{\text{DMA AEN}}$. In Fig. 9.8, this signal is used to enable the DMA address circuitry. Moreover, in Fig. 9.5 we will find that it is used to enable the 8237A to produce its own address and I/O or memory read/write control signals.

NMI Circuitry

In Section 9.2, we indicated that there are three sources for applying a nonmaskable interrupt to the 8088 microprocessor. They are the 8087 numeric coprocessor, memory parity check, and I/O channel check. In Fig. 9.3, the signal mnemonics used to represent these three inputs are N P NPI, $\overline{\text{PCK}}$, and $\overline{\text{I/O CH CK}}$, respectively. These signals are combined in the NMI control logic circuitry to produce the nonmaskable interrupt request (NMI) signal. This output is applied directly to the NMI input at pin 17 of the 8088 (see Fig. 9.2). Let us now look at the operation of the NMI interrupt request control circuit.

The NMI control logic circuitry in Fig. 9.3 includes a *nonmaskable interrupt control register*. This register is implemented with the 74LS74 D-type flip-flop U_{96}. At reset of the PC, the NMI interface is automatically disabled. Note in Fig. 9.3 that the RESET signal is input to a 74LS04 inverter, and the output at pin 2 of this inverter is applied to the clear (CLR) input of the NMI control register flip-flop. Clearing the flip-flop causes its ALLOW NMI output to switch to logic 0. This output is used as the enable input of the 74S08 AND gate (U_{97}) that controls the NMI output. As long as ALLOW NMI is logic 0, the NMI output is held at its inactive 0 logic level, and the NMI interface is disabled.

We will now look at how the NMI interface gets turned on. Looking at Fig. 9.3, we find that the data input (pin 12) of the 74LS74 flip-flop is supplied by XD_7

of the data bus, and its clock input (CLK) at pin 11 is supplied by a chip select signal identified as $\overline{\text{WR NMI REG}}$ (write NMI register). As part of the initialization software of the PC, the NMI control register gets set by executing an instruction that writes a byte with its most significant bit (XD_7) set to logic 1 to any I/O address in the range $00A0_{16}$ through $00BF_{16}$. All these addresses decode to produce the chip select signal $\overline{\text{WR NMI REG}}$ at CLK; therefore, the 1 at XD_7 is loaded into the flip-flop and ALLOW NMI switches to logic 1. This supplies the enable input for the 74S08 AND gate to the NMI output. The NMI interface is now enabled and waiting for one of the NMI interrupt functions to occur.

Now that the NMI interface is enabled, let us look at how the numeric coprocessor, parity check, or I/O channel check interrupt requests are produced. Figure 9.3 shows that the inputs for each of these three functions are combined with the 74LS10 NAND gate U_{84}. If any combination of the NAND gate inputs is logic 0, the output at pin 8 switches to logic 1. This represents an active NMI request. As long as the NMI interface is enabled, this logic 1 is passed to the NMI output and on to the NMI input of the 8088.

Actually, each NMI interrupt input also has an enable signal that allows it to be individually enabled or disabled. For instance, in Fig. 9.3 we see that N P NPI is combined with the signal NP INSTL SW by the 74S00 NAND gate U_{81}. For the numeric coprocessor interrupt to be active, the N P INSTL SW input must be logic 1. N P INSTL SW stands for numerics processor install switch, which is the switch represented by the contacts marked 2–15 on SW1 in Fig. 9.10. Only when this switch is off (open) is the numeric coprocessor interrupt input enabled.

The parity check nonmaskable interrupt input can also be enabled or disabled; however, this part of the circuit is not shown in Fig. 9.3. To enable $\overline{\text{PCK}}$, a logic 0 must be written to bit 4 of output port PB of the 8255A U_{36} (see Fig. 9.10). This produces the signal $\overline{\text{ENB RAM PCK}}$ (enable RAM parity check), which is used to enable the parity check circuits that produce $\overline{\text{PCK}}$ in the RAM circuit (see Fig. 9.7).

Looking at Fig. 9.3, we see that to enable the NMI input for $\overline{\text{I/O CH CK}}$ (I/O channel check) logic 0 must be applied to the $\overline{\text{ENABLE I/O CK}}$ input. This signal is directly supplied by bit 5 of output port PB on the 8255A device U_{36} (see Fig. 9.10). This bit is set to logic 0 through software at power-up.

Up to this point, we have shown how the NMI input is enabled, disabled, or made active. However, since there are three possible sources for the NMI input, another question that must be answered is how does the 8088 know which of the three interrupt inputs has caused the request for service. It turns out that the signals PCK and I/O CH CK are returned to input ports on the 8255A device U_{36} (see Fig. 9.10). For instance, I/O CH CK is applied to input bit 6 on port PC of the 8255A. Therefore, the service routine for NMI can read these inputs through software, determine which has caused the request, and then branch to the part of the service routine that corresponds to the active input.

9.5 INPUT/OUTPUT AND MEMORY CHIP SELECT CIRCUITRY

In the previous section, we found that the chip select signal $\overline{\text{WRT NMI REG}}$ was used as an enable input for the NMI control register. Besides the NMI control register chip select signal, chip selects are needed in the ROM, RAM, DMA, PPI, interval timer, and interrupt controller sections of the PC's system processor board circuitry. These chip selects are all generated by the I/O and memory chip select circuit that is shown in Fig. 9.4(a). Two types of chip select signals are produced, *I/O chip selects* and *memory chip selects,* and they are both generated by decoding of addresses. Let us now look at the operation of the circuits that produce these I/O and memory chip select outputs.

I/O Chip Selects

Earlier we found that in the architecture of the PC LSI peripheral devices, such as the DMA controller, interrupt controller, programmable interval timer, and programmable peripheral interface controller, are located in the I/O address space of the 8088 microprocessor. I/O chip select decoding for these devices takes place in the circuit of Fig. 9.4(a) formed from devices U_{66}, U_{50}, and U_{51}. Let us begin by looking at the operation of this segment of circuitry in detail.

To access a register within one of the peripheral devices, an I/O instruction must be executed to read from or write to the register. The address output on address lines A_0 through A_9 during the I/O bus cycle is used to both chip select the peripheral device and select the appropriate register. Note in Fig. 9.4(a) that address bits XA_8 and XA_9 are applied to enable inputs G_{2B} and G_{2A}, respectively, of the 74LS138 three-line to eight-line decoder device (U_{66}). When these inputs are both at logic 0 and $\overline{\text{AEN}}$ is at logic 1, the decoder is enabled for operation. At the same time, address lines XA_5 through XA_7 apply a 3-bit code to the ABC inputs of the decoder. When U_{66} is enabled, the Y output corresponding to the code $XA_7 XA_6 XA_5$ is switched to its active 0 logic level. These Y signals produce I/O chip select outputs $\overline{\text{DMA CS}}$ (DMA chip select), $\overline{\text{INTR CS}}$ (interrupt request chip select), $\overline{\text{T/C CS}}$ (timer/counter chip select), $\overline{\text{PPI CS}}$ (parallel peripheral interface chip select), $\overline{\text{WRT NMI REG}}$ (NMI register chip select), and $\overline{\text{WRT DMA PG REG}}$ (DMA page register chip select).

For instance, if $XA_7 XA_6 XA_5 = 001$, output Y_1 switches to logic 0 and produces the chip select output $\overline{\text{INTR CS}}$ at pin 14. In Fig. 9.2, we find that this signal is applied to the $\overline{\text{CS}}$ input at pin 1 of the 8259A interrupt controller and enables its microprocessor interface for operation.

At the same time, appropriate lower-order address bits are applied directly to the register select inputs of the peripherals to select the register that is to be accessed. For the 8259A in Fig. 9.2, we find that only one address bit, XA_0 is used, and this signal is applied to register select input A_0 at pin 27.

In this way we see that the individual I/O chip select signals produced in this circuit actually correspond to a range of addresses. The address range for each

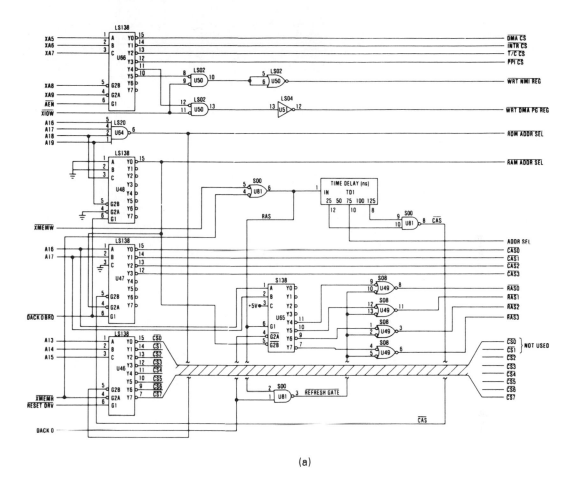

(a)

Address range	Signal	Function	Conditions
0–1F	$\overline{\text{DMA CS}}$	DMA controller	Non DMA bus cycle
20–3F	$\overline{\text{INTR CS}}$	Interrupt controller	Non DMA bus cycle
40–5F	$\overline{\text{T/C CS}}$	Interval timer	Non DMA bus cycle
60–7F	$\overline{\text{PPI CS}}$	Parallel peripheral interface	Non DMA bus cycle
80–9F	$\overline{\text{WRT DMA PG REG}}$	DMA page register	Non DMA bus cycle, XIOW active
A0–BF	$\overline{\text{WRT NMI REG}}$	NMI control register	Non DMA bus cycle, XIOW active

(b)

Figure 9.4 (a) Peripherals/memory chip select circuitry. (Courtesy of International Business Machines Corporation). (b) Peripheral address decoding. (c) ROM address decoding. (d) RAM address decoding.

Address range	Chip select
F0000–F1FFF	$\overline{CS}_0$
F2000–F3FFF	$\overline{CS}_1$
F4000–F5FFF	$\overline{CS}_2$
F6000–F7FFF	$\overline{CS}_3$
F8000–F9FFF	$\overline{CS}_4$
FA000–FCFFF	$\overline{CS}_5$
FC000–FDFFF	$\overline{CS}_6$
FE000–FFFFF	$\overline{CS}_7$

(c)

Address range	Active signal	Condition
00000–3FFFF	$\overline{\text{RAM ADDR SEL}}$	Inactive DACK 0 BRD
00000–0FFFF	$\overline{RAS}_0$, $\overline{CAS}_0$	Active XMEMR or XMEMW
10000–1FFFF	$\overline{RAS}_1$, $\overline{CAS}_1$	Active XMEMR or XMEMW
20000–2FFFF	$\overline{RAS}_2$, $\overline{CAS}_2$	Active XMEMR or XMEMW
30000–3FFFF	$\overline{RAS}_3$, $\overline{CAS}_3$	Active XMEMR or XMEMW

(d)

Figure 9.4   (Continued)

chip select output is shown in Fig. 9.4(b). Here we find that any address in the range 0020_{16} through $003F_{16}$ decodes to produce the $\overline{\text{INTR CS}}$ chip select signal.

The signal $\overline{\text{AEN}}$ is at its active 0 logic level only during DMA bus cycles. When $\overline{\text{AEN}}$ is logic 0, decoder U_{66} is disabled. In this way, we see that only addresses output by the microprocessor will produce an I/O chip select. This is identified as a condition required for the occurrence of all chip selects in Fig. 9.4(b). Looking at the circuit in Fig. 9.4(a), we also find that the NMI control register and DMA page register chip selects are gated with the I/O write control signal $\overline{\text{XIOW}}$ by NOR gates in IC U_{50}. Therefore, as shown in Fig. 9.4(b), for these two chip selects to take place, an additional condition must be satisfied; that is, they are only produced if an I/O write (output) bus cycle is taking place.

Since the upper address lines XA_{10} through XA_{15} are not used in the I/O chip select address decoder circuit, they represent don't-care states. Therefore, more than one range of addresses may be used to access each peripheral. For instance, any address in the range $FC20_{16}$ through $FC3F_{16}$ will also decode to produce the signal $\overline{\text{INTR CS}}$.

Memory Chip Selects

The system processor board of the PC contains both read only memory (ROM) and random access read/write memory (RAM). The ROM part of memory is used to store embedded system software such as the BIOS, power-up diagnostics, and basic interpreter. On the other hand, programs that are typically loaded from disk, such as the operating system and application programs, are stored in the RAM. Here we will just look at the chip select signals that are produced for enabling the memory devices. These chip select signals are also generated in the I/O and memory chip select circuit of Fig. 9.4(a).

Let us begin by examining the circuitry that produces the chip selects needed by the ROM. The output signals produced for ROM in the circuit of Fig. 9.4(a) are ROM address select ($\overline{\text{ROM ADDR SEL}}$) and chip selects $\overline{\text{CS}}_0$ through $\overline{\text{CS}}_7$. Note that the signal $\overline{\text{ROM ADDR SEL}}$ is generated by combining the upper four address bits, A_{16} through A_{19}, with NAND gate U_{64}. If all three of these bits are at logic 1, the output at pin 6, which is $\overline{\text{ROM ADDR SEL}}$ switches to its active 0 logic level. This signal has two functions. First, it is used to enable the ROM chip select decoder U_{46} and, second, it is supplied to the *ROM array* (see Fig. 9.5) where it is used to control the direction of data transfer through the ROM data bus transceiver.

The chip select outputs for the EPROMs, which are labeled $\overline{\text{CS}}_0$ through $\overline{\text{CS}}_7$ in Fig. 9.4(a), are produced by the 74LS138 three-line to eight-line decoder U_{46}. Note that $\overline{\text{ROM ADDR SEL}}$ is applied to the G_{2B} chip enable input of the decoder. This enable signal ensures that the decoder only decodes addresses in the range $F0000_{16}$ through $FFFFF_{16}$. Two other chip select signals, $\overline{\text{XMEMR}}$ and $\overline{\text{RESET DRV}}$, are also applied to the decoder. $\overline{\text{XMEMR}}$ ensures that the decoder is enabled only during memory read operations.

Note that address lines A_{13} through A_{15} are applied to the ABC inputs of the decoder. This 3-bit code is to generate the individual chip selects, $\overline{\text{CS}}_0$ through $\overline{\text{CS}}_7$. As shown in Fig. 9.4(a), chip selects $\overline{\text{CS}}_0$ and $\overline{\text{CS}}_1$ are not used. However, the other six, $\overline{\text{CS}}_2$ through $\overline{\text{CS}}_7$, are each used to enable an individual EPROM in the ROM array (see Fig. 9.5).

For example if the input to the ROM address decoder is $A_{14}A_{13}A_{12} = 010$, chip select output $\overline{\text{CS}}_2$ is active, and a read operation is performed from one of the 8K-byte storage locations in the EPROM that is located in the address range $F4000_{16}$ through $F5FFF_{16}$. The actual storage location in this EPROM that is accessed is selected by the lower address bits, which are applied to the circuitry in the ROM array. The memory address range that corresponds to each of the ROM chip select outputs is given in Fig. 9.4(c). This chart shows that there are a total of 64K addresses decoded by the ROM address decoder circuitry.

We will now look at the circuitry used to produce the chip select, row address select, and column address select signals for the *RAM array* circuit. In

Fig. 9.4(a), the chip select outputs that are used to control the operation of RAM are $\overline{\text{RAM ADDR SEL}}$ (RAM address select) and ADDR SEL (address select). $\overline{\text{RAM ADDR SEL}}$ is produced by the 74LS138 decoder U_{48}. Looking at the circuit diagram, we find that if A_{19} is logic 0 and $\overline{\text{DACK 0 BRD}}$ is logic 1, the decoder is enabled for operation. Moreover, as long as address bit A_{18} is also logic 0, output Y_0 of the decoder switches to logic 0. In this way, we see that $\overline{\text{RAM ADDR SEL}}$ goes active whenever the 8088 outputs an address in the range 00000_{16} through $3FFFF_{16}$. This is the full address range of the RAM that resides on the system processor board. Note that this $\overline{\text{RAM ADDR SEL}}$ is applied to the G_{2A} input of the 74LS138 CAS decoder (U_{47}) and to input G_{2B} of the 74LS138 RAS decoder (U_{65}). It is also sent to the RAM array circuit (see Fig. 9.6), where it is used to enable the data bus transceiver.

The other chip select signal, ADDR SEL, is generated from $\overline{\text{XMEMW}}$ and $\overline{\text{XMEMR}}$ by NAND gate U_{81} and delay line TD_1. If either the memory read or write control input signal is at its active 0 logic level, the output at pin 6 of the NAND gate switches to logic 1, and ADDR SEL becomes active after the time delay set by TD elapses. ADDR SEL is supplied to the RAS/CAS address selector in the RAM array circuit (see Fig. 9.6), where it is used to select between the RAS and CAS parts of the address.

Note that the output at pin 6 of NAND gate U_{81}, which was used to produce ADDR SEL, is also the RAS (row address select) signal. RAS is applied to the G_1 enable input of the 74S138 RAS decoder (U_{65}). The other chip select inputs of this decoder are supplied by the signals $\overline{\text{RAM ADDR SEL}}$ and DACK 0 and must be logic 0 and logic 1, respectively, to enable the device for operation.

Now when U_{65} is enabled, the code at the ABC input is decoded to produce the RAS output. Note that the C input of the decoder is fixed at the 1 logic level and the other two inputs, A and B, are supplied by address bits A_{16} and A_{17}, respectively. For instance, if these two address bits are both logic 0, the input code is 100, and output Y_4 switches to the 0 logic level and generates the signal $\overline{\text{RAS}}_0$. After a short delay, which is set by TD_1, the $\overline{\text{CAS}}$ signal is output at pin 8 of U_{81}. This signal is applied to the G_{2B} input of the CAS decoder U_{47}. Here the other chip select inputs are supplied by $\overline{\text{RAM ADDR SEL}}$ and $\overline{\text{DACK 0 BRD}}$. When enabled, the address at the AB inputs causes the corresponding column address select output to occur. Assuming that A_{16} and A_{17} are still both 0, $\overline{\text{CAS}}_0$ switches to its active 0 logic level. In this way, we see that all RAS chip selects are followed after a short delay by the corresponding CAS chip select. Figure 9.4(d) summarizes the address decoding for the RAM address chip selects.

9.6 MEMORY CIRCUITRY

Earlier we found that the system processor board of the PC is equipped with 48K bytes of ROM and either 64K or 256K bytes of RAM. The ROM array is implemented using EPROM devices and provides for nonvolatile storage of fixed information, such as the BIOS of the PC. On the other hand, RAM is volatile and is used for temporary storage of information such as application programs. This part of the memory subsystem can be implemented with either 64K-bit or 256K-bit dynamic RAM chips. In the previous section, we showed how the ROM and RAM chip select signals are generated on the system processor board. Here we will trace the operation of the ROM array as the 8088 performs an instruction read bus cycle and the operation of the RAM array as a byte of data is read by the MPU.

ROM Array Circuitry

Let us begin by briefly examining the architecture of the ROM array of the PC. The circuitry of the ROM array is shown in Fig. 9.5. Looking at this circuit

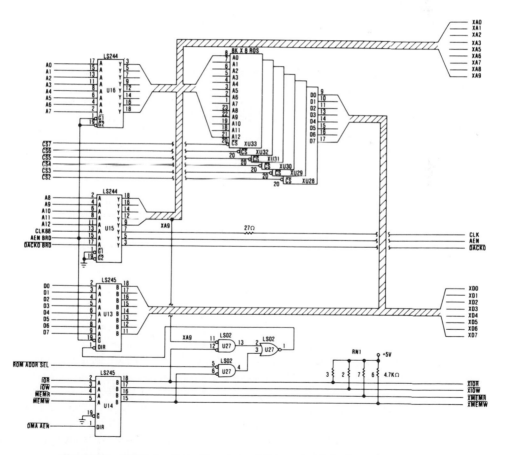

Figure 9.5 ROM circuitry. (Courtesy of International Business Machines Corporation)

diagram, we find that it is implemented with six 8K by 8-bit EPROMs. These devices are labeled XU_{28} through XU_{33}. Note that each of these EPROMs is enabled by one of the ROM chip select signals, $\overline{CS}_2$ through $\overline{CS}_7$, that are generated by the ROM address decoder. For instance, EPROM XU_{28} is enabled by $\overline{CS}_2$. In Fig. 9.4(c), we find that this chip select output is at its active 0 logic level for all memory addresses in the range $F4000_{16}$ through $F5FFF_{16}$. Therefore, EPROM XU_{28} holds the information corresponding to these 8K addresses.

Now that we know how the individual EPROMs are selected, let us look at how a storage location within an EPROM is accessed and its data returned to the MPU. The address output on the lower 13 address lines of the system address bus, A_0 through A_{12}, are used to select the specific byte of data within an EPROM. These address inputs are first buffered with 74LS244 octal buffers U_{15} and U_{16} and then applied to the address inputs of all six EPROMs in parallel. Note that control signal AEN BRD must be at the 0 logic level for the address buffer to be enabled for operation.

The byte of code held at the addressed storage location in the chip selected EPROM is output on data lines D_0 through D_7 for return to the MPU. These data outputs are interfaced to the 8088's system data bus by the 74LS245 bus transceiver U_{13}. During a read bus cycle, data must be transferred from the outputs of the ROM array to the system data bus lines D_0 through D_7.

The direction of data transfer through the data bus transceiver is set by the logic level at its data direction (DIR) input. In Fig. 9.5, we find that the logic level at DIR is determined by the operation of the control logic formed from transceiver U_{14} and three NOR gates of IC U_{27}. The $\overline{IOR}$ and $\overline{MEMW}$ outputs of U_{14}, along with chip select signal $\overline{ROM\ ADDR\ SEL}$ and address bit XA_9, are inputs to the NOR gate circuit. In response to these inputs, the circuit switches DIR to logic 0 during all read bus cycles to storage locations in the address range of the ROM array and for all I/O read cycles from an address where XA_9 is logic 0. Logic 0 at DIR sets the direction of data transfer through U_{13} to be from memory to the 8088's system bus. That is, data are being read from the ROM array.

RAM Array Circuitry

The circuitry of the RAM array is shown in Fig. 9.6. This circuit shows just two of the four banks of RAM ICs that are provided for on the system processor board of the PC. These banks are identified as *bank 0* and *bank 1*. The circuitry for the other two banks, *bank 2* and *bank 3,* is shown in Fig. 9.7. In each bank, eight 64K by 1-bit dynamic RAMs (DRAMs) are used for data storage, and a ninth DRAM is included to hold parity bits for each of the 64K storage locations. In Fig. 9.6, we find that the DRAMs in bank 0 are labeled U_{37} through U_{45}. Device U_{37} is used to store the parity bit, and U_{38} through U_{45} store the bits of the byte of data. The data storage capacity of bank 0 is 64K byes, and all four banks together give the system processor board a maximum storage capacity of 256K bytes.

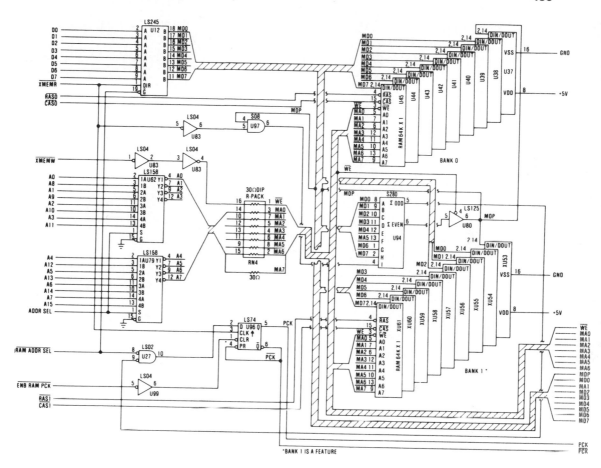

Figure 9.6   RAM circuitry. (Courtesy of International Business Machines Corporation)

Let us now examine how a byte of data is read from the DRAMs in bank 0. Address lines A_0 through A_{15} are applied to inputs of the 74LS158 data selectors U_{62} and U_{79}. These devices are used to multiplex the 16-bit memory address into a byte-wide row address and a byte-wide column address. The multiplexed address outputs of the data selectors are called MA_0 through MA_7 and are applied to address inputs A_0 through A_7 of all DRAMs in parallel. The chip select signal ADDR SEL, which is applied to the select (S) input of both data selectors, is used to select whether the RAS or CAS byte of the address is output on the MA lines.

We have assumed that the storage location to be accessed is located in bank 0. In this case, the RAS and CAS address bytes are output from the address multiplexer synchronously with the occurrence of the active $\overline{RAS_0}$ and $\overline{CAS_0}$ strobe signals, respectively. ADDR SEL initially sets the multiplexer to output

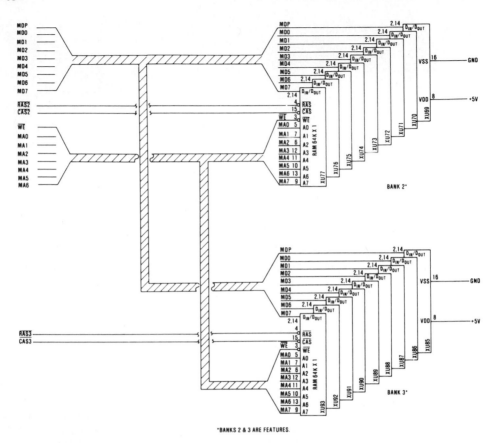

Figure 9.7   RAM banks 2 and 3. (Courtesy of International Business Machines Corporation)

the RAS address byte on the MA line. When RAS_0 switches to logic 0, it signals all DRAMs in bank 0 to accept the row address off of the MA lines. Next, ADDR SEL switches logic levels and causes the column address to be output from the multiplexer. It is accompanied by $\overline{CAS_0}$, which is applied to the $\overline{CAS}$ inputs of all DRAMs in bank 0. Logic 0 at $\overline{CAS}$ causes them to accept the column address from the MA lines. At this point, the complete address of the storage location that is to be accessed has been supplied to the RAM in bank 0.

We are also assuming that a read bus cycle is taking place. For this reason, the $\overline{XMEMW}$ input is logic 1 and signals all DRAMs that a read operation is to take place. Therefore, they all output the bit of data held in the storage location corresponding to the row and column address on their DIN/DOUT lines. The byte of data is passed over data lines MD_0 through MD_7 to the 74LS245 bus transceiver U_{12}. Here a 0 logic level at $\overline{XMEMR}$ sets the transceiver to pass data from the MA lines to system data bus lines D_0 through D_7 during all read cycles.

Moreover, the signal $\overline{\text{RAM ADDR SEL}}$ enables the transceiver for operation during all bus cycles to the RAM array.

In our description of the read cycle, we did not consider the effect of the *parity generator/checker circuitry* that is included in the RAM array of the PC. *Parity* is a technique that is used to improve the reliability of data storage in a RAM subsystem. Whenever data are written into or read from the DRAMs in Fig. 9.6, the byte of data on lines MD_0 through MD_7 is also applied to inputs A through H of the 74S280 parity generator/checker device U_{94}. If the byte has *even parity* (contains an even number of bits at the 1 logic level), the E_{EVEN} output (pin 6) of U_{94} switches to logic 1. However, if parity is odd, E_{EVEN} switches to logic 0. During write bus cycles, this *parity bit* output is supplied to the DIN/DOUT pin of the *parity bit DRAM* over the MDP line and is stored in DRAM along with the byte of data.

On the other hand, during read operations, the parity bit that is read out of the parity bit DRAM on the MDP line is gated by AND gate U_{97} to the ninth input (I) of the 74S280 parity generator/checker. If the 9-bit word read from memory has *odd parity* (an extra 1 is added to even parity words as the parity bit), the E_{ODD} output (pin 5) of U_{94} switches to logic 1 to indicate that parity is correct. E_{ODD} is sent through NOR gate U_{27} to the data input at pin 2 of the 74LS74 parity check interrupt latch U_{96}. As long as no *parity error* has occurred, the $\overline{\text{PCK}}$ output of the latch remains at its inactive 1 logic level. However, if E_{ODD} signals that a parity error has been detected by switching to logic 0, the parity error interrupt latch sets, and the logic 0 that results at $\overline{\text{PCK}}$ issues a nonmaskable interrupt request to the MPU. The NMI service routine must test the logic level of PCK through the 8255A I/O interface to determine if the source of the NMI is PCK. Moreover, at completion of the parity error interrupt service routine, the parity error interrupt latch must be cleared by issuing the signal $\overline{\text{ENB RAM PCK}}$ through the 8255A I/O interface.

9.7 DIRECT MEMORY ACCESS CIRCUITRY

The 8088-based system processor board of the IBM PC supports the direct memory access (DMA) mode of operation for both its memory and I/O address spaces. This DMA capability permits high-speed data transfers to take place between two sections of memory or an I/O device and memory. The bus cycles initiated for these DMA transfers are not under control of the 8088 MPU; instead, they are performed by a special VLSI device known as a *DMA controller*. The DMA circuitry in the PC implements this function through the use of the 8237A-5 DMA controller IC. Looking at the circuit drawing in Fig. 9.8, we find that the 8237A is the device labeled U_{35}. This device provides four independent DMA channels for the PC.

Even though the 8237A performs the actual DMA bus cycles by itself, the 8088 controls are overall operation of the device. There are 16 registers within the

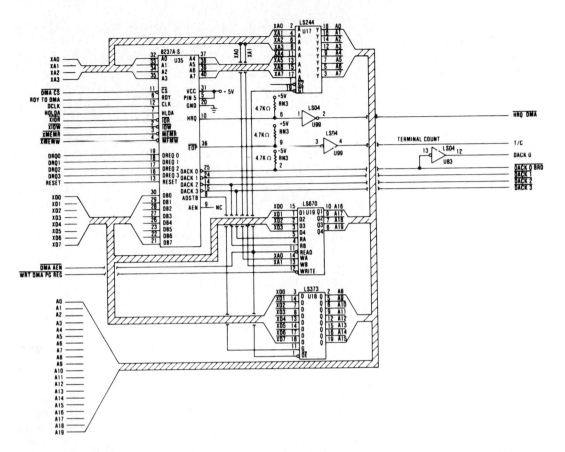

Figure 9.8   Direct memory access circuitry. (Courtesy of International Business Machines Corporation)

8237A that determine how and when the four DMA channels work. Since the microprocessor interface of the 8237A is I/O mapped, the 8088 communicates with these registers by executing I/O instructions. For instance, the 8237A must be configured with operating features such as autoinitialization, address increment or decrement, and fixed or rotating channel priority. These options are selected by loading the command and mode registers within the 8237A through a software initialization routine. Moreover, before a DMA transfer can be performed, the 8088 must send the 8237A information related to the operation that is to take place. This information could include a source base address, destination base address, count of the words of data to be moved, and an operating mode. The modes of DMA operation available with the 8237A are demand transfer mode, single transfer mode, block transfer mode, or cascade mode. Finally, the 8088 can obtain status information about the current DMA bus cycle by reading the contents of registers. For example, it can read the values in the current address register and current count register to determine which data have been transferred.

Let us now look briefly at the signals and operation of the microprocessor interface of the 8237A. In Fig. 9.8, we find that the microprocessor interface of the 8237A is enabled by the signal $\overline{\text{DMA CS}}$, which is applied to its $\overline{\text{CS}}$ input at pin 11. Figure 9.4(b) shows that $\overline{\text{DMA CS}}$ is active whenever an I/O address in the range 0000_{16} through $001F_{16}$ is output on the system address bus. The register to be accessed is selected using the four least significant address lines, XA_0 through XA_3. Data are read from or written into the selected register over system data bus lines XD_0 through XD_7. The 8088 signals the 8237A whether data are to be input or output over the bus with the control signal $\overline{\text{XIOR}}$ or $\overline{\text{XIOW}}$, respectively.

Earlier we pointed out that the four DMA channels of the PC are identified as DMA channels 0 through 3. Moreover, we found that channel 0 is dedicated to RAM refresh and that channel 2 is used by the floppy disk subsystem. Use of a DMA channel is initiated by a request through hardware. In Fig. 9.8, the signals DRQ_0 through DRQ_3 are the hardware request inputs for DMA channels 0 through 3, respectively. DRQ_0 is generated by timer 1 of the 8253 programmable interval timer (see Fig. 9.9) and is used to initiate a DMA 0 refresh cycle for RAM every 15.12 μs. The other three DMA request lines are supplied from the I/O channel and are available for use by other I/O channel devices.

For a DMA request to be active, the DRQ input must be switched to the 1 logic level. Let us assume that a DRQ input has become active, the DMA request input for the active channel is not masked out within the 8237A, and a higher-priority channel is not already active. Then the response of the 8237A to the active DMA request is that it requests to take over control of the system bus by switching its hold request (HRQ) output to logic 1 and then waits in this state until the 8088 signals that it has given up the bus by returning a logic 1 to the hold acknowledge (HLDA) input of the 8237A.

The simulated hold/hold acknowledge handshake that takes place between the 8237A and 8088 is performed by the wait state control logic circuitry that is shown in Fig. 9.3. The HRQ signal that is output at pin 10 of the 8237A is applied to the $\overline{\text{HRQ DMA}}$ input of the wait state control logic circuit. The operation of this circuitry was described in detail in Section 9.3. For this reason, here we will just overview the events that take place in the hold acknowledge handshake sequence.

In response to logic 0 at the $\overline{\text{HRQ DMA}}$ input, the circuit first waits until the 8088 signals that its bus is in the passive state (no bus activity is taking place) and then switches the HOLDA output to logic 1. This signal is returned to the HLDA input at pin 7 of the 8237A, where it signals that the 8088 has given up control of the system bus.

Next, the control logic switches signals AEN BRD and $\overline{\text{AEN}}$ to their active logic levels. These signals are used to tristate the outputs of the 8288 bus controller and system bus address latches. With these outputs floating, the MPU is isolated from devices connected to the system bus. At the same time, they disable the decoder that produces chip selects for the peripherals that are located on the system processor board.

One clock later, the signal $\overline{\text{DMA WAIT}}$ becomes active. This signal is returned through the ready/wait logic of the 8284A to the READY input of the 8088 and ensures that the 8088 cannot initiate a new bus cycle. The signal $\overline{\text{DMA AEN}}$ is now produced by the control logic and sent to the DMA address logic (see Fig. 9.9). Logic 0 at this input enables the address buffers for operation. $\overline{\text{DMA AEN}}$ is also applied to the DIR input of transceiver U_{14} (see Fig. 9.5) and cuts off the I/O and memory read/write control signals from the system bus so that the DMA controller itself can provide them.

At this point, the 8237A is free to take control of the system bus; therefore, it outputs the DMA acknowledge ($\overline{\text{DACK}}_0$ to $\overline{\text{DACK}}_3$) signal corresponding to the device requesting DMA service. DACK_0 is output as $\overline{\text{DACK 0 BRD}}$ to the refresh control circuitry. Logic 0 on this line signals the wait state circuits and RAM chip select decoder that DMA refresh bus cycles are to be initiated. The other three DACK outputs are supplied to the I/O channel.

Now that the 8237A has taken control of the system data bus, let us look at how a block of data is transferred from memory to a device in the I/O address space. To perform this operation, the DMA controller first outputs a 16-bit address on address lines A_0 through A_7 and data lines DB_0 through DB_7. Address bit A_8 through A_{15}, which are output on the data lines, are output in conjunction with a pulse on the address strobe (ADSTB) line at pin 8 of the 8237A. This pulse is used to latch the address into the 74LS373 latch, U_{18}. The four most significant bits of the 20-bit address are not produced by the 8237A; instead, they are generated by three DMA page registers within the 74LS670 register file device, U_{19}. A valid 20-bit source address is now available on system address bus lines A_0 through A_{19}. Next, the memory read ($\overline{\text{MEMR}}$) and I/O write ($\overline{\text{IOW}}$) control signals become active, and the data held at the addressed storage location are read over system data bus lines XD_0 through XD_7 to the I/O device. This completes the first data transfer.

We will assume that during the DMA bus cycle the source or destination address is automatically incremented by the 8237A. In this way, its current value points to the next data element that is to be read from memory or written to memory. Moreover, at completion of the DMA bus cycle, the count in the current word register is decremented by one. The new count stands for the number of data transfers that still remain to be performed.

This basic DMA transfer operation is automatically repeated by the 8237A until the current word register count is decremented from 0000_{16} to FFFF_{16}. At this moment, the DMA operation is complete and the end of process ($\overline{\text{EOP}}$) output is switched to logic 0. $\overline{\text{EOP}}$ is used to tell external circuitry that the DMA operation has run to completion. In Fig. 9.9, we see that $\overline{\text{EOP}}$ is inverted to produce the terminal count (T/C) signal for the I/O channel. In response to T/C, the requesting device removes its DMA request signal, and the 8237A responds by returning control of the system bus to the 8088.

9.8 TIMER CIRCUITRY

The timer circuitry of the IBM PC is shown in Fig. 9.9. This circuitry controls four basic system functions: *time-of-day clock, DRAM refresh, speaker,* and *cassette.* In the PC, the timers are implemented with the 8253-5 programmable interval timer IC. This device is labeled U_{34} in Fig. 9.9. The 8253 provides three independent, programmable, 16-bit counters for use in the microcomputer system. Here we will first look at how the 8253 is interfaced to the 8088 microprocessor and then at how it implements each of the four system functions.

Microprocessor Interface and Clock Inputs

The 8088 MPU communicates with the 8253's internal control registers through the microprocessor interface. In Fig. 9.1(c), we find that the control registers of

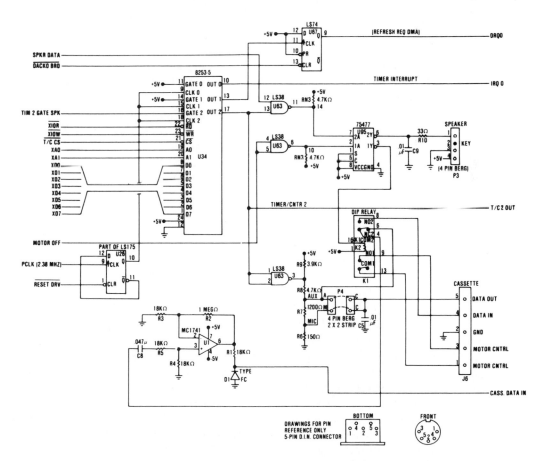

Figure 9.9   Timer circuitry. (Courtesy of International Business Machines Corporation)

the 8253 are located in the range 0040_{16} through 0043_{16} of the PC's I/O address space. Using I/O instructions, we can access the 8253's internal registers to configure the mode of operation and read or load its counters. For example, an input operation from I/O address 0040_{16} reads the current count in counter 0. On the other hand, an output operation to the same address loads an initial value into the count register for counter 0. The same type of operations can be performed to the registers for counters 1 and 2 by using address 0041_{16} or 0042_{16}, respectively. Moreover, the mode of operation for the counters is set up by writing a byte-wide control word to address 0043_{16}. However, the contents of the mode control register cannot be read through software.

Let us now look at how the 8088 performs data transfers to the 8253 over the system bus. The microprocessor interface of the 8253 is enabled by the signal $\overline{\text{T/C CS}}$, which is tied to its $\overline{\text{CS}}$ (chip select) input at pin 21. Figure 9.4(b) shows that this signal is at its 0 active logic level whenever an I/O address in the range 0040_{16} through $005F_{16}$ is output on the system address bus. The internal control register that is to be accessed is selected by a code that is applied to register select inputs A_0 and A_1 over system address bus lines XA_0 and XA_1. In Fig. 9.9, we see that system data bus lines XD_0 through XD_7 connect to the data lines D_0 through D_7 of the 8253. The 8088 tells the PIT whether data are to be read from or written into the selected control register over these lines with logic 0 at $\overline{\text{XIOR}}$ (I/O read) or $\overline{\text{XIOW}}$ (I/O write), respectively.

The signal that is applied to the CLK inputs of the timers is derived from the 2.38-MHz PCLK (peripheral clock) signal. Note that PCLK is first divided by 2 using the 74LS175-D-type flip-flop U_{26}. This generates a 1.19-MHz clock for input to the timers. This signal drives clock inputs CLK_0, CLK_1, and CLK_2 in parallel. Note in Fig.9.9 that the first two of these CLK signals are permanently enabled to the counter by having +5 V connected directly to the $GATE_0$ and $GATE_1$ inputs, respectively. However, CLK_2 is enabled to the counter with signal TIM 2 GATE SPK. This signal must be switched to logic 1 under software control to enable the clock input for counter 2.

Outputs of the PIT

In Fig. 9.9, the three outputs of the 8253 timer are labeled OUT_0, OUT_1, and OUT_2. OUT_0 is produced by timer 0 and is set up to occur at a regular time interval equal to 54.936 ms. This output is applied to the timer interrupt request input (IRQ_0) of the 8259A interrupt controller, where it represents the time-of-day interrupt.

Timer output OUT_1 is generated by timer 1 and also occurs at a regular interval, every 15.12 μs. In Fig. 9.9, we find that this signal is applied to the CLK input (pin 11) of the 74LS74 flip-flop U_{67} and causes the DRQ_0 output to set. Logic 1 at this output sends a request for service to the 8237A DMA controller and asks it to perform a refresh operation for the dynamic RAM subsystem. When the DMA controller has taken control of the system bus and is ready to perform the refresh cycle, it acknowledges this fact by outputting the refresh acknowledge ($\overline{\text{DACK 0 BRD}}$) signal. Logic 0 on this line clears flip-flop U_{67}, thereby removing the refresh request.

The output of the third timer, OUT_2, is used three ways in the PC. First, it is sent as the signal T/C2 OUT to input 5 on port C of the 8255A PIC (see Fig. 9.10). In this way, its logic level can be read through software. Second, it is used as an enable signal for speaker data in the speaker interface. When the speaker is to be used, the 8088 must write logic 1 to bit 0 of port B on the 8255A PIC (see Fig. 9.10). This produces the signal TIM 2 GATE SPK, which enables the clock for timer 2. Pulses are now produced at OUT_2. When a tone is to be produced by the speaker, the 8088 outputs the signal SPKR DATA at pin 1 of port B of the 8255A (see Fig. 9.10). Logic 1 at input SPKR DATA enables the pulses output at OUT_2 to the 75477 driver U_{95}. The filtered output is supplied to the speaker. The frequency of the tone produced by the speaker can be changed by changing the count in timer 2.

The last use of counter 2 is to supply the record tone for the cassette interface. As shown in Fig. 9.9, the PC's cassette interface is through connector J_6. Data that are to be recorded on the tape are output on the DATA OUT line at pin 5 of J_6. In Fig. 9.9, we find that the data to be recorded on the cassette are output from the OUT_2 pin of the 8253 timer and are supplied through inverter U_{63} to a voltage divider. Jumper P_4 is used to select the voltage level for the DATA OUT signal. For instance, if a jumper is installed from A to C, DATA OUT is set for a 0.68-V high signal level and 0 V as the low level.

Data played back from the cassette enter the microcomputer at the DATA IN input at pin 6 of connector J_6. DATA IN is passed through a set of contacts on DIP relay K_1 to the input of an amplifier made with the MC1741 device, U_1. Since it is a high-gain amplifier, the low-level signals read from the tape are saturated to produce a TTL-level signal at output CASS DATA IN. This signal is applied to input 4 at port B of the 8255A (see Fig. 9.10), where it can be read by the 8088 using IN instructions.

The motor of the cassette player is also turned on or off through circuitry shown in Fig. 9.9. When the MOTOR OFF input is switched to logic 0, DIP relay K_1 is activated. This connects the DATA IN signal to the input of the amplifier circuit formed from the MC1741 device U_1. At the same time, the motor control (MOTOR CNTRL) outputs at pins 1 and 3 of J_6 are connected through a relay contact and the motor turns on. MOTOR OFF is provided by output 3 at port B of the 8255A PIC (see Fig. 9.10).

9.9 INPUT/OUTPUT CIRCUITRY

Figure 9.10 shows the I/O circuitry of the IBM PC. Three basic types of functions are performed through this I/O interface. First, using this circuitry, the 8088 inputs data from the keyboard and outputs data to the cassette and speaker.

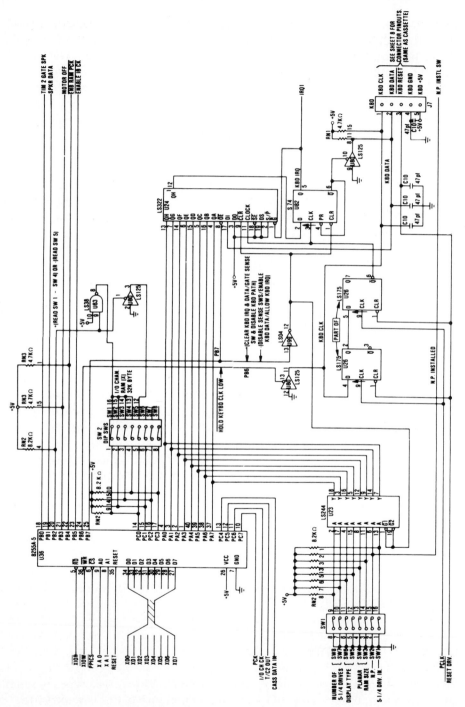

Figure 9.10 I/O circuitry. (Courtesy of International Business Machines Corporation)

Second, through this circuitry, the microprocessor reads the setting of DIP switches to determine system configuration information such as the size of the system memory, number of floppy disk drives, type of monitor used on the system, and whether or not an 8087 numeric coprocessor is installed. Finally, certain I/O ports are used for special functions, such as clearing the parity check flip-flop and reading the state of the parity check flip-flop through software. In this section, we will look at how the 8255A is interfaced to the 8088 MPU and at the different input/output operations that take place through its ports.

8255A Programmable Peripheral Interface

The I/O circuitry of the PC system processor board is designed using the 8255A-5 programmable peripheral interface (PPI) IC. This device, which is labeled U_{36} in Fig. 9.10, has three 8-bit ports for implementing inputs or outputs. In the PC, ports PA and PC are configured to operate as inputs, and the lines of port PB are set up to work as outputs. In Fig. 9.1(d), we find that ports PA, PB, and PC reside at addresses 0060_{16}, 0061_{16}, and 0062_{16}, respectively, in the I/O address space of the 8088.

Figure 9.1(d) also identifies the function of each pin at PA, PB, and PC. Here we find that input port PA is used to both read configuration switches SW1 and communicate with the keyboard. On the other hand, output port PB controls the cassette and speaker. It also supplies enable signals for RAM parity check, I/O channel check, and reading of the configuration switches or keyboard. Finally, we find that input port PC is used to read the I/O channel RAM switches (SW2), parity check signal, I/O channel check signal, terminal count status from timer 2, and cassette data.

The operation of the ports of the 8255A are configurable under software control. This is done by writing a configuration byte to the command/mode control register within the device. In Fig. 9.1(d), we find that the command/mode register is located at address 0063_{16}. When configured by the initialization software of the PC, it is loaded with the value 99_{16}. This configuration code selects mode 0 operation for all three ports.

Loading of the control register, as well as inputting of data from ports PA and PC or outputting of data to port PB, is performed through the 8255A's microprocessor interface. In Fig. 9.10, we see that the microprocessor interface is activated by the $\overline{PPICS}$ (PPI chip select) signal, which is applied to the $\overline{CS}$ input at pin 6 of the 8255A. Figure 9.4(b) shows that this signal is at its active (logic 0) level whenever an I/O address in the range 0060_{16} through $007F_{16}$ is output on the system address bus. However, remember that just four of these addresses, 0060_{16} through 0063_{16}, are used by the 8255A interface. Note that the data bus inputs of the 8255A are tied to lines XD_0 through XD_7 of the system data bus. It is over these lines that the configuration information or input/output data are carried. The 8088 signals the PPI that data are to be read from or written into a register with signals $\overline{\text{XIOR}}$ and $\overline{\text{XIOW}}$, respectively, while the register to be accessed is determined by the register select code on address lines XA_0 and XA_1.

Inputting System Configuration DIP Switch Settings

Let us now look at how the settings of the system configuration DIP switches are input to the 8088 microprocessor. Looking at Fig. 9.10, we see that input port PA, which is at I/O address 0060_{16}, is connected to configuration switch SW1 through the 74LS244 buffer (U_{23}). To read the state of these switches, the keyboard data path must be disabled and the switch path enabled. This is done by writing a 1 to bit PB_7 of the output port. This output is inverted and then applied to the enable inputs of buffer U_{23}. Logic 0 at these inputs enables the buffer and causes the switch setting to pass through to port PA. Now the instruction

```
IN 60H
```

can be used to read the contents of port PA. The byte of data read in can be decoded based on the table in Fig. 9.1(d) to determine the number of floppy disk drives, type of display, presence or absence of an 8087, and size of the RAM on the system board.

EXAMPLE 9.1

The system configuration byte read from input port PA is $7D_{16}$. Describe the PC configuration for these switch settings.

SOLUTION   Expressing the switch setting byte in binary form, we get

$$PA_7PA_6PA_5PA_4PA_3PA_2PA_1PA_0 = 7D_{16} = 01111101_2$$

Referring to the table in Fig. 9.1(d), we find that

$PA_0 = 1$ indicates that the system has floppy disk drive(s)
$PA_1 = 0$ indicates that an 8087 is not installed
$PA_3PA_2 = 11$ indicates that the system processor board has 256K of memory
$PA_5PA_4 = 11$ indicates that the system has a monochrome monitor
$PA_7PA_6 = 01$ indicates that the system has two floppy drives

---

Scanning the Keyboard

The keyboard of the PC is also interfaced to the 8088 through port PA of the 8255A. In Fig. 9.10, we find that the keyboard attaches to the system processor board at connector KB0. The keyboard interface circuit includes devices U_{82},

U_{26}, and U_{24}. At completion of the power-up reset service routine, output PB_7 of the 8255A is switched to logic 0. This disables reading of configuration switch SW1 and enables the keyboard data path and interrupt.

We will now examine how the 8088 determines that a key on the keyboard has been depressed. The keyboard of the PC generates a *keyscan code* whenever one of its keys is depressed. Bits of the keyscan code are input to the system processor board in serial form at the KBD DATA pin of the keyboard connector synchronously with pulses at KBD CLK. Note in Fig. 9.10 that KBD DATA is applied directly to the data input (DI) of the 74LS322 serial-in, parallel-out shift register (U_{24}). On the other hand, KBD CLK is input to the data input at pin 4 of one of the two D-type flip-flops in the 74LS175 device, U_{26}. This flip-flop circuit divides the clock by 4 before outputting it at pin 6. The clock produced at pin 6 of U_{26} is applied to the clock input of the 74S74 keyboard interrupt request flip-flop U_{82}, as well as the CLOCK input of the 74LS322 shift register. CLOCK is used by the shift register to clock in bits of the serial keyscan code from DI. When a byte of data has been received, the Q_H output at pin 12 of the shift register switches to logic 1. Q_H is returned to the data input of the 74S74 flip-flop U_{82}, and when logic 1 is clocked into the device, the keyboard interrupt request signal KBD IRQ becomes active. At the same moment that the interrupt signal is generated, the KBD DATA line is driven to logic 0 by the output at pin 8 of buffer U_{80} and the shift register is disabled.

In response to the IRQ_1 interrupt request, the 8088 initiates a keyscan code service routine. This routine reads the keyscan code by inputting the contents of port PA. After reading the code, it drives output PB_7 to logic 1 to clear the keyboard interrupt request flip-flop and keyscan shift register. Next, the service routine drives PB_7 back to logic 0. This reenables the keyboard interface to accept another character from the keyboard.

Port C Input and Output Functions

The switch configuration identified as SW2 in Fig. 9.10 represents what is called the *I/O channel RAM switches*. The five connected switches are used to identify the amount of read/write memory provided through the I/O channel. The settings of these switches are also read through the 8255A PPI. Once the setting are read from the switches, the total amount of memory can be determined by multiplying the binary value of the switch settings by 32K bytes.

Looking at the hardware in Fig. 9.10, we find that the settings of the five switches are returned to the 8088 over just four input lines, PC_0 through PC_3. To read the settings of switches SW2-1 through SW2-4, a logic 1 must first be written to output PB_2 and then the contents of port PC input. The four least significant bits of this byte are the switch settings. Logic 1 in a bit position indicates that the corresponding switch is in the OFF position (open circuit). Switch SW2-5 is read by switching PB_2 to logic 0 and once again reading the contents of port PC. In this byte, the content of the least significant bit represents the setting of SW2-5. These two bytes can be combined through software to give a single byte that contains all five switch settings.

The four most significant bit lines of port PC are supplied by signals generated elsewhere on the system processor board. PC_5 through PC_7 allow the 8088 to read the state of the RAM parity check (PCK), I/O channel check (I/O CH CK), and timer terminal count (T/C2 OUT) signals through software. On the other hand, CASS DATA IN, which is available at PC_4, is the data input line from the cassette interface.

9.10 INPUT/OUTPUT CHANNEL INTERFACE

The input/output channel is the system expansion bus of the PC. The chassis of the PC has five 62-pin I/O channel card slots. Earlier we pointed out that using these slots special function adapter cards, such as boards to control a monochrome or color display, floppy disk drives, a hard disk drive, expanded memory, or a printer, can be added to the system to expand its configuration.

Figure 9.11(a) shows the electrical interface implemented with the I/O channel. In all, 62 signals are provided in each I/O channel slot. They include an 8-bit data bus, 20-bit address bus, six interrupts, memory and I/O read/write controls, clock and timing signals, a channel check signal, and power and ground pins.

The table in Fig. 9.11(b) lists the mnemonic and name for each of the I/O channel signals. For instance, here we see that the signal AEN stands for address enable. Also identified in this table is whether the signals is an input (I), output (O), or input/output (I/O). Notice that input/output channel ready (I/O CH RDY) is an input signal; input/output write command ($\overline{\text{IOW}}$) is an example of an output; and data bus lines D_0 through D_7 are the only signals that are capable of operating as inputs or outputs.

9.11 HIGH-INTEGRATION PCXT COMPATIBLE PERIPHERAL ICs

The circuitry of the main processor boards of the IBM PC and PCXT has become the architectural standard. Compatible PCs and PCXTs made by other manufacturers must provide an equivalent circuit implementation to ensure 100% hardware compatibility at the bus and 100% software compatibility. Since the introduction of the original IBM PC and PCXT, much work has been done to develop special purpose ICs that simplify the design of PC or PCXT compatible personal computers. The cornerstone of this effort has been the development of high-integration peripheral ICs. The objectives of these peripherals is to reduce the complexity and cost of the circuitry on the main processor board. In this section, we will examine one of the more popular PCXT compatible peripheral ICs and its use in the design of a PCXT main processor board.

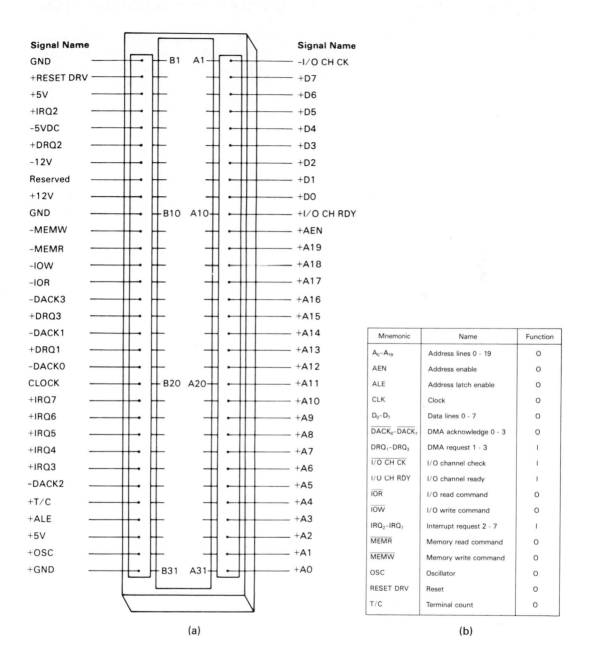

Signal Name				Signal Name
GND	B1	A1		–I/O CH CK
+RESET DRV				+D7
+5V				+D6
+IRQ2				+D5
–5VDC				+D4
+DRQ2				+D3
–12V				+D2
Reserved				+D1
+12V				+D0
GND	B10	A10		+I/O CH RDY
–MEMW				+AEN
–MEMR				+A19
–IOW				+A18
–IOR				+A17
–DACK3				+A16
+DRQ3				+A15
–DACK1				+A14
+DRQ1				+A13
–DACK0				+A12
CLOCK	B20	A20		+A11
+IRQ7				+A10
+IRQ6				+A9
+IRQ5				+A8
+IRQ4				+A7
+IRQ3				+A6
–DACK2				+A5
+T/C				+A4
+ALE				+A3
+5V				+A2
+OSC				+A1
+GND	B31	A31		+A0

(a)

Mnemonic	Name	Function
A_0–A_{19}	Address lines 0 - 19	O
AEN	Address enable	O
ALE	Address latch enable	O
CLK	Clock	O
D_0–D_7	Data lines 0 - 7	O
$\overline{DACK_0}$–$\overline{DACK_7}$	DMA acknowledge 0 - 3	O
DRQ_1–DRQ_3	DMA request 1 - 3	I
$\overline{I/O\ CH\ CK}$	I/O channel check	I
I/O CH RDY	I/O channel ready	I
$\overline{IOR}$	I/O read command	O
$\overline{IOW}$	I/O write command	O
IRQ_2–IRQ_7	Interrupt request 2 - 7	I
$\overline{MEMR}$	Memory read command	O
$\overline{MEMW}$	Memory write command	O
OSC	Oscillator	O
RESET DRV	Reset	O
T/C	Terminal count	O

(b)

Figure 9.11 (a) I/O channel interface. (Courtesy of International Business Machines Corporation). (b) Signal mnemonics, names, and functions.

The 82C100 *Super XT™ Compatible Chip* is a single chip PCXT compatible peripheral IC. This device, which is manufactured by Chips and Technologies, Inc., implements most of the circuitry on the main processor board of a PCXT compatible personal computer. Figure 9.12 is a block diagram of the architecture of a main processor board that uses the 82C100. Here we find that the circuitry includes the 82C100 system controller, buffers for the ROM, RAM, and I/O channel, the ROM subsystem, and RAM subsystem. Notice that the 82C100 attaches to the CPU bus of the microprocessor. In fact, it can be connected to either an 8088 or 8086 MPU. The 82C100 contains most of the hardware functions we examined in earlier sections of this chapter: clock generator, bus controller, interrupt controller, wait state logic, hold/hold acknowledge logic, NMI logic, memory chip select decoders, parity checker/generator, DMA channels, timers, and parallel I/O ports.

As shown in Fig. 9.13, the 82C100 IC is manufactured in a 100-pin plastic flatpack. The signals brought out to each of its pins are identified in Fig. 9.13. For example, address/data bus signals AD_{15} through AD_0 are located at pins 10 through 25, respectively.

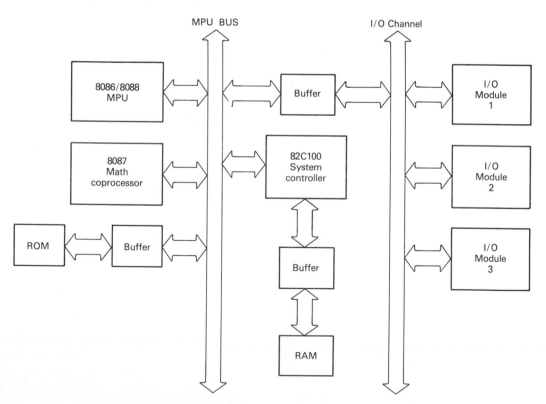

Figure 9.12 Super XT™ main processor board architecture. (Super XT™ is a trademark of Chips and Technologies, Inc.)

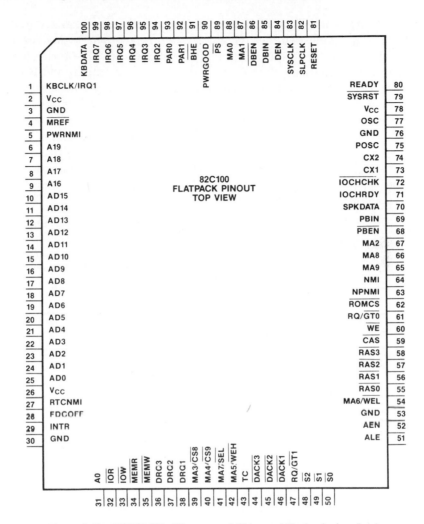

Figure 9.13   82C100 IC. (Courtesy of Chips and Technologies, Inc.)

EXAMPLE 9.2

How many ground pins are provided on the 82C100 IC? What are their pin numbers?

SOLUTION   Looking at the pin layout diagram in Fig. 9.13(b), we find four ground (GND) pins. They are pins 3, 30, 53, and 76.

The functions of all of the 82C100's pins are summarized in the table of Fig. 9.14. This table identifies the pin number, type of pin, symbol of the signal, name of the signal, and gives a brief functional description of the signal at each pin. Three pin types are identified: I for input, O for output, and B for bidirectional. Moreover, the signals are organized into eight groups based on their system level function. These groups are *clocks and reset logic, CPU interface, local bus interface, buffer controls, memory controls, DMA and interrupt controller interface, keyboard and speaker interface,* and *power and grounds.* For instance, pin 73 is the crystal/oscillator input (CX1). This is the pin at which an external crystal must be attached. The system clock (SYSCLK) signal is output at pin 83. Just like for the 8284A clock generator, the frequency of SYSCLK is one-third that of the crystal attached to CX1.

EXAMPLE 9.3

To which pin of the 82C100 is the RESET input of the 8088 connected?

SOLUTION The RESET input of the 8088 is driven by the RESET output of the 82C100. This output is one of the CPU interface signals in Fig. 9.14 and is located at pin 81.

The circuit diagrams in Fig. 9.15 show an 8086-based main processor board for a PCXT compatible personal computer that is designed with the 82C100. Looking at sheet 1, we see that it contains the core microcomputer circuitry, the 8086 MPU, 8087 match coprocessor, the 82C100 system control peripheral, the data bus transceiver, and the RAM address/control signal buffers.

Let us begin our study of the circuit diagram by looking at the connection of the 82C100 to the 8086. Earlier we pointed out that the CPU interface signals identified in Fig. 9.14 are simply connected directly to the equivalent pins of the MPU. Notice in Fig. 9.15 that the $\overline{\text{BHE}}/\text{S}_7$ output of the 8086 is tied to the $\overline{\text{BHE}}$ input of the 82C100, the READY input of the 8086 is connected to the READY output of the 82C100, and so on.

Some of the 82C100's local bus lines are also directly connected to the 8086. For example, address/data bus lines AD_0 through AD_{15} of the 8086 in Fig. 9.15 are directly connected to the AD_0 through AD_{15} lines of the 82C100. Moreover, address/status lines A_{16}/S_3 through A_{19}/S_6 connect to lines A_{16} through A_{19} of the 82C100. The local bus interface signal group also includes a number of outputs. These signals are generated within the 82C100 and are required to control the transfer of address information over the address bus and data over the data bus. All of these signals are supplied to the I/O channel bus. Tracing the signal $\overline{\text{IOR}}$, which is carried by the line labeled $\overline{\text{IORD}}$ from pin 32 of the 82C100 in Fig. 9.15,

82C100 Pin Description

Pin No.	Pin Type	Symbol	Pin Description
Clocks and Reset Logic			
73	I	CX1	**Crystal/oscillator input.** CX1 is an input for a passive crystal circuit or packaged oscillator to generate the initial system timings. This frequency is divided by three to generate the default system clock when the system is powered up. The type of crystal is 14.31818 MHz, parallel resonance, fundamental frequency.
74	O	CX2	**Crystal/oscillator output.** CX2 is the inverted output of CX1. If a crystal is used, then CX2 should be connected to the crystal circuit. If an oscillator is used, then CX2 should be left unconnected.
75	I	POSC	**Optional Oscillator input.** The POSC input is divided by three to generate alternate system timing (other than 4.77 MHz). Typically POSC is a 24 MHz or 30 MHz oscillator with a 50% duty cycle, for 8 MHz or 10 MHz sytems, respectively. The maximum POSC frequency is 30 MHz. System timing is software selectable from the configuration register.
83	O	SYSCLK	**System Clock.** SYSCLK is a continuous running clock with selectable frequency and duty cycle. The duty cycle is either 33% for INTEL 808X CPUs, or 50% for NEC V20/30 CPUs. The SYSCLK frequency is selected from either 1/3 of the POSC or 1/3 of the CX1 frequencies. The default is 4.77 MHz, 33% duty cycle.
82	O	SLPCLK	**Sleep Clock Output.** SLPCLK is similar to SYSCLK, except that SLPCLK can be disabled through software. SLPCLK provides the clock for the CPU and other static devices. In the OFF state it is LOW and the default is enabled.
77	O	OSC	**Oscillator output.** OSC is a continuous running square wave with a 50% duty cycle, derived from the frequency generated by CX1. Normally this is used for the 14.3818 MHz.
90	I	PWRGOOD	**Power Good.** An active high indicator that the power supply is stable, it also starts the clocks and the internal system functions. PWRGOOD is generated by the power supply, by monitoring V_{CC}.
89	I	$\overline{PS}$	**Power Sense.** An active low input which indicates the system configuration is invalid, due to a power loss. An active low level on $\overline{PS}$ and $\overline{SYSRST}$ resets the 82C100 internal ports and configuration registers to their default values. If power has been lost, $\overline{PS}$ must be held low until PWRGOOD is high and $\overline{SYSRST}$ has returned high.

Figure 9.14 Pin functions. (Courtesy of Chips and Technologies, Inc.)

82C100 Pin Description (Continued)

Pin No.	Pin Type	Symbol	Pin Description
79	I	SYSRST	**System Reset.** SYSRST is an active low Schmitt trigger input for power-up reset. SYSRST initializes the 82C100 circuitry (but not the registers which are initialized by PS). This signal also generates the RESET output used to reset the CPU, 8087 and other peripherals. It should be held active until PWRGOOD becomes active.
28	O	FDCOFF	**Floppy Disk Controller OFF.** FDCOFF is a programmable output, normally LOW. If FDCOFF is enabled (by a bit in a configuration register), and sleep mode is entered, the FDCOFF output pin will go high. This condition causes the FDC and other peripherals to be disabled, thus reducing power consumption. FDCOFF should be connected to FDC and other chip enable pins.

CPU Interface

Pin No.	Pin Type	Symbol	Pin Description
81	O	RESET	**RESET.** RESET is an active high output derived from the SYSRST input. RESET should be used to reset the CPU, the 8087, and the external peripherals.
48 49 50	I I I	$\overline{S2}$ $\overline{S1}$ $\overline{S0}$	**Processor Status Signals.** These signals are status inputs from the CPU. S0-S2 should be pulled up with 4.7K-10K resistors.
91	I	$\overline{BHE}$	**Byte High Enable.** $\overline{BHE}$ is an input signal. $\overline{BHE}$ and A0 from the CPU indicate the type of bus transfer.

$\overline{BHE}$	A0	Type
0	0	16 bit transfer
0	1	odd byte transfer
1	0	even byte transfer
1	1	invalid (for 16 bit CPU)

If the 82C100 is used with an 8 bit processor, $\overline{BHE}$ should be tied high through a 4.7K to 10K resistor. The 82C100 uses the "invalid" state to perform the correct bus conversion for an 8 bit processor. $\overline{BHE}$ is floated to the high impedance state during "hold" cycles, so it should be pulled up with 4.7K-10K resistor.

Pin No.	Pin Type	Symbol	Pin Description
80	O	READY	**READY.** READY is an active high, asynchronous output indicates that a memory or I/O transfer can complete. READY is internally synchronized to meet the setup/hold times of the processor.

Figure 9.14 (Continued)

512

82C100 Pin Description (Continued)

Pin No.	Pin Type	Symbol	Pin Description
29	O	INTR	**Interrupt Request.** INTR is an active high output from the internal Interrupt Controller. It should be connected to the INTR pin of the CPU.
64	O	NMI	**Non-Maskable Interrupt.** A LOW to HIGH transition on NMI causes an interrupt at the end of the current instruction. It should be connected to the NMI input of the CPU.
61	B	RQ/$\overline{\text{GT0}}$	**Request/Grant.** These signals are used by bus masters other than the CPU to gain control of the CPU local bus. In the Model 25/30 or XT application, the other bus masters are the 8087 numeric co-processor, and the 82C100 itself. RQ/GT0 has higher priority than RQ/GT1. 808X RQ/GT signals are internally pulled up, so external pullups are not necessary. See the Request/Grant section of this data sheet for more information.
47	B	RQ/$\overline{\text{GT1}}$	

Local Bus Interface

Pin No.	Pin Type	Symbol	Pin Description
6	B	A19	**Address Bits A19-16.** During processor cycles, these are inputs for the high order address bits. During DMA cycles, the 82C100 sources the high order address on these lines. These should be connected directly to the processor address lines and to the system address latches.
7	B	A18	
8	B	A17	
9	B	A16	
10	B	AD15	**Local Address/Data Bus Bits 15:0.** During the T1 phase of a CPU cycle the processor sources the address on these lines. The 82C100 sources the address during hold acknowledge and interrupt acknowledge cycles. AD0-AD7 should be isolated from the 82C100 using bidirectional buffers to prevent bus contention during bus conversion cycles. PBEN enables the buffers and PBIN controls the direction.
11	B	AD14	
12	B	AD13	
13	B	AD12	
14	B	AD11	
15	B	AD10	
16	B	AD9	
17	B	AD8	
18	B	AD7	
19	B	AD6	
20	B	AD5	
21	B	AD4	
22	B	AD3	
23	B	AD2	
24	B	AD1	
25	B	AD0	
31	O	A0	**Address Bit 0.** This signal represents the state of address bit 0. It is latched and should be used throughout the system instead of AD0 that would normally be latched externally from the AD bus. The 82C100 toggles this bit during bus conversion cycles. It should be buffered (in a normal system) but not routed through transparent latches like the other address bits.

Figure 9.14 (Continued)

82C100 Pin Description (Continued)

Pin No.	Pin Type	Symbol	Pin Description
32	O	$\overline{\text{IOR}}$	**I/O Read.** An active low strobe that informs the I/O devices to put their data on the bus. All the commands ($\overline{\text{MEMR}}$, $\overline{\text{MEMW}}$, $\overline{\text{IOR}}$, and $\overline{\text{IOW}}$) can be delayed one cycle through software. The delay is necessary when running the CPU at high speed. Delaying the commands allow more data and address setup time. Default is no delay.
33	O	$\overline{\text{IOW}}$	**I/O Write.** An active low strobe that informs the I/O devices that data is available on the bus.
34	O	$\overline{\text{MEMR}}$	**Memory Read.** An active low strobe that informs the memory devices to put their data on the bus.
35	O	$\overline{\text{MEMW}}$	**Memory Write.** An active low strobe that informs the memory devices that data is available on the bus.
51	O	ALE	**Address Latch Enable.** ALE is used by the address buffer/latch to latch the address. During the second half of a bus conversion cycle, a second ALE will not be generated by the 82C100.
52	O	AEN	**Address Enable.** When high, this signal is an indication to the devices on the I/O channel that DMA is active, meaning the DMA channel has control of the address bus, data bus, and the appropriate command lines.
84	O	DEN	**Data Enable.** Provided to control the output enable of 245 type transceiver. DEN is active during memory and I/O accesses and for INTA cycles. It floats to the high impedance state in "hold acknowledge" cycles. This signal is equivalent to the DEN signal generated by an 8288 bus controller. It is normally not used in XT/Model 30 type applications.
93	B	PAR0	**Parity Bit 0.** The parity bit from the low order byte of the DRAMs. A HIGH means there are an odd number of 1's in memory, including the parity bit itself, thus odd parity.
92	B	PAR1	**Parity Bit 1.** The parity bit from the high order byte of the DRAMs. A HIGH means there are an odd number of 1's in memory, including the parity bit itself, thus odd parity. This signal is not used in 8 bit only systems.
71	I	IOCHRDY	**I/O Channel Ready.** An active high signal from the I/O channel. It is normally HIGH indicating that the addressed device on the channel is ready to complete the data transfer. Slow I/O or memory devices pull this signal LOW to lengthen bus cycles. IOCHRDY should be pulled up with a 4.7K resistor, because if there are no add-in boards present, this signal would float to an undefined state.

Figure 9.14 (Continued)

82C100 Pin Description (Continued)

Pin No.	Pin Type	Symbol	Pin Description
72	I	IOCHCHK	**I/O Channel Check.** This signal goes low when there is parity or other error on memory or devices on the I/O channel. IOCHCHK should be pulled up with a 4.7K resistor, because if there are no add-in boards present, this signal would float to an undefined state.

Buffer Controls

Pin No.	Pin Type	Symbol	Pin Description
86	O	DBEN	**Data Buffer Enable.** DBEN enables the data transceiver between the I/O channel data bus and 82C100.
85	O	DBIN	**Data Buffer Direction.** A HIGH allows data to flow from the I/O channel to the internal bus. Normally low, this means the data direction is to the I/O channel. DBIN is used to control the direction of the buffer for the system data bus.
68	O	PBEN	**Processor Buffer Enable.** An active low signal, PBEN enables the data buffer between the processor and the 82C100. It is high during DMA cycles so that the data bus is tri-stated. PBEN is qualified with DEN to avoid bus contention during T2 cycles.
69	O	PBIN	**Processor Buffer Direction.** A HIGH on PBIN allows data to flow from the processor to the 82C100. PBIN controls the direction of the data buffer on the local data bus.

Memory Controls

Pin No.	Pin Type	Symbol	Pin Description
62	O	ROMCS	**ROM Chip Select.** This signal goes low for memory accesses in the address range F0000H-FFFFFH. It would normally be tied to the chip select inputs of the BIOS ROM(s).

Note: All DRAM signals (MA9-0, RAS3-0, CAS and WE should be buffered if connected to more than 9 memory devices)

Pin No.	Pin Type	Symbol	Pin Description
65	O	MA9	**Multiplex Address Bits 9 and 8.** Should be connected to DRAM address bits 9 and 8.
66	O	MA8	

Note: The following 5 pins have different functions depending on whether static RAMs or Dynamic RAMs are used with the 82C100. The functions change based on a bit in the configuration registers.

Pin No.	Pin Type	Symbol	Pin Description
41	O	MA7/SEL	DRAM: **Multiplex Address Bit 7.** Should be connected to DRAM address bit 7.
			SRAM: **Select.** An active low decode address range 0-640K (00000-9FFFFH).

Figure 9.14   (Continued)

82C100 Pin Description (Continued)

Pin No.	Pin Type	Symbol	Pin Description
54	O	MA6/$\overline{\text{WEL}}$	DRAM: **Multiplex Address Bit 6.** Should be connected to DRAM address bit 6. SRAM: **Write Enable Low Bank.** An active low strobe that writes data to the low byte. Should be connected to the write enable of the low byte static RAMs.
42	O	MA5/$\overline{\text{WEH}}$	DRAM: **Multiplex Address Bit 5.** Should be connected to DRAM address bit 5. SRAM: **Write Enable High Bank.** An active low strobe that writes data to the high byte. Should be connected to the write enable of the high byte static RAMs.
40	O	MA4/$\overline{\text{CS9}}$	DRAM: **Multiplex Address Bit 4.** Should be connected to DRAM address bit 4. SRAM: **Chip Select 9.** An active low chip select for the address range 90000-9FFFFH. Should be connected to the chip selects of the SRAM located at address 90000-9FFFFH.
39	O	MA3/$\overline{\text{CS8}}$	DRAM: **Multiplex Address Bit 3.** Should be connected to DRAM address bit 3. SRAM: **Chip Select 8.** An active low chip select for the address range 80000-8FFFFH. Should be connected to the chip selects of the SRAM located at address 80000-8FFFFH.
67 87 88	O O O	MA2 MA1 MA0	**Multiplexed Address Bits 2-0.** These should be connected to DRAM address bits 2-0.
55 56 57 58	O O O O	$\overline{\text{RAS0}}$ $\overline{\text{RAS1}}$ $\overline{\text{RAS2}}$ RAS3	**RAS3-0.** Active low row address strobes for DRAM banks 0-3. Each bank is 9 bits wide (1 bit for parity). Byte referencing is done using the $\overline{\text{RAS}}$ signal. For more information, see the DRAM Interface section of this data sheet.
59	O	$\overline{\text{CAS}}$	**CAS.** Active low column address strobe for all DRAMs.
60	O	$\overline{\text{WE}}$	**WE.** Active low write enable for all DRAMs.
4	O	$\overline{\text{MREF}}$	**Memory Refresh.** $\overline{\text{MREF}}$ is the output of the independent refresh timer signifying that a refresh cycle is occurring. The refresh rate is programmable from 838 ns to 214 μs.

DMA and Interrupt Controller Interface

36 37 38	I I I	DRQ3 DRQ2 DRQ1	**DMA Request 3-1.** These signals are asynchronous requests used by peripherals to request DMA services. They have a fixed priority: channel 1 is the highest and channel 3 is the lowest. DRQ must be held active HIGH until it is acknowledged by the corresponding DACK.

Figure 9.14 (Continued)

82C100 Pin Description (Continued)

Pin No.	Pin Type	Symbol	Pin Description
44	O	DACK3	**DMA Acknowledge 3-1.** An active low acknowledgement signal generated by the 82C100 as a result of a request for DMA service (via a DRQ line) and a successful arbitration. These lines must be pulled up with 10Kohm resistors.
45	O	DACK2	
46	O	DACK1	
43	O	TC	**Terminal Count.** An active high output pulse from the DMA Controller, indicating the end of a DMA transfer (transfer count register = 0).
94	I	IRQ2	**Interrupt Request 2-7.** Active high asynchronous inputs to the interrupt controller generated by I/O devices. They are edge-triggered, but should be held active HIGH until acknowledged.
95	I	IRQ3	
96	I	IRQ4	
97	I	IRQ5	
98	I	IRQ6	
99	I	IRQ7	
63	I	NPNMI	**Numeric Co-Processor NMI.** An active high signal indicating that an error has occurred during numeric instruction execution. This is an active high, edge-sensitive input. If enabled, will cause an NMI to the CPU. The NMI service routine has to determine which NMI occurred by reading the NMI Status Register.
27	I	RTCNMI	**Real Time Clock NMI.** When the Real Time Clock needs immediate attention, it can generate RTCNMI. This is an active high, edge-sensitive input. If enabled, will cause an NMI to the CPU. The NMI service routine has to determine which NMI occurred by reading the NMI Status Register.
5	I	PWRNMI	**Power Fail NMI.** A monitoring circuit generates PWRNMI when it detects imminent loss of power. This is an active high, edge-sensitive input. If enabled, will cause an NMI to the CPU. The NMI service routine has to determine which NMI occurred by reading the NMI Status Register.
Keyboard and Speaker Interface			
1	B	KBCLK/IRQ1	**Keyboard Clock/Interrupt Request 1.** KBCLK is a bidirectional open drain signal. Defaults to KBCLK when using an XT style keyboard. The 82C100 synchronizes the internal keyboard logic with this signal. It sources the clock for the keyboard when sending serial data to the keyboard and receives the clock when the keyboard is sending data. If an external Model 25/30 style keyboard interface is used (and selected through the Internal Configuration Register), IRQ1 is the shared, active high Interrupt Request 1 input from the keyboard controller, pointing device, and real time clock.
100	B	KBDATA	**Keyboard Data.** KBDATA is an open drain bidirectional serial data to or from the keyboard. This line is unused if a Model 25/30 external keyboard interface is used.

Figure 9.14 (Continued)

82C100 Pin Description (Continued)

Pin No.	Pin Type	Symbol	Pin Description
70	O	SPKDATA	**Speaker Data.** SPKDATA should be buffered, and the output of the buffer should go through a low pass filter. The output of the filter connects to the speaker.

Power and Grounds

Pin No.	Pin Type	Symbol	Pin Description
2,26,78	—	V$_{CC}$	**Power Supply.**
3,30, 53,76	—	GND	**Ground.**

Notes:
1. The 82C100 provides four RAS signals to select which byte will be written. A single CAS and WE is provided for all banks.
2. PAR1 is provided for 16 bit 8086 systems with DRAM. Usage of this is determined by setting of the internal configuration registers.
3. BHE is provided for 8086 systems.
4. A packaged oscillator is assumed for the processor clock if the CPU clock is above 4.77MHz (14.318MHz/3).
5. The following explains the abbreviations used in the pin type/direction column.

Pin	Meaning
I	Input B
B	Input and Output (3-state)
O	Output

Figure 9.14   (Continued)

we find that it is applied to the input at pin 4 of the 74F244 buffer U_{15}. At the output of the buffer (pin 16), the signal is again labeled $\overline{\text{IOR}}$ and connects to pin B_{14} of each of the I/O channel connectors (U_{28} through U_{33}). The ALE output signal is also used in the ROM subsystem. The two local bus inputs of the 82C100, IOCHRDY and $\overline{\text{IOCHCHK}}$, are received from the I/O channel connectors.

The clock input of the 8086 is connected to the *sleep clock* (SLPCLK) output of the 82C100. SLPCLK is the same as the SYSCLK output we mentioned earlier; however, it can be turned on or off under software control. This feature is important for portable PCs. In sheet 1 of Fig. 9.15, we see that a 14.318-MHz crystal is connected between the CX_1 and CX_0 inputs of the 82C100. This makes the frequency of SLPCLK equal to 4.77 MHz.

Next, we will look at the buffer and memory control signals that are produced by the 82C100. In Fig. 9.14, the buffer control signals are found to be $\overline{\text{DBEN}}$, DBIN, $\overline{\text{PBEN}}$, and PBIN. Looking at sheet 1 of Fig. 9.15, we see that $\overline{\text{PBEN}}$ and PBIN control the 74F245 bidirectional transceiver (U_4) that is used to buffer the lower eight lines of the local data bus. Logic 0 at $\overline{\text{PBEN}}$ enables the

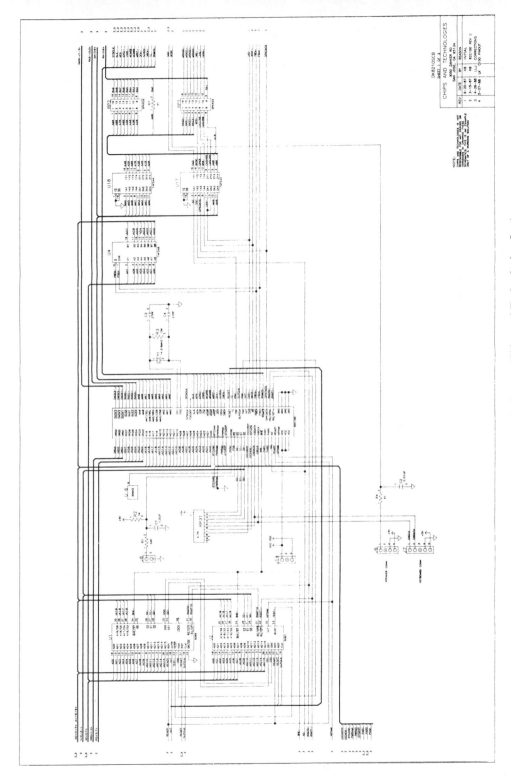

Figure 9.15 Super XT™ circuit diagram (Chips and Technologies, Inc.)

Figure 9.15 (Continued)

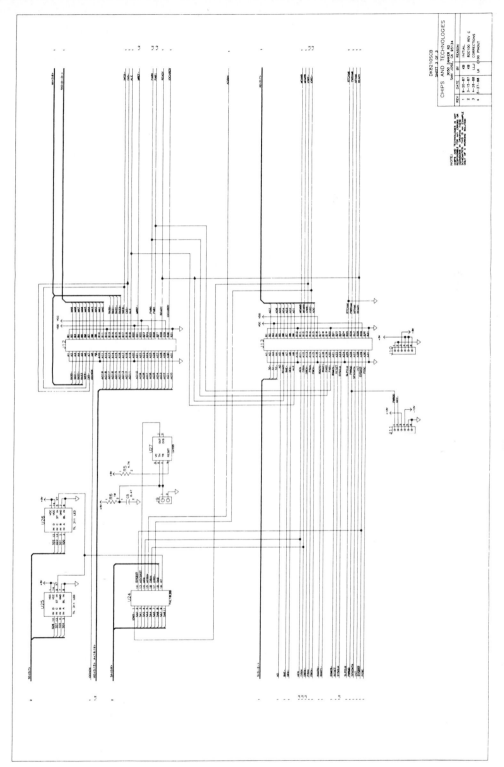

Figure 9.15 (Continued)

device, and the logic level of PBIN selects the direction of data transfer through the transceiver.

On sheet 2 of Fig. 9.15, we find that the ROM subsystem consists of the address latch (U_9, U_{10}, and U_{11}) and ROM array (U_7 and U_8). The address latch is formed from three 74F373 octal latch ICs. Notice that the inputs of the latches are directly supplied by the address lines of the 8086 MPU. Address information is latched synchronously with the ALE output of the 82C100. The latched address is identified as SA_0 through SA_{19}. Lines SA_1 through SA_{15} of this address are applied to the address inputs of both 27C256 EPROMs in parallel. At the output side of EPROM U_8, we see that data outputs Q_0 through Q_7 are applied to the lower eight data bus lines of the 8086, AD_0 through AD_7. Moreover, the data outputs of EPROM U_7 are supplied to data bus lines AD_8 through AD_{15}. Looking at Fig. 9.14, we find that the memory control signals are all outputs of the 82C100. Only one of these signals, *ROM chip select* ($\overline{ROMCS}$), is used in the ROM subsystem. $\overline{ROMCS}$ is used as the output enable signal for both EPROMs.

The rest of the memory control outputs are used in the RAM subsystem. From sheet 2 of Fig. 9.15, we find that the DRAM array is formed from four 9-bit SIM modules. They are labeled R_{19} through R_{22}. Assuming that these SIMs are each organized 256K $\times$ 9 bits, the total data storage capacity of the DRAM arrays is 1MB.

The 82C100 provides the multiplexed row and column addresses, row and column address strobes, and write enable signal that are needed to drive the DRAM array. On sheet 1 of the circuit diagram in Fig. 9.15, we find that the 82C100 outputs the multiplexed RAS/CAS address that is used to select a storage location in the DRAM array over the MA_0 through MA_7 lines. These signals are buffered by the 74F244 octal buffers U_{17} and U_{18} and then sent to the address inputs A_0 through A_9 of all four SIMs. The $\overline{CAS}$ output of the 82C100 is also buffered by U_{17} and applied in parallel to both the $\overline{CAS}$ and $\overline{CAS_0}$ inputs of all four SIMs. This signal is used to strobe the column address into the DRAMs of the SIM modules. On the other hand, individual row address strobe signals, $\overline{RAS_0}$, $\overline{RAS_1}$, $\overline{RAS_2}$, and $\overline{RAS_3}$, are applied to the RAS inputs of SIMs R_{20}, R_{19}, R_{22}, and R_{21}, respectively. Therefore, the row address is only strobed into the RAMs of the appropriate SIM modules. For instance, if just $\overline{RAS_1}$ is at its active 0 logic level, the row address is strobed into the 9 DRAMs of SIM R_{20}. Finally, the $\overline{WE}$ output of the 82C100 is buffered and supplied to the $\overline{WE}$ input of each of the four SIMs in parallel. The logic level of $\overline{WE}$ signals whether the contents of the addressed storage location is to be read from or written into.

The DMA and interrupt interface signals of the 82C100 are all directly connected to the I/O channel interface. Looking at Fig. 9.15, we find that DMA request 3 (DRQ_3) is input from pin B_{16} of the I/O channel connectors and DMA acknowledge 3 ($\overline{DACK_3}$) is output to pin B_{15} on these connectors. Moreover, interrupt request 3 (IRQ_3) is input from pin B_{25} of the I/O channel connectors.

ASSIGNMENTS

Section 9.2

1. Name the three system buses of the PC.
2. What three functions are performed by the clock generator block in Fig. 9.1?
3. What I/O addresses are dedicated to the PPI?
4. What I/O addresses are assigned to the registers of the DMA controller? To the DMA page register?
5. What functions are assigned to timer 0? Timer 1? Timer 2?
6. Is port PA of the PPI configured for the input or output mode of operation? Port PB? Port PC?
7. Over which PPI lines are the state of the memory and system configuration switches input to the microprocessor?
8. Which output port of the PPI is used to turn ON/OFF the cassette motor?
9. Which output port of the PPI is used to output data to the speaker?
10. What are the three sources of the NMI signal?
11. What is assigned to the lowest-priority interrupt request?
12. What I/O device is assigned to priority level 5?

Section 9.3

13. How much I/O channel expansion RAM is supported in the PC?
14. What is the frequency of CLK88? PCLK?
15. At what frequency will the 8087 in the PC run?
16. What are the input and output signals of the 8284A's reset circuitry?
17. To what pin of the 8087 is RESET applied?
18. What are the input and output signals of the 8284A's wait state logic?
19. What does logic 0 at $\overline{\text{DMA WAIT}}$ mean? $\overline{\text{RDY}}$/WAIT?
20. Which devices are attached to the local bus?
21. What devices are used to demultiplex the local bus into the system address bus and system data bus?
22. What device is used to produce the system control bus signals?
23. At what pins of the 8288 are signals $\overline{\text{MEMW}}$ and $\overline{\text{MEMR}}$ output?
24. Overview the interrupt request/acknowledge cycle that takes place between the 8259A and 8088.

Section 9.4

25. What is the source of the signal I/O CH RDY? To what logic level must it be switched to initiate a wait state?
26. What types of bus cycles cause the $\overline{\text{RDY}}$/WAIT output to switch to the 1 logic level? What input signal represents each of the bus cycles?

27. Overview the operation of the hold/hold acknowledge circuitry.

28. What signals are used to represent the three sources of the nonmaskable interrupt?

29. Overview how the NMI interface is enabled for operation.

30. Can the parity check interrupt request be individually enabled/disabled? Explain.

31. Overview how the 8088 determines which of the NMI sources has initiated the request for service.

Section 9.5

32. Trace through the operation of the I/O chip select circuitry when an I/O write takes place to address $A0_{16}$

33. Which I/O chip selects can occur during either an input or output bus cycle?

34. What are the outputs of the ROM chip circuitry?

35. Trace through the operation of the ROM address decoder as address $FA000_{16}$ is applied to the input.

36. At what logic level must address bits A_{18} and A_{19} be for the $\overline{\text{RAM ADDR SEL}}$ output to switch to its active 0 logic level?

37. What $\overline{\text{RAS}}$ output is produced by U_{65} if the address input is 10100_{16}?

38. What $\overline{\text{CAS}}$ output is produced by U_{46} if the address input is 20200_{16}?

Section 9.6

39. Trace through the operation of the ROM circuitry in Fig. 9.5 as a read cycle is performed to address $F4000_{16}$.

40. Overview the operation of the RAM circuitry in Fig. 9.6 as a byte of data is written to the DRAMs in bank 0.

Section 9.7

41. What are the sources of DMA requests for channels 1, 2, and 3?

42. Overview the DMA request/acknowledge handshake sequence.

43. What is the function of the DMA page register?

Section 9.8

44. Overview the operation of the 8253's microprocessor interface as a byte of data is written into the current count register.

45. What frequency clock is applied to the counters?

46. Overview how timer 2 is used to drive the speaker.

Section 9.9

47. Overview the operation of the 8255A's microprocessor interface as a byte of data is input from port PA.

48. What is the function of signal KBD IRQ?

Section 9.10

49. What is the purpose of the I/O channel slots in the system processor board? How many are provided?

50. Which I/O channel connector pin is used to supply the signal I/O channel ready to the system processor board?

Section 9.11

51. How many $+V_{CC}$ power supply pins are provided on the package of the 82C100? What are their pin numbers?

52. What 82C100 signal does the symbol PAR_0 stand for?

53. Is the signal $\overline{PS}$ an input or output of the 82C100?

54. What symbol is used to identify the power fail NMI signal of the 82C100? Is this signal an input or output? What is its pin number?

55. To which pin of the I/O channel connectors in Fig. 9.15 is the AEN output of the 82C100 supplied?

56. To which devices is the PAR_1 signal line of the 82C100 supplied in the circuit of Fig. 9.15?

57. Which one of the local bus interface outputs of the 82C100 is not connected to the I/O channel connectors in Fig. 9.15?

58. To which pin of the I/O channel connectors is the $\overline{IOCHCHK}$ input of the 82C100 connected in the circuit of Fig. 9.15?

59. What frequency signal is applied to the optional oscillator input of the 82C100 in Fig. 9.15?

60. What is the source of the PWRGD (power good) input of the 82C100 in Fig. 9.15?

61. Which transceiver device in Fig. 9.15 is controlled by the signals $\overline{DBEN}$ and DBIN?

62. What is the total storage capacity of the ROM subsystem?

63. To which device and pin is the signal $\overline{MRAS_3}$ applied in the circuit of Fig. 9.15?

64. To which devices and pins is the signal PAR_0 supplied in the circuit of Fig. 9.15?

65. To which pin of the I/O channel connectors in Fig. 9.15 is the 82C100's $\overline{MREF}$ output connected? What signal is output to this pin of the I/O channel interface connector in Fig. 9.11?

66. What is the source of the IRQ_2 input of the 82C100 in Fig. 9.15?

67. What is the source of the numeric coprocessor NMI input of the 82C100 in the circuit of Fig. 9.15?

68. What is the source of the speaker data input of the 82C100 in Fig. 9.15?

69. What is the source and destination of the keyboard data line in the circuit of Fig. 9.15?

Suggested Laboratory Assignments

LABORATORY 1: EXPLORING THE SOFTWARE ARCHITECTURE OF THE 8088 MICROPROCESSOR

Objective

Learn how to:

1. Bring up the DEBUG program.
2. Examine and modify the contents of the 8088's internal registers.
3. Examine and modify the contents of the 8088's code, data, and stack segments of memory.
4. Calculate the physical addresses of storage locations in the memory address space.
5. Examine the contents of the dedicated parts of the 8088's memory address space.

Part 1: Loading the DEBUG Program

Here we will learn how to bring up the DEBUG program from the keyboard of the PC. *Check off each step as it is completed.*

Check	Step	Procedure
✓	1	Turn the PC on and verify that it is running the DOS 3.1 operating system.
	2	Set up the PC to print all displayed information by entering the key sequence

(Ctrl) (PrtSc)

Check	Step	Procedure
✓	3	Insert the diskette that contains the DEBUG program into drive A.
	4	Load DEBUG by issuing the command

A>DEBUG   (↵)

What prompt do you see on the screen? Ans. _____

Check	Step	Procedure
✓	5	Return to the DOS operating system by entering the command

—Q   (↵)

What prompt is now displayed? Ans. _____ >_____

Check	Step	Procedure
	6	Tear off the page(s) of printed information produced and label as "Printout for Laboratory 1, Part 1."

Part 2: Examining and Modifying the Contents of the 8088's Internal Registers

Now we will use the REGISTER command to first examine the initial contents of the 8088's internal registers and then modify the values in the registers and state of the flags.

Check	Step	Procedure
✓	1	Use the REGISTER command to display the current contents of all the 8088's internal registers. List the initial values held in CS, DS, and SS. Ans. _0F9D_, _0F9D_, _0F9D_ _IP0100_ Calculate the physical address of the next instruction to be executed. Ans. _109D_ What is the instruction held at this address? Ans. _255300_ Calculate the physical address of the current top of the stack. Ans. _____
	2	Enter the command

—R AH   (↵)

What happens? Ans. _A H = 00_

Check	Step	Procedure
✓	3	Use a REGISTER command to first display the current contents of CX and then change this value to 10_{16}.
✓	4	Issue a REGISTER command to first display the current contents of IP and then modify its value to 0200_{16}.

Check	Step	Procedure
✓	5	Use the REGISTER command to display the current contents of the flag register and then change the state of the parity flag to represent even parity.
✓	6	Redisplay the contents of all the 8088's internal registers. Compare the displayed register contents to those printed in Step 1. Make a list of those registers whose contents have changed. Ans. _CX, F, IP, Physical address_ What instruction is now pointed to by CS:IP? Ans. _6E_
✓	7	Tear off the page(s) of printed information produced and label as "Printout for Laboratory 1, Part 2."

Part 3: Examining and Modifying the Contents of Memory

Next we explore the memory subsystem of the PC and operation of the memory examine/modify commands provided in DEBUG.

Check	Step	Procedure
✓	1	Use the information printed out in Step 1 of Part 2 to draw a diagram similar to that in Fig. 2.5 to show how the active memory segments are initially mapped. In the diagram, identify the lowest and highest physical address of each segment.

Memory

0F9D	CS
0F9D	DS
0F9D	SS
0F9D	ES

Check	Step	Procedure
✓	2	Use the DUMP command to display the first 256 bytes of the current data segment.
✓	3	Display the next 128 bytes of the code segment.
✓	4	Use the DUMP command to show the last six words pushed to the stack.
✓	5	With the ENTER command, load the first 16 bytes of the current data segment with the value FF_{16}. Before terminating the command, verify that

Check	Step	Procedure
		the memory contents have been changed by stepping back through the memory locations by depressing the − key.
✓	6	Use FILL commands to initialize the 16 storage locations starting at DS:10 with the value 55_{16} and the 16 storage locations starting at address DS:30 with 00_{16}.
✓	7	With a MOVE command, copy the contents of the 16 storage locations starting at DS:00 to the 16 storage locations starting at DS:20.
✓	8	Display the contents of the first 128 bytes of the current data segment with the DUMP command.
✓	9	Use the COMPARE command to compare the contents of the 16 storage locations starting at DS:00 to those starting at DS:10 and then to those starting at DS:20.
✓	10	Execute a SEARCH command to determine which storage locations in the range DS:00 through DS:3F contain the value FF_{16}.
	11	Tear off the page(s) of printed information produced and label as "Printout for Laboratory 1, Part 3."

Part 4: Exploring the Dedicated Use Part of the 8088's Memory Address Space

Figure 2.14 identifies certain parts of the 8088's memory address space as having dedicated functions. Here we will determine the contents of these dedicated address spaces.

Check	Step	Procedure
✓	1	Change the contents of the DS register to 0000_{16}.
	2	Display the vectors stored at addresses 00000_{16} through 00015_{16} of the interrupt pointer table.
	3	Dedicated addresses 00000_{16} through 00003_{16} store a pointer that is the starting address of the service routine for the divide error interrupt. Use the values displayed in Step 2 to calculate the physical address corresponding to this pointer. Ans. _____
✓	4	The address pointer that identifies the starting location of the nonmaskable interrupt (NMI) service routine is held in storage locations 00008_{16} through $0000B_{16}$. Use the value displayed in Step 2 to calculate the physical address represented by this pointer. Ans. _____
✓	5	The overflow interrupt pointer is held at locations 00012_{16} through 00015_{16} in memory. Using the values displayed in Step 2, calculate the physical address represented by this pointer. Ans. _____

LABORATORY 2: ASSEMBLING AND EXECUTING INSTRUCTIONS WITH THE DEBUG

Objective

Learn how to:

1. Code assembly language instructions into machine code.
2. Assemble instructions into the memory of the PC.
3. Unassemble machine code instructions stored in memory.
4. Store and load machine code instructions from diskette.
5. Execute an instruction to determine the operation it performs.

Part 1: Coding Instructions in 8088 Machine Language

Here we will use the general instruction formats of Fig. 3.5 and machine language coding tables in Figs. 3.2 through 3.4 to code assembly language instructions into their equivalent machine code. *Check off each step as it is completed.*

Check	Step	Procedure
✓	1	Encode each of the instructions that follow into machine code.
		(a) MOV AX,BX Ans. _8BC3_
		(b) MOV AX,0AAAAH Ans. _B8AAAA_
		(c) MOV AX,[BX] Ans. _8B07_
		(d) MOV AX,[0004] Ans. _8B0400_
		(e) MOV AX,[BX+SI] Ans. _8B00_
		(f) MOV AX,[SI]+[0004] Ans. _8B84_
✓		(g) MOV AX,[BX][SI]+[0004] Ans. _8B80_
	2	How many bytes are required to store each of the machine code instructions in Step 1?
		(a) Ans. _2_
		(b) Ans. _3_
		(c) Ans. _2_
		(d) Ans. _3_
		(e) Ans. _2_
		(f) Ans. _2_
		(g) Ans. _2_

Part 2: Assembling Instructions and Saving Them on a Floppy Diskette

Next we will learn how to use the ASSEMBLE command to enter assembly language instructions into the memory of the PC, verify the loading of machine code instructions by disassembling with the UNASSEMBLE command, and save the machine code instruction on a data diskette with the WRITE command.

Check	Step	Procedure
	1	For each of the instructions that follow, use DEBUG commands to assemble the instruction at the specified address, verify the loading of the instruction in memory, and then store the instruction at the given file specification on a formatted data diskette.
		(a) MOV AX,BX; CS:100; FILE SPEC =1 00 1
		(b) MOV AX,0AAAAH; CS:110; FILE SPEC = 1 10 1
		(c) MOV AX,[BX]; CS:120; FILE SPEC = 1 20 1
		(d) MOV AX,[0004]; CS:130; FILE SPEC = 1 30 1
		(e) MOV AX,[BX+SI]; CS:140; FILE SPEC = 1 40 1
		(f) MOV AX,[SI]+[0004]; CS:150; FILE SPEC = 1 50 1
		(g) MOV AX,[BX][SI]+[0004]; CS:160; FILE SPEC = 1 60 1
	2	Tear off the page(s) of printed information produced and label as "Printout for Laboratory 2, Part 2."

Part 3: Loading Instructions from Floppy Diskette for Execution with the Trace Command

Next, machine code instructions that were saved on a data diskette will be loaded into memory with LOAD commands and their operation observed by executing them with the TRACE command.

Check	Step	Procedure
	1	Initialize the internal registers of the 8088 as follows:
		$(AX) = 0000H$
		$(BX) = 0001H$
		$(CX) = 0002H$
		$(DX) = 0003H$
		$(SI) = 0010H$
		$(DI) = 0020H$
		$(BP) = 0030H$
		Verify the initialization by displaying the new contents of the registers.
	2	Fill all memory locations in the range DS:00 through DS:1F with 00_{16} and then initialize the word storage locations that follow:
		$(DS:0001H) = BBBBH$
		$(DS:0004H) = CCCCH$
		$(DS:0011H) = DDDDH$
		$(DS:0014H) = EEEEH$
		$(DS:0016H) = FFFFH$
	3	For each of the file specifications that follow, reload the instruction that was saved in Step 1 of Part 2, verify the loading of the instruction, display the contents of the internal registers and memory locations DS:00 through DS:1F, and then execute the instruction with the TRACE command. Describe the operation performed by the instruction.

Check	Step	Procedure
		(a) FILE SPEC = 1 00 1
		Ans. _AX = BX_
		(b) FILE SPEC = 1 10 1
		Ans. _AX = AAAA_
		(c) FILE SPEC = 1 20 1
		Ans. _AX = [BX]_
		(d) FILE SPEC = 1 30 1
		Ans. _AX = 0004_
		(e) FILE SPEC = 1 40 1
		Ans. _AX = [BX + SI]_
		(f) FILE SPEC = 1 50 1
		Ans. _AX = [SI + 6004]_
		(g) FILE SPEC = 1 60 1
		Ans. _AX = [BX SI] + 6004]_
✓	4	Tear off the page(s) of printed information produced and label as "Printout for Laboratory 2, Part 3."

LABORATORY 3: LOADING, EXECUTING, AND DEBUGGING PROGRAMS

Objective

Learn how to:

1. Load a program with the line-by-line assembler, verify its loading with the UNASSEMBLE command, and save the program on a data diskette.
2. Run a program and verify its operation from the results it produces.
3. Load the machine code of an assembled program from a file on a data diskette, run the program, and observe the operation of the program.
4. Debug the operation of a program.

Part 1: Executing a Program That Is Loaded with the ASSEMBLE Command

In this part of the laboratory, we will learn how to enter a program with the line-by-line assembler, verify that the program was entered correctly by disassembling the program with the UNASSEMBLE command, save the program on a data diskette, reload a program from a data diskette, and observe the operation of the program by executing with GO and TRACE commands. *Check off each step as it is completed.*

Check	Step	Procedure
✓	1	Using the ASSEMBLE command, load the block move program of Fig. 3.34(a) into memory starting at address CS:100.

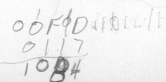

Check	Step	Procedure
✓	2	Verify the loading of the program by displaying it with the UNAS-SEMBLE command. How many bytes of memory does the program take up? Ans. _18_ What is the machine code for the NOP instruction? Ans. _90_ At what address is the NOP instruction stored? Ans. _10B4_
✓	3	Save the program on a formatted data diskette in file specification 1 110 1.
✓	4	Reload the program into memory at CS:100.
	5	Initialize the blocks of data as follows: (a) Use a FILL command to clear all storage locations in the range 1020:0100 through 1020:013F. (b) Verify that this range of memory has been cleared by displaying its contents with a DUMP command. (c) Fill the storage locations from address 1020:0100 through 1020:010F with the value 55_{16}. (d) Verify the initialization of the storage locations from 1020:0100 through 1020:010F with a DUMP command.
✓	6	Run the complete program by issuing a single GO command. What is the starting address in the GO command? Ans. _CS:20F:20E_ What is the ending address? Ans. _SS:215 217_
✓	7	Verify that the block move operation was correctly performed by displaying the contents of memory range 1020:0100 through 1020:013F. Given an overview of the operation performed by the program. Ans. _____
	8	Reinitialize the block of memory as specified in Step 5.
✓	9	Execute the program using the TRACE and GO commands that are shown in Fig. 3.37.
✓	10	Tear off the page(s) of printed information produced and label as "Printout for Laboratory 3, Part 1."

Part 2: Executing a Program Assembled with the IBM MASM Macroassembler

Here we will load a program that was assembled with IBM's 8088 Macroassembler and observe its operation by executing the program with GO and TRACE commands.

Check	Step	Procedure
✓	1	Exit DEBUG with the QUIT command.
✓	2	Insert the "Programs Diskette" into drive B of the PC.

Check	Step	Procedure
✓	3	Use the DOS "TYPE" command to display the source listing in file L3P2.LST that resides on the programs diskette.
		What is the starting address offset from CS: for the first instruction (PUSH DS) of the program? Ans. _001E_
		The last instruction (RET) of the program? Ans. _001C EB_
✓	4	Load the run module L3P2.EXE with the DOS command

```
A>DEBUG  B:L3P2.EXE
```

Check	Step	Procedure
✓	5	Verify loading of the program by unassembling the contents of the current code segment for the offset range found in Step 3.
✓	6	Initialize memory the same way as done in Step 5 of Part 1.
✓	7	Run the program to completion by issuing a single GO command.
✓	8	Verify the operation of the program by displaying the contents of memory range 1020:0100 through 1020:013F.
✓	9	Reinitialize the memory as done in Step 5 of Part 1 and display the contents of the 8088's registers.
	10	Execute the program according to the instructions that follow:

(a) GO from address CS:00 through CS:13.
What has happened to the values in DS, AX, CX, SI, and DI?
Ans. _AX 1020, DS 1020, CX 0100, SI 0100_, _DI 0120_

(b) GO from address CS:13 through CS:1A.

(c) Display the data from 1020:0100 through 1020:013F.
Which byte of data was moved? Ans. _SI_
Where was it moved to? Ans. _AH_

(d) GO from address CS:1A to CS:13.
What has happened to the value in IP? Ans. _001A - 0013_

(e) GO from address CS:13 through CS:1A.
What has happened to the values in SI, DI, and CS? Ans. _SI INCl_,
DI-INCl, CS - NOchange

(f) Display the data from 1020:0100 through 1020:013F.
Which byte of data was moved? Ans. _SI_
Where was it moved to? Ans. _AH_

(g) GO from address CS:1A through CS:1C.
What has happened to the values in SI, DI, and CS? Ans. _____,
_____, _____

(h) Display the data from 1020:0100 through 1020:013F.
Describe the block move operation performed by the program.
Ans. _No change_
_____
_____

How does it differ from that performed in Part I? Ans. _____

Part 3: Debugging a Program

Now we will debug a program that contains an error by executing the program step by step and observing program operation with DEBUG commands.

Check	Step	Procedure
✓	1	Exit DEBUG with the QUIT command.
✓	2	Insert the "Program Diskette" into drive B of the PC.
✓	3	Use the DOS "TYPE" command to display the source listing in file L3P3.LST that resides on the programs diskette. What is the starting address offset from CS: for the first instruction (PUSH DS) of the program? Ans. _00_ The last instruction (RET) of the program? Ans. _1C_
	4	Load the run module L3P3.EXE with the DOS command A>DEBUG B:L3P3.EXE
✓	5	Verify loading of the program by unassembling the contents of the current code segment for the offset range found in Step 3.
✓	6	Initialize memory the same way as done in Step 5 of Part 1.
	7	Execute the program according to the instructions that follow: (a) GO from address CS:00 through CS:13. What has happened to the values in DS, AX, CX, SI, and DI? Ans. _1020_, _1020_, _10_, _100_, _13?_ (b) GO from address CS:13 through CS:1A. (c) Display the data from 1020:0100 through 1020:013F Which byte of data was moved? Ans. _____ Where was it moved to? Ans. _____ (d) GO from address CS:1A to CS:13. What has happened to the value in IP? Ans. _decr._ (e) GO from address CS:13 through CS:1A. (f) Display the data from 1020:0100 through 1020:013F. Which byte of data was moved? Ans. _Next instrus. to be fetch_ Where was it moved to? Ans. _?_ (g) GO from address CS:1A through CS:1C. (h) Display the data from 1020:0100 through 1020:013F. Describe the block move operation performed by the program. Ans. _no change_ How does it differ from the planned operation? Ans. _should have changed_ From the printout of the program's operation, what is the error in the program? Ans. _No pointer at location_

LABORATORY 4: WORKING WITH THE DATA TRANSFER, ARITHMETIC, LOGIC, SHIFT, AND ROTATE INSTRUCTIONS

Objective

Learn how to:

1. Verify the operation of data transfer instructions by executing them with DEBUG.
2. Verify the operation of arithmetic instructions by executing them with DEBUG.
3. Verify the operation of logic instructions by executing them with DEBUG.
4. Verify the operation of shift and rotate instructions by executing them with DEBUG.

Part 1: Data Transfer Instructions

Here we will use DEBUG commands to execute various instructions from the data transfer group to observe the operation that they perform. *Check off each step as it is completed.*

Check	Step	Procedure
✓	1	Assemble the instruction MOV SI,[0ABC] into memory at address CS:100 and verify loading of the instruction. How many bytes of memory does the instruction take up? Ans. _4 bytes_
✓	2	Initialize the word of memory starting at DS:0ABC with the value $FFFF_{16}$ and then verify with a DUMP command that the contents of memory have been updated.
✓	3	Clear the SI register and verify by redisplaying its contents.
✓	4	Execute the instruction with a trace command. Describe the operation performed by the instruction. Ans. _SI=000 → FFFF_
✓	5	Assemble the instruction MOV WORD PTR [SI],ABCD into memory at address CS:100 and then verify loading of the instruction. How many bytes of memory does the instruction take up? Ans. _4 bytes_
✓	6	Initialize the SI register with the value $0ABC_{16}$ and verify by redisplaying its contents.
✓	7	Clear the word of memory starting at DS:0ABC and then verify that the contents of this memory location have been set to zero with a DUMP command.
✓	8	Execute the instruction with a trace command. Describe the operation performed by the instruction. Ans. _No changes_

Check	Step	Procedure
✓	9	Exit DEBUG with the QUIT command.
✓	10	Insert the "Programs Diskette" into drive B of the PC.
✓	11	Use the DOS "TYPE" command to display the source listing in file L4P1.LST that resides on the programs diskette. What is the starting address offset from CS: for the first instruction (PUSH DS) of the program? Ans. _00_ The last instruction (RET) of the program? Ans. _1E_
✓	12	Load the run module L4P1.EXE with the DOS command

```
A>DEBUG  B:L4P1.EXE
```

Check	Step	Procedure
✓	13	Verify loading of the program by unassembling the contents of the current code segment for the offset range found in Step 11.
	14	Execute the program according to the instructions that follow:

(a) GO from address CS:00 through CS:5.

(b) Use TRACE commands to single-step execute instructions through address CS:1E. Explain what operation is performed by each instruction.

INSTRUCTION 1 _Mov AX, 0FC4_
INSTRUCTION 2 _Mov DS, AX_
INSTRUCTION 3 _Mov DX, 00_
INSTRUCTION 4 _XLAT_
INSTRUCTION 5 _Mov [0010], AL_
INSTRUCTION 6 _Mov AL, [0011]_
INSTRUCTION 7 _Mov BX, 0008_
INSTRUCTION 8 _XLAT_
INSTRUCTION 9 _Mov [001], AL_
INSTRUCTION 10 _RETF_

Part 2: Arithmetic Instructions

We will now continue by executing various instructions from the arithmetic group to observe their operation.

Check	Step	Procedure
	1	Assemble the instruction ADC AX,[0ABC] into memory at address CS:100 and verify loading of the instruction. How many bytes of memory does the instruction take up? Ans. _____
	2	Initialize the word of memory starting at DS:0ABC with the value $FFFF_{16}$ and then verify that the contents of memory have been updated with a DUMP command.
	3	Initialize register AX with the value 0001_{16} and verify by redisplaying its contents.
	4	Clear the carry flag.
	5	Execute the instruction with a TRACE command.

Check	Step	Procedure
		Describe the operation performed by the instruction. Ans. _____
		Does a carry occur? Ans. _____
_____	6	Assemble the instruction SBB WORD PTR [SI],ABCD into memory at address CS:100 and then verify loading of the instruction. How many bytes of memory does the instruction take up? Ans. _____
_____	7	Initialize the SI register with the value $0ABC_{16}$ and verify by redisplaying its contents.
_____	8	Initialize the word of memory starting at DS:0ABC with the value $FFFF_{16}$ and then verify that the contents of this memory location have been correctly initialized with a DUMP command.
_____	9	Clear the carry flag.
_____	10	Execute the instruction with a TRACE command. Describe the operation performed by the instruction. Ans. _____
		Does a borrow occur? Ans. _____
_____	11	Exit DEBUG with the QUIT command.
_____	12	Insert the "Programs Diskette" into drive B of the PC.
_____	13	Use the DOS "TYPE" command to display the source listing in file L4P2.LST that resides on the programs diskette. What is the starting address offset from CS: for the first instruction (PUSH DS) of the program? Ans. _____ The last instruction (RET) of the program? Ans. _____
_____	14	Load the run module L4P2.EXE with the DOS command `A>DEBUG  B:L4P2.EXE`
_____	15	Verify loading of the program by unassembling the contents of the current code segment for the offset range found in Step 13.
_____	16	Execute the program according to the instructions that follow: (a) GO from address CS:00 through CS:5. (b) Use TRACE commands to single-step execute instructions through address CS:15. Explain what operation is performed by each instruction. INSTRUCTION 1 _____ INSTRUCTION 2 _____ INSTRUCTION 3 _____ INSTRUCTION 4 _____ INSTRUCTION 5 _____ INSTRUCTION 6 _____

Part 3: Logic Instructions

In this section we will study the operation of various logic instructions by executing them with DEBUG.

Check	Step	Procedure
_____	1	Assemble the instruction OR AX,[0ABC] into memory at address CS:100 and verify loading of the instruction. How many bytes of memory does the instruction take up? Ans. _____
_____	2	Initialize the word of memory starting at DS:0ABC with the value 5555_{16} and then verify that the contents of memory have been updated with a DUMP command.
_____	3	Initialize register AX with the value $AAAA_{16}$ and verify by redisplaying its contents.
_____	4	Execute the instruction with a TRACE command. Describe the operation performed by the instruction. Ans. _____
_____	5	Assemble the instruction XOR WORD PTR [SI],5555 into memory at address CS:100 and then verify loading of the instruction. How many bytes of memory does the instruction take up? Ans. _____
_____	6	Initialize the SI register with the value $0ABC_{16}$ and verify by redisplaying its contents.
_____	7	Initialize the word of memory starting at DS:0ABC with the value $00AA_{16}$ and then verify that the contents of this memory location have been correctly initialized with a DUMP command.
_____	8	Execute the instruction with a TRACE command. Describe the operation performed by the instruction. Ans. _____
_____	9	Assemble the instruction sequence

```
                        NOT AX
                        ADD AX,1
```

into memory starting at address CS:100 and then verify loading of the instructions. How many bytes of memory do they take up? Ans. _____

Check	Step	Procedure
_____	10	Initialize register AX with the value $FFFF_{16}$ and verify by redisplaying its contents.
_____	11	Verify loading of the instructions by disassembling them.
_____	12	Execute the instructions with TRACE commands. Describe the operation performed by each instruction. INSTRUCTION 1 _____ INSTRUCTION 2 _____

Part 4: Shift and Rotate Instructions

Now we will execute various instructions from the shift and rotate groups to observe their operation.

Check	Step	Procedure
_____	1	Assemble the instruction SHL WORD PTR[0ABC],1 into memory at address CS:100 and verify loading of the instruction. How many bytes of memory does the instruction take up? Ans. _____
_____	2	Initialize the word of memory starting at DS:0ABC with the value 5555_{16} and then verify that the contents of memory have been updated with a DUMP command.
_____	3	Clear the carry flag.
_____	4	Execute the instruction with a TRACE command. Describe the operation performed by the instruction. Ans. _____ _____ Does a carry occur? Ans. _____
_____	5	Assemble the instruction ROR WORD PTR [SI],1 into memory at address CS:100 and then verify loading of the instruction. How many bytes of memory does the instruction take up? Ans. _____
_____	6	Initialize the SI register with the value $0ABC_{16}$ and verify by redisplaying its contents.
_____	7	Initialize the word of memory starting at DS:0ABC with the value $AAAA_{16}$ and then verify that the contents of this memory location have been correctly initialized with a DUMP command.
_____	8	Clear the carry flag.
_____	9	Execute the instruction with a TRACE command. Describe the operation performed by the instruction. Ans. _____ _____ Does a carry occur? Ans. _____
_____	10	Exit DEBUG with the QUIT command.
_____	11	Insert the "Programs Diskette" into drive B of the PC.
_____	12	Use the DOS "TYPE" command to display the source listing in file L4P4.LST that resides on the program diskette. What is the starting address offset from CS: for the first instruction (PUSH DS) of the program? Ans. _____ The last instruction (RET) of the program? Ans. _____
_____	13	Load the run module L4P4.EXE with the DOS command ``` A>DEBUG B:L4P4.EXE ```
_____	14	Verify loading of the program by unassembling the contents of the current code segment for the offset range found in Step 12.
_____	15	Execute the program according to the instructions that follow: (a) GO from address CS:00 through CS:5. (b) Use TRACE commands to single-step execute instructions through address CS:10. Explain what operation is performed by each instruction. INSTRUCTION 1 _____ INSTRUCTION 2 _____ INSTRUCTION 3 _____ INSTRUCTION 4 _____

LABORATORY 5: WORKING WITH THE FLAG CONTROL, COMPARE, JUMP, SUBROUTINE, LOOP, AND STRING INSTRUCTIONS

Objective

Learn how to:

1. Verify the operation of flag control instructions by executing them with DEBUG.
2. Verify the operation of the compare instruction by executing it with DEBUG.
3. Verify the operation of jump instructions by executing them with DEBUG.
4. Verify the operation of the subroutine handling instructions by executing them with DEBUG.
5. Verify the operation of the loop handling instructions by executing them with DEBUG.
6. Verify the operation of the string handling instructions by executing them with DEBUG.

Part 1: Flag-Control Instructions

In this part of the lab we will execute a program sequence that includes instructions from the flag-control group to observe the operations that they perform. *Check off each step as it is completed.*

Check	Step	Procedure
_____	1	Assemble the instruction sequence

```
LAHF
MOV   BH,AH
AND   BH,1FH
AND   AH,0E0H
MOV   [200H],BH
SAHF
```

Check	Step	Procedure
		into memory starting at address CS:100 and then verify loading of the instructions. How many bytes of memory do the instructions take up? Ans. _____
_____	2	Initialize the byte of memory at DS:200 with the value 00_{16} and then verify that the contents of memory have been updated with a DUMP command.
_____	3	Clear registers AX and BX and verify by redisplaying their contents.

Check	Step	Procedure
_____	4	Display the current state of the flags. Make SF equal to NG.
_____	5	Execute the instructions one at a time with TRACE commands. Describe the operation performed by each instruction.

INSTRUCTION 1 _____
INSTRUCTION 2 _____
INSTRUCTION 3 _____
INSTRUCTION 4 _____
INSTRUCTION 5 _____
INSTRUCTION 6 _____
Briefly describe the overall operation performed by the instruction sequence.
Ans. _____
_____
_____

Part 2: Compare Instruction

Here we will use DEBUG commands to execute an instruction sequence that involves the compare instruction to observe the operation that it performs.

Check	Step	Procedure
√	1	Assemble the instruction sequence

```
MOV  BX,1111H
MOV  AX,0BBBBH
CMP  BX,AX
```

into memory starting at address CS:100 and then verify loading of the instructions. How many bytes of memory do the instructions take up?
Ans. *8 bytes*

Check	Step	Procedure
√	2	Clear registers AX and BX and verify by redisplaying their contents.
√	3	Display the current state of the flags.
√	4	Execute the instructions one at a time with TRACE commands. Describe the operation performed by each instruction.

INSTRUCTION 1 _*Mov Bx 1111*_____
INSTRUCTION 2 _*Mov A 0BBB*_____
INSTRUCTION 3 _*Cmp BX AX*_____
Briefly describe the overall operation performed by the instruction sequence.
Ans. _____
_____
_____

Part 3: Jump Instructions

Now we will use DEBUG commands to execute and observe the operation of a factorial calculation program that performs both unconditional and conditional jumps.

Check	Step	Procedure
✓	1	Exit DEBUG with the QUIT command.
✓	2	Insert the "Programs Diskette" into drive B of the PC.
✓	3	Use the DOS "TYPE" command to display the source listing in file L5P3.LST that resides on the programs diskette. What is the starting address offset from CS: for the first instruction (PUSH DS) of the program? Ans. __00__ The last instruction (RET) of the program? Ans. __1B__
	4	Load the run module L5P3.EXE with the DOS command

```
A>DEBUG  B:L5P3.EXE
```

Check	Step	Procedure
✓	5	Verify loading of the program by unassembling the contents of the current code segment for the offset range found in Step 3.
✓	6	Execute the program according to the instructions that follow:

    (a) GO from address CS:00 to CS:5.
    (b) Load the number whose factorial is to be calculated (N = 5) into register DX.
    (c) Clear the storage location for the value of the factorial (FACT), which is register CX.
    (d) GO from address CS:5 to CS:10. What is the state of the zero flag? Ans. __NZ__
    (e) Execute the JZ instruction with a TRACE command. Was the jump taken? Ans. __NO__
    (f) GO from address CS:12 to CS:16. What is the current value in AL? Ans. __02__
    (g) Execute the JMP instruction with a TRACE command. Was the jump taken? Ans. __Yes__ What is the address of the next instruction to be executed? Ans. __0E__
    (h) GO from address CS:E to CS:10. What is the state of the zero flag? Ans. __Low reset__
    (i) Execute the JZ instruction with a TRACE command. Was the jump taken? Ans. __NO__
    (j) GO from address CS:12 to CS:16. What is the current value in AL? Ans. __06__
    (k) Execute the JMP instruction with a TRACE command. Was the jump taken? Ans. __Yes__ What is the address of the next instruction to be executed? Ans. __0E__

Check	Step	Procedure

(l) GO from address CS:E to CS:10. What is the state of the zero flag?
Ans. _low_

(m) Execute the JZ instruction with a TRACE command. Was the jump taken? Ans. _no_

(n) GO from address CS:12 to CS:16. What is the current value in AL?
Ans. _0018_

(o) Execute the JMP instruction with a TRACE command. Was the jump taken? Ans. _yes_
What is the address of the next instruction to be executed?
Ans. _000E_

(p) GO from address CS:E to CS:10. What is the state of the zero flag?
Ans. _low_

(q) Execute the JZ instruction with a TRACE command. Was the jump taken? Ans. _No_

(r) GO from address CS:12 to CS:16. What is the current value in AL?
Ans. _0018_

(s) Execute the JMP instruction with a TRACE command. Was the jump taken? Ans. _yes_
What is the address of the next instruction to be executed?
Ans. _000E_

(t) GO from address CS:E to CS:10. What is the state of the zero flag?
Ans. _high (set)_

(u) Execute the JZ instruction with a TRACE command. Was the jump taken? Ans. _yes_

(v) GO from address CS:12 to CS:16. What is the current value in AL?
Ans. _00_

(w) Execute the JMP instruction with a TRACE command. Was the jump taken? Ans. _yes_
What is the address of the next instruction to be executed?
Ans. _0E_

(x) GO from address CS:E to CS:10. What is the state of the zero flag?
Ans. _reset (low)_

(y) Execute the JZ instruction with a TRACE command. Was the jump taken? Ans. _No_
What instruction is to be executed next? Ans. _FEC1_

(z) GO to CS:1C. What is the final value in AL? Ans. _N/A_
At what address is the value in AL stored in memory as FACT?
Ans. _N/A_

(aa) Display the value stored for FACT in memory.

Part 4: Subroutine Handling Instructions

Next we will use DEBUG commands to execute and observe the operation of a program that employs a subroutine.

Check	Step	Procedure
✓	1	Exit DEBUG with the QUIT command.
✓	2	Insert the "Programs Diskette" into drive B of the PC.
✓	3	Use the DOS "TYPE" command to display the source listing in file L5P4.LST that resides on the programs diskette. What is the starting address offset from CS: for the first instruction (PUSH DS) of the program? Ans. _00_ The last instruction (RET) of the program? Ans. _08_
✓	4	Load the run module L5P4.EXE with the DOS command

```
A>DEBUG B:L5P4.EXE
```

Check	Step	Procedure
✓	5	Verify loading of the program by unassembling the contents of the current code segment for the offset range found in Step 3.
	6	Execute the program according to the instructions that follow:

(a) GO from address CS:00 to CS:5. What instruction is to be executed next? Ans. _05_

(b) Load the numbers that follow for use by the arithmetic subroutine.

$$
\begin{aligned}
(AX) &= -32_{10} = \text{FFE0H} \\
(BX) &= 27_{10} = \text{001BH} \\
(CX) &= 10_{10} = \text{000AH} \\
(DX) &= 200_{10} = \text{00C8H}
\end{aligned}
$$

(c) Execute the call instruction with a TRACE command. What instruction is to be executed next? Ans. _Push DX_

(d) GO to address CS:10. What is the sum in DX? Ans. _25_

(e) Check the value of the last word pushed to the stack.

(f) Run the program to completion with a GO command. What is the final value in DX? Ans. _25_ How did the contents of DX become this value? Ans. _we pushed it from the stack_

Part 5: Loop Handling Instructions

Here we will use DEBUG commands to execute and observe the operation of a block search program that performs a loop.

Check	Step	Procedure
✓	1	Exit DEBUG with the QUIT command.
✓	2	Insert the "Programs Diskette" into drive B of the PC.
✓	3	Use the DOS "TYPE" command to display the source listing in file L5P5.LST that resides on the programs diskette.

Check	Step	Procedure
		What is the starting address offset from CS: for the first instruction (PUSH DS) of the program? Ans. _00_
		The last instruction (RET) of the program? Ans. _17_
✓	4	Load the run module L5P5.EXE with the DOS command

```
A>DEBUG B:L5P5.EXE
```

Check	Step	Procedure
✓	5	Verify loading of the program by unassembling the contents of the current code segment for the offset range found in Step 3.
	6	Execute the program according to the instructions that follow:

(a) GO from address CS:00 to CS:12.

(b) Clear all storage locations in the range DS:0 through DS:AF.

(c) Initialize the byte storage location DS:03 with the value AB_{16}.

(d) Display the contents of all storage locations in the range DS:0 through DS:AF.

(e) GO to address CS:15. What is the value in SI? Ans. _03_

What are the states of CF and ZF? Ans. _0_, _0_ What is the next instruction to be executed? Ans. _E0FB_

(f) Execute the LOOPNZ instruction with a TRACE command. Was the loop taken? Ans. _yes_

(g) GO to address CS:15. What is the value in SI? Ans. _____ What are the states of CF and ZF? Ans. _____, _____ What is the next instruction to be executed? Ans. _____

(h) Execute the LOOPNZ instruction with a TRACE command. Was the loop taken? Ans. _____

(i) GO to address CS:15. What is the value in SI? Ans. _____ What are the states of CF and ZF? Ans. _____, _____ What is the next instruction to be executed? Ans. _____

(j) Execute the LOOPNZ instruction with a TRACE command. Was the loop taken? Ans. _____ What is the next instruction to be executed? Ans. _____ Why? Ans. _____

(k) Run the program to completion with a GO command. Overview the operation performed by the program. Ans. _____

Part 6: **String Handling Instructions**

In this part of the laboratory, we will use DEBUG commands to execute and observe the operation of an array comparison program that employs a string instruction.

Check	Step	Procedure
_____	1	Exit DEBUG with the QUIT command.
_____	2	Insert the "Programs Diskette" into drive B of the PC.
_____	3	Use the DOS "TYPE" command to display the source listing in file L5P6.LST that resides on the programs diskette. What is the starting address offset from CS: for the first instruction (PUSH DS) of the program? Ans. _____ The last instruction (RET) of the program? Ans. _____
_____	4	Load the run module L5P6.EXE with the DOS command

$$\text{A>DEBUG B:L5P6.EXE}$$

Check	Step	Procedure
_____	5	Verify loading of the program by unassembling the contents of the current code segment for the offset range found in Step 3.
_____	6	Execute the program according to the instructions that follow: (a) GO from address CS:00 to CS:16. What is the state of the direction flag? Ans. _____ Does this mean that autoincrement or autodecrement addressing will be performed? Ans. _____ What is the state of ZF? Ans. _____ What are the values in the DS, SI, and DI registers? Ans. _____, _____, _____ What is the count in CX? Ans. _____ What is the next instruction to be executed? Ans. _____ (b) Clear all storage locations in the range DS:00 through DS:C7. (c) Fill all storage locations in the range DS:C8 through DS:18F with FF_{16}. (d) Initialize the word storage locations starting at DS:04 with the value $FFFF_{16}$. (e) Display the contents of all storage locations in the range DS:00 through DS:18F. (f) Run the program to completion with a GO command and then display the registers. What is the state of ZF? Ans. _____ What are the values in the DS, SI, and DI registers? Ans. _____, _____, _____ What is the count in CX? Ans. _____ Overview the operation performed by the program. Ans. ____

LABORATORY 6: CALCULATING THE AVERAGE OF A SERIES OF NUMBERS

Objective

Learn how to:

1. Describe a function that is to be performed with a program.
2. Write a program to implement the function.
3. Run the program to verify that it performs the function for which it was written.

Part 1: Description of the Problem

It is required to determine the average of a set of data points stored in a buffer. The number of points in the buffer, the offset address of the beginning of the buffer, and the data segment address are stored in a table called a *parameter table*. Figure L6.1(a) shows an example of the parameters needed for the average program. Notice that the beginning address of this table is $1ABC0_{16}$. This first address holds the number that indicates how many data points are in the buffer. Since a byte is used to specify the number of data points, the size of the buffer is limited to 255 bytes. The offset address of the beginning of the buffer is stored at table locations $1ABC1_{16}$ and $1ABC2_{16}$. This buffer table offset address is taken with respect to the data segment defined by the address in locations $1ABC3_{16}$ and $1ABC4_{16}$. Assuming that the data points are signed 8-bit binary numbers, write a program to find their average.

Part 2: Writing the Program

The average can be found by adding all the signed numbers and then dividing their sum by the number of points that were added. Even though 8-bit data points are being added, the sum that results can be more than 8 bits. Therefore, we will consider a 16-bit result for the sum, and it will be held in register DX. The average that is obtained turns out to be just 8 bits long. It will be available in AL at the completion of the program.

Out plan for the program that will solve this problem is shown in Fig. L6.1(b). This flowchart can be divided into six basic operations, which are initialization, preparing the next point for addition, performing the addition, updating the counter and pointer, testing for the end of the summation, and computing the average.

Initialization involves establishing the data segment and data buffer addresses and loading the data point counter. This is achieved by loading the appro-

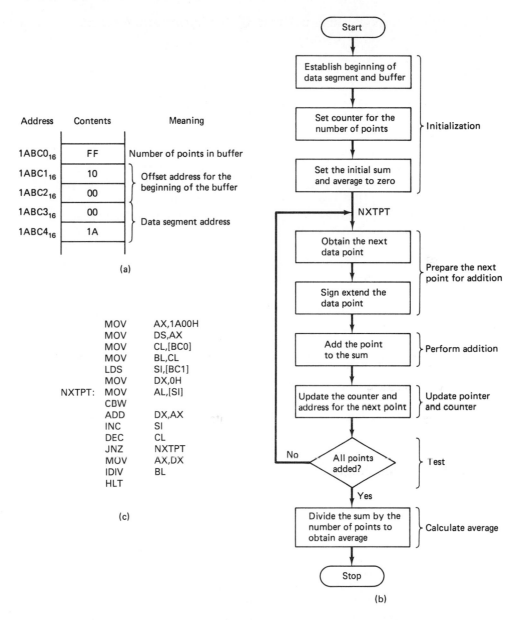

Address	Contents	Meaning
1ABC0$_{16}$	FF	Number of points in buffer
1ABC1$_{16}$	10	Offset address for the beginning of the buffer
1ABC2$_{16}$	00	
1ABC3$_{16}$	00	Data segment address
1ABC4$_{16}$	1A	

(a)

```
        MOV     AX,1A00H
        MOV     DS,AX
        MOV     CL,[BC0]
        MOV     BL,CL
        LDS     SI,[BC1]
        MOV     DX,0H
NXTPT:  MOV     AL,[SI]
        CBW
        ADD     DX,AX
        INC     SI
        DEC     CL
        JNZ     NXTPT
        MOV     AX,DX
        IDIV    BL
        HLT
```

(c)

Start

Establish beginning of data segment and buffer

Set counter for the number of points

Initialization

Set the initial sum and average to zero

NXTPT

Obtain the next data point

Prepare the next point for addition

Sign extend the data point

Add the point to the sum

Perform addition

Update the counter and address for the next point

Update pointer and counter

All points added?

Test

No

Yes

Divide the sum by the number of points to obtain average

Calculate average

Stop

(b)

Figure L6.1 (a) Parameter table for average calculation program. (b) Flowchart for average calculation. (c) Program.

priate registers within the 8088 with parameters from the parameter table. The instructions that perform this initialization are:

```
MOV AX,1A00H
MOV DS,AX
MOV CL,[0BC0H]
MOV BL,CL
LDS SI,[0BC1H]
```

The first two instructions define the data segment in which the parameter table resides. This is achieved by first loading AX with the immediate operand $1A00_{16}$ of a MOV instruction and then copying it into DS.

The instruction that follows this loads CL from the first address in the parameter table. This address is $1ABC0_{16}$ and contains the number of points to be used in forming the average. Looking at Fig. L6.1(a), we see that this value is FF_{16}. The next instruction copies the number in CL into BL for later use. The LDS instruction is used to define the buffer together with the data segment in which it resides. This instruction first loads SI with the offset address of the beginning of the buffer from table locations $1ABC1_{16}$ and $1ABC2_{16}$ and then DS with the address of the data segment in which the data table lies from table locations $1ABC3_{16}$ and $1ABC4_{16}$. The sum must start with zero; therefore, register DX, which is to hold the sum, is loaded with zeros by the instruction

```
MOV DX,0
```

The next operation involves obtaining a byte of data from the buffer, making it into a 16-bit number by sign extension, and adding it to the contents of the DX register. This is accomplished by the following sequence of instructions.

```
NXTPT: MOV AL,[SI]
       CBW
       ADD DX,AX
```

The first instruction loads AL with the element in the buffer that is pointed to by the address in SI. The CBW instruction converts the signed byte in AL to a signed word in AX by extending its sign. Next the 16-bit signed number in AX is added to the sum in DX. Notice that the label NXTPT (next point) has been used on the first instruction.

To prepare for the next addition, we must increment the value in SI such that it points to the next element in the buffer and decrement the count in CL. To do this, we use the following instructions:

```
INC SI
DEC CL
```

If the contents of CL at this point are nonzero, we should go back to obtain and add the next element from the buffer; otherwise, we just proceed with the next instruction in the program. To do this, we execute the following instruction:

```
JNZ NXTPT
```

Execution of this instruction tests the value in ZF that results from the DEC CL instruction. If this flag is not set to one, a jump is initiated to the instruction corresponding to the label NXTPT. Remember that NXTPT is placed at the instruction used to move a byte into AL for addition to the sum. In this way we see that this part of the program will be repeated until all data points have been added. After this is complete, the sum resides in DX.

The average is obtained by dividing the accumulated sum in DX by the number of data points. The count of data points was saved earlier in BL. However, the contents of DX cannot be divided directly. It must first be moved into AX. Once there, the signed divide instruction can be used to do the division. This gives the following instructions:

```
MOV AX,DX
IDIV BL
```

The result of the division, which is the average, is now in AL. The entire average calculation program is shown in Fig. L6.1(c).

Part 3: Running the Program

The source program in Fig. L6.2(a) implements the average calculation routine we just developed, as a procedure. This program was assembled and linked to produce a run module in file LAB6.EXE. The source listing produced by the assembler is shown in Fig. L6.2(b). Now we will execute the program on the IBM PC with 16 arbitrarily selected data points. *Check off each step as it is completed.*

Check	Step	Procedure
_____	1	Load the run module LAB6.EXE in the debugger with the DOS command
		`A>DEBUG B:LAB6.EXE`
_____	2	Verify loading of the program by unassembling the contents of memory starting at the current code segment.
_____	3	Execute the program according to the instructions that follow:
		(a) GO from address CS:0 through CS:A. What are the contents of the data segment register? Ans. _____
		(b) Use DUMP commands to display the contents of the first five data segment storage locations. What is represented by the byte at DS:0? Ans. _____

```
TITLE   LABORATORY 6

        PAGE      ,132

STACK_SEG      SEGMENT      STACK 'STACK'
               DB           64 DUP(?)
STACK_SEG      ENDS

DATA_SEG       SEGMENT      'DATA'
COUNT          DB     16
BUFFER         DD     10000000H
DATA_SEG       ENDS

CODE_SEG       SEGMENT      'CODE'
LAB6    PROC   FAR
        ASSUME CS:CODE_SEG, SS:STACK_SEG, DS:DATA_SEG

;To return to DEBUG program put return address on the stack

        PUSH    DS
        MOV     AX, 0
        PUSH    AX

;Following code implements Laboratory 6

        MOV     AX, DATA_SEG      ;Establish data segment
        MOV     DS, AX
        MOV     CL, COUNT         ;Point count
        MOV     BL, CL
        LDS     SI, BUFFER        ;Pointer for data points
        MOV     DX, 0H            ;Sum = 0
NXTPT:  MOV     AL, [SI]          ;Get a byte size point
        CBW                       ;Convert to word size
        ADD     DX, AX            ;Add to last sum
        INC     SI                ;Point to next point
        DEC     CL                ;All points added ?
        JNZ     NXTPT             ;If not - repeat
        MOV     AX, DX            ;Compute average
        IDIV    BL

        RET                       ;Return to DEBUG program
LAB6    ENDP
CODE_SEG       ENDS

        END     LAB6
```

(a)

```
              TITLE   LABORATORY 6

                      PAGE      ,132

0000                  STACK_SEG      SEGMENT      STACK 'STACK'
0000    40 [                         DB           64 DUP(?)
           ??
                ]

0040                  STACK_SEG      ENDS
```

(b)

Figure L6.2 (a) Source program for average calculation. (b) Source listing produced by assembler. (c) DEBUG sequence.

```
0000                        DATA_SEG    SEGMENT      'DATA'
0000  10                    COUNT       DB      16
0001  00 00 00 10           BUFFER      DD      10000000H
0005                        DATA_SEG    ENDS


0000                        CODE_SEG    SEGMENT      'CODE'
0000                        LAB6  PROC  FAR
                                  ASSUME  CS:CODE_SEG, SS:STACK_SEG, DS:DATA_SEG

                            ;To return to DEBUG program put return address on the stack

0000  1E                            PUSH    DS
0001  B8 0000                       MOV     AX, 0
0004  50                            PUSH    AX

                            ;Following code implements Laboratory 6

0005  B8 ---- R                     MOV     AX, DATA_SEG      ;Establish data segment
0008  8E D8                         MOV     DS, AX
000A  8A 0E 0000 R                  MOV     CL, COUNT         ;Point count
000E  8A D9                         MOV     BL, CL
0010  C5 36 0001 R                  LDS     SI, BUFFER        ;Pointer for data points
0014  BA 0000                       MOV     DX, 0H            ;Sum = 0
0017  8A 04             NXTPT:      MOV     AL, [SI]          ;Get a byte size point
0019  98                            CBW                       ;Convert to word size
001A  03 D0                         ADD     DX, AX            ;Add to last sum
001C  46                            INC     SI                ;Point to next point
001D  FE C9                         DEC     CL                ;All points added ?
001F  75 F6                         JNZ     NXTPT             ;If not - repeat
0021  8B C2                         MOV     AX, DX            ;Compute average
0023  F6 FB                         IDIV    BL

0025  CB                            RET                       ;Return to DEBUG program
0026                        LAB6  ENDP
0026                        CODE_SEG    ENDS

                                  END     LAB6
```

Segments and groups:

Name	Size	align	combine	class
CODE_SEG	0026	PARA	NONE	'CODE'
DATA_SEG	0005	PARA	NONE	'DATA'
STACK_SEG.	0040	PARA	STACK	'STACK'

Symbols:

Name	Type	Value	Attr	
BUFFER	L DWORD	0001	DATA_SEG	
COUNT.	L BYTE	0000	DATA_SEG	
LAB6	F PROC	0000	CODE_SEG	Length =0026
NXTPT.	L NEAR	0017	CODE_SEG	

Warning Severe
Errors   Errors
0   0

(b)

Figure L6.2   (Continued)

```
A>DEBUG B:LAB6.EXE
-U
0D03:0000 1E            PUSH    DS
0D03:0001 B80000        MOV     AX,0000
0D03:0004 50            PUSH    AX
0D03:0005 B8060D        MOV     AX,0D06
0D03:0008 8ED8          MOV     DS,AX
0D03:000A 8A0E0000      MOV     CL,[0000]
0D03:000E 8AD9          MOV     BL,CL
0D03:0010 C5360100      LDS     SI,[0001]
0D03:0014 BA0000        MOV     DX,0000
0D03:0017 8A04          MOV     AL,[SI]
0D03:0019 98            CBW
0D03:001A 03D0          ADD     DX,AX
0D03:001C 46            INC     SI
0D03:001D FEC9          DEC     CL
0D03:001F 75F6          JNZ     0017
-G A

AX=0D06  BX=0000  CX=0035  DX=0000  SP=003C  BP=0000  SI=0000  DI=0000
DS=0D06  ES=0CF3  SS=0D07  CS=0D03  IP=000A   NV UP EI PL NZ NA PO NC
0D03:000A 8A0E0000      MOV     CL,[0000]                        DS:0000=10
-D 0 6
0D06:0000   10 00 00 00 10 63 65                         .....ce
-G 17

AX=0D06  BX=0010  CX=0010  DX=0000  SP=003C  BP=0000  SI=0000  DI=0000
DS=1000  ES=0CF3  SS=0D07  CS=0D03  IP=0017   NV UP EI PL NZ NA PO NC
0D03:0017 8A04          MOV     AL,[SI]                          DS:0000=1C
-E 1000:0 4 5 6 4 5 6 FF FE FF 1 2 0 1 5 5 5
-D 0 F
1000:0000   04 05 06 04 05 06 FF FE-FF 01 02 00 01 05 05 05   ................
-U 17 25
0D03:0017 8A04          MOV     AL,[SI]
0D03:0019 98            CBW
0D03:001A 03D0          ADD     DX,AX
0D03:001C 46            INC     SI
0D03:001D FEC9          DEC     CL
0D03:001F 75F6          JNZ     0017
0D03:0021 8BC2          MOV     AX,DX
0D03:0023 F6FB          IDIV    BL
0D03:0025 CB            RETF
-G 25

AX=0D02  BX=0010  CX=0000  DX=002D  SP=003C  BP=0000  SI=0010  DI=0000
DS=1000  ES=0CF3  SS=0D07  CS=0D03  IP=0025   NV UP EI NG NZ NA PO NC
0D03:0025 CB            RETF
-G

Program terminated normally
-Q

A>
```

(c)

Figure L6.2   (Continued)

Check	Step	Procedure

What is represented by the next four bytes?
Ans. _____

(c) GO to address CS:17. What is represented by the contents of registers
CL, BL, SI, and DX?
CL _____
BL _____
SI _____
DX _____

What data storage location is addressed by DS and SI?
Ans. _____

(d) Load DS:0 through DS:F with the values 4, 5, 6, 4, 5, 6, FF, FE, FF, 1, 2,
0, 1, 5, 5, and 5. Verify loading with a dump command.

(e) GO to address CS:25. What is the sum? Ans. _____ What is the
integer average? Ans. _____ What is the remainder?
Ans. _____

(f) Run the program to completion.

LABORATORY 7: SORTING A TABLE OF DATA

Objective

Learn how to:

1. Describe a function that is to be performed with a program.
2. Write a program to implement the function.
3. Run the program to verify that it performs the function for which it was written.

Part 1: Description of the Problem

It is required to sort an array of 16-bit signed binary numbers so that they are arranged in ascending order. For instance, if the original array is

$$5, 1, 29, 15, 38, 3, -8, -32$$

after sorting, the array that results would be

$$-32, -8, 1, 3, 5, 15, 29, 38$$

Assume that the array of numbers is stored at consecutive memory locations from addresses $A400_{16}$ through $A41E_{16}$ in memory. Write a sort program.

Part 2: Writing the Program

First, we will develop an algorithm that can be used to sort an array of elements A(0), A(1), A(2), through A(N) into ascending order. One way of doing this is to take the first number in the array, which is A(0), and compare it to the second number, A(1). If A(0) is greater than A(1), the two numbers are swapped; otherwise, they are left alone. Next A(0) is compared to A(2) and, based on the result of this comparison, they are either swapped or left alone. This sequence is repeated until A(0) has been compared with all numbers up through A(N). When this is complete, the smallest number will be in the A(0) position.

Now A(1) must be compared to A(2) through A(N) in the same way. After this is done, the second smallest number is in the A(1) position. Up to this point, just two of the N numbers have been put in ascending order. Therefore, the procedure must be continued for A(2) through A(N − 1) to complete the sort.

Figure L7.1(a) illustrates the use of this algorithm for an array with just four numbers. The numbers are A(0) = 5, A(1) = 1, A(2) = 29, and A(3) = −8. During the sort sequence, A(0) = 5 is first compared to A(1) = 1. Since 5 is greater than 1, A(0) and A(1) are swapped. Now A(0) = 1 is compared to A(2) = 29. This time 1 is less than 29; therefore, the numbers are not swapped and A(0) remains equal to 1. Next A(0) = 1 is compared with A(3) = −8. A(0) is greater than A(3). Thus A(0) and A(3) are swapped and A(0) becomes equal to −8. Notice in Fig. L7.1(a) that the lowest of the four numbers now resides in A(0).

The sort sequence in Fig. L7.1(a) continues with A(1) = 5 being compared first to A(2) = 29 and then to A(3) = 1. In the first comparison, A(1) is less than A(2). For this reason, their values are not swapped. But in the second comparison, A(1) is greater than A(3); therefore, the two values are swapped. In this way, the second lowest number, which is 1, is sorted into A(1).

I	0	1	2	3	Status
A(I)	5	1	29	−8	Original array
A(I)	1	5	29	−8	Array after comparing A(0) and A(1)
A(I)	1	5	29	−8	Array after comparing A(0) and A(2)
A(I)	−8	5	29	1	Array after comparing A(0) and A(3)
A(I)	−8	5	29	1	Array after comparing A(1) and A(2)
A(I)	−8	1	29	5	Array after comparing A(1) and A(3)
A(I)	−8	1	5	29	Array after comparing A(2) and A(3)

(a)

Figure L7.1 (a) Sort algorithm demonstration. (b) Flowchart for the sort program. (c) Program.

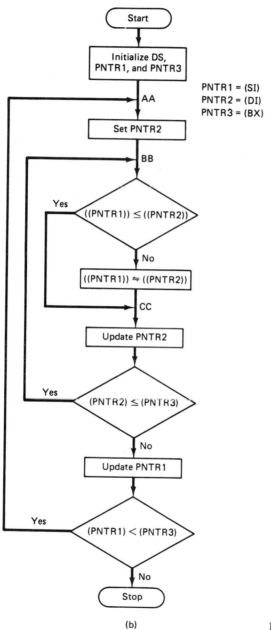

PNTR1 = (SI)
PNTR2 = (DI)
PNTR3 = (BX)

(b)

Figure L7.1 (Continued)

```
           MOV    AX,1A00H
           MOV    DS,AX
           MOV    SI,0400H
           MOV    BX,041EH
     AA:   MOV    DI,SI
           ADD    DI,2H
     BB:   MOV    AX,[SI]
           CMP    AX,[DI]
           JLE    CC
           MOV    DX,[DI]
           MOV    [SI],DX
           MOV    [DI],AX
     CC:   INC    DI
           INC    DI
           CMP    DI,BX
           JBE    BB
           INC    SI
           INC    SI
           CMP    SI,BX
           JB     AA
           HLT
```

(c)   **Figure L7.1**   (Continued)

It just remains to sort A(2) and A(3). Comparing these two values, we see that 29 is greater than 5. This causes the two values to be swapped so that A(2) = 5 and A(3) = 29. As shown in Fig. L7.1(a), the sorting of the array is now complete.

Now we will implement the algorithm on the 8088 microprocessor. The flowchart for its implementation is shown in Fig. L7.1(b).

The first block in the flowchart represents the initialization of data segment register DS and pointers $PNTR_1$ and $PNTR_3$. The DS register is initialized with $1A00_{16}$ to define a data segment starting from memory address $1A000_{16}$. $PNTR_1$ points to the first element in the array. It will be register SI and will be initialized to 0400_{16}. Therefore, the first element of the array is at address $1A400_{16}$. For pointer $PNTR_3$, we will use register BX and will initialize it to $041E_{16}$. It points to the last element in the array, which is at address $1A41E_{16}$. Next, $PNTR_2$, the moving pointer, is initialized so that it points to the second element in the array. Register DI will be used for this pointer. This leads to the following instruction sequence for initialization.

```
        MOV AX,1A00H
        MOV DX,AX
        MOV SI,0400H
        MOV BX,041EH
    AA: MOV DI,SI
        ADD DI,2
```

Notice that DS was loaded via AX with the immediate data $1A00_{16}$ to define a data segment starting at $1A000_{16}$. SI and BX, which are $PNTR_1$ and $PNTR_3$, respectively, are loaded with immediate operands 0400_{16} and $041E_{16}$. In this way they point to the first and last elements of the array, respectively. Finally, register DI, which is $PNTR_2$, is loaded with 0400_{16} from SI and then incremented by two with an ADD instruction so that it points to the second element in the array. This completes the initialization process.

Next, the array element pointed to by $PNTR_1$ is to be compared to the element pointed to by $PNTR_2$. If the element corresponding to $PNTR_1$ is arithmetically less than the element corresponding to pointer $PNTR_2$, the two elements are already in ascending order. But if this is not the case, the two elements must be interchanged. Both of these elements are in memory. However, the 8088 cannot directly compare two values in memory. For this reason, one of the two elements must be moved to a register within the 8088. We will use AX for this purpose. The resulting code is as follows:

```
BB: MOV AX,[SI]
    CMP AX,[DI]
    JLE CC
    MOV DX,[DI]
    MOV [SI],DX
    MOV [DI],AX
CC:
```

The first instruction moves the element pointed to by $PNTR_1$ into AX. The second instruction compares the value in AX with the element pointed to by $PNTR_2$. The result of this comparison is reflected in the status flags. The jump on less-than or equal-to instruction that follows checks if the first element is arithmetically less than or equal to the second element. If the result of this check is yes, control is transferred to CC. CC is a label to be used in the segment of program that will follow. If the check fails, the two elements must be interchanged. In this case, the instructions executed next move the element pointed to by $PNTR_2$ into the location pointed to by $PNTR_1$. Then the copy of the original value pointed to by $PNTR_1$, which is saved in AX, is moved to the location pointed to by $PNTR_2$.

To continue sorting through the rest of the element in the array, we update $PNTR_2$ so that it points to the next element in the array. This comparison should be repeated until the first element has been compared to each of the other elements in the array. This condition is satisfied when $PNTR_2$ points to the last element in the array. That is, $PNTR_2$ equals $PNTR_3$. This part of the program can be done with the code that follows:

```
CC: INC DI
    INC DI
    CMP DI,BX
    JBE BB
```

The first two instructions update $PNTR_2$ such that it points to the next element. The third instruction compares $PNTR_2$ to $PNTR_3$ to determine whether or not they are equal. If they are equal to each other, the first element has been compared to the last element and we are ready to continue with the second element. Otherwise, we must repeat from the label BB. This test is done with the jump on below or equal instruction. Notice that label BB corresponds to the beginning of the part of the program that compares the elements of the array. Once we fall through the JBE instruction, we have placed the smallest number in the array into the position pointed to by $PNTR_1$. To process the rest of the elements in the array in a similar way, $PNTR_1$ must be moved over the entire range of elements and the foregoing procedure repeated. This can be done by implementing the code that follows:

```
INC SI
INC SI
CMP SI,BX
JB  AA
HLT
```

The first two instructions increment pointer $PNTR_1$ so that it points to the next element in the array. The third instruction checks if all the elements have been sorted. The fourth instruction passes control back to the sorting sequence of instructions if $PNTR_1$ does not point to the last element. However, if all elements of the array have been sorted, we come to a halt at the end of the program. The entire program appears in Fig. L7.1(c).

Part 3: Running the Program

The sort algorithm we just developed is implemented by the source program in Fig. L7.2(a). This program was assembled and linked to produce a run module in file LAB7.EXE. The source listing produced by the assembler during the assembly process is shown in Fig. L7.2(b). Now we will run the program on the IBM PC for an arbitrary set of data points. *Check off each step as it is completed.*

Check	Step	Procedure
_____	1	Load the program LAB7.EXE with the DOS command `A >DEBUG  B:LAB7.EXE`
_____	2	Verify loading of the program by unassembling the contents of memory starting at the current code segment.
_____	3	Execute the program according to the instructions that follow: (a) Enter the following 16 data values as 16-bit numbers starting at address 1A00:400. $5,0,-3,1,12,-20,77,2,9,-2,53,-5,1,28,15,19.$

Check	Step	Procedure
		(b) Verify the 16 data values by dumping from the address 1A00:400.
		(c) Execute the program from the start until CS:2D.
		(d) Dump the 16 data values starting from the address 1A00:400. Are the numbers sorted? Ans. _____
		(e) Execute the program to completion.

```
TITLE   LABORATORY 7

        PAGE    ,132

STACK_SEG    SEGMENT      STACK 'STACK'
             DB           64 DUP(?)
STACK_SEG    ENDS


CODE_SEG     SEGMENT      'CODE'
LAB7    PROC  FAR
        ASSUME  CS:CODE_SEG, SS:STACK_SEG

;To return to DEBUG program put return address on the stack

        PUSH    DS
        MOV     AX, 0
        PUSH    AX

;Following code implements Laboratory 7

        MOV     AX, 1A00H        ;Establish data segment
        MOV     DS, AX
        MOV     SI, 400H         ;Establish PNTR1
        MOV     BX, 41EH         ;Establish PNTR3
AA:     MOV     DI, SI           ;Establish PNTR2
        ADD     DI, 2
BB:     MOV     AX, [SI]         ;Compare two elements
        CMP     AX, [DI]
        JLE     CC               ;No interchange if equal/less
        MOV     DX, [DI]         ;Otherwise interchange
        MOV     [SI], DX
        MOV     [DI], AX
CC:     INC     DI               ;Update PNTR2
        INC     DI
        CMP     DI, BX           ;Last element ?
        JBE     BB               ;If no
        INC     SI               ;Update PNTR1
        INC     SI
        CMP     SI, BX           ;Last comparison ?
        JB      AA               ;If no
DONE:   NOP

        RET                      ;Return to DEBUG program
LAB7    ENDP
CODE_SEG     ENDS

        END     LAB7
```

(a)

Figure L7.2 (a) Source program for sorting a table of data. (b) Source listing produced by the assembler.

```
                              TITLE   LABORATORY 7

                                      PAGE    ,132

0000                          STACK_SEG        SEGMENT      STACK 'STACK'
0000    40 [                                   DB           64 DUP(?)
            ??
               ]


0040                          STACK_SEG        ENDS


0000                          CODE_SEG         SEGMENT      'CODE'
0000                          LAB7    PROC     FAR
                                      ASSUME   CS:CODE_SEG, SS:STACK_SEG

                              ;To return to DEBUG program put return address on the stack

0000  1E                              PUSH     DS
0001  B8 0000                         MOV      AX, 0
0004  50                              PUSH     AX

                              ;Following code implements Laboratory 7

0005  B8 1A00                         MOV      AX, 1A00H          ;Establish data segment
0008  8E D8                           MOV      DS, AX
000A  BE 0400                         MOV      SI, 400H           ;Establish PNTR1
000D  BB 041E                         MOV      BX, 41EH           ;Establish PNTR3
0010  8B FE              AA:          MOV      DI, SI             ;Establish PNTR2
0012  83 C7 02                        ADD      DI, 2
0015  8B 04              BB:          MOV      AX, [SI]           ;Compare two elements
0017  3B 05                           CMP      AX, [DI]
0019  7E 06                           JLE      CC                 ;No interchange if equal/less
001B  8B 15                           MOV      DX, [DI]           ;Otherwise interchange
001D  89 14                           MOV      [SI], DX
001F  89 05                           MOV      [DI], AX
0021  47                 CC:          INC      DI                 ;Update PNTR2
0022  47                              INC      DI
0023  3B FB                           CMP      DI, BX             ;Last element ?
0025  76 EE                           JBE      BB                 ;If no
0027  46                              INC      SI                 ;Update PNTR1
0028  46                              INC      SI
0029  3B F3                           CMP      SI, BX             ;Last comparison ?
002B  72 E3                           JB       AA                 ;If no
002D  90                 DONE:        NOP

002E  CB                              RET                         ;Return to DEBUG program
002F                          LAB7    ENDP
002F                          CODE_SEG         ENDS

                                      END      LAB7

Segments and groups:

              N a m e            Size    align   combine class

CODE_SEG . . . . . . . . . . . . .   002F    PARA    NONE    'CODE'
STACK_SEG. . . . . . . . . . . .     0040    PARA    STACK   'STACK'
```

(b)

Figure L7.2   (Continued)

Symbols:

N a m e	Type	Value	Attr	
AA	L NEAR	0010	CODE_SEG	
BB	L NEAR	0015	CODE_SEG	
CC	L NEAR	0021	CODE_SEG	
DONE	L NEAR	002D	CODE_SEG	
LAB7	F PROC	0000	CODE_SEG	Length =002F

Warning Errors	Severe Errors
0	0

(b)

Figure L7.2 (Continued)

LABORATORY 8: GENERATING ELEMENTS FOR A MATHEMATICAL SERIES

Objective

Learn how to:

1. Describe a function that is to be performed with a program.
2. Write a program to implement the function.
3. Run the program to verify that it performs the function for which it was written.

Part 1: Description of the Problem

Write a program to generate the first ten elements of a Fibonacci series. In this series, the first and second elements are zero and one, respectively. Each element that follows is obtained by adding the previous two elements. Use a subroutine to generate the next element from the previous two elements. Store the elements of the series starting at address FIBSER.

Part 2: Writing the Program

Our plan for the solution of this problem is shown in Fig. L8.1(a). This flowchart shows the use of a subroutine to generate an element of the series, store it in memory, and prepare for generation of the next element.

The first step in the solution is initialization. It involves setting up a data segment, generating the first two numbers of the series, and storing them at memory locations with offset addresses FIBSER and FIBSER+1. Then a pointer must be established to address the locations for other terms of the series. This

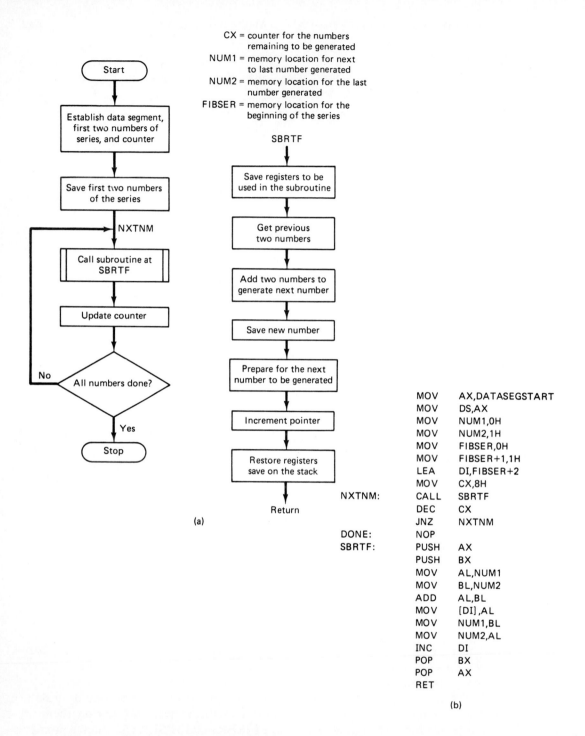

CX = counter for the numbers remaining to be generated
NUM1 = memory location for next to last number generated
NUM2 = memory location for the last number generated
FIBSER = memory location for the beginning of the series

```
          MOV    AX,DATASEGSTART
          MOV    DS,AX
          MOV    NUM1,0H
          MOV    NUM2,1H
          MOV    FIBSER,0H
          MOV    FIBSER+1,1H
          LEA    DI,FIBSER+2
          MOV    CX,8H
NXTNM:    CALL   SBRTF
          DEC    CX
          JNZ    NXTNM
DONE:     NOP
SBRTF:    PUSH   AX
          PUSH   BX
          MOV    AL,NUM1
          MOV    BL,NUM2
          ADD    AL,BL
          MOV    [DI],AL
          MOV    NUM1,BL
          MOV    NUM2,AL
          INC    DI
          POP    BX
          POP    AX
          RET
```

(b)

Figure L8.1 (a) Flowchart for generation of a Fibonacci series. (b) Program.

address will be held in the DI register. Finally, a counter with initial value equal to 8 can be set up in CX to keep track of how many numbers remain to be generated. The instructions needed for initialization are

```
MOV AX,DATASEGSTART
MOV DS,AX
MOV NUM1,0
MOV NUM2,1
MOV FIBSER,0
MOV FIBSER+1,1
LEA DI,FIBSER+2
MOV CX,8
```

Notice that the data segment address defined by variable DATASEGSTART is first moved into AX, and then DS is loaded from AX with another MOV operation. Next the memory locations assigned to NUM$_1$ and NUM$_2$ are loaded with immediate data 0000_{16} and 0001_{16}, respectively. The same values are then copied into the storage locations for the first two series elements, FIBSER and FIBSER+1. Now DI is loaded with the address of FIBSER+2, which is a pointer to the storage location of the third element of the series. Finally, CX is loaded with 8.

To generate the next term in the series, we call a subroutine. This subroutine generates and stores the elements. Before returning to the main program, it also updates memory locations NUM$_1$ and NUM$_2$ with the values of the immediate past two elements. After this, the counter in CX is decremented to record that a series element has been generated and stored. This process must be repeated until the counter becomes equal to zero. This leads to the following assembly language code:

```
NXTNM: CALL SBRTF
       DEC CX
       JNZ NXTNM
DONE:  NOP
```

The call is to the subroutine labeled SBRTF. After the subroutine runs to completion, program control returns to the DEC CX statement. This statement causes the count in CX to be decremented by one. Next, a conditional jump instruction tests the zero flag to determine if the result after decrementing CX is zero. If CX is not zero, control is returned to the CALL instruction at NXTNM. If it is zero, the program is complete and execution halts.

The subroutine itself is given next.

```
SBRTF: PUSH AX
       PUSH BX
       MOV  AL,NUM1
```

```
MOV   BL,NUM2
ADD   AL,BL
MOV   [DI],AL
MOV   NUM1,BL
MOV   NUM2,AL
INC   DI
POP   BX
POP   AX
RET
```

First, we save the contents of AX and BX on the stack. Then NUM_1 and NUM_2 are copied into AL and BL, respectively. They are then added together to form the next element. The resulting sum is produced in AL. Now the new element is stored in memory indirectly through DI. Remember that DI holds a pointer to the storage location of the next element of the series in memory. Then the second element, which is held in BL, becomes the new first element by copying it into NUM_1. The sum, which is in AL, becomes the new second term by copying it into NUM_2. Finally, DI is incremented by one so that it points to the next element of the series. The registers saved on the stack are restored and then we return back to the main program.

Notice that both the subroutine call and its return have Near-proc operands. The entire program is presented in Fig. L8.1(b).

Part 3: Running the Program

Figure L8.2(a) shows a source program that implements the Fibonacci series generation routine written as a procedure. This program was assembled and linked to produce a run module called LAB8.EXE. The source listing produced by the assembler is given in Fig. L8.2(b). Now we will verify the operation of the program by generating the first ten numbers of the series by executing it on the IBM PC. *Check off each step as it is completed.*

Check	Step	Procedure
_____	1	Load the program LAB8.EXE with the DOS command A>DEBUG B:LAB8.EXE
_____	2	Verify loading of the program by unassembling the contents of memory starting at the current code segment.
_____	3	Execute the program according to the instructions that follow: (a) GO from CS:0 to CS:2C. (b) DUMP the data memory from 1A00:0 to 1A00:C. (c) Verify that the series of numbers starting at location 1A00:2 until 1A00:B satisfies the rules of Fibonnaci series. (d) What is contained in locations 1A00:0 and 1A00:1? Ans. _____ (e) Execute the program to completion.

```
TITLE   LABORATORY 8

        PAGE    ,132

STACK_SEG       SEGMENT     STACK 'STACK'
                DB          64 DUP(?)
STACK_SEG       ENDS


DATASEGMENT     =       1A00H


DATA_SEG        SEGMENT     'DATA'
NUM1            DB          ?
NUM2            DB          ?
FIBSER          DB          10 DUP(?)
DATA_SEG        ENDS


CODE_SEG        SEGMENT     'CODE'
LAB8    PROC    FAR
        ASSUME  CS:CODE_SEG, SS:STACK_SEG, DS:DATA_SEG

;To return to DEBUG program put return address on the stack

        PUSH    DS
        MOV     AX, 0
        PUSH    AX

;Following code implements Laboratory 8

        MOV     AX, DATASEGMENT     ;Establish data segment
        MOV     DS, AX
        MOV     NUM1, 0             ;Initialize first number
        MOV     NUM2, 1             ;Initialize second number
        MOV     FIBSER, 0           ;First number in series
        MOV     FIBSER+1, 1         ;Second number in series
        LEA     DI, FIBSER+2        ;Pointer to next element
        MOV     CX, 8               ;Initialize count
NXTNM:  CALL    SBRTF               ;Generate next element
        DEC     CX
        JNZ     NXTNM               ;If not done
DONE:   NOP
        RET

SBRTF   PROC    NEAR
        PUSH    AX                  ;Save registers used
        PUSH    BX
        MOV     AL, NUM1            ;Generate next element
        MOV     BL, NUM2
        ADD     AL, BL
        MOV     [DI], AL
        MOV     [DI], AL            ;Save next element
        MOV     NUM1, BL            ;Prepare for next call
        MOV     NUM2, AL
        INC     DI
        POP     BX                  ;Restore registers
        POP     AX
        RET
SBRTF   ENDP

LAB8    ENDP
CODE_SEG        ENDS

        END     LAB8
```

(a)

Figure L8.2 (a) Source program for generating a Fibonacci series. (b) Source listing produced by the assembler.

```
                              TITLE   LABORATORY 8

                                      PAGE    ,132

0000                          STACK_SEG    SEGMENT      STACK 'STACK'
0000    40 [                               DB           64 DUP(?)
            ??
                ]

0040                          STACK_SEG    ENDS


= 1A00                        DATASEGMENT  =       1A00H


0000                          DATA_SEG     SEGMENT      'DATA'
0000    ??                    NUM1         DB           ?
0001    ??                    NUM2         DB           ?
0002    0A [                  FIBSER       DB           10 DUP(?)
            ??
                ]

000C                          DATA_SEG     ENDS


0000                          CODE_SEG     SEGMENT      'CODE'
0000                          LAB8    PROC  FAR
                                      ASSUME  CS:CODE_SEG, SS:STACK_SEG, DS:DATA_SEG

                              ;To return to DEBUG program put return address on the stack

0000  1E                              PUSH   DS
0001  B8 0000                         MOV    AX, 0
0004  50                              PUSH   AX

                              ;Following code implements Laboratory 8

0005  B8 1A00                         MOV    AX, DATASEGMENT    ;Establish data segment
0008  8E D8                           MOV    DS, AX
000A  C6 06 0000 R 00                 MOV    NUM1, 0            ;Initialize first number
000F  C6 06 0001 R 01                 MOV    NUM2, 1            ;Initialize second number
0014  C6 06 0002 R 00                 MOV    FIBSER, 0          ;First number in series
0019  C6 06 0003 R 01                 MOV    FIBSER+1, 1        ;Second number in series
001E  8D 3E 0004 R                    LEA    DI, FIBSER+2       ;Pointer to next element
0022  B9 0008                         MOV    CX, 8              ;Initialize count
0025  E8 002D R          NXTNM: CALL   SBRTF                    ;Generate next element
0028  49                              DEC    CX
0029  75 FA                           JNZ    NXTNM              ;If not done
002B  90                DONE:  NOP
002C  CB                              RET

002D                          SBRTF   PROC   NEAR
002D  50                              PUSH   AX                 ;Save registers used
002E  53                              PUSH   BX
002F  A0 0000 R                       MOV    AL, NUM1           ;Generate next element
0032  8A 1E 0001 R                    MOV    BL, NUM2
0036  02 C3                           ADD    AL, BL
0038  88 05                           MOV    [DI], AL
003A  88 05                           MOV    [DI], AL           ;Save next element
003C  88 1E 0000 R                    MOV    NUM1, BL           ;Prepare for next call
```

(b)

Figure L8.2 (Continued)

```
0040  A2 0001 R           MOV     NUM2, AL
0043  47                  INC     DI
0044  5B                  POP     BX                  ;Restore registers
0045  5B                  POP     AX
0046  C3                  RET
0047              SBRTF   ENDP

0047              LAB8    ENDP
0047              CODE_SEG        ENDS

                  END     LAB8
```

Segments and groups:

N a m e	Size	align	combine	class
CODE_SEG	0047	PARA	NONE	'CODE'
DATA_SEG	000C	PARA	NONE	'DATA'
STACK_SEG.	0040	PARA	STACK	'STACK'

Symbols:

N a m e	Type	Value	Attr	
DATASEGMENT.	Number	1A00		
DONE	L NEAR	002B	CODE_SEG	
FIBSER	L BYTE	0002	DATA_SEG	Length =000A
LAB8	F PROC	0000	CODE_SEG	Length =0047
NUM1	L BYTE	0000	DATA_SEG	
NUM2	L BYTE	0001	DATA_SEG	
NXTNM.	L NEAR	0025	CODE_SEG	
SBRTF.	N PROC	002D	CODE_SEG	Length =001A

```
Warning Severe
Errors  Errors
  0       0
```

(b)

Figure L8.2   (Continued)

LABORATORY 9: EXPLORING THE MEMORY SUBSYSTEM OF THE IBM PC

Objective

Learn how to:

1. Explore the implemented and unimplemented parts of the memory space in the IBM PC.
2. Explore the R/W memory and ROM parts of the implemented memory.
3. Determine the ROM BIOS release date.
4. Explore the relationship between the display memory contents and the corresponding character displays.
5. Execute a routine to test the memory space.

Part 1: IBM PC Memory

The microprocessor in the IBM PC is capable of accessing 1M byte of memory. The address range 0_{16} through $BFFFF_{16}$ is for R/W memory and $C0000_{16}$ to $FFFFF_{16}$ is meant for the ROM. Not all the ROM or R/W memory address space is implemented in a particular PC. Here we will explore various address ranges to determine if they are implemented and, if a range is implemented, whether it is R/W memory or ROM. *Check off each step as it is completed.*

Check	Step	Procedure
_____	1	Load the DEBUG program by entering A>DEBUG (↵)
_____	2	Perform the debug operations that follow: (a) Dump the 128 memory locations starting at address 100:0. (b) Dump the 128 memory locations starting at address 4000:0. (c) Dump the 128 memory locations starting at address B000:0. (d) Dump the 128 memory locations starting at address F600:0. (e) Comparing the displays produced for steps (a), (b), (c), and (d), can you identify an unimplemented area of memory (depends on the memory in your PC)? Ans. _____
_____	3	Try writing 55H to the 128 locations starting at 100:0, 4000:0, B000:0, and F600:0. To verify writing, dump the contents of these locations. Are there locations that you were not able to write to? Ans. _____ If yes, what are these locations? Ans. _____ Looking at the display in Step 2, can you conclude which part of the memory appears to be unimplemented and which part is ROM? Ans. _____
_____	4	Dump the 8-byte memory contents starting at address F000:FFF5. What do you see? Ans. _____ This is the ROM BIOS release date.
_____	5	Quit the DEBUG program.

Part 2: Monochrome Display Memory

A part of the PC's memory known as the monochrome display memory starts at address B000:0. Here we will study the relationship between the contents of this memory and information displayed on the screen. For every character displayed on the screen, there are two consecutive bytes in display memory. The first byte, which is located at the even address, is the ASCII code for the character. The contents of the second byte, which is at the odd address, select display attributes for the character. The attributes available for characters displayed on the monochrome display are normal, blinking, underlined, intensified, and reverse-video. By performing the steps that follow, we will examine the relationship between the contents of the character and attribute bytes and displayed information.

Check	Step	Procedure
_____	1	Clear the screen by issuing the command
		A>CLS (↵)
		(This operation must be performed; otherwise, the steps that follow may not produce the desired result.)
_____	2	Load the debugger by entering
		A>B:DEBUG (↵)
_____	3	DUMP the contents of memory locations B000:0 to B000:BF. At what memory address does the display message A>B:DEBUG start? Ans. _____ Why? Ans. _____
_____	4	Perform the DEBUG operations that follow.
		(a) Enter the ASCII characters of the word NORMAL separated and terminated by the hexadecimal code 07H starting at address B000:0. What is displayed at the top left corner of the screen? Ans. _____
		(b) Enter the ASCII characters of the word BLINKING separated and terminated by the hexadecimal code 87H starting at address B000:0. What is displayed at the top left corner of the screen? Ans. _____
		(c) Enter the ASCII characters of the word UNDERLINED separated and terminated by the hexadecimal code 01H starting at address B000:0. What is displayed at the top left corner of the screen? Ans. _____
		(d) Enter the ASCII characters of the word INTENSIFIED separated and terminated by the hexadecimal code 0FH starting at address B000:0. What is displayed at the top left corner of the screen? Ans. _____
		(e) Enter the ASCII characters of the word REVERSEVIDEO separated and terminated by the hexadecimal code 70H starting at address B000:0. What is displayed at the top left corner of the screen? Ans. _____
		(f) What are the addresses of the memory locations that contain the ASCII code and attributes of a character displayed on line 20 at column 50? Ans. _____
_____	5	Quit the DEBUG program.

Part 3: Memory Test Program

Figure L9.1(a) shows a source program that writes the pattern 0755 to the 128-byte memory block starting at location B000:0. After writing the pattern, the storage locations are read and their contents compared with the pattern. In this way, we

```
TITLE   LABORATORY 9

        PAGE     ,132

STACK_SEG    SEGMENT      STACK 'STACK'
             DB           64 DUP(?)
STACK_SEG    ENDS


PATTERN      =       0755H
MEM_START    =       0H
MEM_STOP     =       7FH
DSEG_ADDR    =       0B000H


CODE_SEG     SEGMENT      'CODE'
LAB9    PROC    FAR
        ASSUME  CS:CODE_SEG, SS:STACK_SEG

;To return to DEBUG program put return address on the stack

        PUSH    DS
        MOV     AX, 0
        PUSH    AX

;Following code implements Laboratory 9

        MOV     AX, DSEG_ADDR         ;Establish data segment
        MOV     DS, AX
        MOV     SI, MEM_START         ;Next memory address
        MOV     CX, (MEM_STOP-MEM_START+1)/2   ;No of locations
AGAIN:  MOV     WORD PTR [SI], PATTERN ;Write the pattern
        MOV     AX, [SI]              ;Read it back
        CMP     AX, PATTERN          ;Same ?
        JNE     BADMEM
        INC     SI                   ;Repeat for next location
        INC     SI
        LOOP    AGAIN
        MOV     DX, 1234H            ;Code for test passed
        JMP     DONE
BADMEM: MOV     DX, 0BADH            ;Code for test failed
DONE:   NOP

        RET                          ;Return to DEBUG program
LAB9    ENDP
CODE_SEG     ENDS

        END     LAB9
```

(a)

```
                    TITLE   LABORATORY 9

                        PAGE     ,132

0000                    STACK_SEG    SEGMENT      STACK 'STACK'
0000    40 [                         DB           64 DUP(?)
            ??
            ]

0040                    STACK_SEG    ENDS
```

(b)

Figure L9.1 (a) Source program for Laboratory 9. (b) Source listing produced by assembler.

572

```
= 0755                    PATTERN      =      0755H
= 0000                    MEM_START    =      0H
= 007F                    MEM_STOP     =      7FH
= B000                    DSEG_ADDR    =      0B000H


0000                      CODE_SEG     SEGMENT        'CODE'
0000                      LAB9    PROC    FAR
                                  ASSUME  CS:CODE_SEG, SS:STACK_SEG

                          ;To return to DEBUG program put return address on the stack

0000  1E                          PUSH    DS
0001  B8 0000                     MOV     AX, 0
0004  50                          PUSH    AX

                          ;Following code implements Laboratory 9

0005  B8 B000                     MOV     AX, DSEG_ADDR            ;Establish data segment
0008  8E D8                       MOV     DS, AX
000A  BE 0000                     MOV     SI, MEM_START           ;Next memory address
000D  B9 0040                     MOV     CX, (MEM_STOP-MEM_START+1)/2   ;No of locations
0010  C7 04 0755        AGAIN:    MOV     WORD PTR [SI], PATTERN   ;Write the pattern
0014  8B 04                       MOV     AX, [SI]                ;Read it back
0016  3D 0755                     CMP     AX, PATTERN             ;Same ?
0019  75 0A                       JNE     BADMEM
001B  46                          INC     SI                      ;Repeat for next location
001C  46                          INC     SI
001D  E2 F1                       LOOP    AGAIN
001F  BA 1234                     MOV     DX, 1234H               ;Code for test passed
0022  EB 04 90                    JMP     DONE
0025  BA 0BAD          BADMEM:    MOV     DX, 0BADH               ;Code for test failed
0028  90               DONE:      NOP


0029  CB                          RET                             ;Return to DEBUG program
002A                     LAB9    ENDP
002A                     CODE_SEG     ENDS

                                  END     LAB9
```

Segments and groups:

N a m e	Size	align	combine	class
CODE_SEG	002A	PARA	NONE	'CODE'
STACK_SEG.	0040	PARA	STACK	'STACK'

Symbols:

N a m e	Type	Value	Attr	
AGAIN.	L NEAR	0010	CODE_SEG	
BADMEM	L NEAR	0025	CODE_SEG	
DONE	L NEAR	0028	CODE_SEG	
DSEG_ADDR.	Number	B000		
LAB9	F PROC	0000	CODE_SEG	Length =002A
MEM_START.	Number	0000		
MEM_STOP	Number	007F		
PATTERN.	Number	0755		

Warning	Severe
Errors	Errors
0	0

(b)

Figure L9.1 (Continued)

test to determine if each memory location is readable and writable. A listing of the program is shown in Fig. L9.1(b). The run module is available as LAB9.EXE. Now we will execute this program and verify if the memory passes the test.

Check	Step	Procedure
_____	1	Clear the screen by issuing the command in Part 2, Step 1.
_____	2	Load the run module LAB9.EXE in the debugger.
_____	3	Run the program by executing it to the end. What happens to the top line of the display? Ans. _____ Why? Ans. _____
_____	4	DUMP the register contents of DX. What is the significance of the value in DX with respect to the state of the memory block? Ans. _____
_____	5	DUMP the memory contents starting at address B000:0. What do they signify? Ans. _____

LABORATORY 10: EXPLORING THE INPUT/OUTPUT SUBSYSTEM OF THE IBM PC

Objective

Learn how to:

1. Input and output to the I/O peripherals of the IBM PC.
2. Write a program to control the speaker of the IBM PC.
3. Program the 8253 timer for speaker tone control.
4. Write a keyboard and display control program.
5. Execute the keyboard/control program and understand how it uses IBM PC software interrupts.

Part 1: Input/Output Ports of the IBM PC

In the IBM PC, peripherals such as the 8255A, 8253, 8237A, and 8259A are located in the 8088's I/O address space. For this reason, they are accessed using IN and OUT instructions. Here we will explore the registers of just one of these devices. Moreover, we will write to an area where no port is implemented to see what happens when we try to read or write to a nonexistent port. Finally, we will read a timer register to see that it changes with time. *Check off each step as it is completed.*

Check	Step	Procedure
_____	1	Load the debugger.
_____	2	Assemble the following instructions:

```
XOR  AL,AL
MOV  DX,300H
IN   AL,DX
MOV  AL,55H
OUT  DX,AL
IN   AL,DX
```

Check	Step	Procedure
_____	3	Perform the following debug operations:

(a) Execute the first three instructions of the program. What value is now in AL? Ans. _____

(b) Execute the next two instructions. What do they do? Ans. _____

_____

(c) Execute the last instruction. What do you get in AL? Ans. _____
What is your conclusion? Ans. _____

_____

Check	Step	Procedure
_____	4	Assemble and execute the instructions that follow to read the port for timer 2 on the 8253. This timer is read on port 42H.

```
MOV  AL,40H
OUT  43,AL
IN   AL,42H
MOV  CL,AL
IN   AL,42H
```

What are the contents of CL? Ans. _____ AL? Ans. _____

Check	Step	Procedure
_____	5	Execute the instructions in Step 4 one more time.

What do you read in CL? Ans. _____ AL? Ans. _____
Are they different from Step 4? Ans. _____
If so, why? Ans. _____

_____

Check	Step	Procedure
_____	6	Quit the debugger.

Part 2: Writing a Speaker Control Program

A flowchart for a program that will produce a tone at the speaker is shown in Fig. L10.1. Let us first calculate the count that needs to be loaded into the 8253 timer to set the tone frequency to 1.5 kHz. This is done with the expression

$$NNNN = 1.19 \text{ MHz}/f = 1.19 \text{ MHz}/1.5 \text{ kHz}$$

$$= 793$$

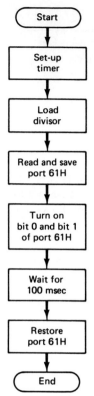

Figure L10.1 Flowchart for tone generation program.

Expressing in hexadecimal form, we get

$$NNNN = 319_{16}$$

Thus, to generate the 1.5-kHz tone, we must first load the timer with the divisor 319_{16}. To do this, the mode of the 8253 must be first set to accept the divisor. The instructions needed to set the mode are

```
MOV AL,0B6H
OUT 43H,AL    ;SET MODE TO ACCEPT DIVISOR
```

Now the divisor is loaded into the timer with the instructions

```
MOV AX,319H
OUT 42H,AL    ;LOAD LSBYTE OF DIVISOR
MOV AL,AH
OUT 42H,AL    ;LOAD MSBYTE OF DIVISOR
```

Next we enable both the timer and the AND gate by first reading the state of the output port at address 61_{16}, setting bits 0 and 1 to logic 1, and then writing the byte back to the output port. This is done with the sequence of instructions

```
IN   AL,61H
MOV  AH,AL
OR   AL,3
OUT  61H,AL
```

Notice that the current value of port 61_{16} has been saved in the AH register.

Now the speaker is turned on and the 1.5-kHz tone is being generated. However, if the tone is to be produced for approximately 100 ms, a software delay can be inserted in the program. When the delay is complete, the speaker is turned off. The software delay is produced by the instruction sequence

```
        MOV CX,5064H   ;4 CLOCK CYCLES
DELAY:  NOP            ;3 CLOCK CYCLES
        NOP            ;3 CLOCK CYCLES
        LOOP DELAY     ;17 CLOCK CYCLES
```

The count loaded into CX by the MOV instruction determines the duration of the time delay. The value 5064_{16} is found from the time it takes to execute the instructions in the loop. The total number of clock cycles in the loop are given by the expression

$$\text{\#CYC} = 4 + (X - 1)(3 + 3 + 17) + 12$$

Here the 4 represents the execution of the MOV instruction once; the 12 represents the execution of the instructions that must be executed just after the loop to turn the tone back off; and the expression $(X - 1)(3 + 3 + 17)$ represents the repeated execution of the 3 instruction loop $X - 1$ times. Here X stands for the count loaded into CX. In the IBM PC, each clock cycle has a duration of 210 ns. Thus a 100-ms delay is defined by the expression

$$\text{DELAY} = \text{\#CYC (CLOCK CYCLE DURATION)}$$

$$100 \text{ ms} = (4 + [X - 1][3 + 3 + 17] + 12) \, 210 \text{ ns}$$

Solving this expression for X, we get

$$X \cong 20{,}708$$

and converting to hexadecimal form gives

$$X = 5064_{16}$$

After the delay is complete, we must turn the speaker back off. This is done by writing the byte saved in AH back to the output port at address 61_{16}. We do this with the instructions

```
MOV AL,AH
OUT 61H,AL
```

The complete source program is shown in Fig. L10.2(a) and the listing produced by the assembler is shown in Fig. L10.2(b).

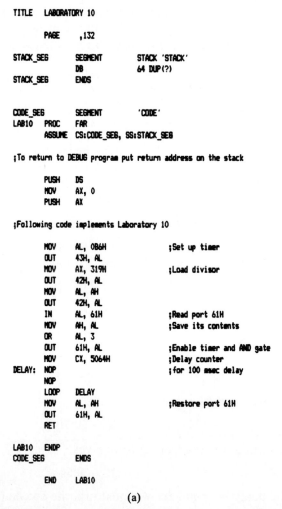

```
TITLE   LABORATORY 10

        PAGE     ,132

STACK_SEG    SEGMENT      STACK 'STACK'
             DB           64 DUP(?)
STACK_SEG    ENDS


CODE_SEG     SEGMENT      'CODE'
LAB10   PROC     FAR
        ASSUME  CS:CODE_SEG, SS:STACK_SEG

;To return to DEBUG program put return address on the stack

        PUSH    DS
        MOV     AX, 0
        PUSH    AX

;Following code implements Laboratory 10

        MOV     AL, 0B6H           ;Set up timer
        OUT     43H, AL
        MOV     AX, 319H           ;Load divisor
        OUT     42H, AL
        MOV     AL, AH
        OUT     42H, AL
        IN      AL, 61H            ;Read port 61H
        MOV     AH, AL             ;Save its contents
        OR      AL, 3
        OUT     61H, AL            ;Enable timer and AND gate
        MOV     CX, 5064H          ;Delay counter
DELAY:  NOP                        ;for 100 msec delay
        NOP
        LOOP    DELAY
        MOV     AL, AH             ;Restore port 61H
        OUT     61H, AL
        RET

LAB10   ENDP
CODE_SEG     ENDS

        END     LAB10
```

(a)

Figure L10.2   (a) Source program for Laboratory 10. (b) Source listing produced by the assembler.

```
                        TITLE    LABORATORY 10

                            PAGE      ,132

0000                            STACK_SEG    SEGMENT      STACK 'STACK'
0000        40 [                             DB           64 DUP(?)
              ??
                ]


0040                            STACK_SEG    ENDS


0000                            CODE_SEG     SEGMENT      'CODE'
0000                            LAB10  PROC  FAR
                                       ASSUME  CS:CODE_SEG, SS:STACK_SEG

                                ;To return to DEBUG program put return address on the stack

0000   1E                               PUSH    DS
0001   B8 0000                          MOV     AX, 0
0004   50                               PUSH    AX

                                ;Following code implements Laboratory 10

0005   B0 B6                            MOV     AL, 0B6H          ;Set up timer
0007   E6 43                            OUT     43H, AL
0009   B8 0319                          MOV     AX, 319H          ;Load divisor
000C   E6 42                            OUT     42H, AL
000E   8A C4                            MOV     AL, AH
0010   E6 42                            OUT     42H, AL
0012   E4 61                            IN      AL, 61H           ;Read port 61H
0014   8A E0                            MOV     AH, AL            ;Save its contents
0016   0C 03                            OR      AL, 3
0018   E6 61                            OUT     61H, AL           ;Enable timer and AND gate
001A   B9 5064                          MOV     CX, 5064H         ;Delay counter
001D   90                       DELAY:  NOP                       ;for 100 msec delay
001E   90                               NOP
001F   E2 FC                            LOOP    DELAY
0021   8A C4                            MOV     AL, AH            ;Restore port 61H
0023   E6 61                            OUT     61H, AL
0025   CB                               RET

0026                            LAB10  ENDP
0026                            CODE_SEG     ENDS

                                       END     LAB10

Segments and groups:

              N a m e           Size    align   combine class

CODE_SEG . . . . . . . . . . . .   0026    PARA    NONE    'CODE'
STACK_SEG. . . . . . . . . . .     0040    PARA    STACK   'STACK'

Symbols:

              N a m e           Type    Value   Attr

DELAY. . . . . . . . . . . . .    L NEAR  001D    CODE_SEG
LAB10. . . . . . . . . . . . .    F PROC  0000    CODE_SEG      Length =0026

Warning Severe
Errors  Errors
0       0
```

(b)

Figure L10.2 (Continued)

Part 3: Output Port for the Speaker in the IBM PC

As described in Part 2, I/O address 61H points to the output port that controls the speaker and other peripherals, such as the cassette and keyboard. Bit 0 on the port enables the timer to supply a clock signal, and bit 1 is used to enable the clock signal to the speaker. We will first read the status of these bits on the port and then change them to drive the speaker. Finally, we will run the program developed in Part 2.

Check	Step	Procedure
——	1	Load the DEBUG program.
——	2	Assemble and execute the instruction needed to input the contents of port 61H into the AL register. What are these contents? Ans. _____ What do bits 0 and 1 indicate with respect to the 8253 timer clock and the enable bit for the clock to the speaker? Ans. _____
——	3	Change the contents of AL so that the two least significant bits are logic 1. What are the new contents of AL? Ans. _____
——	4	Assemble and execute the instruction needed to output the new contents of AL to the output port 61H. What happens and why? Ans. _____
——	5	Reload AL with the original contents as read in Step 2. Again, assemble and execute an instruction to output the contents in AL to the output port 61H. What happens and why? Ans. _____
——	6	Load the program LAB10.EXE.
——	7	Unassemble the program to verify its loading.
——	8	Execute the program. What happens? Ans. _____
——	9	Change the program so that the divisor loaded into the 8253 is one-fourth the original value. Execute the program again. What is the difference when compared to the operation observed in Step 8? Ans. _____
——	10	Change the program so that the tone interval is doubled. Execute the program. Describe the difference when compared to the results observed in Steps 8 and 9. Ans. _____

LABORATORY 11: EXPLORING THE INTERRUPT SUBSYSTEM OF THE IBM PC

Objective

Learn how to:

1. Determine the address of an interrupt service routine.
2. Explore the code of an interrupt service routine.
3. Execute software interrupt service routines to determine the equipment attached to the PC and the amount of RAM.
4. Execute the software interrupt service routines for print screen and the system boot.
5. Use the interrupt 21 function calls to read and set date and time.

Part 1: Interrupt Vector Table

The PC's interrupt vector table is located in the first 1024 bytes of RAM memory, that is, from address 00000H through 003FFH. Each vector takes up 4 bytes of memory; therefore, there are 256 vectors in the interrupt vector table. Here we will explore the contents of the interrupt vector table and use this information to calculate the starting address for several interrupt service routines. *Check off each step as it is completed.*

Check	Step	Procedure
_____	1	Load the DEBUG program.
_____	2	Dump the contents of the memory locations starting at 0:0. Compute the starting addresses of the service routines for the following interrupt types:
		Interrupt type 2 (NMI) _____
		Interrupt type 8 (Timer) _____
		Interrupt type 9 (Keyboard) _____
		Interrupt type 10 _____
		Interrupt type 11 _____
		Interrupt type 12 _____
		Interrupt type 13 _____
		Interrupt type 14 (Diskette) _____
		Interrupt type 15 _____

Part 2: Exploring the Code of an Interrupt Service Routine

Now we know the starting address of several interrupt service routines in ROM. Next we will examine the instruction sequence in the NMI service routine.

Check	Step	Procedure
_____	1	Unassemble the code for the service routine for NMI.
_____	2	What is the address of the last instruction in the NMI service routine? Ans. _____
_____	3	Does this service routine invoke another software interrupt? Ans. _____ If yes, which one? Ans. _____
_____	4	Does this service routine call another routine? Ans. _____ If yes, where is that routine located? Ans. _____
_____	5	Describe the operation implemented by the first four instructions of the service routine? Ans. _____
_____	6	From the hardware discussion in Chapter 9, determine the conditions of the hardware that will enforce bypassing of the rest of the instructions (those after the first 4) of the NMI routine and returning to the invocation address. Ans. _____
_____	7	Now determine the conditions of the hardware that will enforce executing the rest of the instructions of the service routine. Ans. _____
_____	8	After the first four instructions are executed, SI is loaded with an offset to a memory location. The value loaded into SI depends on the contents of AL. If AL contains 40H, what value is loaded into SI? Ans. _____
_____	9	Display the memory contents pointed to by the condition met in Step 8. What is the message in the ASCII code area of the display? Ans. _____
		What does this indicate? Ans. _____
_____	10	Display the memory contents pointed to by the offset in SI if the contents of AL are not equal to 40H. What does this indicate? Ans. _____

Part 3: Determining the PC Equipment and RAM Implementation

The service routines for INT 11H and INT 12H are used to determine what equipment is attached to the PC and how much RAM is implemented. Execution of the service routine for INT 11H returns a word in AX. The bits of this word indicate what type of equipment is attached to the PC. The bits of the word are encoded as follows:

Bit 0 =   1 if the PC has floppy disk drives attached

Bit 3, 2 =   system board R/W memory size (00 = 16K, 01 = 32K, 10 = 48K, 11 = 64K)

Bit 5, 4 =   video mode (00 = unused, 01 = 40X25 BW using color card, 10 = 80X25 BW using color card, 11 = 80X25 BW using monochrome card)

Bit 7. 6 =   number of floppy disk drives (00 = 1, 01 = 2, 10 = 3, 11 = 4 only if bit 0 = 1)

Bit 11, 10, 9 = number of RS 232 cards

Bit 15, 14 =   number of printers attached

Other bits =   don't care

By executing the service routine for INT 12H, a number is returned in AX that indicates the number of K bytes of R/W memory in the system.

Check	Step	Procedure
_____	1	Load the DEBUG program.
_____	2	Display the contents of all registers. What is the value in AX? Ans. _____
_____	3	Assemble the instruction INT 11H at the current code segment address. Execute the instruction and then display the registers. What are the new contents of AX? Ans. _____ What do the contents of AX indicate with respect to the following equipment? (a) Floppy disk drives present or not _____ (b) System board RAM size _____ (c) Video mode _____ (d) Number of floppy disk drives _____ (e) Number of RS232 cards _____ (f) Number of printers attached _____
_____	4	Assemble the instruction INT 12H at the current code segment address. Execute the instruction and then display the new contents of the registers. What is the value in AX? Ans. _____
_____	5	How much R/W memory is in the PC? Ans. _____
_____	6	Quit the debugger.

Part 4: Print Screen and System Boot Interrupts

Now we will examine the operation of two other interrupt service routines. The INT 5H service routine can be used to print what is displayed on the screen. On the other hand, the service routine for INT 19H is used to boot the system. Here we will execute these interrupts to observe the functions that they perform.

Check	Step	Procedure
_____	1	Load the DEBUG program.
_____	2	Assemble the instruction INT 5H at the current memory location pointed to by CS:IP. Execute the instruction and then describe what happens. Ans. _____
_____	3	Assemble the instruction INT 19H at the memory location pointed to by CS:IP. Execute this instruction. What happens? Ans. _____ _____

Part 5: The INT 21H Function Calls

INT 21H is provided to invoke DOS operations for a wide variety of functions, such as character I/O, file management, date and time setting and reading. Here we will learn to use the time setting and reading functions. To call any function, the register AH is loaded with the function number and then the instruction INT 21H is executed. If the specified function cannot be performed, DOS returns FF_{16} in the AH register.

Check	Step	Procedure
_____	1	Read the program in Fig. L11.1 and determine the following:
		(a) Function number and AH contents to read date. Ans. _____
		(b) Function number and AH contents to read time. Ans. _____
		(c) Function number and AH contents to set date. Ans. _____
		(d) Function number and AH contents to set time. Ans. _____
		(e) What date is set by the program? Ans. _____
		(f) What time is set by the program? Ans. _____

```
mov ah,2ah        ; get date, AL=day of the week, CX=year, DH=month, DL=day
int 21h           ;
                  ;
mov ah,2ch        ; get time, CH=hour, CL=minutes, DH=seconds,
int 21h           ; DL=hundredths of a second
                  ;
mov ah,2bh        ; set date as follows:
                  ;
mov cx,07c3       ; cx = year
                  ;
mov dh,0a         ; dh = month
                  ;
mov dl,0a         ; dl = day
int 21h           ;
                  ;
mov ah,2d         ; set time as follows:
                  ;
mov ch,11h        ; ch = hour
                  ;
mov dh,10h        ; dh = seconds
                  ;
mov cl,32h        ; cl = minutes
                  ;
mov dl,4ah        ; dl = hundredths
int 21h           ;
```

Figure L11.1   Program for Laboratory 11, Part 5.

_____	2	Load the DEBUG program.
_____	3	Assemble the program starting at the address specified by the current CS:IP.
_____	4	Execute the program up to the point where it reads the date. What date is read? Ans. _____

Check	Step	Procedure
_____	5	Execute the program up to the point where it reads the time. What time is read? Ans. _____
_____	6	Execute the program up to the point where it sets the new date. Display the contents of AX. AX = _____
_____	7	Execute the program up to the point where it sets the new time. Display the contents of AX. AX = _____
_____	8	Quit the debugger. Do you think a new date and time are set? Ans. _____
_____	9	Use DOS commands TIME and DATE to verify that the new date and time are set.

Answers to Selected Assignments

CHAPTER 1

Section 1.2

1. Original PC.
2. Mainframe computer, minicomputer, and microcomputer.
3. Very large scale integration.

Section 1.3

7. Microprocessing unit (MPU).
9. Keyboard; mouse and joy stick.
11. Primary storage and secondary storage memory.
13. Read-only memory (ROM) and random access read/write memory (RAM).
15. DOS is loaded from either the diskette or hard disk into RAM. Since RAM is volatile, the operating system is lost whenever power is turned off.

Section 1.4

17. 4004, 8088, 8086.
19. 30,000, 270,000.

21. Event controller and data controller.

24. Real mode and protected mode.

26. Memory management, protection, and multitasking.

CHAPTER 2

Section 2.2

1. Software.

4. Instructions encoded in machine language are coded in 0s and 1s, while assembly language instructions are written in alphanumeric symbols such as MOV, ADD, or SUB.

6. The data that are to be processed during execution of an instruction; source operand and destination operand.

8. An assembler is a program that is used to convert an assembly language source program to its equivalent program in machine code. A compiler is a program that converts a program written in a high-level language to equivalent machine code.

9. The machine code output of an assembler or compiler is called object code. The assembly or high-level language code that is input to an assembler or compiler is called source code.

11. A real-time application is one in which the tasks required by the application must be completed before any other input to the program occurs that can alter its operation.

Section 2.3

13. Bus interface unit and execution unit.

15. 4 bytes; 6 bytes.

Section 2.4

17. Aid to the assembly language programmer for understanding the 8088's software operation.

20. 1,048,576 (1M) bytes.

Section 2.5

21. $FFFFF_{16}$ and 00000_{16}.

24.

Address	Contents
A001	78
A002	56
A003	34
A004	12

Section 2.6

25. Unsigned integer, signed integer, unpacked BCD, packed BCD, ASCII.

27. (0A000H) = F4H   (0A001H) = 01H

29. **(a)** 00000010,00001001; 00101001.   **(b)** 00001000, 00001000; 10001000.

31. NEXT I

Section 2.7

34. Code segment (CS) register, stack segment (SS) register, data segment (DS) register, and extra segment (ES) register.

36. Instructions of the program can be stored anywhere in the memory address space.

Section 2.8

37. Pointers to service routines.

Section 2.9

40. The instruction is fetched from memory, decoded within the 8088, operands are read from memory or internal registers, the operation specified by the instruction is performed on the data, and results are written back to either memory or an internal register.

Section 2.10

42. Accumulator (A) register, base (B) register, count (C) register, and data (D) register.

44. DH and DL.

Section 2.11

47. Base pointer (BP) and stack pointer (SP).

50. The address in SI is the offset to a source operand and DI contains the offset to a destination operand.

Section 2.12

51.

Flag	Type
CF	Status
PF	Status
AF	Status
ZF	Status
SF	Status
OF	Status
TF	Control
IF	Control
DF	Control

53. Instructions can be used to test the state of these flags and, based on their setting, modify the sequence in which instructions of the program are executed.

55. Instructions are provided that can load the complete register or modify specific flag bits.

Section 2.13

57. Offset and base.

59. **(a)** ? = 0123H.
   (b) ? = 2210H.
   (c) ? = 3570H.
   (d) ? = 2600H.

60. $021AC_{16}$.

Section 2.14

63. The stack is the area of memory that is used to temporarily store information (parameters) that is to be passed to subroutines and other information such as the contents of IP and CS that is needed to return from a called subroutine to the main part of the program.

65. 128 words.

Section 2.15

68. 64K bytes.

Section 2.16

71.

Instruction	Source	Destination
(a)	Register	Register
(b)	Register	Immediate
(c)	Register indirect	Register
(d)	Register indirect	Direct
(e)	Register	Based
(f)	Register	Indexed
(g)	Register	Based indexed

CHAPTER 3

Section 3.2

1. $0000001111000010_2 = 03C2H$.

2. **(a)** $1000100100010101_2 = 8915H$.
   (b) $1000100100011000_2 = 8918H$.
   (c) $10001010010101011100010000_2 = 8A5710H$.

Section 3.3

4. 3 bytes.

Section 3.4

7. Yes.

8. Error.

9. −R CX   (↵)
     CX XXXX
     :0010   (↵)

11. −R (↵)

Section 3.5

12. −D CS:0000 000F   (↵)

16. −F CS:100 105 1   (↵)
      −F CS:106 10B 22   (↵)
      −F CS:10C 111 33   (↵)
      −F CS:112 117 44   (↵)
      −F CS:118 11D 55   (↵)
      −E CS:105   (↵)
      CS:0115 XX.FF   (↵)
      −E CS:113   (↵)
      CS:0113 XX.FF   (↵)
      −D CS:100 11D   (↵)
      −S CS:100 11D FF   (↵)

Section 3.6

17. −E CS:100 32 0E 34 12   (↵)
      −U CS:100 103   (↵)
      −W CS:100 1 50 1   (↵)

Section 3.8

21. −L CS:300 1 50 1   (↵)
      −U CS:300 303   (↵)
      −R CX   (↵)
      CX XXXX
      :000F   (↵)
      −E DS:1234 FF   (↵)
      −T =CS:300   (↵)
      −D DS:1234 1235   (↵)

Section 3.9

23. A syntax error is an error in the rules of coding the program. On the other hand, an execution error is an error in the logic of the planned solution for the problem.

CHAPTER 4

Section 4.2

1. Data transfer instructions, arithmetic instructions, logic instructions, shift instructions, and rotate instructions.

Section 4.3

3. (a) Value 0110H is moved into AX.
   (b) 0110H is copied into DI.
   (c) 10H is copied into BL.
   (d) 0110H is copied into memory address DS:0100H.
   (e) 0110H is copied into memory address DS:0120H.
   (f) 0110H is copied into memory address DS:0114H.
   (g) 0110H is copied into memory address DS:0124H.

5. MOV [1010],ES

7. (a) Contents of AX and BX are swapped.
   (b) Contents of BX and DI are swapped.
   (c) Contents of memory location DATA and register AX are swapped.
   (d) Contents of the memory location pointed to by BX + DI are swapped with that of register AX.

9. AL is loaded from address $10000_{16} + 0100_{16} + 0010_{16} = 10110_{16}$.

11.

```
NAME:  PUSH AX              ;SAVE FLAGS AND REGISTERS IN STACK
       PUSH DS
       PUSH BX
       PUSHF
       MOV AX,DATA_SEG      ;ESTABLISH THE DATA SEGMENT
       MOV DS,AX
       MOV AL,MEM1          ;GET THE GIVEN CODE AT MEM1
       MOV BX,OFFSET_TABL1
       XLAT                 ;TRANSLATE
       MOV MEM1,AL          ;SAVE NEW CODE AT MEM1
       MOV AL,MEM2          ;REPEAT FOR THE SECOND CODE AT MEM2
       MOV BX,OFFSET_TABL2
       XLAT
       MOV MEM2,AL
       POPF                 ;RESTORE FLAGS AND REGISTERS FROM
                            ;STACK
```

```
POP  BX
POP  DS
POP  AX
RET                        ;SUBROUTINE ENDS
```

Section 4.4

13. **(a)** (AX) = 00FFH
    (b) (SI) = 0011H
    (c) (DS:100H) = 11H
    (d) (DL) = 20H
    (e) (DL) = 1FH
    (f) (DS:220H) = 2FH
    (g) (DS:210H) = C0H
    (h) (AX) = 039CH
       (DX) = 0000H
    (i) (AL) = F0H
       (AH) = 07H
    (j) (AL) = 02H
       (AH) = 00H
    (k) (AL) = 08H
       (AH) = 00H

15. SBB AX,[BX]

17. (AH) = remainder = 3_{16}, (AL) = quotient = 12_{16}; therefore, (AX) = 0312_{16}.

19. AAS

21. (AX) = 7FFFH, (DX) = 0000H

Section 4.5

23. **(a)** 0FH is ANDed with the contents of the memory address DS:300H.
    (b) Contents of DX are ANDed with the contents of the storage location pointed to by SI.
    (c) Contents of AX is ORed with the contents of the memory location pointed to by BX + DI.
    (d) F0H is ORed with the contents of the memory location pointed to by BX + DI + 10H.
    (e) Contents of the memory location pointed to by SI + BX are exclusive-ORed with the contents of AX.
    (f) The bits of memory location DS:300H are inverted.
    (g) The bits of the word memory location pointed to by BX + DI are inverted.

25. AND DX,0080H

27. The new contents of AX are the 2's complement of the old contents.

Section 4.6

29. **(a)** Contents of DX are shifted left by a number of bit positions equal to the contents of

CL. LSBs are filled with 0s, and CF equals the value of the last bit shifted out of the MSB position.

(b) Contents of the byte-wide memory location DS:400H are shifted left by a number of bit positions equal to the contents of CL. LSBs are filled with 0s, and CF equals the value of the last bit shifted out of the MSB position.

(c) Contents of the byte-wide memory location pointed to by DI are shifted right by one bit position. MSB is filled with 0, and CF equals the value shifted out of the LSB position.

(d) Contents of the byte-wide memory location pointed to by DI + BX are shifted right by a number of bit positions equal to the contents of CL. MSBs are filled with 0s, and CF equals the value of the last bit shifted out of the LSB position.

(e) Contents of the word-wide memory location pointed to by BX + DI are shifted right by one bit position. MSB is filled with the value of the original MSB, and CF equals the value shifted out of the LSB position.

(f) Contents of the word-wide memory location pointed to by BX + DI + 10H are shifted right by a number of bit positions equal to the contents of CL. MSBs are filled with the value of the original MSB, and CF equals the value of the last bit shifted out of the LSB position.

31. SHL CX,1

33. The original contents of AX must have the four most significant bits equal to 0.

Section 4.7

35. (a) Contents of DX are rotated left by a number of bit positions equal to the contents of CL. As each bit is rotated out of the MSB position, the LSB position and CF are filled with this value.

(b) Contents of the byte-wide memory location DS:400H are rotated left by a number of bit positions equal to the contents of CL. As each bit is rotated out of the MSB position, it is loaded into CF, and the prior contents of CF are loaded into the LSB position.

(c) Contents of the byte-wide memory location pointed to by DI are rotated right by one bit position. As the bit is rotated out of the LSB position, the MSB position and CF are filled with this value.

(d) Contents of the byte-wide memory location pointed to by DI + BX are rotated right by a number of bit positions equal to the contents of CL. As each bit is rotated out of the LSB position, the MSB position and CF are filled with this value.

(e) Contents of the word-wide memory location pointed to by BX + DI are shifted right by one bit position. As the bit is rotated out the LSB location, it is loaded into CF, and the prior contents of CF are loaded into the MSB position.

(f) Contents of the word-wide memory location pointed to by BX + DI + 10H are rotated right by a number of bit positions equal to the contents of CL. As each bit is rotated out of the LSB position, it is loaded into CF, and the prior contents of CF are loaded into the MSB position.

37. RCL WORD PTR [BX],1

CHAPTER 5

Section 5.2

1. Executing the first instruction causes the contents of the status register to be copied into AH. The second instruction causes the value of the flags to be saved in memory at the location pointed to by BX + DI.

3. STC, CLC.

5.
```
CLI
LAHF
MOV AX,0
MOV DS,AX
MOV BX,0A000H
MOV [BX],AH
CLC
```

Section 5.3

7. **(a)** The byte of data in AL is compared with the byte of data in memory at address DS:100H by subtraction, and the status flags are set or reset to reflect the results.
   (b) The word contents of the data storage memory location pointed to by SI are compared with the contents of AX by subtraction, and the status flags are set or reset to reflect the results.
   (c) The immediate data 1234H are compared with the word contents of the memory location pointed to by the value in DI by subtraction, and the status flags are set or reset to reflect the results.

9.

Instruction	ZF	CF
Initial state	0	0
MOV BX,1111H	0	0
MOV AX,0BBBBH	0	0
CMP BX,AX	0	1

Section 5.4

11. IP; CS; and IP.

13. Intersegment.

15. **(a)** 1075H:310H.
    (b) 1075H:1000H.
    (c) 1075H:1000H.

17. SF = 0.

19. **(a)** Intrasegment; Short-label; if the carry flag is set, a jump is performed by adding the value 10H to the current value in IP.
    (b) Intrasegment; Near-label; if PF is not set, a jump is performed by loading IP with the value assigned to PARITY_ERROR.

(c) Intersegment; Memptr32; if the overflow flag is set, a jump is performed by loading the two words of the 32-bit pointer addressed by the value in BX into IP and CS, respectively.

21. (a) $1000_{16} = 2^{12} = 4096$ times.

(b)
```
                    MOV CX,11H
          DLY: DEC CX
               JNZ DLY
     NXT:  ___
```

(c)
```
                    MOV AX,0FFFFH
         DLY1: MOV CX,0
         DLY2: DEC CX
               JNZ DLY2
               DEC AX
               JNZ DLY1
     NXT:  ___
```

23.
```
               MOV AX,DATA_SEG  ;ESTABLISH DATA SEGMENT
               MOV DS,AX
               MOV CX,64H       ;SET UP ARRAY COUNTER
               MOV SI,0A000H    ;SET UP SOURCE ARRAY POINTER
               MOV DI,0B000H    ;SET UP DESTINATION ARRAY
                                ;POINTER
      GO_ON:   MOV AX,[SI]
               CMP AX,[DI]      ;COMPARE THE NEXT ELEMENT
               JNE MIS_MATCH    ;SKIP ON A MISMATCH
               ADD SI,2         ;UPDATE POINTERS AND COUNTER
               ADD DI,2
               DEC CX
               JNZ GO_ON        ;REPEAT FOR THE NEXT ELEMENT
               MOV FOUND,0      ;IF ARRAYS ARE IDENTICAL, SAVE
                                ;A ZERO
               JMP DONE
  MIS_MATCH:   MOV FOUND,SI     ;ELSE, SAVE THE MISMATCH ADDRESS
      DONE:  ___
```

25. ;For the given binary number B, the BCD number's digits are
;D0 = R(B/10)
;D1 = R(Q(B/10)/10)
;D2 = R(Q(Q(B/10)/10)/10)
;D3 = R(Q(Q(Q(B/10)/10)/10)/10)
;where R and Q stand for the remainder and the quotient.

```
          MOV SI,0       ;RESULT = 0
          MOV CH,4       ;COUNTER
          MOV BX,10      ;DIVISOR
          MOV AX,DX      ;GET THE BINARY NUMBER
          MOV DX,0       ;FOR DIVISION MAKE (DX) = 0
```

```
NEXTDIGIT:
            DIV  BX            ;COMPUTE THE NEXT BCD DIGIT
            CMP  DX,9          ;INVALID IF >9
            JG   INVALID
            MOV  CL,12         ;POSITION AS MOST SIGNIFICANT DIGIT
            SHL  DX,CL
            OR   SI,DX
            DEC  CH            ;REPEAT FOR ALL FOUR DIGITS
            JZ   DONE
            MOV  CL,4          ;PREPARE FOR NEXT DIGIT
            SHR  SI,CL
            JMP  NEXTDIGIT
   INVALID:MOV  DX,0FFFFH      ;INVALID CODE
            JMP  DONE1
   DONE:MOV  DX,SI
   DONE1:____
```

Section 5.5

27. The call instruction saves the value in the instruction pointer (and may be both the instruction pointer and the segment register) in addition to performing the jump operation.

29. IP; IP and CS.

31. **(a)** 1075H:1000H.

    (b) 1075H:1000H.

    (c) 1000H:0100H.

33. **(a)** The value in the DS register is pushed onto the top of the stack.

    (b) The word of data in memory pointed to by SI is pushed onto the top of the stack.

    (c) The word at the top of the stack is popped into the DI register.

    (d) The word at the top of the stack is popped into the memory location pointed to by BX + DI.

    (e) The word at the top of the stack is popped into the status register.

35.
```
;FOR THE DECIMAL NUMBER = D₃D₂D₁D₀
;THE BINARY NUMBER = 10 (10 (10 (0+D₃) +D₂) +D₁) + D₀
```

with $D_3 D_2 D_1 D_0$ and binary number $= 10(10(10(0+D_3)+D_2)+D_1)+D_0$

```
                MOV  BX,0        ;RESULT = 0
                MOV  SI,10       ;MULTIPLIER = 10
                MOV  CH,4        ;NUMBER OF DIGITS = 4
                MOV  CL,4        ;ROTATE COUNTER = 4
                MOV  DI,DX
   NXTDIGIT:    MOV  AX,DI       ;GET THE DECIMAL NUMBER
                ROL  AX,CL       ;ROTATE TO EXTRACT THE DIGIT
                MOV  DI,AX       ;SAVE THE ROTATED DECIMAL NUMBER
                AND  AX,0FH      ;EXTRACT THE DIGIT
                ADD  AX,BX       ;ADD TO THE LAST RESULT
                DEC  CH
```

```
                    JZ    DONE          ;SKIP IF THIS IS THE LAST DIGIT
                    MUL   SI            ;MULTIPLY BY 10
                    MOV   BX,AX         ;AND SAVE
                    JMP   NXTDIGIT      ;REPEAT FOR THE NEXT DIGIT
          DONE:     ___                 ;RESULT = (AX)
```

37. ;ASSUME THAT THE OFFSET OF A[I] IS AI1ADDR
   ;AND THE OFFSET OF B[I] IS BI1ADDR

```
                    MOV   AX,DATA_SEG   ;INITIALIZE DATA SEGMENT
                    MOV   DS,AX
                    MOV   CX,98
                    MOV   SI,AI1ADDR    ;SOURCE ARRAY POINTER
                    MOV   DI,BI1ADDR    ;DESTINATION ARRAY POINTER
                    MOV   AX,[SI]
                    MOV   [DI],AX       ;B[1] = A[1]
          MORE:MOV  AX,[SI]             ;STORE A[I] INTO AX
                    ADD   SI,2          ;INCREMENT POINTER
                    MOV   BX,[SI]       ;STORE A[I+1] INTO BX
                    ADD   SI,2
                    MOV   CX,[SI]       ;STORE A[I+2] INTO CX
                    ADD   SI,2
                    CALL  ARITH         ;CALL ARITHMETIC SUBROUTINE
                    MOV   [DI],AX
                    SUB   SI,4
                    ADD   DI,2
                    LOOP  MORE          ;LOOP BACK FOR NEXT ELEMENT
                    ADD   SI,4
          DONE:MOV  AX,[SI]             ;B[100] = A[100]
                    MOV   [DI],AX
                    HLT
```

   ;Subroutine for the arithmetic
   ;(AX) ← ((AX) − 5(BX) + 9)CX))/4

```
          ARITH:    PUSHF               ;SAVE FLAGS AND REGISTERS IN STACK
                    PUSH  BX
                    PUSH  CX
                    PUSH  DX
                    PUSH  DI
                    MOV   DX,CX
                    MOV   DI,CX         ;KEEP COPY OF A[I+2]
                    MOV   CL,3
                    SAL   DX,CL         ;8A[I+2]
                    ADD   DX,DI         ;9A[I+2]
                    MOV   CL,2
                    MOV   DI,BX         ;SAVE COPY OF A[I+1]
```

```
        SAL    BX,CL    ;4A[I+1]
        ADD    BX,DI    ;5A[I+1]
        SUB    AX,BX    ;A[I] - 5A[I+1]
        ADD    AX,DX    ;A[I] - 5A[I+1] + 9A[I+2]
        SAR    AX,CL    ;DIVIDE BY 4
        POP    DI       ;RESTORE FLAGS AND REGISTERS
        POP    DX
        POP    CX
        POP    BX
        POPF
        RET             ;RETURN
```

Section 5.6

39. ZF.

41. 127 bytes.

43.

```
        MOV    AL,1
        MOV    CX,N
        JCXZ   DONE     ;N = 0 CASE
        LOOPZ  DONE     ;N = 1 CASE
        INC    CX       ;RESTORE N
AGAIN:  MUL    CL
        LOOP   AGAIN
DONE:   MOV    FACT,AL
```

Section 5.7

45. DF.

47. (a) CLD
        MOVSB
     (b) CLD
        LODSW
     (c) STD
        CMPSB

49.

```
        MOV    SI,OFFSET DATASEG1_ASCII_CHAR ;ASCII OFFSET
        MOV    DI,OFFSET DATASEG2_EBCDIC_CHAR ;EBCDIC OFFSET
        MOV    BX,OFFSET DATASEG3_ASCII_TO_EBCDIC ;TRANSLA-
                              ;TION TABLE OFFSET
        CLD                   ;SELECT AUTOINCREMENT MODE
        MOV    CL,100         ;BYTE COUNT
        MOV    AX,DATASEG1 ;ASCII SEGMENT
        MOV    DS,AX
        MOV    AX,DATASEG2 ;EBCDIC SEGMENT
        MOV    ES,AX
```

```
NEXTBYTE:
          LODS   BYTE          ;GET THE ASCII
          MOV    DX,DATASEG3   ;TRANSLATION TABLE SEGMENT
          MOV    DS,DX
          XLAT                 ;TRANSLATE
          STOS   BYTE          ;SAVE EBCDIC
          MOV    DX,DATASEG1   ;ASCII SEGMENT FOR NEXT ASCII
          MOV    DS,DX         ;ELEMENT
          LOOP   NEXTBYTE
DONE:            ____
```

CHAPTER 6

Section 6.2

1. HMOS.

3. 17.

5. IM byte.

Section 6.3

7. The logic level of input MN/$\overline{MX}$.

9. $\overline{WR}$; $\overline{LOCK}$.

11. $\overline{SSO}$

Section 6.4

13. 20 bit, 8 bit; 20 bit, 16 bit.

15. A_0, D_{15}.

17. $\overline{BHE}$.

19. $\overline{WR}$.

21. HOLD, HLDA.

Section 6.5

23. HOLD, HLDA, $\overline{WR}$, IO/$\overline{M}$, DT/$\overline{R}$, $\overline{DEN}$, ALE, and $\overline{INTA}$, in minimum mode are $\overline{RQ/GT}_{1.0}$, $\overline{LOCK}$, $\overline{S}_2-\overline{S}_0$, QS_1, and QS_0, respectively, in the maximum mode.

25. $\overline{MRDC}$, $\overline{MWTC}$, $\overline{AMWC}$, $\overline{IORC}$, $\overline{IOWC}$, $\overline{AIOWC}$, $\overline{INTA}$, and MCE/$\overline{PDEN}$.

27. 101_2.

29. 10_2.

Section 6.6

31. +4.5 V to +5.5 V.

33. + 2.0V

Section 6.7

35. 5 MHz and 8 MHz

37. CLK, PCLK, and OSC; 10 MHz, 5 MHz, and 30 MHz.

Section 6.8

39. 4: T_1, T_2, T_3, and T_4.

40. 800 ns.

42. An extension of the current bus cycle by a period equal to one or more T states because the READY input is tested and found to be logic 0.

Section 6.9

46. Two bus cycles must take place to write the word of data to memory. During the first bus cycle, the least significant byte of the word is written to the byte storage location at address $A0000_{16}$. Next the 8088 automatically increments the address so that it points to the byte storage location $A0001_{16}$. The most significant byte of the word is written into this storage location with a second write bus cycle. During both bus cycles, address information is applied to the memory subsystem over address lines A_0 through A_{19} and data are transferred over data bus lines D_0 through D_7. $\overline{\text{BHE}} = 0$, $A_0 = 0$, $\overline{\text{WR}} = 0$, $\text{M}/\overline{\text{IO}} = 1$, $\text{DT}/\overline{\text{R}} = 1$, $\overline{\text{DEN}} = 0$.

47. High bank; $\overline{\text{BHE}}$.

49. $\overline{\text{BHE}} = 0$, $A_0 = 0$, $\overline{\text{WR}} = 0$, $\text{M}/\overline{\text{IO}} = 1$, $\text{DT}/\overline{\text{R}} = 1$, DEN $= 0$.

Section 6.10

51. 01.

Section 6.11

53. $\text{IO}/\overline{\text{M}}$.

55. $\overline{S}_2\overline{S}_1\overline{S}_0 = 100$; $\overline{\text{MRDC}}$.

57. $\overline{S}_3\overline{S}_4 = 10$, $\overline{S}_2\overline{S}_1\overline{S}_0 = 110$; $\overline{\text{MWTC}}$, $\overline{\text{AMWC}}$.

Section 6.12

59. Address is output on A_0 through A_{19}, $\overline{\text{BHE}}$, is output, $\text{M}/\overline{\text{IO}}$ and $\text{DT}/\overline{\text{R}}$ are set to the appropriate logic levels.

61. READY.

Section 6.13

63. The 8288 bus controller produces the appropriately timed command and control signals needed to control transfers over the data bus. The address bus latch is used to latch and buffer the lower bits of the address. The address decoder decodes the higher-order address bits to produce chip enable signals. The bank write control logic determines to which memory banks $\overline{\text{MWTC}}$ is applied during write bus cycles. The data bus transceiver/buffer controls the direction of data transfers between the MPU and memory subsystem and supplies buffering for the data bus lines.

65. Octal D-type latch.

69. $\overline{\text{DEN}}$ = 0, DT/$\overline{\text{R}}$ = 1.

71. $\overline{\text{G}}$ = 0, DIR = 1, CAB = X, CBA = X, SAB = 1, and SBA = X.

73. Y_5 = 0.

Section 6.14

75. Programmable logic array.

77. Fuse link.

79. EPROM technology.

81. 10 dedicated inputs, 2 dedicated outputs, 6 programmable I/Os, and 64 product terms.

83. The 16R8 has registered outputs.

Section 6.15

84. When the power supply for the memory device is turned off, its data contents are not lost.

86. Ultraviolet light.

88. We are assuming that external decode logic has already produced active signals for $\overline{\text{CE}}$ and $\overline{\text{OE}}$. Next the address is applied to the A inputs of the EPROM and decoded within the device to select the storage location to be accessed. After a delay equal to t_{ACC}, the data at this storage location are available at the D outputs.

90. The access time of the 2764A is 250 ns and that of the 2764A-1 is 170 ns. That is, the 2764-1 is a faster device.

92. 1 ms.

Section 6.16

94. Volatile.

96. 64K × 16.

98. Higher density and lower power.

101. Additional circuitry must be acquired to perform the refresh function.

Section 6.17

104. 128.

CHAPTER 7

Section 7.2

1. Isolated I/O and memory mapped I/O

3. Memory mapped I/O.

Section 7.3

5. Address lines A_0 through A_{15} and $\overline{BHE}$ carry the address of the I/O port to be accessed; address lines A_{16} through A_{19} are held at the 0 logic level. Data bus lines D_0 through D_{15} carry the data that are transferred between the MPU and I/O port.

7. In the 8086's I/O interface, the 8 bit data bus is replaced by a 16 bit data bus, AD_0 through AD_{15}; control signal IO/$\overline{M}$ is replaced by M/$\overline{IO}$; and status signal $\overline{SSO}$ is replaced by $\overline{BHE}$.

9. 8288.

11. $\overline{S}_2\overline{S}_1\overline{S}_0$; 001.

Section 7.4

13. 16 bits.

15. 32K word-wide I/O ports.

17. 2;1.

Section 7.5

19.

```
MOV  AX,1AH
IN   DX,AX
```

21.

```
MOV  AL,0FH
MOV  DX,1000H
OUT  DX,AL
```

23.

```
IN   AL,0B0H
AND  AL,01H
SHR  AL,1
JC   ACTIVE_INPUT
```

Section 7.6

25. Address is output in T_1; data are read in T_3.

28. 1200 ns.

Section 7.7

29. $800E_{16}$.

31. Sets all outputs at port 2 ($0_{16}-0_{23}$) to logic 1.

Section 7.8

33. Port 4.

35.

```
        MOV  AX,0A000H
        MOV  DS,AX
        MOV  DX,8002H
        IN   AL,DX
        MOV  [0000H],AL
        MOV  DX,8004H
        IN   AL,DX
        MOV  [0001H],AL
```

Section 7.9

37. Handshaking.

39. First, the address is clocked into the address latch. Address bits $A_{3L}A_{2L}A_{1L} = 000$, $A_{0L} = 0$, and $A_{15L} = 1$ enables the decoder and switches the P_0 output to 0. This output activates one input of the NOR gate that drives the CLK input of the Port 0 latch. Later in the bus cycle, the byte of data is output on data bus lines D_0 through D_7. DT/$\overline{R}$ is logic 1 and $\overline{DEN}$ equals 0. Therefore, the transceiver is set for transmit (output) mode of operation and the byte of data is passed to the data inputs of Port 0. Finally, the write pulse at $\overline{WR}$ supplies the second input of the NOR gate at the CLK input. Since both inputs of the gate are now logic 0, the output switches to 1. As $\overline{WR}$ returns to logic 1, the clock pulse is complete and the data is latched into outputs O_0 through O_7 of Port 0.

Section 7.10

41. Parallel I/O.

43. Port A = mode 1 output; port B = mode 1 output.

45. Mode 0 selects simple I/O operation. This means that the lines of the port can be configured as level-sensitive inputs or latched outputs. Port A and port B can be configured as 8-bit input or output ports, and port C can be configured for operation as two independent 4-bit input or output ports.

Mode 1 operation represents what is known as strobed I/O. In this mode, ports A and B are configured as two independent byte-wide I/O ports, each of which has a 4-bit control/data port associated with it. The control/data ports are formed from port C's lower and upper nibbles, respectively. When configured in this way, data applied to an input port must be strobed in with a signal produced in external hardware. An output port is provided with handshake signals that indicate when new data are available at its outputs and when an external device has read these values.

Mode 2 represents strobed bidirectional I/O. The key difference is that now the port works as either input or output, and control signals are provided for both functions. Only port A can be configured to work in this way.

47.

```
        MOV  AX,0
        MOV  DS,AX
        MOV  AL,92H
        MOV  BX,100H
        MOV  [BX],AL
```

49.
```
                              MOV  AL,3
                              MOV  DX,100H
                              OUT  DX,AL
```

Section 7.11

51. The value at the inputs of port A of I/O device 2 are read into AL.

53.
```
              IN   AL,08      ;READ PORT A
              MOV  BL,AL      ;SAVE IN BL
              IN   AL,0AH     ;READ PORT B
              ADD  AL,BL      ;ADD THE TWO NUMBERS
              OUT  0CH,AL     ;OUTPUT TO PORT C
```

Section 7.12

55. $A_0 = 0$, $A_2A_1 = 01$, and $A_5A_4A_3 = 010$; 00012_{16}.

57.
```
                              MOV  CX,0408H
                              MOV  AL, [CX]
                              MOV  BL,AL
                              MOV  AL,040AH
                              MOV  AL, [CX]
                              ADD  AL,BL
                              MOV  CX,040CH
                              MOV  [CX],AL
```

Section 7.13

58. CLK_2, $GATE_2$, and OUT_2.

60. $\overline{CS} = 0$, $\overline{RD} = 1$, $\overline{WR} = 0$, $A_1 = 1$, and $A_0 = 1$.

62.
```
MOV AL,12H
MOV [1002H],AL
```

64. 54.9 ms; 32.8 ms.

65. 838 ns; 500 ns.

66. 3.43 ms.

Section 7.14

69. No.

71. 27.

73. $DMA + 8_{16}$.

76. $0F_{16}$.

CHAPTER 8

Section 8.2

1. Hardware interrupts, software interrupts, internal interrupts, software interrupts, and reset.

3. Software interrupts, external hardware interrupts, nonmaskable interrupt, and internal interrupts.

5. Higher priority.

Section 8.3

7. 4 bytes.

9. Overflow.

11. $IP_{40} \rightarrow$ (40H) and $CS_{40} \rightarrow$ (A2H).

Section 8.4

13. Arithmetic; overflow flag.

Section 8.5

15.

```
        CLI   ;DISABLE INTERRUPTS AT ENTRY POINT OF
              ;UNINTERRUPTIBLE SUBROUTINE
          .
          .
          .
          .
              ;BODY OF SUBROUTINE
        STI   ;REENABLE INTERRUPTS
        RET   ;RETURN TO MAIN PROGRAM
```

Section 8.6

17. INTR is the interrupt request signal that must be applied to the 8088 MPU by external interrupt interface circuitry to request service for an interrupt-driven device. When this request is acknowledged by the MPU, it outputs an interrupt acknowledge bus status code on $\overline{S_2}\overline{S_1}\overline{S_0}$, and this code is decoded by the 8288 bus controller to produce the $\overline{INTRA}$ signal. $\overline{INTRA}$ is the signal that is used to signal the external device that its request for service has been granted.

19. D_0 through D_7.

Section 8.7

21. When the 8088 microprocessor recognizes an interrupt request, it checks whether the interrupts are enabled. It does this by checking the IR flag. If the IR flag is set, an interrupt acknowledge cycle is initiated. During the cycle $\overline{INTA}$ and $\overline{LOCK}$ signals are inserted. This tells the external interrupt hardware that the interrupt request has been accepted. Following the acknowledge bus cycle, the 8088 initiates a cycle to read interrupt vector type. During this cycle an $\overline{\text{INTA}}$ signal is again inserted to get the vector type presented by the external interrupt hardware. Finally, the interrupt vector words corresponding to the type number are fetched from memory and loaded into IP and CS.

23. 1.8 μs; 6 bytes.

Section 8.8

25. $D_0 = $ 0 ICW$_4$ not needed
$\quad$ $D_1 = $ 1 Single-device
$\quad$ $D_3 = $ 0 Edge-triggered
$\quad$ and assuming that all other bits are logic 0 gives ICW$_1$ = 00000010$_2$ = 02$_{16}$

27. $D_0 = 1$ $\qquad$ Use with the 8086
$\quad$ $D_1 = 0$ $\qquad$ Normal end of interrupt
$\quad$ $D_3D_2 = 11$ $\quad$ Buffered-mode master
$\quad$ $D_4 = 0$ $\qquad$ Disable special fully nested mode and assuming that the rest of the bits are
$\qquad\qquad\qquad\quad$ 0, we get ICW$_4$ = 00001101$_2$ = 0D$_{16}$

29. MOV AL, [0A001H]

Section 8.9

33. 22.

Section 8.10

35. Vectored subroutine call.
37. CS$_{80}$ → (142H); IP$_{80}$ → (140H).

Section 8.11

39. NMI is different from the external hardware interrupts in three ways: NMI is not masked out by IF; NMI is initiated from the NMI input lead instead of from the INTR input; and the NMI input is edge triggered instead of level sensitive like INTR. Therefore, its occurrence is latched inside the 8088 or 8086 as it switches to its active 1 logic level.

Section 8.12

41. 8284.
43. FFFF0H.

Section 8.13

45. Divide error, single step, breakpoint, overflow error.
47. Single step mode; CS$_1$:IP$_1$.

CHAPTER 9

Section 9.2

1. System address bus, system data bus, and system control bus.
3. 060H, 061H, 062H, and 063H.
6. Port A = input; port B = output; and port C = input.
8. PB_3.
11. Printer.

Section 9.3

13. 384K bytes.
14. CLK88 = 4.77 MHz; PCLK = 2.385 MHz.
17. Pin 21.
20. 8259A and 8087.
22. 8288.
23. $\overline{MEMR}$ = pin 7 and $\overline{MEMW}$ = pin 8.

Section 9.4

25. I/O channel cards; 0.
26. I/O channel cards (I/O CH RDY), I/O reads or writes ($\overline{XIOR}$ and $\overline{XIOW}$); DMA cycles (DACK 0 BRD or AEN BRD).
28. N P NPI, $\overline{PCK}$, and $\overline{I/O\ CH\ CK}$.
30. Yes. Output PB_4 of 8255A U_{36} is the enable RAM parity check ($\overline{ENB\ RAM\ PCK}$) signal.

Section 9.5

33. DMA controller chip select, interrupt controller chip select, interval timer chip select, and parallel peripheral interface chip select.
34. $\overline{CS_0}$, $\overline{CS_1}$, $\overline{CS_2}$, $\overline{CS_3}$, $\overline{CS_4}$, $\overline{CS_5}$, $\overline{CS_6}$, $\overline{CS_7}$.
36. $A_{19}A_{18}$ = 00.
37. $\overline{RAS_1}$.

Section 9.7

41. DMA requests for channels 1, 2, and 3 are supplied by I/O channel devices.
43. The DMA page register is used to generate the four most significant bits of the 20-bit DMA address.

Section 9.8

45. 1.19 MHz.

Section 9.9

48. KBD IRQ is an output that is used as an interrupt to the MPU and when active it signals that a keyscan code needs to be read.

Section 9.10

50. A_{10}.

Section 9.11

51. 3; pins 2, 26, and 78.
53. Input.
55. A_{11}.
57. DEN.
59. 30 MHz.
61. 74F245 U_{23}.
63. Pin 27 of R_{21}.
65. B_{19}; $-DACK_0$.
67. Pin 32 of the 8087 (U_2).
69. The KBDATA line of the 82C100 is tied to pin 2 of keyboard connector J_7.

Bibliography

BRADLEY, DAVID J. *Assembly Language Programming for the IBM Personal Computer.* Englewood Cliffs, N.J.: Prentice-Hall, 1984.

CIARCIA, STEVEN. "The Intel 8086," *Byte,* November 1979.

COFFRON, JAMES W. *Programming the 8086/8088.* Berkeley, Calif.: Sybex, 1983.

INTEL CORPORATION. *Components Data Catalog.* Santa Clara, Calif.: Intel Corporation, 1980.

———. *iAPX86,88 User's Manual.* Santa Clara, Calif.: Intel Corporation, July 1981.

———. *MCS-86® User's Manual.* Santa Clara, Calif.: Intel Corporation, February 1979.

———. *Peripheral Design Handbook,* Santa Clara, Calif.: Intel Corporation, April 1978.

MORSE, STEPHEN P. *The 8086 Primer.* Rochelle Park, N.J.: Hayden Book Company, 1978.

NORTON, PETER. *Inside the IBM PC.* Bowie, MD.: Robert J. Brady, 1983.

RECTOR, RUSSELL, and GEORGE ALEXY. *The 8086 Book.* Berkeley, Calif.: Osborne/McGraw-Hill, 1980.

SCANLON, LEO J. *IBM PC Assembly Language.* Bowie, Md.: Robert J. Brady, 1983.

SCHNEIDER, AL. *Fundamentals of IBM PC Assembly Language.* Blue Ridge Summit, Pa.: Tab Books, 1984.

SINGH, AVTAR, and WALTER A. TRIEBEL. *IBM PC/8088 Assembly Language Programming.* Englewood Cliffs, N.J.: Prentice-Hall, 1985.

SINGH, AVTAR, and WALTER A. TRIEBEL. *The 8088 Microprocessor: Programming, Interfacing, Software, Hardware, and Applications.* Englewood Cliffs, N.J.: Prentice-Hall, 1989.

SINGH, AVTAR, and WALTER A. TRIEBEL. *The 8086 and 80286 Microprocessors; Hargware, Software, and Interfacing.* Englewood Cliffs, N.J.: Prentice-Hall, 1990.

TRIEBEL, WALTER A. *Integrated Digital Electronics.* Englewood Cliffs, N.J.: Prentice-Hall, 1979.

TRIEBEL, WALTER A., and ALFRED E. CHU. *Handbook of Semiconductor and Bubble Memories.* Englewood Cliffs, N.J.: Prentice-Hall, 1982.

TRIEBEL, WALTER A., and AVTAR SINGH. *The 8086 Microprocessor: Architecture, Software, and Interface Techniques.* Englewood Cliffs, N.J.: Prentice-Hall, 1985.

WILLEN, DAVID C., and JEFFREY I. KRANTZ. *8088 Assembly Language Programming: the IBM PC.* Indianapolis, Ind.: Howard W. Sams, 1983.

INDEX